STUDENT STUDY GUIDE

Richard N. Aufmann
Palomar College

Vernon C. Barker
Palomar College

Richard D. Nation
Palomar College

Christine S. Verity

COLLEGE ALGEBRA

FIFTH EDITION

Aufmann/Barker/Nation

HOUGHTON MIFFLIN COMPANY   BOSTON NEW YORK

Senior Sponsoring Editor: Lynn Cox
Senior Development Editor: Dawn Nuttall
Assistant Editor: Melissa Parkin
Editorial Assistant: Noel Kamm
Senior Manufacturing Coordinator: Florence Cadran
Senior Marketing Manager: Danielle Potvin

Printed in the U.S.A.

ISBN: 0-618-386726

4 5 6 7 8 9 VHG 08 07 06 05

Contents

Preface

The *Student Study Guide* for the Aufmann/Barker/Nation *College Algebra*, Fifth Edition text contains *Study Tips*, a *Solutions Manual*, and *Chapter Tests* with *Solutions to Chapter Tests*.

The *Study Tips* explain how to best utilize the text and your time in order to succeed in this course.

The *Solutions Manual* provides complete, worked-out solutions to the following text exercises:
- odd-numbered section exercises
- all *Prepare for Section* exercises (found within the section exercises)
- all *Chapter True/False Exercises*
- all *Chapter Review Exercises*
- all *Chapter Test* exercises
- all *Cumulative Review Exercises*

The *Chapter Tests* contain one practice test for each chapter in the text. They are modeled after the Chapter Tests found at the end of each chapter in the text and can be used to provide additional practice for an in-class chapter test. The *Chapter Tests* are immediately followed by *Solutions to Chapter Tests*.

Study Tips

STUDY TIPS

The skills you will learn in any mathematics course will be important in your future career—no matter what career you choose. In your textbook, we have provided you with the tools to master these skills. There's no mystery to success in this course; a little hard work and attention to your instructor will pay off. Here are a few tips to help ensure your success in this class.

Know Your Instructor's Requirements

To do your best in this course, you must know exactly what your instructor requires. If you don't, you probably will not meet his or her expectations and are not likely to earn a good grade in the course.

Instructors ordinarily explain course requirements during the first few days of class. Course requirements may be stated in a *syllabus*, which is a printed outline of the main topics of the course, or they may be presented orally. When they are listed in a syllabus or on other printed pages, keep them in a safe place. When they are presented orally, make sure to take complete notes. In either case, understand them completely and follow them exactly.

Attend Every Class

Attending class is vital if you are to succeed in this course. Your instructor will provide not only information but also practice in the skills you are learning. Be sure to arrive on time. You are responsible for everything that happens in class, even if you are absent. If you *must* be absent from a class session:

1. Deliver due assignments to the instructor as soon as possible.
2. Contact a classmate to learn about assignments or tests announced in your absence.
3. Hand copy or photocopy notes taken by a classmate while you were absent.

Take Careful Notes in Class

You need a notebook in which to keep class notes and records about assignments and tests. Make sure to take complete and well-organized notes. Your instructor will explain text material that may be difficult for you to understand on your own and may supply important information that is not provided in the textbook. Be sure to include in your notes everything that is written on the chalkboard.

Information recorded in your notes about assignments should explain exactly what they are, how they are to be done, and when they are due. Information about tests should include exactly what text material and topics will be covered on each test and the dates on which the tests will be given.

Survey the Chapter

Before you begin reading a chapter, take a few minutes to survey it. Glancing through the chapter will give you an overview of its contents and help you see how the pieces fit together as you read.

Begin by reading the chapter title. The title summarizes what the chapter is about. Next, read the section headings. The section headings summarize the major topics presented in the chapter. Then read the topic headings that appear in green within each section. The topic headings describe the concepts for that section. Keep these headings in mind as you work through the material. They provide direction as you study.

Use the Textbook to learn the Material

For each concept studied, read very carefully all of the material from the topic heading to the examples provided for that concept. As you read, note carefully the formulas and words printed in **boldface** type. It is important for you to know these formulas and the definitions of these words.

You will note that each example references an exercise. The example is worked out for you; the exercise, which is highlighted in red in the section's exercise set, is left for you to do. After studying the example, do the exercise. Immediately look up the answer to this exercise in the Solutions section at the back of the text. If your answer is correct, continue. If your answer is incorrect, check your solution against the one given in the Solutions section. It may be helpful to review the worked-out example also. Determine where you made your mistakes.

Next, do the other problems in the exercise set that correspond to the concept just studied. The answers to all the odd-numbered exercises appear in the answer section in the back of the text, and the solutions appear in this Study Guide. Check your answers to the exercises against these.

If you have difficulty solving problems in the exercise set, review the material in the text. Many examples are solved within the text material. Review the solutions to these problems. Reread the examples provided for the concept. If, after checking these sources and trying to find your mistakes, you are still unable to solve a problem correctly, make a note of the exercise number so that you can ask someone for help with that problem.

Review Material

Reviewing material is the repetition that is essential for learning. Much of what we learn is soon forgotten unless we review it. If you find that you do not remember information that you studied previously, you probably have not reviewed it sufficiently. *You will remember best what you review most.*

One method of reviewing material is to begin a study session by reviewing a concept you have studied previously. For example, before trying to solve a new type of problem, spend a few minutes solving a kind of problem you already know how to solve. Not only will you provide yourself with the review practice you need, but you are also likely to put yourself in the right frame of mind for learning how to solve the new type of problem.

Use the End-of-Chapter Material

To help you review the material presented within a chapter, a Chapter Review appears at the end of each chapter. In the Chapter Review, the main concepts of each section are summarized. Included are important definitions and formulas. After completing a chapter, be sure to read the Chapter Review. Use it to check your understanding of the material presented and to determine what concepts you need to review. Return to any section that contains a concept you need to study again.

Each chapter ends with Chapter Review Exercises and a Chapter Test. The problems these contain summarize what you should have learned when you have finished the chapter. Do these exercises as you prepare for an examination. Check your answers against those in the back of the text. Answers to the odd-numbered Chapter Review Exercises and all the Chapter Test exercises are provided there. For any problem you answer incorrectly, review the material corresponding to that concept in the textbook. Determine *why* your answer was wrong.

Finding Good Study Areas

Find a place to study where you are comfortable and can concentrate well. Many students find the campus library to be a good place. You might select two or three places at the college library where you like to study. Or there may be a small, quiet lounge on the third floor of a building where you find you can study well. Take the time to find places that promote good study habits.

Determining When to Study

Spaced practice is generally superior to massed practice. For example, four half-hour study periods will produce more learning than one two-hour study session. The following suggestions may help you decide when to study.

1. A free period immediately before class is the best time to study about the lecture topic for the class.
2. A free period immediately after class is the best time to review notes taken during the class.
3. A brief period of time is good for reciting or reviewing information.

4. A long period of an hour or more is good for doing challenging activities such as learning to solve a new type of problem.

5. Free periods just before you go to sleep are good times for learning information. (There is evidence that information learned just before sleep is remembered longer than information learned at other times.)

Determining How Much to Study

Instructors often advise students to spend twice as much time outside of class studying as they spend in the classroom. For example, if a course meets for three hours each week, instructors customarily advise students to study for six hours each week outside of class.

Any mathematics course requires the learning of skills, which are abilities acquired through practice. It is often necessary to practice a skill more than a teacher requires. For example, this textbook may provide 50 practice problems on a specific concept, and the instructor may assign only 25 of them. However, some students may need to do 30, 40, or all 50 problems.

If you are an accomplished athlete, musician, or dancer, you know that long hours of practice are necessary to acquire a skill. Do not cheat yourself of the practice you need to develop the abilities taught in this course.

Study followed by reward is usually productive. Schedule something enjoyable to do following study sessions. If you know that you only have two hours to study because you have scheduled an enjoyable activity for yourself, you may be inspired to make the best use of the two hours that you have set aside for studying.

Keep Up to Date with Course Work

College terms start out slowly. Then they gradually get busier and busier, reaching a peak of activity at final examination time. If you fall behind in the work for a course, you will find yourself trying to catch up at a time when you are very busy with all of your other courses. Don't fall behind—keep up to date with course work.

Keeping up with course work is doubly important for a course in which information and skills learned early in the course are needed to learn information and skills later in the course. Any mathematics course falls into this category. Skills must be learned immediately and reviewed often.

Your instructor gives assignments to help you acquire a skill or understand a concept. Do each assignment as it is assigned, or you may well fall behind and have great difficulty catching up. Keeping up with course work also makes it easier to prepare for each exam.

Be Prepared for Tests

The Chapter Test at the end of a chapter should be used to prepare for an examination. Additional Chapter Tests are also provided in this Study Guide. We suggest that you try a Chapter Test a few days before your actual exam. Do these exercises in a quiet place, and try to complete the exercises in the same amount of time as you will be allowed for your exam. When completing the exercises, practice the strategies of successful test takers: 1) look over the entire test before you begin to solve any problem; 2) write down any rules or formulas you may need so they are readily available; 3) read the directions carefully; 4) work the problems that are easiest for you first; 5) check your work, looking particularly for careless errors.

When you have completed the exercises in the Chapter Test, check your answers. If you missed a question, review the material in the appropriate section and then rework some of the exercises from that concept. This will strengthen your ability to perform the skills in that concept.

Get Help for Academic Difficulties

If you do have trouble in this course, teachers, counselors, and advisers can help. They usually know of study groups, tutors, or other sources of help that are available. They may suggest visiting an office of academic skills, a learning center, a tutorial service or some other department or service on campus.

Students who have already taken the course and who have done well in it may be a source of assistance. If they have a good understanding of the material, they may be able to help by explaining it to you.

Solutions Manual

Chapter P
Preliminary Concepts

Section P.1

1. $-\frac{1}{5}$: rational, real; 0: integer, rational, real; –44: integer, rational, real; π : irrational, real; 3.14: rational, real;

5.05005000500005…: irrational, real; $\sqrt{81} = 9$: integer, rational, prime, real; 53: integer, rational, prime, real

3. Let $x = 1, 2, 3, 4$. Then $\{2x \mid x$ is a positive integer$\} = \{2, 4, 6, 8\}$

5. Let $x = 1, 2, 3, 4$. (Recall 0 is not a natural number.) Then $\{y \mid y = 2x + 1, x$ is a natural number$\} = \{3, 5, 7, 9\}$

7. Let $x = 0, 1, 2, 3$. (We could have used $x = -3, -2, -1, 0$.) Then $\{z \mid z = |x|, x$ is an integer$\} = \{0, 1, 2, 3\}$

9. $A \cup B = \{-3, -2, -1, 0, 1, 2, 3, 4, 6\}$

11. $A \cap C = \{0, 1, 2, 3\}$

13. $B \cap D = \varnothing$

15. $(B \cup C) = \{-2, 0, 1, 2, 3, 4, 5, 6\}$
$D \cap (B \cup C) = \{1, 3\}$

17. $(B \cup C) \cap (B \cup D) = \{-2, 0, 1, 2, 3, 4, 5, 6\} \cap \{-3, -2, -1, 0, 1, 2, 3, 4, 6\} = \{-2, 0, 1, 2, 3, 4, 6\}$

19. $\{x \mid -2 < x < 3\}$

21. $\{x \mid -5 \le x \le -1\}$

23. $\{x \mid x \ge 2\}$

25. $(3, 5)$

27. $[-2, \infty)$

29. $[0, 1]$

31. -5

33. $3(4) = 12$

35. $\pi^2 + 10$

37. $|x - 4| + |x + 5| = 4 - x + x + 5 = 9$

39. $|2x| - |x - 1| = 2x - (1 - x)$
$= 2x - 1 + x$
$= 3x - 1$

41. $|x - 3|$

43. $|x - -2| = 4$
$|x + 2| = 4$

45. $|m - n|$

47. $|a - 4| < 5$

49. $|x + 2| > 4$

51.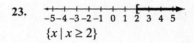

65.

67. $-(-2)^3 = -(-8) = 8$

69. $2(3)(-2)(-1) = 12$

71. $-2(3)^2(-2)^2 = -2(9)(4) = -72$

73. $3(-2) - (-1)[3 - (-2)]^2 = 3(-2) - (-1)[3 + 2]^2 = (3)(-2) - (-1)[5]^2 = (3)(-2) - (-1)(25) = -6 + 25 = 19$

75. $\dfrac{3^2 + (-2)^2}{3 + (-2)} = \dfrac{9 + 4}{1} = \dfrac{13}{1} = 13$

77. $\dfrac{3(-2)}{3} - \dfrac{2(-1)}{-2} = \dfrac{-6}{3} - \dfrac{-2}{-2} = -2 - 1 = -3$

79. $(ab^2)c = a(b^2c)$
Associative Property of Multiplication

81. $4(2a - b) = 8a - 4b$
Distributive Property

83. $(3x)y = y(3x)$
Commutative Property of Multiplication

85. $1 \cdot (4x) = 4x$
Identity Property of Multiplication

87. $x^2 + 1 = x^2 + 1$
Reflexive Property of Equality

89. If $2x + 1 = y$ and $3x - 2 = y$, then $2x + 1 = 3x - 2$
Transitive Property of Equality

91. $4 \cdot \frac{1}{4} = 1$
Inverse Property of Multiplication

93. $3(2x)$
$6x$

95. $3(2 + x)$
$3x + 6$

97. $\frac{2}{3}a + \frac{5}{6}a$
$\frac{4}{6}a + \frac{5}{6}a$
$\frac{9}{6}a$
$\frac{3}{2}a$

99. $2 + 3(2x - 5)$
$2 + 6x - 15$
$6x - 13$

101. $5 - 3(4x - 2y)$
$5 - 12x + 6y$
$-12x + 6y + 5$

103. $3(2a - 4b) - 4(a - 3b)$
$6a - 12b - 4a + 12b$
$6a - 4a - 12b + 12b$
$2a$

105. $5a - 2[3 - 2(4a + 3)]$
$5a - 2(3 - 8a - 6)$
$5a - 2(-8a - 3)$
$5a + 16a + 6$
$21a + 6$

107. Area $= \frac{1}{2}bh = \frac{1}{2}(3 \text{ in})(4 \text{ in}) = 6 \text{ in}^2$

109. Profit $= -0.5x^2 + 120x - 2000$
$= -0.5(110)^2 + 120(110) - 2000$
$= -0.5(110)^2 + 120(110) - 2000$
$= -0.5(12100) + 120(110) - 2000$
$= -6050 + 13200 - 2000$
$= 5150$
The profit for selling 110 bicycles is $5,150.

111. Heart rate $= 65 + \dfrac{53}{4t + 1}$
$= 65 + \dfrac{53}{4(10) + 1}$
$= 65 + \frac{53}{41}$
≈ 66
Heart rate is about 66 beats per minute.

113. Height $= -16t^2 + 80t + 4$
$= -16(2)^2 + 80(2) + 4$
$= -16(4) + 80(2) + 4$
$= -64 + 160 + 4$
$= 100$
After 2 seconds, the ball will have a height of 100 feet.

Connecting Concepts

115. For any set A,
$A \cup A = A$.

117. For any set A,
$A \cap \varnothing = \varnothing$.

119. If A and B are two sets and $A \cup B = A$, then all elements of B are contained in A. So B is a subset of A.

121. No.
$(8 \div 4) \div 2 = 2 \div 2 = 1$
$8 \div (4 \div 2) = 8 \div 2 = 4$

123. All but the multiplicative inverse property

125.
$$\left| \frac{x+7}{|x|+|x-1|} \right| = \frac{|x+7|}{\||x|+|x-1|\|} = \frac{x+7}{|x-(x-1)|} = \frac{x+7}{|1|} = x+7$$

127. $|x-2| < |x-6|$

129. $|x-3| > |x+7|$

131. $2 < |x-4| < 7$

Prepare for Section P.2

133. $2^2 \cdot 2^3 = 4 \cdot 8 = 32$
Alternate method: $2^2 \cdot 2^3 = 2^{2+3} = 2^5 = 32$

134. $\frac{4^3}{4^5} = 4^{3-5} = 4^{-2} = \frac{1}{4^2} = \frac{1}{16}$

Alternate method: $\frac{4^3}{4^5} = \frac{1}{4^{5-3}} = \frac{1}{4^2} = \frac{1}{16}$

135. $(2^3)^2 = 8^2 = 64$

Alternate method: $(2^3)^2 = 2^{3(2)} = 2^6 = 64$

136. $3.14(10^5) = 3.14(100,000) = 314,000$

Alternate method: To multiply by 10^5, move the decimal point 5 places to the right.
Thus, $3.14(10^5) = 3\,14000. = 314,000$

137. False
$3^4 \cdot 3^2 = 3^6$, not 9^6.

138. False
$(3+4)^2 = 7^2 = 49$ but $3^2 + 4^2 = 9+16 = 25$.

Section P.2

1. $-5^3 = -(5^3) = -125$

3. $\left(\frac{2}{3}\right)^0 = 1$

5. $4^{-2} = \frac{1}{4^2} = \frac{1}{16}$

7. $\frac{1}{2^{-5}} = 2^5 = 32$

9. $\frac{2^{-3}}{6^{-3}} = \left(\frac{2}{6}\right)^{-3} = \left(\frac{1}{3}\right)^{-3} = \left(\frac{3}{1}\right)^3 = 3^3 = 27$

11. $-2x^0 = -2$

13. $2x^{-4} = 2\left(x^{-4}\right) = \frac{2}{x^4}$

15. $(-2ab^4)(-3a^2b^4) = (-2)(-3)a^{1+2}b^{4+4} = 6a^3b^8$

17. $\frac{6a^4}{8a^8} = \frac{6}{8}a^{4-8} = \frac{3}{4}a^{-4} = \frac{3}{4a^4}$

19. $\frac{12x^3y^4}{18x^5y^2} = \frac{12}{18}x^{3-5}y^{4-2} = \frac{2}{3}x^{-2}y^2 = \frac{2y^2}{3x^2}$

21. $\frac{36a^{-2}b^3}{3ab^4} = \frac{36}{3}a^{-2-1}b^{3-4} = 12a^{-3}b^{-1} = \frac{12}{a^3b}$

23. $(-2m^3n^2)(-3mn^2)^2 = (-2m^3n^2)(9m^2n^4)$
$= (-2)(9)m^{3+2}n^{2+4}$
$= -18m^5n^6$

25.
$$(x^{-2}y)^2(xy)^{-2} = (x^{-4}y^2)(x^{-2}y^{-2})$$
$$= x^{-4-2}y^{2-2}$$
$$= x^{-6}y^0$$
$$= \frac{1}{x^6}$$

27.
$$\left(\frac{3a^2b^3}{6a^4b^4}\right)^2 = \frac{9a^4b^6}{36a^8b^8}$$
$$= \frac{9}{36}a^{4-8}b^{6-8}$$
$$= \frac{1}{4}a^{-4}b^{-2}$$
$$= \frac{1}{4a^4b^2}$$

29.
$$\frac{(-4x^2y^3)^2}{(2xy^2)^3} = \frac{16x^4y^6}{8x^3y^6}$$
$$= 2x^{4-3}y^{6-6}$$
$$= 2x$$

31.
$$\left(\frac{a^{-2}b}{a^3b^{-4}}\right)^2 = \frac{a^{-4}b^2}{a^6b^{-8}}$$
$$= a^{-4-6}b^{2-(-8)}$$
$$= a^{-4-6}b^{2+8}$$
$$= a^{-10}b^{10}$$
$$= \frac{b^{10}}{a^{10}}$$

33. $2,011,000,000,000 = 2.011 \times 10^{12}$

35. $0.000000000562 = 5.62 \times 10^{-10}$

37. $3.14 \times 10^7 = 31,400,000$

39. $-2.3 \times 10^{-6} = -0.0000023$

41.
$$(3 \times 10^{12})(9 \times 10^{-5}) = (3)(9) \times 10^{12-5}$$
$$= 27 \times 10^7$$
$$= 2.7 \times 10^8$$

43.
$$\frac{9 \times 10^{-3}}{6 \times 10^8} = \frac{9}{6} \times 10^{-3-8}$$
$$= 1.5 \times 10^{-11}$$

45.
$$\frac{(3.2 \times 10^{-11})(2.7 \times 10^{18})}{1.2 \times 10^{-5}} = \frac{(3.2)(2.7)}{1.2} \times 10^{-11+18-(-5)}$$
$$= 7.2 \times 10^{-11+18+5}$$
$$= 7.2 \times 10^{12}$$

47.
$$\frac{(4.0 \times 10^{-9})(8.4 \times 10^5)}{(3.0 \times 10^{-6})(1.4 \times 10^{18})} = \frac{(4.0)(8.4)}{(3.0)(1.4)} \times 10^{-9+5+6-18}$$
$$= 8 \times 10^{-16}$$

49. $4^{3/2} = \sqrt{4}^3 = 2^3 = 8$

51. $-64^{2/3} = -\sqrt[3]{64}^2 = -4^2 = -16$

53. $9^{-3/2} = \frac{1}{9^{3/2}} = \frac{1}{\sqrt{9}^3} = \frac{1}{3^3} = \frac{1}{27}$

55. $\left(\frac{4}{9}\right)^{1/2} = \sqrt{\frac{4}{9}} = \frac{\sqrt{4}}{\sqrt{9}} = \frac{2}{3}$

57. $\left(\frac{1}{8}\right)^{-4/3} = 8^{4/3} = \sqrt[3]{8}^4 = 2^4 = 16$

59. $(4a^{2/3}b^{1/2})(2a^{1/3}b^{3/2}) = (4)(2)a^{2/3+1/3}b^{1/2+3/2} = 8a^{3/3}b^{4/2} = 8ab^2$

61. $(-3x^{2/3})(4x^{1/4}) = (-3)(4)x^{2/3+1/4} = -12x^{8/12+3/12} = -12x^{11/12}$

63. $(81x^8 y^{12})^{1/4} = 81^{1/4} x^{8/4} y^{12/4} = \sqrt[4]{81}x^2 y^3 = 3x^2 y^3$

65. $\dfrac{16z^{3/5}}{12z^{1/5}} = \dfrac{16z^{3/5-1/5}}{12} = \dfrac{4z^{2/5}}{3}$

67. $(2x^{2/3}y^{1/2})(3x^{1/6}y^{1/3}) = (2)(3)x^{2/3+1/6}y^{1/2+1/3} = 6x^{5/6}y^{5/6}$

69. $\dfrac{9a^{3/4}b}{3a^{2/3}b^2} = \dfrac{9a^{3/4-2/3}b^{1-2}}{3} = 3a^{9/12-8/12}b^{-1} = \dfrac{3a^{1/12}}{b}$

71. $\sqrt{45} = \sqrt{3^2 \cdot 5} = 3\sqrt{5}$ 　　　**73.** $\sqrt[3]{24} = \sqrt[3]{2^3 \cdot 3} = 2\sqrt[3]{3}$ 　　　**75.** $\sqrt[3]{-135} = \sqrt[3]{(-3)^3 \cdot 5}$
$$= -3\sqrt[3]{5}$$

77. $\sqrt{24x^2 y^3} = \sqrt{2^2 x^2 y^2} \cdot \sqrt{6y} = 2|xy|\sqrt{6y}$ 　　　**79.** $\sqrt[3]{16a^3 y^7} = \sqrt[3]{2^3 a^3 y^6} \cdot \sqrt[3]{2y} = 2ay^2\sqrt[3]{2y}$

81. $2\sqrt{32} - 3\sqrt{98} = 2\sqrt{16} \cdot \sqrt{2} - 3\sqrt{49} \cdot \sqrt{2} = 2(4)\sqrt{2} - 3(7)\sqrt{2} = 8\sqrt{2} - 21\sqrt{2} = -13\sqrt{2}$

83. $-8\sqrt[4]{48} + 2\sqrt[4]{243} = -8\sqrt[4]{16 \cdot 3} + 2\sqrt[4]{81 \cdot 3} = -8\sqrt[4]{16} \cdot \sqrt[4]{3} + 2\sqrt[4]{81} \cdot \sqrt[4]{3} = -8\sqrt[4]{2^4} \cdot \sqrt[4]{3} + 2\sqrt[4]{3^4} \cdot \sqrt[4]{3}$
$$= -8(2)\sqrt[4]{3} + 2(3)\sqrt[4]{3} = -16\sqrt[4]{3} + 6\sqrt[4]{3} = -10\sqrt[4]{3}$$

85. $4\sqrt[3]{32y^4} + 3y\sqrt[3]{108y} = 4\sqrt[3]{8y^3 \cdot 4y} + 3y\sqrt[3]{27 \cdot 4y} = 4\sqrt[3]{8y^3} \cdot \sqrt[3]{4y} + 3y\sqrt[3]{27} \cdot \sqrt[3]{4y}$
$$= 4\sqrt[3]{2^3 y^3} \cdot \sqrt[3]{4y} + 3y\sqrt[3]{3^3} \cdot \sqrt[3]{4y} = 4(2y)\sqrt[3]{4y} + 3y(3)\sqrt[3]{4y} = 8y\sqrt[3]{4y} + 9y\sqrt[3]{4y} = 17y\sqrt[3]{4y}$$

87. $x\sqrt[3]{8x^3 y^4} - 4y\sqrt[3]{64x^6 y} = x\sqrt[3]{8x^3 y^3 \cdot y} - 4y\sqrt[3]{64x^6 \cdot y} = x\sqrt[3]{8x^3 y^3} \cdot \sqrt[3]{y} - 4y\sqrt[3]{64x^6} \cdot \sqrt[3]{y}$
$$= x\sqrt[3]{2^3 x^3 y^3} \cdot \sqrt[3]{y} - 4y\sqrt[3]{4^3 x^6} \cdot \sqrt[3]{y} = x(2xy)\sqrt[3]{y} - 4y(4x^2)\sqrt[3]{y}$$
$$= 2x^2 y\sqrt[3]{y} - 16x^2 y\sqrt[3]{y} = -14x^2 y\sqrt[3]{y}$$

89. $(\sqrt{5} + 3)(\sqrt{5} + 4) = \sqrt{5}^2 + 4\sqrt{5} + 3\sqrt{5} + (3)(4) = 5 + 7\sqrt{5} + 12 = 17 + 7\sqrt{5}$

91. $(\sqrt{2} - 3)(\sqrt{2} + 3) = \sqrt{2}^2 + 3\sqrt{2} - 3\sqrt{2} + (-3)(3) = 2 - 9 = -7$

93. $(3\sqrt{z} - 2)(4\sqrt{z} + 3) = (3)(4)\sqrt{z}^2 + 3(3\sqrt{z}) - 2(4\sqrt{z}) + (-2)(3) = 12z + 9\sqrt{z} - 8\sqrt{z} - 6 = 12z + \sqrt{z} - 6$

95. $(\sqrt{x} + 2)^2 = \sqrt{x}^2 + 2(\sqrt{x})(2) + 2^2 = x + 4\sqrt{x} + 4$

97. $(\sqrt{x-3} + 2)^2 = \sqrt{x-3}^2 + 2(\sqrt{x-3})(2) + 2^2 = x - 3 + 4\sqrt{x-3} + 4 = x + 4\sqrt{x-3} + 1$

99. $\dfrac{2}{\sqrt{2}} = \dfrac{2}{\sqrt{2}} \cdot \dfrac{\sqrt{2}}{\sqrt{2}} = \dfrac{2\sqrt{2}}{\sqrt{2}^2} = \dfrac{2\sqrt{2}}{2} = \dfrac{\cancel{2}\sqrt{2}}{\cancel{2}} = \sqrt{2}$

101. $\sqrt{\dfrac{5}{18}} = \sqrt{\dfrac{5}{2 \cdot 3^2}} = \sqrt{\dfrac{5}{2 \cdot 3^2}} \cdot \sqrt{\dfrac{2}{2}} = \sqrt{\dfrac{5 \cdot 2}{2^2 \cdot 3^2}} = \dfrac{\sqrt{5 \cdot 2}}{\sqrt{2^2 \cdot 3^2}} = \dfrac{\sqrt{10}}{2 \cdot 3} = \dfrac{\sqrt{10}}{6}$

103. $\dfrac{3}{\sqrt[3]{2}} = \dfrac{3}{\sqrt[3]{2}} \cdot \dfrac{\sqrt[3]{2^2}}{\sqrt[3]{2^2}} = \dfrac{3\sqrt[3]{2^2}}{\sqrt[3]{2^3}} = \dfrac{3\sqrt[3]{4}}{2}$

105. $\dfrac{4}{\sqrt[3]{8x^2}} = \dfrac{4}{\sqrt[3]{2^3 x^2}} = \dfrac{4}{2\sqrt[3]{x^2}} = \dfrac{\overset{2}{\cancel{4}}}{\cancel{2}\sqrt[3]{x^2}} = \dfrac{2}{\sqrt[3]{x^2}} = \dfrac{2}{\sqrt[3]{x^2}} \cdot \dfrac{\sqrt[3]{x}}{\sqrt[3]{x}} = \dfrac{2\sqrt[3]{x}}{\sqrt[3]{x^3}} = \dfrac{2\sqrt[3]{x}}{x}$

107. $\dfrac{3}{\sqrt{3}+4} = \dfrac{3}{\sqrt{3}+4} \cdot \dfrac{\sqrt{3}-4}{\sqrt{3}-4} = \dfrac{3(\sqrt{3}-4)}{(\sqrt{3}+4)(\sqrt{3}-4)} = \dfrac{3(\sqrt{3}-4)}{\sqrt{3}^2 - 4^2} = \dfrac{3(\sqrt{3}-4)}{3-16} = \dfrac{3\sqrt{3}-12}{-13} = -\dfrac{3\sqrt{3}-12}{13}$

109. $\dfrac{6}{2\sqrt{5}+2} = \dfrac{6}{2(\sqrt{5}+1)} = \dfrac{\overset{3}{\cancel{6}}}{\cancel{2}(\sqrt{5}+1)} = \dfrac{3}{\sqrt{5}+1} = \dfrac{3}{\sqrt{5}+1} \cdot \dfrac{\sqrt{5}-1}{\sqrt{5}-1} = \dfrac{3(\sqrt{5}-1)}{(\sqrt{5}+1)(\sqrt{5}-1)} = \dfrac{3(\sqrt{5}-1)}{\sqrt{5}^2 - 1}$

$= \dfrac{3(\sqrt{5}-1)}{5-1} = \dfrac{3\sqrt{5}-3}{4}$

111. $\dfrac{3}{\sqrt{5}+\sqrt{x}} = \dfrac{3}{\sqrt{5}+\sqrt{x}} \cdot \dfrac{\sqrt{5}-\sqrt{x}}{\sqrt{5}-\sqrt{x}} = \dfrac{3(\sqrt{5}-\sqrt{x})}{(\sqrt{5}+\sqrt{x})(\sqrt{5}-\sqrt{x})} = \dfrac{3\sqrt{5}-3\sqrt{x}}{(\sqrt{5})^2-(\sqrt{x})^2} = \dfrac{3\sqrt{5}-3\sqrt{x}}{5-x}$

113. $\dfrac{\$6.40 \times 10^{12}}{2.89 \times 10^8 \text{ people}} = \dfrac{\$6.40}{2.89} \times 10^{12-8} \Big/ \text{person} \approx \$2.21 \times 10^4 \text{ / person}$

115. $\dfrac{1 \text{ seed}}{3.2 \times 10^{-8} \text{ ounce}} \cdot \dfrac{1 \text{ ounce}}{\text{package}}$

$\dfrac{1}{3.2 \times 10^{-8}} \cdot 1 = \dfrac{1}{3.2} \times 10^8$

$= 0.3125 \times 10^8$

$= 3.13 \times 10^7 \text{ seeds per package}$

117. Red shift $= \dfrac{\lambda_r - \lambda_s}{\lambda_s}$

$= \dfrac{5.13 \times 10^{-7} - 5.06 \times 10^{-7}}{5.06 \times 10^{-7}}$

$= \dfrac{(5.13 - 5.06) \times 10^{-7}}{5.06 \times 10^{-7}}$

$= \dfrac{0.07}{5.06} \cdot \dfrac{10^{-7}}{10^{-7}}$

$= 1.38 \times 10^{-2}$

119. $\dfrac{1 \text{ sec}}{3 \times 10^8 \text{ m}} \cdot 1.5 \times 10^{11} \text{ m} \cdot \dfrac{1 \text{ min}}{60 \text{ sec}}$

$\dfrac{1}{3 \times 10^8} \cdot 1.5 \times 10^{11} \cdot \dfrac{1}{60} = \dfrac{(1)(1.5)(1) \times 10^{11}}{3(60) \times 10^8}$

$= \dfrac{1.5}{180} \times 10^{11-8}$

$\approx 0.008 \times 10^3$

$\approx 8 \text{ minutes}$

121. Evaluate R when $x = 20$.

$R = 1250x(2^{-0.007x}) = 1250(20)(2^{-0.007(20)}) = 25,000(2^{-0.14}) \approx 25,000(0.907519) \approx 22,688$

When the company sells 20 thousand phones, the revenue is \$22,688.

123. Evaluate P when $n = 50$. $P = 5.9(2^{0.0119n}) = 5.9(2^{0.0119(50)}) = 5.9(2^{0.595}) \approx 5.9(1.510) \approx 8.91$

In 2050, the world's population will be approximately 8.91 billion.

125. **a.** Evaluate P when $d = 10$. $P = 10^{2-d/40} = 10^{2-10/40} = 10^{2-0.25} = 10^{1.75} \approx 56$

The amount of light that will pass to a depth of 10 feet below the ocean's surface is about 56%.

b. Evaluate P when $d = 25$. $P = 10^{2-d/40} = 10^{2-25/40} = 10^{2-0.625} = 10^{1.375} \approx 24$

The amount of light that will pass to a depth of 25 feet below the ocean's surface is about 24%.

Connecting Concepts

127. No, if a and b are nonzero numbers and $a < b$, then the statement $a^{-1} < b^{-1}$ is not a true statement. Let $a = 2$ and $b = 3$. Then $a < b$, but $a^{-1} = 2^{-1} = \frac{1}{2}$ and $b^{-1} = 3^{-1} = \frac{1}{3}$. $\frac{1}{2} > \frac{1}{3}$ so $a^{-1} > b^{-1}$.

129. $a^{2/5}a^p = a^2$

$\dfrac{2}{5} + p = 2$

$p = 2 - \dfrac{2}{5}$

$p = \dfrac{8}{5}$

131. $\dfrac{x^{-3/4}}{x^{3p}} = x^4$

$-\dfrac{3}{4} - 3p = 4$

$-3p = \dfrac{19}{4}$

$p = -\dfrac{19}{12}$

133. $\dfrac{\sqrt{4+h}-2}{h} = \dfrac{\sqrt{4+h}-2}{h} \cdot \dfrac{\sqrt{4+h}+2}{\sqrt{4+h}+2} = \dfrac{(\sqrt{4+h}-2)(\sqrt{4+h}+2)}{h(\sqrt{4+h}+2)} = \dfrac{(\sqrt{4+h})^2 - 2^2}{h(\sqrt{4+h}+2)} = \dfrac{4+h-4}{h(\sqrt{4+h}+2)}$

$= \dfrac{h}{h(\sqrt{4+h}+2)} = \dfrac{\cancel{h}}{\cancel{h}(\sqrt{4+h}+2)} = \dfrac{1}{\sqrt{4+h}+2}$

135. $\dfrac{\sqrt{n^2+1}-n}{1} = \dfrac{\sqrt{n^2+1}-n}{1} \cdot \dfrac{\sqrt{n^2+1}+n}{\sqrt{n^2+1}+n} = \dfrac{(\sqrt{n^2+1}-n)(\sqrt{n^2+1}+n)}{\sqrt{n^2+1}+n} = \dfrac{(\sqrt{n^2+1})^2 - n^2}{\sqrt{n^2+1}+n} = \dfrac{n^2+1-n^2}{\sqrt{n^2+1}+n} = \dfrac{1}{\sqrt{n^2+1}+n}$

137. $\left(\sqrt{2}^{\sqrt{2}}\right)^{\sqrt{2}} = \sqrt{2}^{(\sqrt{2})(\sqrt{2})} = \sqrt{2}^{(\sqrt{2})^2} = \sqrt{2}^2 = 2$

Prepare for Section P.3

138. $-3(2a - 4b)$

$-6a + 12b$

139. $5 - 2(2x - 7)$

$5 - 4x + 14$

$-4x + 19$

140.
$$2x^2 + 3x - 5 + x^2 - 6x - 1$$
$$2x^2 + x^2 + 3x - 6x - 5 - 1$$
$$(2+1)x^2 + (3-6)x - (5+1)$$
$$3x^2 - 3x - 6$$

141.
$$4x^2 - 6x - 1 - 5x^2 + x$$
$$4x^2 - 5x^2 - 6x + x - 1$$
$$(4-5)x^2 + (-6+1)x - 1$$
$$-x^2 - 5x - 1$$

142.
$$4 - 3x - 2x^2 \overset{?}{=} -2x^2 - 4x + 4$$
$$-2x^2 - 3x + 4 \overset{?}{=} -2x^2 - 4x + 4$$
False.

143.
$$\frac{12+15}{4} = \frac{27}{4}$$
$$= 6\frac{3}{4} \neq 18$$
False.

Section P.3

1. D **3.** H **5.** G **7.** B **9.** J

11.
a. $x^2 + 2x - 7$
b. 2
c. 1, 2, −7
d. 1
e. x^2, $2x$, −7

13.
a. $x^3 - 1$
b. 3
c. 1, −1
d. 1
e. x^3, −1

15.
a. $2x^4 + 3x^3 + 4x^2 + 5$
b. 4
c. 2, 3, 4, 5
d. 2
e. $2x^4, 3x^3, 4x^2, 5$

17. 3 **19.** 5 **21.** 2

23. $(3x^2 + 4x + 5) + (2x^2 + 7x - 2) = 5x^2 + 11x + 3$

25. $(4w^3 - 2w + 7) + (5w^3 + 8w^2 - 1) = 9w^3 + 8w^2 - 2w + 6$

27. $(r^2 - 2r - 5) - (3r^2 - 5r + 7) = r^2 - 2r - 5 - 3r^2 + 5r - 7 = -2r^2 + 3r - 12$

29. $(u^3 - 3u^2 - 4u + 8) - (u^3 - 2u + 4) = u^3 - 3u^2 - 4u + 8 - u^3 + 2u - 4 = -3u^2 - 2u + 4$

31. $(2x^2 + 7x - 8)(4x - 5) = 8x^3 - 10x^2 + 28x^2 - 35x - 32x + 40 = 8x^3 + 18x^2 - 67x + 40$

33.
$$
\begin{array}{r}
3x^2 - 2x + 5 \\
2x^2 - 5x + 2 \\
\hline
+ 6x^2 - 4x + 10 \\
-15x^3 + 10x^2 - 25x \\
+ 6x^4 - 4x^3 + 10x^2 \\
\hline
6x^4 - 19x^3 + 26x^2 - 29x + 10
\end{array}
$$

35. $(2x + 4)(5x + 1) = 10x^2 + 2x + 20x + 4 = 10x^2 + 22x + 4$

37. $(y + 2)(y + 1) = y^2 + y + 2y + 2 = y^2 + 3y + 2$

39. $(4z - 3)(z - 4) = 4z^2 - 16z - 3z + 12 = 4z^2 - 19z + 12$

41. $(a + 6)(a - 3) = a^2 - 3a + 6a - 18 = a^2 + 3a - 18$

43. $(5x - 11y)(2x - 7y) = 10x^2 - 35xy - 22xy + 77y^2$
$$= 10x^2 - 57xy + 77y^2$$

45. $(9x + 5y)(2x + 5y) = 18x^2 + 45xy + 10xy + 25y^2$
$$= 18x^2 + 55xy + 25y^2$$

47. $(3p + 5q)(2p - 7q) = 6p^2 - 21pq + 10pq - 35q^2$
$$= 6p^2 - 11pq - 35q^2$$

49. $(4d - 1)^2 - (2d - 3)^2 = (16d^2 - 8d + 1) - (4d^2 - 12d + 9) = 16d^2 - 8d + 1 - 4d^2 + 12d - 9 = 12d^2 + 4d - 8$

51.
$$r^2 - rs + s^2$$
$$\underline{\qquad\qquad r + s}$$
$$+ r^2s - rs^2 + s^3$$
$$\underline{r^3 - r^2s + rs^2 \qquad}$$
$$r^3 \qquad\quad + s^3$$

53. $(3c - 2)(4c + 1)(5c - 2) = (12c^2 - 5c - 2)(5c - 2)$
$$12c^2 - 5c - 2$$
$$\underline{\qquad\qquad 5c - 2}$$
$$-24c^2 + 10c + 4$$
$$\underline{60c^3 - 25c^2 - 10c \qquad}$$
$$60c^3 - 49c^2 \qquad + 4$$

55. $(3x + 5)(3x - 5) = 9x^2 - 25$

57. $(3x^2 - y)^2 = 9x^4 - 6x^2y + y^2$

59. $(4w + z)^2 = 16w^2 + 8wz + z^2$

61. $[(x + 5) + y][(x + 5) - y] = (x + 5)^2 - y^2$
$$= x^2 + 10x + 25 - y^2$$

63. $x^2 + 7x - 1 = 3^2 + 7(3) - 1 = 9 + 21 - 1 = 29$

65. $-x^2 + 5x - 3 = -(-2)^2 + 5(-2) - 3 = -4 - 10 - 3 = -17$

67. $3x^3 - 2x^2 - x + 3 = 3(-1)^3 - 2(-1)^2 - (-1) + 3 = 3(-1) - 2(1) + 1 + 3 = -3 - 2 + 1 + 3 = -1$

69. $1 - x^5 = 1 - (-2)^5 = 1 - (-32) = 1 + 32 = 33$

71. Substitute the given value of v into $0.016v^2$. Then simplify

    a. $0.016 v^2$
$0.016(10)^2 = 1.6$
The air resistance is 1.6 pounds.

    b. $0.016 v^2$
$0.016(15)^2 = 3.6$
The air resistance is 3.6 pounds.

73. Substitute the given value of h and r into $\pi r^2 h$. Then simplify

    a. $\pi r^2 h$
$\pi(3)^2(8) = 72\pi$
The volume is 72π in^3.

    b. $\pi r^2 h$
$\pi(5)^2(12) = 300\pi$
The volume 300π cm^3.

75. Substitute the given value of v into $0.005x^2 - 0.32x + 12$.

    a. $0.005x^2 - 0.32x + 12$
$0.005(20)^2 - 0.32(20) + 12 = 7.6$
The reaction time is 7.6 hundredths of a second or 0.076 seconds.

    b. $0.005x^2 - 0.32x + 12$
$0.005(50)^2 - 0.32(50) + 12 = 8.5$
The reaction time is 8.5 hundredths of a second or 0.085 seconds.

77. $\dfrac{1}{2}n^2 - \dfrac{1}{2}n = \dfrac{1}{2}(150)^2 - \dfrac{1}{2}(150) = 11{,}175$ chess matches

79. **a.** $1.9 \times 10^{-6}(4000)^2 - 3.9 \times 10^{-3}(4000) = 14.8$ sec

81. Evaluate $-16t^2 + 4.7881t + 6$ when $t = 0.5$
height $= -16t^2 + 4.7881t + 6$
$= -16(0.5)^2 + 4.7881(0.5)t + 6$
$= 4.39$
Yes. The ball is approximately 4.4 feet high when it crosses homeplate.

    b. $1.9 \times 10^{-6}(8000)^2 - 3.9 \times 10^{-3}(8000) = 90.4$ sec

83. $2^{11} \cdot 3^6 \cdot 5^3 \cdot 7^2 \cdot 11 \cdot 13$
$= 2 \cdot 3 \cdot (2^2) \cdot 5 \cdot (2 \cdot 3) \cdot 7 \cdot (2^3) \cdot (3^2) \cdot (2 \cdot 5) \cdot 11 \cdot (2^2 \cdot 3) \cdot 13 \cdot (2 \cdot 7) \cdot (3 \cdot 5)$
$= 2 \cdot 3 \cdot 4 \cdot 5 \cdot 6 \cdot 7 \cdot 8 \cdot 9 \cdot 10 \cdot 11 \cdot 12 \cdot 13 \cdot 14 \cdot 15$
$= 15!$
$n = 15$

Connecting **C**oncepts

85. $(a - b)^3 = a^3 - 3a^2 b + 3ab^2 - b^3$

87. $(y + 2)^3 = y^3 + 3y^2 (2) + 3y(2)^2 + 2^3 = y^3 + 6y^2 + 12y + 8$

89. $(3x + 5y)^3 = (3x)^3 + 3(3x)^2 5y + 3(3x)(5y)^2 + (5y)^3 = 27x^3 + 135x^2 y + 225xy^2 + 125y^3$

Prepare for **S**ection **P.4**

90. $\dfrac{6x^3}{2x} = 3x^{3-1} = 3x^2$

91. $(-12x^4)3x^2 = (-12)(3)x^{4+2} = -36x^6$

92. **a.** $x^6 = (x^2)^3$

b. $x^6 = (x^3)^2$

93. $6a^3 b^4 \cdot ? = 18a^3 b^7 = 6a^3 b^4 (3b^3)$
Thus, $? = 3b^3$

94. $-3(5a - ?) = -15a + 21 = -3(5a - 7)$
Thus, $? = 7$

95. $2x(3x - ?) = 6x^2 - 2x = 2x(3x - 1)$
Thus, $? = 1$

Section P.4

1. $5x + 20 = 5(x + 4)$

3. $-15x^2 - 12x = -3x(5x + 4)$

5. $10x^2 y + 6xy - 14xy^2 = 2xy(5x + 3 - 7y)$

7. $(x - 3)(a + b) + (x - 3)(a + 3b) = (x - 3)(a + b + a + 3b) = (x - 3)(2a + 4b)$

9. $x^2 + 7x + 12 = (x + 3)(x + 4)$

11. $a^2 - 10a - 24 = (a - 12)(a + 2)$

13. $6x^2 + 25x + 4 = (6x + 1)(x + 4)$

15. $51x^2 - 5x - 4 = (17x + 4)(3x - 1)$

17. $6x^2 + xy - 40y^2 = (3x + 8y)(2x - 5y)$

19. $x^4 + 6x^2 + 5 = (x^2 + 5)(x^2 + 1)$

21. $6x^4 + 23x^2 + 15 = (6x^2 + 5)(x^2 + 3)$

23. $b^2 - 4ac = 26^2 - 4(8)(15) = 196 = 14^2$
The trinomial is factorable over the integers

25. $b^2 - 4ac = (-5)^2 - 4(4)(6) = -71$
The trinomial is not factorable over the integers.

27. $b^2 - 4ac = (-14)^2 - 4(6)(5) = 76$
The trinomial is not factorable over the integers.

29. $x^4 - x^2 - 6 = (x^2 - 3)(x^2 + 2)$

31. $x^2 y^2 - 2xy - 8 = (xy - 4)(xy + 2)$

33. $3x^4 + 11x^2 - 4 = (3x^2 - 1)(x^2 + 4)$

35. $3x^6 + 2x^3 - 8 = (3x^3 - 4)(x^3 + 2)$

37. $x^2 - 9 = (x - 3)(x + 3)$

39. $4a^2 - 49 = (2a - 7)(2a + 7)$

41. $1 - 100x^2 = (1 - 10x)(1 + 10x)$

43. $x^4 - 9 = (x^2 - 3)(x^2 + 3)$

45. $(x + 5)^2 - 4 = (x + 5 - 2)(x + 5 + 2) = (x + 3)(x + 7)$

47. $x^2 + 10x + 25 = (x + 5)^2$

49. $a^2 - 14a + 49 = (a - 7)^2$

51. $4x^2 + 12x + 9 = (2x + 3)^2$

53. $z^4 + 4z^2w^2 + 4w^4 = (z^2 + 2w^2)^2$

55. $x^3 - 8 = (x - 2)(x^2 + 2x + 4)$

57. $8x^3 - 27y^3 = (2x - 3y)(4x^2 + 6xy + 9y^2)$

59. $8 - x^6 = (2 - x^2)(4 + 2x^2 + x^4)$

61. $(x - 2)^3 - 1 = [(x - 2) - 1][(x - 2)^2 + (x - 2) + 1] = (x - 3)(x^2 - 4x + 4 + x - 2 + 1) = (x - 3)(x^2 - 3x + 3)$

63. $3x^3 + x^2 + 6x + 2 = x^2(3x + 1) + 2(3x + 1) = (3x + 1)(x^2 + 2)$

65. $ax^2 - ax + bx - b = ax(x - 1) + b(x - 1) = (x - 1)(ax + b)$

67. $6w^3 + 4w^2 - 15w - 10 = 2w^2(3w + 2) - 5(3w + 2) = (3w + 2)(2w^2 - 5)$

69. $18x^2 - 2 = 2(9x^2 - 1) = 2(3x - 1)(3x + 1)$

71. $16x^4 - 1 = (4x^2 - 1)(4x^2 + 1) = (2x - 1)(2x + 1)(4x^2 + 1)$

73. $12ax^2 - 23axy + 10ay^2 = a(12x^2 - 23xy + 10y^2) = a(3x - 2y)(4x - 5y)$

75. $3bx^3 + 4bx^2 - 36x - 4b = bx^2(3x + 4) - b(3x + 4) = (3x + 4)(bx^2 - b) = b(3x + 4)(x^2 - 1) = b(3x + 4)(x - 1)(x + 1)$

77. $72bx^2 + 24bxy + 2by^2 = 2b(36x^2 + 12xy + y^2) = 2b(6x + y)^2$

79. $(w - 5)^3 + 8 = [(w - 5) + 2][(w - 5)^2 - 2(w - 5) + 4] = (w - 3)(w^2 - 10w + 25 - 2w + 10 + 4) = (w - 3)(w^2 - 12w + 39)$

81. $x^2 + 6xy + 9y^2 - 1 = (x + 3y)^2 - 1 = (x + 3y - 1)(x + 3y + 1)$

83. $8x^2 + 3x - 4$ is not factorable over the integers.

85. $5x(2x - 5)^2 - (2x - 5)^3 = (2x - 5)^2[5x - (2x - 5)] = (2x - 5)^2(5x - 2x + 5) = (2x - 5)^2(3x + 5)$

87. $4x^2 + 2x - y - y^2 = 4x^2 - y^2 + 2x - y = (2x - y)(2x + y) + (2x - y) = (2x - y)(2x + y + 1)$

••• **Connecting Concepts**

89. $x^2 + kx + 16 = (x + 4)^2 = x^2 + 8x + 16$, thus $k = 8$

91. $x^2 + 16x + k = (x + \sqrt{k})^2 = x^2 + 2x\sqrt{k} + k \Rightarrow 16x = 2x\sqrt{k} \Rightarrow 8 = \sqrt{k} \Rightarrow k = 64$

93. $x^{4n} - 1 = (x^{2n} - 1)(x^{2n} + 1) = (x^n - 1)(x^n + 1)(x^{2n} + 1)$

95. $A = \pi R^2 - \pi r^2 = \pi(R^2 - r^2) = \pi(R - r)(R + r)$

97. $A = (2r)^2 - \pi r^2 = r^2(4 - \pi)$

99.
$$1+\frac{1}{2-\frac{1}{3}}=1+\frac{1}{2-\frac{1}{3}}\cdot\left(\frac{3}{3}\right)$$
$$=1+\frac{1\cdot 3}{2\cdot 3-\frac{1}{3}\cdot 3}$$
$$=1+\frac{3}{6-1}=1+\frac{3}{5}$$
$$=1\frac{3}{5}\ \text{or}\ \frac{8}{5}$$

100.
$$\left(\frac{w}{x}\right)^{-1}\left(\frac{y}{z}\right)^{-1}=\left(\frac{x}{w}\right)\left(\frac{z}{y}\right)$$
$$=\frac{xz}{wy}$$

101.
$x^2+2x-3=(x+3)(x-1)$
$x^2+7x+12=(x+4)(x+3)$
The common factor is $x+3$.

102.
$(2x-3)(3x+2)-(2x-3)(x+2)$
$=(2x-3)[(3x+2)-(x+2)]$
$=(2x-3)(2x)$
$=2x(2x-3)$

103. $x^2-5x-6=(x-6)(x+1)$

104. $x^3-64=(x-4)(x^2+4x+16)$

Section P.5

1.
$$\frac{x^2-x-20}{3x-15}=\frac{(x+4)(x-5)}{3(x-5)}=\frac{x+4}{3}$$

3.
$$\frac{x^3-9x}{x^3+x^2-6x}=\frac{x(x^2-9)}{x(x^2+x-6)}=\frac{x(x-3)(x+3)}{x(x+3)(x-2)}=\frac{x-3}{x-2}$$

5.
$$\frac{a^3+8}{a^2-4}=\frac{(a+2)(a^2-2a+4)}{(a-2)(a+2)}=\frac{a^2-2a+4}{a-2}$$

7.
$$\frac{x^2+3x-40}{-(x^2-3x-10)}=\frac{(x-5)(x+8)}{-(x-5)(x+2)}=-\frac{x+8}{x+2}$$

9.
$$\frac{4y^3-8y^2+7y-14}{-y^2-5y+14}=\frac{4y^2(y-2)+7(y-2)}{-(y^2+5y-14)}=\frac{(y-2)(4y^2+7)}{-(y+7)(y-2)}=-\frac{4y^2+7}{y+7}$$

11.
$$\left(-\frac{4a}{3b^2}\right)\left(\frac{6b}{a^4}\right)=-\frac{24ab}{3a^4b^2}=-\frac{8}{a^3b}$$

13.
$$\left(\frac{6p^2}{5q^2}\right)^{-1}\left(\frac{2p}{3q^2}\right)^2=\frac{5q^2}{6p^2}\cdot\frac{4p^2}{9q^4}=\frac{10}{27q^2}$$

15.
$$\frac{x^2+x}{2x+3}\cdot\frac{3x^2+19x+28}{x^2+5x+4}=\frac{x(x+1)}{2x+3}\cdot\frac{(3x+7)(x+4)}{(x+4)(x+1)}=\frac{x(3x+7)}{2x+3}$$

17.
$$\frac{3x-15}{2x^2-50}\cdot\frac{2x^2+16x+30}{6x+9}=\frac{3(x-15)}{2(x^2-25)}\cdot\frac{2(x^2+8x+15)}{3(2x+3)}=\frac{3(x-15)}{2(x-5)(x+5)}\cdot\frac{2(x+3)(x+5)}{3(2x+3)}=\frac{x+3}{2x+3}$$

19.
$$\frac{12y^2 + 28y + 15}{6y^2 + 35y + 25} \div \frac{2y^2 - y - 3}{3y^2 + 11y - 20} = \frac{(6y+5)(2y+3)}{(6y+5)(y+5)} \cdot \frac{(3y-4)(y+5)}{(2y-3)(y+1)} = \frac{(2y+3)(3y-4)}{(2y-3)(y+1)}$$

21.
$$\frac{a^2 + 9}{a^2 - 64} \div \frac{a^3 - 3a^2 + 9a - 27}{a^2 + 5a - 24} = \frac{a^2 + 9}{(a-8)(a+8)} \cdot \frac{(a-3)(a+8)}{a^2(a-3) + 9(a-3)} = \frac{a^2 + 9}{(a-8)(a+8)} \cdot \frac{(a-3)(a+8)}{(a-3)(a^2+9)} = \frac{1}{a-8}$$

23.
$$\frac{p+5}{r} + \frac{2p-7}{r} = \frac{p+5+2p-7}{r} = \frac{3p-2}{r}$$

25.
$$\frac{x}{x-5} + \frac{7x}{x+3} = \frac{x(x+3) + 7x(x-5)}{(x-5)(x+3)} = \frac{x^2 + 3x + 7x^2 - 35x}{(x-5)(x+3)} = \frac{8x^2 - 32x}{(x-5)(x+3)} = \frac{8x(x-4)}{(x-5)(x+3)}$$

27.
$$\frac{5y-7}{y+4} - \frac{2y-3}{y+4} = \frac{(5y-7) - (2y-3)}{y+4} = \frac{5y - 7 - 2y + 3}{y+4} = \frac{3y-4}{y+4}$$

29.
$$\frac{4z}{2z-3} + \frac{5z}{z-5} = \frac{4z(z-5) + 5z(2z-3)}{(2z-3)(z-5)} = \frac{4z^2 - 20z + 10z^2 - 15z}{(2z-3)(z-5)} = \frac{14z^2 - 35z}{(2z-3)(z-5)} = \frac{7z(2z-5)}{(2z-3)(z-5)}$$

31.
$$\frac{x}{x^2 - 9} - \frac{3x-1}{x^2 + 7x + 12} = \frac{x}{(x-3)(x+3)} - \frac{3x-1}{(x+3)(x+4)} = \frac{x(x+4) - (3x-1)(x-3)}{(x-3)(x+3)(x+4)}$$
$$= \frac{(x^2 + 4x) - (3x^2 - 10x + 3)}{(x-3)(x+3)(x+4)} = \frac{x^2 + 4x - 3x^2 + 10x - 3}{(x-3)(x+3)(x+4)} = \frac{-2x^2 + 14x - 3}{(x-3)(x+3)(x+4)}$$

33.
$$\frac{1}{x} + \frac{2}{3x-1} \cdot \frac{3x^2 + 11x - 4}{x-5} = \frac{1}{x} + \frac{2}{3x-1} \cdot \frac{(3x-1)(x+4)}{(x-5)} = \frac{1}{x} + \frac{2(x+4)}{x-5} = \frac{1(x-5) + x[2(x+4)]}{x(x-5)}$$
$$= \frac{x - 5 + 2x^2 + 8x}{x(x-5)} = \frac{2x^2 + 9x - 5}{x(x-5)} = \frac{(2x-1)(x+5)}{x(x-5)}$$

35.
$$\frac{q+1}{q-3} - \frac{2q}{q-3} \div \frac{q+5}{q-3} = \frac{q+1}{q-3} - \frac{2q}{q-3} \cdot \frac{q-3}{q+5} = \frac{q+1}{q-3} - \frac{2q}{q+5} = \frac{(q+1)(q+5) - 2q(q-3)}{(q-3)(q+5)}$$
$$= \frac{q^2 + 6q + 5 - 2q^2 + 6q}{(q-3)(q+5)} = \frac{-q^2 + 12q + 5}{(q-3)(q+5)}$$

37.
$$\frac{1}{x^2 + 7x + 12} + \frac{1}{x^2 - 9} + \frac{1}{x^2 - 16} = \frac{1}{(x+3)(x+4)} + \frac{1}{(x-3)(x+3)} + \frac{1}{(x-4)(x+4)}$$
$$= \frac{1(x-3)(x-4) + 1(x-4)(x+4) + 1(x-3)(x+3)}{(x+3)(x+4)(x-3)(x-4)}$$
$$= \frac{x^2 - 7x + 12 + x^2 - 16 + x^2 - 9}{(x+3)(x+4)(x-3)(x-4)} = \frac{3x^2 - 7x - 13}{(x+3)(x+4)(x-3)(x-4)}$$

39.
$$\left(1 + \frac{2}{x}\right)\left(3 - \frac{1}{x}\right) = \left(\frac{x}{x} + \frac{2}{x}\right)\left(\frac{3x}{x} - \frac{1}{x}\right) = \left(\frac{x+2}{x}\right)\left(\frac{3x-1}{x}\right) = \frac{(x+2)(3x-1)}{x^2}$$

41.
$$\frac{4 + \frac{1}{x}}{1 - \frac{1}{x}} = \frac{\left(4 + \frac{1}{x}\right)x}{\left(1 - \frac{1}{x}\right)x} = \frac{4x+1}{x-1}$$

43.
$$\frac{\frac{x}{y} - 2}{y - x} = \frac{\left(\frac{x}{y} - 2\right)y}{(y-x)y} = \frac{x - 2y}{y(y-x)}$$

45.
$$\frac{5-\dfrac{1}{x+2}}{1+\dfrac{3}{1+\dfrac{3}{x}}}=\frac{5-\dfrac{1}{x+2}}{1+\dfrac{3}{\dfrac{1(x)}{x}+\dfrac{3}{x}}}=\frac{5-\dfrac{1}{x+2}}{1+\dfrac{3}{\dfrac{x+3}{x}}}=\frac{5-\dfrac{1}{x+2}}{1+3\div\dfrac{x+3}{3}}=\frac{5-\dfrac{1}{x+2}}{1+3\cdot\dfrac{x}{x+3}}=\frac{5-\dfrac{1}{x+2}}{1+\dfrac{3x}{x+3}}=\frac{\dfrac{5(x+2)}{x+2}-\dfrac{1}{x+2}}{\dfrac{1(x+3)}{x+3}+\dfrac{3x}{x+3}}$$

$$=\frac{\dfrac{5(x+2)-1}{x+2}}{\dfrac{1(x+3)+3x}{x+3}}=\frac{\dfrac{5x+10-1}{x+2}}{\dfrac{x+3+3x}{x+3}}=\frac{\dfrac{5x+9}{x+2}}{\dfrac{4x+3}{x+3}}=\frac{5x+9}{x+2}\div\frac{4x+3}{x+3}=\frac{5x+9}{x+2}\cdot\frac{x+3}{4x+3}=\frac{(5x+9)(x+3)}{(x+2)(4x+3)}$$

47.
$$\frac{1+\dfrac{1}{b-2}}{1-\dfrac{1}{b+3}}=\frac{\left(1+\dfrac{1}{b-2}\right)}{\left(1-\dfrac{1}{b+3}\right)}\cdot\frac{(b-2)(b+3)}{(b-2)(b+3)}=\frac{1(b-2)(b+3)+1(b+3)}{1(b-2)(b+3)-1(b-2)}=\frac{b^2+b-6+b+3}{b^2+b-6-b+2}=\frac{b^2+2b-3}{b^2-4}=\frac{(b+3)(b-1)}{(b-2)(b+2)}$$

49.
$$\frac{1-\dfrac{1}{x^2}}{1+\dfrac{1}{x}}=\frac{\left(1-\dfrac{1}{x^2}\right)}{\left(1+\dfrac{1}{x}\right)}\cdot\frac{x^2}{x^2}=\frac{x^2-1}{x^2+x}=\frac{(x-1)(x+1)}{x(x+1)}=\frac{x-1}{x}$$

51.
$$2-\frac{m}{1-\dfrac{1-m}{-m}}=2-\frac{m}{1+\dfrac{1-m}{m}}=2-\frac{m}{\dfrac{1(m)}{m}+\dfrac{1-m}{m}}=2-\frac{m}{\dfrac{m+1-m}{m}}=2-\frac{m}{\dfrac{1}{m}}=2-\frac{(m)}{\left(\dfrac{1}{m}\right)}\cdot\frac{m}{m}=2-m^2$$

53.
$$\frac{\left(\dfrac{1}{x}-\dfrac{x-4}{x+1}\right)}{\dfrac{x}{x+1}}\cdot\frac{x(x+1)}{x(x+1)}=\frac{x+1-x(x-4)}{x(x)}=\frac{x+1-x^2+4x}{x^2}=\frac{-x^2+5x+1}{x^2}$$

55.
$$\frac{\left(\dfrac{1}{x+3}-\dfrac{2}{x-1}\right)}{\left(\dfrac{x}{x-1}+\dfrac{3}{x+3}\right)}\cdot\frac{(x+3)(x-1)}{(x+3)(x-1)}=\frac{1(x-1)-2(x+3)}{x(x+3)+3(x-1)}=\frac{x-1-2x-6}{x^2+3x+3x-3}=\frac{-x-7}{x^2+6x-3}$$

57.
$$\frac{\dfrac{x^2+3x-10}{x^2+x-6}}{\dfrac{x^2-x-30}{2x^2-15x+18}}=\frac{\dfrac{(x-2)(x+5)}{(x-2)(x+3)}}{\dfrac{(x+5)(x-6)}{(2x-3)(x-6)}}=\frac{\dfrac{x+5}{x+3}}{\dfrac{x+5}{2x-3}}=\frac{x+5}{x+3}\div\frac{x+5}{2x-3}=\frac{x+5}{x+3}\cdot\frac{2x-3}{x+5}=\frac{2x-3}{x+3}$$

59.
$$\frac{a^{-1}+b^{-1}}{a-b}=\frac{\dfrac{1}{a}+\dfrac{1}{b}}{a-b}=\frac{\dfrac{1b}{ab}+\dfrac{1a}{ab}}{a-b}=\frac{\dfrac{b+a}{ab}}{a-b}=\frac{b+a}{ab}\div(a-b)=\frac{b+a}{ab}\cdot\frac{1}{a-b}=\frac{a+b}{ab(a-b)}$$

61.
$$\frac{a^{-1}b-ab^{-1}}{a^2+b^2}=\frac{\dfrac{b}{a}-\dfrac{a}{b}}{a^2+b^2}=\frac{\dfrac{(b)b}{(b)a}-\dfrac{a(a)}{b(a)}}{a^2+b^2}=\frac{\dfrac{b^2}{ab}-\dfrac{a^2}{ab}}{a^2+b^2}=\frac{\dfrac{b^2-a^2}{ab}}{a^2+b^2}=\frac{b^2-a^2}{ab}\div a^2+b^2$$

$$=\frac{b^2-a^2}{ab}\cdot\frac{1}{a^2+b^2}=\frac{b^2-a^2}{ab(a^2+b^2)}=\frac{(b-a)(b+a)}{ab(a^2+b^2)}$$

63. a. $\dfrac{2}{\dfrac{1}{180}+\dfrac{1}{110}}=\dfrac{2}{\dfrac{110+180}{180(110)}}=2\div\dfrac{290}{180(110)}$ **b.** $\dfrac{2}{\dfrac{1}{v_1}+\dfrac{1}{v_2}}=\dfrac{2}{\dfrac{v_2+v_1}{v_1v_2}}=\dfrac{2v_1v_2}{v_2+v_1}=\dfrac{2v_1v_2}{v_1+v_2}$

$=2\cdot\dfrac{(180)(110)}{290}\approx136.55$ mph (to the nearest hundredth)

65.

Evaluate $z=\dfrac{\lambda_0-\lambda_s}{\lambda_s}$ when $\lambda_0=390.5\times10^{-9}$ and $\lambda_s=375.4\times10^{-9}$

$z=\dfrac{390.5\times10^{-9}-375.4\times10^{-9}}{375.4\times10^{-9}}=\dfrac{15.1\times10^{-9}}{375.4\times10^{-9}}\approx0.040$

67.

Evaluate $v=c\left[\dfrac{(z+1)^2-1}{(z+1)^2+1}\right]$ when $c=3\times10^5$ and $z=0.032$.

$v=3\times10^5\left[\dfrac{(0.032+1)^2-1}{(0.032+1)^2+1}\right]=3\times10^5\left[\dfrac{0.065024}{2.065024}\right]\approx9446$

The relative speed is 9446 kilometers per second.

69. $\dfrac{1}{x}+\dfrac{1}{x+1}=\dfrac{x+1+x}{x(x+1)}=\dfrac{2x+1}{x(x+1)}$

71.

$\dfrac{1}{x-2}+\dfrac{1}{x}+\dfrac{1}{x+2}=\dfrac{x(x+2)+(x-2)(x+2)+x(x-2)}{x(x-2)(x+2)}=\dfrac{x^2+2x+x^2-4+x^2-2x}{x(x-2)(x+2)}=\dfrac{3x^2-4}{x(x-2)(x+2)}$

Connecting Concepts

73. $\dfrac{(x+5)-x(x+5)^{-1}}{x+5}\cdot\dfrac{x+5}{x+5}=\dfrac{(x+5)^2-x}{(x+5)^2}=\dfrac{x^2+10x+25-x}{(x+5)^2}=\dfrac{x^2+9x+25}{(x+5)^2}$

75.

$\dfrac{x^{-1}-4y}{(x^{-1}-2y)(x^{-1}+2y)}=\dfrac{\dfrac{1}{x}-4y}{\left(\dfrac{1}{x}-2y\right)\left(\dfrac{1}{x}+2y\right)}=\dfrac{\dfrac{1-4xy}{x}}{\left(\dfrac{1-2xy}{x}\right)\left(\dfrac{1+2xy}{x}\right)}\cdot\dfrac{x^2}{x^2}=\dfrac{x(1-4xy)}{(1-2xy)(1+2xy)}$

77.

$R\left[\dfrac{1-\dfrac{1}{(1+i)^n}}{i}\right]=R\left[\dfrac{\dfrac{(1+i)^n-1}{(1+i)^n}}{i}\right]=R\left[\dfrac{(1+i)^n-1}{i(1+i)^n}\right]$

Prepare for Section P.6

79. $(2-3x)(4-5x)=8-10x-12x+15x^2$

$=15x^2-22x+8$

80. $(2-5x)^2=2^2+2(2)(-5x)+(-5x)^2$

$=4-20x+25x^2$

$=25x^2-20x+4$

81. $\sqrt{96}=\sqrt{16\cdot6}=4\sqrt{6}$

82. $\left(2+3\sqrt{5}\right)\left(3-4\sqrt{5}\right) = 6-8\sqrt{5}+9\sqrt{5}-12\left(\sqrt{5}\right)^2 = 6+\sqrt{5}-60 = -54+\sqrt{5}$

83. $\dfrac{5+\sqrt{2}}{3-\sqrt{2}} = \dfrac{5+\sqrt{2}}{3-\sqrt{2}} \cdot \dfrac{3+\sqrt{2}}{3+\sqrt{2}} = \dfrac{15+8\sqrt{2}+2}{9-2} = \dfrac{17+8\sqrt{2}}{7}$

84. **a.** $81-x^2$ is a difference of perfect squares with integer coefficients, which does factor over the integers.

$81-x^2 = (9-x)(9+x)$

b. $9+z^2$ is a sum of perfect squares with integer coefficients. If there is no common factor, sums of perfect squares with integer coefficients are not factorable over the integers.

Section P.6

1. $\sqrt{-81} = i\sqrt{81} = 9i$

3. $\sqrt{-98} = i\sqrt{98} = 7i\sqrt{2}$

5. $\sqrt{16}+\sqrt{-81} = 4+i\sqrt{81}$
$= 4+9i$

7. $5+\sqrt{-49} = 5+i\sqrt{49} = 5+7i$

9. $8-\sqrt{-18} = 8-i\sqrt{18} = 8-3i\sqrt{2}$

11. $(5+2i)+(6-7i) = 5+2i+6-7i$
$= (5+6)+(2i-7i)$
$= 11-5i$

13. $(-2-4i)-(5-8i) = -2-4i-5+8i$
$= (-2-5)+(-4i+8i)$
$= -7+4i$

15. $(1-3i)+(7-2i) = 1-3i+7-2i$
$= (1+7)+(-3i-2i)$
$= 8-5i$

17. $(-3-5i)-(7-5i) = -3-5i-7+5i$
$= (-3-7)+(-5i+5i)$
$= -10$

19. $8i-(2-8i) = 8i-2+8i$
$= -2+(8i+8i)$
$= -2+16i$

21. $5i \cdot 8i = 40i^2$
$= 40(-1)$
$= -40$

23. $\sqrt{-50} \cdot \sqrt{-2} = i\sqrt{50} \cdot i\sqrt{2} = 5i\sqrt{2} \cdot i\sqrt{2}$
$= 5i^2\left(\sqrt{2}\right)^2 = 5(-1)(2)$
$= -10$

25. $3(2+5i)-2(3-2i) = 6+15i-6+4i$
$= (6-6)+(15i+4i)$
$= 19i$

27. $(4+2i)(3-4i) = 4(3-4i)+(2i)(3-4i)$
$= 12-16i+6i-8i^2$
$= 12-16i+6i-8(-1)$
$= 12-16i+6i+8$
$= (12+8)+(-16i+6i)$
$= 20-10i$

29. $(-3-4i)(2+7i) = -3(2+7i)-4i(2+7i)$
$= -6-21i-8i-28i^2$
$= -6-21i-8i-28(-1)$
$= -6-21i-8i+28$
$= (-6+28)+(-21i-8i)$
$= 22-29i$

31.
$$(4-5i)(4+5i) = 4(4+5i) - 5i(4+5i)$$
$$= 16 + 20i - 20i - 25i^2$$
$$= 16 + 20i - 20i - 25(-1)$$
$$= 16 + 20i - 20i + 25$$
$$= (16+25) + (20i - 20i)$$
$$= 41$$

33.
$$(3+\sqrt{-4})(2-\sqrt{-9}) = (3+i\sqrt{4})(2-i\sqrt{9})$$
$$= (3+2i)(2-3i)$$
$$= 3(2-3i) + 2i(2-3i)$$
$$= 6 - 9i + 4i - 6i^2$$
$$= 6 - 9i + 4i - 6(-1)$$
$$= 6 - 9i + 4i + 6$$
$$= (6+6) + (-9i + 4i)$$
$$= 12 - 5i$$

35.
$$(3+2\sqrt{-18})(2+2\sqrt{-50}) = (3+2i\sqrt{18})(2+2i\sqrt{50}) = [3+2i(3\sqrt{2})][2+2i(5\sqrt{2})] = (3+6i\sqrt{2})(2+10i\sqrt{2})$$
$$= 3(2+10i\sqrt{2}) + 6i\sqrt{2}(2+10i\sqrt{2}) = 6 + 30i\sqrt{2} + 12i\sqrt{2} + 60i^2(\sqrt{2})^2$$
$$= 6 + 30i\sqrt{2} + 12i\sqrt{2} + 60(-1)(2) = 6 + 30i\sqrt{2} + 12i\sqrt{2} - 120$$
$$= (6-120) + (30i\sqrt{2} + 12i\sqrt{2}) = -114 + 42i\sqrt{2}$$

37.
$$\frac{6}{i} = \frac{6}{i} \cdot \frac{i}{i} = \frac{6i}{i^2} = \frac{6i}{-1} = -6i$$

39.
$$\frac{6+3i}{i} = \frac{6+3i}{i} \cdot \frac{i}{i} = \frac{6i+3i^2}{i^2} = \frac{6i+3(-1)}{-1} = \frac{6i-3}{-1} = 3 - 6i$$

41.
$$\frac{1}{7+2i} = \frac{1}{7+2i} \cdot \frac{7-2i}{7-2i} = \frac{1(7-2i)}{(7+2i)(7-2i)} = \frac{7-2i}{49-4i^2} = \frac{7-2i}{49-4(-1)} = \frac{7-2i}{49+4} = \frac{7-2i}{53} = \frac{7}{53} - \frac{2}{53}i$$

43.
$$\frac{2i}{1+i} = \frac{2i}{1+i} \cdot \frac{1-i}{1-i} = \frac{2i(1-i)}{(1+i)(1-i)} = \frac{2i-2i^2}{1-i^2} = \frac{2i-2(-1)}{1-(-1)} = \frac{2i+2}{1+1} = \frac{2+2i}{2} = \frac{2}{2} + \frac{2}{2}i = 1 + i$$

45.
$$\frac{5-i}{4+5i} = \frac{5-i}{4+5i} \cdot \frac{4-5i}{4-5i} = \frac{(5-i)(4-5i)}{(4+5i)(4-5i)} = \frac{5(4-5i) - i(4-5i)}{4(4-5i) + 5i(4-5i)} = \frac{20-25i-4i+5i^2}{16-20i+20i-25i^2}$$
$$= \frac{20-25i-4i+5(-1)}{16-25(-1)} = \frac{20-25i-4i-5}{16+25} = \frac{(20-5)+(-25i-4i)}{16+25} = \frac{15-29i}{41} = \frac{15}{41} - \frac{29}{41}i$$

47.
$$\frac{3+2i}{3-2i} = \frac{3+2i}{3-2i} \cdot \frac{3+2i}{3+2i} = \frac{(3+2i)^2}{(3-2i)(3+2i)} = \frac{3^2 + 2(3)(2i) + (2i)^2}{3^2 - (2i)^2} = \frac{9+12i+4i^2}{9-4i^2} = \frac{9+12i+4(-1)}{9-4(-1)}$$
$$= \frac{9+12i-4}{9+4} = \frac{5+12i}{13} = \frac{5}{13} + \frac{12}{13}i$$

49.
$$\frac{-7+26i}{4+3i} = \frac{-7+26i}{4+3i} \cdot \frac{4-3i}{4-3i} = \frac{(-7+26i)(4-3i)}{(4+3i)(4-3i)} = \frac{-7(4-3i) + 26i(4-3i)}{4^2 - (3i)^2} = \frac{-28+21i+104i-78i^2}{16-9i^2}$$
$$= \frac{-28+21i+104i-78(-1)}{16-9(-1)} = \frac{-28+21i+104i+78}{16+9} = \frac{50+125i}{25} = \frac{50}{25} + \frac{125}{25}i = 2 + 5i$$

51.
$$(3-5i)^2 = 3^3 + 2(3)(-5i) + (-5i)^2$$
$$= 9 - 30i + 25i^2$$
$$= 9 - 30i + 25(-1)$$
$$= 9 - 30i - 25$$
$$= -16 - 30i$$

53.
$$(1+2i)^3 = (1+2i)(1+2i)^2$$
$$= (1+2i)[1^2 + 2(1)(2i) + (2i)^2]$$
$$= (1+2i)[1 + 4i + 4i^2]$$
$$= (1+2i)[1 + 4i + 4(-1)]$$
$$= (1+2i)[1 + 4i - 4]$$
$$= (1+2i)(-3+4i)$$
$$= 1(-3+4i) + 2i(-3+4i)$$
$$= -3 + 4i - 6i + 8i^2$$
$$= -3 + 4i - 6i - 8$$
$$= -11 - 2i$$

55. Use the Powers of i Theorem.
The remainder of $15 \div 4$ is 3.
$$i^{15} = i^3 = -i$$

57. Use the Powers of i Theorem.
The remainder of $40 \div 4$ is 0.
$$-i^{40} = -(i^0) = -1$$

59. Use the Powers of i Theorem.
The remainder of $25 \div 4$ is 1.
$$\frac{1}{i^{25}} = \frac{1}{i} = \frac{1}{i} \cdot \frac{i}{i} = \frac{i}{i^2} = \frac{i}{-1} = -i$$

61. Use the Powers of i Theorem.
The remainder of $34 \div 4$ is 2.
$$i^{-34} = \frac{1}{i^{34}} = \frac{1}{i^2} = \frac{1}{-1} = -1$$

63. Use $a = 3$, $b = -3$, $c = 3$.
$$\frac{-b + \sqrt{b^2 - 4ac}}{2a} = \frac{-(-3) + \sqrt{(-3)^2 - 4(3)(3)}}{2(3)}$$
$$= \frac{3 + \sqrt{9 - 36}}{6} = \frac{3 + \sqrt{-27}}{6}$$
$$= \frac{3 + i\sqrt{27}}{6} = \frac{3 + 3i\sqrt{3}}{6}$$
$$= \frac{3}{6} + \frac{3\sqrt{3}}{6}i = \frac{1}{2} + \frac{\sqrt{3}}{2}i$$

65. Use $a = 2$ $b = 6$, $c = 6$.
$$\frac{-b + \sqrt{b^2 - 4ac}}{2a} = \frac{-(6) + \sqrt{(6)^2 - 4(2)(6)}}{2(2)}$$
$$= \frac{-6 + \sqrt{36 - 48}}{4} = \frac{-6 + \sqrt{-12}}{4}$$
$$= \frac{-6 + i\sqrt{12}}{4} = \frac{-6 + 2i\sqrt{3}}{4}$$
$$= \frac{-6}{4} + \frac{2i\sqrt{3}}{4} = -\frac{3}{2} + \frac{\sqrt{3}}{2}i$$

67. Use $a = 4$, $b = -4$, $c = 2$.
$$\frac{-b + \sqrt{b^2 - 4ac}}{2a} = \frac{-(-4) + \sqrt{(-4)^2 - 4(4)(2)}}{2(4)}$$
$$= \frac{4 + \sqrt{16 - 32}}{8} = \frac{4 + \sqrt{-16}}{8}$$
$$= \frac{4 + i\sqrt{16}}{8} = \frac{4 + 4i}{8}$$
$$= \frac{4}{8} + \frac{4i}{8} = \frac{1}{2} + \frac{1}{2}i$$

Connecting **C**oncepts

69. $x^2 + 16 = x^2 + 4^2 = (x + 4i)(x - 4i)$

71. $z^2 + 25 = z^2 + 5^2 = (z + 5i)(z - 5i)$

73. $4x^2 + 81 = (2x)^2 + 9^2 = (2x + 9i)(2x - 9i)$

75. If $x = 1 + 2i$, then $x^2 - 2x + 5 = (1 + 2i)^2 - 2(1 + 2i) + 5 = 1 + 4i + 4i^2 - 2 - 4i + 5 = 1 + 4i + 4(-1) - 2 - 4i + 5$
$$= 1 + 4i - 4 - 2 - 4i + 5 = (1 - 4 - 2 + 5) + (4i - 4i) = 0$$

77. Verify that $(-1 + i\sqrt{3})^3 = 8$.

$(-1 + i\sqrt{3})^3 = (-1 + i\sqrt{3})(-1 + i\sqrt{3})^2 = (-1 + i\sqrt{3})[(-1)^2 + 2(-1)(i\sqrt{3}) + (i\sqrt{3})^2]$

$\quad = (-1 + i\sqrt{3})[1 - 2i\sqrt{3} + 3i^2] = (-1 + i\sqrt{3})[1 - 2i\sqrt{3} + 3(-1)] = (-1 + i\sqrt{3})[1 - 2i\sqrt{3} - 3]$

$\quad = (-1 + i\sqrt{3})(-2 - 2i\sqrt{3}) = -1(-2 - 2i\sqrt{3}) + i\sqrt{3}(-2 - 2i\sqrt{3}) = 2 + 2i\sqrt{3} - 2i\sqrt{3} - 2i^2(\sqrt{3})^2$

$\quad = 2 + 2i\sqrt{3} - 2i\sqrt{3} - 2(-1)(3) = 2 + 2i\sqrt{3} - 2i\sqrt{3} + 6 = (2 + 6) + (2i\sqrt{3} - 2i\sqrt{3})$

$\quad = 8$

Verify that $(-1 - i\sqrt{3})^3 = 8$.

$(-1 - i\sqrt{3})^3 = (-1 - i\sqrt{3})(-1 - i\sqrt{3})^2 = (-1 - i\sqrt{3})[(-1)^2 + 2(-1)(-i\sqrt{3}) + (-i\sqrt{3})^2]$

$\quad = (-1 - i\sqrt{3})[1 + 2i\sqrt{3} + 3i^2] = (-1 - i\sqrt{3})[1 + 2i\sqrt{3} + 3(-1)] = (-1 - i\sqrt{3})[1 + 2i\sqrt{3} - 3]$

$\quad = (-1 - i\sqrt{3})(-2 + 2i\sqrt{3}) = -1(-2 + 2i\sqrt{3}) - i\sqrt{3}(-2 + 2i\sqrt{3}) = 2 - 2i\sqrt{3} + 2i\sqrt{3} - 2i^2(\sqrt{3})^2$

$\quad = 2 - 2i\sqrt{3} + 2i\sqrt{3} - 2(-1)(3) = 2 - 2i\sqrt{3} + 2i\sqrt{3} + 6 = (2 + 6) + (-2i\sqrt{3} + 2i\sqrt{3})$

$\quad = 8$

79. $i + i^2 + i^3 + i^4 + \ldots + i^{28} = 7(i + i^2 + i^3 + i^4) = 7(i + (-1) + (-i) + 1) = 7(0) = 0$

·········· **Chapter P True/False Exercises**

1. True

2. False, if $a = \dfrac{1}{2}$, then $\left(\dfrac{1}{2}\right)^2 = \dfrac{1}{4} < \dfrac{1}{2}$.

3. True

4. False, $\sqrt{2} + (-\sqrt{2}) = 0$ which is a rational number.

5. False, let $x = 2, y = 4, z = 6$.

$(x \oplus y) \oplus z = \dfrac{2 + 4}{2} \oplus 6 = \left(\dfrac{6}{2}\right) \oplus 6 = 3 \oplus 6 = \dfrac{3 + 6}{2} = \dfrac{9}{2}$

$x \oplus (y \oplus z) = 2 \oplus \dfrac{4 + 6}{2} = 2 \oplus \left(\dfrac{10}{2}\right) = 2 \oplus 5 = \dfrac{2 + 5}{2} = \dfrac{7}{2}$

$\dfrac{9}{2} \neq \dfrac{7}{2}$ therefore $(x \oplus y) \oplus z \neq x \oplus (y \oplus z)$

6. False, $x > a$ is written as (a, ∞).

7. False, $\sqrt{(-2)^2} = \sqrt{4} = 2 \neq -2$

8. False, $(a + b)^2 = a^2 + 2ab + b^2$

9. False, if $a = 1$ and $b = 2$, then $\sqrt[3]{1^3 + 2^3} \neq 1 + 2$

10. False; $\sqrt{-2}\sqrt{-8} = i\sqrt{2} \cdot i\sqrt{8} = i^2\sqrt{16} = -4$

·········· **Chapter Review**

1. Integer, rational number, real number, prime number [P.1]

2. Irrational number, real number [P.1]

3. Rational number, real number [P.1]

4. Rational number, real number [P.1]

5. $A \cup B = \{1, 2, 3, 5, 7, 11\}$ [P.1]

6. $A \cap B = \{5\}$ [P.1]

7. Distributive Property [P.1]

8. Commutative Property of Addition [P.1]

9. Associative Property of Multiplication [P.1]

10. Closure Property of Addition [P.1]

11. Identity Property of Addition [P.1]

12. Identity Property of Multiplication [P.1]

13. Symmetric Property of Equality [P.1]

14. Transitive Property of Equality [P.1]

15. $-4 < x \leq 2$ [P.1]

$(-4, 2]$

16. $x \leq -1$ or $x > 3$ [P.1]

$(-\infty, -1] \cup (3, \infty)$

17. $[-3, 2)$ [P.1]

$-3 \leq x < 2$

18. $(-1, \infty)$ [P.1]

$x > -1$

19. $|7| = 7$ [P.1]

20. $|2 - \pi| = -(2 - \pi) = \pi - 2$, because $\pi > 2$ [P.1]

21. $|4 - \pi| = 4 - \pi$, [P.1] because $4 > \pi$

22. $|-11| = 11$ [P.1]

23. $|-3 - 14| = 17$ [P.1]

24. $\left|\sqrt{5} - (-\sqrt{2})\right| = \sqrt{5} + \sqrt{2}$ [P.1]

25. $-5^2 + (-11) = -25 - 11 = -36$ [P.1]

26. $\dfrac{\left(2^2 \cdot 3^{-2}\right)^2}{3^{-1}2^3} = \dfrac{2^4 3^{-4}}{3^{-1}2^3} = 2^{4-3}3^{-4-(-1)} = 2^{4-3}3^{-4+1} = 2^1 3^{-3} = \dfrac{2}{3^3} = \dfrac{2}{27}$ [P.1]

27. $(3x^2y)(2x^3y)^2 = 3x^2y \cdot 4x^6y^2 = 12x^8y^3$ [P.2]

28. $\left(\dfrac{2a^2b^3c^{-2}}{3ab^{-1}}\right)^2 = \left(\dfrac{2ab^4}{3c^2}\right)^2 = \dfrac{4a^2b^8}{9c^4}$ [P.2]

29. $25^{1/2} = \sqrt{25} = 5$ [P.2]

30. $-27^{2/3} = -\left(\sqrt[3]{27}\right)^2 = -(3)^2 = -9$ [P.2]

31. $x^{2/3} \cdot x^{3/4} = x^{2/3 + 3/4} = x^{8/12 + 9/12} = x^{17/12}$ [P.2]

32. $\left(\dfrac{8x^{5/4}}{x^{1/2}}\right)^{2/3} = \left(8x^{5/4 - 1/2}\right)^{2/3} = \left(8x^{5/4 - 2/4}\right)^{2/3} = \left(8x^{3/4}\right)^{2/3} = 8^{2/3}x^{(3/4)(2/3)} = (2^3)^{2/3}x^{(3/4)(2/3)} = 2^2 x^{1/2} = 4x^{1/2}$ [P.2]

33. $\left(\dfrac{x^2y}{x^{1/2}y^{-3}}\right)^{1/2} = \left(x^{2 - 1/2}y^{1 - (-3)}\right)^{1/2} = \left(x^{4/2 - 1/2}y^{1+3}\right)^{1/2} = \left(x^{3/2}y^4\right)^{1/2} = x^{(3/2)(1/2)}y^{4(1/2)} = x^{3/4}y^2$ [P.2]

34. $\left(x^{1/2} - y^{1/2}\right)\left(x^{1/2} + y^{1/2}\right) = x - y$ [P.2]

35. $\sqrt{48a^2b^7} = \sqrt{16a^2b^6 \cdot 3b} = 4ab^3\sqrt{3b}$ [P.2]

36. $\sqrt{12a^3b} = \sqrt{4a^2 \cdot 3ab} = 2a\sqrt{3ab}$ [P.2]

37. $\sqrt{72x^2y} = \sqrt{36x^2 \cdot 2y} = 6x\sqrt{2y}$ [P.2]

38. $\sqrt{18x^3y^5} = \sqrt{9x^2y^4 \cdot 2xy} = 3xy^2\sqrt{2xy}$ [P.2]

39. $\sqrt{\dfrac{54xy^3}{10x}} = \sqrt{\dfrac{27y^3}{5}} = \dfrac{\sqrt{9y^2 \cdot 3y}}{\sqrt{5}} = \dfrac{3y\sqrt{3y}}{\sqrt{5}} \cdot \dfrac{\sqrt{5}}{\sqrt{5}} = \dfrac{3y\sqrt{15y}}{5}$ [P.2]

40. $-\sqrt{\dfrac{24xyz^3}{15z^6}} = -\sqrt{\dfrac{8xy}{5z^3}} = -\dfrac{2\sqrt{2xy}}{z\sqrt{5z}} \cdot \dfrac{\sqrt{5z}}{\sqrt{5z}} = -\dfrac{2\sqrt{10xyz}}{5z^2}$ [P.2]

41. $\dfrac{7x}{\sqrt[3]{2x^2}} = \dfrac{7x}{\sqrt[3]{2x^2}} \cdot \dfrac{\sqrt[3]{2^2x}}{\sqrt[3]{2^2x}} = \dfrac{7x\sqrt[3]{4x}}{2x} = \dfrac{7\sqrt[3]{4x}}{2}$ [P.2]

42.

$$\frac{5y}{\sqrt[3]{9y}} = \frac{5y}{\sqrt[3]{3^2 y}} \cdot \frac{\sqrt[3]{3y^2}}{\sqrt[3]{3y^2}} = \frac{5y\sqrt[3]{3y^2}}{3y} = \frac{5\sqrt[3]{3y^2}}{3} \text{ [P.2]}$$

43.

$$\sqrt[3]{-135x^2 y^7} = \sqrt[3]{-27y^6 \cdot 5x^2 y} = -3y^2 \sqrt[3]{5x^2 y} \text{ [P.2]}$$

44.

$$\sqrt[3]{-250xy^6} = \sqrt[3]{-125y^6 \cdot 2x} = -5y^2 \sqrt[3]{2x} \text{ [P.2]}$$

45. $620{,}000 = 6.2 \times 10^5$ [P.2]

46. $0.0000017 = 1.7 \times 10^{-6}$ [P.2]

47. $3.5 \times 10^4 = 35{,}000$ [P.2]

48. $4.31 \times 10^{-7} = 0.000000431$ [P.2]

49. $(2a^2 + 3a - 7) + (-3a^2 - 5a + 6) = [2a^2 + (-3a^2)] + [3a + (-5a)] + [(-7) + 6] = -a^2 - 2a - 1$ [P.3]

50. $(5b^2 - 11) - (3b^2 - 8b - 3) = 5b^2 - 11 - 3b^2 + 8b + 3$ [P.3]
$$= 2b^2 + 8b - 8$$

51. [P.3]

$$
\begin{array}{r}
2x^2 + 3x - 5 \\
3x^2 - 2x + 4 \\
\hline
+ 8x^2 + 12x - 20 \\
- 4x^3 - 6x^2 + 10x \\
6x^4 + 9x^3 - 15x^2 \\
\hline
6x^4 + 5x^3 - 13x^2 + 22x - 20
\end{array}
$$

52. $(3y-5)^3 = (3y-5)^2(3y-5) = (9y^2 - 30y + 25)(3y - 5) = 27y^3 - 45y^2 - 90y^2 + 150y + 75y - 125 = 27y^3 - 135y^2 + 225y - 125$ [P.3]

53. $3x^2 + 30x + 75 = 3(x^2 + 10x + 25) = 3(x+5)^2$ [P.4]

54. $25x^2 - 30xy + 9y^2 = (5x - 3y)^2$ [P.4]

55. $20a^2 - 4b^2 = 4(5a^2 - b^2)$ [P.4]

56. $16a^3 + 250 = 2(8a^3 + 125) = 2(2a + 5)(4a^2 - 10a + 25)$ [P.4]

57.

$$\frac{6x^2 - 19x + 10}{2x^2 + 3x - 20} = \frac{(3x-2)(2x-5)}{(2x-5)(x+4)} = \frac{3x-2}{x+4} \text{ [P.5]}$$

58.

$$\frac{4x^3 - 25x}{8x^4 + 125x} = \frac{x(4x^2 - 25)}{x(8x^3 + 125)} = \frac{x(2x-5)(2x+5)}{x(2x+5)(4x^2 - 10x + 25)} = \frac{2x-5}{4x^2 - 10x + 25} \text{ [P.5]}$$

59.

$$\frac{10x^2 + 13x - 3}{6x^2 - 13x - 5} \cdot \frac{6x^2 + 5x + 1}{10x^2 + 3x - 1} = \frac{(2x+3)(5x-1)}{(2x-5)(3x+1)} \cdot \frac{(2x+1)(3x+1)}{(2x+1)(5x-1)} = \frac{2x+3}{2x-5} \text{ [P.5]}$$

60.

$$\frac{15x^2 + 11x - 12}{25x^2 - 9} \div \frac{3x^2 + 13x + 12}{10x^2 + 11x + 3} = \frac{15x^2 + 11x - 12}{25x^2 - 9} \cdot \frac{10x^2 + 11x + 3}{3x^2 + 13x + 12} = \frac{(5x-3)(3x+4)}{(5x-3)(5x+3)} \cdot \frac{(5x+3)(2x+1)}{(3x+4)(x+3)} = \frac{2x+1}{x+3} \text{ [P.5]}$$

61.

$$\frac{x}{x^2 - 9} + \frac{2x}{x^2 + x - 12} = \frac{x}{(x-3)(x+3)} + \frac{2x}{(x+4)(x-3)} = \frac{x(x+4) + 2x(x+3)}{(x-3)(x+3)(x+4)} = \frac{x^2 + 4x + 2x^2 + 6x}{(x-3)(x+3)(x+4)} \text{ [P.5]}$$
$$= \frac{3x^2 + 10x}{(x-3)(x+3)(x+4)} = \frac{x(3x+10)}{(x-3)(x+3)(x+4)}$$

62.

$$\frac{3x}{x^2 + 7x + 12} - \frac{x}{2x^2 + 5x - 3} = \frac{3x}{(x+3)(x+4)} - \frac{x}{(2x-1)(x+3)} = \frac{3x(2x-1) - x(x+4)}{(x+3)(x+4)(2x-1)} \text{ [P.5]}$$
$$= \frac{6x^2 - 3x - x^2 - 4x}{(x+3)(x+4)(2x-1)} = \frac{5x^2 - 7x}{(x+3)(x+4)(2x-1)} = \frac{x(5x-7)}{(x+3)(x+4)(2x-1)}$$

63.
$$\dfrac{2+\dfrac{1}{x-5}}{3-\dfrac{2}{x-5}} = \dfrac{\left(2+\dfrac{1}{x-5}\right)}{\left(3-\dfrac{2}{x-5}\right)} \cdot \dfrac{x-5}{x-5} = \dfrac{2(x-5)+1}{3(x-5)-2} = \dfrac{2x-10+1}{3x-15-2} = \dfrac{2x-9}{3x-17} \quad [P.5]$$

64.
$$\dfrac{1}{2+\dfrac{3}{1+\dfrac{4}{x}}} = \dfrac{1}{2+\dfrac{3}{\dfrac{x}{x}+\dfrac{4}{x}}} = \dfrac{1}{2+\dfrac{3}{\dfrac{x+4}{x}}} = \dfrac{1}{2+\left(3\div\dfrac{x+4}{x}\right)} = \dfrac{1}{2+\left(3\cdot\dfrac{x}{x+4}\right)} = \dfrac{1}{2+\dfrac{3x}{x+4}} \cdot \dfrac{x+4}{x+4} = \dfrac{x+4}{2(x+4)+3x} = \dfrac{x+4}{2x+8+3x} = \dfrac{x+4}{5x+8} \quad [P.5]$$

65. $5+\sqrt{-64} = 5+8i \quad [P.6]$

66.
$$2+\sqrt{-18} = 2+i\sqrt{18} \quad [P.6]$$
$$= 2+i\sqrt{9\cdot 2}$$
$$= 2+3i\sqrt{2}$$

67.
$$(2-3i)+(4+2i) = 2-3i+4+2i \quad [P.6]$$
$$= (2+4)+(-3i+2i)$$
$$= 6-i$$

68.
$$(4+7i)-(6-3i) = 4+7i-6+3i \quad [P.6]$$
$$= (4-6)+(7i+3i)$$
$$= -2+10i$$

69.
$$2i(3-4i) = 6i-8i^2 \quad [P.6]$$
$$= 6i-8(-1)$$
$$= 6i+8$$
$$= 8+6i$$

70.
$$(4-3i)(2+7i) = 4(2+7i)-3i(2+7i) \quad [P.6]$$
$$= 8+28i-6i-21i^2$$
$$= 8+22i-21(-1)$$
$$= 8+22i+21$$
$$= 29+22i$$

71.
$$(3+i)^2 = 3^2+2(3)(i)+i^2 \quad [P.6]$$
$$= 9+6i+(-1)$$
$$= 8+6i$$

72. Use the Powers of i Theorem. [P.6]
The remainder of $345\div 4$ is 1
$$i^{345} = i^1 = i$$

73.
$$\dfrac{4-6i}{2i} = \dfrac{2(2-3i)}{2i} = \dfrac{\cancel{2}(2-3i)}{\cancel{2}i} = \dfrac{2-3i}{i} = \dfrac{2-3i}{i}\cdot\dfrac{i}{i} = \dfrac{2i-3i^2}{i^2} = \dfrac{2i-3(-1)}{-1} = \dfrac{2i+3}{-1} = -3-2i \quad [P.6]$$

74.
$$\dfrac{2-5i}{3+4i} = \dfrac{2-5i}{3+4i}\cdot\dfrac{3-4i}{3-4i} = \dfrac{(2-5i)(3-4i)}{(3+4i)(3-4i)} = \dfrac{2(3-4i)-5i(3-4i)}{(3)^2-(4i)^2} = \dfrac{6-8i-15i+20i^2}{9-16i^2} = \dfrac{6-8i-15i+20(-1)}{9-16(-1)} \quad [P.6]$$
$$= \dfrac{6-8i-15i-20}{9+16} = \dfrac{-14-23i}{25} = -\dfrac{14}{25}-\dfrac{23}{25}i$$

Chapter Test

1. The distributive property [P.1]

2. $A\cup B = \{0, 1, 2, 3, 4, 5, 6, 7, 8, 9\}$ [P.1]

3. $|-12-(-5)| = |-12+5| = |-7| = 7$ [P.1]

4.
$$\left(-2x^0 y^{-2}\right)^2\left(-3x^2 y^{-1}\right)^{-2} = \left(4y^{-4}\right)\left(3^{-2}x^{-4}y^2\right) = \dfrac{4}{9x^4 y^2}$$
[P.2]

5.
$$\dfrac{\left(2a^{-1}bc^{-2}\right)^2}{\left(3^{-1}b\right)\left(2^{-1}ac^{-2}\right)^3} = \dfrac{2^2 a^{-2}b^2 c^{-4}}{\left(3^{-1}b\right)\left(2^{-3}a^3 c^{-6}\right)} = \dfrac{2^2\cdot 2^3\cdot 3^1\cdot b^2 c^6}{ba^3 a^2 c^4} = \dfrac{2^5\cdot 3\cdot bc^2}{a^5} = \dfrac{96bc^2}{a^5} \quad [P.2]$$

6. $0.00137 = 1.37 \times 10^{-3}$ [P.2]

7. $\dfrac{x^{1/3} y^{-3/4}}{x^{-1/2} y^{3/2}} = x^{1/3 - (-1/2)} \, y^{-3/4 - 3/2} = x^{1/3 + 1/2} \, y^{-3/4 - 3/2} = x^{2/6 + 3/6} \, y^{-3/4 - 6/4} = x^{5/6} \, y^{-9/4} = \dfrac{x^{5/6}}{y^{9/4}}$ [P.2]

8. $3x\sqrt[3]{81xy^4} - 2y\sqrt[3]{3x^4 y} = 3x\sqrt[3]{27y^3 \cdot 3xy} - 2y\sqrt[3]{x^3 \cdot 3xy} = 3x \cdot 3y\sqrt[3]{3xy} - 2y \cdot x\sqrt[3]{3xy} = 9xy\sqrt[3]{3xy} - 2xy\sqrt[3]{3xy} = 7xy\sqrt[3]{3xy}$ [P.2]

9. $\dfrac{x}{\sqrt[4]{2x^3}} = \dfrac{x}{\sqrt[4]{2x^3}} \cdot \dfrac{\sqrt[4]{2^3 x}}{\sqrt[4]{2^3 x}} = \dfrac{x\sqrt[4]{2^3 x}}{\sqrt[4]{2^4 x^4}} = \dfrac{x\sqrt[4]{8x}}{2x} = \dfrac{\sqrt[4]{8x}}{2}$ [P.2]

10. $\dfrac{3}{\sqrt{x}+2} = \dfrac{3}{\sqrt{x}+2} \cdot \dfrac{\sqrt{x}-2}{\sqrt{x}-2} = \dfrac{3\sqrt{x}-6}{x-4}$ [P.2]

11. $(x - 2y)(x^2 - 2x + y) = x^3 - 2x^2 + xy - 2x^2 y + 4xy - 2y^2 = x^3 - 2x^2 + 5xy - 2x^2 y - 2y^2$ [P.3]

12.   If $y = -3, \ 3y^3 - 2y^2 - y + 2 = 3(-3)^3 - 2(-3)^2 - (-3) + 2 = 3(-27) - 2(9) + 3 + 2 = -81 - 18 + 3 + 2 = -94$ [P.4]

13. $7x^2 + 34x - 5 = (7x - 1)(x + 5)$ [P.4]

14. $3ax - 12bx - 2a + 8b = (3ax - 12bx) - (2a - 8b) = 3x(a - 4b) - 2(a - 4b) = (a - 4b)(3x - 2)$ [P.4]

15. $16x^4 - 2xy^3 = 2x(8x^3 - y^3) = 2x(2x - y)(4x^2 + 2xy + y^2)$ [P.4]

16. $\dfrac{x^2 - 2x - 15}{25 - x^2} = \dfrac{(x - 5)(x + 3)}{(5 - x)(5 + x)} = \left(\dfrac{x - 5}{5 - x}\right)\left(\dfrac{x + 3}{x + 5}\right) = -1 \cdot \left(\dfrac{x + 3}{x + 5}\right) = -\dfrac{x + 3}{x + 5}$ [P.5]

17. $\dfrac{x}{x^2 + x - 6} - \dfrac{2}{x^2 - 5x + 6} = \dfrac{x}{(x - 2)(x + 3)} - \dfrac{2}{(x - 2)(x - 3)} = \dfrac{x(x - 3) - 2(x + 3)}{(x - 2)(x + 3)(x - 3)}$ [P.5]

$= \dfrac{x^2 - 3x - 2x - 6}{(x - 2)(x + 3)(x - 3)} = \dfrac{x^2 - 5x - 6}{(x - 2)(x + 3)(x - 3)} = \dfrac{(x - 6)(x + 1)}{(x - 2)(x + 3)(x - 3)}$

18. $\dfrac{2x^2 + 3x - 2}{x^2 - 3x} \div \dfrac{2x^2 - 7x + 3}{x^3 - 3x^2} = \dfrac{2x^2 + 3x - 2}{x^2 - 3x} \cdot \dfrac{x^3 - 3x^2}{2x^2 - 7x + 3} = \dfrac{(2x - 1)(x + 2)}{x(x - 3)} \cdot \dfrac{x^2(x - 3)}{(2x - 1)(x - 3)} = \dfrac{x(x + 2)}{x - 3}$ [P.5]

19. $\dfrac{3}{a + b} \cdot \dfrac{a^2 - b^2}{2a - b} - \dfrac{5}{a} = \dfrac{3}{a + b} \cdot \dfrac{(a - b)(a + b)}{2a - b} - \dfrac{5}{a} = \dfrac{3(a - b)}{2a - b} - \dfrac{5}{a} = \dfrac{3a(a - b) - 5(2a - b)}{a(2a - b)} = \dfrac{3a^2 - 3ab - 10a + 5b}{a(2a - b)}$ [P.5]

20. $x - \dfrac{x}{x + \dfrac{1}{2}} = x - \dfrac{x}{\dfrac{2x}{2} + \dfrac{1}{2}} = x - \dfrac{x}{\dfrac{2x + 1}{2}} = x - x \div \dfrac{2x + 1}{2} = x - x \cdot \dfrac{2}{2x + 1} = x - \dfrac{2x}{2x + 1}$

$= \dfrac{x(2x + 1)}{2x + 1} - \dfrac{2x}{2x + 1} = \dfrac{2x^2 + x}{2x + 1} - \dfrac{2x}{2x + 1} = \dfrac{2x^2 + x - 2x}{2x + 1} = \dfrac{2x^2 - x}{2x + 1} = \dfrac{x(2x - 1)}{2x + 1}$ [P.5]

21. $7 + \sqrt{-20} = 7 + 2i\sqrt{5}$ [P.6]

22. $(4-3i)-(2-5i)=4-3i-2+5i$ [P.6]   **23.** $(2+5i)(1-4i)=2(1-4i)+5i(1-4i)$ [P.6]

$\qquad\qquad\qquad\quad = (4-2)+(-3i+5i)$ $\qquad\qquad\qquad\qquad\quad = 2-8i+5i-20i^2$

$\qquad\qquad\qquad\quad = 2+2i$ $\qquad\qquad\qquad\qquad\quad = 2-8i+5i-20(-1)$

$\qquad\qquad\qquad\qquad\qquad\qquad\qquad\qquad\qquad\qquad\qquad\qquad\quad = 2-8i+5i+20$

$\qquad\qquad\qquad\qquad\qquad\qquad\qquad\qquad\qquad\qquad\qquad\qquad\quad = (2+20)+(-8i+5i)$

$\qquad\qquad\qquad\qquad\qquad\qquad\qquad\qquad\qquad\qquad\qquad\qquad\quad = 22-3i$

24. $\dfrac{3+4i}{5-i}=\dfrac{3+4i}{5-i}\cdot\dfrac{5+i}{5+i}=\dfrac{(3+4i)(5+i)}{(5-i)(5+i)}=\dfrac{3(5+i)+4i(5+i)}{5^2-i^2}=\dfrac{15+3i+20i+4i^2}{25-i^2}=\dfrac{15+3i+20i+4(-1)}{25-(-1)}$ [P.6]

$\qquad = \dfrac{15+3i+20i-4}{25+1}=\dfrac{(15-4)+(3i+20i)}{26}=\dfrac{11+23i}{26}=\dfrac{11}{26}+\dfrac{23}{26}i$

25.   Use the Powers of i Theorem. [P.6]

The remainder of $97\div 4$ is 1.

$i^{97}=i^1=i$

Chapter 1
Equations and Inequalities

Section 1.1

1.
$$2x + 10 = 40$$
$$2x = 40 - 10$$
$$2x = 30$$
$$x = 15$$

3.
$$5x + 2 = 2x - 10$$
$$5x - 2x = -10 - 2$$
$$3x = -12$$
$$x = -4$$

5.
$$2(x - 3) - 5 = 4(x - 5)$$
$$2x - 6 - 5 = 4x - 20$$
$$2x - 11 = 4x - 20$$
$$2x - 4x = -20 + 11$$
$$-2x = -9$$
$$x = \frac{9}{2}$$

7.
$$4(2r - 17) + 5(3r - 8) = 0$$
$$8r - 68 + 15r - 40 = 0$$
$$23r - 108 = 0$$
$$23r = 108$$
$$r = \frac{108}{23}$$

9.
$$\frac{3}{4}x + \frac{1}{2} = \frac{2}{3}$$
$$12 \cdot \left(\frac{3}{4}x + \frac{1}{2} \right) = 12 \cdot \left(\frac{2}{3} \right)$$
$$9x + 6 = 8$$
$$9x = 8 - 6$$
$$9x = 2$$
$$x = \frac{2}{9}$$

11.
$$\frac{2}{3}x - 5 = \frac{1}{2}x - 3$$
$$6 \cdot \left(\frac{2}{3}x - 5 \right) = 6 \cdot \left(\frac{1}{2}x - 3 \right)$$
$$4x - 30 = 3x - 18$$
$$4x - 3x = -18 + 30$$
$$x = 12$$

13.
$$0.2x + 0.4 = 3.6$$
$$0.2x = 3.6 - 0.4$$
$$0.2x = 3.2$$
$$x = 16$$

15.
$$x + 0.08(60) = 0.20(60 + x)$$
$$x + 4.8 = 12 + 0.20x$$
$$x - 0.20x = 12 - 4.8$$
$$0.80x = 7.2$$
$$x = 9$$

17.
$$3(x + 5)(x - 1) = (3x + 4)(x - 2)$$
$$3\left(x^2 + 4x - 5 \right) = 3x^2 - 2x - 8$$
$$3x^2 + 12x - 15 = 3x^2 - 2x - 8$$
$$12x + 2x = -8 + 15$$
$$14x = 7$$
$$x = \frac{1}{2}$$

19.
$$5[x - (4x - 5)] = 3 - 2x$$
$$5(x - 4x + 5) = 3 - 2x$$
$$5(-3x + 5) = 3 - 2x$$
$$-15x + 25 = 3 - 2x$$
$$-15x + 2x = 3 - 25$$
$$-13x = -22$$
$$x = \frac{22}{13}$$

21.
$$\frac{40 - 3x}{5} = \frac{6x + 7}{8}$$
$$40 \cdot \left(\frac{40 - 3x}{5} \right) = 40 \cdot \left(\frac{6x + 7}{8} \right)$$
$$8(40 - 3x) = 5(6x + 7)$$
$$320 - 24x = 30x + 35$$
$$-24x - 30x = 35 - 320$$
$$-54x = -285$$
$$x = \frac{95}{18}$$

23.
$$-3(x - 5) = -3x + 15$$
$$-3x + 15 = -3x + 15$$
Identity

25.
$$2x + 7 = 3(x - 1)$$
$$2x + 7 = 3x - 3$$
$$2x - 3x = -3 - 7$$
$$-x = -10$$
$$x = 10$$
Conditional equation

27.
$$\frac{4x + 8}{4} = x + 8$$
$$4x + 8 = 4(x + 8)$$
$$4x + 8 = 4x + 32$$
$$8 = 32$$
Contradiction

29.
$$3[x - 2(x - 5)] - 1 = -3x + 29$$
$$3[x - 2x + 10] - 1 = -3x + 29$$
$$3[-x + 10] - 1 = -3x + 29$$
$$-3x + 30 - 1 = -3x + 29$$
$$-3x + 29 = -3x + 29$$
Identity

31.
$$2x - 8 = -x + 9$$
$$3x = 17$$
$$x = \frac{17}{3}$$
Conditional equation

33.
$$|x| = 4$$
$$x = 4 \quad \text{or} \quad x = -4$$

35.
$$|x - 5| = 2$$
$$x - 5 = 2 \quad \text{or} \quad x - 5 = -2$$
$$x = 7 \qquad\qquad x = 3$$

37. $|2x-5|=11$

$2x-5=11$ or $2x-5=-11$

$2x=16$ $\quad$ $2x=-6$

$x=8$ $\quad$ $x=-3$

39. $|2x+6|=10$

$2x+6=10$ or $2x+6=-10$

$2x=4$ $\quad$ $2x=-16$

$x=2$ $\quad$ $x=-8$

41. $\left|\dfrac{x-4}{2}\right|=8$

$\dfrac{x-4}{2}=8$ or $\dfrac{x-4}{2}=-8$

$x-4=8(2)$ $\quad$ $x-4=-8(2)$

$x-4=16$ $\quad$ $x-4=-16$

$x=20$ $\quad$ $x=-12$

43. $|2x+5|=-8$

$|2x+5|\ge 0$

$-8\ge 0$

Contradiction. There is no solution.

45. $2|x+3|+4=34$

$2|x+3|=30$

$|x+3|=15$

$x+3=15$ or $x+3=-15$

$x=12$ $\quad$ $x=-18$

47. $|2x-a|=b,\;\; b>0$

$2x-a=b$ or $2x-a=-b$

$2x=a+b$ $\quad$ $2x=a-b$

$x=\dfrac{a+b}{2}$ $\quad$ $x=\dfrac{a-b}{2}$

49. $0.35x+5.7=\text{Revenue}$

$0.35x+5.7=12$

$0.35x=6.3$

$x=\dfrac{6.3}{0.35}=18$

$1990+18=2008$

The revenue first exceeded \$12 billion in 2008.

51. $d=|210-50t|$

$60=210-50t$ or $-60=210-50t$

$-150=-50t$ $\quad$ $-270=-50t$

$t=3$ $\quad$ $t=5.4$

5.4 hours = 5 hours 24 minutes

Ruben will be exactly 60 miles from Barstow after 3 hours and after 5 hours and 24 minutes.

53. $45x+550=\text{Cost}$

$45x+550=3800$

$45x=3250$

$x\approx 72$

Rounded to the nearest yard, 72 sq yards can be carpeted for \$3800.

55. $100-\dfrac{42,000}{500,000}t=\text{Percent remaining}$

$100-\dfrac{42,000}{500,000}t=25$

$100-\dfrac{21}{250}t=25$

$-\dfrac{21}{250}t=-75$

$t\approx 892.857142857\text{ seconds}$

$892.857142857\text{ sec}\cdot\left(\dfrac{1\text{ min}}{60\text{ sec}}\right)\approx 15\text{ min}$

57. $\max=0.85(220-a)$ $\quad$ $\min=0.65(220-a)$

$=0.85(220-25)$ $\quad$ $=0.65(220-25)$

$=0.85(195)$ $\quad$ $=0.65(195)$

$=165.75$ $\quad$ $=126.75$

The maximum exercise heart rate for a person who is 25 years of age is 166 beats per minute (to the nearest beat).

The minimum exercise heart rate for a person who is 25 years of age is 127 beats per minute (to the nearest beat).

59. $ax + b = c$

$ax = c - b$

$x = \dfrac{c - b}{a}, \ a \neq 0$

61. $|x + 4| = x + 4$

if $x + 4 \geq 0$ if $x + 4 < 0$

     $x \geq -4$ $x < -4$

  $x + 4 = x + 4$ $x + 4 = -(x + 4)$

an identity $x + 4 = -x - 4$

                           $2x = -8$

                            $x = -4$

The case $x + 4 < 0$ has no solution since there is no real number x such that $x < -4$ and $x = -4$.

$\{x \mid x \geq -4\}$

63. $|x + 7| = -(x + 7)$

if $x + 7 \geq 0$ if $x + 7 < 0$

     $x \geq -7$ $x < -7$

  $x + 7 = -(x + 7)$ $x + 7 = x + 7$

  $x + 7 = -x - 7$ an identity

       $2x = -14$

        $x = -7$

$\{x \mid x \leq -7\}$

65. $|2x + 7| = 2x + 7$

if $2x + 7 \geq 0$ if $2x + 7 < 0$

     $x \geq -\dfrac{7}{2}$ $x < -\dfrac{7}{2}$

$2x + 7 = 2x + 7$ $2x + 7 = -(2x + 7)$

an identity $2x + 7 = -2x - 7$

                        $4x = -14$

                        $x = -\dfrac{7}{2}$

The case $2x + 7 < 0$ has no solution since there is no real number x such that $x < -\dfrac{7}{2}$ and $x = -\dfrac{7}{2}$.

$\left\{x \mid x \geq -\dfrac{7}{2}\right\}$

Prepare for Section 1.2

67. $32 - x$

$32 - 8\dfrac{1}{2} = 23\dfrac{1}{2}$

68. $\dfrac{1}{2} bh$

$\dfrac{1}{2} \cdot \dfrac{2}{3} \cdot \dfrac{4}{5} = \dfrac{4}{15}$

69. $2l + 2w = 2(l + w)$

The distributive property

70. $\left(\dfrac{1}{2} b\right) h = \dfrac{1}{2} bh$

The associative property of multiplication

71. $\dfrac{2}{5}x + \dfrac{1}{3}x = \dfrac{6}{15}x + \dfrac{5}{15}x = \dfrac{11}{15}x$

72. $\dfrac{1}{\dfrac{1}{a} + \dfrac{1}{b}} = \dfrac{1}{\dfrac{1}{a} \cdot \dfrac{b}{b} + \dfrac{1}{b} \cdot \dfrac{a}{a}} = \dfrac{1}{\dfrac{b}{ab} + \dfrac{a}{ab}} = \dfrac{1}{\dfrac{b + a}{ab}} = \dfrac{ab}{a + b}$

Section 1.2

1.
$$V = \frac{1}{3}\pi r^2 h$$
$$3V = \pi r^2 h$$
$$\frac{3V}{\pi r^2} = h$$

3.
$$I = \Pr t$$
$$\frac{I}{\Pr} = t$$

5.
$$F = \frac{Gm_1 m_2}{d^2}$$
$$Fd^2 = Gm_1 m_2$$
$$\frac{Fd^2}{Gm_2} = m_1$$

7.
$$a_n = a_1 + (n-1)d$$
$$a_n - a_1 = (n-1)d$$
$$\frac{a_n - a_1}{n-1} = d$$

9.
$$S = \frac{a_1}{1-r}$$
$$S(1-r) = a_1$$
$$S - Sr = a_1$$
$$S - a_1 = Sr$$
$$\frac{S - a_1}{S} = r$$

11.
$$\text{qb rating} = \frac{100}{6}[0.05(66.33-30)+0.25(7.11-3)+0.2(4.57)+(2.375-0.25(3.21))]$$
$$= 88.8$$

13.
$$\text{SMOG} = \sqrt{42} + 3$$
$$= 9.5$$

15.
$$\text{GFI} = 0.4(23.0+5)$$
$$= 11.2$$

17. Let x = the number
$$\frac{1}{5}x + \frac{1}{4}x = \frac{1}{2}x - 5$$
$$20\left(\frac{1}{5}x + \frac{1}{4}x\right) = 20\left(\frac{1}{2}x - 5\right)$$
$$4x + 5x = 10x - 100$$
$$9x = 10x - 100$$
$$100 = x$$

19.
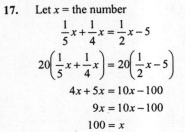

$$P = 2L + 2W$$
$$174 = 2(2W - 3) + 2W$$
$$174 = 4W - 6 + 2W$$
$$180 = 6W$$
$$W = 30 \text{ ft}$$
$$L = 2W - 3 = 2(30) - 3 = 60 - 3 = 57 \text{ ft}$$

21.

$$3x + 3x + x = 84$$
$$7x = 84$$
$$x = 12$$
$$3x = 3(12) = 36$$

The shortest side is 12 cm. The longer sides are each 36 cm.

23.

$$d = 6t \longrightarrow$$

$$\longleftarrow d = 2(160 - t)$$

Let t = the time to run to the end of the track.
Let $160 - t$ = the time in seconds to jog back.

$$6t = 2(160 - t)$$
$$6t = 320 - 2t$$
$$8t = 320$$
$$t = 40$$
$$d = 6(40) = 240 \text{ meters}$$

27. Let $x + y + z$ = the distance to Jon's house, where x = the distance uphill, y = the distance down hill, and z = the distance on level ground. Note that x, the distance uphill on the way to Jon's house equals the distance down hill on the way home, and that z, the distance down hill on the way to Jon's house equals the distance uphill on the way home. Also note that y is the distance on level ground on the way to Jon's house and on the way home.

$$rt = d \Rightarrow t = \frac{d}{r}$$

		rate	time	distance
To Jon's house	Up	4	$\frac{x}{4}$	x
	Level	6	$\frac{y}{6}$	y
	Down	12	$\frac{z}{12}$	z
Back home	Up	12	$\frac{x}{12}$	x
	Level	6	$\frac{y}{6}$	y
	Down	4	$\frac{z}{4}$	z

$$\frac{x}{4} + \frac{y}{6} + \frac{z}{12} + \frac{x}{12} + \frac{y}{6} + \frac{z}{4} = 1$$

$$12\left(\frac{x}{4} + \frac{y}{6} + \frac{z}{12} + \frac{x}{12} + \frac{y}{6} + \frac{z}{4}\right) = 12(1)$$

$$3x + 2y + z + x + 2y + 3z = 12$$
$$4x + 4y + 4z = 12$$
$$4(x + y + z) = 12$$
$$x + y + z = 3$$

The distance to Jon's house is 3 miles.

25.

$$d = 240(t + 3) \longrightarrow$$

$$\longleftarrow d = 600t$$

Let t = the time (in hours) of the second plane.

Let $t + 3$ = the time (in hours) of the first plane.

$$d = 240(t + 3)$$
$$d = 600t$$

$$240(t + 3) = 600t$$
$$240t + 720 = 600t$$
$$720 = 360t$$
$$2 = t$$
$$t = 2 \text{ hours}$$

29. Let x = the score on the next test.

$$\frac{80 + 82 + 94 + 71 + x}{5} = 85$$

$$\frac{327 + x}{5} = 85$$

$$327 + x = 425$$

$$x = 98$$

A score of 98 will produce an average of 85.

31. Let x = the number of sunglasses.
Profit = Revenue − Cost
$17,884 = 29.99x - 8.95x$
$17,884 = 21.04x$
$x = 850$

The manufacturer must sell 850 sunglasses to make a profit of $17,884.

33. Let x = cost last year.
$x - 0.20x = 750$
$0.80x = 750$
$x = 937.50$
The cost of a computer last year was $937.50.

35. Let x = amount invested at 8%.
$(14,000 - x)$ = amount invested at 6.5%.
$0.08x + 0.065(14,000 - x) = 1024$
$0.08x + 910 - 0.065x = 1024$
$0.015x = 114$
$x = 7600$
$14,000 - x = 6400$

$7600 was invested at 8%.
$6400 was invested at 6.5%.

37

5.5%	2500
8%	x
7%	$2500 + x$

$0.055(2500) + 0.08x = 0.07(2500 + x)$
$137.5 + 0.08x = 175 + 0.07x$
$0.01x = 37.5$
$x = 3700$

$3750 additional investment.

39.

1.00	x
0.45	$200 - x$
0.50	200

$x + 0.45(200 - x) = 0.50(200)$
$x + 90 - 0.45x = 100$
$0.55x = 10$
$x = 18\dfrac{2}{11}$ g pure silver

41.

0	x
0.12	160
0.20	$160 - x$

$0.12(160) - 0 = 0.20(160 - x)$
$19.2 = 32 - 0.20x$
$0.20x = 12.8$
$x = 64$

64 liters of water

43.

14	x
25	$3000 - x$

$14x + 25(3000 - x) = 61,800$
$14x + 75,000 - 25x = 61,800$
$-11x = -13,200$
$x = 1200$
$3000 - x = 1800$

1200 tickets at $14 each
1800 tickets at $25 each

45.

$12	x
$9	$20 - x$
$10	20

$12x + 9(20 - x) = 10(20)$
$12x + 180 - 9x = 200$
$3x = 20$
$x = 6\dfrac{2}{3}$

$6\dfrac{2}{3}$ lb of $12 coffee

$20 - 6\dfrac{2}{3} = 13\dfrac{1}{3}$ lb of $9 coffee

47.

1.00	x
$\dfrac{14}{24}$ or $\dfrac{7}{12}$	15
$\dfrac{18}{24}$ or $\dfrac{3}{4}$	$15 + x$

$$x + \frac{7}{12}(15) = \frac{3}{4}(15 + x)$$

$$12 \cdot \left[x + \frac{7}{12}(15) \right] = 12 \cdot \left[\frac{3}{4}(15 + x) \right]$$

$$12x + 7(15) = 9(15 + x)$$

$$12x + 105 = 135 + 9x$$

$$3x = 30$$

$$x = 10$$

10 g of pure gold

51. Let x = price of book
$10.10 - x$ = price of bookmark.

$$x = 10 + (10.10 - x)$$

$$2x = 20.10$$

$$x = 10.05$$

$$10.10 - 10.05 = 0.05$$

The price of the book is \$10.05.
The price of the bookmark is \$0.05.

49. Let t = the time it takes both electricians working together to wire the house.

The first electrician does $\dfrac{1}{14}$ of the job every hour.

The second electrician does $\dfrac{1}{18}$ of the job every hour.

$$\frac{1}{14}t + \frac{1}{18}t = 1$$

$$126\left[\frac{1}{14}t + \frac{1}{18}t \right] = 126 \cdot 1$$

$$9t + 7t = 126$$

$$16t = 126$$

$$t = 7.875 \text{ hours}$$

Connecting Concepts

53.

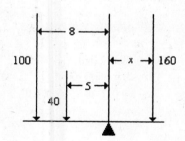

$$8(100) + 40(5) = 160x$$

$$800 + 200 = 160x$$

$$1000 = 160x$$

$$6.25 = x$$

6.25 ft

55.

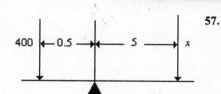

$$400(0.5) = 5x$$

$$200 = 5x$$

$$40 = x$$

A 40-lb force is needed to lift 400 lbs.

57.

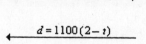

$$1865t = 1100(2 - t)$$

$$1865t = 2200 - 1100t$$

$$2965t = 2200$$

$$t \approx 0.741989$$

$$d = 1865t$$

$$d \approx 1383.81$$

The distance to the target is 1384 feet (to the nearest foot).

59.

$$\frac{1}{6}x + \frac{1}{12}x + \frac{1}{7}x + 5 + \frac{1}{2}x + 4 = x$$

$$84\left[\frac{1}{6}x + \frac{1}{12}x + \frac{1}{7}x + 5 + \frac{1}{2}x + 4\right] = 84x$$

$$14x + 7x + 12x + 420 + 42x + 336 = 84x$$

$$75x + 756 = 84x$$

$$756 = 9x$$

$$84 = x$$

Diophantus was 84 years old when he died.

●●●●●●●●●●●●●●●●●●●●●●●●●●●●●●●●●●●

61. $x^2 - x - 42 = (x+6)(x-7)$

62. $6x^2 - x - 15 = (2x+3)(3x-5)$

63. $3 + \sqrt{-16} = 3 + 4i$

64. $\dfrac{-(-2) - \sqrt{(-2)^2 - 4(-3)(5)}}{2(-3)} = \dfrac{2 - \sqrt{64}}{-6} = 1$

65. $\dfrac{-(-3) + \sqrt{(-3)^2 - 4(2)(1)}}{2(2)} = \dfrac{3 + \sqrt{1}}{4} = 1$

66. $(3-i)^2 - 6(3-i) + 10 = 9 - 6i + i^2 - 18 + 6i + 10$
$$= 0$$

Section 1.3

1.
$$x^2 - 2x - 15 = 0$$
$$(x+3)(x-5) = 0$$
$$x+3 = 0 \quad \text{or} \quad x-5 = 0$$
$$x = -3 \qquad\qquad x = 5$$

3.
$$2x^2 - x = 1$$
$$2x^2 - x - 1 = 0$$
$$(2x+1)(x-1) = 0$$
$$2x+1 = 0 \quad \text{or} \quad x-1 = 0$$
$$2x = -1 \qquad\qquad x = 1$$
$$x = -\frac{1}{2}$$

5.
$$8x^2 + 189x - 72 = 0$$
$$(8x-3)(x+24) = 0$$
$$8x-3 = 0 \quad \text{or} \quad x+2 = 0$$
$$8x = 3 \qquad\qquad x = -24$$
$$x = \frac{3}{8}$$

7.
$$3x^2 - 7x = 0$$
$$x(3x-7) = 0$$
$$x = 0 \quad \text{or} \quad 3x-7 = 0$$
$$3x = 7$$
$$x = \frac{7}{3}$$

9.
$$(x-5)^2 - 9 = 0$$
$$[(x-5)-3][(x-5)+3] = 0$$
$$(x-8)(x-2) = 0$$
$$x-8 = 0 \quad \text{or} \quad x-2 = 0$$
$$x = 8 \qquad\qquad x = 2$$

11.
$$x^2 = 81$$
$$x = \pm\sqrt{81}$$
$$x = \pm 9$$

13.
$$2x^2 = 48$$
$$x^2 = 24$$
$$x = \pm\sqrt{24}$$
$$x = \pm 2\sqrt{6}$$

15.
$$3x^2 + 12 = 0$$
$$3x^2 = -12$$
$$x^2 = -4$$
$$x = \pm\sqrt{-4}$$
$$x = \pm 2i$$

17.
$$(x-5)^2 = 36$$
$$x - 5 = \pm\sqrt{36}$$
$$x - 5 = \pm 6$$
$$x = 5 \pm 6$$
$$x = 5 + 6 \quad \text{or} \quad x = 5 - 6$$
$$x = 11 \qquad\qquad x = -1$$

19.
$$(x-3)^2 + 16 = 0$$
$$(x-3)^2 = -16$$
$$x - 3 = \pm\sqrt{-16}$$
$$x - 3 = \pm 4i$$
$$x = 3 \pm 4i$$

21.
$$x^2 + 6x + 1 = 0$$
$$x^2 + 6x + 9 = -1 + 9$$
$$(x+3)^2 = 8$$
$$x + 3 = \pm\sqrt{8}$$
$$x = -3 \pm 2\sqrt{2}$$
$$x = -3 + 2\sqrt{2} \quad \text{or} \quad x = -3 - 2\sqrt{2}$$

23.
$$x^2 - 2x - 15 = 0$$
$$x^2 - 2x + 1 = 15 + 1$$
$$(x-1)^2 = 16$$
$$x - 1 = \pm\sqrt{16}$$
$$x = 1 \pm 4$$
$$x = 1 + 4 \quad \text{or} \quad x = 1 - 4$$
$$x = 5 \qquad\qquad x = -3$$

25.
$$x^2 + 4x + 5 = 0$$
$$x^2 + 4x + 4 = -5 + 4$$
$$(x+2)^2 = -1$$
$$x + 2 = \pm\sqrt{-1}$$
$$x + 2 = \pm i$$
$$x = -2 \pm i$$
$$x = -2 - i \quad \text{or} \quad x = -2 + i$$

27.
$$x^2 + 3x - 1 = 0$$
$$x^2 + 3x + \frac{9}{4} = 1 + \frac{9}{4}$$
$$\left(x + \frac{3}{2}\right)^2 = \frac{13}{4}$$
$$x + \frac{3}{2} = \pm\sqrt{\frac{13}{4}}$$
$$x = -\frac{3}{2} \pm \frac{\sqrt{13}}{2}$$
$$x = \frac{-3 + \sqrt{13}}{2}, \quad \text{or} \quad x = \frac{-3 - \sqrt{13}}{2}$$

29.
$$2x^2 + 4x - 1 = 0$$
$$2x^2 + 4x = 1$$
$$x^2 + 2x = \frac{1}{2}$$
$$x^2 + 2x + 1 = \frac{1}{2} + 1$$
$$(x+1)^2 = \frac{3}{2}$$
$$x + 1 = \pm\sqrt{\frac{3}{2}}$$
$$x = -1 \pm \sqrt{\frac{3}{2}} = -1 \pm \sqrt{\frac{3}{2} \cdot \frac{2}{2}}$$
$$x = -1 \pm \frac{\sqrt{6}}{\sqrt{4}} = -1 \pm \frac{\sqrt{6}}{2} = -\frac{2}{2} \pm \frac{\sqrt{6}}{2}$$
$$x = \frac{-2 + \sqrt{6}}{2}, \quad \text{or} \quad x = \frac{-2 - \sqrt{6}}{2}$$

31.
$$3x^2 - 8x + 1 = 0$$
$$3x^2 - 8x = -1$$
$$x^2 - \frac{8}{3}x = -\frac{1}{3}$$
$$x^2 - \frac{8}{3}x + \frac{16}{9} = -\frac{1}{3} + \frac{16}{9}$$
$$\left(x - \frac{4}{3}\right)^2 = \frac{13}{9}$$
$$x - \frac{4}{3} = \pm\sqrt{\frac{13}{9}}$$
$$x = \frac{4}{3} = \pm\frac{\sqrt{13}}{3}$$
$$x = \frac{4 + \sqrt{13}}{3} \quad \text{or} \quad x = \frac{4 - \sqrt{13}}{3}$$

33. $x^2 - 2x - 15 = 0$, $a = 1$, $b = -2$, $c = -15$

$$x = \frac{-b \pm \sqrt{b^2 - 4ac}}{2a}$$

$$x = \frac{-(-2) \pm \sqrt{(-2)^2 - 4(1)(-15)}}{2(1)}$$

$$x = \frac{2 \pm \sqrt{4 + 60}}{2} = \frac{2 \pm \sqrt{64}}{2} = \frac{2 \pm 8}{2}$$

$$x = \frac{2 + 8}{2} = \frac{10}{2} = 5 \quad \text{or} \quad x = \frac{2 - 8}{2} = \frac{-6}{2} = -3$$

$x = 5$ or $x = -3$

35. $x^2 + x - 1 = 0$

$$x = \frac{-1 \pm \sqrt{1^2 - 4(1)(-1)}}{2(1)}$$

$$x = \frac{-1 \pm \sqrt{1 + 4}}{2} = \frac{-1 \pm \sqrt{5}}{2}$$

$$x = \frac{-1 + \sqrt{5}}{2} \quad \text{or} \quad x = \frac{-1 - \sqrt{5}}{2}$$

37. $2x^2 + 4x + 1 = 0$

$$x = \frac{-4 \pm \sqrt{4^2 - 4(2)(1)}}{2(2)}$$

$$x = \frac{-4 \pm \sqrt{16 - 8}}{4} = \frac{-4 \pm \sqrt{8}}{4}$$

$$x = \frac{-4 \pm 2\sqrt{2}}{4} = \frac{-2 \pm \sqrt{2}}{2}$$

$$x = \frac{-2 + \sqrt{2}}{2}, \quad \text{or} \quad x = \frac{-2 - \sqrt{2}}{2}$$

39. $3x^2 - 5x + 3 = 0$

$$x = \frac{-(-5) \pm \sqrt{(-5)^2 - 4(3)(3)}}{2(3)}$$

$$x = \frac{5 \pm \sqrt{25 - 36}}{6} = \frac{5 \pm \sqrt{-11}}{6}$$

$$x = \frac{5 \pm i\sqrt{11}}{6}$$

$$x = \frac{5}{6} + \frac{\sqrt{11}}{6}i, \quad \text{or} \quad x = \frac{5}{6} - \frac{\sqrt{11}}{6}i$$

41. $\frac{1}{2}x^2 + \frac{3}{4}x - 1 = 0$

$$4\left(\frac{1}{2}x^2 + \frac{3}{4}x - 1\right) = 4(0)$$

$$2x^2 + 3x - 4 = 0$$

$$x = \frac{-3 \pm \sqrt{3^2 - 4(2)(-4)}}{2(2)}$$

$$x = \frac{-3 \pm \sqrt{9 + 32}}{4}$$

$$x = \frac{-3 \pm \sqrt{41}}{4}$$

$$x = \frac{-3 + \sqrt{41}}{4}, \quad \text{or} \quad x = \frac{-3 - \sqrt{41}}{4}$$

43. $24x^2 - 22x - 35 = 0$

$$x = \frac{-(-22) \pm \sqrt{(-22)^2 - 4(24)(-35)}}{2(24)}$$

$$x = \frac{22 \pm \sqrt{484 + 3360}}{48}$$

$$x = \frac{22 \pm \sqrt{3844}}{48}$$

$$= \frac{22 \pm 62}{48}$$

$$x = -\frac{5}{6}, \quad \text{or} \quad x = \frac{7}{4}$$

45. $0.5x^2 + 0.6x - 0.8 = 0$

$$x = \frac{-0.6 \pm \sqrt{(0.6)^2 - 4(0.5)(-0.8)}}{2(0.5)}$$

$$x = \frac{-0.6 \pm \sqrt{0.36 + 0.6}}{1}$$

$$x = -0.6 \pm \sqrt{1.96}$$

$$= -0.6 \pm 1.4$$

$$x = -2, \quad \text{or} \quad x = \frac{4}{5}$$

47.
$$2x^2 - 5x - 7 = 0$$
$$b^2 - 4ac = (-5)^2 - 4(2)(-7)$$
$$= 25 + 56 = 81$$
Two distinct real numbers

49.
$$3x^2 - 2x + 10 = 0$$
$$b^2 - 4ac = (-2)^2 - 4(3)(10)$$
$$= 4 - 120 = -116$$
Two distinct nonreal complex numbers

51.
$$x^2 - 20x + 100 = 0$$
$$b^2 - 4ac = (-20)^2 - 4(1)(100)$$
$$= 400 - 400 = 0$$
One real number

53.
$$24x^2 + 10x - 21 = 0$$
$$b^2 - 4ac = (10)^2 - 4(24)(-21)$$
$$= 100 + 2016 = 2116$$
Two distinct real numbers

55.
$$12x^2 + 15x + 7 = 0$$
$$b^2 - 4ac = (15)^2 - 4(12)(7)$$
$$= 225 - 336 = -111$$
Two distinct nonreal complex numbers

57.

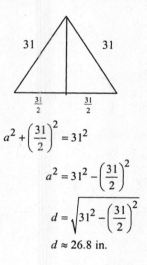

$$a^2 + \left(\frac{31}{2}\right)^2 = 31^2$$
$$a^2 = 31^2 - \left(\frac{31}{2}\right)^2$$
$$d = \sqrt{31^2 - \left(\frac{31}{2}\right)^2}$$
$$d \approx 26.8 \text{ in.}$$

59.
$$\frac{a}{b} = \frac{4}{3}$$
$$a = \frac{4b}{3}$$
$$a^2 + b^2 = c^2$$
$$\left(\frac{4b}{3}\right)^2 + b^2 = 54^2$$
$$\frac{16b^2}{9} + b^2 = 2916$$
$$\frac{25b^2}{9} = 2916$$
$$b^2 = 1049.76$$
$$b = 32.4$$
$$a = \frac{4(32.4)}{3} = 43.2$$
The TV is 32.4 in. high and 43.2 in. wide.

61.
$$19,000 = 38t^2 + 291t + 15,208$$
$$0 = 38t^2 + 291t - 3792$$
$$a = 38, \ b = 291, \ c = -3292$$
$$t = \frac{-291 \pm \sqrt{291^2 - 4(38)(-3292)}}{2(38)}$$
$$= \frac{-291 \pm \sqrt{585065}}{76} \approx \frac{-291 \pm 764.8954}{76}$$
$$t \approx 6.23 \text{ or } t \approx -13.89 \text{ (not } 0 \leq t \leq 14)$$
6.23 years after 1990 is 1996.

63.
$$518,000 = -0.01x^2 + 168x - 120,000$$
$$0 = -0.01x^2 + 168x - 638,000$$
$$a = -0.01, \ b = 168, \ c = -638,000$$
$$x = \frac{-168 \pm \sqrt{168^2 - 4(-0.01)(-638,000)}}{2(-0.01)}$$
$$= \frac{-168 \pm \sqrt{2704}}{-0.02} = \frac{-168 \pm 52}{-0.02}$$
$$x = \frac{-168 + 52}{-0.02} \qquad \text{or} \qquad x = \frac{-168 - 52}{-0.02}$$
$$= \frac{-116}{-0.02} = 5800 \qquad\qquad = \frac{-220}{-0.02} = 11000$$
5,800 or 11,000 racquets must be sold.

65. Let w = width of region

Then $\dfrac{132 - 3w}{2}$ = length.

$$\text{Area} = \text{length(width)}$$
$$576 = \dfrac{132 - 3w}{2} \cdot w$$
$$1152 = 132w - 3w^2$$
$$3w^2 - 132w + 1152 = 0$$
$$3(w^2 - 44w + 384) = 0$$
$$w^2 - 44w + 384 = 0$$
$$(w - 32)(w - 12) = 0$$

$w - 32 = 0$ or $w - 12 = 0$

$w = 32$ $w = 12$

$\dfrac{132 - 3w}{2} = \dfrac{132 - 3(32)}{2}$ $\dfrac{132 - 3w}{2} = \dfrac{132 - 3(12)}{2}$

$= 18$ $= 48$

The region is either 32 feet wide and 18 feet long, or 12 feet wide and 48 feet long.

67. Solve $D = -45x^2 + 190x + 200$ for x with $D = 250$.

$$250 = -45x^2 + 190x + 200$$
$$0 = -45x^2 + 190x - 50$$
$$a = -45, \; b = 190, \; c = -50$$
$$x = \dfrac{-190 \pm \sqrt{190^2 - 4(-45)(-50)}}{2(-45)}$$
$$= \dfrac{-190 \pm \sqrt{27100}}{-90} \approx \dfrac{-190 \pm 164.2}{-90}$$

$x \approx \dfrac{-190 + 164.2}{-90}$ or $x \approx \dfrac{-190 - 164.2}{-90}$

$\approx \dfrac{-25.8}{-90}$ $\approx \dfrac{-354.2}{-90}$

≈ 0.3 mile ≈ 3.9 miles

69. Solve $h = -16t^2 + 25.3t + 20$ for t where $h = 17$.

$$17 = -16t^2 + 25.3t + 20$$
$$0 = -16t^2 + 25.3t + 3$$
$$t = \dfrac{-25.3 \pm \sqrt{(25.3)^2 - 4(-16)(3)}}{2(-16)}$$
$$= \dfrac{-25.3 \pm \sqrt{832.09}}{-32}$$

$t = 1.7$ or $t = -0.11$

He was in the air for 1.7 s.

71. Solve $h = -16t^2 + 220t$ for t where $h = 350$.

$$350 = -16t^2 + 220t$$
$$0 = -16t^2 + 220t - 350$$
$$a = -16, \; b = 220, \; c = -350$$
$$t = \dfrac{-220 \pm \sqrt{220^2 - 4(-16)(-350)}}{2(-16)}$$
$$= \dfrac{-220 \pm \sqrt{26000}}{-32} \approx \dfrac{-220 \pm 161.245}{-32}$$

$t \approx \dfrac{-220 + 161.245}{-32}$ or $t \approx \dfrac{-220 - 161.245}{-32}$

$\approx \dfrac{-58.755}{-32}$ $\approx \dfrac{-381.245}{-32}$

≈ 1.8 seconds ≈ 11.9 seconds

73. Solve $s = 103.9t$ for t where $s = 360$ to find the time it takes the ball to reach the fence.

$$360 = 103.9t$$
$$t \approx 3.465 \text{ seconds}$$

Next, evaluate $h = -16t^2 + 50t + 4.5$ where $t = 3.465$ to determine if the ball is at least 10 feet in the air when it reaches the fence.

$$h = -16(3.465)^2 + 50(3.465) + 4.5$$
$$h \approx -14.3$$

No, the ball will not clear the fence.

75. Solve $h = \frac{1}{2}n(n-1)$ for n where $h = 36$.

$$36 = \tfrac{1}{2}n(n-1)$$
$$72 = n(n-1) = n^2 - n$$
$$0 = n^2 - n - 72 = (n-9)(n+8)$$

$n - 9 = 0$ or $n + 8 = 0$

$n = 9$ people $n = -8$ (no)

77. Solve $P = -0.0016t^2 + 0.225t + 6.201$ for t where $P = 11$.

$$11 = -0.0016t^2 + 0.225t + 6.201$$

$$0 = -0.0016t^2 + 0.225t - 4.799$$

$$a = -0.0016, \ b = 0.225, \ c = -4.799$$

$$t = \frac{-0.225 \pm \sqrt{(0.225)^2 - 4(-0.0016)(-4.799)}}{2(-0.0016)}$$

$$= \frac{-0.225 \pm \sqrt{0.0199114}}{-0.0032} \approx \frac{-0.225 \pm 0.14110776}{-0.0032}$$

$$t \approx \frac{-0.225 + 0.14110776}{-0.0032} \quad \text{or} \quad t \approx \frac{-0.225 - 0.14110776}{-0.0032}$$

$$\approx 26.2 \qquad\qquad\qquad \approx 114.4$$

The percent of U.S. citizens that are divorced will first reach 11% 26.2 years from 1980, which is in 2006.

79. a. If $t = 0$ represents the year 1995, then the year 2006 is represented by $t = 11$.

Evaluate $A = 0.05t^2 + 2.25t + 14$ for $t = 11$.

$$A = 0.05(11)^2 + 2.25(11) + 14$$

$$= 0.05(121) + 2.25(11) + 14$$

$$= 6.05 + 24.75 + 14$$

$$= 44.8 \text{ million pounds}$$

b. Solve $A = 0.05t^2 + 2.25t + 14$ for t where $A = 50$.

$$50 = 0.05t^2 + 2.25t + 14$$

$$0 = 0.05t^2 + 2.25t - 36$$

$$a = 0.05, \ b = 2.25, \ c = -36$$

$$t = \frac{-2.25 \pm \sqrt{2.25^2 - 4(0.05)(-36)}}{2(0.05)}$$

$$= \frac{-2.25 \pm \sqrt{5.0625 + 7.2}}{0.1}$$

$$= \frac{-2.25 \pm \sqrt{12.2625}}{0.1} \approx \frac{-2.25 \pm 3.50}{0.1}$$

$$t \approx \frac{-2.25 + 3.50}{0.1} \quad \text{or} \quad t \approx \frac{-2.25 - 3.50}{0.1}$$

$$\approx 12.5 \qquad\qquad\qquad \approx -57.5$$

$$\text{(not } 0 \le t \le 15)$$

12.5 years from 1995 will be in 2007.

Connecting **C**oncepts

81. a.

$$\frac{l}{w} = \frac{l+w}{l}$$

$$l^2 = w(l+w)$$

$$l^2 = lw + w^2$$

$$l^2 - lw - w^2 = 0$$

Use quadratic formula solving for l in terms of w.

$$l = \frac{-(-w) \pm \sqrt{(-w)^2 - 4(1)(-w^2)}}{2(1)}$$

$$= \frac{w \pm \sqrt{5w^2}}{2}$$

$$= \frac{w \pm w\sqrt{5}}{2}$$

$$= \left(\frac{1+\sqrt{5}}{2}\right)w \quad \text{positive solution only}$$

b. $l = \left(\dfrac{1+\sqrt{5}}{2}\right)(101)$

$$= 163.4 \text{ ft}$$

c. Answers will vary.

83. $\dfrac{-5}{2} + 6 = \dfrac{7}{2}; \ -\dfrac{b}{a} = -\dfrac{(-7)}{2} = \dfrac{7}{2}$

$$\left(\frac{-5}{2}\right)(6) = -15; \ \frac{c}{a} = \frac{(-30)}{2} = -15$$

Yes, $\dfrac{-5}{2}$ and 6 are roots of $2x^2 - 7x - 30 = 0$.

85.

$(1+i)+(1-i) = 2; \ -\dfrac{b}{a} = -\dfrac{(-2)}{1} = 2$

$(1+i)(1-i) = 1-i^2 = 1+1 = 2; \ \dfrac{c}{a} = \dfrac{(2)}{1} = 2$

Yes, $1+i$ and $1-i$ are roots of $x^2 - 2x + 2 = 0$.

·······························

87.
$x^3 - 16x$
$x(x^2 - 16)$
$x(x+4)(x-4)$

88.
$x^4 - 36x^2$
$x^2(x^2 - 36)$
$x^2(x+6)(x-6)$

89.
$8^{2/3} = (\sqrt[3]{8})^2$
$\quad = 2^2$
$\quad = 4$

90.
$16^{3/2} = (\sqrt{16})^3$
$\quad = 4^3$
$\quad = 64$

91.
$(1+\sqrt{x-5})^2$
$1^2 + 2\sqrt{x-5} + (\sqrt{x-5})^2$
$1 + 2\sqrt{x-5} + x - 5$
$x + 2\sqrt{x-5} - 4$

92.
$(2-\sqrt{x+3})^2$
$2^2 - 2(2)\sqrt{x+3} + (\sqrt{x+3})^2$
$4 - 4\sqrt{x+3} + x + 3$
$x - 4\sqrt{x+3} + 7$

Section 1.4

1.
$x^3 - 25x = 0$
$x(x^2 - 25) = 0$
$x(x-5)(x+5) = 0$
$x = 0, \ x = 5, \ \text{or} \ x = -5$

3.
$x^3 - 2x^2 - x + 2 = 0$
$x^2(x-2) - (x-2) = 0$
$(x-2)(x^2 - 1) = 0$
$(x-2)(x-1)(x+1) = 0$
$x = 2, \ x = 1, \ \text{or} \ x = -1$

5.
$2x^5 - 18x^3 = 0$
$2x^3(x^2 - 9) = 0$
$2x^3(x-3)(x+3) = 0$
$x = 0, \ x = 3, \ \text{or} \ x = -3$

7.
$x^4 - 3x^3 - 40x^2 = 0$
$x^2(x^2 - 3x - 40) = 0$
$x^2(x+5)(x-8) = 0$
$x = 0, \ x = -5, \ \text{or} \ x = 8$

9.
$x^4 - 16x^2 = 0$
$x^2(x^2 - 16) = 0$
$x^2(x-4)(x+4) = 0$
$x = 0, \ x = 4, \ \text{or} \ x = -4$

11.
$x^3 - 8 = 0$
$(x-2)(x^2 + 2x + 4) = 0$
$x = 2, \ \text{or} \ x^2 + 2x + 4 = 0$

$x = \dfrac{-2 \pm \sqrt{2^2 - 4(1)(4)}}{2}$

$x = \dfrac{-2 \pm \sqrt{-12}}{2} = \dfrac{-2 \pm 2i\sqrt{3}}{2} = -1 \pm i\sqrt{3}$

$x = -1 + i\sqrt{3} \ \text{or} \ x = -1 - i\sqrt{3}$

Thus the solutions are $2, -1 + i\sqrt{3}, \ -1 - i\sqrt{3}$

13.
$\dfrac{3}{x+2} = \dfrac{5}{2x-7}$

$3(2x-7) = 5(x+2)$
$6x - 21 = 5x + 10$
$6x - 5x = 10 + 21$
$x = 31$

15. $\dfrac{30}{10+x} = \dfrac{20}{10-x}$

$$30(10-x) = 20(10+x)$$
$$300 - 30x = 200 + 20x$$
$$-30x - 20x = 200 - 300$$
$$-50x = -100$$
$$x = 2$$

17. $\dfrac{3x}{x+4} = 2 - \dfrac{12}{x+4}$

$$(x+4)\cdot\left(\dfrac{3x}{x+4}\right) = (x+4)\cdot\left(2 - \dfrac{12}{x+4}\right)$$
$$3x = 2(x+4) - 12$$
$$3x = 2x + 8 - 12$$
$$3x = 2x - 4$$
$$3x - 2x = -4$$
$$x = -4$$

No solution because each side is undefined when $x = -4$.

19. $2 + \dfrac{9}{r-3} = \dfrac{3r}{r-3}$

$$(r-3)\cdot\left(2 + \dfrac{9}{r-3}\right) = (r-3)\cdot\left(\dfrac{3r}{r-3}\right)$$
$$2(r-3) + 9 = 3r$$
$$2r - 6 + 9 = 3r$$
$$2r + 3 = 3r$$
$$2r - 3r = -3$$
$$-r = -3$$
$$r = 3$$

No solution because each side is undefined when $r = 3$.

21. $\dfrac{5}{x-3} - \dfrac{3}{x-2} = \dfrac{4}{x-3}$

$$(x-3)(x-2)\cdot\left(\dfrac{5}{x-3} - \dfrac{3}{x-2}\right) = (x-3)(x-2)\cdot\left(\dfrac{4}{x-3}\right)$$
$$5(x-2) - 3(x-3) = 4(x-2)$$
$$5x - 10 - 3x + 9 = 4x - 8$$
$$2x - 1 = 4x - 8$$
$$2x - 4x = -8 + 1$$
$$-2x = -7$$
$$x = \dfrac{7}{2}$$

23. $\dfrac{x}{x-3} = \dfrac{x+4}{x+2}$

$$x(x+2) = (x+4)(x-3)$$
$$x^2 + 2x = x^2 + x - 12$$
$$2x - x = -12$$
$$x = -12$$

25. $\dfrac{x+3}{x+5} = \dfrac{x-3}{x-4}$

$$(x+3)(x-4) = (x-3)(x+5)$$
$$x^2 - x - 12 = x^2 + 2x - 15$$
$$-x - 2x = -15 + 12$$
$$-3x = -3$$
$$x = 1$$

27. $\sqrt{x-4} - 6 = 0$

$$\sqrt{x-4} = 6$$
$$x - 4 = 36$$
$$x = 40$$

Check $\sqrt{40-4} - 6 = 0$

$$\sqrt{36} - 6 = 0$$
$$6 - 6 = 0$$
$$0 = 0$$

The solution is 40.

29. $x = 3 + \sqrt{3-x}$

$$x - 3 = \sqrt{3-x}$$
$$(x-3)^2 = (\sqrt{3-x})^2$$
$$x^2 - 6x + 9 = 3 - x$$
$$x^2 - 5x + 6 = 0$$
$$(x-3)(x-2) = 0$$
$$x = 3 \text{ or } x = 2$$

Check $\quad 3 = 3 + \sqrt{3-3}\qquad 2 = 3 + \sqrt{3-2}$

$\qquad\qquad 3 = 3 + 0 \qquad\qquad\ 2 = 3 + 1$

$\qquad\qquad 3 = 3 \qquad\qquad\qquad 2 = 4 \text{ (No)}$

The solution is 3.

31.

$$\sqrt{3x-5}-\sqrt{x+2}=1$$
$$(\sqrt{3x-5})^2=(1+\sqrt{x+2})^2$$
$$3x-5=1+2\sqrt{x+2}+x+2$$
$$2x-8=2\sqrt{x+2}$$
$$(x-4)^2=(\sqrt{x+2})^2$$
$$x^2-8x+16=x+2$$
$$x^2-9x+14=0$$
$$(x-7)(x-2)=0$$

$$x=7, \text{ or } x=2$$

Check
$$\sqrt{3(7)-5}-\sqrt{7+2}=1$$
$$\sqrt{16}-\sqrt{9}=1$$
$$4-3=1$$
$$1=1$$

$$\sqrt{3(2)-5}-\sqrt{2+2}=1$$
$$\sqrt{1}-\sqrt{4}=1$$
$$1-2=1$$
$$-1=1 \quad (No)$$

The solution is 7.

33.

$$\sqrt{2x+11}-\sqrt{2x-5}=2$$
$$(\sqrt{2x+11})^2=(2+\sqrt{2x-5})^2$$
$$2x+11=4+4\sqrt{2x-5}+2x-5$$
$$12=4\sqrt{2x-5}$$
$$(3)^2=(\sqrt{2x-5})^2$$
$$9=2x-5$$
$$14=2x$$
$$7=x$$

Check $\sqrt{2(7)+11}-\sqrt{2(7)-5}=2$
$$\sqrt{25}-\sqrt{9}=2$$
$$5-3=2$$
$$2=2$$

7 checks as the solution.

35.

$$\sqrt{x+7}+\sqrt{x-5}=6$$
$$(\sqrt{x+7})^2=(6-\sqrt{x-5})^2$$
$$x+7=36-12\sqrt{x-5}+x-5$$
$$12\sqrt{x-5}=24$$
$$(\sqrt{x-5})^2=(2)^2$$
$$x-5=4$$
$$x=9$$

Check $\sqrt{9+7}+\sqrt{9-5}=6$
$$\sqrt{16}+\sqrt{4}=6$$
$$4+2=6$$
$$6=6$$

9 checks as a solution.

37.

$$2x=\sqrt{4x+15}$$
$$(2x)^2=(\sqrt{4x+15})^2$$
$$4x^2=4x+15$$
$$4x^2-4x-15=0$$
$$(2x+3)(2x-5)=0$$
$$x=-\frac{3}{2}, \text{ or } x=\frac{5}{2}$$

Check $2\left[-\frac{3}{2}\right]=\sqrt{4\left[-\frac{3}{2}\right]+15}$ $2\left[\frac{5}{2}\right]=\sqrt{4\left[\frac{5}{2}\right]+15}$
$$-3=\sqrt{-6+15} \qquad 5=\sqrt{10+15}$$
$$-3=\sqrt{9} \qquad\qquad 5=\sqrt{25}$$
$$-3=3 \quad (No) \qquad 5=5$$

The solution is $\frac{5}{2}$.

39.

$$\sqrt[3]{2x^2+5x-3}=\sqrt[3]{x^2+3}$$

$$\left[\sqrt[3]{2x^2+5x-3}\right]^3=\left[\sqrt[3]{x^2+3}\right]^3$$

$$2x^2+5x-3=x^2+3$$

$$x^2+5x-6=0$$

$$(x-1)(x+6)=0$$

$$x=1, \text{ or } x=-6$$

Check $\sqrt[3]{2(1)^2+5-3}=\sqrt[3]{(1)^2+3}$

$$\sqrt[3]{4}=\sqrt[3]{4}$$

$$\sqrt[3]{2(-6)^2+5(-6)-3}=\sqrt[3]{(-6)^2+3}$$

$$\sqrt[3]{39}=\sqrt[3]{39}$$

The solutions are 1 and –6.

41.

$$x^4-9x^2+14=0$$

Let $u=x^2$.

$$u^2-9u+14=0$$

$$(u-7)(u-2)=0$$

$$u=7 \qquad \text{or} \qquad u=2$$

$$x^2=7 \qquad\qquad x^2=2$$

$$x=\pm\sqrt{7} \qquad\qquad x=\pm\sqrt{2}$$

The solutions are $\sqrt{7},\ -\sqrt{7},\ \sqrt{2},\ -\sqrt{2}$.

43.

$$2x^4-11x^2+12=0$$

Let $u=x^2$.

$$2u^2-11u+12=0$$

$$(2u-3)(u-4)=0$$

$$u=\frac{3}{2} \qquad \text{or} \qquad u=4$$

$$x^2=\frac{3}{2} \qquad\qquad x^2=4$$

$$x=\pm\sqrt{\frac{3}{2}}=\pm\frac{\sqrt{6}}{2} \qquad x=\pm2$$

The solutions are $\dfrac{\sqrt{6}}{2},-\dfrac{\sqrt{6}}{2},\ 2,-2$.

45.

$$x^6+x^3-6=0$$

Let $u=x^3$.

$$u^2+u-6=0$$

$$(u-2)(u+3)=0$$

$$u=2 \qquad \text{or} \qquad u=-3$$

$$x^3=2 \qquad\qquad x^3=-3$$

$$x=\sqrt[3]{2} \qquad\qquad x=\sqrt[3]{-3}=-\sqrt[3]{3}$$

The solutions are $\sqrt[3]{2}$ and $-\sqrt[3]{3}$.

47.

$$x^{1/2}-3x^{1/4}+2=0$$

Let $u=x^{1/4}$.

$$u^2-3u+2=0$$

$$(u-1)(u-2)=0$$

$$u=1 \qquad \text{or} \qquad u=2$$

$$x^{1/4}=1 \qquad\qquad x^{1/4}=2$$

$$x=1 \qquad\qquad x=16$$

The solutions are 1 and 16.

49.

$$3x^{2/3}-11x^{1/3}-4=0$$

Let $u=x^{1/3}$.

$$3u^2-11u-4=0$$

$$(3u+1)(u-4)=0$$

$$u=-\frac{1}{3} \qquad \text{or} \qquad u=4$$

$$x^{1/3}=-\frac{1}{3} \qquad\qquad x^{1/3}=4$$

$$x=-\frac{1}{27} \qquad\qquad x=64$$

The solutions are $-\dfrac{1}{27}$ and 64.

51. $9x^4 = 30x^2 - 25$

Let $u = x^2$.

$9u^2 - 30u + 25 = 0$

$(3u - 5)(3u - 5) = 0$

$u = \dfrac{5}{3}$

$x^2 = \dfrac{5}{3}$

$x = \pm\sqrt{\dfrac{5}{3}} = \pm\dfrac{\sqrt{15}}{3}$

The solutions are $\dfrac{\sqrt{15}}{3}$ and $-\dfrac{\sqrt{15}}{3}$.

53. $x^{2/5} - 1 = 0$

$x^{2/5} = 1$

$(x^{2/5})^{5/2} = \pm(1)^{5/2}$

$x = \pm 1$

The solutions are 1 and -1.

55. $9x - 52\sqrt{x} + 64 = 0$

Let $\sqrt{x} = u$.

$9u^2 - 52u + 64 = 0$

$(9u - 16)(u - 4) = 0$

$u = \dfrac{16}{9}$ or $u = 4$

$\sqrt{x} = \dfrac{16}{9}$ $\qquad \sqrt{x} = 4$

$\qquad\qquad\qquad x = 16$

$x = \dfrac{256}{81}$

The solutions are $\dfrac{256}{81}$ and 16.

57. Let x = the number of hours the assistant would take to build the fence working alone.

The worker does $\frac{1}{8}$ of the job per hour; the assistant does $\frac{1}{x}$ of the job per hour.

worker	$\frac{1}{8}$	5
assistant	$\frac{1}{x}$	5

$\left(\dfrac{1}{8}\right)(5) + \left(\dfrac{1}{x}\right)(5) = 1$

$\dfrac{5}{8} + \dfrac{5}{x} = 1$

$8x\left(\dfrac{5}{8} + \dfrac{5}{x}\right) = 1(8x)$

$5x + 40 = 8x$

$40 = 3x$

$\dfrac{40}{3} = x$

$x = 13\dfrac{1}{3}$ hours

59. Let x = number of games the golfer needs to play.

$88 = \dfrac{4(92) + 86x}{4 + x}$

$88(4 + x) = 368 + 86x$

$352 + 88x = 368 + 86x$

$2x = 16$

$x = 8$ games

61. $\text{SMOG} = \sqrt{w} + 3$

$6 = \sqrt{w} + 3$

$3 = \sqrt{w}$

$9 = w$

9 words with three or more syllables.

63.

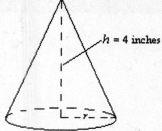

$$L = \pi r \sqrt{r^2 + h^2}$$

$$15\pi = \pi r \sqrt{r^2 + 4^2}$$

$$15 = r \sqrt{r^2 + 16}$$

$$225 = r^2(r^2 + 16)$$

$$0 = r^4 + 16r^2 - 225$$

Let $u = r^2$.

$$u^2 + 16u - 225 = 0$$

$$(u + 25)(u - 9) = 0$$

$$u = 9 \quad \text{or} \quad u = -25 \ (\text{No})$$

$$r^2 = 9$$

$$r = 3$$

The radius is 3 in.

67.

$$d = 1.5 \sqrt{h}$$

$$14 = 1.5\sqrt{h}$$

$$\frac{2}{3}(14) = \sqrt{h}$$

$$\frac{28}{3} = \sqrt{h}$$

$$\frac{784}{9} = h$$

The height is approximately 87 ft.

65.

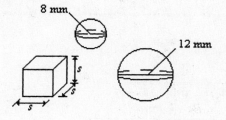

$$d_1 = 8 \text{ mm}, \quad d_2 = 12 \text{ mm}$$

$$V_c = s^3 \qquad V_s = \frac{4}{3}\pi r^3$$

$$s^3 = \frac{4}{3}\pi (4)^3 + \frac{4}{3}\pi (6)^3 = \frac{4}{3}\pi (64 + 216) \approx 1172.86$$

$$s \approx 10.5 \text{ mm}$$

The side is approximately 10.5 mm.

69.

a. $s = \dfrac{1}{2}(a+b+c) = \dfrac{1}{2}(10+7+15) = 16$

$r = \dfrac{abc}{4\sqrt{s(s-a)(s-b)(s-c)}}$

$r = \dfrac{(10)(7)(15)}{4\sqrt{16(16-10)(16-7)(16-15)}}$

$r = \dfrac{10(7)(15)}{4\sqrt{16(6)(9)(1)}} = \dfrac{10(7))(15)}{4 \cdot 4 \cdot \sqrt{6} \cdot 3} \approx 8.93$

The radius is approximately 8.93 in.

b. $a = \text{side}, a = b = c, r = 5$

$s = \dfrac{1}{2}(a+b+c) = \dfrac{1}{2}(a+a+a) = \dfrac{3a}{2}$

$r = \dfrac{abc}{4\sqrt{s(s-a)(s-b)(s-c)}} = \dfrac{a \cdot a \cdot a}{4\sqrt{s(s-a)(s-a)(s-a)}}$

$5 = \dfrac{a \cdot a \cdot a}{4\sqrt{\dfrac{3}{2}a\left[\dfrac{3}{2}a-a\right]\left[\dfrac{3}{2}a-a\right]\left[\dfrac{3}{2}a-a\right]}}$

$5 = \dfrac{a^3}{4\sqrt{\dfrac{3}{2}a\left[\dfrac{a}{2}\right]\left[\dfrac{a}{2}\right]\left[\dfrac{a}{2}\right]}} = \dfrac{a^3}{4\dfrac{\sqrt{3a^4}}{16}} = \dfrac{a^3}{\dfrac{4a^2\sqrt{3}}{4}}$

$a = 5\sqrt{3}$

Each side is $5\sqrt{3}$ in.

71.

$T = \dfrac{\sqrt{s}}{4} + \dfrac{s}{1100}$

$T = \dfrac{\sqrt{7100}}{4} + \dfrac{7100}{1100}$

$T \approx 27.5$ seconds

73. $\{x \mid x > 5\}$

74. $3(-3)^2 - 2(-3) + 5 = 38$

75. $\dfrac{7+3}{7-2} = 2$

76. $10x^2 + 9x - 9 = (3x+5)(5x-3)$

77. $\dfrac{x-3}{2x-7}, \ 2x-7 \neq 0$

It is undefined for $x = \dfrac{7}{2}$.

78. $2x^2 - 11x + 15 = 0$

$(2x-5)(x-3) = 0$

$2x-5 = 0 \quad x-3 = 0$

$x = \dfrac{5}{2} \quad\quad x = 3$

Section 1.5

1. $2x+3<11$
$2x<11-3$
$2x<8$
$x<4$

$\{x|x<4\}$

3. $x+4>3x+16$
$-2x>12$
$x<-6$

$\{x|x<-6\}$

5. $-3(x+2)\le 5x+7$
$-3x-6\le 5x+7$
$-8x\le 13$
$x\ge -\dfrac{13}{8}$

$\left\{x\Big|x\ge -\dfrac{13}{8}\right\}$

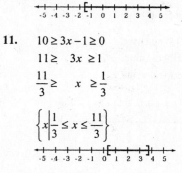

7. $-4(3x-5)>2(x-4)$
$-12x+20>2x-8$
$-14x>-28$
$x<2$

$\{x|x<2\}$

9. $4x+1>-2$ and $4x+1\le 17$
$4x>-3$ and $4x\le 16$
$x>-\dfrac{3}{4}$ and $x\le 4$

$\left\{x\Big|x>-\dfrac{3}{4}\right\}\cap\{x|x\le 4\}=\left\{x\Big|-\dfrac{3}{4}<x\le 4\right\}$

11. $10\ge 3x-1\ge 0$
$11\ge \quad 3x\ \ge 1$
$\dfrac{11}{3}\ge \quad x\ \ge \dfrac{1}{3}$

$\left\{x\Big|\dfrac{1}{3}\le x\le \dfrac{11}{3}\right\}$

13. $x+2<-1$ or $x+3\ge 2$
$x<-3$ or $x\ge -1$

$\{x|x<-3\}\cup\{x|x\ge -1\}=\{x|x<-3\ \text{ or }\ x\ge -1\}$

15. $-4x+5>9$ or $4x+1<5$
$-4x>4$ or $4x<4$
$x<-1$ or $x<1$

$\{x|x<-1\}\cup\{x|x<1\}=\{x|x<1\}$

17. $|2x-1|>4$
$2x-1<-4$ or $2x-1>4$
$2x<-3$ or $2x>5$
$x<-\dfrac{3}{2}$ or $x>\dfrac{5}{2}$

$\left(-\infty,-\dfrac{3}{2}\right)\cup\left(\dfrac{5}{2},\infty\right)$

19. $|x+3|\ge 5$
$x+3\le -5$ or $x+3\ge 5$
$x\le -8$ $\quad x\ge 2$
$(-\infty,-8]\cup[2,\infty)$

21. $|3x-10|\le 14$
$-14\le 3x-10\le 14$
$-4\le \ 3x\ \le 24$
$-\dfrac{4}{3}\le \ \ x\ \ \le 8$
$\left[-\dfrac{4}{3},8\right]$

23. $|4-5x|\ge 24$
$4-5x\le -24$ or $4-5x\ge 24$
$-5x\le -28$ $\quad -5x\ge 20$
$x\ge \dfrac{28}{5}$ $\quad x\le -4$
$(-\infty,-4]\cup\left[\dfrac{28}{5},\infty\right)$

25. $|x-5|\ge 0$
(Note: The absolute value of *any* real number is greater than or equal to 0.)
$(-\infty,\infty)$

27. $|x-4|\le 0$
(Note: No absolute value is less than 0.)
$x-4=0$
$x=4$
$\{4\}$

29. $x^2 + 7x > 0$

$x(x + 7) > 0$

The product $x(x + 7)$ is positive.

$x = 0$ is a critical value.

$x + 7 = 0 \Rightarrow x = -7$ is a critical value.

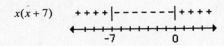

$x(x + 7)$

$(-\infty, -7) \cup (0, \infty)$

31. $x^2 - 16 \le 0$

$(x - 4)(x + 4) \le 0$

The product $(x - 4)(x + 4)$ is negative or zero.

$x - 4 = 0 \Rightarrow x = 4$ is a critical value.

$x + 4 = 0 \Rightarrow x = -4$ is a critical value.

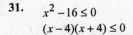

$(x - 4)(x + 4)$

$[-4, 4]$

33. $x^2 + 7x + 10 < 0$

$(x + 5)(x + 2) < 0$

The product $(x + 5)(x + 2)$ is negative.

$x + 5 = 0 \Rightarrow x = -5$ is a critical value.

$x + 2 = 0 \Rightarrow x = -2$ is a critical value.

$(x + 5)(x + 2)$

$(-5, -2)$

35. $x^2 - 3x \ge 28$

$x^2 - 3x - 28 \ge 0$

$(x - 7)(x + 4) \ge 0$

The product $(x - 7)(x + 4)$ is positive or zero.

$x - 7 = 0 \Rightarrow x = 7$ is a critical value.

$x + 4 = 0 \Rightarrow x = -4$ is a critical value.

$(x - 7)(x + 4)$

$(-\infty, -4] \cup [7, \infty)$

37. $\dfrac{x + 4}{x - 1} < 0$

The quotient $\dfrac{x + 4}{x - 1}$ is negative.

$x + 4 = 0 \Rightarrow x = -4$

$x - 1 = 0 \Rightarrow x = 1$

The critical values are -4 and 1.

$\dfrac{x + 4}{x - 1}$

$(-4, 1)$

39. $\dfrac{x - 5}{x + 8} \ge 3$

$\dfrac{x - 5}{x + 8} - 3 \ge 0$

$\dfrac{x - 5 - 3(x + 8)}{x + 8} \ge 0$

$\dfrac{x - 5 - 3x - 24}{x + 8} \ge 0$

$\dfrac{-2x - 29}{x + 8} \ge 0$

The quotient $\dfrac{-2x - 29}{x + 8}$ is positive or zero.

$-2x - 29 = 0 \Rightarrow x = -\dfrac{29}{8}$

$x + 8 = 0 \Rightarrow x = -8$

The critical values are $-\dfrac{29}{2}$ and -8.

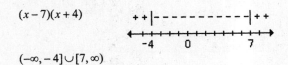

$\dfrac{-2x - 29}{x + 8}$

The denominator cannot equal zero $\Rightarrow x \ne -8$.

$\left[-\dfrac{29}{2}, -8 \right)$

41.
$$\frac{x}{2x+7} \geq 4$$

$$\frac{x}{2x+7} - 4 \geq 0$$

$$\frac{x - 4(2x+7)}{2x+7} \geq 0$$

$$\frac{x - 8x - 28}{2x+7} \geq 0$$

$$\frac{-7x - 28}{2x+7} \geq 0$$

The quotient $\dfrac{-7x-28}{2x+7}$ is positive or zero.

$$-7x - 28 = 0 \Rightarrow x = -4$$

$$2x + 7 = 0 \Rightarrow x = -\frac{7}{2}$$

The critical values are -4 and $-\dfrac{7}{2}$.

$$\frac{-7x-28}{2x+7}$$

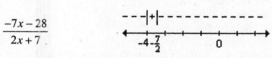

The denominator cannot equal zero $\Rightarrow x \neq -\dfrac{7}{2}$.

$$\left[-4, -\frac{7}{2}\right)$$

43.
$$\frac{(x+1)(x-4)}{x-2} < 0$$

The quotient $\dfrac{(x+1)(x-4)}{x-2}$ is negative.

$$x + 1 = 0 \Rightarrow x = -1$$

$$x - 4 = 0 \Rightarrow x = 4$$

$$x - 2 = 0 \Rightarrow x = 2$$

The critical values are -1, 4, and 2.

$$\frac{(x+1)(x-4)}{x-2}$$

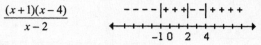

$$(-\infty, -1) \cup (2, 4)$$

45.
$$\frac{x+2}{x-5} \leq 2$$

$$\frac{x+2}{x-5} - 2 \leq 0$$

$$\frac{x+2-2(x-5)}{x-5} \leq 0$$

$$\frac{x+2-2x+10}{x-5} \leq 0$$

$$\frac{-x+12}{x-5} \leq 0$$

The quotient $\dfrac{-x+12}{x-5}$ is negative or zero.

$$-x + 12 = 0 \Rightarrow x = 12$$

$$x - 5 = 0 \Rightarrow x = 5$$

The critical values are 12 and 5.

$$\frac{-x+12}{x-5}$$

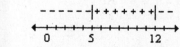

The denominator cannot equal zero $\Rightarrow x \neq 5$.

$$(-\infty, 5) \cup [12, \infty)$$

47.
$$\frac{6x^2 - 11x - 10}{x} > 0$$

$$\frac{(3x+2)(2x-5)}{x} > 0$$

The quotient $\dfrac{(3x+2)(2x-5)}{x}$ is positive.

$$3x + 2 = 0 \Rightarrow x = -\frac{2}{3}$$

$$2x - 5 = 0 \Rightarrow x = \frac{5}{2}$$

$$x = 0$$

The critical values are $-\dfrac{2}{3}, \dfrac{5}{2}$, and 0.

$$\frac{(3x+2)(2x-5)}{x}$$

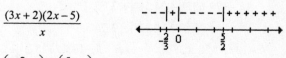

$$\left(-\frac{2}{3}, 0\right) \cup \left(\frac{5}{2}, \infty\right)$$

49.

$$\frac{x^2 - 6x + 9}{x - 5} \le 0$$

$$\frac{(x-3)(x-3)}{x-5} \le 0$$

The quotient $\dfrac{(x-3)(x-3)}{x-5}$ is negative or zero.

$x - 3 = 0 \Rightarrow x = 3$

$x - 5 = 0 \Rightarrow x = 5$

The critical values are 3 and 5.

$$\frac{(x-3)(x-3)}{x-5}$$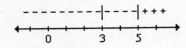

The denominator cannot equal zero $\Rightarrow x \ne 5$.

$(-\infty, 5) \cup \{3\}$

53. Let h = the height of the package.

$$\text{length} + \text{girth} \le 130$$

$$\text{length} + 2(\text{width}) + 2(\text{height}) \le 130$$

$$34 + 2(22) + 2h \le 130$$

$$34 + 44 + 2h \le 130$$

$$78 + 2h \le 130$$

$$2h \le 52$$

$$h \le 26$$

The height must be more than 0 but less than or equal to 26 inches.

57.

$$68 \le \quad F \quad \le 104$$

$$68 \le \frac{9}{5}C + 32 \le 104$$

$$36 \le \quad \frac{9}{5}C \quad \le 72$$

$$\frac{5}{9}(36) \le \frac{5}{9}\left(\frac{9}{5}C\right) \le \frac{5}{9}(72)$$

$$20° \le \quad C \quad \le 40°$$

61. Solve $\left| h - (2.47f + 54.10) \right| \le 3.72$ for h where $f = 32.24$.

$$\left| h - (2.47f + 54.10) \right| \le 3.72$$

$$\left| h - [2.47(32.24) + 54.10] \right| \le 3.72$$

$$\left| h - (79.6328 + 54.10) \right| \le 3.72$$

$$\left| h - 133.7328 \right| \le 3.72$$

$h - 133.7328 \le 3.72$ or $h - 133.7328 \ge -3.72$

$\quad h \le 137.4528 \qquad\qquad h \ge 130.0128$

The height, to the nearest 0.1 cm, is from 130.0 cm to 137.5 cm.

51.
Plan A: $5 + 0.01x$
Plan B: $1 + 0.08x$

$$5 + 0.01x < 1 + 0.08x$$

$$4 < 0.07x$$

$$57.1 < x$$

Plan A is less expensive if you use more than 57 checks.

55.
Plan A: $100 + 8x$
Plan B: $250 + 3.5x$

$$100 + 8x > 250 + 3.5x$$

$$4.5x > 150$$

$$x > 33.3$$

Plan A pays better if at least 34 sales are made.

59.

$$36 < x + (x + 2) + (x + 4) < 54$$

$$36 < \quad 3x + 6 \quad < 54$$

$$30 < \quad 3x \quad < 48$$

$$10 < \quad x \quad < 16$$

x must be even, thus $x = 12$ or $x = 14$.
Therefore, the numbers are $\{12, 14, 16\}$ or $\{14, 16, 18\}$.

63.

$$R = 420x - 2x^2$$

$$420x - 2x^2 > 0$$

$$2x(210 - x) > 0$$

The product is positive.

$$2x = 0 \Rightarrow x = 0$$

$$210 - x = 0 \Rightarrow x = 210$$

Critical values are 0 and 210.

$2x(210 - x)$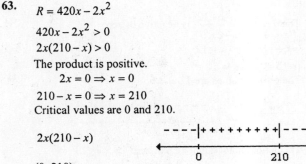

$(0, 210)$

65.
$$\frac{14.25x + 350,000}{x} < 50$$

$$14.25x + 350,000 < 50x$$

$$-35.75x < -350,000$$

$$x > 9790.2$$

At least 9791 books must be published.

··

67. $28 - 0.15 \le \quad C \quad \le 28 + 0.15$

$27.85 \le 2\pi r \quad \le 28.15$

$$\frac{27.85}{2\pi} \le \quad r \quad \le \frac{28.15}{2\pi}$$

$4.432 \le \quad r \quad \le 4.480$

The radius of the cylinder must be between 4.432 inches and 4.480 inches.

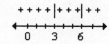

69.
$$\frac{(x-3)^2}{(x-6)^2} > 0$$

The quotient is positive.

$x - 3 = 0 \Rightarrow x = 3$

$x - 6 = 0 \Rightarrow x = 6$

Critical values are 3 and 6.

$$\frac{(x-3)^2}{(x-6)^2}$$

$(-\infty, 3) \cup (3, 6) \cup (6, \infty)$

71.
$$\frac{(x-4)^2}{(x+3)^3} \ge 0$$

The quotient is positive or zero.

$x - 4 = 0 \Rightarrow x = 4$

$x + 3 = 0 \Rightarrow x = -3$

Critical values are 4 and -3.

$$\frac{(x-4)^2}{(x+3)^3}$$

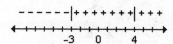

Denominator not $0 \Rightarrow x \ne -3$.

$(-3, \infty)$

73. $1 < |x| < 5$

if $x \ge 0 \quad 1 < \quad x < 5$

if $x < 0 \quad 1 < -x < 5$

$\qquad -1 > \quad x > -5$

$(-5, -1) \cup (1, 5)$

75. $3 \le |x| < 7$

if $x \ge 0 \quad 3 \le \quad x < 7$

if $x < 0 \quad 3 \le -x < 7$

$\qquad -3 \ge \quad x > -7$

$(-7, -3] \cup [3, 7)$

77. $0 < |x - \alpha| < \delta, \quad \delta > 0$

if $x - a \ge 0 \quad 0 < \quad x - a \quad < \delta$

$\qquad\qquad\qquad \alpha < \quad x \quad < \delta + \alpha$

if $x - a < 0 \quad 0 < -(x - a) < \delta$

$\qquad\qquad\qquad 0 > \quad x - a \quad > -\delta$

$\qquad\qquad\qquad a > \quad x \quad > a - \delta$

$(a - \delta, a) \cup (a, a + \delta)$

Connecting Concepts

79. $s = -16t^2 + v_0t + s_0, \quad s > 48, v_0 = 64, s_0 = 0$

$-16t^2 + 64t > 48$

$-16t^2 + 64t - 48 > 0$

$-16(t^2 - 4t + 3) > 0$

$-16(t-1)(t-3) > 0$

The product is positive.
The critical values are 1 and 3.

$(t-1)(t-3)$

$- - - - - - |+ + + + + + +| - - -$

$\quad\quad\quad\quad\quad 1 \quad\quad\quad 3$

1 second $< t <$ 3 seconds
The ball is higher than 48 ft between 1 and 3 seconds.

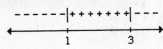

Prepare for Section 1.6

81. $1820 = k(28)$

$65 = k$

82. $20 = \dfrac{k}{1.5^2}$

$45 = k$

83. $k\dfrac{3}{5^2}$

$(225)\dfrac{3}{5^2} = 27$

84. $k\dfrac{4.5 \cdot 32}{8^2}$

$(12.5)\dfrac{4.5 \cdot 32}{8^2} = 28.125$

85.   The area becomes 4 times as large.

86.   No. The volume becomes 9 times as large.

Section 1.6

1. $d = kt$

3. $y = \dfrac{k}{x}$

5. $m = knp$

7. $V = klwh$

9. $A = ks^2$

11. $F = \dfrac{km_1m_2}{d^2}$

13. $y = kx$

$64 = k \cdot 48$

$\dfrac{64}{48} = k$

$\dfrac{4}{3} = k$

15. $r = kt^2$

$144 = k \cdot 108^2$

$\dfrac{144}{108^2} = k$

$\dfrac{2^4 \cdot 3^2}{2^4 \cdot 3^6} = k$

$\dfrac{1}{81} = k$

17.
$$T = krs^2$$
$$210 = k \cdot 30 \cdot 5^2$$
$$\frac{210}{30 \cdot 5^2} = k$$
$$\frac{7}{25} = k$$
$$0.28 = k$$

19.
$$V = klwh$$
$$240 = k \cdot 8 \cdot 6 \cdot 5$$
$$\frac{240}{8 \cdot 6 \cdot 5} = k$$
$$1 = k$$

21.
$$V = kT$$
$$0.85 = k \cdot 270$$
$$\frac{0.85}{270} = k$$
$$\frac{0.17}{54} = k$$

Thus $V = \frac{0.17}{54}T = \frac{0.17}{54} \cdot 324 = (0.17)6 = 1.02$ liters

23.
$$s = k \cdot q$$
$$34 = k \cdot 51$$
$$\frac{2}{3} = k$$
$$p = \frac{2}{3} \cdot 93$$
$$p = 62 \text{ semester hours}$$

25.
$$j = k \cdot d^3$$
$$6 = k \cdot (4)^3$$
$$\frac{3}{32} = k$$
$$p = \frac{3}{32} \cdot (5)^3$$
$$p \approx 11.7 \text{ fl oz}$$

27.
$$T = k\sqrt{l}$$
$$1.8 = k\sqrt{3}$$
$$\frac{1.8}{\sqrt{3}} = k$$
$$1.03923 \approx k$$

a.
$$T = \frac{1.8}{\sqrt{3}}\sqrt{10}$$
$$= \frac{1.8\sqrt{30}}{3}$$
$$= 0.6\sqrt{30}$$
$$\approx 3.3 \text{ seconds}$$

b.
$$T = k\sqrt{l}$$
$$\frac{T}{k} = \sqrt{l}$$
$$\frac{2}{1.03923} = \sqrt{l}$$
$$\frac{4}{1.03923^2} = \sqrt{l}$$
$$3.7 \text{ ft} \approx l$$

29.

$$r = \frac{k}{t}$$

$$30 = \frac{k}{64}$$

$$1920 = k$$

$$r = \frac{1920}{48}$$

$r = 40$ revolutions per minute

31.

$$l = \frac{k}{d^2}$$

$$28 = \frac{k}{8^2}$$

$$28 \cdot 64 = k$$

$$1792 = k$$

$$l = \frac{1792}{4^2} = \frac{1792}{16}$$

$l = 112$ decibels

33.

a. $\;\;V = kr^2h$

$$V_1 = k(3r)^2h$$

$$= 9(kr^2h)$$

$$= 9V$$

Thus the new volume is 9 times the original volume.

b. $\quad V_2 = kr^2(3h)$

$$= 3(kr^2h)$$

$$= 3V$$

Thus the new volume is 3 times the original volume.

c. $\quad V_3 = k(3r)^2(3h)$

$$= k9r^2 \cdot 3 \cdot h$$

$$= 27(kr^2h)$$

$$= 27V$$

Thus the new volume is 27 times the original volume.

35.

$$V = \frac{knT}{P}$$

$$V_1 = \frac{k(3n)T}{\left(\frac{1}{2}p\right)}$$

$$= 6\left(\frac{knT}{p}\right)$$

$$= 6V$$

Thus the new volume is 6 times larger than the original volume.

37. For Randy Johnson,

$$ERA = \frac{kr}{i}$$

$$2.32 = \frac{k(67)}{(260)}$$

$$9.00 = k$$

For Tom Glavine,

$$ERA = \frac{9(74)}{(224.2)}$$

$$= 2.97$$

39.

$$F = \frac{kws^2}{r}$$

$$2800 = \frac{k \cdot 1800 \cdot 45^2}{425}$$

$$\frac{2800 \cdot 425}{1800 \cdot 45^2} = k$$

$$\frac{14 \cdot 425}{9 \cdot 45^2} = k$$

$$0.3264746 \approx k$$

Thus $F = \dfrac{(0.3264746) \cdot 1800 \cdot 55^2}{450}$

$$\approx 3950 \text{ pounds}$$

Connecting Concepts

41.

$$T = kd^{3/2}$$

$$365 = k \cdot 93^{3/2}$$

$$\frac{365}{93^{3/2}} = k$$

Thus $\quad 686 = \dfrac{365}{93^{3/2}} \cdot d^{3/2}$

$$\frac{686 \cdot 93^{3/2}}{365} = d^{3/2}$$

$$\left(\frac{686 \cdot 93^{3/2}}{365}\right)^{2/3} = d$$

$$93\left(\frac{686}{365}\right)^{2/3} = d$$

142 million miles $\approx d$

1. False, $(-3)^2 = 9$, therefore $x = -3$ is also a solution.

2. False, $x = \sqrt{12 - x^2}$ has solution 3.

$x^2 = 12 - x$ has solutions 3 and -4.

3. True

4. True

5. False, $100 > 1$ but $\dfrac{1}{100} \not> \dfrac{1}{1}$.

6. False, the discriminant is $b^2 - 4ac$.

7. False, if $a = 1$, $b = 1$, and $c = 2$, then

$\sqrt{a} + \sqrt{b} = \sqrt{1} + \sqrt{1} = 1 + 1 = 2 = c$,

but $a + b = 1 + 1 = 2 \neq c^2$.

8. True

9. False, $3x^2 - 48 = 0$ also has roots of 4 and -4.

10. True

1. $x - 2(5x - 3) = -3(-x + 4)$ [1.1]

$x - 10x + 6 = 3x - 12$

$-9x + 6 = 3x - 12$

$-12x = -18$

$x = \dfrac{3}{2}$

2. $3x - 5(2x - 7) = -4(5 - 2x)$ [1.1]

$3x - 10x + 35 = -20 + 8x$

$-7x + 35 = -20 + 8x$

$-15x = -55$

$x = \dfrac{11}{3}$

3. $\dfrac{4x}{3} - \dfrac{4x - 1}{6} = \dfrac{1}{2}$ [1.1]

$6\left(\dfrac{4x}{3} - \dfrac{4x - 1}{6}\right) = 6\left(\dfrac{1}{2}\right)$

$2(4x) - (4x - 1) = 3$

$8x - 4x + 1 = 3$

$4x + 1 = 3$

$4x = 2$

$x = \dfrac{1}{2}$

4. $\dfrac{3x}{4} - \dfrac{2x - 1}{8} = \dfrac{3}{2}$ [1.1]

$8\left(\dfrac{3x}{4} - \dfrac{2x - 1}{8}\right) = 8\left(\dfrac{3}{2}\right)$

$2(3x) - (2x - 1) = 4(3)$

$6x - 2x + 1 = 12$

$4x + 1 = 12$

$4x = 11$

$x = \dfrac{11}{4}$

5. $\dfrac{x}{x + 2} + \dfrac{1}{4} = 5$ [1.5]

$4(x + 2)\left(\dfrac{x}{x + 2} + \dfrac{1}{4}\right) = 5(4)(x + 2)$

$4x + x + 2 = 20(x + 2)$

$5x + 2 = 20x + 40$

$-15x = 38$

$x = -\dfrac{38}{15}$

6. $\dfrac{y - 1}{y + 1} - 1 = \dfrac{2}{y}$ [1.4]

$y(y + 1)\left(\dfrac{y - 1}{y + 1} - 1\right) = y(y + 1)\left(\dfrac{2}{y}\right)$

$y(y - 1) - y(y + 1) = 2(y + 1)$

$y^2 - y - y^2 - y = 2y + 2$

$-4y = 2$

$y = -\dfrac{1}{2}$

7. $x^2 - 5x + 6 = 0$ [1.3]

$(x - 2)(x - 3) = 0$

$x - 2 = 0$ or $x - 3 = 0$

$x = 2$ $x = 3$

8. $6x^2 + x - 12 = 0$ [1.3]

$(3x - 4)(2x + 3) = 0$

$3x - 4 = 0$ or $2x + 3 = 0$

$3x = 4$ $2x = -3$

$x = \dfrac{4}{3}$ $x = -\dfrac{3}{2}$

9. $3x^2 - x - 1 = 0$ [1.3]

$x = \dfrac{-(-1) \pm \sqrt{(-1)^2 - 4(3)(-1)}}{2(3)}$

$x = \dfrac{1 \pm \sqrt{13}}{6}$

$x = \dfrac{1 + \sqrt{13}}{6}$ or $x = \dfrac{1 - \sqrt{13}}{6}$

10. $x^2 - x + 1 = 0$ [1.3]

$x = \dfrac{-(-1) \pm \sqrt{(-1)^2 - 4(1)(1)}}{2(1)}$

$x = \dfrac{1 \pm \sqrt{-3}}{2} = \dfrac{1 \pm i\sqrt{3}}{2}$

$x = \dfrac{1}{2} + \dfrac{\sqrt{3}}{2}i$ or $x = \dfrac{1}{2} - \dfrac{\sqrt{3}}{2}i$

11. $3x^3 - 5x^2 = 0$ [1.4]

$x^2(3x - 5) = 0$

$x^2 = 0 \Rightarrow x = 0$

$3x - 5 = 0 \Rightarrow x = \dfrac{5}{3}$

$x = 0$ or $x = \dfrac{5}{3}$

12. $2x^3 - 8x = 0$ [1.4]

$2x(x^2 - 4) = 0$

$2x(x - 2)(x + 2) = 0$

$x = 0, \ x = 2, \ $ or $\ x = -2$

13. $6x^4 - 23x^2 + 20 = 0$ [1.4]

Let $u = x^2$.

$6u^2 - 23u + 20 = 0$

$(3u - 4)(2u - 5) = 0$

$u = \dfrac{4}{3}$ or $u = \dfrac{5}{2}$

$x^2 = \dfrac{4}{3}$ $\qquad x^2 = \dfrac{5}{2}$

$x = \pm\sqrt{\dfrac{4}{3}}$ $\qquad x = \pm\sqrt{\dfrac{5}{2}}$

$x = \pm\dfrac{2}{\sqrt{3}}\left(\dfrac{\sqrt{3}}{\sqrt{3}}\right)$ $\qquad x = \pm\dfrac{\sqrt{5}}{\sqrt{2}}\left(\dfrac{\sqrt{2}}{\sqrt{2}}\right)$

$x = \pm\dfrac{2\sqrt{3}}{3}$ $\qquad x = \pm\dfrac{\sqrt{10}}{2}$

14. $3x + 16\sqrt{x} - 12 = 0$ [1.4]

Let $u = \sqrt{x}$.

$3u^2 + 16u - 12 = 0$

$(3u - 2)(u + 6) = 0$

$u = \dfrac{2}{3}$ or $u = -6$

$\sqrt{x} = \dfrac{2}{3}$ $\qquad \sqrt{x} = -6$

$\qquad\qquad\qquad$ No solution.

$x = \dfrac{4}{9}$

Thus, $x = \dfrac{4}{9}$.

15. $\sqrt{x^2 - 15} = \sqrt{-2x}$ [1.4]

$\left[\sqrt{x^2 - 15}\right]^2 = \left[\sqrt{-2x}\right]^2$

$x^2 - 15 = -2x$

$x^2 + 2x - 15 = 0$

$(x + 5)(x - 3) = 0$

$x = -5$ or $x = 3$

Check $\sqrt{(-5)^2 - 15} = \sqrt{-2(-5)}$

$\sqrt{10} = \sqrt{10}$

$\sqrt{3^2 - 15} = \sqrt{-2(3)}$

$\sqrt{-6} = \sqrt{-6}$

The solutions are -5 and 3.

16. $\sqrt{x^2 - 24} = \sqrt{2x}$ [1.4]

$\left[\sqrt{x^2 - 24}\right]^2 = \left[\sqrt{2x}\right]^2$

$x^2 - 24 = 2x$

$x^2 - 2x - 24 = 0$

$(x - 6)(x + 4) = 0$

$x = 6$ or $x = -4$

Check $\sqrt{(6)^2 - 24} = \sqrt{2(6)}$

$\sqrt{36 - 24} = \sqrt{12}$

$\sqrt{12} = \sqrt{12}$

$\sqrt{(-4)^2 - 24} = \sqrt{2(-4)}$

$\sqrt{16 - 24} = \sqrt{-8}$

$\sqrt{-8} = \sqrt{-8}$

The solutions are 6 and -4.

17.

$$\sqrt{3x+4}+\sqrt{x-3}=5$$

$$\sqrt{3x+4}=5-\sqrt{x-3}$$

$$\left[\sqrt{3x+4}\right]^2=\left[5-\sqrt{x-3}\right]^2$$

$$3x+4=25-10\sqrt{x-3}+x-3$$

$$2x-18=-10\sqrt{x-3}$$

$$x-9=-5\sqrt{x-3}$$

$$(x-9)^2=\left[-5\sqrt{x-3}\right]^2$$

$$x^2-18x+81=25(x-3)$$

$$x^2-18x+81=25x-75$$

$$x^2-43x+156=0$$

$$(x-4)(x-39)=0$$

$$x=4 \quad \text{or} \quad x=39$$

Check $\quad \sqrt{3(4)+4}+\sqrt{4-3}=5$

$$\sqrt{16}+\sqrt{1}=5$$

$$4+1=5$$

$$5=5$$

$$\sqrt{3(39)+4}+\sqrt{39-3}=5$$

$$\sqrt{121}+\sqrt{36}=5$$

$$11+6=5$$

$$17=5 \quad \text{(No)}$$

The solution is 4. [1.4]

18.

$$\sqrt{2x+2}-\sqrt{x+2}=\sqrt{x-6}$$

$$\left[\sqrt{2x+2}-\sqrt{x+2}\right]^2=\left[\sqrt{x-6}\right]^2$$

$$2x+2-2\sqrt{(2x+2)(x+2)}+x+2=x-6$$

$$-2\sqrt{(2x+2)(x+2)}=-2(x+5)$$

$$\sqrt{(2x+2)(x+2)}=x+5$$

$$\left[\sqrt{(2x+2)(x+2)}\right]^2=[x+5]^2$$

$$(2x+2)(x+2)=x^2+10x+25$$

$$2x^2+4x+2x+4=x^2+10x+25$$

$$x^2-4x-21=0$$

$$(x-7)(x+3)=0$$

$$x=7 \quad \text{or} \quad x=-3$$

Check $\quad \sqrt{2(7)+2}-\sqrt{7+2}=\sqrt{7-6}$

$$\sqrt{16}-\sqrt{9}=\sqrt{1}$$

$$4-3=1$$

$$1=1$$

$$\sqrt{2(-3)+2}-\sqrt{-3+2}=\sqrt{-3-6}$$

$$\sqrt{-4}-\sqrt{-1}=\sqrt{-9}$$

$$2i-i=3i$$

$$i=3i \quad \text{(No)}$$

The solution is 7. [1.4]

19.

$$\sqrt{4-3x}-\sqrt{5-x}=\sqrt{5+x} \qquad [1.4]$$

$$\left[\sqrt{4-3x}-\sqrt{5-x}\right]^2=\left[\sqrt{5+x}\right]^2$$

$$-2\sqrt{(4-3x)(5-x)}=5x-4$$

$$\left[-2\sqrt{(4-3x)(5-x)}\right]^2=[5x-4]^2$$

$$4(4-3x)(5-x)=25x^2-40x+16$$

$$4(20-19x+3x^2)=25x^2-40x+16$$

$$0=13x^2+36x-64$$

$$0=(13x-16)(x+4)$$

$$x=\frac{16}{13} \quad \text{or} \quad x=-4$$

Check $\quad \sqrt{4-3\left(\dfrac{16}{13}\right)}-\sqrt{5-\dfrac{16}{13}}=\sqrt{5+\dfrac{16}{13}}$

$$\sqrt{\frac{52}{13}-\left(\frac{48}{13}\right)}-\sqrt{\frac{65}{13}-\frac{16}{13}}=\sqrt{\frac{65}{13}+\frac{16}{13}}$$

$$\sqrt{\frac{4}{13}}-\sqrt{\frac{49}{13}}=\sqrt{\frac{81}{13}}$$

$$\frac{2}{\sqrt{13}}-\frac{7}{\sqrt{13}}=\frac{9}{\sqrt{13}} \quad \text{(No)}$$

$$\sqrt{4-3(-4)}-\sqrt{5-(-4)}=\sqrt{5-4}$$

$$\sqrt{16}-\sqrt{9}=\sqrt{1}$$

$$4-3=1$$

$$1=1$$

The solution is −4.

20.

$$\sqrt{3x+9}-\sqrt{2x+4}=\sqrt{x+1} \qquad [1.4]$$

$$\left[\sqrt{3x+9}-\sqrt{2x+4}\right]^2=\left[\sqrt{x+1}\right]^2$$

$$3x+9-2\sqrt{(3x+9)(2x+4)}+2x+4=x+1$$

$$-2\sqrt{(3x+9)(2x+4)}=-4x-12$$

$$\left[\sqrt{(3x+9)(2x+4)}\right]^2=[2x+6]^2$$

$$(3x+9)(2x+4)=4x^2+24x+36$$

$$6x^2+30x+36=4x^2+24x+36$$

$$2x^2+6x=0$$

$$2x(x+3)=0$$

$x=0$ or $x=-3$

Check $\sqrt{3(0)+9}-\sqrt{2(0)+4}=\sqrt{0+1}$

$$\sqrt{9}-\sqrt{4}=\sqrt{1}$$

$$3-2=1$$

$$1=1$$

$$\sqrt{3(-3)+9)}-\sqrt{2(-3)+4}=\sqrt{-3+1}$$

$$\sqrt{0}-\sqrt{-2}=\sqrt{-2}$$

$$0-\sqrt{-2}=\sqrt{-2}$$

$$-\sqrt{-2}=\sqrt{-2} \quad \text{(No)}$$

The solution is 0.

21.

$$\frac{1}{(y+3)^2}=1 \quad [1.4]$$

$$1=(y+3)^2$$

$$1=y^2+6y+9$$

$$0=y^2+6y+8$$

$$0=(y+2)(y+4)$$

$$y=-2 \quad \text{or} \quad y=-4$$

22.

$$\frac{1}{(2s-5)^2}=4 \quad [1.4]$$

$$1=4(4s^2-20s+25)$$

$$1=16s^2-80s+100$$

$$0=16s^2-80s+99$$

$$0=(4s-11)(4s-9)$$

$$s=\frac{11}{4} \quad \text{or} \quad s=\frac{9}{4}$$

23.

$$|x-3|=2 \quad [1.1]$$

$$x-3=2 \quad \text{or} \quad x-3=-2$$

$$x=5 \qquad\qquad x=1$$

24.

$$|x+5|=4 \quad [1.1]$$

$$x+5=4 \quad \text{or} \quad x+5=-4$$

$$x=-1 \qquad\qquad x=-9$$

25.

$$|2x+1|=5 \quad [1.1]$$

$$2x+1=5 \quad \text{or} \quad 2x+1=-5$$

$$2x=4 \qquad\qquad 2x=-6$$

$$x=2 \qquad\qquad x=-3$$

26.

$$|3x-7|=8 \quad [1.1]$$

$$3x-7=8 \quad \text{or} \quad 3x-7=-8$$

$$3x=15 \qquad\qquad 3x=-1$$

$$x=5 \qquad\qquad x=-\frac{1}{3}$$

27.

$$(x+2)^{1/2}+x(x+2)^{3/2}=0 \quad [1.4]$$

$$(x+2)^{1/2}\left[1+x(x+2)\right]=0$$

$$(x+2)^{1/2}\left[1+x^2+2x\right]=0$$

$$(x+2)^{1/2}(x^2+2x+1)=0$$

$$(x+2)^{1/2}(x+1)^2=0$$

$$(x+2)^{1/2}=0 \quad \text{or} \quad (x+1)^2=0$$

$$x+2=0 \qquad\qquad x+1=0$$

$$x=-2 \qquad\qquad x=-1$$

28.

$$x^2(3x-4)^{1/4}+(3x-4)^{5/4}=0 \quad [1.4]$$

$$(3x-4)^{1/4}(x^2+3x-4)=0$$

$$(3x-4)^{1/4}=0 \quad \text{or} \quad x^2+3x-4=0$$

$$3x-4=0 \qquad\qquad (x+4)(x-1)=0$$

$$3x=4 \qquad\qquad x+4=0 \quad \text{or} \quad x-1=0$$

$$x=\frac{4}{3} \qquad\qquad x=-4 \qquad\qquad x=1$$

29.

$$-3x+4\geq-2 \quad [1.5]$$

$$-3x\geq-2-4$$

$$-3x\geq-6$$

$$x\leq2$$

$$(-\infty, 2]$$

30.

$$-2x+7\leq5x+1 \quad [1.5]$$

$$-7x\leq-6$$

$$x\geq\frac{6}{7}$$

$$\left[\frac{6}{7}, \infty\right)$$

31. $x^2 + 3x - 10 \leq 0$ [1.5]

$(x+5)(x-2) \leq 0$

The product is negative or zero.

$x + 5 = 0 \Rightarrow x = -5$

$x - 2 = 0 \Rightarrow x = 2$

Critical values are −5 and 2.

$(x+5)(x-2)$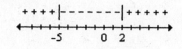

$[-5, 2]$

32. $x^2 - 2x - 3 > 0$ [1.5]

$(x+1)(x-3) > 0$

The product is positive.

$x + 1 = 0 \Rightarrow x = -1$

$x - 3 = 0 \Rightarrow x = 3$

Critical values are −1 and 3.

$(x+1)(x-3)$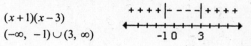

$(-\infty, -1) \cup (3, \infty)$

33. $61 \leq \frac{9}{5}C + 32 \leq 95$ [1.5]

$29 \leq \quad \frac{9}{5}C \quad \leq 63$

$\frac{145}{9} \leq \quad C \quad \leq 35$

$\left[\frac{145}{9}, 35\right]$

34. $30 < \frac{5}{9}(F - 32) < 65$ [1.5]

$54 < \quad F - 32 \quad < 117$

$86 < \quad\quad F \quad\quad < 149$

$(86, 149)$

35. $x^3 - 7x^2 + 12x \leq 0$ [1.5]

$x(x^2 - 7x + 12) \leq 0$

$x(x-3)(x-4) \leq 0.$

The product is negative or zero.

$x = 0$

$x - 3 = 0 \Rightarrow x = 3$

$x - 4 = 0 \Rightarrow x = 4$

The critical values are 0, 3, and 4.

$x(x-3)(x-4)$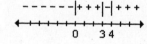

$(-\infty, 0] \cup [3, 4]$

36. $x^3 + 4x^2 - 21x > 0$ [1.5]

$x(x^2 + 4x - 21) > 0$

$x(x+7)(x-3) > 0.$

The product is positive.

$x = 0$

$x + 7 = 0 \Rightarrow x = -7$

$x - 3 = 0 \Rightarrow x = 3$

The critical values are 0, −7, and 3.

$x(x+7)(x-3)$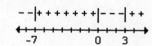

$(-7, 0) \cup (3, \infty)$

37. $\frac{x+3}{x-4} > 0$ [1.5]

The quotient is positive.

$x + 3 = 0 \Rightarrow x = -3$

$x - 4 = 0 \Rightarrow x = 4$

The critical values are −3 and 4.

$\frac{x+3}{x-4}$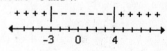

$(-\infty, -3) \cup (4, \infty)$

38. $\frac{x(x-5)}{x+7} \leq 0$ [1.5]

The quotient is negative or zero.

$x = 0$

$x - 5 = 0 \Rightarrow x = 5$

$x + 7 = 0 \Rightarrow x = -7$

The critical values are 0, 5 and −7.

$\frac{x(x-5)}{x+7}$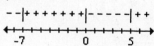

Denominator $\neq 0 \Rightarrow x \neq -7$.

$(-\infty, -7) \cup [0, 5]$

39.

$$\frac{2x}{3-x} \le 10 \quad [1.5]$$

$$\frac{2x}{3-x} - 10 \le 0$$

$$\frac{2x - 10(3-x)}{3-x} \le 0$$

$$\frac{2x - 30 + 10x}{3-x} \le 0$$

$$\frac{12x - 30}{3-x} \le 0$$

The quotient is negative or zero.

$$12x - 30 = 0 \Rightarrow x = \frac{5}{2}$$

$$3 - x = 0 \Rightarrow x = 3$$

The critical values are $\frac{5}{2}$ and 3.

$$\frac{12x - 30}{3-x}$$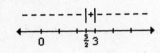

Denominator $\ne 0 \Rightarrow x \ne 3$.

$$\left(-\infty, \ \frac{5}{2}\right] \cup (3, \infty)$$

40.

$$\frac{x}{5-x} \ge 1 \quad [1.5]$$

$$\frac{x}{5-x} - 1 \ge 0$$

$$\frac{x - (5-x)}{5-x} \ge 0$$

$$\frac{x - 5 + x}{5-x} \ge 0$$

$$\frac{2x - 5}{5-x} \ge 0$$

The quotient is positive or zero.

$$2x - 5 = 0 \Rightarrow x = \frac{5}{2}$$

$$5 - x = 0 \Rightarrow x = 5$$

The critical values are $\frac{5}{2}$ and 5.

$$\frac{2x - 5}{5-x}$$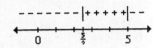

Denominator $\ne 0 \Rightarrow x \ne 5$.

$$\left[\frac{5}{2}, \ 5\right)$$

41. $|3x - 4| < 2 \quad [1.5]$

$$-2 < 3x - 4 < 2$$

$$2 < \ 3x \ < 6$$

$$\frac{2}{3} < \ \ x \ \ < 2$$

$$\left(\frac{2}{3}, \ 2\right)$$

42. $|2x - 3| \ge 1 \quad [1.5]$

$$2x - 3 \ge 1 \quad \text{or} \quad 2x - 3 \le -1$$

$$2x \ge 4 \qquad \qquad 2x \le 2$$

$$x \ge 2 \qquad \qquad x \le 1$$

$$(-\infty, 1] \cup [2, \infty)$$

43. $0 < |x - 2| < 1 \quad [1.5]$

If $x - 2 \ge 0$, then $2 < \ x \ < 3$.

If $x - 2 < 0$, then $0 < x - 2 < -1$

$$2 > \ x \ > 1.$$

$$(1, 2) \cup (2, 3)$$

44. $0 < |x - a| < b \quad [1.5]$

If $x - a \ge 0$, then $a < \ x \ < a + b$.

If $x - a < 0$, then $0 < x - a < -b$

$$a > \ x \ > a - b.$$

$$[a - b, \ a) \cup (a, \ a + b]$$

45.

$$V = \pi r^2 h \quad [1.2]$$

$$\frac{V}{\pi r^2} = h$$

46.

$$P = \frac{A}{1 + rt} \quad [1.2]$$

$$P(1 + rt) = A$$

$$P + Prt = A$$

$$Prt = A - P$$

$$t = \frac{A - P}{Pr}$$

47.

$$A = \frac{h}{2}(b_1 + b_2) \quad [1.2]$$

$$2A = h(b_1 + b_2)$$

$$2A = hb_1 + hb_2$$

$$2A - hb_2 = hb_1$$

$$\frac{2A - hb_2}{h} = b_1$$

48.

$$P = 2(l + w) \quad [1.2]$$

$$P = 2l + 2w$$

$$P - 2l = 2w$$

$$\frac{P - 2l}{2} = w$$

49.

$$e = mc^2 \quad [1.2]$$

$$\frac{e}{c^2} = m$$

50.

$$F = G\frac{m_1 m_2}{s^2} \quad [1.2]$$

$$Fs^2 = Gm_1 m_2$$

$$\frac{Fs^2}{Gm_2} = m_1$$

51. Let x = the number [1.2]

$$\frac{1}{2}x - \frac{1}{4}x = 4 + \frac{1}{5}x$$

$$20\left(\frac{1}{2}x - \frac{1}{4}x\right) = 20\left(4 + \frac{1}{5}x\right)$$

$$10x - 5x = 80 + 4x$$

$$5x = 80 + 4x$$

$$x = 80$$

52.

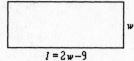

$l = 2w - 9$

$$P = 54$$
$$54 = 2l + 2w$$
$$54 = 2(2w - 9) + 2w$$
$$54 = 4w - 18 + 2w$$
$$72 = 6w$$
$$12 = w$$
$$2w - 9 = 2(12) - 9 = 24 - 9 = 15$$

width = 12 ft, length = 15 ft [1.2]

53.

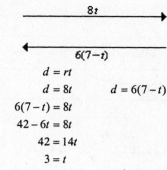

$8t$

$6(7 - t)$

$$d = rt$$
$$d = 8t \qquad d = 6(7 - t)$$
$$6(7 - t) = 8t$$
$$42 - 6t = 8t$$
$$42 = 14t$$
$$3 = t$$

$d = 8(3) = 24$ nautical miles [1.2]

54. Let x = cost last year

Cost = last year + raise

Let x = the number.

$$21 = x + 0.05x$$
$$21 = 1.05x$$
$$\frac{21}{1.05} = x$$
$$20 = x$$

The cost last year was $20.00 . [1.2]

55.

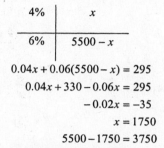

4%	x
6%	$5500 - x$

$$0.04x + 0.06(5500 - x) = 295$$
$$0.04x + 330 - 0.06x = 295$$
$$-0.02x = -35$$
$$x = 1750$$
$$5500 - 1750 = 3750$$

$1750 in the 4% account

$3750 in the 6% account [1.2]

56. Let x = price of battery

$x + 20$ = price of calculator

$$x + x + 20 = 21$$
$$2x + 20 = 21$$
$$2x = 1$$
$$x = 0.50$$
$$x + 20 = 20.50$$

Price of calculator is $20.50.

Price of battery is $0.50.   [1.2]

57. Let x = monthly maintenance cost per owner

$$18x = 24(x - 12)$$
$$18x = 24x - 288$$
$$-6x = -288$$
$$x = 48$$
$$18x = 864$$

The total monthly maintenance cost is $864. [1.2]

58.

$$P = 40$$
$$A = 96$$
$$40 = 2l + 2w$$
$$20 = l + w$$
$$l = 20 - w$$
$$96 = lw$$
$$96 = (20 - w)w$$
$$96 = 20w - w^2$$
$$w^2 - 20w + 96 = 0$$
$$(w - 12)(w - 8) = 0$$
$$w = 12 \qquad \text{or} \quad w = 8$$
$$l = 20 - 12 \quad \text{or} \quad l = 20 - 8$$
$$l = 8 \qquad\qquad l = 12$$

Length = 8 in. and width = 12 in.,
or length = 12 in. and width = 8 in. [1.2]

59.

	Time	Part completed In 1 hour
Mason	$x - 9$	$\dfrac{1}{x-9}$
Apprentice	x	$\dfrac{1}{x}$

$$6\left(\frac{1}{x} + \frac{1}{x-9}\right) = 1$$

$$6x(x-9)\left(\frac{1}{x} + \frac{1}{x-9}\right) = 1x(x-9)$$

$$6(x-9) + 6x = x^2 - 9x$$

$$6x - 54 + 6x = x^2 - 9x$$

$$0 = x^2 - 21x + 54$$

$$0 = (x-18)(x-3)$$

$$x = 18 \quad \text{or} \quad x = 3$$

(Note : $x = 3 \Rightarrow$ mason's time $= -6$ hours. Thus $x \neq 3$.)

Apprentice takes 18 hours to build the wall. [1.4]

60.

Let x = number of adult tickets

$4526 - x$ = number of student tickets

$$8x + 2(4526 - x) = 33,196$$

$$8x + 9052 - 2x = 33,196$$

$$6x = 24,144$$

$$x = 4024$$

$$4526 - x = 502$$

4024 adult tickets, 502 student tickets [1.2]

61.

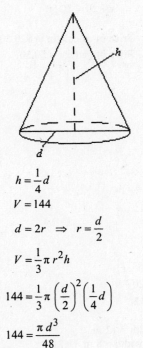

$$h = \frac{1}{4}d$$

$$V = 144$$

$$d = 2r \implies r = \frac{d}{2}$$

$$V = \frac{1}{3}\pi r^2 h$$

$$144 = \frac{1}{3}\pi \left(\frac{d}{2}\right)^2 \left(\frac{1}{4}d\right)$$

$$144 = \frac{\pi d^3}{48}$$

$$\frac{144(48)}{\pi} = d^3$$

$$d \approx 13 \text{ ft} \qquad [1.2]$$

62.

$$R = 72x - 2x^2, \ R > 576$$

$$72x - 2x^2 > 576$$

$$0 > 2x^2 - 72x + 576$$

$$2x^2 - 72x + 576 < 0$$

$$x^2 - 36x + 288 < 0$$

$$(x-24)(x-12) < 0$$

The product is negative.

$$x - 24 = 0 \Rightarrow x = 24$$

$$x - 12 = 0 \Rightarrow x = 12$$

Critical values are 24 and 12.

$(x-24)(x-12)$

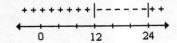

$(12, 24)$

The revenue is greater than \$576
when the price is between \$12 and \$24. [1.5]

63. **a.** $|B - 218| > 48$ [1.5]

   b. $|B - 218| > 48$

   $B - 218 > 48$ or $B - 218 < -48$

   $B > 266$ $B < 170$

   $(0,\ 170) \cup (266,\ \infty)$ [1.5]

64. Let x = the fee for the second apartment.

$|x - 575| < 150$

$x - 575 < 150$ or $x - 575 > -150$

$x < 725$ $x > 425$

The second apartment costs more than \$425 but less than \$725. [1.5]

65. Let h = the height of the package.

$$\text{length} + \text{girth} \le 165$$

$$\text{length} + 2(\text{width}) + 2(\text{height}) \le 165$$

$$42 + 2(38) + 2h \le 165$$

$$42 + 76 + 2h \le 165$$

$$118 + 2h \le 165$$

$$2h \le 47$$

$$h \le 23.5$$

The height must be more than 0 but less than or equal to 23.5 inches. [1.5]

66. Let x = the score on the fifth test.

$$68 \le \frac{82 + 72 + 64 + 95 + x}{5} \le 79$$

$$68 \le \frac{313 + x}{5} \le 79$$

$$340 \le 313 + x \le 395$$

$$27 \le x \le 82$$

The student needs to earn a score in the interval [27, 82] to receive a C grade for the course. [1.5]

67. Let C = the circumference, r = the radius, and d = the diameter.

$$C = 2\pi r = \pi d$$

$$29.5 \le C \le 30.0$$

$$29.5 \le \pi d \le 30.0$$

$$\frac{29.5}{\pi} \le d \le \frac{30.0}{\pi}$$

$$9.39 \le d \le 9.55$$

The diameter of the basketball is from 9.39 to 9.55 inches. [1.5]

68.
$$300 = -45x^2 + 190x + 200$$

$$45x^2 - 190x + 100 = 0$$

$$9x^2 - 38x + 20 = 0$$

$$x = \frac{-(-38) \pm \sqrt{(-38)^2 - 4(9)(20)}}{2(9)}$$

$$= \frac{38 \pm \sqrt{724}}{18}$$

$$x \approx 0.6 \text{ or } x \approx 3.6$$

More than 0.6 mi but less than 3.6 mi from the city center. [1.5]

69.
$$A = \frac{km}{r^2}$$

$$9.8 = \frac{k(5.98 \times 10^{26})}{(6,370,000)^2}$$

$$9.8(6,370,000)^2 = k(5.98 \times 10^{26})$$

$$\frac{9.8(6,370,000)^2}{5.98 \times 10^{26}} = k$$

$$k \approx 6.6497 \times 10^{-13}$$

$$A = \frac{6.6497 \times 10^{-13}\, m}{r^2}$$

$$A = \frac{(6.6497 \times 10^{-13})(7.46 \times 10^{24})}{(1,740,000)^2}$$

$$A \approx 1.64 \text{ meters/sec}^2 \qquad [1.6]$$

70.
$$L = \frac{kd^4}{h^2}$$

$$4 = \frac{k(1.5)^4}{8^2}$$

$$4(8^2) = k(1.5)^4$$

$$\frac{4(8^2)}{(1.5)^4} = k$$

$$k \approx 50.5679$$

$$L = \frac{50.5679 d^4}{h^2}$$

$$L = \frac{50.5679(4)^4}{12^2}$$

$$L \approx 89.9 \text{ tons} \qquad [1.6]$$

••

1. $3(2x-5)+1=-2(x-5)$ [1.1]

$6x-15+1=-2x+10$

$6x-14=-2x+10$

$8x=24$

$x=3$

2. $|x-3|=8$ [1.1]

$x-3=8$ or $x-3=-8$

$x=11$ $x=-5$

3. $6x^2-13x-8=(3x-8)(2x+1)=0$ [1.3]

$3x-8=0$ or $2x+1=0$

$x=\frac{8}{3}$ $x=-\frac{1}{2}$

4. $2x^2-8x+1=0 \Rightarrow x^2-4x=-\frac{1}{2}$ [1.3]

$x^2-4x+4=-\frac{1}{2}+4 \Rightarrow (x-2)^2=\frac{7}{2}$

$x-2=\pm\sqrt{\frac{7}{2}}=\pm\frac{\sqrt{7}}{\sqrt{2}}=\pm\frac{\sqrt{7\cdot2}}{\sqrt{2\cdot2}}=\pm\frac{\sqrt{14}}{2}$

$x=2\pm\frac{\sqrt{14}}{2}=\frac{4}{2}\pm\frac{\sqrt{14}}{2}=\frac{4\pm\sqrt{14}}{2}$

5. $3x^2-5x-1=0$ [1.3]

$a=3,\ b=-5,\ c=-1$

$x=\dfrac{-(-5)\pm\sqrt{(-5)^2-4(3)(-1)}}{2(3)}$

$=\dfrac{5\pm\sqrt{25+12}}{6}=\dfrac{5\pm\sqrt{37}}{6}$

6. $2x^2+3x+1=0$ [1.3]

$a=2,\ b=3,\ c=1$

$b^2-4ac=(3)^2-4(2)(1)=9-8=1$

The discriminant, 1, is a positive number. Therefore, there are two real solutions.

7. $ax-c=c(x-d)$

$ax-c=cx-cd$

$ax-cx=c-cd$

$x(a-c)=c-cd$

$x=\dfrac{c-cd}{a-c},\ a\neq c$ [1.2]

8. $\sqrt{x-2}-1=\sqrt{3-x}$

$\left(\sqrt{x-2}-1\right)^2=\left(\sqrt{3-x}\right)^2$

$x-2-2\sqrt{x-2}+1=3-x$

$2x-4=2\sqrt{x-2}$

$x-2=\sqrt{x-2}$

$(x-2)^2=\left(\sqrt{x-2}\right)^2$

$x^2-4x+4=x-2$

$x^2-5x+6=0$

$(x-3)(x-2)=0$

$x-3=0 \Rightarrow x=3$

$x-2=0 \Rightarrow x=2$

Check $\sqrt{2-2}-1=\sqrt{3-2}$

$-1=1$ (No)

$\sqrt{3-2}-1=\sqrt{3-3}$

$1-1=0$

$0=0$

The solution is 3. [1.4]

9. $3x^{2/3} + 10x^{1/3} - 8 = 0$ [1.4]

Let $u = x^{1/3}$

$3u^2 + 10u - 8 = 0$

$(3u - 2)(u + 4) = 0$

$u = \dfrac{2}{3}$ or $u = -4$

$x^{1/3} = \dfrac{2}{3}$ $x^{1/3} = -4$

$\left(x^{1/3}\right)^3 = \left(\dfrac{2}{3}\right)^3$ $\left(x^{1/3}\right)^3 = (-4)^3$

$x = \dfrac{8}{27}$ $x = -64$

10. $\dfrac{3}{x+2} - \dfrac{3}{4} = \dfrac{5}{x+2}$ [1.4]

$4(x+2)\left(\dfrac{3}{x+2} - \dfrac{3}{4}\right) = 4(x+2)\left(\dfrac{5}{x+2}\right)$

$4(3) - 3(x+2) = 4(5)$

$12 - 3x - 6 = 20$

$-3x = 14$

$x = -\dfrac{14}{3}$

11. a. $2x - 5 \le 11$ or $-3x + 2 > 14$

$\qquad 2x \le 16 \qquad\qquad -3x > 12$

$\qquad x \le 8 \qquad\qquad\quad x < -4$

$\{x \mid x \le 8\} \cup \{x \mid x < -4\} = \{x \mid x \le 8\}$ [1.5]

b. $2x - 1 < 9$ and $-3x + 1 \le 7$

$\qquad 2x < 10 \qquad\qquad -3x \le 6$

$\qquad x < 5 \qquad\qquad\quad x \ge -2$

$\{x \mid x < 5\} \cap \{x \mid x \ge -2\} = [-2, 5)$ [1.5]

12. $\dfrac{x^2 + x - 12}{x + 1} \ge 0$

$\dfrac{(x + 4)(x - 3)}{x + 1} \ge 0$

The quotient is positive or zero.

$x + 4 = 0 \Rightarrow x = -4$

$x - 3 = 0 \Rightarrow x = 3$

$x + 1 = 0 \Rightarrow x = -1$

Critical values are -4, 3, and -1.

$\dfrac{(x + 4)(x - 3)}{x + 1}$ $- - -|+ + +|- - - -|+ + +$

$\qquad\qquad\qquad\qquad$ $-4 \quad -1\ 0 \qquad 3$

Denominator $\ne 0 \Rightarrow x \ne -1$.

$[-4, -1) \cup [3, \infty)$ [1.5]

13. $\left| x - 11\dfrac{5}{32} \right| \le \dfrac{9}{32}$

$-\dfrac{9}{32} \le x - 11\dfrac{5}{32} \le \dfrac{9}{32}$

$10\dfrac{7}{8} \le x \le 11\dfrac{7}{16}$

The range is from $10\dfrac{7}{8}$ in. to $11\dfrac{7}{16}$ in. [1.5]

14. Let $x =$ the rate of the current.

Rate with current $= 5 + x$.

Rate against current $= 5 - x$.

$d = rt$

$21 = (5 + x)t \qquad\qquad 9 = (5 - x)t$

$\dfrac{21}{5 + x} = t \qquad\qquad \dfrac{9}{5 - x} = t$

$\dfrac{21}{5 + x} = \dfrac{9}{5 - x}$

$21(5 - x) = 9(5 + x)$

$105 - 21x = 45 + 9x$

$60 = 30x$

$2 = x$

The current is 2 mph. [1.2]

15.

x	0.20	Remove x amount of 20%
x	1.00	Add x amount of 100%

$6(0.20) - x(0.20) + x(1.00) = 6(0.50)$

$1.2 + 0.8x = 3$

$0.8x = 1.8$

$x = 2.25$ liters [1.2]

16. Let x = number of hours the assistant needs to cover the parking lot.

$$6\left[\frac{1}{10}+\frac{1}{x}\right]=1$$

$$10x(6)\left[\frac{1}{10}+\frac{1}{x}\right]=10x(1)$$

$$6x+60=10x$$

$$-4x=-60$$

$$x=15$$

The assistant takes 15 hours to cover the parking lot. [1.4]

17.
$$10+0.18x>18+0.10x$$
$$0.08x>8$$
$$x>100$$

If you drive more than 100 miles, then company A is less expensive. [1.5]

18.
$$0.5=-0.0002348x^2+0.0375x$$
$$0.0002348x^2-0.0375x+0.5=0$$
$$x=\frac{-(-0.0375)\pm\sqrt{(-0.0375)^2-4(0.0002348)(0.5)}}{2(0.0002348)}$$
$$=\frac{0.0375\pm\sqrt{0.00094}}{0.00047}$$
$$=\frac{0.0375\pm0.0306}{0.0004696}$$
$$x\approx145.0\text{ or }x\approx14.7$$

More than 14.7 ft but less than 145.0 ft from a side line. [1.5]

19.
$$200=\frac{4500x}{2x^2+25}$$
$$200(2x^2+25)=4500x$$
$$400x^2-4500x+5000=0$$
$$4x^2-45x+50=0$$
$$(x-10)(4x-5)=0$$
$$x-10=0\qquad 4x-5=0$$
$$x=10\qquad\quad x=1.25$$

More than 1.25 mi but less than 10 mi from the city center. [1.5]

20.
$$v=\frac{k}{\sqrt{d}}$$
$$4=\frac{k}{\sqrt{3000}}$$
$$k=4\sqrt{3000}=40\sqrt{30}$$
$$v=\frac{40\sqrt{30}}{\sqrt{2500}}=\frac{40\sqrt{30}}{50}$$
$$v=\frac{4\sqrt{30}}{5}\approx4.4\text{ miles/second }[1.6]$$

•••

Cumulative Review

1. $4+3(-5)=4-15=-11$ [P.1]

2. $0.00017=1.7\times10^{-4}$ [P.2]

3. $(3x-5)^2-(x+4)(x-4)=(9x^2-30x+25)-(x^2-16)$ [P.3]
$$=9x^2-30x+25-x^2+16$$
$$=8x^2-30x+41$$

4. $8x^2+19x-15=(8x-5)(x+3)$ [P.4]

5. $\dfrac{7x-3}{x-4}-5=\dfrac{7x-3-5x+20}{x-4}=\dfrac{2x+17}{x-4}$ [P.5]

6. $a^{2/3}\cdot a^{1/4}=a^{2/3+1/4}=a^{11/12}$ [P.2]

7. $(2+5i)(2-5i)=4-25i^2=4+25=29$ [P.6]

8. $2(3x-4)+5=17$ [1.1]
$$2(3x-4)=12$$
$$6x=20$$
$$x=\frac{10}{3}$$

9.
$$2x^2 - 4x = 3 \quad [1.3]$$
$$2x^2 - 4x - 3 = 0$$
$$x = \frac{-(-4) \pm \sqrt{(-4)^2 - 4(2)(-3)}}{2(2)} = \frac{4 \pm 2\sqrt{10}}{4} = \frac{2 \pm \sqrt{10}}{2}$$

10.
$$|2x - 6| = 4 \quad [1.1]$$
$$2x - 6 = 4 \qquad 2x - 6 = -4$$
$$2x = 10 \quad \text{or} \qquad 2x = 2$$
$$x = 5 \qquad\qquad x = 1$$

11.
$$x = 3 + \sqrt{9 - x} \quad [1.4]$$
$$x - 3 = \sqrt{9 - x}$$
$$(x - 3)^2 = \left(\sqrt{9 - x}\right)^2$$
$$x^2 - 6x + 9 = 9 - x$$
$$x^2 - 5x = x(x - 5) = 0$$
$$x = 0 \quad \text{or} \quad x = 5$$

Check 0:
$$0 = 3 + \sqrt{9 - 0}$$
$$0 = 3 + \sqrt{9}$$
$$0 = 3 + 3$$
$$0 = 6$$
No

Check 5:
$$5 = 3 + \sqrt{9 - 5}$$
$$5 = 3 + \sqrt{4}$$
$$5 = 3 + 2$$
$$5 = 5$$

12. $x^3 - 36x = x(x^2 - 36) = x(x + 6)(x - 6) = 0$
The solutions are 0, –6, 6. [1.4]

13.
$$2x^4 - 11x^2 + 15 = 0 \quad \text{Let } u = x^2.$$
$$2u^2 - 11u + 15 = (2u - 5)(u - 3) = 0$$
$$2u - 5 = 0 \qquad\qquad \text{or} \quad u - 3 = 0$$
$$u = x^2 = \frac{5}{2} \qquad\qquad\qquad u = 3$$
$$\qquad\qquad\qquad\qquad\qquad\qquad x^2 = 3$$
$$x = \pm\sqrt{\frac{5}{2}} = \pm\frac{\sqrt{10}}{2} \qquad\qquad x = \pm\sqrt{3}$$
The solutions are $-\dfrac{\sqrt{10}}{2}, \dfrac{\sqrt{10}}{2}, -\sqrt{3}, \sqrt{3}$ [1.4]

14.
$$3x - 1 > 2 \quad \text{or} \quad -3x + 5 \geq 8$$
$$3x > 3 \qquad\qquad -3x \geq 3$$
$$x > 1 \qquad\qquad x \leq -1$$
The solution is $\{x \mid x \leq -1 \text{ or } x > 1\}$. [1.5]

15.
$$|x - 6| \geq 2 \Rightarrow x - 6 \geq 2 \qquad \text{or} \qquad x - 6 \leq -2$$
$$x \geq 8 \qquad\qquad\qquad x \leq 4$$
The solution is $(-\infty, 4] \cup [8, \infty)$. [1.5]

16.
$$\frac{x - 2}{2x - 3} \geq 4 \Rightarrow \frac{x - 2}{2x - 3} - 4 \geq 0 \Rightarrow \frac{x - 2}{2x - 3} - \frac{4(2x - 3)}{2x - 3} \geq 0 \Rightarrow \frac{x - 2 - 8x + 12}{2x - 3} \geq 0 \Rightarrow \frac{-7x + 10}{2x - 3} \geq 0$$

Solve $-7x + 10 = 0$ and $2x - 3 - 0$ to find the critical values.
$$-7x + 10 = 0 \qquad\qquad 2x - 3 = 0$$
$$x = \frac{10}{7} \qquad\qquad\qquad x = \frac{3}{2}$$

The critical values are $\dfrac{10}{7}$ and $\dfrac{3}{2}$. The intervals are $\left(-\infty, \dfrac{10}{7}\right), \left(\dfrac{10}{7}, \dfrac{3}{2}\right)$ and $\left(\dfrac{3}{2}, \infty\right)$

Test 0, in the interval $\left(-\infty, \dfrac{10}{7}\right)$: $\dfrac{0 - 2}{2(0) - 3} \geq 4 \Rightarrow \dfrac{-2}{-3} \geq 4 \Rightarrow \dfrac{2}{3} \geq 4$, which is false.

Test 1.45, in the interval $\left(\dfrac{10}{7}, \dfrac{3}{2}\right)$: $\dfrac{1.45 - 2}{2(1.45) - 3} \geq 4 \Rightarrow \dfrac{-0.55}{-0.1} \geq 4 \Rightarrow 5.5 \geq 4$, which is true.

Test 2, in the interval $\left(\dfrac{3}{2}, \infty\right)$: $\dfrac{2 - 2}{2(2) - 3} \geq 4 \Rightarrow \dfrac{0}{1} \geq 4 \Rightarrow 0 \geq 4$, which is false.

The denominator cannot equal zero $\Rightarrow x \neq \dfrac{3}{2}$.

The solution is $\left\{x \mid \dfrac{10}{7} \leq x < \dfrac{3}{2}\right\}$. [1.5]

17.

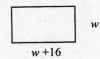

w

$w + 16$

$$\text{Perimeter} = 2(\text{Length}) + 2(\text{Width})$$
$$200 = 2(w+16) + 2w$$
$$200 = 2w + 32 + 2w$$
$$168 = 4w$$
$$42 = w$$
$$w = 42$$
$$w + 16 = 58$$

The width is 42 feet; length is 58 feet. [1.2]

18. Let x = time for assistant to do the job alone.

The worker does $\frac{1}{10}$ of the job per hour.

The assistant does $\frac{1}{x}$ of the job per hour.

$$6\left(\frac{1}{10}\right) + 6\left(\frac{1}{x}\right) = 1$$
$$\frac{6}{10} + \frac{6}{x} = 1$$
$$10x\left(\frac{6}{10} + \frac{6}{x}\right) = 1(10x)$$
$$6x + 60 = 10x$$
$$60 = 4x$$
$$x = 15$$

The assistant takes 15 hours working alone. [1.5]

19. Let x = the score on the fourth test.

$$80 \le \frac{86+72+94+x}{4} < 90 \quad \text{and} \quad 0 \le x \le 100$$
$$80 \le \frac{252+x}{4} < 90$$
$$320 \le 252 + x < 360$$
$$68 \le x < 108$$
$$[68, 108) \cap [0, 100] = [68, 100]$$

The fourth test score must be from 68 to 100. [1.5]

20.

$$\frac{600p}{100-p} \ge 100$$
$$600p \ge 100(100-p)$$
$$600p \ge 10,000 - 100p$$
$$700p \ge 10,000$$
$$p \ge 14.3$$

and $\dfrac{600p}{100-p} \le 180$

$$600p \le 180(100-p)$$
$$600p \le 18,000 - 180p$$
$$780p \le 18,000$$
$$p \le 23.1$$

They can expect to ticket from 14.3% to 23.1% of the speeders. [1.5]

Chapter 2
Functions and Graphs

1.

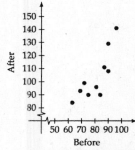

3. **a.**

b.
$$\text{average} = \frac{(84-63)+(99-72)+(111-87)+(129-90)+(108-90)+(141-96)+(93-69)+(96-81)+(90-75)+(90-84)}{10}$$

$$= \frac{21+27+24+39+18+45+24+15+15+6}{10} = \frac{234}{10} = 23.4$$

The average increase in heart rate is 23.4 beats per minute.

5.
$$d = \sqrt{(-8-6)^2 + (11-4)^2}$$
$$= \sqrt{(-14)^2 + (7)^2}$$
$$= \sqrt{196 + 49}$$
$$= \sqrt{245}$$
$$= 7\sqrt{5}$$

7.
$$d = \sqrt{(-10-(-4))^2 + (15-(-20))^2}$$
$$= \sqrt{(-6)^2 + (35)^2}$$
$$= \sqrt{36 + 1225}$$
$$= \sqrt{1261}$$

9.
$$d = \sqrt{(0-5)^2 + (0-(-8))^2}$$
$$= \sqrt{(-5)^2 + (8)^2}$$
$$= \sqrt{25 + 64}$$
$$= \sqrt{89}$$

11.
$$d = \sqrt{(\sqrt{12} - \sqrt{3})^2 + (\sqrt{27} - \sqrt{8})^2}$$
$$= \sqrt{(2\sqrt{3} - \sqrt{3})^2 + (3\sqrt{3} - 2\sqrt{2})^2}$$
$$= \sqrt{(\sqrt{3})^2 + (3\sqrt{3} - 2\sqrt{2})^2}$$
$$= \sqrt{3 + (27 - 12\sqrt{6} + 8)}$$
$$= \sqrt{3 + 27 - 12\sqrt{6} + 8}$$
$$= \sqrt{38 - 12\sqrt{6}}$$

13.
$$d = \sqrt{(-a-a)^2 + (-b-b)^2}$$
$$= \sqrt{(-2a)^2 + (-2b)^2}$$
$$= \sqrt{4a^2 + 4b^2}$$
$$= \sqrt{4(a^2 + b^2)}$$
$$= 2\sqrt{a^2 + b^2}$$

15.
$$d = \sqrt{(-2x-x)^2 + (3x-4x)^2} \text{ with } x < 0$$
$$= \sqrt{(-3x)^2 + (-x)^2}$$
$$= \sqrt{9x^2 + x^2}$$
$$= \sqrt{10x^2}$$
$$= -x\sqrt{10} \quad \text{(Note: since } x < 0, \sqrt{x^2} = -x\text{)}$$

17.
$$\sqrt{(4-x)^2 + (6-0)^2} = 10$$
$$\left(\sqrt{(4-x)^2 + (6-0)^2}\right)^2 = 10^2$$
$$16 - 8x + x^2 + 36 = 100$$
$$x^2 - 8x - 48 = 0$$
$$(x-12)(x+4) = 0$$
$$x = 12 \quad \text{or} \quad x = -4$$
The points are $(12, 0)$, $(-4, 0)$.

19.
$$M = \left(\frac{x_1 + x_2}{2}, \frac{y_1 + y_2}{2}\right)$$
$$= \left(\frac{1+5}{2}, \frac{-1+5}{2}\right)$$
$$= \left(\frac{6}{2}, \frac{4}{2}\right)$$
$$= (3, 2)$$

21.
$$M = \left(\frac{6+6}{2}, \frac{-3+11}{2}\right)$$
$$= \left(\frac{12}{2}, \frac{8}{2}\right)$$
$$= (6, 4)$$

23.
$$M = \left(\frac{1.75 + (-3.5)}{2}, \frac{2.25 + 5.57}{2}\right)$$
$$= \left(-\frac{1.75}{2}, \frac{7.82}{2}\right)$$
$$= (-0.875, 3.91)$$

25.

27.
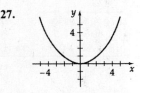

29.
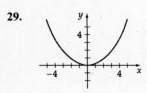

31.
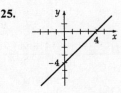

33.
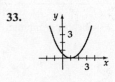

35.
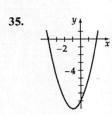

37.

39. Intercepts: $\left(0, \frac{12}{5}\right), (6, 0)$

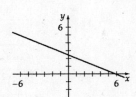

41. $\left(0, \sqrt{5}\right), \left(0, -\sqrt{5}\right), (5, 0)$

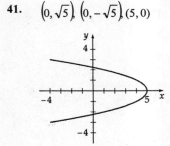

$$x = -y^2 + 5$$

43. $(0, 4), (0, -4), (-4, 0)$

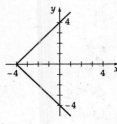

$x = |y| - 4$

45. $(0, \pm 2), (\pm 2, 0)$

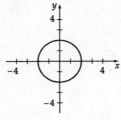

$x^2 + y^2 = 4$

47. $(0, \pm 4), (\pm 4, 0)$

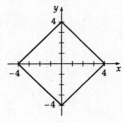

$|x| + |y| = 4$

49. center $(0, 0)$, radius 6

51. center $(1, 3)$, radius 7

53. center $(-2, -5)$, radius 5

55. center $(8, 0)$, radius $\frac{1}{2}$

57. $(x - 4)^2 + (y - 1)^2 = 2^2$

59. $\left(x - \dfrac{1}{2}\right)^2 + \left(y - \dfrac{1}{4}\right)^2 = \left(\sqrt{5}\right)^2$

61.
$$(x - 0)^2 + (y - 0)^2 = r^2$$
$$(-3 - 0)^2 + (4 - 0)^2 = r^2$$
$$(-3)^2 + 4^2 = r^2$$
$$9 + 16 = r^2$$
$$25 = 5^2 = r^2$$
$$(x - 0)^2 + (y - 0)^2 = 5^2$$

63.
$$(x + 2)^2 + (y - 5)^2 = r^2$$
$$(x - 1)^2 + (y - 3)^2 = r^2$$
$$(4 - 1)^2 + (-1 - 3)^2 = r^2$$
$$3^2 + (-4)^2 = r^2$$
$$9 + 16 = r^2$$
$$25 = 5^2 = r^2$$
$$(x - 1)^2 + (y - 3)^2 = 5^2$$

65.
$$x^2 - 6x \quad + y^2 = -5$$
$$x^2 - 6x + 9 + y^2 = -5 + 9$$
$$(x - 3)^2 + y^2 = 2^2$$
center $(3, 0)$, radius 2

67.
$$x^2 - 14x \quad + y^2 + 8y \quad = -56$$
$$x^2 - 14x + 49 + y^2 + 8y + 16 = -56 + 49 + 16$$
$$(x - 7)^2 + (y + 4)^2 = 3^2$$
center $(7, -4)$, radius 3

69.
$$4x^2 + 4x \qquad + 4y^2 = 63$$
$$x^2 + x \qquad + y^2 = \frac{63}{4}$$
$$x^2 + x + \frac{1}{4} \quad + y^2 = \frac{63}{4} + \frac{1}{4}$$
$$\left(x + \frac{1}{2}\right)^2 + y^2 = 16$$
$$\left(x + \frac{1}{2}\right)^2 + (y - 0)^2 = 4^2$$
center $\left(-\dfrac{1}{2}, 0\right)$, radius 4

71.
$$x^2 - x \quad + y^2 + \frac{3}{2}y \quad = \frac{15}{4}$$
$$x^2 - x + \frac{1}{4} + y^2 + \frac{3}{2}y + \frac{9}{4} = \frac{15}{4} + \frac{1}{4} + \frac{9}{4}$$
$$\left(x - \frac{1}{2}\right)^2 + \left(y + \frac{3}{2}\right)^2 = \left(\frac{5}{2}\right)^2$$

center $\left(\frac{1}{2}, -\frac{3}{2}\right)$, radius $\frac{5}{2}$

73.
$$d = \sqrt{(-4-2)^2 + (11-3)^2}$$
$$= \sqrt{36 + 64}$$
$$= \sqrt{100}$$
$$= 10$$

Since the diameter is 10, the radius is 5.
The center is the midpoint of the line segment from (2,3) to (-4,11).
$$\left(\frac{2 + (-4)}{2}, \frac{3 + 11}{2}\right) = (-1, 7) \text{ center}$$
$$(x+1)^2 + (y-7)^2 = 5^2$$

75. Since it is tangent to the x-axis, its radius is 11.
$$(x-7)^2 + (y-11)^2 = 11^2$$

··

77.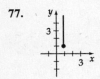

79.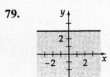

81.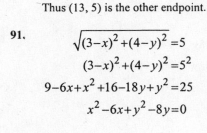

83.

85.

87.
$$\left(\frac{x+5}{2}, \frac{y+1}{2}\right) = (9, 3)$$

therefore $\dfrac{x+5}{2} = 9 \quad$ and $\dfrac{y+1}{2} = 3$
$$x + 5 = 18 \qquad y + 1 = 6$$
$$x = 13 \qquad\quad y = 5$$

Thus (13, 5) is the other endpoint.

89.
$$\left(\frac{x + (-3)}{2}, \frac{y + (-8)}{2}\right) = (2, -7)$$

therefore $\dfrac{x-3}{2} = 2$ and $\dfrac{y-8}{2} = -7$
$$x - 3 = 4 \qquad y - 8 = -14$$
$$x = 7 \qquad\quad y = -6$$

Thus (7, −6) is the other endpoint.

91.
$$\sqrt{(3-x)^2 + (4-y)^2} = 5$$
$$(3-x)^2 + (4-y)^2 = 5^2$$
$$9 - 6x + x^2 + 16 - 18y + y^2 = 25$$
$$x^2 - 6x + y^2 - 8y = 0$$

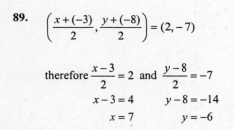
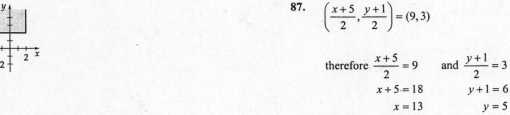

93.

$$\sqrt{(4-x)^2+(0-y)^2}+\sqrt{(-4-x)^2+(0-y)^2}=10$$

$$(4-x)^2+(0-y)^2=100-20\sqrt{(-4-x)^2+(0-y)^2}+(-4-x)^2+(-y)^2$$

$$16-8x+x^2+y^2=100-20\sqrt{(-4-x)^2+(-y)^2}+16+8x+x^2+y^2$$

$$-16x-100=-20\sqrt{(-4-x)^2+(-y)^2}$$

$$4x+25=5\sqrt{(-4-x)^2+(-y)^2}$$

$$16x^2+200x+625=25\left[(-4-x)^2+(-y)^2\right]$$

$$16x^2+200x+625=25\left[16+8x+x^2+y^2\right]$$

$$16x^2+200x+625=400+200x+25x^2+25y^2$$

Simplifying yields $9x^2+25y^2=225$.

95. The center is (-3,3). The radius is 3.

$$(x+3)^2+(y-3)^2=3^2$$

•••

97. x^2+3x-4

$(-3)^2+3(-3)-4=9-9-4=-4$

98. $D=\{-3,-2,-1,0,2\}$

$R=\{1,2,4,5\}$

99. $d=\sqrt{(3-(-4))^2+(-2-1)^2}=\sqrt{49+9}=\sqrt{58}$

100. $2x-6\geq0$

$2x\geq6$

$x\geq3$

101. $x^2-x-6=0$

$(x+2)(x-3)=0$

$x+2=0 \quad x-3=0$

$x=-2 \quad x=3$

$-2, 3$

102. $a=3x+4, \quad a=6x-5$

$3x+4=6x-5$

$9=3x$

$3=x$

$a=3(3)+4=13$

Section 2.2

1. Given $f(x) = 3x - 1$,

a. $f(2) = 3(2) - 1$
$= 6 - 1$
$= 5$

b. $f(-1) = 3(-1) - 1$
$= -3 - 1$
$= -4$

c. $f(0) = 3(0) - 1$
$= 0 - 1$
$= -1$

d. $f\left(\dfrac{2}{3}\right) = 3\left(\dfrac{2}{3}\right) - 1$
$= 2 - 1$
$= 1$

e. $f(k) = 3(k) - 1$
$= 3k - 1$

f. $f(k+2) = 3(k+2) - 1$
$= 3k + 6 - 1$
$= 3k + 5$

3. Given $A(w) = \sqrt{w^2 + 5}$,

a. $A(0) = \sqrt{(0)^2 + 5}$
$= \sqrt{5}$

b. $A(2) = \sqrt{(2)^2 + 5}$
$= \sqrt{9}$
$= 3$

c. $A(-2) = \sqrt{(-2)^2 + 5}$
$= \sqrt{9}$
$= 3$

d. $A(4) = \sqrt{4^2 + 5}$
$= \sqrt{21}$

e. $A(r+1) = \sqrt{(r+1)^2 + 5}$
$= \sqrt{r^2 + 2r + 1 + 5}$
$= \sqrt{r^2 + 2r + 6}$

f. $A(-c) = \sqrt{(-c)^2 + 5}$
$= \sqrt{c^2 + 5}$

5. Given $f(x) = \dfrac{1}{|x|}$,

a. $f(2) = \dfrac{1}{|2|} = \dfrac{1}{2}$

b. $f(-2) = \dfrac{1}{|-2|} = \dfrac{1}{2}$

c. $f\left(-\dfrac{3}{5}\right) = \dfrac{1}{\left|-\dfrac{3}{5}\right|}$
$= \dfrac{1}{3/5}$
$= 1 \div \dfrac{3}{5} = 1 \cdot \dfrac{5}{3} = \dfrac{5}{3}$

d. $f(2) + f(-2) = \dfrac{1}{2} + \dfrac{1}{2} = 1$

e. $f(c^2 + 4) = \dfrac{1}{|c^2 + 4|} = \dfrac{1}{c^2 + 4}$

f. $f(2 + h) = \dfrac{1}{|2 + h|}$

7. Given $s(x) = \dfrac{x}{|x|}$,

a. $s(4) = \dfrac{4}{|4|} = \dfrac{4}{4} = 1$

b. $s(5) = \dfrac{5}{|5|} = \dfrac{5}{5} = 1$

c. $s(-2) = \dfrac{-2}{|-2|} = \dfrac{-2}{2} = -1$

d. $s(-3) = \dfrac{-3}{|-3|} = \dfrac{-3}{3} = -1$

e. Since $t > 0, |t| = t$.
$s(t) = \dfrac{t}{|t|} = \dfrac{t}{t} = 1$

f. Since $t < 0, |t| = -t$.
$s(t) = \dfrac{t}{|t|} = \dfrac{t}{-t} = -1$

9. a. Since $x = -4 < 2$, use $P(x) = 3x + 1$.
$P(-4) = 3(-4) + 1 = -12 + 1 = -11$

b. Since $x = \sqrt{5} \geq 2$, use $P(x) = -x^2 + 11$.
$P(\sqrt{5}) = -(\sqrt{5})^2 + 11 = -5 + 11 = 6$

c. Since $x = c < 2$, use $P(x) = 3x + 1$.
$P(c) = 3c + 1$

d. Since $k \geq 1$, then $x = k + 1 \geq 2$,
so use $P(x) = -x^2 + 11$.
$P(k+1) = -(k+1)^2 + 11 = -(k^2 + 2k + 1) + 11$
$= -k^2 - 2k - 1 + 11$
$= -k^2 - 2k + 10$

11. $2x + 3y = 7$
$3y = -2x + 7$
$y = -\dfrac{2}{3}x + \dfrac{7}{3}$, y is a function of x.

13. $-x + y^2 = 2$
$y^2 = x + 2$
$y = \pm\sqrt{x + 2}$, y is a not function of x.

15. $y = 4 \pm \sqrt{x}$, y is not a function of x since for each $x > 0$ there are two values of x.

17. $y = \sqrt[3]{x}$, y is a function of x.

19. $y^2 = x^2$

$y = \pm\sqrt{x^2}$, y is a not function of x.

21. Function; each x is paired with exactly one y.

23. Function; each x is paired with exactly one y.

25. Function; each x is paired with exactly one y.

27. $f(x) = 3x - 4$ Domain is the set of all real numbers.

29. $f(x) = x^2 + 2$ Domain is the set of all real numbers.

31. $f(x) = \dfrac{4}{x+2}$ Domain is $\{x \mid x \neq -2\}$

33. $f(x) = \sqrt{7+x}$ Domain is $\{x \mid x \geq -7\}$

35. $f(x) = \sqrt{4-x^2}$ Domain is $\{x \mid -2 \leq x \leq 2\}$

37. $f(x) = \dfrac{1}{\sqrt{x+4}}$ Domain is $\{x \mid x > -4\}$

39.

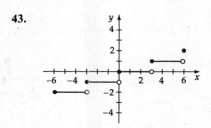

Domain: the set of all real numbers

41.

Domain: the set of all real numbers

43.

Domain: $\{x \mid -6 \leq x \leq 6\}$

45.

Domain: $\{x \mid -3 \leq x \leq 3\}$

47. **a.** $C(2.8) = 0.37 - 0.34\text{int}(1-2.8)$

$= 0.37 - 0.34\text{int}(-1.8)$

$= 0.37 - 0.34(-2)$

$= 0.37 + 0.68$

$= \$1.05$

b.

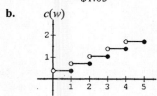

49. **a.** Yes; every vertical line intersects the graph in one point.

b. Yes; every vertical line intersects the graph in one point.

c. No; some vertical lines intersect the graph at more than one point.

d. Yes; every vertical line intersects the graph in at most one point.

51. Decreasing on $(-\infty, 0]$; increasing on $[0, \infty)$

53. Increasing on $(-\infty, \infty)$

55. Decreasing on $(-\infty, -3]$; increasing on $[-3, 0]$; decreasing on $[0, 3]$; increasing on $[3, \infty)$

57. Constant on $(-\infty, 0]$; increasing on $[0, \infty)$

59. Decreasing on $(-\infty, 0]$; constant on $[0, 1]$; increasing on $[1, \infty)$

61. g and F are one-to-one since every horizontal line intersects the graph at one point.
f, V, and p are not one-to-one since some horizontal lines intersect the graph at more than one point.

63. a.
$$2l + 2w = 50$$
$$2w = 50 - 2l$$
$$w = 25 - l$$

b.
$$A = lw$$
$$A = l(25 - l)$$
$$A = 25l - l^2$$

65. $v(t) = 80{,}000 - 6500t, \quad 0 \le t \le 10$

67. a.
$$C(x) = 5(400) + 22.80x$$
$$= 2000 + 22.80x$$

b. $R(x) = 37.00x$

c.
$$P(x) = 37.00x - C(x)$$
$$= 37.00 - [2000 + 22.80x]$$
$$= 37.00x - 2000 - 22.80x$$
$$= 14.20x - 2000$$

Note x is a natural number.

69.
$$\frac{15}{3} = \frac{15 - h}{r}$$
$$5 = \frac{15 - h}{r}$$
$$5r = 15 - h$$
$$h = 15 - 5r$$
$$h(r) = 15 - 5r$$

71.
$$d = \sqrt{(3t)^2 + (50)^2}$$
$$d = \sqrt{9t^2 + 2500} \text{ meters}, \ 0 \le t \le 60$$

73.
$$d = \sqrt{(45 - 8t)^2 + (6t)^2} \text{ miles}$$
where t is the number of hours after 12:00 noon

75. a.

Circle	Square
$C = 2\pi r$	$C = 4s$
$x = 2\pi r$	$20 - x = 4s$
$r = \dfrac{x}{2\pi}$	$s = 5 - \dfrac{x}{4}$
$\text{Area} = \pi r^2 = \pi\left(\dfrac{x}{2\pi}\right)^2$	$\text{Area} = s^2 = \left(5 - \dfrac{x}{4}\right)^2$
$= \dfrac{x^2}{4\pi}$	$= 25 - \dfrac{5}{2}x + \dfrac{x^2}{16}$

$$\text{Total Area} = \frac{x^2}{4\pi} + 25 - \frac{5}{2}x + \frac{x^2}{16}$$
$$= \left(\frac{1}{4\pi} + \frac{1}{16}\right)x^2 - \frac{5}{2}x + 25$$

b.

x	0	4	8	12	16	20
Total Area	25	17.27	14.09	15.46	21.37	31.83

c. Domain: $[0, 20]$.

77. a.

Left side triangle	Right side triangle
$c^2 = 20^2 + (40 - x)^2$	$c^2 = 30^2 + x^2$
$c = \sqrt{400 + (40 - x)^2}$	$c = \sqrt{900 + x^2}$

$$\text{Total length} = \sqrt{900 + x^2} + \sqrt{400 + (40 - x)^2}$$

b.

x	0	10	20	30	40
Total Length	74.72	67.68	64.34	64.79	70

c. Domain: $(0, 40)$.

79.

x	5	10	12.5	15	20
$Y(x)$	275	375	385	390	394

answers accurate to nearest apple

81.
$$f(c) = c^2 - c - 5 = 1$$
$$c^2 - c - 6 = 0$$
$$(c-3)(c+2) = 0$$
$$c - 3 = 0 \quad \text{or} \quad c + 2 = 0$$
$$c = 3 \qquad\qquad c = -2$$

83. 1 is not in the range of $f(x)$, since

$1 = \dfrac{x-1}{x+1}$ only if $x + 1 = x - 1$ or $1 = -1$.

85. Set the graphing utility to "dot" mode.
```
Y1◘int X/abs X
Y2 =
Y3 =
Y4 =
Y5 =
Y6 =
Y7 =
Y8 =
```

WINDOW FORMAT
```
Xmin=-4. 7
Xmax=4. 7
Xscl=1
Ymin=-5
Ymax=2
Yscl=1
```

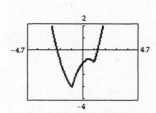

87.
```
Y1◘ X²-2abs X-3
Y2 =
Y3 =
Y4 =
Y5 =
Y6 =
Y7 =
Y8 =
```

WINDOW FORMAT
```
Xmin=-4. 7
Xmax=4. 7
Xscl=1
Ymin=-5
Ymax=1
Yscl=1
```

89.
```
Y1◘ abs (X²-1)-
abs (X-2)
Y2 =
Y3 =
Y4 =
Y5 =
Y6 =
Y7 =
```

WINDOW FORMAT
```
Xmin=-4.7
Xmax=4.7
Xscl=1
Ymin=-4.7
Ymax=4.7
Yscl=1
```

Connecting Concepts

91. $f(x)\Big|_2^3 = (9-3) - (4-2) = 6 - 2 = 4$

93. $f(x)\Big|_0^2 = (16 - 12 - 2) - 0 = 2$

95.
a. $f(1,7) = 3(1) + 5(7) - 2 = 3 + 35 - 2 = 36$
b. $f(0,3) = 3(0) + 5(3) - 2 = 13$
c. $f(-2,4) = 3(-2) + 5(4) - 2 = 12$
d. $f(4,4) = 3(4) + 5(4) - 2 = 30$
e. $f(k,2k) = 3(k) + 5(2k) - 2 = 13k - 2$
f. $f(k+2, k-3) = 3(k+2) + 5(k-3) - 2 = 3k + 6 + 5k - 15 - 2 = 8k - 11$

97. $s = \dfrac{5 + 8 + 11}{2} = 12$

$A(5,8,11) = \sqrt{12(12-5)(12-8)(12-11)}$

$\qquad\qquad = \sqrt{12(7)(4)(1)} = \sqrt{336} = 4\sqrt{21}$

99.
$$a^2 + 3a - 3 = a$$
$$a^2 + 2a - 3 = 0$$
$$(a-1)(a+3) = 0$$
$$a = 1 \quad \text{or} \quad a = -3$$

101.

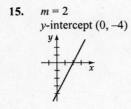

Prepare for **Section 2.3**

103. $d = 5 - (-2) = 7$

104. The product of any number and its negative reciprocal is -1.

$$-7 \cdot \frac{1}{7} = -1$$

105. $\dfrac{-4-4}{2-(-3)} = \dfrac{-8}{5}$

106. $y - 3 = -2(x - 3)$
$y - 3 = -2x + 6$
$\quad y = -2x + 9$

107. $3x - 5y = 15$
$-5y = -3x + 15$
$\quad y = \dfrac{3}{5}x - 3$

108. $y = 3x - 2(5 - x)$
$0 = 3x - 2(5 - x)$
$0 = 3x - 10 + 2x$
$10 = 5x$
$\quad 2 = x$

Section 2.3

1. $m = \dfrac{y_2 - y_1}{x_2 - x_1} = \dfrac{7 - 4}{1 - 3} = \dfrac{3}{-2} = -\dfrac{3}{2}$

3. $m = \dfrac{2 - 0}{0 - 4} = -\dfrac{1}{2}$

5. The line does not have a slope since $x_2 = x_1 = 0$.

7. $m = \dfrac{-2 - 4}{-4 - (-3)} = \dfrac{-6}{-1} = 6$

9. $m = \dfrac{\frac{7}{2} - \frac{1}{2}}{\frac{7}{3} - (-4)} = \dfrac{\frac{6}{2}}{\frac{19}{3}} = 3 \cdot \dfrac{3}{19} = \dfrac{9}{19}$

11. $m = \dfrac{f(3 + h) - f(3)}{3 + h - 3} = \dfrac{f(3 + h) - f(3)}{h}$

13. $m = \dfrac{f(h) - f(0)}{h - 0} = \dfrac{f(h) - f(0)}{h}$

15. $m = 2$
y-intercept $(0, -4)$

17. $m = -\dfrac{1}{3}$
y-intercept $(0, 4)$

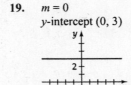

19. $m = 0$
y-intercept $(0, 3)$

21. $m = 2$
y-intercept $(0, 0)$

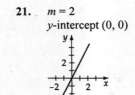

23. $m = -2$
 y-intercept $(0, 5)$

25. $m = -\dfrac{3}{4}$
 y-intercept $(0, 4)$

27. Use $y = mx + b$ with $m = 1$, $b = 3$.
 $y = x + 3$

29. Use $y = mx + b$ with $m = \dfrac{3}{4}$, $b = \dfrac{1}{2}$.

 $y = \dfrac{3}{4}x + \dfrac{1}{2}$

31. Use $y = mx + b$ with $m = 0$, $b = 4$.
 $y = 4$

33. $y - 2 = -4(x - (-3))$
 $y - 2 = -4x - 12$
 $y = -4x - 10$

35. $m = \dfrac{4 - 1}{-1 - 3}$

 $= \dfrac{3}{-4} = -\dfrac{3}{4}$

 $y - 1 = -\dfrac{3}{4}(x - 3)$

 $y = -\dfrac{3}{4}x + \dfrac{9}{4} + \dfrac{4}{4}$

 $y = -\dfrac{3}{4}x + \dfrac{13}{4}$

37. $m = \dfrac{-1 - 11}{2 - 7}$

 $= \dfrac{-12}{-5} = \dfrac{12}{5}$

 $y - 11 = \dfrac{12}{5}(x - 7)$

 $y - 11 = \dfrac{12}{5}x - \dfrac{84}{5}$

 $y = \dfrac{12}{5}x - \dfrac{84}{5} + \dfrac{55}{5}$

 $= \dfrac{12}{5}x - \dfrac{29}{5}$

39. $f(x) = 2x + 3 = -1$
 $2x = -4$
 $x = -2$

41. $f(x) = 1 - 4x = 3$
 $-4x = 2$
 $x = -\dfrac{1}{2}$

43. $f(x) = 3 - \dfrac{x}{2} = 5$

 $-\dfrac{x}{2} = 2$

 $x = 2(-2)$

 $x = -4$

45. $f(x) = 3x - 12$
 $3x - 12 = 0$
 $3x = 12$
 $x = 4$
The x-intercept of the graph of $f(x)$ is $(4, 0)$.

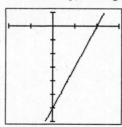

Xmin $= -4$, Xmax $= 6$, Xscl $= 2$,
Ymin $= -12.2$, Ymax $= 2$, Yscl $= 2$

47.
$$f(x)=\frac{1}{4}x+5$$
$$\frac{1}{4}x+5=0$$
$$\frac{1}{4}x=-5$$
$$x=-20$$

The x-intercept of the graph of $f(x)$ is $(-20,0)$.

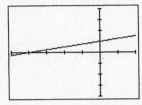

Xmin $=-30$, Xmax $=30$, Xscl $=10$,
Ymin $=-10$, Ymax $=10$, Yscl $=1$

51. Algebraic method: $f_1(x)=f_2(x)$
$$2x-4=-x+12$$
$$3x=16$$
$$x=\frac{16}{3}$$

Graphical method: Graph $y=2x-4$ and
$$y=-x+12$$

They intersect at $x=5\frac{1}{3}$, $y=6\frac{2}{3}$.

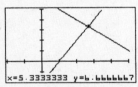

Xmin $=-4$, Xmax $=10$, Xscl $=2$,
Ymin $=-2$, Ymax $=10$, Yscl $=2$

55. **a.**
$$m=\frac{29-13}{20-9}\approx1.45$$
$$H(c)-13=1.45(c-9)$$
$$H(c)=1.45c$$

b. $H(18)=1.45(18)\approx26$ mpg

49. Algebraic method: $f_1(x)=f_2(x)$
$$4x+5=x+6$$
$$3x=1$$
$$x=\frac{1}{3}$$

Graphical method: Graph $y=4x+5$ and
$$y=x+6$$

They intersect at $x=\frac{1}{3}$, $y=6\frac{1}{3}$.

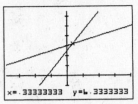

Xmin $=-7.8$, Xmax $=7.8$, Xscl $=2$,
Ymin $=-2$, Ymax $=10$, Yscl $=2$

53.
$$m=\frac{1505-1482}{28-20}=2.875$$

The value of the slope indicates that the speed of sound in water increases 2.875 ft per s for a one-degree increase in temperature.

57. **a.**
$$m=\frac{63,000-38,000}{2010-2000}=2500$$
$$N(t)-63,000=2500(t-2010)$$
$$N(t)=2500t-4,962,000$$

b.
$$60,000=2500t-4,962,000$$
$$5,022,000=2500t$$
$$2008.8=t$$

The number of jobs will exceed 60,000 in 2008.

59.

a. $m = \dfrac{240-180}{18-16} = 30$

$B(d) - 180 = 30(d - 16)$

$B(d) = 30d - 300$

b. The value of the slope means that a 1-inch increase in the diameter of a log 32 ft long results in an increase of 30 board-feet of lumber that can be obtained from the log.

c. $B(19) = 30(19) - 300 = 270$ board feet

61. Line A represents Michelle

Line B represents Amanda

Line C represents the distance between Michelle and Amanda.

63.

a. Find the slope of the line.

$m = \dfrac{180-110}{108-70} = \dfrac{70}{38} \approx 1.842$

Use the point-slope formula to find the equation.

$y - y_1 = m(x - x_1)$

$y - 110 = 1.842(x - 70)$

$y - 110 = 1.842x - 128.94$

$y = 1.842x - 18.94$

b. $y = 1.842(90) - 18.94$

$y = 165.78 - 18.94$

$y = 146.84 \approx 147$

65. $P(x) = 92.50x - (52x + 1782)$

$P(x) = 92.50x - 52x - 1782$

$P(x) = 40.50x - 1782$

$40.50x - 1782 = 0$

$40.50x = 1782$

$x = \dfrac{1782}{40.50}$

$x = 44$, the break-even point

67. $P(x) = 259x - (180x + 10,270)$

$P(x) = 259x - 180x - 10,270$

$P(x) = 79x - 10,270$

$79x - 10,270 = 0$

$79x = 10.270$

$x = \dfrac{10.270}{79}$

$x = 130$, the break-even point

69.

a. $C(0) = 8(0) + 275 = 0 + 275 = \$275$

b. $C(1) = 8(1) + 275 = 8 + 275 = \$283$

c. $C(10) = 8(10) + 275 = 80 + 275 = \$355$

d. The marginal cost is the slope of $C(x) = 8x + 275$, which is 8 (dollars).

71.

a. $C(t) = 19,500.00 + 6.75t$

b. $R(t) = 55.00t$

c. $P(t) = R(t) - C(t)$

$P(t) = 55.00t - (19,500.00 + 6.75t)$

$P(t) = 55.00t - 19,500.00 - 6.75t$

$P(t) = 48.25t - 19,500.00$

d. $48.25t = 19,500.00$

$t = \dfrac{19,500.00}{48.25}$

$t = 404.1451$ days ≈ 405 days

73. The graph of $3x + y = -24$ has $m = -\dfrac{3}{4}$.

$y - 3 = -\dfrac{3}{4}(x - 1)$

$y = -\dfrac{3}{4}x + \dfrac{3}{4} + 3$

$y = -\dfrac{3}{4}x + \dfrac{15}{4}$

75. The graph of $x + y = 4$ has $m = -1$.
Thus we use a slope of 1.
$$y - 2 = 1(x - 1)$$
$$y = x - 1 + 2$$
$$y = x + 1$$

77. The equation of the line through $(0,0)$ and $P(3,4)$ has slope $\dfrac{4}{3}$.

The path of the rock is on the line through $P(3,4)$ with slope $-\dfrac{3}{4}$, so $y - 4 = -\dfrac{3}{4}(x - 3)$.

$$y - 4 = -\frac{3}{4}x + \frac{9}{4}$$
$$y = -\frac{3}{4}x + \frac{9}{4} + 4$$
$$y = -\frac{3}{4}x + \frac{25}{4}$$

The point where the rock hits the wall at $y = 10$ is the point of intersection of $y = -\dfrac{3}{4}x + \dfrac{25}{4}$ and $y = 10$.

$$-\frac{3}{4}x + \frac{25}{4} = 10$$
$$-3x + 25 = 40$$
$$-3x = 15$$
$$x = -5 \text{ feet}$$

Therefore the rock hits the wall at $(-5, 10)$.
The x-coordinate is -5.

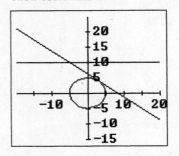

79. **a.** $h = 1$ so $Q(2 + h, [2 + h]^2 + 1) = Q(3, 3^2 + 1) = Q(3, 10)$

$$m = \frac{10 - 5}{3 - 2} = \frac{5}{1} = 5$$

b. $h = 0.1$ so $Q(2 + h, [2 + h]^2 + 1) = Q(2.1, 2.1^2 + 1) = Q(2.1, 5.41)$

$$m = \frac{5.41 - 5}{2.1 - 2} = \frac{0.41}{0.1} = 4.1$$

c. $h = 0.01$ so $Q(2 + h, [2 + h]^2 + 1) = Q(2.01, 2.01^2 + 1) = Q(2.01, 5.0401)$

$$m = \frac{5.0401 - 5}{2.01 - 2} = \frac{0.0401}{0.01} = 4.01$$

d. As h approaches 0, the slope of PQ seems to be approaching 4.

e. $x_1 = 2, y_1 = 5, x_2 = 2 + h, y_2 = [2 + h]^2 + 1$

$$m = \frac{y_2 - y_1}{x_2 - x_1} = \frac{[2 + h]^2 + 1 - 5}{(2 + h) - 2} = \frac{(4 + 4h + h^2) + 1 - 5}{h} = \frac{4h + h^2}{h} = 4 + h$$

81.
$$m = \frac{(x + h)^2 - x^2}{x + h - x} = \frac{x^2 + 2xh + h^2 - x^2}{h} = \frac{2xh + h^2}{h} = \frac{h(2x + h)}{h} = 2x + h$$

83. Substitute $\dfrac{y_2 - y_1}{x_2 - x_1}$ for m in the point-slope form $y - y_1 = m(x - x_1)$ to yield $y - y_1 = \dfrac{y_2 - y_1}{x_2 - x_1}(x - x_1)$, the two-point form.

85.
$$y - 1 = \frac{3-1}{4-5}(x-5)$$
$$y - 1 = \frac{2}{-1}(x-5)$$
$$y = -2(x-5)$$
$$y - 1 = -2x + 10$$
$$y = -2x + 10 + 1$$
$$y = -2x + 11$$

87. Use $\dfrac{x}{a} + \dfrac{y}{b} = 1$ with $a = 3$ and $b = 5$.
$$\frac{x}{3} + \frac{y}{5} = 1$$
$$15\left(\frac{x}{3} + \frac{y}{5}\right) = 15(1)$$
$$5x + 3y = 15$$

89. Use $\dfrac{x}{a} + \dfrac{y}{b} = 1$ with $b = 3a$.
$$\frac{x}{a} + \frac{y}{3a} = 1 \quad \text{Since } (5, 2) \text{ is on the line,}$$
$$\frac{5}{a} + \frac{2}{3a} = 1$$
$$3a\left(\frac{5}{a} + \frac{2}{3a}\right) = 3a(1)$$
$$15 + 2 = 3a$$
$$17 = 3a$$
$$\frac{17}{3} = a$$

Thus $\dfrac{x}{\left(\dfrac{17}{3}\right)} + \dfrac{y}{3\left(\dfrac{17}{3}\right)} = 1$
$$\frac{3x}{17} + \frac{y}{17} = 1$$
$$3x + y = 17$$

91.
$$\frac{3(1+h)^3 - 3}{1 + h - 1} = \frac{3(1 + 3h + 3h^2 + h^3) - 3}{h}$$
$$= \frac{3 + 9h + 9h^2 + 3h^3 - 3}{h}$$
$$= \frac{9h + 9h^2 + 3h^3}{h}$$
$$= \frac{h(9 + 9h + 3h^2)}{h}$$
$$= 9 + 9h + 3h^2$$

93. The slope of the line through $(3, 9)$ and (x, y) is $\dfrac{15}{2}$, so $\dfrac{y-9}{x-3} = \dfrac{15}{2}$.

Therefore
$$2(y-9) = 15(x-3)$$
$$2y - 18 = 15x - 45$$
$$2y - 15x + 27 = 0 \quad \text{Substitute } y = x^2 \text{ into this equation.}$$
$$2x^2 - 15x + 27 = 0$$
$$(2x - 9)(x - 3) = 0$$
$$x = \frac{9}{2} \quad \text{or} \quad x = 3$$

If $x = \dfrac{9}{2}$, $y = x^2 = \left(\dfrac{9}{2}\right)^2 = \dfrac{81}{4} \Rightarrow \left(\dfrac{9}{2}, \dfrac{81}{4}\right)$.

If $x = 3$, $y = x^2 = (3)^2 = 9 \Rightarrow (3, 9)$, but this is the point itself.

The point $\left(\dfrac{9}{2}, \dfrac{81}{4}\right)$ is on the graph of $y = x^2$, and the slope of the line containing $(3, 9)$ and $\left(\dfrac{9}{2}, \dfrac{81}{4}\right)$ is $\dfrac{15}{2}$.

•••

95. $3x^2+10x-8=(3x-2)(x+4)$

96. $x^2-8x=x^2-8x+16=(x-4)^2$

97. $f(-3)=2(-3)^2-5(-3)-7$
$\quad\quad =18+15-7$
$\quad\quad =26$

98. $2x^2-x-1=0$
$(2x+1)(x-1)=0$
$2x+1=0 \quad x-1=0$
$\quad x=-\dfrac{1}{2} \quad\quad x=1$

99. $x^2+3x-2=0$
$x=\dfrac{-3\pm\sqrt{(3)^2-4(1)(-2)}}{2(1)}$
$\quad =\dfrac{-3\pm\sqrt{17}}{2}$

100. $53=-16t^2+64t+5$
$16t^2-64t+48=0$
$\quad t^2-4t+3=0$
$\quad (t-1)(t-3)=0$
$\quad t=1,3$

Section 2.4

1. d   **3.** b   **5.** g   **7.** c

9. $f(x)=(x^2+4x)+1$
$\quad\quad =(x^2+4x+4)+1-4$
$\quad\quad =(x+2)^2-3$ standard form,
vertex $(-2,-3)$, axis of symmetry $x=-2$

11. $f(x)=(x^2-8x)+5$
$\quad\quad =(x^2-8x+16)+5-16$
$\quad\quad =(x-4)^2-11$ standard form,
vertex $(4,-11)$, axis of symmetry $x=4$

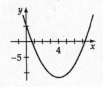

13. $f(x)=(x^2+3x)+1$
$\quad\quad =\left(x^2+3x+\dfrac{9}{4}\right)+1-\dfrac{9}{4}$
$\quad\quad =\left(x+\dfrac{3}{2}\right)^2+\dfrac{4}{4}-\dfrac{9}{4}$
$\quad\quad =\left(x+\dfrac{3}{2}\right)^2-\dfrac{5}{4}$ standard form,
vertex $\left(-\dfrac{3}{2},-\dfrac{5}{4}\right)$, axis of symmetry $x=-\dfrac{3}{2}$

15. $f(x)=-x^2+4x+2$
$\quad\quad =-(x^2-4x)+2$
$\quad\quad =-(x^2-4x+4)+2+4$
$\quad\quad =-(x-2)^2+6$ standard form,
vertex $(2,6)$, axis of symmetry $x=2$

17.

$$f(x) = -3x^2 + 3x + 7$$
$$= -3(x^2 - 1x) + 7$$
$$= -3\left(x^2 - 1x + \frac{1}{4}\right) + 7 + \frac{3}{4}$$
$$= -3\left(x - \frac{1}{2}\right)^2 + \frac{28}{4} + \frac{3}{4}$$
$$= -3\left(x - \frac{1}{2}\right)^2 + \frac{31}{4} \quad \text{standard form,}$$

vertex $\left(\dfrac{1}{2}, \dfrac{31}{4}\right)$, axis of symmetry $x = \dfrac{1}{2}$

19.

$$x = \frac{-b}{2a} = \frac{10}{2(1)} = 5$$
$$y = f(5) = (5)^2 - 10(5)$$
$$= 25 - 50 = -25$$
vertex $(5, -25)$
$$f(x) = (x - 5)^2 - 25$$

21.

$$x = \frac{-b}{2a} = \frac{0}{2(1)} = 0$$
$$y = f(0) = (0)^2 - 10 = -10$$
vertex $(0, -10)$
$$f(x) = x^2 - 10$$

23.

$$x = \frac{-b}{2a} = \frac{-6}{2(-1)} = \frac{-6}{-2} = 3$$
$$y = f(3) = -(3)^2 + 6(3) + 1$$
$$-9 + 18 + 1$$
$$= 10$$
vertex $(3, 10)$
$$f(x) = -(x - 3)^2 + 10$$

25.

$$x = \frac{-b}{2a} = \frac{3}{2(2)} = \frac{3}{4}$$
$$y = f\left(\frac{3}{4}\right) = 2\left(\frac{3}{4}\right)^2 - 3\left(\frac{3}{4}\right) + 7$$
$$= 2\left(\frac{9}{16}\right) - \frac{9}{4} + 7$$
$$= \frac{9}{8} - \frac{9}{4} + 7$$
$$= \frac{9}{8} - \frac{18}{8} + \frac{56}{8}$$
$$= \frac{47}{8}$$
vertex $\left(\frac{3}{4}, \frac{47}{8}\right)$
$$f(x) = 2\left(x - \frac{3}{4}\right)^2 + \frac{47}{8}$$

27.

$$x = \frac{-b}{2a} = \frac{-1}{2(-4)} = \frac{1}{8}$$
$$y = f\left(\frac{1}{8}\right) = -4\left(\frac{1}{8}\right)^2 + \left(\frac{1}{8}\right) + 1$$
$$= -4\left(\frac{1}{64}\right) + \frac{1}{8} + 1$$
$$= -\frac{1}{16} + \frac{1}{8} + 1$$
$$= -\frac{1}{16} + \frac{2}{16} + \frac{16}{16}$$
$$= \frac{17}{16}$$
vertex $\left(\frac{1}{8}, \frac{17}{16}\right)$
$$f(x) = -4\left(x - \frac{1}{8}\right)^2 + \frac{17}{16}$$

29.
$$f(x)=x^2-2x-1$$
$$=(x^2-2x)-1$$
$$=(x^2-2x+1)-1-1$$
$$=(x-1)^2-2$$
vertex $(1, -2)$
The y-value of the vertex is -2.
The parabola opens up since $a=1>0$.
Thus the range is $\{y|y\geq-2\}$

$$f(x)=2=x^2-2x-1$$
$$0=x^2-2x-3$$
$$0=(x-3)(x+1)$$
$$x-3=0 \quad \text{or} \quad x+1=0$$
$$x=3 \qquad\qquad x=-1$$

31.
$$f(x)=-2x^2+5x-1$$
$$=-2\left(x^2-\frac{5}{2}x\right)-1$$
$$=-2\left(x^2-\frac{5}{2}x+\frac{25}{16}\right)-1+2\left(\frac{25}{16}\right)$$
$$=-2\left(x-\frac{5}{4}\right)^2-\frac{8}{8}+\frac{25}{8}$$
$$=-2\left(x-\frac{5}{4}\right)^2+\frac{17}{8}$$
vertex $\left(\frac{5}{4}, \frac{17}{8}\right)$

The y-value of the vertex is $\frac{17}{8}$.

The parabola opens down since $a=-2<0$.

Thus the range is $\left\{y\middle|y\leq\frac{17}{8}\right\}$.

$$f(x)=2=-2x^2+5x-1$$
$$2x^2-5x+3=0$$
$$(2x-3)(x-1)=0$$
$$2x-3=0 \quad \text{or} \quad x-1=0$$
$$x=\frac{3}{2} \qquad\qquad x=1$$

33.
$$f(x)=x^2+3x+6$$
$$=(x^2+3x)+6$$
$$=\left(x^2+3x+\frac{9}{4}\right)+6-\frac{9}{4}$$
$$=\left(x+\frac{3}{2}\right)^2+6-\frac{9}{4}$$
$$=\left(x+\frac{3}{2}\right)^2+\frac{24}{4}-\frac{9}{4}$$
$$=\left(x+\frac{3}{2}\right)^2+\frac{15}{4}$$
vertex $\left(-\frac{3}{2}, \frac{15}{4}\right)$

The y-value of the vertex is $\frac{15}{4}$.

The parabola opens up since $a=1>0$.

Thus the range is $\left\{y\middle|y\geq\frac{15}{4}\right\}$.

No, $3\notin\left\{y\middle|y\geq\frac{15}{4}\right\}$.

35.
$$f(x)=x^2+8x$$
$$=(x^2+8x+16)-16$$
$$=(x+4)^2-16$$
minimum value of -16 when $x=-4$

37.
$$f(x) = -x^2 + 6x + 2$$
$$= -(x^2 - 6x) + 2$$
$$= -(x^2 - 6x + 9) + 2 + 9$$
$$= -(x-3)^2 + 11$$
maximum value of 11 when $x = 3$

39.
$$f(x) = 2x^2 + 3x + 1$$
$$= 2\left(x^2 + \frac{3}{2}x\right) + 1$$
$$= 2\left(x^2 + \frac{3}{2}x + \frac{9}{16}\right) + 1 - 2\left(\frac{9}{16}\right)$$
$$= 2\left(x + \frac{3}{4}\right)^2 + \frac{8}{8} - \frac{9}{8}$$
$$= 2\left(x + \frac{3}{4}\right)^2 - \frac{1}{8}$$
minimum value of $-\frac{1}{8}$ when $x = -\frac{3}{4}$

41.
$$f(x) = 5x^2 - 11$$
$$= 5(x^2) - 11$$
$$= 5(x-0)^2 - 11$$
minimum value of -11 when $x = 0$

43.
$$f(x) = -\frac{1}{2}x^2 + 6x + 17$$
$$= -\frac{1}{2}(x^2 - 12x) + 17$$
$$= -\frac{1}{2}(x^2 - 12x + 36) + 17 + 18$$
$$= -\frac{1}{2}(x-6)^2 + 35$$
maximum value of 35 when $x = 6$

45.
$$h(x) = -\frac{3}{64}x^2 + 27 = -\frac{3}{64}(x-0)^2 + 27$$

a. The maximum height of the arch is 27 feet.

b.
$$h(10) = -\frac{3}{64}(10)^2 + 27$$
$$= -\frac{3}{64}(100) + 27$$
$$= -\frac{75}{16} + 27$$
$$= -\frac{75}{16} + \frac{432}{16}$$
$$= \frac{357}{16} = 22\frac{5}{16} \quad \text{feet}$$

c.
$$h(x) = 8 = -\frac{3}{64}x^2 + 27$$
$$8 - 27 = -\frac{3}{64}x^2$$
$$-19 = -\frac{3}{64}x^2$$
$$64(-19) = -3x^2$$
$$\frac{64(-19)}{-3} = x^2$$
$$\sqrt{\frac{64(-19)}{-3}} = x$$
$$8\sqrt{\frac{19}{3}} = x$$
$$\frac{8\sqrt{19}\sqrt{3}}{3} = x$$
$$\frac{8\sqrt{57}}{3} = x$$
$$20.1 \approx x$$
$h(x) = 8$ when $x \approx 20.1$ feet

47.

a.
$$3w + 2l = 600$$
$$3w = 600 - 2l$$
$$w = \frac{600 - 2l}{3}$$

b.
$$A = w \cdot l$$
$$A = \left(\frac{600 - 2l}{3}\right) l$$
$$= 200l - \frac{2}{3}l^2$$

c.
$$A = -\frac{2}{3}(l^2 - 300l)$$
$$A = -\frac{2}{3}(l^2 - 300l + 150^2) + 15,000$$
In standard form,
$$A = -\frac{2}{3}(l - 150)^2 + 15,000$$

The maximum area of 15,000 ft^2 is produced when

$l = 150$ ft and the width $w = \dfrac{600 - 2(150)}{3} = 100$ ft.

94

49. a.

$$T(t) = -0.7t^2 + 9.4t + 59.3$$

$$= -0.7\left(t^2 - \frac{9.4}{0.7}t\right) + 59.3$$

$$= -0.7\left(t^2 - \frac{94}{7}t\right) + 59.3$$

$$= -0.7\left(t^2 - \frac{94}{7}t + \left[\frac{47}{7}\right]^2\right) + 59.3 + 0.7\left[\frac{47}{7}\right]^2$$

$$\approx -0.7\left(t - \frac{47}{7}\right)^2 + 90.857$$

$$\approx -0.7\left(t - 6\frac{5}{7}\right)^2 + 91$$

The temperature is a maximum when

$$t = \frac{47}{7} = 6\frac{5}{7} \text{ hours after 6:00 A.M.}$$

Note $\frac{5}{7}$ (60 minutes) ≈ 43 minutes.

Thus the temperature is a maximum at 12:43 P.M.

b. The maximum temperature is approximately 91°F.

51.

$$N(t) = 1.43t^2 - 11.44t + 47.68$$

$$N(t) = 1.43(t^2 - 8t) + 47.68$$

$$N(t) = 1.43(t-4)^2 + 24.8$$

minimum at $t = 4$, or 1993 for 2500 homes

53.

$$h(x) = -0.002x^2 - 0.03x + 8$$

$$h(39) = -0.002(39)^2 - 0.03(39) + 8 = 3.788 > 3$$

Solve for x using quadratic formula.

$$-0.002x^2 - 0.03x + 8 = 0$$

$$x^2 + 15x - 4000 = 0$$

$$x = \frac{-15 \pm \sqrt{(15)^2 - 4(1)(-4000)}}{2(1)}$$

$$= \frac{-15 \pm \sqrt{16,225}}{2}, \text{ use positive value of } x$$

$$x \approx 56.2$$

Yes, the conditions are satisfied.

55. a.

$$E(v) = -0.018v^2 + 1.476v + 3.4$$

$$= -0.018\left(v^2 - \frac{1.476}{0.018}v\right) + 3.4$$

$$= -0.018(v^2 - 82v) + 3.4$$

$$= -0.018\left(v^2 - 82v + 41^2\right) + 3.4 + 0.018(41)^2$$

$$= -0.018(v - 41)^2 + 33.658$$

The maximum fuel efficiency is obtained at a speed of 41 mph.

b. The maximum fuel efficiency for this car, to the nearest mile per gallon, is 34 mpg.

57. Let $y = 0$, then $0 = x^2 + 6x$

$$0 = x(x + 6)$$

$$x = 0 \quad \text{or} \quad x + 6 = 0$$

$$x = -6$$

The x-intercepts are $(0, 0)$ and $(-6, 0)$.

Let $x = 0$, then $f(x) = 0^2 + 6(0) = 0$

The y-intercept is $(0, 0)$.

59. Let $y = 0$, then $0 = -3x^2 + 5x - 6$

$$x = \frac{-5 \pm \sqrt{5^2 - 4(-3)(-6)}}{2(-3)}$$

Since the discriminant $5^2 - 4(-3)(-6) = -47$ is negative, there are no x-intercepts.

Let $x = 0$, then $f(x) = -3(0)^2 + 5(0) - 6 = -6$

The y-intercept is $(0, -6)$.

61.

$$-\frac{b}{2a} = -\frac{296}{2(-0.2)} = 740$$

$$R(740) = 296(740) - 0.2(740)^2 = 109,520$$

Thus, 740 units yield a maximum revenue of $109,520.

63.

$$-\frac{b}{2a} = -\frac{1.7}{2(-0.01)} = 85$$

$$P(85) = -0.01(85)^2 + 1.7(85) - 48 = 24.25$$

Thus, 85 units yield a maximum profit of $24.25.

Copyright © Houghton Mifflin Company. All rights reserved.

65. $P(x) = R(x) - C(x)$

$= x(102.50 - 0.1x) - (52.50x + 1840)$

$= -0.1x^2 + 50x - 1840$

The break-even points occur when $R(x) = C(x)$ or $P(x) = 0$.

Thus, $0 = -0.1x^2 + 50x - 1840$

$x = \dfrac{-50 \pm \sqrt{50^2 - 4(-0.1)(-1840)}}{2(-0.1)}$

$= \dfrac{-50 \pm \sqrt{1764}}{-0.2}$

$= \dfrac{-50 \pm 42}{-0.2}$

$x = 40 \quad \text{or} \quad x = 460$

The break-even points occur when $x = 40$ or $x = 460$.

69. $h(t) = -16t^2 + 128t$

a. $-\dfrac{b}{2a} = -\dfrac{128}{2(-16)} = 4 \text{ seconds}$

b. $h(4) = -16(4)^2 + 128(4) = 256 \text{ feet}$

c. $0 = -16t^2 + 128t$

$0 = -16t(t - 8)$

$-16t = 0 \quad \text{or} \quad t - 8 = 0$

$t = 0 \qquad\qquad t = 8$

The projectile hits the ground at $t = 8$ seconds.

67.   Let x = the number of people that take the tour.

a. $R(x) = x(15.00 + 0.25(60 - x))$

$= x(15.00 + 15 - 0.25x)$

$= -0.25x^2 + 30.00x$

b. $P(x) = R(x) - C(x)$

$= (-0.25x^2 + 30.00x) - (180 + 2.50x)$

$= -0.25x^2 + 27.50x - 180$

c. $-\dfrac{b}{2a} = -\dfrac{27.50}{2(-0.25)} = 55$

$P(55) = -0.25(55)^2 + 27.50(55) - 180$

$= \$576.25$

d.   The maximum profit occurs when $x = 55$.

71. $y(x) = -0.014x^2 + 1.19x + 5$

$-\dfrac{b}{2a} = -\dfrac{1.19}{2(-0.014)} = 42.5$

$y(42.5) = -0.014(42.5)^2 + 1.19(42.5) + 5$

$= 30.2875 \approx 30 \text{ feet}$

73.

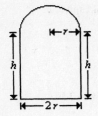

The perimeter is $48 = \pi r + h + 2r + h$.

Solve for h.

$$48 - \pi r - 2r = 2h$$

$$\frac{1}{2}(48 - \pi r - 2r) = h$$

Area = semicircle + rectangle

$$A = \frac{1}{2}\pi r^2 + 2rh$$

$$= \frac{1}{2}\pi r^2 + 2r\left(\frac{1}{2}\right)(48 - \pi r - 2r)$$

$$= \frac{1}{2}\pi r^2 + r(48 - \pi r - 2r)$$

$$= \frac{1}{2}\pi r^2 + 48r - \pi r^2 - 2r^2$$

$$= \left(\frac{1}{2}\pi - \pi - 2\right)r^2 + 48r$$

$$= \left(-\frac{1}{2}\pi - 2\right)r^2 + 48r$$

Graph the function A to find that its maximum occurs when $r \approx 6.72$ feet.

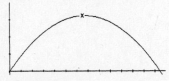

Maximum
X=6.7211927   Y=161.30856

Xmin = 0, Xmax = 14, Xscl = 1
Ymin = –50, Ymax = 200, Yscl = 50

$$h = \frac{1}{2}(48 - \pi r - 2r)$$

$$\approx \frac{1}{2}(48 - \pi(6.72) - 2(6.72))$$

$$\approx 6.72 \text{ feet}$$

Hence the optimal window has its semicircular radius equal to its height.

Note: Using calculus it can be shown that the exact value of $r = h = \dfrac{48}{\pi + 4}$.

75. $f(x) = x^2 - (a + b)x + ab$

a. x-intercepts occur when $y = 0$.

$$0 = x^2 - (a + b)x + ab$$
$$0 = (x - a)(x - b)$$
$$x - a = 0 \quad \text{or} \quad x - b = 0$$
$$x = a \qquad\qquad x = b$$

Thus the x-intercepts are $(a, 0)$ and $(b, 0)$.

b. $-\dfrac{b}{2a} = \dfrac{(a + b)}{2(1)} = \dfrac{a + b}{2}$ which is the x-coordinate of

the midpoint of the segment joining $(a, 0)$ and $(b, 0)$.

77. Let $f(x) = ax^2 + bx + c$. We know

$$f(2) = a(2)^2 + b(2) + c = 1 \qquad (1)$$
$$f(0) = a(0)^2 + b(0) + c = 4$$

This implies $c = 4$ and from Equation (1) we have

$$4a + 2b + 4 = 1 \quad \text{or} \quad 4a + 2b = -2 \qquad (2)$$

The x-value of the vertex is 2, and by the vertex formula we

have $2 = \dfrac{-b}{2a}$, which implies $b = -4a$.

Substituting $-4a$ for b in Equation (2) gives us

$$4a + 2(-4a) = -3$$
$$4a - 8a = -3$$
$$-4a = -3$$
$$a = \frac{3}{4}$$

Substituting $\dfrac{3}{4}$ for a in Equation (2) gives us

$$4\left(\frac{3}{4}\right) + 2b = -3$$
$$3 + 2b = -3$$
$$2b = -6$$
$$b = -3$$

Thus the desired quadratic function is

$$f(x) = \frac{3}{4}x^2 - 3x + 4.$$

79. $P = 32 = 2x + 2w$

$16 = x + w$

a. $w = 16 - x$

b. Area $A = xw$

$$A = x(16 - x)$$
$$A = 16x - x^2$$

81. The discriminant is $b^2 - 4(1)(-1) = b^2 + 4$, which is always positive. Thus the equation has two real zeros for all values of b.

83. Increasing the constant c increases the height of each point on the graph by c units.

85. Let $x =$ one number. Then $8 - x =$ the other number. $P = x(8 - x) = 8x - x^2$, vertex at $x = \dfrac{-b}{2a} = \dfrac{-8}{-2} = 4$.

Thus, $x = 4$ and $8 - x = 4$. The numbers are 4 and 4 .

87. $x_1 = x, \quad y_1 = x^3, \quad x_2 = x + h, \quad y_2 = (x + h)^3$

$$m = \frac{y_2 - y_1}{x_2 - x_1} = \frac{(x + h)^3 - x^3}{x + h - x} = \frac{x^3 + 3hx^2 + 3h^2x + h^3 - x^3}{h} = \frac{3hx^2 + 3h^2x + h^3}{h} = \frac{h(3x^2 + 3hx + h^2)}{h} = 3x^2 + 3hx + h^2$$

89.

$f(x) = x^2 + 4x - 6$

$-\dfrac{b}{2a} = -\dfrac{4}{2(1)} = -2$

$x = -2$

90.

$f(3) = \dfrac{3(3)^4}{(3)^2 + 1} = \dfrac{243}{10} = 24.3$

$f(-3) = \dfrac{3(-3)^4}{(-3)^2 + 1} = \dfrac{243}{10} = 24.3$

$f(3) = f(-3)$

91.

$f(-2) = 2(-2)^3 - 5(-2) = -16 + 10 = -6$

$-f(2) = -[2(2)^3 - 5(2)] = -[16 - 10] = -6$

$f(-2) = -f(2)$

92.

$f(-2) - g(-2) = (-2)^2 - [-2 + 3] = 4 - 1 = 3$

$f(-1) - g(-1) = (-1)^2 - [-1 + 3] = 1 - 2 = -1$

$f(0) - g(0) = (0)^2 - [0 + 3] = 0 - 3 = -3$

$f(1) - g(1) = (1)^2 - [1 + 3] = 1 - 4 = -3$

$f(2) - g(2) = (2)^2 - [2 + 3] = 4 - 5 = -1$

93.

$\dfrac{-a + a}{2} = 0, \quad \dfrac{b + b}{2} = b$

midpoint is $(0, b)$

94.

$\dfrac{-a + a}{2} = 0, \quad \dfrac{-b + b}{2} = 0$

midpoint is $(0, 0)$

Section 2.5

1.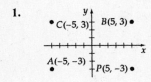

3.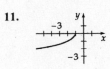

5.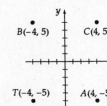

7.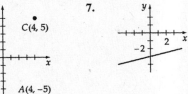

9.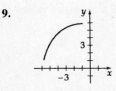

11.

13. Replacing x by $-x$ leaves the equation unaltered. Thus the graph is symmetric with respect to the y-axis.

15. Not symmetric with respect to either axis. (neither)

17. Symmetric with respect to both the x- and the y-axes.

19. Symmetric with respect to both the x- and the y-axes.

21. Symmetric with respect to both the x- and the y-axes.

23. No, since $(-y) = 3(-x) - 2$ simplifies to $(-y) = -3x - 2$, which is not equivalent to the original equation $y = 3x - 2$.

25. Yes, since $(-y) = -(-x)^3$ implies $-y = x^3$ or $y = -x^3$, which is the original equation.

27. Yes, since $(-x)^2 + (-y)^2 = 10$ simplifies to the original equation.

29. Yes, since $-y = \dfrac{-x}{|-x|}$ simplifies to the original equation.

31.

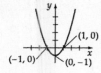

symmetric with
respect to the *y*-axis

33.

symmetric with
respect to the origin

35.

symmetric with
respect to the origin

37.

symmetric with
respect to the line $x = 4$

39.

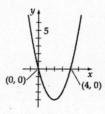

symmetric with
respect to the line $x = 2$

41.

no symmetry

43. Even since $g(-x) = (-x)^2 - 7 = x^2 - 7 = g(x)$.

45. Odd, since $F(-x) = (-x)^5 + (-x)^3$
$$= -x^5 - x^3$$
$$= -F(x).$$

47. Even   **49.** Even   **51.** Even   **53.** Even   **55.** Neither

57.

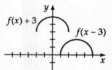

59. a. $f(x+2)$

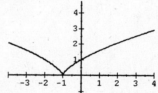

b. $f(x)+2$

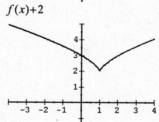

100   Chapter 2: Functions and Graphs

61. **a.** $f(x+3)$

$(-2-3,5)=(-5,5)$
$(0-3,-2)=(-3,-2)$
$(1-3,0)=(-2,0)$

b. $f(x)+1$

$(-2,5+1)=(-2,6)$
$(0,-2+1)=(0,-1)$
$(1,0+1)=(1,1)$

63. **a.** $f(-x)$

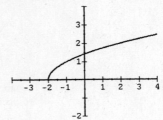

b. $-f(x)$

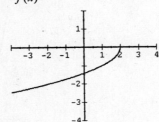

65. **a.** $f(-x)$

$(--1,3)=(1,3)$
$(-2,-4)$

b. $-f(x)$

$(-1,-3)$
$(2,--4)=(2,4)$

67.

69.

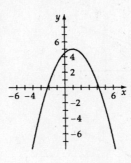

71. **a.**

b.

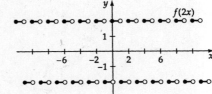

73. **a.**

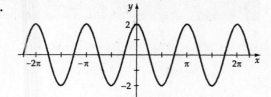

$y = h(2x)$

b.

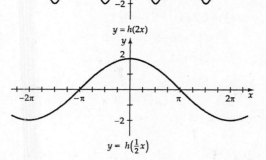

$y = h\left(\frac{1}{2}x\right)$

75.

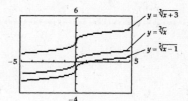

77.

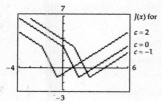

79.

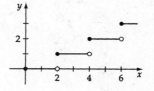

81.

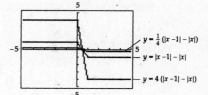

83. **a.**

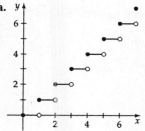

b.

c.

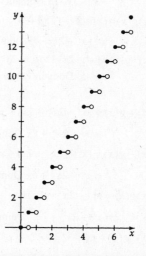

Connecting Concepts

85. **a.**

$$f(x) = \frac{2}{(x+1)^2 + 1} + 1$$

b.

$$f(x) = -\frac{2}{(x-2)^2 + 1}$$

87. $(2x^2+3x-4)-(x^2+3x-5)=x^2+1$

88. $(3x^2-x+2)(2x-3)=6x^3-2x^2+4x-9x^2+3x-6$

$=6x^3-11x^2+7x-6$

89. $f(3a)=2(3a)^2-5(3a)+2$

$=18a^2-15a+2$

90. $f(2+h)=2(2+h)^2-5(2+h)+2$

$=2h^2+8h+8-5h-10+2$

$=2h^2+3h$

91. Domain: all real numbers except $x=1$

92. $2x-8=0$

$x=4$

Domain: $x\geq4$

Section 2.6

1. $f(x)+g(x)=(x^2-2x-15)+(x+3)$

$=x^2-x-12$ Domain all real numbers

$f(x)-g(x)=(x^2-2x-15)-(x+3)$

$=x^2-3x-18$ Domain all real numbers

$f(x)g(x)=(x^2-2x-15)(x+3)$

$=x^3+x^2-21x-45$ Domain all real numbers

$f(x)/g(x)=(x^2-2x-15)/(x+3)$

$=x-5$ Domain $\{x|x\neq-3\}$

3. $f(x)+g(x)=(2x^2+8)+(x+4)$

$=3x+12$ Domain all real numbers

$f(x)-g(x)=(2x+8)-(x+4)$

$=x+4$ Domain all real numbers

$f(x)g(x)=(2x+8)(x+4)$

$=2x^2+16x+32$ Domain all real numbers

$f(x)/g(x)=(2x+8)/(x+4)$

$=[2(x+4)]/(x+4)$

$=2$ Domain $\{x|x\neq-4\}$

5. $f(x)+g(x)=(x^3-2x^2+7x)+x$

$=x^3-2x^2+8x$ Domain all real numbers

$f(x)-g(x)=(x^3-2x^2+7x)-x$

$=x^3-2x^2+6x$ Domain all real numbers

$f(x)g(x)=(x^3-2x^2+7x)x$

$=x^4-2x^3+7x^2$ Domain all real numbers

$f(x)/g(x)=(x^3-2x^2+7x)/x$

$=x^2-2x+7$ Domain $\{x\,|\,x\neq0\}$

7. $f(x)+g(x)=(2x^2+4x-7)+(2x^2+3x-5)$

$=4x^2+7x-12$ Domain all real numbers

$f(x)-g(x)=(2x^2+4x-7)-(2x^2+3x-5)$

$=x-2$ Domain all real numbers

$f(x)g(x)=(2x^2+4x-7)(2x^2+3x-5)$

$=4x^4+6x^3-10x^2+8x^3+12x^2-20x-14x^2-21x+35$

$=4x^4+14x^3-12x^2-41x+35$ Domain all real numbers

$f(x)/g(x)=(2x^2+4x-7)/(2x^2+3x-5)$

$=1+\dfrac{x-2}{2x^2+3x-5}$ Domain $\left\{x|x\neq1,x\neq-\dfrac{5}{2}\right\}$

9. $f(x) + g(x) = \sqrt{x-3} + x$ Domain $\{x \mid x \geq 3\}$

$f(x) - g(x) = \sqrt{x-3} - x$ Domain $\{x \mid x \geq 3\}$

$f(x)g(x) = x\sqrt{x-3}$ Domain $\{x \mid x \geq 3\}$

$f(x)/g(x) = \dfrac{\sqrt{x-3}}{x} + x$ Domain $\{x \mid x \geq 3\}$

11. $f(x) + g(x) = \sqrt{4-x^2} + 2 + x$ Domain $\{x \mid -2 \leq x \leq 2\}$

$f(x) - g(x) = \sqrt{4-x^2} - 2 - x$ Domain $\{x \mid -2 \leq x \leq 2\}$

$f(x)g(x) = \left(\sqrt{4-x^2}\right)(2+x)$ Domain $\{x \mid -2 \leq x \leq 2\}$

$f(x)/g(x) = \dfrac{\sqrt{4-x^2}}{2+x}$ Domain $\{x \mid -2 \leq x \leq 2\}$

13. $(f+g)(x) = x^2 - x - 2$

$(f+g)(5) = (5)^2 - (5) - 2$

$= 25 - 5 - 2$

$= 18$

15. $(f+g)(x) = x^2 - x - 2$

$(f+g)\left(\dfrac{1}{2}\right) = \left(\dfrac{1}{2}\right)^2 - \left(\dfrac{1}{2}\right) - 2$

$= \dfrac{1}{4} - \dfrac{1}{2} - 2$

$= -\dfrac{9}{4}$

17. $(f-g)(x) = x^2 - 5x + 6$

$(f-g)(-3) = (-3)^2 - 5(-3) + 6$

$= 9 + 15 + 6$

$= 30$

19. $(f-g)(x) = x^2 - 5x + 6$

$(f-g)(-1) = (-1)^2 - 5(-1) + 6$

$= 1 + 5 + 6$

$= 12$

21. $(fg)(x) = \left(x^2 - 3x + 2\right)(2x - 4)$

$= 2x^3 - 6x^2 + 4x - 4x^2 + 12x - 8$

$= 2x^3 - 10x^2 + 16x - 8$

$(fg)(7) = 2(7)^3 - 10(7)^2 + 16(7) - 8$

$= 686 - 490 + 112 - 8$

$= 300$

23. $(fg)(x) = 2x^3 - 10x^2 + 16x - 8$

$(fg)\left(\dfrac{2}{5}\right) = 2\left(\dfrac{2}{5}\right)^3 - 10\left(\dfrac{2}{5}\right)^2 + 16\left(\dfrac{2}{5}\right) - 8$

$= \dfrac{16}{125} - \dfrac{40}{25} + \dfrac{32}{5} - 8$

$= \dfrac{-384}{125} = -3.072$

25. $\left(\dfrac{f}{g}\right)(x) = \dfrac{x^2 - 3x + 2}{2x - 4}$

$\left(\dfrac{f}{g}\right)(x) = \dfrac{1}{2}x - \dfrac{1}{2}$

$\left(\dfrac{f}{g}\right)(-4) = \dfrac{1}{2}(-4) - \dfrac{1}{2}$

$= -2 - \dfrac{1}{2}$

$= -2\dfrac{1}{2} \text{ or } -\dfrac{5}{2}$

27. $\left(\dfrac{f}{g}\right)(x) = \dfrac{1}{2}x - \dfrac{1}{2}$

$\left(\dfrac{f}{g}\right)\left(\dfrac{1}{2}\right) = \dfrac{1}{2}\left(\dfrac{1}{2}\right) - \dfrac{1}{2}$

$= \dfrac{1}{4} - \dfrac{1}{2}$

$= -\dfrac{1}{4}$

29. $\dfrac{f(x+h) - f(x)}{h} = \dfrac{[2(x+h)+4] - (2x+4)}{h}$

$= \dfrac{2x + 2(h) + 4 - 2x - 4}{h}$

$= \dfrac{2h}{h}$

$= 2$

31. $\dfrac{f(x+h)-f(x)}{h}=\dfrac{[(x+h)-6]-(x^2-6)}{h}$

$\qquad\qquad\quad=\dfrac{x^2+2x(h)+(h)^2-6-x^2+6}{h}$

$\qquad\qquad\quad=\dfrac{2x(h)+h^2}{h}$

$\qquad\qquad\quad=2x+h$

33. $\dfrac{f(x+h)-f(x)}{h}=\dfrac{2(x+h)^2+4(x+h)-3-(2x^2+4x-3)}{h}$

$\qquad\qquad\quad=\dfrac{2x^2+4xh+2h^2+4x+4h-3-2x^2-4x+3}{h}$

$\qquad\qquad\quad=\dfrac{4xh+2h^2+4h}{h}$

$\qquad\qquad\quad=4x+2h+4$

35. $\dfrac{f(x+h)-f(x)}{h}=\dfrac{-4(x+h)^2+6-(-4x^2+6)}{h}$

$\qquad\qquad\quad=\dfrac{-4x^2-8xh-4h^2+6+4x^2-6}{h}$

$\qquad\qquad\quad=\dfrac{-8xh-4h^2}{h}$

$\qquad\qquad\quad=-8x-4h$

37. $(g\circ f)(x)=g[f(x)]$

$\qquad\quad=g[3x+5]$

$\qquad\quad=2[3x+5]$

$\qquad\quad=6x+10-7$

$\qquad\quad=6x+3$

$(f\circ g)(x)=f[g(x)]$

$\qquad\quad=f[2x-7]$

$\qquad\quad=3[2x-7]+5$

$\qquad\quad=6x-21+5$

$\qquad\quad=6x-16$

39. $(g\circ f)(x)=g\left[x^2+4x-1\right]$

$\qquad\quad=\left[x^2+4x-1\right]+2$

$\qquad\quad=x^2+4x+1$

$(f\circ g)(x)=f[x+2]$

$\qquad\quad=[x+2]^2+4[x+2]-1$

$\qquad\quad=x^2+4x+4+4x+8-1$

$\qquad\quad=x^2+8x+11$

41. $(g\circ f)(x)=g[f(x)]$

$\qquad\quad=g\left[x^3+2x\right]$

$\qquad\quad=-5\left[x^3+2x\right]$

$\qquad\quad=-5x^3-10x$

$(f\circ g)(x)=f[g(x)]$

$\qquad\quad=f[-5x]$

$\qquad\quad=[-5x]^3+2[-5x]$

$\qquad\quad=-125x^3-10x$

43. $(g\circ f)(x)=g[f(x)]$

$\qquad\quad=g\left[\dfrac{2}{x+1}\right]$

$\qquad\quad=3\left[\dfrac{2}{x+1}\right]-5$

$\qquad\quad=\dfrac{6}{x+1}-\dfrac{5(x+1)}{x+1}$

$\qquad\quad=\dfrac{6-5x-5}{x+1}$

$\qquad\quad=\dfrac{1-5x}{x+1}$

$(f\circ g)(x)=f[g(x)]$

$\qquad\quad=f[3x-5]$

$\qquad\quad=\dfrac{2}{[3x-5]+1}$

$\qquad\quad=\dfrac{2}{3x-4}$

45.

$$(g \circ f)(x) = g[f(x)]$$

$$= g\left[\frac{1}{x^2}\right]$$

$$= \sqrt{\left[\frac{1}{x^2}\right] - 1}$$

$$= \sqrt{\frac{1 - x^2}{x^2}}$$

$$= \frac{\sqrt{1 - x^2}}{|x|}$$

$$(f \circ g)(x) = f[g(x)]$$

$$= f\left[\sqrt{x - 1}\right]$$

$$= \frac{1}{\left[\sqrt{x - 1}\right]^2}$$

$$= \frac{1}{x - 1}$$

47.

$$(g \circ f)(x) = g\left[\frac{3}{|5 - x|}\right]$$

$$= -\frac{2}{\left[\frac{3}{|5 - x|}\right]}$$

$$= \frac{-2|5 - x|}{3}$$

$$(f \circ g)(x) = f\left[-\frac{2}{x}\right]$$

$$= \frac{3}{\left|5 - \left[-\frac{2}{x}\right]\right|}$$

$$= \frac{3}{\left|5 + \frac{2}{x}\right|}$$

$$= \frac{3}{\frac{|5x + 2|}{|x|}}$$

$$= \frac{3|x|}{|5x + 2|}$$

Use the results to work Exercises 49 to 63.

49.

$$(g \circ f)(x) = 4x^2 + 2x - 6$$

$$(g \circ f)(4) = 4(4)^2 + 2(4) - 6$$

$$= 64 + 8 - 6$$

$$= 66$$

51.

$$(f \circ g)(x) = 2x^2 - 10x + 3$$

$$(f \circ g)(-3) = 2(-3)^2 - 10(-3) + 3$$

$$= 18 + 30 + 3$$

$$= 51$$

53.

$$(g \circ h)(x) = 9x^4 - 9x^2 - 4$$

$$(g \circ h)(0) = 9(0)^4 - 9(0)^2 - 4$$

$$= -4$$

55.

$$(f \circ f)(x) = 4x + 9$$

$$(f \circ f)(8) = 4(8) + 9$$

$$= 41$$

57.

$$(h \circ g)(x) = -3x^4 + 30x^3 - 75x^2 + 4$$

$$(h \circ g)\left(\frac{2}{5}\right) = -3\left(\frac{2}{5}\right)^4 + 30\left(\frac{2}{5}\right)^3 - 75\left(\frac{2}{5}\right)^2 + 4$$

$$= -\frac{48}{625} + \frac{240}{125} - \frac{300}{25} + 4$$

$$= \frac{-48 + 1200 - 7500 + 2500}{625}$$

$$= -\frac{3848}{625}$$

59.

$$(g \circ f)(x) = 4x^2 + 2x - 6$$

$$(g \circ f)(\sqrt{3}) = 4(\sqrt{3})^2 + 2(\sqrt{3}) - 6$$

$$= 12 + 2\sqrt{3} - 6$$

$$= 6 + 2\sqrt{3}$$

61.

$$(g \circ f)(x) = 4x^2 + 2x - 6$$

$$(g \circ f)(2c) = 4(2c)^2 + 2(2c) - 6$$

$$= 16c^2 + 4c - 6$$

63.

$$(g \circ h)(x) = 9x^4 - 9x^2 - 4$$

$$(g \circ h)(k + 1) = 9(k + 1)^4 - 9(k + 1)^2 - 4$$

$$= 9(k^4 + 4k^3 + 6k^2 + 4k + 1) - 9k^2 - 18k - 9 - 4$$

$$= 9k^4 + 36k^3 + 54k^2 + 36k + 9 - 9k^2 - 18k - 13$$

$$= 9k^4 + 36k^3 + 45k^2 + 18k - 4$$

65. **a.** $r = 1.5t$ and $A = \pi r^2$

so $A(t) = \pi[r(t)]^2$

$= \pi(1.5t)^2$

$= 2.25\pi(2)^2$

$= 9\pi$ square feet

≈ 28.27 square feet

b. $r = 1.5t$

$h = 2r = 2(1.5t) = 3t$ and

$V = \dfrac{1}{3}\pi r^2 h$ so

$V(t) = \dfrac{1}{3}\pi(1.5t)^2[3t]$

$= 2.25\pi t^3$

Note: $V = \dfrac{1}{3}\pi r^2 h = \dfrac{1}{3}(\pi r^2) = \dfrac{1}{3}hA$

$= \dfrac{1}{3}(3t)(2.25\pi t^2) = 2.25\pi t^3$

$V(3) = 2.25\pi(3)^3$

$= 60.75\pi$ cubic feet

≈ 190.85 cubic feet

67. **a.**   Since $d^2 + 4^2 = s^2$,

$d^2 = s^2 - 16$

$d = \sqrt{s^2 - 16}$

$d = \sqrt{(48-t)^2 - 16}$ $\cdot\ s = 48 - t$

$= \sqrt{2304 - 96t + t^2 - 16}$

$= \sqrt{t^2 - 96t + 2288}$

b. $s(35) = 48 - 35 + 13$

$d(35) = \sqrt{35^2 - 96(35) + 2288}$

$= \sqrt{153} \approx 12.37$ ft

69. $(Y \circ F)(x) = Y(F(x))$ converts x inches to yards.

F takes x inches to feet, and then Y takes feet to yards.

71. **a.**   On $[0, 1]$, $a = 0$

$\Delta t = 1 - 0 = 1$

$C(a + \Delta t) = C(1) = 99.8$

$C(a) = C(0) = 0$

Average rate of change $= \dfrac{C(1) - C(0)}{1} = 99.8 - 0 = 99.8$

This is identical to the slope of the line through

$(0, C(0))$ and $(1, C(1))$ since $m = \dfrac{C(1) - C(0)}{1 - 0} = C(1) - C(0)$

b.   On $[0, 0.5]$, $a = 0$

$\Delta t = 0.5$

Average rate of change $= \dfrac{C(0.5) - C(0)}{0.5} = \dfrac{78.1 - 0}{0.5} = 156.2$

c.   On $[1, 2]$, $a = 1$

$\Delta t = 2 - 1 = 1$

Average rate of change $= \dfrac{C(2) - C(1)}{1} = \dfrac{50.1 - 99.8}{1} = -49.7$

d.   On $[1, 1.5]$, $a = 1$

$\Delta t = 1.5 - 1 = 0.5$

Average rate of change $= \dfrac{C(1.5) - C(1)}{0.5} = \dfrac{84.4 - 99.8}{0.5} = \dfrac{-15.4}{0.5} = -30.8$

71. **e.** On $[1, 1.25]$, $a = 1$

$\Delta t = 1.25 - 1 = 0.25$

Average rate of change $= \dfrac{C(1.25) - C(1)}{0.25} = \dfrac{95.7 - 99.8}{0.25} = \dfrac{-4.1}{0.25} = -16.4$

f. On $[1, 1 + \Delta t]$, $Con\,(1 + \Delta t) = 25(1 + \Delta t)^3 - 150(1 + \Delta t)^2 + 225(1 + \Delta t)$

$= 25(1 + 3(\Delta t) + 3(\Delta t)^3) - 150(1 + 2(\Delta t) + (\Delta t)^2) + 225(1 + \Delta t)$

$= 25 + 75(\Delta t) + 75(\Delta t)^2) + 25(\Delta t)^3 - 150 - 300(\Delta t) - 150(\Delta t)^2 + 225 + 225(\Delta t)$

$= 100 - 75(\Delta t)^2 + 25(\Delta t)^3$

$Con(1) = 100$

Average rate of change $= \dfrac{Con(1 + \Delta t) - Con(1)}{\Delta t} = \dfrac{100 - 75(\Delta t)^2 + 25(\Delta t)^3 - 100}{\Delta t}$

$= \dfrac{-75(\Delta t)^2 + 25(\Delta t)^3}{\Delta t}$

$= -75(\Delta t) + 25(\Delta t)^2$

As Δt approaches 0, the average rate of change over $[1, 1 + \Delta t]$ seems to approach 0.

Connecting Concepts

73.

$(g \circ f)(x) = g[f(x)]$

$= g[2x + 3]$

$= 5(2x + 3) + 12$

$= 10x + 15 + 12$

$= 10x + 27$

$(g \circ f)(x) = (f \circ g)(x)$

$(f \circ g)(x) = f[g(x)]$

$= f[5x + 12]$

$= 2(5x + 12) + 3$

$= 10x + 24 + 3$

$= 10x + 27$

75.

$(g \circ f)(x) = g[f(x)]$

$= g\left[\dfrac{6x}{x-1}\right]$

$= \dfrac{5\left(\dfrac{6x}{x-1}\right)}{\dfrac{6x}{x-1} - 2}$

$= \dfrac{\dfrac{30x}{x-1}}{\dfrac{6x-2x+2}{x-1}} = \dfrac{\dfrac{30x}{x-1}}{\dfrac{4x+2}{x-1}}$

$= \dfrac{30x}{x-1} \cdot \dfrac{x-1}{2(2x+1)}$

$= \dfrac{15x}{2x+1}$

$(g \circ f)(x) = (f \circ g)(x)$

$(f \circ g)(x) = f[g(x)]$

$= f\left[\dfrac{5x}{x-2}\right]$

$= \dfrac{6\left(\dfrac{5x}{x-2}\right)}{\dfrac{5x}{x-2} - 1}$

$= \dfrac{\dfrac{30x}{x-2}}{\dfrac{5x-x+2}{x-2}} = \dfrac{\dfrac{30x}{x-2}}{\dfrac{4x+2}{x-2}}$

$= \dfrac{30x}{x-2} \cdot \dfrac{x-2}{2(2x+1)}$

$= \dfrac{15x}{2x+1}$

77. $(g \circ f)(x) = g[f(x)]$ $(f \circ g)(x) = f[g(x)]$

$= g[2x+3]$ $= f\left[\dfrac{x-3}{2}\right]$

$= \dfrac{[2x+3]-3}{2}$ $= 2\left[\dfrac{x-3}{2}\right]+3$

$= \dfrac{2x}{2}$ $= x-3+3$

$= x$ $= x$

79. $(g \circ f)(x) = g[f(x)]$ $(f \circ g)(x) = f[g(x)]$

$= g\left[\dfrac{4}{x+1}\right]$ $= f\left[\dfrac{4-x}{x}\right]$

$= \dfrac{4-\left[\dfrac{4}{x+1}\right]}{\left[\dfrac{4}{x+1}\right]}$ $= \dfrac{4}{\left[\dfrac{4-x}{x}\right]+1}$

$= \dfrac{\dfrac{4x+4-4}{x+1}}{\dfrac{4}{x+1}}$ $= \dfrac{4}{\dfrac{4-x+x}{x}}$

$= \dfrac{4x}{x+1} \cdot \dfrac{x+1}{4}$ $= \dfrac{4}{\dfrac{4}{x}}$

$= x$ $= 4 \cdot \dfrac{x}{4}$

$= x$

81. $(g \circ f)(x) = g[f(x)]$ $(f \circ g)(x) = f[g(x)]$

$= g\left[x^3-1\right]$ $= f\left[\sqrt[3]{x+1}\right]$

$= \sqrt[3]{\left[x^3-1\right]+1}$ $= \left[\sqrt[3]{x+1}\right]^3 - 1$

$= \sqrt[3]{x^3}$ $= x+1-1$

$= x$ $= x$

••   ████ **P**repare for **S**ection **2.7** ████

83. Slope: $-\dfrac{1}{3}$; y-intercept: $(0, 4)$ **84.** $3x-4y=12$

$y = \dfrac{3}{4}x - 3$

Slope: $\dfrac{3}{4}$; y-intercept: $(0, -3)$

85. $y = -0.45x + 2.3$ **86.** $y+4 = -\dfrac{2}{3}(x-3)$

$y = -\dfrac{2}{3}x - 2$

87. $f(2) = 3(2)^2 + 4(2) - 1 = 12 + 8 - 1 = 19$ **88.** $|f(x_1) - y_1| + |f(x_2) - y_2| = \left|(2)^2 - 3 - (-1)\right| + \left|(4)^2 - 3 - 14\right|$

$= |4-3+1| + |16-3-14|$

$= 2+1$

$= 3$

Section 2.7

1. The scatter diagram suggests no relationship between x and y.

3. The scatter diagram suggests a linear relationship between x and y.

5. Figure A more approximates a graph that can be modeled by an equation than does Figure B. Thus Figure A has a coefficient of determination closer to 1.

7. Enter the data on your calculator. The technique for a TI-83 calculator is illustrated here.

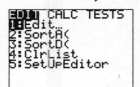 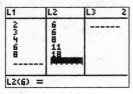 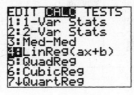 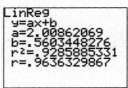

$y = 2.00862069x + 0.5603448276$

9. Enter the data on your calculator. The technique for a TI-83 calculator is illustrated here.

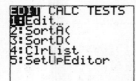 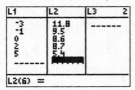 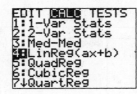 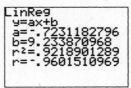

$y = -0.7231182796x + 9.233870968$

11. Enter the data on your calculator. The technique for a TI-83 calculator is illustrated here.

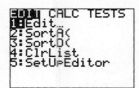 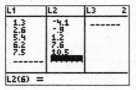 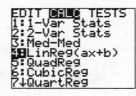 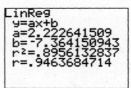

$y = 2.222641509x - 7.364150943$

13. Enter the data on your calculator. The technique for a TI-83 calculator is illustrated here.

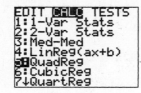 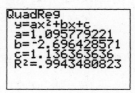

$y = 1.095779221x^2 - 2.69642857x + 1.136363636$

15.   Enter the data on your calculator. The technique for a TI-83 calculator is illustrated here.

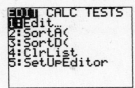 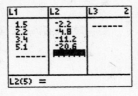 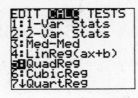 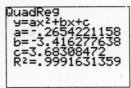

$y = -0.2987274717x^2 - 3.20998141x + 3.416463667$

17.   Enter the data on your calculator. The technique for a TI-83 calculator is illustrated here.

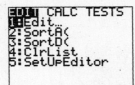 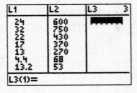 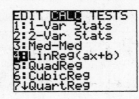 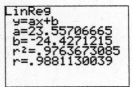

a. $y = 23.55706665x - 24.4271215$

b. $y = 23.55706665(54) - 24.4271215 \approx 1247.7$ cm

19.   Enter the data on your calculator. The technique for a TI-83 calculator is illustrated here.

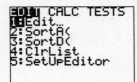 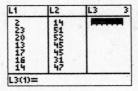 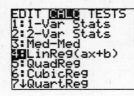 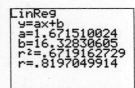

a. $y = 1.671510024x + 16.32830605$

b. $y = 1.671510024(18) + 16.32830605 \approx 46.4$ cm

21.   Enter the data on your calculator. The technique for a TI-83 calculator is illustrated here.

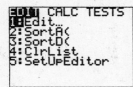  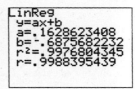

a. $y = 0.1628623408x - 0.6875682232$

b. $y = 0.1628623408(158) - 0.6875682232 \approx 25$

23.   Enter the data on your calculator. The technique for a TI-83 calculator is illustrated here.

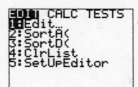 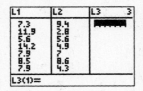 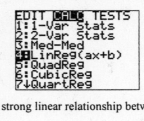 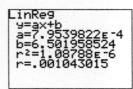

The value of r is close to 0. Therefore, no, there is not a strong linear relationship between the current and the torque.

25.   Enter the data on your calculator. The technique for a TI-83 calculator is illustrated here.

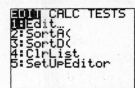 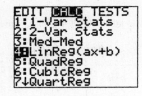 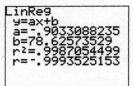 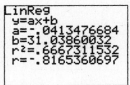

a.   The value of r is close to −1, so, yes, there is a strong linear correlation.

b. $y = -0.9033088235x + 78.62573529$

c. $y = -0.9033088235(25) + 78.62573529 \approx 56$ years

27.   Enter the data on your calculator. The technique for a TI-83 calculator is illustrated here.

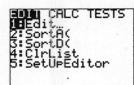 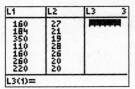 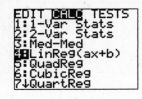

$r^2 \approx 0.667$ The coefficient of determination means that approximately 66.7% of the variation in EPA mileage estimates can be attributed to the horsepower of a car.

29.   Enter the data on your calculator. The technique for a TI-83 calculator is illustrated here.

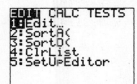 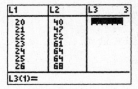 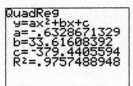 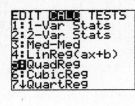

$y = -0.6328671329x^2 + 33.6160839x - 379.4405594$

31.   Enter the data on your calculator. The technique for a TI-83 calculator is illustrated here.

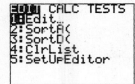 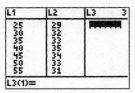 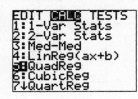 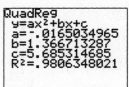

a. $y = -0.0165034965x^2 + 1.366713287x + 5.685314685$

b. $y = -0.0165034965(50)^2 + 1.366713287(50) + 5.685314685 \approx 32.8$ mpg

33. **a.** Enter the data on your calculator. The technique for a TI-83 calculator is illustrated here.

5-lb ball

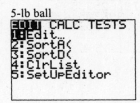 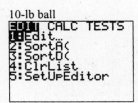 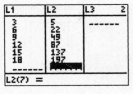 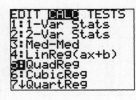 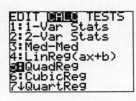

$y = 0.6130952381t^2 - 0.0714285714t + 0.1071428571$

10-lb ball

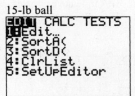 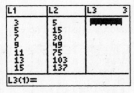 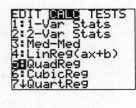

$y = 0.6091269841t^2 - 0.0011904762t - 0.3$

15-lb ball

$y = 0.5922619048t^2 + 0.3571428571t - 1.520833333$

b. All the regression equations are approximately the same. Therefore, there is one equation of motion.

35. Enter the data on your calculator. The technique for a TI-83 calculator is illustrated here.
Compute r for the linear regression model and R^2 for the quadratic model.

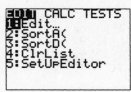 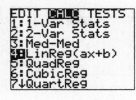 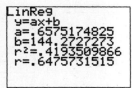 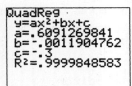 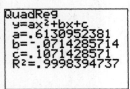

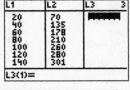 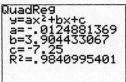

The quadratic regression model is the better fit for this data. R^2 is closer to 1 for the quadratic model than r^2 is for the linear model.

1. False. Let $f(x) = x^2$. Then $f(3) = f(-3) = 9$, but $3 \neq -3$.

2. False. Let $f(x) = 2x$ and $g(x) = x^2$. Then $(f \circ g)(x) = f(x^2) = 2x^2$, but $(g \circ f)(x) = g(2x) = (2x)^2 = 4x^2$.

3. True

4. True

5. False. Let $f(x) = 3x$. $[f(x)]^2 = [3x]^2 = 9x^2$, whereas $f[f(x)] = f(3x) = 3(3x) = 9x$.

6. False. Let $f(x) = x^2$. Then $\dfrac{f(2)}{f(1)} = \dfrac{2^2}{1^2} = \dfrac{4}{1} = 4 \neq \dfrac{2}{1}$.

7. True

8. False. Let $f(x) = |x|$. Then $f(-1+3) = f(2) = 2$, whereas $f(-1) + f(3) = 1 + 3 = 4$.

9. True   10. True   11. True   12. True   13. True

14. False. The coefficient of determination is r^2 and therefore always non-negative.

1. $d = \sqrt{(7-(-3))^2 + (11-2)^2}$ [2.1]

    $= \sqrt{10^2 + 9^2} = \sqrt{100+81} = \sqrt{181}$

2. $d = \sqrt{(-3-5)^2 + (-8-(-4))^2}$ [2.1]

    $= \sqrt{(-8)^2 + (-4)^2} = \sqrt{64+16} = \sqrt{80} = 4\sqrt{5}$

3. $\left(\dfrac{2+(-3)}{2}, \dfrac{8+12}{2} \right) = \left(\dfrac{-1}{2}, \dfrac{20}{2} \right) = \left(-\dfrac{1}{2}, 10 \right)$ [2.1]

4. $\left(\dfrac{-4+8}{2}, \dfrac{7+(-11)}{2} \right) = \left(\dfrac{4}{2}, \dfrac{-4}{2} \right) = (2, -2)$ [2.1]

5. center $(3, -4)$, radius 9 [2.1]

6.
$$x^2 + 10x + y^2 + 4y = -20 \qquad [2.1]$$
$$x^2 + 10x + 25 + y^2 + 4y + 4 = -20 + 25 + 4$$
$$(x+5)^2 + (y+2)^2 = 9$$
center $(-5, -2)$, radius 3

7. $(x-2)^2 + (y+3)^2 = 5^2$ [2.1]

8.
$$(x+5)^2 + (y-1)^2 = r^2 \quad [2.1]$$
$$(3+5)^2 + (1-1)^2 = r^2$$
$$8^2 + 0^2 = r^2$$
$$8^2 = r^2$$
$$(x+5)^2 + (y-1)^2 = 8^2$$

9.

   a. $f(1)=3(1)^2+4(1)-5$ [2.2]
$$=3(1)+4-5$$
$$=3+4-5$$
$$=2$$

   b. $f(-3)=3(-3)^2+4(-3)-5$
$$=3(9)-12-5$$
$$=27-12-5$$
$$=10$$

   c. $f(t)=3t^2+4t-5$

   d. $f(x+h)=3(x+h)^2+4(x+h)-5$
$$=3(x^2+2xh+h^2)+4x+4h-5$$
$$=3x^2+6xh+3h^2+4x+4h-5$$

   e. $3f(t)=3(3t^2+4t-5)$
$$=9t^2+12t-15$$

   f. $f(3t)=3(3t)^2+4(3t)-5$
$$=3(9t^2)+12t-5$$
$$=27t^2+12t-5$$

10.

   a. $g(3)=\sqrt{64-3^2}$ [2.2]
$$=\sqrt{64-9}$$
$$=\sqrt{55}$$

   b. $g(-5)=\sqrt{64-(-5)^2}$
$$=\sqrt{64-25}$$
$$=\sqrt{39}$$

   c. $g(8)=\sqrt{64-(8)^2}$
$$=\sqrt{64-64}$$
$$=\sqrt{0}$$
$$=0$$

   d. $g(-x)=\sqrt{64-(-x)^2}$
$$=\sqrt{64-x^2}$$

   e. $2g(t)=2\sqrt{64-t^2}$

   f. $g(2t)=\sqrt{64-(2t)^2}$
$$=\sqrt{64-4t^2}$$
$$=\sqrt{4(16-t^2)}$$
$$=2\sqrt{16-t^2}$$

11.

   a. $(f\circ g)(3)=f[g(3)]$ [2.6]
$$=f[3-8]$$
$$=f[-5]$$
$$=(-5)^2+4(-5)$$
$$=25-20$$
$$=5$$

   b. $(g\circ f)(-3)=g[f(-3)]$
$$=g[(-3)^2+4(-3)]$$
$$=g[9-12]$$
$$=g[-3]$$
$$=[-3]-8$$
$$=-11$$

   c. $(f\circ g)(x)=f[g(x)]$
$$=f[x-8]$$
$$=(x-8)^2+4(x-8)$$
$$=x^2-16x+64+4x-32$$
$$=x^2-12x+32$$

   d. $(g\circ f)(x)=g[f(x)]$
$$=g[x^2+4x]$$
$$=[x^2+4x]-8$$
$$=x^2+4x-8$$

12.

   a. $(f\circ g)(-5)=f[g(-5)]$ [2.6]
$$=f[|(-5)-1|]$$
$$=f[6]$$
$$=2(6)^2+7$$
$$=72+7$$
$$=79$$

   b. $(g\circ f)(-5)=g[f(-5)]$
$$=g[2(-5)^2+7]$$
$$=g[57]$$
$$=|57-1|$$
$$=56$$

   c. $(f\circ g)(x)=f[g(x)]$
$$=f[|x-1|]$$
$$=2(|x-1|)^2+7$$
$$=2(x-1)^2+7$$
$$=2(x^2-2x+1)+7$$
$$=2x^2-4x+2+7$$
$$=2x^2-4x+9$$

   d. $(g\circ f)(x)=g[f(x)]$
$$=g[2x^2+7]$$
$$=|2x^2+7-1|$$
$$=|2x^2+6|$$
$$=2x^2+6$$

13.

$$\frac{f(x+h)-f(x)}{h}=\frac{4(x+h)^2-3(x+h)-1-(4x^2-3x-1)}{h} \quad [2.6]$$

$$=\frac{4(x^2+2xh+h^2)-3x-3h-1-4x^2+3x+1}{h}$$

$$=\frac{4x^2+8xh+4h^2-3x-3h-1-4x^2+3x+1}{h}$$

$$=\frac{8xh+4h^2-3h}{h}$$

$$=\frac{h(8x+4h-3)}{h}$$

$$=8x+4h-3$$

14.

$$\frac{g(x+h)-g(x)}{h}=\frac{(x+h)^3-(x+h)-(x^3-x)}{h} \quad [2.6]$$

$$=\frac{x^3+3x^2h+3xh^2+h^3-x-h-x^3+x}{h}$$

$$=\frac{3x^2h+3xh^2+h^3-h}{h}$$

$$=\frac{h(3x^2+3xh+h^2-1)}{h}$$

$$=3x^2+3xh+h^2-1$$

15.

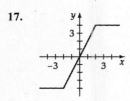

f is increasing on $[3, \infty)$
f is decreasing on $(-\infty, 3]$ [2.2]

16.

f is increasing on $[0, \infty)$
f is decreasing on $(-\infty, 0]$ [2.2]

17.

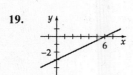

f is increasing on $[-2, 2]$
f is constant on $(-\infty, -2] \cup [2, \infty)$ [2.2]

18.

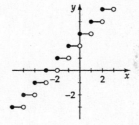

f is constant on $\dots$, $[-6, -5)$, $[-5, -4)$, $[-4, -3)$, $[-3, -2)$,
$[-2, -1)$, $[-1, 0)$, $[0, 1)$, $\dots$ [2.2]

19.

f is increasing on $(-\infty, \infty)$ [2.2]

20.

f is increasing on $(-\infty, \infty)$ [2.2]

21. Domain $\{x | x \text{ is a real number}\}$ [2.2]

22. Domain $\{x | x \le 6\}$ [2.2]

23. Domain $\{x | -5 \le x \le 5\}$ [2.2]

24. Domain $\{x | x \ne -3, \ x \ne 5\}$ [2.2]

25. $m = \dfrac{-7-3}{4-(-1)} = \dfrac{-10}{5} = -2$ [2.3]

$y - 3 = -2(x+1)$ point - slope form

$y - 3 = -2x - 2$

$y = -2x + 1$

26. $m = \dfrac{11-0}{7-0} = \dfrac{11}{7}$ [2.3]

$y - 0 = \dfrac{11}{7}(x-0)$

$y = \dfrac{11}{7}x$

27. $3x - 4y = 8$ [2.3]

$-4y = -3x + 8$

$y = \dfrac{3}{4}x - 2$

Slope of parallel line is $\dfrac{3}{4}$.

$y - 11 = \dfrac{3}{4}(x - 2)$

$y - 11 = \dfrac{3}{4}x - \dfrac{3}{2}$

$y = \dfrac{3}{4}x - \dfrac{3}{2} + 11$

$y = \dfrac{3}{4}x - \dfrac{3}{2} + \dfrac{22}{2}$

$y = \dfrac{3}{4}x + \dfrac{19}{2}$

28. $2x = -5y + 10$ [2.3]

$5y = -2x + 10$

$y = -\dfrac{2}{5}x + 2$

Slope of perpendicular line is $\dfrac{5}{2}$.

$y - (-7) = \dfrac{5}{2}[x - (-3)]$

$y + 7 = \dfrac{5}{2}(x + 3)$

$y + 7 = \dfrac{5}{2}x + \dfrac{15}{2}$

$y = \dfrac{5}{2}x + \dfrac{15}{2} - 7$

$y = \dfrac{5}{2}x + \dfrac{15}{2} - \dfrac{14}{2}$

$y = \dfrac{5}{2}x + \dfrac{1}{2}$

29. $f(x) = (x^2 + 6x) + 10$ [2.4]

$f(x) = (x^2 + 6x + 9) + 10 - 9$

$f(x) = (x + 3)^2 + 1$

30. $f(x) = (2x^2 + 4x) + 5$ [2.4]

$f(x) = 2(x^2 + 2x) + 5$

$f(x) = 2(x^2 + 2x + 1) + 5 - 2$

$f(x) = 2(x + 1)^2 + 3$

31. $f(x) = -x^2 - 8x + 3$ [2.4]

$f(x) = -(x^2 + 8x) + 3$

$f(x) = -(x^2 + 8x + 16) + 3 + 16$

$f(x) = -(x + 4)^2 + 19$

32. $f(x) = (4x^2 - 6x) + 1$ [2.4]

$f(x) = 4\left(x^2 - \dfrac{3}{2}x\right) + 1$

$f(x) = 4\left(x^2 - \dfrac{3}{2}x + \dfrac{9}{16}\right) + 1 - \dfrac{9}{4}$

$f(x) = 4\left(x - \dfrac{3}{4}\right)^2 + \dfrac{4}{4} - \dfrac{9}{4}$

$f(x) = 4\left(x - \dfrac{3}{4}\right)^2 - \dfrac{5}{4}$

33.
$$f(x) = -3x^2 + 4x - 5 \quad [2.4]$$
$$f(x) = -3\left(x^2 - \frac{4}{3}x\right) - 5$$
$$f(x) = -3\left(x^2 - \frac{4}{3}x + \frac{4}{9}\right) - 5 + \frac{4}{3}$$
$$f(x) = -3\left(x - \frac{2}{3}\right)^2 - \frac{15}{3} + \frac{4}{3}$$
$$f(x) = -3\left(x - \frac{2}{3}\right)^2 - \frac{11}{3}$$

34.
$$f(x) = x^2 - 6x + 9 \quad [2.4]$$
$$f(x) = (x^2 - 6x) + 9$$
$$f(x) = (x^2 - 6x + 9) + 9 - 9$$
$$f(x) = (x - 3)^2 + 0$$

35.
$$\frac{-b}{2a} = \frac{-(-6)}{2(3)} = \frac{6}{6} = 1 \quad [2.4]$$
$$f(1) = 3(1)^2 - 6(1) + 11$$
$$= 3(1) - 6 + 11$$
$$= 3 - 6 + 11$$
$$= 8$$
Thus the vertex is (1, 8).

36.
$$\frac{-b}{2a} = \frac{0}{2(4)} = 0 \quad [2.4]$$
$$f(0) = 4(0)^2 - 10$$
$$= 0 - 101$$
$$= -10$$
Thus the vertex is $(0, -10)$.

37.
$$\frac{-b}{2a} = \frac{-(60)}{2(-6)} = \frac{-60}{-12} = 5 \quad [2.4]$$
$$f(5) = -6(5)^2 + 60(5) + 11$$
$$= -6(25) + 300 + 11$$
$$= -150 + 300 + 11$$
$$= 161$$
Thus the vertex is (5, 161).

38.
$$\frac{-b}{2a} = \frac{-(-8)}{2(-1)} = \frac{8}{-2} = -4 \quad [2.4]$$
$$f(-4) = 14 - 8(-4) - (-4)^2$$
$$= 14 + 32 - 16$$
$$= 30$$
Thus the vertex is $(-4, 30)$.

39.
$$d = \frac{|mx_1 + b - y_1|}{\sqrt{1 + m^2}}, \quad y = 2x - 3, \quad (x_1, y_1) = (1, 3) \quad [2.3]$$
$$d = \frac{|2(1) + (-3) - 3|}{\sqrt{1 + 2^2}}$$
$$d = \frac{|2 - 3 - 3|}{\sqrt{1 + 4}}$$
$$d = \frac{|-4|}{\sqrt{5}}$$
$$d = \frac{4}{\sqrt{5}} = \frac{4\sqrt{5}}{5}$$

40.
a. Revenue $= 13x$
b. Profit = Revenue − Cost
$$P = 13x - (0.5x + 1050)$$
$$P = 13x - 0.5x - 1050$$
$$P = 12.5x - 1050$$
c. Break even $\Rightarrow$ Revenue = Cost
$$13x = 0.5x + 1050$$
$$12.5x = 1050$$
$$x = 84$$
The company must ship 84 parcels. [2.5]

41.
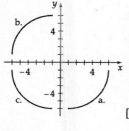
[2.5]

42.
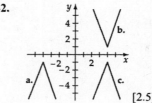
[2.5]

43. The graph of $y = x^2 - 7$ is symmetric with respect to the y-axis. [2.5]

---

44. The graph of $x = y^2 + 3$ is symmetric with respect to the x-axis. [2.5]

45. The graph of $y = x^3 - 4x$ is symmetric with respect to the origin. [2.5]

46. The graph of $y^2 = x^2 + 4$ is symmetric with respect to the x-axis, y-axis, and the origin. [2.5]

47. The graph of $\dfrac{x^2}{3^2} + \dfrac{y^2}{4^2} = 1$ is symmetric with respect to the x-axis, y-axis, and the origin. [2.5]

48. The graph of $xy = 8$ is symmetric with respect to the origin. [2.5]

49. The graph of $|y| = |x|$ is symmetric with respect to the x-axis, y-axis, and the origin. [2.5]

50. The graph of $|x + y| = 4$ is symmetric with respect to the origin. [2.5]

51.

    a.   Domain all real numbers
             Range $\{y|y \le 4\}$
    b. g is an even function [2.5]

52.

    a.   Domain all real numbers
             Range all real numbers
    b. g is neither even nor odd [2.5]

53.

    a.   Domain all real numbers
             Range $\{y|y \ge 4\}$
    b. g is an even function [2.5]

54.

    a.   Domain $\{x|-4 \le x \le 4\}$
             Range $\{y|0 \le y \le 4\}$
    b. g is an even function [2.5]

55.

    a.   Domain all real numbers
             Range all real numbers
    b. g is an odd function [2.5]

56.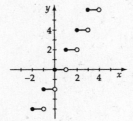

    a.   Domain all real numbers
             Range $\{y|y$ is an even integer$\}$
    b. g is neither even nor odd [2.5]

57. $F(x) = x^2 + 4x - 7$ [2.5]

$F(x) = (x^2 + 4x) - 7$

$F(x) = (x^2 + 4x + 4) - 7 - 4$

$F(x) = (x + 2)^2 - 11$

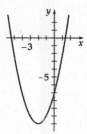

58. $A(x) = x^2 - 6x - 5$ [2.5]

$A(x) = (x^2 - 6x) - 5$

$A(x) = (x^2 - 6x + 9) - 5 - 9$

$A(x) = (x - 3)^2 - 14$

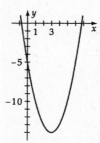

59. $P(x) = 3x^2 - 4$ [2.5]

$P(x) = 3(x - 0)^2 - 4$

60. $G(x) = 2x^2 - 8x + 3$ [2.5]

$G(x) = 2(x^2 - 4x) + 3$

$G(x) = 2(x^2 - 4x + 4) + 3 - 8$

$G(x) = 2(x - 2)^2 - 5$

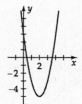

61. $W(x) = -4x^2 - 6x + 6$ [2.5]

$W(x) = -4\left(x^2 + \dfrac{3}{2}x\right) + 6$

$W(x) = -4\left(x^2 + \dfrac{3}{2}x + \dfrac{9}{16}\right) + 6 + \dfrac{9}{4}$

$W(x) = -4\left(x + \dfrac{3}{4}\right)^2 + \dfrac{24}{4} + \dfrac{9}{4}$

$W(x) = -4\left(x + \dfrac{3}{4}\right)^2 + \dfrac{33}{4}$

62. $T(x) = -2x^2 - 10x$ [2.5]

$T(x) = -2(x^2 + 5x)$

$T(x) = -2\left(x^2 + 5x + \dfrac{25}{4}\right) + \dfrac{25}{2}$

$T(x) = -2\left(x + \dfrac{5}{2}\right)^2 + \dfrac{25}{2}$

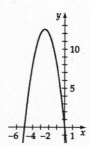

63.

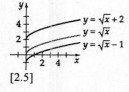

[2.5]

64.

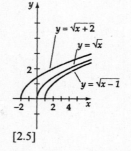

[2.5]

120   Chapter 2: Functions and Graphs

65.

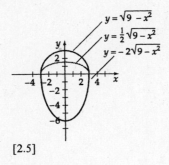

$y = \sqrt{9 - x^2}$
$y = \frac{1}{2}\sqrt{9 - x^2}$
$y = -2\sqrt{9 - x^2}$

[2.5]

66.

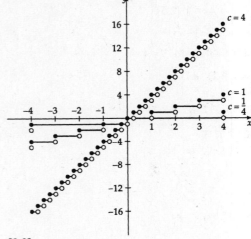

[2.2]

67.

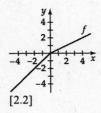

[2.2]

68.

[2.2]

69.

$(f+g)(x) = x^2 - 9 + x + 3$ [2.6]
$\qquad = x^2 + x - 6$
The domain is all real numbers.

$(f-g)(x) = x^2 - 9 - (x+3)$
$\qquad = x^2 - 9 - x - 3$
$\qquad = x^2 - x - 12$
The domain is all real numbers.

$(fg)(x) = (x^2 - 9)(x+3)$
$\qquad = x^3 + 3x^2 - 9x - 27$
The domain is all real numbers.

$\left(\dfrac{f}{g}\right)(x) = \dfrac{x^2 - 9}{x+3}$
$\qquad = \dfrac{(x-3)(x+3)}{x+3}$
$\qquad = x - 3$
The domain is $\left\{x \mid x \neq -3\right\}$.

70.

$(f+g)(x) = x^3 + 8 + x^2 - 2x + 4$ [2.6]
$\qquad = x^3 + x^2 - 2x + 12$
The domain is all real numbers.

$(f-g)(x) = x^3 + 8 - (x^2 - 2x + 4)$
$\qquad = x^3 + 8 - x^2 + 2x - 4$
$\qquad = x^3 - x^2 + 2x + 4$
The domain is all real numbers.

$(fg)(x) = (x^3 + 8)(x^2 - 2x + 4)$
$\qquad = x^5 - 2x^4 + 4x^3 + 8x^2 - 16x + 32$
The domain is all real numbers.

$\left(\dfrac{f}{g}\right)(x) = \dfrac{x^3 + 8}{x^2 - 2x + 4}$
$\qquad = \dfrac{(x+2)(x^2 - 2x + 4)}{x^2 - 2x + 4}$
$\qquad = x + 2$

The domain is restricted when $x^2 - 2x + 4 = 0$.

$x = \dfrac{-(-2) \pm \sqrt{(-2)^2 - 4(1)(4)}}{2(1)}$

$x = \dfrac{2 \pm \sqrt{4 - 16}}{2}$

$x = \dfrac{2 \pm \sqrt{-12}}{2}$ which is not a real number

Therefore the domain is all real numbers.

71. Let x = one of the numbers and $50 - x$ = the other number. Their product is given by

$$y = x(50 - x) = 50x - x^2 = -x^2 + 50x.$$

Now y takes on its maximum value when

$$x = \frac{-b}{2a} = \frac{-50}{2(-1)} = \frac{-50}{-2} = 25.$$

Thus the two numbers are 25 and $(50 - 25) = 25$. That is, both numbers are 25. [2.4]

72. Let x = the smaller number. Let $x + 10$ equal the larger number. The sum of their squares y is given by

$$y = x^2 + (x+10)^2$$
$$= x^2 + x^2 + 20x + 100$$
$$= 2x^2 + 20x + 100$$

Now y takes on its minimum value when

$$x = \frac{-b}{2a} = \frac{-20}{2(2)} = \frac{-20}{4} = -5$$

Thus the numbers are -5 and $(-5 + 10) = 5$. [2.4]

73. $s(t) = 3t^2$ [2.4]

a. Average velocity $= \dfrac{3(4)^2 - 3(2)^2}{4-2}$

$= \dfrac{3(16) - 3(4)}{2}$

$= \dfrac{48 - 12}{2}$

$= \dfrac{36}{2} = 18$ ft/sec

b. Average velocity $= \dfrac{3(3)^2 - 3(2)^2}{3-2}$

$= \dfrac{3(9) - 3(4)}{1}$

$= \dfrac{27 - 12}{1} = 15$ ft/sec

c. Average velocity $= \dfrac{3(2.5)^2 - 3(2)^2}{2.5-2}$

$= \dfrac{3(6.25) - 3(4)}{0.5}$

$= \dfrac{18.75 - 12}{0.5}$

$= \dfrac{6.75}{0.5} = 13.5$ ft/sec

d. Average velocity $= \dfrac{3(2.01)^2 - 3(2)^2}{2.01-2}$

$= \dfrac{3(4.0401) - 3(4)}{0.01}$

$= \dfrac{12.1203 - 12}{0.01}$

$= \dfrac{0.1203}{0.01} = 12.03$ ft/sec

e. It appears that the average velocity of the ball approaches 12 ft/sec.

74. $s(t) = 2t^2 + t$ [2.4]

a. Average velocity $= \dfrac{2(5)^2 + 5 - [2(3)^2 + 3]}{5-3}$

$= \dfrac{2(25) + 5 - [2(9) + 3]}{2}$

$= \dfrac{50 + 5 - [18 + 3]}{2}$

$= \dfrac{50 + 5 - 18 - 3}{2}$

$= \dfrac{34}{2} = 17$ ft/sec

b. Average velocity $= \dfrac{2(4)^2 + 4 - [2(3)^2 + 3]}{4-3}$

$= \dfrac{2(16) + 4 - [2(9) + 3]}{1}$

$= \dfrac{32 + 4 - [18 + 3]}{1}$

$= \dfrac{32 + 4 - 18 - 3}{1}$

$= \dfrac{15}{1} = 15$ ft/sec

c. Average velocity $= \dfrac{2(3.5)^2 + 3.5 - [2(3)^2 + 3]}{3.5-3}$

$= \dfrac{2(12.25) + 3.5 - [2(9) + 3]}{0.5}$

$= \dfrac{24.5 + 3.5 - [18 + 3]}{0.5}$

$= \dfrac{24.5 + 3.5 - 18 - 3}{0.5}$

$= \dfrac{7}{0.5} = 14$ ft/sec

d. Average velocity $= \dfrac{2(3.01)^2 + 3.01 - [2(3)^2 + 3]}{3.01-3}$

$= \dfrac{2(9.0601) + 3.01 - [2(9) + 3]}{0.01}$

$= \dfrac{18.1202 + 3.01 - [18 + 3]}{0.01}$

$= \dfrac{18.1202 + 3.01 - 18 - 3}{0.01}$

$= \dfrac{0.1302}{2} = 13.02$ ft/sec

e. It appears that the average velocity of the ball approaches 13 ft/sec.

75. **a.** Enter the data on your calculator. The technique for a TI-83 calculator is illustrated here. [2.7]

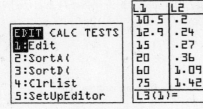

$$y = 0.018024687x + 0.00050045744$$

b. Yes, a linear model of this data is reasonable. The value of $r = 0.999$ is very close to 1.

c. $y = 0.018024687(100) + 0.00050045744$

≈ 1.8 seconds

76. **a.** Enter the data on your calculator. The technique for a TI-83 calculator is illustrated here. [2.7]

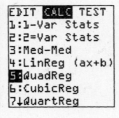

$$y = 0.0047952048x^2 - 1.756843157x + 180.4065934$$

b. Empty $\Rightarrow y = 0 \Rightarrow$ the graph intersects the x-axis.

Graph the equation, and notice that it never intersects the x-axis.

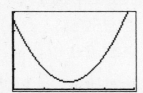

Xmin = 0, Xmax = 400, Xscl = 100
Ymin = 0, Ymax = 200, Xscl = 50

Thus, no, on the basis of this model, the can never empties.

c. The regression line is a model of the data and is not based on physical principles.

Chapter **T**est

1.

$$\text{midpoint} = \left(\frac{x_1 + x_2}{2}, \frac{y_1 + y_2}{2} \right) = \left(\frac{-2+4}{2}, \frac{3+(-1)}{2} \right) = \left(\frac{2}{2}, \frac{2}{2} \right) = (1, 1) \ [2.1]$$

$$\text{length} = d = \sqrt{(x_1 - x_2)^2 + (y_1 - y_2)^2} = \sqrt{(-2-4)^2 + (3-(-1))^2} = \sqrt{(-6)^2 + 4^2} = \sqrt{36+16} = \sqrt{52} = 2\sqrt{13}$$

2.

$x = 2y^2 - 4 \ [2.1]$

$y = 0 \Rightarrow x = 2(0)^2 - 4 = -4$

Thus the x-intercept is $(-4, 0)$.

$x = 0 \Rightarrow 0 = 2y^2 - 4$

$4 = 2y^2$

$2 = y^2$

$\pm\sqrt{2} = y$

Thus the y-intercepts are $(0, -\sqrt{2})$

and $(0, \sqrt{2})$.

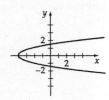

3. $y = |x+2| + 1$ [2.1]

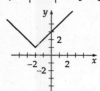

4.
$$x^2 - 4x + y^2 + 2y - 4 = 0 \quad [2.1]$$
$$(x^2 - 4x) + (y^2 + 2y) = 4$$
$$(x^2 - 4x + 4) + (y^2 + 2y + 1) = 4 + 4 + 1$$
$$(x-2)^2 + (y+1)^2 = 9$$

center $(2, -1)$, radius 3

5.
$$x^2 - 16 \geq 0$$
$$(x-4)(x+4) \geq 0$$

The product is positive or zero.
The critical values are 4 and -4.

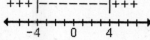

The domain is $\{x | x \geq 4 \text{ or } x \leq -4\}$. [2.2]

6.

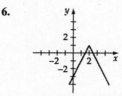

a. increasing on $(-\infty, 2]$
b. never constant
c. decreasing on $[2, \infty)$ [2.2]

7. **a.** $R = 12x$

b. $P = \text{revenue} - \text{cost}$
$P = 12x - (6.75x + 875)$
$P = 11.25x - 875$

c. break-even $\Rightarrow P = 0$
$0 = 11.25x - 875$
$875 = 11.25x$
$78 \approx x$
78 parcels must be sent to break even. [2.4]

8.

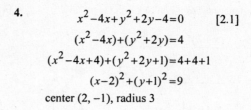

[2.5]

9. **a.** $f(x) = x^4 - x^2$ [2.5]
$f(-x) = (-x)^4 - (-x)^2 = x^4 - x^2 = f(x)$
$f(x)$ is an even function.

b. $f(x) = x^3 - x$
$f(-x) = (-x)^3 - (-x) = -x^3 + x$
$\qquad = -(x^3 - x) = -f(x)$
$f(x)$ is an odd function.

c. $f(x) = x - 1$
$f(-x) = -x - 1 \neq f(x)$ not an even function
$f(-x) = -x - 1 \neq -f(x)$ not an odd function

10. $3x - 2y = 4$ [2.3]
$-2y = -3x + 4$
$y = \dfrac{3}{2}x - 2$

Slope of perpendicular line is $-\dfrac{2}{3}$.
$y - y_1 = m(x - x_1)$
$y + 2 = -\dfrac{2}{3}(x - 4)$
$y + 2 = -\dfrac{2}{3}x + \dfrac{8}{3}$
$y = -\dfrac{2}{3}x + \dfrac{8}{3} - \dfrac{6}{3}$
$y = -\dfrac{2}{3}x + \dfrac{2}{3}$

11. $-\dfrac{b}{2a} = -\dfrac{-4}{2(1)} = 2$ [2.4]

$f(2) = 2^2 - 4(2) - 8$
$\qquad = 4 - 8 - 8$
$\qquad = -12$
The minimum value of the function is -12.

12. $(f+g)(x) = f(x) + g(x)$ [2.6]
$\qquad = (x^2 - 1) + (x - 2)$
$\qquad = x^2 + x - 3$
$\left(\dfrac{f}{g}\right)(x) = \dfrac{f(x)}{g(x)}$
$\qquad = \dfrac{x^2 - 1}{x - 2}, \ x \neq 2$

13. $f(x) = x^2 + 1$ [2.6]

$$\frac{f(x+h) - f(x)}{h} = \frac{(x+h)^2 + 1 - (x^2 + 1)}{h}$$

$$= \frac{x^2 + 2xh + h^2 + 1 - x^2 - 1}{h}$$

$$= \frac{2xh + h^2}{h} = \frac{h(2x + h)}{h}$$

$$= 2x + h$$

14. $f(x) = x^2 - 2x \quad g(x) = 2x + 5$ [2.6]

$$(f \circ g)(x) = f[g(x)] = f(2x+5)$$

$$= (2x+5)^2 - 2(2x+5)$$

$$= 4x^2 + 20x + 25 - 4x - 10$$

$$= 4x^2 + 16x + 15$$

15. $s(t) = 5t^2$ [2.6]

a. Average velocity $= \dfrac{5(3)^2 - 5(2)^2}{3 - 2}$

$$= \frac{5(9) - 5(4)}{1}$$

$$= 45 - 20$$

$$= 25 \text{ ft/sec}$$

b. Average velocity $= \dfrac{5(2.5)^2 - 5(2)^2}{2.5 - 2}$

$$= \frac{5(6.25) - 5(4)}{0.5}$$

$$= \frac{31.25 - 20}{0.5}$$

$$= 22.5 \text{ ft/sec}$$

c. Average velocity $= \dfrac{5(2.01)^2 - 5(2)^2}{2.01 - 2}$

$$= \frac{5(4.0401) - 5(4)}{0.01}$$

$$= \frac{20.2005 - 20}{0.01}$$

$$= 20.05 \text{ ft/sec}$$

16. **a.** Enter the data on your calculator. The technique for a TI-83 calculator is illustrated here. [2.7]

EDIT CALC TESTS
1:Edit
2:SortA(
3:SortD(
4:ClrList
5:SetUpEditor

L1	L2	L3	3
93.2	28		
92.3	26		
91.9	39		
89.5	56		
89.6	56		
90.5	36		
L3(1)=			

EDIT **CALC** TEST
1:1-Var Stats
2:2-Var Stats
3:Med-Med
4:LinReg (ax+b)
5:QuadReg
6:CubicReg
7↓QuartReg

LinReg
y=ax+b
a=-7.98245614
b=767.122807
r2=.805969575
r=-.8977580826

$y = -7.98245614x + 767.122807$

b. $y = -7.98245614(89) + 767.122807$

≈ 57 calories

---

1. Commutative Property of Addition [P.1]

2. $\frac{6}{\pi}, \sqrt{2}$ are not rational numbers

   [P.1]

3. $3+4(2x-9)$ [P.1]

   $3+8x-36$

   $8x-33$

4. $(-4xy^2)^3(-2x^2y^4) = (-64x^3y^6)(-2x^2y^4)$ [P.2]

   $= (-64)(-2)(x^{3+2}y^{6+4}) = 128x^5y^{10}$

5. $\dfrac{24a^4b^3}{18a^4b^5} = \dfrac{4a^{4-4}b^{3-5}}{3} = \dfrac{4b^{-2}}{3} = \dfrac{4}{3b^2}$ [P.2]

6. $(2x+3)(3x-7) = 6x^2 - 5x - 21$ [P.3]

7. $\dfrac{x^2+6x-27}{x^2-9} = \dfrac{(x+9)(x-3)}{(x+3)(x-3)} = \dfrac{x+9}{x+3}$ [P.5]

8. $\dfrac{4}{2x-1} - \dfrac{2}{x-1} = \dfrac{4(x-1)}{(2x-1)(x-1)} - \dfrac{2(2x-1)}{(2x-1)(x-1)} = \dfrac{4x-4-4x+2}{(2x-1)(x-1)} = \dfrac{-2}{(2x-1)(x-1)}$ [P.5]

9. $6 - 2(2x-4) = 14 \Rightarrow 6 - 4x + 8 = 14 \Rightarrow -4x = 0 \Rightarrow x = 0$ [1.1]

10. $x^2 - x - 1 = 0 \Rightarrow x = \dfrac{-(-1) \pm \sqrt{(-1)^2 - 4(1)(-1)}}{2(1)} = \dfrac{1 \pm \sqrt{1+4}}{2} = \dfrac{1 \pm \sqrt{5}}{2}$ [1.3]

11. $(2x-1)(x+3) = 4 \Rightarrow 2x^2 + 5x - 3 = 4 \Rightarrow 2x^2 + 5x - 7 = (2x+7)(x-1) = 0 \Rightarrow x = -\dfrac{7}{2}$ or $x = 1$ [1.3]

12. $3x + 2y = 15$ [1.1]

    $3x = -2y + 15$

    $x = -\dfrac{2}{3}y + 5$

13. $x^4 - x^2 - 2 = 0$ [1.4]

    Let $u = x^2$.

    $u^2 - u - 2 = 0$

    $(u-2)(u+1) = 0$

    $u - 2 = 0$ or $u + 1 = 0$

    $u = 2$ $u = -1$

    $x^2 = 2$ $x^2 = -1$

    $x = \pm\sqrt{2}$ $x = \pm i$

14. $3x - 1 < 5x + 7$ [1.5]

    $-2x < 8$

    $x > -4$

15. distance $= \sqrt{[-2-2]^2 + [-4-(-3)]^2} = \sqrt{(-4)^2 + (-1)^2} = \sqrt{16+1} = \sqrt{17}$ [2.1]

16. $G(x) = 2x^3 - 4x - 7$ [2.2]

    $G(-2) = 2(-2)^3 - 4(-2) - 7 = 2(-8) + 8 - 7 = -15$

17. The slope is $m = \dfrac{-1-(-3)}{-2-2} = \dfrac{-1+3}{-2-2} = \dfrac{2}{-4} = -\dfrac{1}{2}$ [2.3]

    The equation is $y - (-3) = -\dfrac{1}{2}(x-2) \Rightarrow y = -\dfrac{1}{2}x - 2$

18.

0	x
0.08	60
0.03	$60 + x$

$0.08(60) + 0x = 0.03(60 + x)$

$\quad 4.8 = 1.8 + 0.03x$

$\quad\quad 3 = 0.03x$

$\quad 100 = x$

100 ounces of water [1.1]

Chapter 3
Polynomial and Rational Functions

1.

$$5x^2 - 9x + 10 + \frac{-10}{x+3}$$

$$x+3 \overline{)5x^3 + 6x^2 - 17x + 20}$$
$$\underline{5x^3 + 15x^2}$$
$$-9x^2 - 17x$$
$$\underline{-9x^2 - 27x}$$
$$10x + 20$$
$$\underline{10x + 30}$$
$$-10$$

3.

$$x^3 + 2x^2 - x + 1 + \frac{1}{x-2}$$

$$x-2 \overline{)x^4 \qquad -5x^2 + 3x - 1}$$
$$\underline{x^4 - 2x^3}$$
$$2x^3 - 5x^2$$
$$\underline{2x^3 - 4x^2}$$
$$-x^2 + 3x$$
$$\underline{-x^2 + 2x}$$
$$x - 1$$
$$\underline{x - 2}$$
$$1$$

5.

$$x^2 + 4x + 10 + \frac{25}{x-3}$$

$$x-3 \overline{)x^3 + x^2 - 2x - 5}$$
$$\underline{x^3 - 3x^2}$$
$$4x^2 - 2x$$
$$\underline{4x^2 - 12x}$$
$$10x - 5$$
$$\underline{10x - 30}$$
$$25$$

7.

$$x^3 + 7x^2 + 31x + 119 + \frac{475}{x-4}$$

$$x-4 \overline{)x^4 + 3x^3 + 3x^2 - 5x - 1}$$
$$\underline{x^4 - 4x^3}$$
$$7x^3 + 3x^2$$
$$\underline{7x^3 - 28x^2}$$
$$31x^2 - 5x$$
$$\underline{31x^2 - 124x}$$
$$119x - 1$$
$$\underline{119x - 476}$$
$$475$$

9.

$$x^4 + 2x^3 + 2x + 1 - \frac{8}{x-1}$$

$$x-1 \overline{)x^5 + x^4 - 2x^3 + 2x^2 - 3x - 7}$$
$$\underline{x^5 - x^4}$$
$$2x^4 - 2x^3$$
$$\underline{2x^4 - 2x^3}$$
$$0 + 2x^2 - 3x$$
$$\underline{2x^2 - 2x}$$
$$-x - 7$$
$$\underline{-x - 1}$$
$$-8$$

11.

$$\begin{array}{r|rrrr} 2 & 4 & -5 & 6 & -7 \\ & & 8 & 6 & 24 \\ \hline & 4 & 3 & 12 & 17 \end{array}$$

$$4x^2 + 3x + 12 + \frac{17}{x-2}$$

13.

$$\begin{array}{r|rrrr} -1 & 4 & 0 & -2 & 3 \\ & & -4 & 4 & -2 \\ \hline & 4 & -4 & 2 & 1 \end{array}$$

$$4x^2 - 4x + 2 + \frac{1}{x+1}$$

15.
```
4 | 1   0   -10   0    5    -1
        4   16   24   96   404
    1   4    6   24   101   403
```

$$x^4 + 4x^3 + 6x^2 + 24x + 101 + \frac{403}{x-4}$$

17.
```
1 | 1   0   0   0   0   -1
        1   1   1   1    1
    1   1   1   1   1    0
```

$$x^4 + x^3 + x^2 + x + 1$$

19.
```
1/2 | 8   -4   6   -3
          4    0    3
      8   0    6    0
```

$$8x^2 + 6$$

21.
```
2 | 1   0   1   0    1    0    1    0    4
        2   4   10   20   42   84   170  340
    1   2   5   10   21   42   85   170  344
```

$$x^7 + 2x^6 + 5x^5 + 10x^4 + 21x^3 + 42x^2 + 85x + 170 + \frac{344}{x-2}$$

23.
```
-3 | 1   0   0    0    0     1     -10
        -3   9   -27   81   -243   726
     1  -3   9   -27   81   -242   716
```

$$x^5 - 3x^4 + 9x^3 - 27x^2 + 81x - 242 + \frac{716}{x+3}$$

25.
```
2 | 3   1    1    -5
        6   14    30
    3   7   15    25
```

$$P(c) = P(2) = 25$$

27.
```
-2 | 4   0   -6    0    5
        -8   16  -20   40
     4  -8   10  -20   45
```

$$P(c) = P(-2) = 45$$

29.
```
10 | -2   -2    -1     -20
         -20   -220   -2210
     -2  -22   -221   -2230
```

$$P(c) = P(10) = -2230$$

31.
```
3 | -1   0    0    0    1
        -3   -9   -27  -81
    -1  -3   -9   -27  -80
```

$$P(c) = P(3) = -80$$

33.
```
3 | 1   -10    0     0     2
        3    -21   -63   -189
    1   -7   -21   -63   -187
```

$$P(c) = P(3) = -187$$

35.
```
2 | 1   2   -5   -6
        2   8    6
    1   4   3    0
```

A remainder of 0 implies that $x - 2$ is a factor of $P(x)$.

37.
```
-1 | 2   1   -3   -1
        -2   1    2
     2  -1   -2   1
```

A remainder of 1 implies that $x+1$ is not a factor of $P(x)$.

39.
```
-3 | 1   0   -25   0    144
        -3   9    48  -144
     1  -3  -16   48    0
```

A remainder of 0 implies that $x + 3$ is a factor of $P(x)$.

41.
```
5 | 1   2   -22   -50   -75   0
        5   35    65    75   0
    1   7   13    15    0    0
```

A remainder of 0 implies that $x - 5$ is a factor of $P(x)$.

43.
```
1/4 | 16   -8   9   14   4
            4   -1   2    4
      16   -4   8   16   8
```

A remainder of 8 implies that $x-1/4$ is not a factor of $P(x)$.

45.
```
2 | 3   -8   -10   28
        6    -4   -28
    3   -2   -14    0
```

47.
```
1 | 1   0   0   0   -1
        1   1   1    1
    1   1   1   1    0
```

49.
```
-2 | 3   8   10   2   -20
        -6  -4  -12   20
     3   2   6   -10   0
```

51.
```
11 | 2   -18   -50   66
         22    44   -66
     2   4    -6    0
```

53.
```
2/3 | 3   -8   4
           2   -4
      3   -6   0
```

55.

$$\begin{array}{r|rrrr} 2 & 1 & 1 & 1 & -14 \\ & & 2 & 6 & 14 \\ \hline & 1 & 3 & 7 & 0 \end{array}$$

A remainder of 0 implies that $x - 2$ is a factor of $P(x)$.

$P(x) = (x - 2)(x^2 + 3x + 7)$

56.

$$\begin{array}{r|rrrrr} 4 & 1 & -1 & -9 & -11 & -4 \\ & & 4 & 12 & 12 & 4 \\ \hline & 1 & 3 & 3 & 1 & 0 \end{array}$$

A remainder of 0 implies that $x - 4$ is a factor of $P(x)$.

$P(x) = (x - 4)(x^3 + 3x^2 + 3x + 1)$

59. **a.**

$$\begin{array}{r|rrr} 8 & 38 & 291 & 15{,}208 \\ & & 304 & 4{,}760 \\ \hline & 38 & 595 & 19{,}968 \end{array}$$

$19,968

b.

$$\begin{array}{r|rrr} 11 & 38 & 291 & 15{,}208 \\ & & 418 & 7{,}799 \\ \hline & 38 & 709 & 23{,}007 \end{array}$$

$23,007

61. **a.**

$$\begin{array}{r|rrrr} 8 & 1 & -3 & 2 & 0 \\ & & 8 & 40 & 336 \\ \hline & 1 & 5 & 42 & 336 \end{array}$$

336 ways

b.

$$\begin{aligned} P(8) &= 8^3 - 3(8)^2 + 2(8) \\ &= 512 - 3(64) + 2(8) \\ &= 512 - 192 + 16 \\ &= 336 \text{ ways} \end{aligned}$$

They are the same.

63. **a.**

$$\begin{array}{r|rrr} 8 & 1.5 & 0.5 & 0 \\ & & 12 & 100 \\ \hline & 1.5 & 12.5 & 100 \end{array}$$

100 cards

b.

$$\begin{array}{r|rrr} 20 & 1.5 & 0.5 & 0 \\ & & 30 & 610 \\ \hline & 1.5 & 30.5 & 610 \end{array}$$

610 cards

65. **a.**

$$\begin{array}{r|rrr} 2 & -45 & 190 & 200 \\ & & -90 & 200 \\ \hline & -45 & 100 & 400 \end{array}$$

400 people per square mile

b.

$$\begin{array}{r|rrr} 4 & -45 & 190 & 200 \\ & & -180 & 40 \\ \hline & -45 & 10 & 240 \end{array}$$

240 people per square mile

67. **a.**

$$\begin{array}{r|rrrr} 6 & 1 & 1 & 10 & -8 \\ & & 6 & 42 & 312 \\ \hline & 1 & 7 & 52 & 304 \end{array}$$

304 cubic inches

b.

$$\begin{array}{r|rrrr} 9 & 1 & 1 & 10 & -8 \\ & & 9 & 90 & 900 \\ \hline & 1 & 10 & 100 & 892 \end{array}$$

892 cubic inches

• •

69. $5(1)^{48} + 6(1)^{10} - 5(1) + 7 = 5 + 6 - 5 + 7 = 13$

Connecting Concepts

71.

$$\begin{array}{r|rrrr} i & 1 & -3 & 1 & -3 \\ & & i & -1 - 3i & 3 \\ \hline & 1 & -3 + i & -3i & 0 \end{array}$$

A remainder of 0 implies that $x - i$ is a factor of $x^3 - 3x^2 + x - 3$.

•••

73. $P(x) = x^2 - 4x + 6$

$-\dfrac{b}{2a} = -\dfrac{-4}{2(1)} = -\dfrac{-4}{2} = 2$

$P(2) = (2)^2 - 4(2) + 6$

$\quad = 4 - 8 + 6 = 2$

The minimum value is 2.

74. $P(x) = -2x^2 - x + 1$

$-\dfrac{b}{2a} = -\dfrac{-1}{2(-2)} = -\dfrac{-1}{-4} = -\dfrac{1}{4}$

$P\left(-\dfrac{1}{4}\right) = -2\left(-\dfrac{1}{4}\right)^2 - \left(-\dfrac{1}{4}\right) + 1$

$\quad = -2\left(\dfrac{1}{16}\right) - \left(-\dfrac{1}{4}\right) + 1$

$\quad = -\dfrac{1}{8} + \dfrac{2}{8} + \dfrac{8}{8} = \dfrac{9}{8}$

The maximum value is $\dfrac{9}{8}$.

75. $P(x) = x^2 + 2x + 7$ is a parabola that opens up. The x-value of the vertex is

$$-\frac{b}{2a} = -\frac{2}{2(1)} = -\frac{2}{2} = -1$$

The graph decreases from the left until it reaches the vertex, and then it increases.

$P(x)$ increases on the interval $[-1, \infty)$.

76. $P(x) = -2x^2 + 4x + 5$ is a parabola that opens downward. The x-value of the vertex is

$$-\frac{b}{2a} = -\frac{4}{2(-2)} = -\frac{4}{-4} = 1$$

The graph increases from the left until it reaches the vertex, and then it decreases.

$P(x)$ decreases on the interval $[1, \infty)$.

77. $x^4 - 5x^2 + 4$

$(x^2 - 4)(x^2 - 1)$

$(x + 2)(x - 2)(x + 1)(x - 1)$

78. $P(x) = 6x^2 - x - 2$

$\quad 0 = 6x^2 - x - 2$

$\quad 0 = (3x - 2)(2x + 1)$

$3x - 2 = 0 \quad$ or $\quad 2x + 1 = 0$

$\qquad x = \dfrac{2}{3} \qquad\qquad x = -\dfrac{1}{2}$

The x-intercepts are $\left(\dfrac{2}{3}, 0\right)$ and $\left(-\dfrac{1}{2}, 0\right)$.

Section 3.2

1. Since $a_n = 3$ is positive and $n = 4$ is even, the graph of P goes up to its far left and up to its far right.

3. Since $a_n = 5$ is positive and $n = 5$ is odd, the graph of P goes down to its far left and up to its far right.

5. $P(x) = -4x^2 - 3x + 2$

Since $a_n = -4$ is negative and $n = 2$ is even, the graph of P goes down to its far left and down to its far right.

7. $P(x) = \dfrac{1}{2}x^3 + \dfrac{5}{2}x^2 - 1$

Since $a_n = \dfrac{1}{2}$ is positive and $n = 3$ is odd, the graph of P goes down to its far left and up to its far right.

9. Up to the far left and down to the far right $\Rightarrow a < 0$.

11. The coordinates of the vertex of a parabola whose equation is $P(x) = ax^2 + bx + c$ are $\left(\dfrac{-b}{2a}, P\left(\dfrac{-b}{2a}\right)\right)$.

For $P(x) = x^2 + 4x - 1, a = 1, b = 4,$ and $c = -1$.

$$\frac{-b}{2a} = \frac{-4}{2(1)} = -2$$

$$P(-2) = (-2)^2 + 4(-2) - 1 = -5$$

The coordinates of the vertex are $(-2, -5)$. Because $a = 1$, a positive number, the graph of the parabola opens up. Therefore, the minimum value of the function is the y-value of the vertex.
The minimum value of the function is -5.

13. The coordinates of the vertex of a parabola whose equation is $P(x) = ax^2 + bx + c$ are $\left(\dfrac{-b}{2a}, P\left(\dfrac{-b}{2a}\right)\right)$.

For $P(x) = -x^2 - 8x + 1, a = -1, b = -8,$ and $c = 1$.

$$\frac{-b}{2a} = \frac{-(-8)}{2(-1)} = -4$$

$$P(-4) = -(-4)^2 - 8(-4) + 1 = 17$$

The coordinates of the vertex are $(-4, 17)$. Because $a = -1$, a negative number, the graph of the parabola opens down. Therefore, the maximum value of the function is the y-value of the vertex.
The maximum value of the function is 17.

15.

  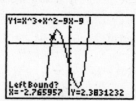 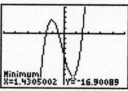

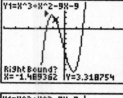 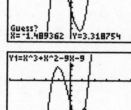 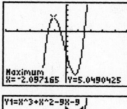 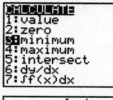

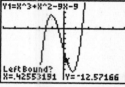 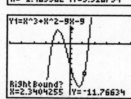 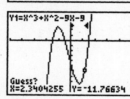

 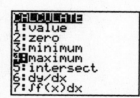 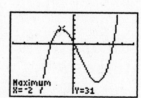

On a TI-83 calculator, the CALC feature is located above the TRACE key.

There is a relative maximum of $y \approx 5.0$ at $x \approx -2.1$. There is a relative minimum of $y \approx -16.9$ at $x \approx 1.4$.

17.

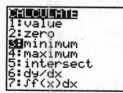 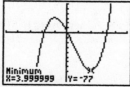

The step-by-step technique for a TI-83 calculator is illustrated in the solution to Exercise **15**.
The CALC feature is located above the TRACE key.

There is a relative maximum of $y \approx 31.0$ at $x \approx -2.0$. There is a relative minimum of $y \approx -77.0$ at $x \approx 4$.

19.

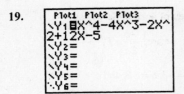
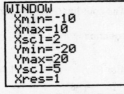

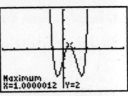

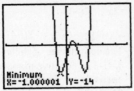

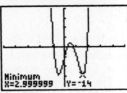

The step-by-step technique for a TI-83 calculator is illustrated in the solution to Exercise **15**.
The CALC feature is located above the TRACE key.

There is a relative maximum of $y \approx 2.0$ at $x \approx 1.0$. There is a relative minimum of $y \approx -14.0$ at $x \approx -1.0$, and another relative minimum of $y \approx -14.0$ at $x \approx 3.0$.

21.
$$P(x) = x^3 - 2x^2 - 15x$$
$$0 = x(x^2 - 2x - 15)$$
$$0 = x(x - 5)(x + 3)$$
The zeros are $0,\ 5,\ -3$.

23.
$$P(x) = x^4 - 13x^2 + 36$$
$$0 = (x^2 - 9)(x^2 - 4)$$
$$0 = (x + 3)(x - 3)(x + 2)(x - 2)$$
The zeros are $-3,\ 3,\ -2,\ 2$.

25.
$$P(x) = x^5 - 5x^3 + 4x$$
$$0 = x(x^4 - 5x^2 + 4)$$
$$0 = x(x^2 - 4)(x^2 - 1)$$
$$0 = x(x + 2)(x - 2)(x + 1)(x - 1)$$
The zeros are $0,\ -2,\ 2,\ -1,\ 1$.

27.
$$P(x) = 2x^3 + 3x^2 - 23x - 42$$

3	2	3	−23	−42
		6	27	12
	2	9	4	−30

4	2	3	−23	−42
		8	44	84
	2	11	21	42

$P(3)$ is negative; $P(4)$ is positive.
Therefore $P(x)$ has a zero between 3 and 4.

29.
$$P(x) = 3x^3 + 7x^2 + 3x + 7$$

−3	3	7	3	7
		−9	6	−27
	3	−2	9	−20

−2	3	7	3	7
		−6	−2	−2
	3	1	1	5

$P(-3)$ is negative; $P(-2)$ is positive.
Therefore $P(x)$ has a zero between −3 and −2.

31.
$$P(x) = 4x^4 + 7x^3 - 11x^2 + 7x - 15$$

1	4	7	−11	7	−15
		4	11	0	7
	4	11	0	7	−8

$1\frac{1}{2} = 1.5$	4	7	−11	7	−15
		6	19.5	12.75	29.625
	4	13	8.5	19.75	14.625

$P(1)$ is negative; $P(1.5)$ is positive.
Therefore $P(x)$ has a zero between 1 and 1.5.

33. $P(x) = (x-1)(x+1)(x-3)$

$0 = (x-1)(x+1)(x-3)$

$x-1=0$ or $x+1=0$ or $x-3=0$

$x=1$ $x=-1$ $x=3$

The exponents on $(x+1)$, $(x-1)$, and $(x-3)$ are odd integers. Therefore the graph of $P(x)$ will cross the x-axis at $(-1, 0)$, $(1, 0)$, and $(3, 0)$.

35. $P(x) = -(x-3)^2(x-7)^5$

$0 = -(x-3)^2(x-7)^5$

$x-3=0$ or $x-7=0$

$x=3$ $x=7$

The exponent on $(x-7)$ is an odd integer. Therefore the graph of $P(x)$ will cross the x-axis at $(7, 0)$.

The exponent on $(x-3)$ is an even integer. Therefore the graph of $P(x)$ will intersect but not cross the x-axis at $(3, 0)$.

37. $P(x) = (2x-3)^4(x-1)^{15}$

$0 = (2x-3)^4(x-1)^{15}$

$2x-3=0$ or $x-1=0$

$x=\dfrac{3}{2}$ $x=1$

The exponent on $(x-1)$ is an odd integer. Therefore the graph of $P(x)$ will cross the x-axis at $(1, 0)$.

The exponent on $(2x-3)$ is an even integer. Therefore the graph of $P(x)$ will intersect but not cross the x-axis at $\left(\dfrac{3}{2}, 0\right)$.

39. $P(x) = x^3 - 6x^2 + 9x$

$0 = x(x^2 - 6x + 9)$

$0 = x(x-3)^2$

$x=0$ or $x-3=0$

$x=3$

The exponent on x is an odd integer. Therefore the graph of $P(x)$ will cross the x-axis at $(0, 0)$

The exponent on $(x-3)$ is an even integer. Therefore the graph of $P(x)$ will intersect but not cross the x-axis at $(3, 0)$.

41.   Let $P(x) = 0$.

$x^3 - x^2 - 2x = 0$

$x(x^2 - x - 2) = 0$

$x(x-2)(x+1) = 0$

$x=0, \ x=2, \ x=-1$

The graph crosses the x-axis at $(0, 0)$, $(2, 0)$, and $(-1, 0)$.

Let $x=0$. $P(0) = 0^3 - 0^2 - 2(0) = 0$

The y-intercept is $(0, 0)$.

x^3 has a positive coefficient and an odd exponent. Therefore, the graph goes down to the far left and up to the far right.

43.   Let $P(x) = 0$.

$-x^3 - 2x^2 + 5x - 6 = 0$

$x^3 + 2x^2 - 5x + 6 = 0$

$$\begin{array}{r|rrrr} 2 & 1 & 2 & -5 & -6 \\ & & 2 & 8 & 6 \\ \hline & 1 & 4 & 3 & 0 \end{array}$$

$(x-2)(x^2 + 4x + 3) = 0$

$(x-2)(x+3)(x+1) = 0$

$x=2, \ x=-3, \ x=-1$

The graph crosses the x-axis at $(2, 0)$, $(-3, 0)$, and $(-1, 0)$.

Let $x=0$. $P(0) = -(0)^3 - 2(0)^2 + 5(0) + 6 = 6$

The y-intercept is $(0, 6)$.

$-x^3$ has a negative coefficient and an odd exponent. Therefore, the graph goes up to the far left and down to the far right.

45. Let $P(x) = 0$.

$$x^4 - 4x^3 + 2x^2 + 4x - 3 = 0$$

```
1 |  1   -4    2    4   -3
  |       1   -3   -1    3
  ------------------------
     1   -3   -1    3    0
```

```
3 |  1   -3   -1    3
  |       3    0   -3
  --------------------
     1    0   -1    0
```

$$(x-1)(x-3)(x^2-1) = 0$$
$$(x-1)(x-3)(x+1)(x-1) = 0$$
$$(x-1)^2(x-3)(x+1) = 0$$

$x = 1, \; x = 3, \; x = -1$

The graph intersects the x-axis but does not cross it at $(1, 0)$.
The graph crosses the x-axis at $(3, 0)$ and $(-1, 0)$.
Let $x = 0$.

$$P(0) = (0)^4 - 4(0)^3 + 2(0)^2 + 4(0) - 3 = -3$$

The y-intercept is $(0, -3)$.

x^4 has a positive coefficient and an even exponent.
Therefore, the graph goes up to the far left and up to the far right.

47. a. Volume = length $\times$ width $\times$ height

$$V(x) = (15 - 2x)(10 - 2x)x$$
$$= [15(10 - 2x) - 2x(10 - 2x)]x$$
$$= [150 - 30x - 20x + 4x^2]x$$
$$= [4x^2 - 50x + 150]x$$
$$= 4x^3 - 50x^2 + 150x$$

b.

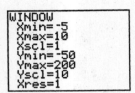

$x = 1.96$ inches (to the nearest 0.01 inch) maximizes the volume of the box.

49. Use a graphing utility to graph
$y = (22 - 4x)(16 - 2x)x$.

Then use the maximum feature of the graphing utility to determine the x-and y-coordinates of the relative maximum.

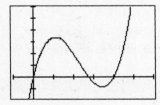

Xmin $= -2$, Xmax $= 12$, Xscl $= 2$
Ymin $= -200$, Ymax $= 600$, Yscl $= 100$

The value of $x \approx 2.137$ inches will produce a box of maximum volume $V \approx 337.1$ cubic inches.

51.

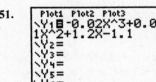

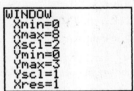

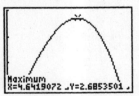

$\$464,000$

53.

a. $x \approx 18$. 18 years after 1900 is in the year 1918.

b. Between 1950 and 1970, the relative minimum rate was 9.5 marriages per thousand population.

55.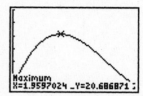

a. 20.69 milligrams

b. 1.968 hours $\times$ 60 minutes per hour $\approx$ 118 minutes after taking the medication

57. a. $D(x) = (-0.0025)(4x^3 - 3 \cdot 8x^2)$

$D(3) = (-0.0025)[4(3)^3 - 3 \cdot 8(3)^2] = (-0.0025)[4(27) - 3 \cdot 8(9)] = (-0.0025)(108 - 216)$

$D(3) = (-0.0025)(-108) = 0.27$ foot $= 0.27$ foot $\times$ 12 inches per foot $= 3.24$ inches

b.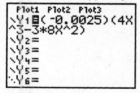

The beam achieves its maximum deflection, 4 feet from the end. The maximum deflection is
0.32 foot $\times$ 12 inches per foot $= 3.84$ inches.

c. The formula is valid on the interval (0, 4]. Therefore, $D(5)$ cannot be determined by using the formula. However, 5 feet from one end of an 8-foot beam is 3 feet from the other end. Thus, the deflection at $x = 5$ is the same as the deflection where $x = 3$, which is 3.24 inches.

Connecting **C**oncepts

59.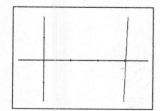

Xmin = –1, Xmax = 4, Xscl = 1
Ymin = –2, Ymax = 2, Yscl = 1

There is a real zero between 3 and 4.

61. $P(x - 3)$ shifts the graph horizontally three points to the right.
$(2 + 3, 0) = (5, 0)$

63. Shift the graph of $y = x^3$ horizontally two units to the right and vertically upward 1 unit.

•••

65. $P(x) = 6x^2 - 25x + 14$

$0 = 6x^2 - 25x + 14$

$0 = (3x - 2)(2x - 7)$

$3x - 2 = 0 \quad \text{or} \quad 2x - 7 = 0$

$\qquad x = \frac{2}{3} \qquad\qquad x = \frac{7}{2}$

66.

$$\begin{array}{r|rrrr} -2 & 2 & 3 & 4 & -7 \\ & & -4 & 2 & -12 \\ \hline & 2 & -1 & 6 & -19 \end{array}$$

$2x^2 - x + 6 - \frac{19}{x+2}$

67.

$$\begin{array}{r|rrrrr} 3 & 3 & 0 & -21 & -3 & -5 \\ & & 9 & 27 & 18 & 45 \\ \hline & 3 & 9 & 6 & 15 & 40 \end{array}$$

$3x^3 + 9x^2 + 6x + 15 + \frac{40}{x-3}$

68. 1, 2, 3, 4, 6, 12

69. $\pm 1, \ \pm 3, \ \pm 9, \ \pm 27$

70. $P(x) = 4x^3 - 3x^2 - 2x + 5$

$P(-x) = 4(-x)^3 - 3(-x)^2 - 2(-x) + 5$

$P(-x) = -4x^3 - 3x^2 + 2x + 5$

Section 3.3

1. $P(x) = (x-3)^2(x+5)$

The zeros are:
−5 (multiplicity 1), 3 (multiplicity 2).

3. $P(x) = x^2(3x+5)^2$

The zeros are:
$-\frac{5}{3}$ (multiplicity 2), 0 (multiplicity 2).

5. $P(x) = (x^2 - 4)(x+3)^2$

$\qquad = (x+2)(x-2)(x+3)^2$

The zeros are:
−3 (multiplicity 2), −2 (multiplicity 1), 2 (multiplicity 1).

7. $P(x) = x^3 + 3x^2 - 6x - 8$

$p = \pm$ factors of $8 = \pm 1, \ \pm 2, \ \pm 4, \ \pm 8$

$q = \pm$ factors of $1 = \pm 1$

$\frac{p}{q} = $ possible rational zeros $= \pm 1, \ \pm 2, \ \pm 4, \ \pm 8$

9. $P(x) = 2x^3 + x^2 - 25x + 12$

$p = \pm$ factors of $12 = \pm 1, \ \pm 2, \ \pm 3, \ \pm 4, \ \pm 6, \ \pm 12$

$q = \pm$ factors of $2 = \pm 1, \ \pm 2$

$\frac{p}{q} = $ possible rational zeros $= \pm 1, \ \pm 2, \ \pm 3, \ \pm 4, \ \pm 6, \ \pm 12, \ \pm \frac{1}{2}, \ \pm \frac{3}{2}$

11. $P(x) = 6x^4 + 23x^3 + 19x^2 - 8x - 4$

$p = \pm$ factors of $4 = \pm 1, \ \pm 2, \ \pm 4$

$q = \pm$ factors of $6 = \pm 1, \ \pm 2, \ \pm 3, \ \pm 6$

$\frac{p}{q} = $ possible rational zeros $= \pm 1, \ \pm 2, \ \pm 4, \pm \frac{1}{2}, \pm \frac{1}{3}, \pm \frac{1}{6}, \pm \frac{2}{3}, \pm \frac{4}{3}$

13. $P(x) = 4x^4 - 12x^3 - 3x^2 + 12x - 7$

$p = \pm$ factors of $7 = \pm 1, \ \pm 7$

$q = \pm$ factors of $4 = \pm 1, \ \pm 2, \ \pm 4$

$\frac{p}{q} = $ possible rational zeros $= \pm 1, \ \pm 7, \ \pm \frac{1}{2}, \ \pm \frac{7}{2}, \ \pm \frac{1}{4}, \ \pm \frac{7}{4}$

15. $P(x) = x^5 - 32$

 $p = \pm$ factors of $32 = \pm 1, \ \pm 2, \ \pm 4, \ \pm 8, \ \pm 16, \ \pm 32$

 $q = \pm$ factors of $1 = \pm 1$

 $\dfrac{p}{q} =$ possible rational zeros $= \pm 1, \ \pm 2, \ \pm 4, \ \pm 8, \ \pm 16, \ \pm 32$

17.

```
 1 | 1    3   -6   -6
   |      1    4
   |_____
     1    4   -2
```
Don't finish dividing. 1 is not an upper bound.

```
 2 | 1    3   -6   -6
   |      2   10    8
   |_____
     1    5    4    2
```
The smallest integer that is an upper bound is 2.

```
-1 | 1    3   -6   -6
   |     -1
   |_____
     1    2
```
Don't finish dividing. −1 is not a lower bound.

```
-2 | 1    3   -6   -6
   |     -2
   |_____
     1    1
```
Don't finish dividing. −2 is not a lower bound.

```
-3 | 1    3   -6   -6
   |     -3    0
   |_____
     1    0   -6
```
Don't finish dividing. −3 is not a lower bound.

```
-4 | 1    3   -6   -6
   |     -4    4
   |_____
     1   -1   -2
```
Don't finish dividing. −4 is not a lower bound.

```
-5 | 1    3   -6   -6
   |     -5   10  -20
   |_____
     1   -2    4  -26
```
The largest integer that is a lower bound is −5.

19.

```
 3 | 2    1  -25   10
   |      6   21
   |_____
     2    7   -4
```
Don't finish dividing. 3 is not an upper bound.

```
 4 | 2    1  -25   10
   |      8   36   44
   |_____
     2    9   11   54
```
The smallest integer that is an upper bound is 4.

```
-3 | 2    1  -25   10
   |     -6   15
   |_____
     2   -5  -10
```
Don't finish dividing. −3 is not a lower bound.

```
-4 | 2    1  -25   10
   |     -8   28  -12
   |_____
     2   -7    3   -2
```
The largest integer that is a lower bound is −4.

21.

```
 1 | 6   23   19   -8   -4
   |      6   29   48   40
   |_____
     6   29   48   40   36
```
The smallest integer that is an upper bound is 1.

```
-3 | 6   23   19   -8   -4
   |    -18
   |_____
     6    5
```
Don't finish dividing. −3 is not a lower bound.

```
-4 | 6   23   19   -8   -4
   |    -24    4  -92  400
   |_____
     6   -1   23 -100  396
```
The largest integer that is a lower bound is −4.

23.

```
 3 | -4   12    3  -12    7
   |     -12    0
   |_____
    -4    0    3
```
Don't finish dividing. 3 is not an upper bound.

```
 4 | -4   12    3  -12     7
   |     -16  -16  -52  -256
   |_____
    -4   -4  -13  -64  -249
```
The smallest integer that is an upper bound is 4.

```
-1 | -4   12    3  -12    7
   |       4  -16   13   -1
   |_____
    -4   16  -13    1    6
```
−1 is not a lower bound.

```
-2 | -4   12    3  -12     7
   |       8  -40   74  -124
   |_____
    -4   20  -37   62  -117
```
The largest integer that is a lower bound is −2.

25.

1	1	0	0	0	0	−32
		1	1	1	1	1
	1	1	1	1	1	−31

1 is not an upper bound.

2	1	0	0	0	0	−32
		2	4	8	16	32
	1	2	4	8	16	0

The smallest integer that is an upper bound is 2.

−1	1	0	0	0	0	−32
		−1	1	−1	1	−1
	1	−1	1	−1	1	−33

The largest integer that is a lower bound is −1.

27. $P(x) = x^3 + 3x^2 - 6x - 8$ has 1 change in sign $\Rightarrow$ one positive zero.

$P(-x) = -x^3 + 3x^2 + 6x - 8$ has 2 changes in sign $\Rightarrow$ two or no negative zeros.

29. $P(x) = 2x^3 + x^2 - 25x + 12$ has 2 changes in sign $\Rightarrow$ two or no positive zeros.

$P(-x) = -2x^3 + x^2 + 25x + 12$ has 1 change in sign $\Rightarrow$ one negative zero.

31. $P(x) = 6x^4 + 23x^3 + 19x^2 - 8x - 4$ has 1 change in sign $\Rightarrow$ one positive zero.

$P(-x) = 6x^4 - 23x^3 + 19x^2 + 8x - 4$ has 3 changes in sign $\Rightarrow$ three or one negative zero.

33. $P(x) = 4x^4 - 12x^3 - 3x^2 + 12x - 7$ has 3 changes in sign $\Rightarrow$ three or one positive zeros.

$P(-x) = 4x^4 + 12x^3 - 3x^2 - 12x - 7$ has 1 change in sign $\Rightarrow$ one negative zero.

35. $P(x) = x^5 - 32$ has 1 change in sign $\Rightarrow$ one positive zero.

$P(-x) = -x^5 - 32$ has no changes in sign $\Rightarrow$ no negative zeros.

37. $P(x) = x^3 + 3x^2 - 6x - 8$

one positive and two or no negative real zeros

$\dfrac{p}{q} = \pm 1, \ \pm 2, \ \pm 4, \ \pm 8$

2	1	3	−6	−8
		2	10	8
	1	5	4	0

$x^2 + 5x + 4 = (x + 4)(x + 1) = 0 \Rightarrow x = -4, \ -1$

The zeros of $P(x)$ are 2, −4, and −1.

39. $P(x) = 2x^3 + x^2 - 25x + 12$ has two or no positive and one negative real zero.

$\dfrac{p}{q} = \pm 1, \ \pm 2, \ \pm 3, \ \pm 4, \ \pm 6, \ \pm 12, \ \pm\dfrac{1}{2}, \ \pm\dfrac{3}{2}$

3	2	1	−25	12
		6	21	−12
	2	7	−4	0

$2x^2 + 7x - 4 = (2x - 1)(x + 4) = 0 \Rightarrow x = \dfrac{1}{2}, \ -4$. The zeros of $P(x)$ are 3, $\dfrac{1}{2}$, −4.

41. $P(x) = 6x^4 + 23x^3 + 19x^2 - 8x - 4$

one positive and three or one negative real zero

$$
\begin{array}{r|rrrrr}
-2 & 6 & 23 & 19 & -8 & -4 \\
   &   & -12 & -22 & 6 & 4 \\
\hline
   & 6 & 11 & -3 & -2 & 0
\end{array}
$$

$$
\begin{array}{r|rrrr}
-2 & 6 & 11 & -3 & -2 \\
   &   & -12 & 2 & 2 \\
\hline
   & 6 & -1 & -1 & 0
\end{array}
$$

$6x^2 - x - 1 = (3x+1)(2x-1) = 0 \Rightarrow x = -\frac{1}{3}, \ \frac{1}{2}$

The zeros of $P(x)$ are -2 (multiplicity 2), $-\frac{1}{3}, \ \frac{1}{2}$.

43. $P(x) = 2x^4 - 9x^3 - 2x^2 + 27x - 12$

$$
\begin{array}{r|rrrrr}
4 & 2 & -9 & -2 & 27 & -12 \\
  &   & 8 & -4 & -24 & 12 \\
\hline
  & 2 & -1 & -6 & 3 & 0
\end{array}
$$

$$
\begin{array}{r|rrrr}
\frac{1}{2} & 2 & -1 & -6 & 3 \\
            &   & 1 & 0 & -3 \\
\hline
            & 2 & 0 & -6 & 0
\end{array}
$$

$2x^2 - 6 = 0 \Rightarrow 2(x^2 - 3) = 0 \Rightarrow x = \pm\sqrt{3}$

The zeros of $P(x)$ are $4, \ \frac{1}{2}, \ \sqrt{3}, \ -\sqrt{3}$.

45. $P(x) = x^3 - 8x^2 + 8x + 24$

two or no positive and one negative real zero

$\dfrac{p}{q} = \pm1, \ \pm2, \ \pm3, \ \pm4, \ \pm6, \ \pm8, \ \pm12, \ \pm24$

$$
\begin{array}{r|rrrr}
6 & 1 & -8 & 8 & 24 \\
  &   & 6 & -12 & -24 \\
\hline
  & 1 & -2 & -4 & 0
\end{array}
$$

$x^2 - 2x - 4 = 0$

$x = \dfrac{-(-2) \pm \sqrt{(-2)^2 - 4(1)(-4)}}{2(1)}$

$= \dfrac{2 \pm \sqrt{20}}{2} = \dfrac{2 \pm 2\sqrt{5}}{2} = 1 \pm \sqrt{5}$

The zeros of $P(x)$ are $6, \ 1 + \sqrt{5}, \ 1 - \sqrt{5}$.

47. $P(x) = 2x^4 - 19x^3 + 51x^2 - 31x + 5$

four, two or no positive and no negative real zeros

$\dfrac{p}{q} = \pm1, \ \pm5, \ \pm\dfrac{1}{2}, \ \pm\dfrac{5}{2}$

$$
\begin{array}{r|rrrrr}
5 & 2 & -19 & 51 & -31 & 5 \\
  &   & 10 & -45 & 30 & -5 \\
\hline
  & 2 & -9 & 6 & -1 & 0
\end{array}
$$

$$
\begin{array}{r|rrrr}
\frac{1}{2} & 2 & -9 & 6 & -1 \\
            &   & 1 & -4 & 1 \\
\hline
            & 2 & -8 & 2 & 0
\end{array}
$$

$2x^2 - 8x + 2 = 2(x^2 - 4x + 1) = 0$

$x = \dfrac{-(-4) \pm \sqrt{(-4)^2 - 4(1)(1)}}{2(1)} = \dfrac{4 \pm \sqrt{12}}{2} = \dfrac{4 \pm 2\sqrt{3}}{2} = 2 \pm \sqrt{3}$

The zeros of $P(x)$ are $5, \ \frac{1}{2}, \ 2+\sqrt{3}, \ 2-\sqrt{3}$.

49. $P(x) = 3x^6 - 10x^5 - 29x^4 + 34x^3 + 50x^2 - 24x - 24$

three or one positive and three or one negative real zeros

$$
\begin{array}{r|rrrrrrr}
1 & 3 & -10 & -29 & 34 & 50 & -24 & -24 \\
  &   & 3 & -7 & -36 & -2 & 48 & 24 \\
\hline
  & 3 & -7 & -36 & -2 & 48 & 24 & 0
\end{array}
$$

$$
\begin{array}{r|rrrrrr}
-1 & 3 & -7 & -36 & -2 & 48 & 24 \\
   &   & -3 & 10 & 26 & -24 & -24 \\
\hline
   & 3 & -10 & -26 & 24 & 24 & 0
\end{array}
$$

$$
\begin{array}{r|rrrrr}
-2 & 3 & -10 & -26 & 24 & 24 \\
   &   & -6 & 32 & -12 & -24 \\
\hline
   & 3 & -16 & 6 & 12 & 9
\end{array}
\qquad
\begin{array}{r|rrrr}
-\frac{2}{3} & 3 & -16 & 6 & 12 \\
             &   & -2 & 12 & -12 \\
\hline
             & 3 & -18 & 18 & 0
\end{array}
$$

$3x^2 - 18x + 18 = 3(x^2 - 6x + 6) = 0 \Rightarrow x^2 - 6x + 6 = 0$

$x = \dfrac{-(-6) \pm \sqrt{(-6)^2 - 4(1)(6)}}{2(1)} = \dfrac{6 \pm \sqrt{12}}{2} = \dfrac{6 \pm 2\sqrt{3}}{2} = 3 \pm \sqrt{3}$

The zeros of $P(x)$ are $1, -1, -2, -\frac{2}{3}, 3+\sqrt{3}, 3-\sqrt{3}$.

51. $P(x) = x^3 - 3x - 2$

one positive and two or no negative real zeros

$\dfrac{p}{q} = \pm 1, \ \pm 2$

$$
\begin{array}{r|rrrr}
2 & 1 & 0 & -3 & -2 \\
  &   & 2 & 4 & 2 \\
\hline
  & 1 & 2 & 1 & 0
\end{array}
$$

$x^2 + 2x + 1 = (x+1)^2 = 0 \Rightarrow x = -1$

The zeros of $P(x)$ are 2, -1 (multiplicity 2).

53. $P(x) = x^4 - 5x^2 - 2x = x(x^3 - 5x - 2)$

one positive and two or no negative real zeros

$\dfrac{p}{q} = \pm 1, \ \pm 2$

$$
\begin{array}{r|rrrr}
-2 & 1 & 0 & -5 & -2 \\
   &   & -2 & 4 & 2 \\
\hline
   & 1 & -2 & -1 & 0
\end{array}
$$

$x^2 - 2x - 1 = 0$

$x = \dfrac{-(-2) \pm \sqrt{(-2)^2 - 4(1)(-1)}}{2(1)}$

$= \dfrac{2 \pm \sqrt{8}}{2} = \dfrac{2 \pm 2\sqrt{2}}{2} = 1 \pm \sqrt{2}$

The zeros of $P(x)$ are 0, -2, $1 + \sqrt{2}$, $1 - \sqrt{2}$.

55. $P(x) = x^4 + x^3 - 3x^2 - 5x - 2$

one positive and three or one negative real zeros

$\dfrac{p}{q} = \pm 1, \ \pm 2$

$$
\begin{array}{r|rrrrr}
-1 & 1 & 1 & -3 & -5 & -2 \\
   &   & -1 & 0 & 3 & 2 \\
\hline
   & 1 & 0 & -3 & -2 & 0
\end{array}
$$

$$
\begin{array}{r|rrrr}
-1 & 1 & 0 & -3 & -2 \\
   &   & -1 & 1 & 2 \\
\hline
   & 1 & -1 & -2 & 0
\end{array}
$$

$x^2 - x - 2 = (x-2)(x+1) = 0 \Rightarrow x = 2, \ -1$

The zeros of $P(x)$ are 2, -1 (multiplicity 3).

57. $P(x) = 2x^4 - 17x^3 + 4x^2 + 35x - 24$

three or one positive and one negative real zeros

$\dfrac{p}{q} = \pm 1, \ \pm 2, \ \pm 3, \ \pm 4, \ \pm 6, \ \pm 8, \ \pm 12, \ \pm 24, \ \pm \dfrac{1}{2}, \ \pm \dfrac{3}{2}$

$$
\begin{array}{r|rrrrr}
1 & 2 & -17 & 4   & 35 & -24 \\
  &   & 2   & -15 & -11 & 24 \\
\hline
  & 2 & -15 & -11 & 24 & 0
\end{array}
$$

$$
\begin{array}{r|rrrr}
1 & 2 & -15 & -11 & 24 \\
  &   & 2   & -13 & -24 \\
\hline
  & 2 & -13 & -24 & 0
\end{array}
$$

$2x^2 - 13x - 24 = (2x+3)(x-8) = 0$

$\Rightarrow x = -\dfrac{3}{2}, \ 8$

The zeros of $P(x)$ are 1 (multiplicity 2), $-\dfrac{3}{2}$, 8.

59. The original cube's dimensions are $n \times n \times n$.

The resulting solid measures $n \cdot n \cdot (n-2)$.

$n \cdot n \cdot (n-2) = 567$

$n^2(n-2) = 567$

$n^3 - 2n^2 - 567 = 0$

$$
\begin{array}{r|rrrr}
9 & 1 & -2 & 0 & -567 \\
  &   & 9 & 63 & 567 \\
\hline
  & 1 & 7 & 63 & 0
\end{array}
$$

$n = 9$ inches.

61. $[(x)(x+1)(x+2)] - [(2)(1)(x)] = 112$

$x(x^2 + 3x + 2) - 2x = 112$

$x^3 + 3x^2 + 2x - 2x = 112$

$x^3 + 3x^2 - 112 = 0$

$$
\begin{array}{r|rrrr}
4 & 1 & 3 & 0 & -112 \\
  &   & 4 & 28 & 112 \\
\hline
  & 1 & 7 & 28 & 0
\end{array}
$$

$x = 4$ inches

63.

a. $P(5) = \dfrac{5^3 + 5(5) + 6}{6} = \dfrac{125 + 25 + 6}{6} = \dfrac{156}{6} = 26$ pieces

b. $\dfrac{n^3 + 5n + 6}{6} = 64$

$n^3 + 5n + 6 = 384$

$n^3 + 5n - 372 = 0$

$$
\begin{array}{r|rrrr}
7 & 1 & 0 & 5 & -372 \\
  &   & 7 & 49 & 378 \\
\hline
  & 1 & 7 & 54 & 0
\end{array}
$$

At least 7 cuts are needed to produce 64 pieces.

65.

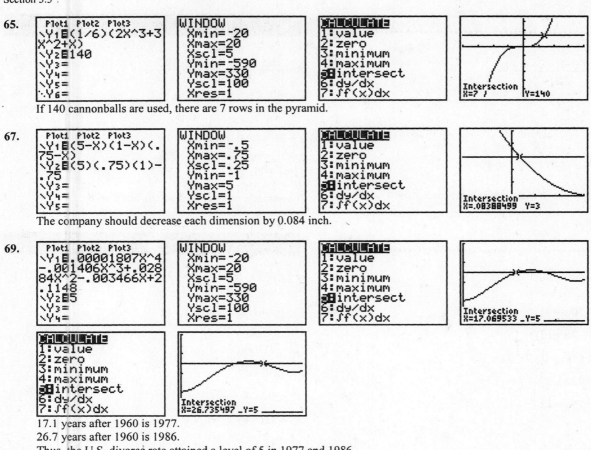

If 140 cannonballs are used, there are 7 rows in the pyramid.

67.

The company should decrease each dimension by 0.084 inch.

69.

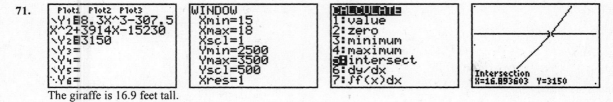

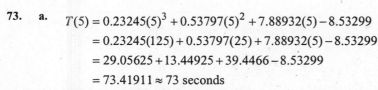

17.1 years after 1960 is 1977.

26.7 years after 1960 is 1986.

Thus, the U.S. divorce rate attained a level of 5 in 1977 and 1986.

71.

The giraffe is 16.9 feet tall.

73. **a.** $T(5) = 0.23245(5)^3 + 0.53797(5)^2 + 7.88932(5) - 8.53299$

$\qquad = 0.23245(125) + 0.53797(25) + 7.88932(5) - 8.53299$

$\qquad = 29.05625 + 13.44925 + 39.4466 - 8.53299$

$\qquad = 73.41911 \approx 73$ seconds

b. 5 minutes = 5(60) = 300 minutes

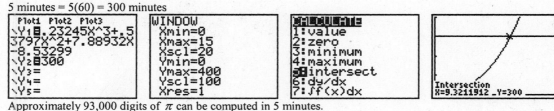

Approximately 93,000 digits of π can be computed in 5 minutes.

75.

$$B = \left(\frac{\text{max of } (|-5|,|-28|,|15|)}{|2|} + 1 \right)$$

$$= \left(\frac{28}{2} + 1 \right)$$

$$= 15$$

$|-3| = 3 < 15$

$\left| \frac{1}{2} \right| = \frac{1}{2} < 15$

$|5| = 5 < 15$

The absolute value of each zero is less than B.

77.

$$B = \left(\frac{\text{max of } (|-2|,|9|,|2|,|-10|)}{|1|} + 1 \right)$$

$$= \left(\frac{10}{1} + 1 \right)$$

$$= 11$$

$|1 + 3i| = \sqrt{10} < 11$

$|1 - 3i| = \sqrt{10} < 11$

$|1| = 1 < 11$

$|-1| = 1 < 11$

The absolute value of each zero is less than B.

79. $3 + 2i$

80. $2 - i\sqrt{5}$

81.

$(x-1)(x-3)(x-4)$

$(x-1)(x^2 - 7x + 12)$

$x(x^2 - 7x + 12) - 1(x^2 - 7x + 12)$

$x^3 - 7x^2 + 12x - x^2 + 7x - 12$

$x^3 - 8x^2 + 19x - 12$

82.

$(x - (2+i))(x - (2-i))$

$(x - 2 - i)(x - 2 + i)$

$((x-2) - i)((x-2) + i)$

$(x-2)^2 - i^2$

$x^2 - 4x + 4 - (-1)$

$x^2 - 4x + 4 + 1$

$x^2 - 4x + 5$

83.

$x^2 + 9 = 0$

$x^2 = -9$

$x = \pm\sqrt{-9}$

$x = \pm 3i$

The solutions are $3i$ and $-3i$.

84.

$x^2 - x + 5 = 0$

$$x = \frac{-(-1) \pm \sqrt{(-1)^2 - 4(1)(5)}}{2(1)}$$

$$= \frac{1 \pm \sqrt{1 - 20}}{2} = \frac{1 \pm \sqrt{-19}}{2}$$

$$= \frac{1 \pm i\sqrt{19}}{2} = \frac{1}{2} \pm \frac{\sqrt{19}}{2} i$$

The solutions are $\frac{1}{2} + \frac{\sqrt{19}}{2} i$ and $\frac{1}{2} - \frac{\sqrt{19}}{2} i$

Section 3.4

1.
$$P(x) = x^4 + x^3 - 2x^2 + 4x - 24$$

2	1	1	−2	4	−24
		2	6	8	24
	1	3	4	12	0

−3	1	3	4	12
		−3	0	−12
	1	0	4	0

$x^2 + 4 = 0 \Rightarrow x^2 = -4 \Rightarrow x = \pm\sqrt{-4} \Rightarrow x = \pm 2i$

The zeros are $2, -3, 2i, -2i$.

$P(x) = (x-2)(x+3)(x-2i)(x+2i)$

3.
$$P(x) = 2x^4 + x^3 + 39x^2 + 136x - 78$$

$\frac{1}{2}$	2	1	39	136	−78
		1	1	20	78
	2	2	40	156	0

−3	2	2	40	156
		−6	12	−156
	2	−4	52	0

$2x^2 - 4x + 52 = 2(x^2 - 2x + 26) = 0$

$x = \dfrac{-(-2)\pm\sqrt{(-2)^2-4(1)(26)}}{2(1)}$

$= \dfrac{2\pm\sqrt{-100}}{2} = \dfrac{2\pm 10i}{2} = 1 \pm 5i$

The zeros are $\frac{1}{2}, -3, 1+5i, 1-5i$.

$P(x) = \left(x-\frac{1}{2}\right)(x+3)(x-1-5i)(x-1+5i)$

5.
$$P(x) = x^5 - 9x^4 + 34x^3 - 58x^2 + 45x - 13$$

1	1	−9	34	−58	45	−13
		1	−8	26	−32	13
	1	−8	26	−32	13	0

1	1	−8	26	−32	13
		1	−7	19	−13
	1	−7	19	−13	0

1	1	−7	19	−13
		1	−6	13
	1	−6	13	0

$x^2 - 6x + 13 = 0$

$x = \dfrac{-(-6)\pm\sqrt{(-6)^2-4(1)(13)}}{2(1)} = \dfrac{6\pm\sqrt{36-52}}{2}$

$= \dfrac{6\pm\sqrt{-16}}{2} = \dfrac{6\pm 4i}{2} = 3 \pm 2i$

The zeros are 1 (multiplicity 3), $3+2i, 3-2i$.

$P(x) = (x-1)^3(x-3-2i)(x-3+2i)$

7.
$$P(x) = 2x^4 - x^3 - 15x^2 + 23x + 15$$

−3	2	−1	−15	23	15
		−6	21	−18	−15
	2	−7	6	5	0

$-\frac{1}{2}$	2	−7	6	5
		−1	4	−5
	2	−8	10	0

$2x^2 - 8x + 10 = 2(x^2 - 4x + 5) = 0$

$x = \dfrac{-(-4)\pm\sqrt{(-4)^2-4(1)(5)}}{2(1)}$

$= \dfrac{4\pm\sqrt{-4}}{2} = \dfrac{4\pm 2i}{2} = 2 \pm i$

The zeros are $-3, -\frac{1}{2}, 2+i, 2-i$.

$P(x) = (x+3)\left(x+\frac{1}{2}\right)(x-2-i)(x-2+i)$

9. $P(x) = 2x^4 - 14x^3 + 33x^2 - 46x + 40$

$$
\begin{array}{r|rrrrr}
4 & 2 & -14 & 33 & -46 & 40 \\
  &   & 8 & -24 & 36 & -40 \\
\hline
  & 2 & -6 & 9 & -10 & 0
\end{array}
$$

$$
\begin{array}{r|rrrr}
2 & 2 & -6 & 9 & -10 \\
  &   & 4 & -4 & 10 \\
\hline
  & 2 & -2 & 5 & 0
\end{array}
$$

$2x^2 - 2x + 5 = 0$

$x = \dfrac{-(-2)\pm\sqrt{(-2)^2-4(2)(5)}}{2(2)}$

$= \dfrac{2\pm\sqrt{-36}}{4} = \dfrac{2\pm 6i}{4} = \dfrac{1}{2}\pm\dfrac{3}{2}i$

The zeros are $4, 2, \frac{1}{2}+\frac{3}{2}i, \frac{1}{2}-\frac{3}{2}i$.

$P(x) = (x-4)(x-2)\left(x-\frac{1}{2}-\frac{3}{2}i\right)\left(x-\frac{1}{2}+\frac{3}{2}i\right)$

11.

$$
\begin{array}{r|rrrr}
1+i & 2 & -5 & 6 & -2 \\
    &   & 2+2i & -5-i & 2 \\
\hline
    & 2 & -3+2i & 1-i & 0
\end{array}
$$

$$
\begin{array}{r|rrr}
1-i & 2 & -3+2i & 1-i \\
    &   & 2-2i & -1+i \\
\hline
    & 2 & -1 & 0
\end{array}
$$

$2x - 1 = 0 \Rightarrow x = \frac{1}{2}$

The remaining zeros are $1-i, \frac{1}{2}$.

13.

$$
\begin{array}{r|rrrr}
-i & 1 & 3 & 1 & 3 \\
   &   & -i & -1-3i & -3 \\
\hline
   & 1 & 3-i & -3i & 0
\end{array}
$$

$$
\begin{array}{r|rrr}
i & 1 & 3-i & -3i \\
  &   & i & 3i \\
\hline
  & 1 & 3 & 0
\end{array}
$$

$x + 3 = 0 \Rightarrow x = -3$

The remaining zeros are $i, -3$.

15.

$$
\begin{array}{r|rrrrr}
2-3i & 1 & -4 & 14 & -4 & 13 \\
     &   & 2-3i & -13 & 2-3i & -13 \\
\hline
     & 1 & -2-3i & 1 & -2-3i & 0
\end{array}
$$

$$
\begin{array}{r|rrrr}
2+3i & 1 & -2-3i & 1 & -2-3i \\
     &   & 2+3i & 0 & 2+3i \\
\hline
     & 1 & 0 & 1 & 0
\end{array}
$$

$x^2 + 1 = 0 \Rightarrow x^2 = -1 \Rightarrow x = \pm i$

The remaining zeros are $2+3i, i, -i$.

17.

$$
\begin{array}{r|rrrrr}
1+3i & 1 & -4 & 19 & -30 & 50 \\
     &   & 1+3i & -12-6i & 25+15i & -50 \\
\hline
     & 1 & -3+3i & 7-6i & -5+15i & 0
\end{array}
$$

$$
\begin{array}{r|rrrr}
1-3i & 1 & -3+3i & 7-6i & -5+15i \\
     &   & 1-3i & -2+6i & 5-15i \\
\hline
     & 1 & -2 & 5 & 0
\end{array}
$$

$x^2 - 2x + 5 = 0 \Rightarrow x = \dfrac{-(-2)\pm\sqrt{(-2)^2-4(1)(5)}}{2(1)} = \dfrac{2\pm\sqrt{-16}}{2} = \dfrac{2\pm 4i}{2} = 1\pm 2i$

The remaining zeros are $1-3i, 1+2i, 1-2i$.

19.

$$
\begin{array}{r|rrrrrr}
-2i & 1 & -3 & 7 & -13 & 12 & -4 \\
    &   & -2i & -4+6i & 12-6i & -12+2i & 4 \\
\hline
    & 1 & -3-2i & 3+6i & -1-6i & 2i & 0
\end{array}
$$

$$
\begin{array}{r|rrrrr}
2i & 1 & -3-2i & 3+6i & -1-6i & 2i \\
   &   & 2i & -6i & 6i & -2i \\
\hline
   & 1 & -3 & 3 & -1 & 0
\end{array}
$$

$$
\begin{array}{r|rrrr}
1 & 1 & -3 & 3 & -1 \\
  &   & 1 & -2 & 1 \\
\hline
  & 1 & -2 & 1 & 0
\end{array}
$$

$x^2 - 2x + 1 = (x-1)^2 = 0 \Rightarrow x = 1$

The remaining zeros are $2i, 1$ (multiplicity 3)

21.

$$\begin{array}{r|rrrrr} 5+2i & 1 & -17 & 112 & -333 & 337 \\ & & 5+2i & -64-14i & 268+26i & -337 \\ \hline & & & & & 0 \end{array}$$

$$\begin{array}{r|rrrr} 5-2i & 1 & -12+2i & 48-14i & -65+26i \\ & & 5-2i & -35+14i & 65-26i \\ \hline & 1 & -7 & 13 & 0 \end{array}$$

$$x^2 - 7x + 13 = 0 \Rightarrow x = \frac{-(-7) \pm \sqrt{(-7)^2 - 4(1)(13)}}{2(1)} = \frac{7 \pm \sqrt{-3}}{2} = \frac{7 \pm i\sqrt{3}}{2} = \frac{7}{2} \pm \frac{\sqrt{3}}{2}i$$

The remaining zeros are $5 - 2i$, $\frac{7}{2} + \frac{\sqrt{3}}{2}i$, $\frac{7}{2} - \frac{\sqrt{3}}{2}i$.

23.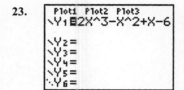

$$\begin{array}{r|rrrr} 1.5 & 2 & -1 & 1 & -6 \\ & & 3 & 3 & 6 \\ \hline & 2 & 2 & 4 & 0 \end{array}$$

$$2x^2 + 2x + 4 = 2(x^2 + x + 2) = 0 \Rightarrow x = \frac{-1 \pm \sqrt{(1)^2 - 4(1)(2)}}{2(1)} = \frac{-1 \pm \sqrt{-7}}{2} = \frac{-1 \pm i\sqrt{7}}{2} = -\frac{1}{2} \pm \frac{\sqrt{7}}{2}i$$

The solutions are 1.5, $-\frac{1}{2} + \frac{\sqrt{7}}{2}i$, $-\frac{1}{2} - \frac{\sqrt{7}}{2}i$.

25.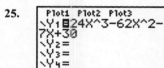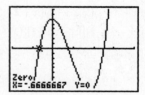

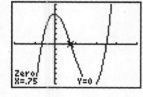 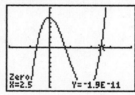

The solutions are $-0.\overline{6}$, 0.75, 2.5 or $-\frac{2}{3}$, $\frac{3}{4}$, $\frac{5}{2}$.

27.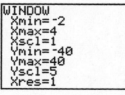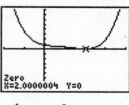

$$\begin{array}{r|rrrrr} 2 & 1 & -4 & 5 & -4 & 4 \\ & & 2 & -4 & 2 & -4 \\ \hline & 1 & -2 & 1 & -2 & 0 \end{array}$$

$$\begin{array}{r|rrrr} 2 & 1 & -2 & 1 & -2 \\ & & 2 & 0 & 2 \\ \hline & 1 & 0 & 1 & 0 \end{array}$$

$$x^2 + 1 = 0 \Rightarrow x^2 = -1 \Rightarrow x = \pm\sqrt{-1} = \pm i$$

The solutions are 2 (multiplicity 2), i, $-i$.

29.

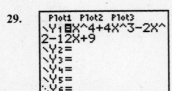 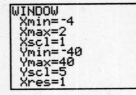  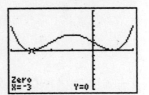

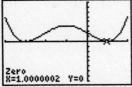

The solutions are –3 (multiplicity 2), 1 (multiplicity 2).

31.
$$P(x) = (x-4)(x+3)(x-2)$$
$$P(x) = (x-4)(x^2 + x - 6)$$
$$P(x) = x(x^2 + x - 6) - 4(x^2 + x - 6)$$
$$P(x) = x^3 + x^2 - 6x - 4x^2 - 4x + 24$$
$$P(x) = x^3 - 3x^2 - 10x + 24$$

33.
$$P(x) = (x-3)(x-2i)(x+2i)$$
$$P(x) = (x-3)(x^2 - [2i]^2)$$
$$P(x) = (x-3)(x^2 - 4i^2)$$
$$P(x) = (x-3)(x^2 - 4[-1])$$
$$P(x) = (x-3)(x^2 + 4)$$
$$P(x) = x(x^2 + 4) - 3(x^2 + 4)$$
$$P(x) = x^3 + 4x - 3x^2 - 12$$
$$P(x) = x^3 - 3x^2 + 4x - 12$$

35.
$$P(x) = [x - (3+i)][x - (3-i)][x - (2+5i)][x - (2 = 5i)]$$
$$P(x) = (x-3-i)(x-3+i)(x-2-5i)(x-2+5i)$$
$$P(x) = [(x-3) - i][(x-3) + i][(x-2) - 5i][(x-2) + 5i]$$
$$P(x) = [(x-3)^2 - i^2][(x-2)^2 - 25i^2]$$
$$P(x) = [(x^2 - 6x + 9) - (-1)][(x^2 - 4x + 4) - (25[-1])]$$
$$P(x) = [(x^2 - 6x + 9) + 1][(x^2 - 4x + 4) + 25]$$
$$P(x) = (x^2 - 6x + 9 + 1)(x^2 - 4x + 4 + 25)$$
$$P(x) = (x^2 - 6x + 10)(x^2 - 4x + 29)$$
$$P(x) = x^2(x^2 - 4x + 29) - 6x(x^2 - 4x + 29) + 10(x^2 - 4x + 29)$$
$$P(x) = x^4 - 4x^3 + 29x^2 - 6x^3 + 24x^2 - 174x + 10x^2 - 40x + 290$$
$$P(x) = x^4 - 10x^3 + 63x^2 - 214x + 290$$

37. $P(x) = [x-(6+5i)][x-(6-5i)](x-2)(x-3)(x-5)$

$P(x) = [x-6-5i][x-6+5i](x-2)(x^2-8x+15)$

$P(x) = [(x-6)^2 - (5i)^2][x(x^2-8x+15) - 2(x^2-8x+15)]$

$P(x) = [(x^2-12x+36)-(25i^2)](x^3-8x^2+15x-2x^2+16x-30)$

$P(x) = [(x^2-12x+36)-(25[-1])](x^3-10x^2+31x-30)$

$P(x) = (x^2-12x+36+25)(x^3-10x^2+31x-30)$

$P(x) = (x^2-12x+61)(x^3-10x^2+31x-30)$

$P(x) = x^2(x^3-10x^2+31x-30)-12x(x^3-10x^2+31x-30)+61(x^3-10x^2+31x-30)$

$P(x) = x^5-10x^4+31x^3-30x^2-12x^4+120x^3-372x^2+360x+61x^3-610x^2+1891x-1830$

$P(x) = x^5-22x^4+212x^3-1012x^2+2251x-1830$

39. Note: $4x-3=0$ if and only if $x=\frac{3}{4}$. Therefore, if $x=\frac{3}{4}$ (that is , $\frac{3}{4}$ is a zero), then $4x-3=0$.

$P(x) = \left(x-\frac{3}{4}\right)[x-(2+7i)][x-(2-7i)]$

$P(x) = (4x-3)[x-2-7i][x-2+7i]$

$P(x) = (4x-3)[(x-2)^2 - (7i)^2]$

$P(x) = (4x-3)[(x^2-4x+4)-49i^2]$

$P(x) = (4x-3)[(x^2-4x+4)-49(-1)]$

$P(x) = (4x-3)(x^2-4x+4+49)$

$P(x) = (4x-3)(x^2-4x+53)$

$P(x) = 4x(x^2-4x+53)-3(x^2-4x+53)$

$P(x) = 4x^3-16x^2+212x-3x^2+12x-159$

$P(x) = 4x^3-19x^2+224x-159$

41. If $2-5i$ is a zero, then $2+5i$ is also a zero.

$P(x) = [x-(2-5i)][x-(2+5i)](x+4)$

$P(x) = [x-2+5i][x-2-5i](x+4)$

$P(x) = [(x-2)^2 - (5i)^2](x+4)$

$P(x) = [x^2-4x+4-25i^2](x+4)$

$P(x) = [x^2-4x+4-25(-1)](x+4)$

$P(x) = [x^2-4x+4+25](x+4)$

$P(x) = (x^2-4x+29)(x+4)$

$P(x) = x^2(x+4)-4x(x+4)+29(x+4)$

$P(x) = x^3+4x^2-4x^2-16x+29x+116$

$P(x) = x^3+13x+116$

43. If $4+3i$ and $5-i$ are zeros, then $4-3i$ and $5+i$ are also zeros.

$P(x) = [x-(4+3i)][x-(4-3i)][x-(5-i)][x-(5+i)]$

$P(x) = (x^2-8x+25)(x^2-10x+26)$

$P(x) = x^4-10x^3+26x^2-8x^3+80x^2-208x+25x^2-250x+650$

$P(x) = x^4-18x^3+131x^2-458x+650$

45. $P(x) = (x+2)(x-1)(x-3)[x-(1+4i)][x-(1-4i)]$

$P(x) = (x^2+x-2)(x-3)[x-1-4i][x-1+4i]$

$P(x) = [x^3-2x^2-5x+6][(x-1)^2 - (4i)^2]$

$P(x) = (x^3-2x^2-5x+6)[x^2-2x+1-16i^2]$

$P(x) = (x^3-2x^2-5x+6)[x^2-2x+1+16]$

$P(x) = (x^3-2x^2-5x+6)[x^2-2x+17]$

$P(x) = x^5-4x^4+16x^3-18x^2-97x+102$

47.
$$P(x) = a(x+1)(x-2)(x-3)$$
$$P(1) = a(1+1)(1-2)(1-3)$$
$$12 = a(2)(-1)(-2)$$
$$12 = 4a$$
$$3 = a$$
$$P(x) = 3(x+1)(x-2)(x-3)$$
$$P(x) = (3x+3)(x^2-5x+6)$$
$$P(x) = 3x(x^2-5x+6)+3(x^2-5x+6)$$
$$P(x) = 3x^3-15x^2+18x+3x^2-15x+18$$
$$P(x) = 3x^3-12x^2+3x+18$$

49.
$$P(x) = a(x-3)(x+5)[x-(2+i)][x-(2-i)]$$
$$P(x) = a(x^2+2x-15)[x-20-i][x-2+i]$$
$$P(x) = a(x^2+2x-15)[(x-2)^2-i^2]$$
$$P(x) = a(x^2+2x-15)[x^2-4x+4-(-1)]$$
$$P(x) = a(x^2+2x-15)[x^2-4x+4+1]$$
$$P(x) = a(x^2+2x-15)(x^2-4x+5)$$
$$P(1) = a(1^2+2[1]-15)(1^2-4[1]+5)$$
$$48 = a(1+2-15)(1-4+5)$$
$$48 = a(-12)(2)$$
$$48 = -24a$$
$$-2 = a$$
$$P(x) = -2(x^2+2x-15)(x^2-4x+5)$$
$$P(x) = -2[x^2(x^2-4x+5)+2x(x^2-4x+5)-15(x^2-4x+5)]$$
$$P(x) = -2[x^4-4x^3+5x^2+2x^3-8x^2+10x-15x^2+60x-75]$$
$$P(x) = -2(x^4-2x^3-18x^2+70x-75)$$
$$P(x) = -2x^4+4x^3+36x^2-140x+150$$

51. $P(x) = x^3 - x^2 - ix^2 - 9x + 9 + 9i = x^3 + (-1-i)x^2 - 9x + (9+9i)$

$$
\begin{array}{r|rrrr}
1+i & 1 & -1-i & -9 & 9+9i \\
    &   & 1+i & 0 & -9-9i \\
\hline
    & 1 & 0   & -9 & 0
\end{array}
\qquad
\begin{array}{r|rrr}
1-i & 1 & 0   & -9 \\
    &   & 1-i & -2i \\
\hline
    & 1 & 1-i & -9-2i
\end{array}
$$

Zero remainder implies $1+i$ is a zero.   Non-zero remainder implies $1-i$ is not a zero.

The Conjugate Pair Theorem does not apply because some of the coefficients of the polynomial function are not real numbers.

53. $\dfrac{x^2-9}{x^2-2x-15} = \dfrac{(x+3)(x-3)}{(x+3)(x-5)} = \dfrac{x-3}{x-5}$

54. $\dfrac{-1+4}{(-1)^2-2(-1)-5} = \dfrac{3}{1+2-5} = \dfrac{3}{-2} = -\dfrac{3}{2}$

55.
$$\frac{2(-3)^2 + 4(-3) - 5}{-3 + 6} = \frac{2(9) - 12 - 5}{3}$$
$$= \frac{18 - 12 - 5}{3} = \frac{1}{3}$$

56.
$$2x^3 + x^2 - 15x = 0$$
$$x(2x^2 + x - 15) = 0$$
$$x(2x - 5)(x + 3) = 0$$
$$x = 0 \quad \text{or} \quad 2x - 5 = 0 \quad \text{or} \quad x + 3 = 0$$
$$x = \frac{5}{2} \qquad\qquad x = -3$$

57. The degree of the numerator, $x^3 + 3x^2 - 5$, is 3; the degree of the denominator, $x^2 - 4$, is 2.

58.
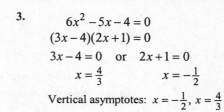

Section 3.5

1.
$$x^2 + 3x = 0$$
$$x(x + 3) = 0$$
$$x = 0 \quad \text{or} \quad x + 3 = 0$$
$$x = -3$$
Vertical asymptotes: $x = 0, x = -3$

3.
$$6x^2 - 5x - 4 = 0$$
$$(3x - 4)(2x + 1) = 0$$
$$3x - 4 = 0 \quad \text{or} \quad 2x + 1 = 0$$
$$x = \frac{4}{3} \qquad\qquad x = -\frac{1}{2}$$
Vertical asymptotes: $x = -\frac{1}{2},\ x = \frac{4}{3}$

5. Horizontal asymptote: $y = \frac{4}{1} = 4$

7. Horizontal asymptote: $y = \frac{15,000}{500} = 30$

9. Vertical asymptote: $x = -4$
Horizontal asymptote: $y = 0$

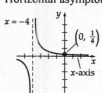

11. Vertical asymptote: $x = 3$
Horizontal asymptote: $y = 0$

13. Vertical asymptote: $x = 0$
Horizontal asymptote: $y = 0$

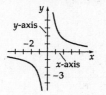

15. Vertical asymptote: $x = -4$
Horizontal asymptote: $y = 1$

17. Vertical asymptote: $x = 2$
Horizontal asymptote: $y = -1$

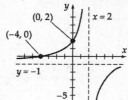

19. Vertical asymptotes: $x = 3, x = -3$
Horizontal asymptote: $y = 0$

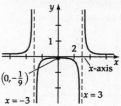

21. Vertical asymptotes: $x = -3, x = 1$
Horizontal asymptote: $y = 0$

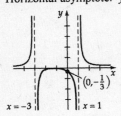

23. Vertical asymptote: $x = -2$
Horizontal asymptote: $y = 1$

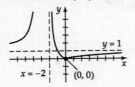

25. Vertical asymptote: none
Horizontal asymptote: $y = 0$

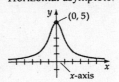

27. Vertical asymptotes: $x = 3, x = -3$
Horizontal asymptote: $y = 2$

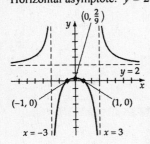

29. Vertical asymptotes:
$x = -1 + \sqrt{2}, x = -1 - \sqrt{2}$
Horizontal asymptote: $y = 1$

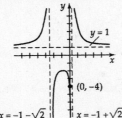

31.

$$\begin{array}{r|rrr} -4 & 3 & 5 & -1 \\ & & -12 & 28 \\ \hline & 3 & -7 & 27 \end{array}$$

$F(x) = 3x - 7 + \dfrac{27}{x + 4}$

Slant asymptote: $y = 3x - 7$

33. $\dfrac{x^3 - 1}{x^2} = \dfrac{x^3}{x^2} - \dfrac{1}{x^2} = x - \dfrac{1}{x^2}$

Slant asymptote: $y = x$

35. $F(x) = \dfrac{x^2 - 4}{x} = x - \dfrac{4}{x}$

Slant asymptote: $y = x$
Vertical asymptote: $x = 0$

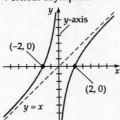

37.

$$\begin{array}{r|rrr} -3 & 1 & -3 & -4 \\ & & -3 & 18 \\ \hline & 1 & -6 & 14 \end{array}$$

$F(x) = \dfrac{x^2 - 3x - 4}{x + 3} = x - 6 + \dfrac{14}{x + 3}$

Slant asymptote: $y = x - 6$
Vertical asymptote: $x = -3$

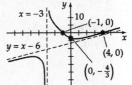

39.

$$\begin{array}{r|rrr} 4 & 2 & 5 & 3 \\ & & 8 & 52 \\ \hline & 2 & 13 & 55 \end{array}$$

$F(x) = \dfrac{2x^2 + 5x + 3}{x - 4} = 2x + 13 + \dfrac{55}{x - 4}$

Slant asymptote: $y = 2x + 13$
Vertical asymptote: $x = 4$

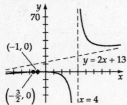

41.

$$\begin{array}{r|rrr} -2 & 1 & -1 & 0 \\ & & -2 & 6 \\ \hline & 1 & -3 & 6 \end{array}$$

$F(x) = \dfrac{x^2 - x}{x + 2} = x - 3 + \dfrac{6}{x + 2}$

Slant asymptote: $y = x - 3$
Vertical asymptote: $x = -2$

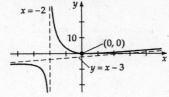

43.

$$\begin{array}{r} x \\ x^2 - 4 \overline{\smash{\big)}\, x^3 \quad\quad + 1} \\ \underline{x^3 - 4x} \\ 4x + 1 \end{array}$$

$F(x) = \dfrac{x^3 + 1}{x^2 - 4} = x + \dfrac{4x + 1}{x^2 - 4}$

Slant asymptote: $y = x$
Vertical asymptotes: $x = 2, x = -2$

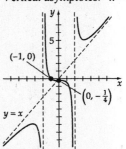

45.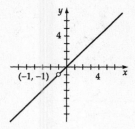

47.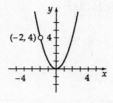

49.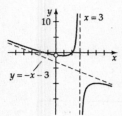

51.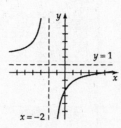

53. **a.**
$$\overline{C}(1000) = \frac{0.43(1000) + 76,000}{1000} = \frac{430 + 76,000}{1000} = \frac{76,430}{1000} = \$76.43$$

$$\overline{C}(10,000) = \frac{0.43(10,000) + 76,000}{10,000} = \frac{4,300 + 76,000}{10,000} = \frac{80,300}{10,000} = \$8.03$$

$$\overline{C}(100,00) = \frac{0.43(100,000) + 76,000}{100,000} = \frac{43,000 + 76,000}{100,000} = \frac{119,000}{100,000} = \$1.19$$

b. $y = 0.43$. As the number of golf balls that are produced increases, the average cost per golf ball approaches \$0.43.

55. **a.**
$$C(40) = \frac{2000(40)}{100 - 40} = \frac{80,000}{60} = \$1,333.33$$

b.
$$C(80) = \frac{2000(80)}{100 - 80} = \frac{160,000}{20} = \$8,000$$

c.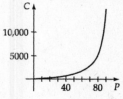

57. **a.**
$$R(0) = \frac{17(0)^2 + 128(0) + 5900}{38(0)^2 + 291(0) + 15,208} = \frac{5900}{15,208} = 0.387954 \approx 38.8\%$$

$$R(7) = \frac{17(7)^2 + 128(7) + 5900}{38(7)^2 + 291(7) + 15,208} = \frac{7629}{19,107} = 0.39928 \approx 39.9\%$$

$$R(12) = \frac{17(12)^2 + 128(12) + 5900}{38(12)^2 + 291(12) + 15,208} = \frac{9884}{24,172} = 0.40890 \approx 40.9\%$$

b. $\dfrac{17}{38} \approx 44.7\%$

59. **a.**

$$P(1) = \frac{420(1)}{0.6(1)^2 + 15} = \frac{420}{15.6} \approx 26.923 \text{ thousand} = 26,923$$

$$P(4) = \frac{420(4)}{0.6(4)^2 + 15} = \frac{1680}{24.6} \approx 68.293 \text{ thousand} = 68,293$$

$$P(10) = \frac{420(10)}{0.6(10)^2 + 15} = \frac{4200}{75} = 56 \text{ thousand} = 56,000$$

b.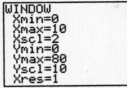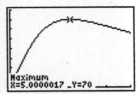

5 years after June 1, 1996 is in the year 2001.

c. $(n < m)$ The population will approach zero.

61. **a.**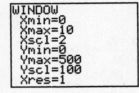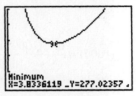

$r \approx 3.8$ centimeters

b. No. The degree of the numerator is not exactly one more than the degree of the denominator.

c. As the radius r increases without bound, the surface area approaches twice the area of a circle with radius r.

Since $V = \pi r^2 h$, then $h = \frac{V}{\pi r^2}$. $h \to 0$ as $r \to \infty$ so as the radius increases without bound, the surface area of the can approaches the area of the top and bottom of the can, two circles with radius r.

● ●

Connecting Concepts

63. Horizontal asymptote: $y = 2$

$$2 = \frac{2x^2 + 3x + 4}{x^2 + 4x + 7}$$

$$2x^2 + 8x + 14 = 2x^2 + 3x + 4$$

$$5x + 10 = 0$$

$$x = -2$$

The graph of $F(x)$ intersects its horizontal asymptote at $(-2, 2)$.

65. Horizontal asymptote: $y = 1$

$$1 = \frac{x^3 + x^2 + 4x + 1}{x^3 + 1}$$

$$x^3 + 1 = x^3 + x^2 + 4x + 1$$

$$x^2 + 4x = 0$$

$$x(x + 4) = 0$$

$$x = 0, \text{ or } x = -4$$

The graph of F intersects its horizontal asymptote at $(0, 1)$ and $(-4, 1)$.

● ●

Chapter 3 True/False Exercises

1. False, consider $x^3 - x^2 - ix^2 - 9x + 9 + 9i$.

$$
\begin{array}{r|rrrr}
1+i & 1 & -1-i & -9 & 9+9i \\
    &   & 1+i & 0 & -9-9i \\
\hline
    & 1 & 0 & -9 & 0
\end{array}
\qquad
\begin{array}{r|rrr}
1-i & 1 & 0 & -9 \\
    &   & 1-i & -2i \\
\hline
    & 1 & 1-i & -9-2i
\end{array}
$$

2. False, Descartes' Rule of Signs indicates that $x^3 - x^2 + x - 1$ has three or one positive zeros.

3. True   **4.** True

5. False, $f(x) = \dfrac{x}{x^2+1}$ does not have a vertical asymptote.

6. False, because $F(x) = \dfrac{(x-2)^2}{(x-3)(x-2)} = \dfrac{x-2}{x-3},\ x \neq 2.$

7. True   **8.** True

9. True   **10.** True

11. True   **12.** False, x^2+1 does not have a real zero.

••••••••••••••••••••••••••••••••••••••

1.
$$
\begin{array}{r|rrrr}
3 & 4 & -11 & 5 & -2 \\
  &   & 12 & 3 & 24 \\
\hline
  & 4 & 1 & 8 & 22
\end{array}
\qquad 4x^2 + x + 8 + \dfrac{22}{x-3}
$$
[3.1]

2.
$$
\begin{array}{r|rrrr}
1 & 5 & 0 & -18 & 2 \\
  &   & 5 & 5 & -13 \\
\hline
  & 5 & 5 & -13 & -11
\end{array}
\qquad 5x^2 + 5x - 13 + \dfrac{-11}{x-1}
$$
[3.1]

3.
$$
\begin{array}{r|rrrr}
-2 & 3 & 0 & -5 & 1 \\
   &   & -6 & 12 & -14 \\
\hline
   & 3 & -6 & 7 & -13
\end{array}
\qquad 3x^2 - 6x + 7 + \dfrac{-13}{x+2}
$$
[3.1]

4.
$$
\begin{array}{r|rrrr}
\frac{1}{2} & 2 & 7 & 16 & -10 \\
            &   & 1 & 4 & 10 \\
\hline
            & 2 & 8 & 20 & 0
\end{array}
\qquad 2x^2 + 8x + 20
$$
[3.1]

5.
$$
\begin{array}{r|rrrr}
5 & 3 & -10 & -36 & 55 \\
  &   & 15 & 25 & -55 \\
\hline
  & 3 & 5 & -11 & 0
\end{array}
\qquad 3x^2 + 5x - 11
$$
[3.1]

6.
$$
\begin{array}{r|rrrrr}
-7 & 1 & 9 & 6 & -65 & -63 \\
   &   & -7 & -14 & 56 & 63 \\
\hline
   & 1 & 2 & -8 & -9 & 0
\end{array}
\qquad x^3 + 2x^2 - 8x - 9
$$
[3.1]

7.
$$
\begin{array}{r|rrrr}
4 & 1 & 2 & -5 & 1 \\
  &   & 4 & 24 & 76 \\
\hline
  & 1 & 6 & 19 & 77
\end{array}
\qquad P(4) = 77
$$
[3.1]

8.
$$
\begin{array}{r|rrrr}
-1 & -4 & 0 & -10 & 8 \\
   &   & 4 & -4 & 14 \\
\hline
   & -4 & 4 & -14 & 22
\end{array}
\qquad P(-1) = 22
$$
[3.1]

9.
$$
\begin{array}{r|rrrrr}
-2 & 6 & 0 & -12 & 8 & 1 \\
   &   & -12 & 24 & -24 & 32 \\
\hline
   & 6 & -12 & 12 & -16 & 33
\end{array}
\qquad P(-2) = 33
$$
[3.1]

10.
$$
\begin{array}{r|rrrrrr}
3 & 5 & -8 & 2 & -6 & 0 & -9 \\
  &   & 15 & 21 & 69 & 189 & 567 \\
\hline
  & 5 & 7 & 23 & 63 & 189 & 558
\end{array}
\qquad P(3) = 558
$$
[3.1]

11.
$$
\begin{array}{r|rrrr}
3 & 1 & 2 & -26 & 33 \\
  &   & 3 & 15 & -33 \\
\hline
  & 1 & 5 & -11 & 0
\end{array}
$$
[3.1]

12.
$$
\begin{array}{r|rrrrr}
-4 & 2 & 8 & -8 & -31 & 4 \\
   &   & -8 & 0 & 32 & -4 \\
\hline
   & 2 & 0 & -8 & 1 & 0
\end{array}
$$
[3.1]

13.
$$
\begin{array}{r|rrrrrr}
1 & 1 & -1 & 0 & -2 & 1 & 1 \\
  &   & 1 & 0 & 0 & -2 & -1 \\
\hline
  & 1 & 0 & 0 & -2 & -1 & 0
\end{array}
$$
[3.1]

14.
$$
\begin{array}{r|rrrr}
\frac{1}{2} & 2 & 3 & -8 & 3 \\
            &   & 1 & 2 & -3 \\
\hline
            & 2 & 4 & -6 & 0
\end{array}
$$
[3.1]

15.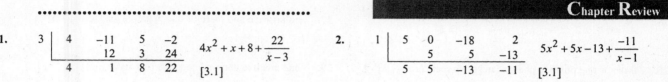
[3.2]

16.
[3.2]

17.
[3.2]

18.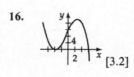
[3.2]

19.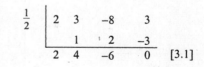
[3.2]

20.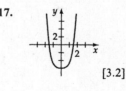
[3.2]

21. $\dfrac{p}{q} = \pm 1, \pm 2, \pm 3, \pm 6$ [3.3]

22. $\dfrac{p}{q} = \pm 1, \pm 2, \pm 3, \pm 5, \pm 6, \pm 10, \pm 15, \pm 30, \pm \dfrac{1}{2}, \pm \dfrac{3}{2}, \pm \dfrac{5}{2}, \pm \dfrac{15}{2}$ [3.3]

23. $\dfrac{p}{q} = \pm 1, \pm 2, \pm 3, \pm 4, \pm 6, \pm 12, \pm \dfrac{1}{3}, \pm \dfrac{2}{3}, \pm \dfrac{4}{3}, \pm \dfrac{1}{5}, \pm \dfrac{2}{5}, \pm \dfrac{3}{5}, \pm \dfrac{4}{5}, \pm \dfrac{6}{5}, \pm \dfrac{12}{5}, \pm \dfrac{1}{15}, \pm \dfrac{2}{15}, \pm \dfrac{4}{15}$ [3.3]

24. $\dfrac{p}{q} = \pm 1, \pm 2, \pm 4, \pm 8, \pm 16, \pm 32, \pm 64$ [3.3]

25. $\dfrac{p}{q} = \pm 1$ [3.3]

26. $\dfrac{p}{q} = \pm 1, \ \pm 2, \ \pm \dfrac{1}{6}, \ \pm \dfrac{1}{3}, \ \pm \dfrac{1}{2}, \ \pm \dfrac{2}{3}$ [3.3]

27. no positive and three or one negative real zeros [3.3]

28. three or one positive and one negative real zeros [3.3]

29. one positive and one negative real zeros [3.3]

30. five, three or one positive and no negative real zeros [3.3]

31.
$$
\begin{array}{r|rrrr}
1 & 1 & 6 & 3 & -10 \\
  &   & 1 & 7 & 10 \\
\hline
  & 1 & 7 & 10 & 0
\end{array}
$$
$x^2 + 7x + 10 = 0$
$(x + 5)(x + 2) = 0$
$x = -5 \ \text{ or } \ x = -2$

The zeros of $x^3 + 6x^2 + 3x - 10$ are $1, -5$, and -2. [3.3]

32.
$$
\begin{array}{r|rrrr}
2 & 1 & -10 & 31 & -30 \\
  &   & 2 & -16 & 30 \\
\hline
  & 1 & -8 & 15 & 0
\end{array}
$$
$x^2 - 8x + 15 = 0$
$(x - 5)(x - 3) = 0$
$x = 5 \ \text{ or } \ x = 3$

The zeros of $x^3 - 10x^2 + 31x - 30$ are $2, 5$, and 3. [3.3]

33.
$$
\begin{array}{r|rrrrr}
-2 & 6 & 35 & 72 & 60 & 16 \\
   &   & -12 & -46 & -52 & -16 \\
\hline
   & 6 & 23 & 26 & 8 & 0
\end{array}
\qquad
\begin{array}{r|rrrr}
-2 & 6 & 23 & 26 & 8 \\
   &   & -12 & -22 & -8 \\
\hline
   & 6 & 11 & 4 & 0
\end{array}
$$
$6x^2 + 11x + 4 = 0$
$(3x + 4)(2x + 1) = 0$
$x = -\dfrac{4}{3} \ \text{ or } \ x = -\dfrac{1}{2}$

The zeros of $6x^4 + 35x^3 + 72x^2 + 60x + 16$ are -2 (multiplicity 2), $-4/3$, and $-1/2$. [3.3]

34.
$$
\begin{array}{r|rrrrr}
-\tfrac{1}{2} & 2 & 7 & 5 & 7 & 3 \\
   &   & -1 & -3 & -1 & -3 \\
\hline
   & 2 & 6 & 2 & 6 & 0
\end{array}
\qquad
\begin{array}{r|rrrr}
-3 & 2 & 6 & 2 & 6 \\
   &   & -6 & 0 & -6 \\
\hline
   & 2 & 0 & 2 & 0
\end{array}
$$
$2x^2 + 2 = 0$
$2x^2 = -2$
$x^2 = -1$
$x = \pm\sqrt{-1}$
$x = \pm i$

The zeros of $2x^4 + 7x^3 + 5x^2 + 7x + 3$ are $-1/2, -3, i$, and $-i$. [3.4]

35.
$$
\begin{array}{r|rrrrr}
1 & 1 & -4 & 6 & -4 & 1 \\
  &   & 1 & -3 & 3 & -1 \\
\hline
  & 1 & -3 & 3 & -1 & 0
\end{array}
\qquad
\begin{array}{r|rrrr}
1 & 1 & -3 & 3 & -1 \\
  &   & 1 & -2 & 1 \\
\hline
  & 1 & -2 & 1 & 0
\end{array}
$$
$x^2 - 2x + 1 = 0$
$(x - 1)(x - 1) = 0$
$x = 1 \ \text{ or } \ x = 1$

The zero of $x^4 - 4x^3 + 6x^2 - 4x + 1$ is 1 (multiplicity 4). [3.3]

36.

$$-\frac{1}{2} \begin{array}{|rrrr} 2 & -7 & 22 & 13 \\ & -1 & 4 & -13 \\ \hline 2 & -8 & 26 & 0 \end{array} \qquad \begin{array}{l} 2x^2 - 8x + 26 = 0 \\ 2(x^2 - 4x + 13) = 0 \end{array}$$

$$x = \frac{-(-4) \pm \sqrt{(-4)^2 - 4(1)(13)}}{2(1)} = \frac{4 \pm \sqrt{16 - 52}}{2} = \frac{4 \pm \sqrt{-36}}{2} = \frac{4 \pm 6i}{2} = 2 \pm 3i$$

The zeros of $2x^3 - 7x^2 + 22x + 13$ are $-1/2$, $2 + 3i$, and $2 - 3i$. [3.4]

37.

$$1 - 2i \begin{array}{|rrrrr} 1 & -4 & 6 & -4 & 15 \\ & 1 - 2i & -7 + 4i & 7 + 6i & 15 \\ \hline 1 & -3 - 2i & -1 + 4i & 3 + 6i & 0 \end{array}$$

$$1 + 2i \begin{array}{|rrrr} 1 & -3 - 2i & -1 + 4i & 3 + 6i \\ & 1 + 2i & -2 - 4i & -3 - 6i \\ \hline 1 & 2 & 3 & 0 \end{array}$$

$$x^2 - 2x - 3 = (x - 3)(x + 1) = 0$$
$$x = 3, \ x = -1$$

The remaining zeros are $1 + 2i$, 3, and -1. [3.4]

38.

$$2 + i \begin{array}{|rrrrr} 1 & -1 & -17 & 55 & -50 \\ & 2 + i & 1 + 3i & -35 - 10i & 50 \\ \hline 1 & 1 + i & -16 + 3i & 20 - 10i & 0 \end{array}$$

$$2 - i \begin{array}{|rrrr} 1 & 1 + i & -16 + 3i & 20 - 10i \\ & 2 - i & 6 - 3i & -20 + 10i \\ \hline 1 & 3 & -10 & 0 \end{array}$$

$$x^2 + 3x - 10 = (x + 5)(x - 2) = 0$$
$$x = -5, \ x = 2$$

The remaining zeros are $2 - i$, -5, and 2. [3.4]

39.
$$(x-4)(x+3)(2x-1) = (x^2 - x - 12)(2x - 1)$$
$$= 2x^3 - x^2 - 2x^2 + x - 24x + 12$$
$$= 2x^3 - 3x^2 - 23x + 12 \qquad [3.4]$$

40.
$$(x-2)(x+3)(x-i)(x+i) = (x^2 + x - 6)(x^2 + 1)$$
$$= x^4 + x^2 + x^3 + x - 6x^2 - 6$$
$$= x^4 + x^3 - 5x^2 + x - 6 \qquad [3.4]$$

41.
$$(x-1)(x-2)(x-5i)(x+5i) = (x^2 - 3x + 2)(x^2 + 25)$$
$$= x^4 + 25x^2 - 3x^3 - 75x + 2x^2 + 50$$
$$= x^4 - 3x^3 + 27x^2 - 75x + 50 \qquad [3.4]$$

42.
$$(x+2)(x+2)[x-(1+3i)][x-(1-3i)] = (x^2 + 4x + 4)(x^2 - 2x + 10)$$
$$= x^4 - 2x^3 + 10x^2 + 4x^3 - 8x^2 + 40x + 4x^2 - 8x + 40$$
$$= x^4 + 2x^3 + 6x^2 + 32x + 40 \qquad [3.4]$$

43. $x + 2 = 0 \Rightarrow$ vertical asymptote : $x = -2$

$\dfrac{3}{1} = 3 \Rightarrow$ horizontal asymptote : $y = 3$ [3.5]

44. $x^2 + 2x - 3 = 0$

$(x + 3)(x - 1) = 0 \Rightarrow$ vertical asymptotes : $x = -3, x = 1$

$\dfrac{2}{1} = 2 \Rightarrow$ horizontal asymptote: $y = 2$ [3.5]

45. $x + 1 = 0 \Rightarrow$ vertical asymptote : $x = -1$

$$\begin{array}{r|rrr} -1 & 2 & 5 & 11 \\ & & -2 & -3 \\ \hline & 2 & 3 & 8 \end{array}$$

$f(x) = 2x + 3 + \dfrac{8}{x+1}$

$\Rightarrow$ slant asymptote: $y = 2x + 3$ [3.5]

46. $2x^2 + x + 7 = 0$

$$x = \frac{-1 \pm \sqrt{1^2 - 4(1)(7)}}{2(1)} = \frac{-1 \pm \sqrt{1 - 28}}{2} = \frac{-1 \pm \sqrt{-27}}{2}$$

x is not a real number $\Rightarrow$ vertical asymptote : none

$\dfrac{6}{2} = 3 \Rightarrow$ horizontal asymptote : $y = 3$ [3.5]

47. 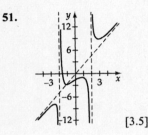 [3.5]

48. 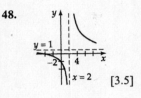 [3.5]

49. 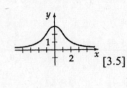 [3.5]

50. 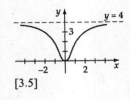 [3.5]

51. 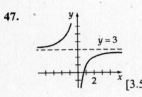 [3.5]

52. 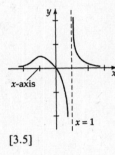 [3.5]

53. 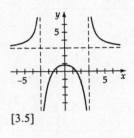 [3.5]

54. 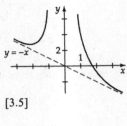 [3.5]

55. **a.** $$C(5000) = \frac{5.75(5000) + 34,200}{5000} = \frac{62,950}{5000} = \$12.59$$

$$C(50,000) = \frac{5.75(50,000) + 34,200}{50,000} = \frac{321,700}{50,000} \approx \$6.43$$

     b. $y = 5.75$. As the number of skateboards that are produced increases, the average cost per skateboard approaches $5.75. [3.5]

56. **a.** $$F(1) = \frac{60}{1^2 + 2(1) + 1} = \frac{60}{4} = 15°F$$

     b. $$F(4) = \frac{60}{4^2 + 2(4) + 1} = \frac{60}{25} = 2.4°F$$

     c. $F(t) \to 0°F$ as $t \to \infty$. [3.5]

57. **a.** As the radius of the blood vessel gets smaller, the resistance gets larger.

     b. As the radius of the blood vessel gets larger, the resistance gets smaller. [3.5]

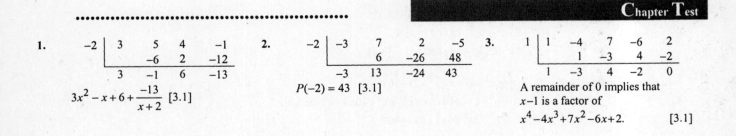

Chapter Test

1. $$\begin{array}{r|rrrr} -2 & 3 & 5 & 4 & -1 \\ & & -6 & 2 & -12 \\ \hline & 3 & -1 & 6 & -13 \end{array}$$

$3x^2 - x + 6 + \dfrac{-13}{x+2}$ [3.1]

2. $$\begin{array}{r|rrrr} -2 & -3 & 7 & 2 & -5 \\ & & 6 & -26 & 48 \\ \hline & -3 & 13 & -24 & 43 \end{array}$$

$P(-2) = 43$ [3.1]

3. $$\begin{array}{r|rrrrr} 1 & 1 & -4 & 7 & -6 & 2 \\ & & 1 & -3 & 4 & -2 \\ \hline & 1 & -3 & 4 & -2 & 0 \end{array}$$

A remainder of 0 implies that $x - 1$ is a factor of $x^4 - 4x^3 + 7x^2 - 6x + 2$.   [3.1]

4. $P(x) = -3x^3 + 2x^2 - 5x + 2$ [3.2]

Since $A_n = -3$ is negative and
$n = 3$ is odd, the graph of P goes up to
the far left and down to the far right.

5. $3x^3 + 7x^2 - 6x = 0$ [3.2]

$x(3x^2 + 7x - 6) = 0$

$x(3x - 2)(x + 3) = 0$

$x = 0, \quad 3x - 2 = 0, \text{ or } x + 3 = 0$

$$x = \frac{2}{3} \qquad x = -3$$

The zeros of $3x^3 + 7x^2 - 6x = 0$

are 0, $\dfrac{2}{3}$, and -3. [3.2]

6. $P(x) = 2x^3 - 3x^2 - x + 1$ [3.2]

$$
\begin{array}{r|rrrr}
1 & 2 & -3 & -1 & 1 \\
  &   & 2 & -1 & -2 \\
\hline
  & 2 & -1 & -2 & -1 \\
\end{array}
$$

$$
\begin{array}{r|rrrr}
2 & 2 & -3 & -1 & 1 \\
  &   & 4 & 2 & 2 \\
\hline
  & 2 & 1 & 1 & 3 \\
\end{array}
$$

Because $P(1)$ and $P(2)$ have different
signs, P must have a real zero between
1 and 2. [3.2]

7. $P(x) = (x^2 - 4)^2(2x - 3)(x + 1)^3$

$P(x) = (x - 2)^2(x + 2)^2(2x - 3)(x + 1)^3$

The zeros of P are 2 (multiplicity 2), -2 (multiplicity 2),
$\dfrac{3}{2}$ (multiplicity 1), and -1 (multiplicity 3) [3.3]

8. $p = \pm 1, \pm 3$

$q = \pm 1, \pm 2, \pm 3, \pm 6$

$\dfrac{p}{q} = \pm 1, \pm 3, \pm \dfrac{1}{2}, \pm \dfrac{3}{2}, \pm \dfrac{1}{3}, \pm \dfrac{1}{6}$ [3.3]

9.

$$
\begin{array}{r|rrrrr}
4 & 2 & 5 & -23 & -38 & 24 \\
  &   & 8 & 52 & 116 & 312 \\
\hline
  & 2 & 13 & 29 & 78 & 336 \\
\end{array}
$$

upper bound: 4

$$
\begin{array}{r|rrrrr}
-5 & 2 & 5 & -23 & -38 & 24 \\
   &   & -10 & 25 & -10 & 240 \\
\hline
   & 2 & -5 & 2 & -48 & 264 \\
\end{array}
$$

lower bound: -5 [3.3]

10. $P(x) = x^4 - 3x^3 + 2x^2 - 5x + 1$

$P(-x) = x^4 + 3x^3 + 2x^2 + 5x + 1$

four, two, or no positive and no negative real zeros [3.3]

11.

$$
\begin{array}{r|rrrr}
\frac{1}{2} & 2 & -3 & -11 & 6 \\
            &   & 1 & -1 & -6 \\
\hline
            & 2 & -2 & -12 & 0 \\
\end{array}
$$

$2x^2 - 2x - 12 = 0$

$2(x + 2)(x - 3) = 0$

$x = -2 \quad \text{or} \quad x = 3$

The zeros of $2x^3 - 3x^2 - 11x + 6$ are $1/2, -2,$ and 3. [3.3]

12.

$$
\begin{array}{r|rrrrr}
2 + 3i & 6 & -5 & 12 & 207 & 130 \\
       &   & 12 + 18i & -40 + 57i & -227 + 30i & -130 \\
\hline
       & 6 & 7 + 18i & -28 + 57i & -20 + 30i & 0 \\
\end{array}
$$

$$
\begin{array}{r|rrrr}
2 - 3i & 6 & 7 + 18i & -28 + 57i & -20 + 30i \\
       &   & 12 - 18i & 38 - 57i & 20 - 30i \\
\hline
       & 6 & 19 & 10 & 0 \\
\end{array}
$$

$6x^2 + 19x + 10 = 0$

$(3x + 2)(2x + 5) = 0$

$3x + 2 = 0 \qquad 2x + 5 = 0$

$x = -2/3 \qquad x = -5/2$

The zeros of $6x^4 - 5x^3 + 12x^2 + 207x + 130$
are $2 + 3i$, $2 - 3i$, $-2/3$, and $-5/2$. [3.4]

13. $P(x) = x(x^4 - 6x^3 + 14x^2 - 14x + 5)$

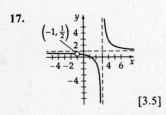

$$\begin{array}{r|rrrrr} 1 & 1 & -6 & 14 & -14 & 5 \\ & & 1 & -5 & 9 & -5 \\ \hline & 1 & -5 & 9 & -5 & 0 \end{array}$$

$$\begin{array}{r|rrrr} 1 & 1 & -5 & 9 & -5 \\ & & 1 & -4 & 5 \\ \hline & 1 & -4 & 5 & 0 \end{array}$$

$x^2 - 4x + 5 = 0$

$$x = \frac{-(-4) \pm \sqrt{(-4)^2 - 4(1)(5)}}{2(1)}$$

$$x = \frac{4 \pm \sqrt{16 - 20}}{2} = \frac{4 \pm \sqrt{-4}}{2}$$

$$x = \frac{4 \pm 2i}{2} = 2 \pm i$$

The zeros of $x^5 - 6x^4 + 14x^3 - 14x^2 + 5x$ are 0, 1 (multiplicity 2), $2+i$, and $2-i$. [3.4]

14. $P(x) = [x-(1+i)][x-(1-i)](x-3)(x)$ [3.4]

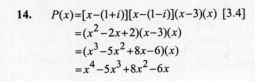

$= (x^2 - 2x + 2)(x - 3)(x)$

$= (x^3 - 5x^2 + 8x - 6)(x)$

$= x^4 - 5x^3 + 8x^2 - 6x$

15. $f(x) = \dfrac{3x^2 - 2x + 1}{x^2 - 5x + 6}$

$x^2 - 5x + 6 = 0$

$(x-3)(x-2) = 0$

$x = 3 \quad x = 2$

vertical asymptotes: $x = 3, x = 2$ [3.5]

16. $f(x) = \dfrac{3x^2 - 2x + 1}{2x^2 - 1}$

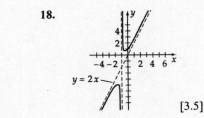

horizontal asymptote: $y = \dfrac{3}{2}$ [3.5]

17.

[3.5]

18.

[3.5]

19. a.

$w(t) = \dfrac{70t + 120}{t + 40}$

$w(1) = \dfrac{70(1) + 120}{1 + 40} = \dfrac{70 + 120}{41} = \dfrac{190}{41} \approx 5$ words per minute

$w(10) = \dfrac{70(10) + 120}{10 + 40} = \dfrac{700 + 120}{50} = \dfrac{820}{50} \approx 16$ words per minute

$w(20) = \dfrac{70(20) + 120}{20 + 40} = \dfrac{1400 + 120}{60} = \dfrac{1520}{60} \approx 25$ words per minute

b.

As $t \to \infty$, $w(t) \to \dfrac{70}{1} = 70$ words per minute [3.5]

20. length $= 25 - 2(2x) = 25 - 4x$

width $= 18 - 2x$

height $= x$

volume $=$ length $\times$ width $\times$ height

$\qquad = (25 - 4x)(18 - 2x)(x)$

$\qquad = (450 - 122x + 8x^2)(x)$

$\qquad = 450x - 122x^2 + 8x^3$

$\qquad = 8x^3 - 122x^2 + 450x$

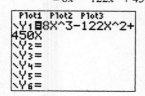

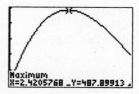

The value of x (to the nearest 0.001 inch) that will produce a box with the maximum volume is 2.42 inches. The maximum volume (to the nearest 0.1 cubic inch) is 487.9 cubic inches. [3.3]

1.

$$\frac{3 + 4i}{1 - 2i} = \frac{3 + 4i}{1 - 2i} \cdot \frac{1 + 2i}{1 + 2i} = \frac{3 + 10i + 8i^2}{1^2 - 4i^2} \quad [\text{P.6}]$$

$$= \frac{3 + 10i + 8(-1)}{1 - 4(-1)} = \frac{3 + 10i - 8}{1 + 4}$$

$$= \frac{-5 + 10i}{5} = -1 + 2i$$

2.

$$x^2 - x - 1 = 0$$

$$a = 1,\ b = -1,\ c = -1$$

$$x = \frac{-(-1) \pm \sqrt{(-1)^2 - 4(1)(-1)}}{2(1)} = \frac{1 \pm \sqrt{5}}{2}$$

$$x = \frac{1 - \sqrt{5}}{2},\ x = \frac{1 + \sqrt{5}}{2} \quad [1.3]$$

3.

$$\sqrt{2x + 5} - \sqrt{x - 1} = 2$$

$$\sqrt{2x + 5} = 2 + \sqrt{x - 1}$$

$$\left(\sqrt{2x + 5}\right)^2 = \left(2 + \sqrt{x - 1}\right)^2$$

$$2x + 5 = 4 + 4\sqrt{x - 1} + x - 1$$

$$2x + 5 = 3 + 4\sqrt{x - 1} + x$$

$$x + 2 = 4\sqrt{x - 1}$$

$$(x + 2)^2 = \left(4\sqrt{x - 1}\right)^2$$

$$x^2 + 4x + 4 = 16(x - 1)$$

$$x^2 + 4x + 4 = 16x - 16$$

$$x^2 - 12x + 20 = 0$$

$$(x - 2)(x - 10) = 0$$

$$x = 2,\ x = 10$$

Check 2:

$$\sqrt{2(2) + 5} - \sqrt{(2) - 1} = 2$$

$$\sqrt{4 + 5} - \sqrt{2 - 1} = 2$$

$$\sqrt{9} - \sqrt{1} = 2$$

$$3 - 1 = 2$$

$$2 = 2$$

$$\text{Yes}$$

Check 10:

$$\sqrt{2(10) + 5} - \sqrt{(10) - 1} = 2$$

$$\sqrt{20 + 5} - \sqrt{10 - 1} = 2$$

$$\sqrt{25} - \sqrt{9} = 2$$

$$5 - 3 = 2$$

$$2 = 2$$

$$\text{Yes}$$

The solutions are $x = 2,\ x = 10$. [1.4]

4. $|x - 3| \le 11$ $\qquad$ [1.5]

$$-11 \le x - 3 \le 11$$

$$-8 \le \ x \ \le 14$$

$$\{x \mid -8 \le x \le 14\}$$

5.

$$d = \sqrt{(2 - 7)^2 + [5 - (-11)]^2} \quad [2.1]$$

$$= \sqrt{(2 - 7)^2 + (5 + 11)^2}$$

$$= \sqrt{(-5)^2 + (16)^2}$$

$$= \sqrt{25 + 256}$$

$$= \sqrt{281}$$

6. Translate the graph of $y = x^2$ two units to the right and four units up. [2.5]

7.
$$P(x) = x^2 - 2x - 3$$

$$\frac{P(a+h) - P(a)}{h} = \frac{[(a+h)^2 - 2(a+h) - 3] - (a^2 - 2a - 3)}{h} = \frac{a^2 + 2ah + h^2 - 2a - 2h - 3 - a^2 + 2a + 3}{h}$$

$$= \frac{2ah + h^2 - 2h}{h} = 2a + h - 2 \qquad [2.6]$$

8.
$$f(x) = 2x^2 + 5x - 3 \qquad [2.6]$$
$$g(x) = 4x - 7$$
$$(f \circ g)(x) = f[g(x)]$$
$$= f(4x - 7)$$
$$= 2(4x - 7)^2 + 5(4x - 7) - 3$$
$$= 2(16x^2 - 56x + 49) + 5(4x - 7) - 3$$
$$= 32x^2 - 112x + 98 + 20x - 35 - 3$$
$$= 32x^2 - 92x + 60$$

9.
$$(f - g)(x) = f(x) - g(x) \qquad [2.6]$$
$$= x^3 - 2x + 7 - (x^2 - 3x - 4)$$
$$= x^3 - 2x + 7 - x^2 + 3x + 4$$
$$= x^2 - x^2 + x + 11$$

10.

$$-2 \,\big|\, \begin{array}{ccccc} 4 & 0 & -2 & -4 & -5 \\ & -8 & 16 & -28 & 64 \\ \hline 4 & -8 & 14 & -32 & 59 \end{array}$$

$$4x^3 - 8x^2 + 14x - 32 + \frac{59}{x+2} \quad [3.1]$$

11.

$$3 \,\big|\, \begin{array}{ccccc} 2 & 0 & -3 & 4 & -6 \\ & 6 & 18 & 45 & 147 \\ \hline 2 & 6 & 15 & 49 & 141 \end{array}$$

$$P(3) = 141 \quad [3.1]$$

12. The leading term has a negative coefficient. The graph of $P(x)$ goes down to the far right. [3.2]

13.

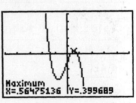

The relative maximum (to the nearest 0.0001) is 0.3997. [3.2]

14.
$$P(x) = 3x^4 - 4x^3 - 11x^2 + 16x - 4 \qquad [3.3]$$
$$p = \pm \text{ factors of } 4 = \pm 1, \ \pm 2, \ \pm 4$$
$$q = \pm \text{ factors of } 3 = \pm 1, \ \pm 3$$
$$\frac{p}{q} = \pm 1, \ \pm 2, \ \pm 4, \ \pm\frac{1}{3}, \ \pm\frac{2}{3}, \ \pm\frac{4}{3}$$

15. $P(x) = x^3 + x^2 + 2x + 4$ has no changes of sign. There are no positive real zeros.

$P(-x) = -x^3 + x^2 - 2x + 4$ has three changes of sign. There are three or one negative real zeros. [3.3]

16.
$$P(x) = x^3 + x + 10$$

no positive and one negative real zeros

$$\frac{p}{q} = \pm 1, \ \pm 2, \ \pm 5, \ \pm 10$$

$$-2 \,\big|\, \begin{array}{cccc} 1 & 0 & 1 & 10 \\ & -2 & 4 & -10 \\ \hline 1 & -2 & 5 & 0 \end{array}$$

$$x = \frac{-(-2) \pm \sqrt{(-2)^2 - 4(1)(5)}}{2(1)} = \frac{2 \pm \sqrt{-16}}{2} = \frac{2 \pm 4i}{2} = 1 \pm 2i$$

The zeros are $-2, \ 1 - 2i, \ 1 + 2i$. [3.4]

17. If $3 + i$ is a zero of $P(x)$, then $3 - i$ is also a zero.
$$P(x) = [x - (3+i)][x - (3-i)](x+2)$$
$$= [x - 3 - i][x - 3 + i](x + 2)$$
$$= [(x-3)^2 - i^2](x + 2)$$
$$= [x^2 - 6x + 9 - (-1)](x + 2)$$
$$= [x^2 - 6x + 9 + 1](x + 2)$$
$$= (x^2 - 6x + 10)(x + 2)$$
$$= x^2(x + 2) - 6x(x + 2) + 10(x + 2)$$
$$= x^3 + 2x^2 - 6x^2 - 12x + 10x + 20$$
$$= x^3 - 4x^2 - 2x + 20 \qquad [3.4]$$

18.

$P(x) = x^3 - 2x^2 + 9x - 18$

three or one positive and no negative real zeros

$\dfrac{p}{q} = \pm 1, \ \pm 2, \ \pm 3, \ \pm 6, \ \pm 9, \ \pm 18$

$$
\begin{array}{c|cccc}
2 & 1 & -2 & 9 & -18 \\
  &   & 2 & 0 & 18 \\
\hline
  & 1 & 0 & 9 & 0
\end{array}
$$

$x^2 + 9 = 0$

$\quad x^2 = -9$

$\quad x = \pm\sqrt{-9}$

$\quad x = \pm 3i$

$P(x) = (x - 2)(x + 3i)(x - 3i)$ [3.4]

19.

$F(x) = \dfrac{4x^2}{x^2 + x - 6}$

Vertical asymptotes:

$\quad x^2 + x - 6 = 0$

$\quad (x + 3)(x - 2) = 0$

$\quad x = -3, \ x = 2$

Horizontal asymptote:

$y = \dfrac{4}{1} \Rightarrow y = 4$ [3.5]

20.

$F(x) = \dfrac{x^3 + 4x^2 + 1}{x^2 + 4}$

$$
\require{enclose}
\begin{array}{r}
x + 4 \\
x^2 + 4 \enclose{longdiv}{x^3 + 4x^2 + 1} \\
\underline{x^3 + 4x } \\
4x^2 - 4x + 1 \\
\underline{4x^2 + 16} \\
-4x - 15
\end{array}
$$

The slant asymptote is $y = x + 4$.   [3.5]

Chapter 4
Exponential and Logarithmic Functions

1. If $f(3) = 7$, then $f^{-1}(7) = 3$.

3. If $h^{-1}(-3) = -4$, then $h(-4) = -3$.

5. If 3 is in the domain of f^{-1}, then $f[f^{-1}(3)] = 3$.

7. The domain of the inverse function f^{-1} is the <u>range</u> of f.

9.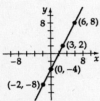
Yes, the inverse is a function.

11.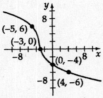
Yes, the inverse is a function.

13.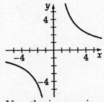
Yes, the inverse is a function.

15.
No, the inverse relation is not a function.

17. $f(x) = 4x;\ g(x) = \frac{x}{4}$

$f[g(x)] = f\left(\frac{x}{4}\right) = 4\left(\frac{x}{4}\right) = x$

$g[f(x)] = g(4x) = \frac{4x}{4} = x$

Yes, f and g are inverses of each other.

19. $f(x) = 4x - 1;\ g(x) = \frac{1}{4}x + \frac{1}{4}$

$f[g(x)] = f\left(\frac{1}{4}x + \frac{1}{4}\right)$

$\qquad = 4\left(\frac{1}{4}x + \frac{1}{4}\right) - 1 = x + 1 - 1$

$\qquad = x$

$g[f(x)] = g(4x - 1)$

$\qquad = \frac{1}{4}(4x - 1) + \frac{1}{4} = x - \frac{1}{4} + \frac{1}{4}$

$\qquad = x$

Yes, f and g are inverses of each other.

21. $f(x) = -\frac{1}{2}x - \frac{1}{2};\ g(x) = -2x + 1$

$f[g(x)] = f(-2x + 1)$

$\qquad = -\frac{1}{2}(-2x + 1) - \frac{1}{2} = x - \frac{1}{2} - \frac{1}{2}$

$\qquad = x - 1$

$\qquad \neq x$

No, f and g are not inverses of each other.

23. The inverse of $\{(-3,\ 1),\ (-2,\ 2),\ (1,\ 5),\ (4,\ -7)\}$ is $\{(1,\ -3),\ (2,\ -2),\ (5,\ 1),\ (-7,\ 4)\}$.

25. The inverse of $\{(0, 1), (1, 2), (2, 4), (3, 8), (4, 16)\}$ is $\{(1, 0), (2, 1), (4, 2), (8, 3), (16, 4)\}$.

27. $f(x) = 2x + 4$

$x = 2y + 4$

$x - 4 = 2y$

$\frac{1}{2}x - 2 = y$

$f^{-1}(x) = \frac{1}{2}x - 2$

29. $f(x) = 3x - 7$

$x = 3y - 7$

$x + 7 = 3y$

$\frac{1}{3}x + \frac{7}{3} = y$

$f^{-1}(x) = \frac{1}{3}x + \frac{7}{3}$

31. $f(x) = -2x + 5$

$x = -2y + 5$

$x - 5 = -2y$

$-\frac{1}{2}x + \frac{5}{2} = y$

$f^{-1}(x) = -\frac{1}{2}x + \frac{5}{2}$

33.
$$f(x) = \frac{2x}{x-1}, \; x \neq 1$$
$$x = \frac{2y}{y-1}$$
$$x(y-1) = xy - x = 2y$$
$$xy - 2y = y(x-2) = x$$
$$y = \frac{x}{x-2}$$
$$f^{-1}(x) = \frac{x}{x-2}, \; x \neq 2$$

35.
$$f(x) = \frac{x-1}{x+1}, \; x \neq -1$$
$$x = \frac{y-1}{y+1}$$
$$x(y+1) = xy + x = y - 1$$
$$xy - y = -x - 1$$
$$y - xy = y(1-x) = x + 1$$
$$y = \frac{x+1}{1-x}$$
$$f^{-1}(x) = \frac{x+1}{1-x}, \; x \neq 1$$

37.
$$f(x) = x^2 + 1, \; x \geq 0$$
$$x = y^2 + 1$$
$$x - 1 = y^2$$
$$\sqrt{x-1} = y$$
$$f^{-1}(x) = \sqrt{x-1}, \; x \geq 1$$
Note: Do not use $\pm$ with the radical because the domain of f, and thus the range of f^{-1}, is nonnegative.

39.
$$f(x) = \sqrt{x-2}, \; x \geq 2$$
$$x = \sqrt{y-2}$$
$$x^2 = y - 2$$
$$x^2 + 2 = y$$
$$f^{-1}(x) = x^2 + 2, \; x \geq 0$$
Note: The range of f is nonnegative, therefore the domain of f^{-1} is also nonnegative.

41.
$$f(x) = x^2 + 4x, \; x \geq -2$$
$$x = y^2 + 4y$$
$$x + 4 = y^2 + 4y + 4$$
$$x + 4 = (y+2)^2$$
$$\sqrt{x+4} = y + 2$$
$$y = \sqrt{x+4} - 2$$
$$f^{-1}(x) = \sqrt{x+4} - 2, \; x \geq -4$$
Note: The range of f is non-negative, therefore the domain of f^{-1} is also non-negative.

43.
$$f(x) = x^2 + 4x - 1, \; x \leq -2$$
$$x = y^2 + 4y - 1$$
$$x + 1 = y^2 + 4y$$
$$x + 1 + 4 = y^2 + 4y + 4$$
$$x + 5 = (y+2)^2$$
$$-\sqrt{x+5} = y + 2$$
$$-\sqrt{x+5} - 2 = y$$
$$f^{-1}(x) = -\sqrt{x+5} - 2, \; x \geq -5$$
Note: Because the range of f is non-positive, the range of f^{-1} must also be non-positive.

45.
$$V(x) = x^3$$
$$x = y^3$$
$$\sqrt[3]{x} = y$$
$$V^{-1}(x) = \sqrt[3]{x}$$
$V^{-1}(x)$ finds the length of a side of a cube given the volume.

47. Yes, a conversion function is always a one-to-one function. Yes, a conversion function always has an inverse function. A conversion function is a nonconstant linear function. All nonconstant linear functions have inverses which are also functions.

49.
$$s(x) = 2x + 24$$
$$x = 2y + 24$$
$$x - 24 = 2y$$
$$\tfrac{1}{2}x - 12 = y$$
$$s^{-1}(x) = \tfrac{1}{2}x - 12$$

51.
$$E(s) = 0.05s + 2500$$
$$s = 0.05y + 2500$$
$$s - 2500 = 0.05y$$
$$\frac{1}{0.05}s - \frac{2500}{0.05} = y$$
$$20s - 50{,}000 = y$$
$$E^{-1}(s) = 20s - 50{,}000$$
From the monthly earnings, the executive can find the value of the software sold.

53.
$$f(x) = 2x - 1$$
$$f(22102917) = 2(22102917) - 1$$
$$= 44205833$$

Find the inverse:
$$f(x) = 2x - 1$$
$$x = 2y - 1$$
$$x + 1 = 2y$$
$$\frac{x+1}{2} = y$$
$$f^{-1}(x) = \frac{x+1}{2}$$

Apply the inverse to the code:
$$f^{-1}(44205833) = \frac{44205833 + 1}{2}$$
$$= \frac{44205834}{2}$$
$$= 22102917$$

55. $f(2) = 7$, $f(5) = 12$, and $f(4) = c$. Because f is an increasing linear function, and 4 is between 2 and 5, then $f(4)$ is between $f(2)$ and $f(5)$. Thus, c is between 7 and 12.

57. f is a linear function, therefore f^{-1} is a linear function.
$$f(2) = 3 \Rightarrow f^{-1}(3) = 2$$
$$f(5) = 9 \Rightarrow f^{-1}(9) = 5$$
Since 6 is between 3 and 9, $f^{-1}(6)$ is between 2 and 5.

59. g is a linear function, therefore g^{-1} is a linear function.
$$g^{-1}(3) = 4 \Rightarrow g(4) = 3$$
$$g^{-1}(7) = 8 \Rightarrow g(8) = 7$$
Since 5 is between 4 and 8, $g(5)$ is between 3 and 7.

Connecting Concepts

61.
$$f(x) = ax + b, \quad a \neq 0$$
$$y = ax + b$$
$$x = ay + b$$
$$x - b = ay$$
$$\frac{x-b}{a} = y$$
Thus $f^{-1}(x) = \frac{x-b}{a}, \quad a \neq 0$

63. The reflection of f across the line given by $y = x$ yields f. Thus f is its own inverse.

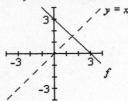

65. There is at most one point where each horizontal line intersects the graph of the function. The function is a one-to-one function.

67. A horizontal line intersects the graph of the function at more than one point. Thus, the function is not a one-to-one function.

Prepare for Section 4.2

69. $2^3 = 2 \cdot 2 \cdot 2 = 8$

70. $3^{-4} = \frac{1}{3^4} = \frac{1}{3 \cdot 3 \cdot 3 \cdot 3} = \frac{1}{81}$

71. $\dfrac{2^2 + 2^{-2}}{2} = \dfrac{4 + \frac{1}{4}}{2} = \dfrac{16+1}{8} = \dfrac{17}{8}$

72. $\dfrac{3^2 - 3^{-2}}{2} = \dfrac{9 - \frac{1}{9}}{2} = \dfrac{81-1}{18} = \dfrac{80}{18} = \dfrac{40}{9}$

73.

$$f(x)=10^x$$

$$f(-1)=10^{-1}=\frac{1}{10}$$

$$f(0)=10^0=1$$

$$f(1)=10^1=10$$

$$f(2)=10^2=100$$

74.

$$f(x)=\left(\frac{1}{2}\right)^x$$

$$f(-1)=\left(\frac{1}{2}\right)^{-1}=2$$

$$f(0)=\left(\frac{1}{2}\right)^0=1$$

$$f(1)=\left(\frac{1}{2}\right)^1=\frac{1}{2}$$

$$f(2)=\left(\frac{1}{2}\right)^2=\frac{1}{4}$$

Section 4.2

1.

$$f(0)=3^0=1$$

$$f(4)=3^4=81$$

3.

$$g(-2)=10^{-2}=\frac{1}{100}$$

$$g(3)=10^3=1000$$

5.

$$h(2)=\left(\frac{3}{2}\right)^2=\frac{9}{4}$$

$$h(-3)=\left(\frac{3}{2}\right)^{-3}=\frac{8}{27}$$

7.

$$j(-2)=\left(\frac{1}{2}\right)^{-2}=4$$

$$j(4)=\left(\frac{1}{2}\right)^4=\frac{1}{16}$$

9.

$$f(3.2)=2^{3.2}\approx9.19$$

11.

$$g(2.2)=e^{2.2}\approx9.03$$

13.

$$h(\sqrt{2})=5^{\sqrt{2}}\approx9.74$$

15.

$f(x)=5^x$ is a basic exponential graph.

$g(x)=1+5^{-x}$ is the graph of $f(x)$ reflected across the y-axis and moved up 1 unit.

$h(x)=5^{x+3}$ is the graph of $f(x)$ moved to the left 3 units.

$k(x)=5^x+3$ is the graph of $f(x)$ moved up 3 units.

a. $k(x)$ **b.** $g(x)$ **c.** $h(x)$ **d.** $f(x)$

17. $f(x)=3^x$

19. $f(x)=10^x$

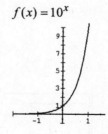

21. $f(x)=\left(\frac{3}{2}\right)^x$

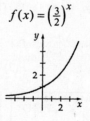

23. $f(x)=\left(\frac{1}{3}\right)^x$

25. Shift the graph of f vertically upward 2 units.

27. Shift the graph of f horizontally to the right 2 units.

29. Reflect the graph of f across the y-axis.

31. Stretch the graph of f vertically away from the x-axis by a factor of 2.

33. Reflect the graph of f across the y-axis, and then shift this graph vertically upward 2 units.

35. $f(x) = \dfrac{3^x + 3^{-x}}{2}$

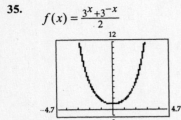

No horizontal asymptote

37. $f(x) = \dfrac{e^x - e^{-x}}{2}$

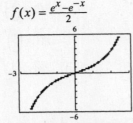

No horizontal asymptote.

39. $f(x) = -e^{(x-4)}$

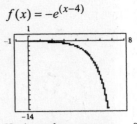

Horizontal asymptote: $y = 0$

41. $f(x) = \dfrac{10}{1 + 0.4e^{-0.5x}}$, with $x \geq 0$

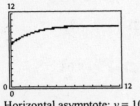

Horizontal asymptote: $y = 10$

43. a. $f(x) = 1.353(1.9025)^x \Rightarrow f(7) = 1.353(1.9025)^7 \approx 122$ million connections

b.
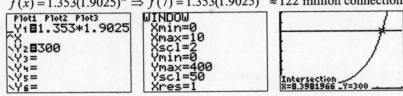

8 years after January 1, 1998 is in 2006.

45. a. $d(p) = 25 + 880e^{-0.18p} \Rightarrow d(8) = 25 + 880e^{-0.18(8)} \approx 233$ items per month

$d(p) = 25 + 880e^{-0.18p} \Rightarrow d(18) = 25 + 880e^{-0.18(18)} \approx 59$ items per month

b. As $p \to \infty$, $d(p) \to 25$. The demand will approach 25 items per month.

47. a. $P(t) = 1 - e^{-0.75t} \Rightarrow P(1) = 1 - e^{-0.75(1)} \approx 0.53$

b. $P(t) = 1 - e^{-0.75t} \Rightarrow P(3) = 1 - e^{-0.75(3)} \approx 0.89$

c.
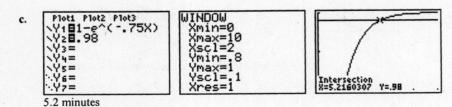

5.2 minutes

d. There is a 98% probability that at least one customer will arrive during the period between 10:00 AM and 10:05.2 AM.

49. **a.**
$$P(x) = \frac{12^x e^{-12}}{x!} \Rightarrow P(9) = \frac{12^9 e^{-12}}{9!} \approx 0.087 = 8.7\%$$

  b.
$$P(x) = \frac{12^x e^{-12}}{x!} \Rightarrow P(18) = \frac{12^{18} e^{-12}}{18!} \approx 0.026 = 2.6\%$$

51. **a.**
$$P(t) = 100 \cdot 2^{2t} \Rightarrow P(3) = 100 \cdot 2^{2(3)} = 100 \cdot 2^6 = 100 \cdot 64 = 6,400 \text{ bacteria}$$
$$P(t) = 100 \cdot 2^{2t} \Rightarrow P(6) = 100 \cdot 2^{2(6)} = 100 \cdot 2^{12} = 100 \cdot 4096 = 409,600 \text{ bacteria}$$

  b.
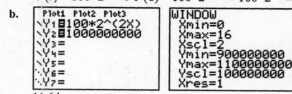

11.6 hours

53. **a.**
$$N(t) = 138,000(1.39)^t \Rightarrow N(4) = 138,000(1.39)^4 \approx 515,000 \text{ people}$$

  b.
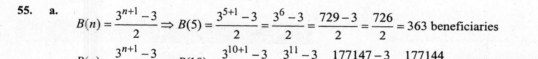

7.2 years after January 1, 1990 is in the year 1997.

55. **a.**
$$B(n) = \frac{3^{n+1} - 3}{2} \Rightarrow B(5) = \frac{3^{5+1} - 3}{2} = \frac{3^6 - 3}{2} = \frac{729 - 3}{2} = \frac{726}{2} = 363 \text{ beneficiaries}$$

$$B(n) = \frac{3^{n+1} - 3}{2} \Rightarrow B(10) = \frac{3^{10+1} - 3}{2} = \frac{3^{11} - 3}{2} = \frac{177147 - 3}{2} = \frac{177144}{2} = 88,572 \text{ beneficiaries}$$

  b.
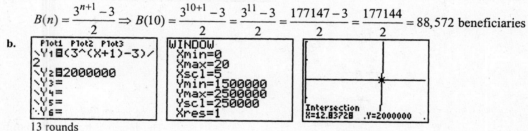

13 rounds

57. **a.**
$$T(t) = 65 + 115e^{-0.042t} \Rightarrow T(10) = 65 + 115e^{-0.042(10)} = 65 + 115e^{-0.42} \approx 141° \text{ F}$$

  b.
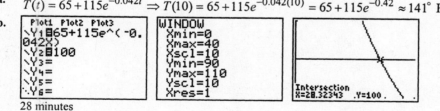

28 minutes

59. **a.**
$$f(n) = (27.5)2^{(n-1)/12} \Rightarrow f(40) = (27.5)2^{(40-1)/12} = (27.5)2^{39/12} = (27.5)2^{3.25} \approx 261.63 \text{ vibrations per second}$$

  b. No. The function $f(n)$ is not a linear function. Therefore, the graph of $f(n)$ does not increase at a constant rate.

61. $\sinh(x) = \dfrac{e^x - e^{-x}}{2}$ is an odd function. That is, prove

$\sinh(-x) = -\sinh(x)$.

Proof: $\sinh(x) = \dfrac{e^x - e^{-x}}{2}$

$\sinh(-x) = \dfrac{e^{-x} - e^x}{2}$

$\sinh(-x) = \dfrac{-e^{-x} + e^x}{2}$

$\sinh(-x) = \dfrac{\left(e^x - e^{-x}\right)}{2}$

$\sinh(-x) = -F(x)$

63.

65.

domain: $(-\infty, \infty)$

67.

domain: $[0, \infty)$

68. $2^x = 16$

$2^x = 2^4$

$x = 4$

69. $3^{-x} = \dfrac{1}{3^x} = \dfrac{1}{27}$

$\dfrac{1}{3^x} = \dfrac{1}{3^3}$

$x = 3$

70. $x^4 = 625$

$x^4 = 5^4$

$x = 5$

71. $f(x) = \dfrac{2x}{x+3}$

$x = \dfrac{2y}{y+3}$

$xy + 3x = 2y$

$3x = 2y - xy = y(2-x)$

$\dfrac{3x}{2-x} = y$

$f^{-1}(x) = \dfrac{3x}{2-x}$

72. $g(x) = \sqrt{x-2}$

$x - 2 \geq 0$

$x \geq 2$

The domain is $\{x \mid x \geq 2\}$.

73. The domain is the set of all positive real numbers.

Section 4.3

1. $\log 10 = 1 \Rightarrow 10^1 = 10$

3. $\log_8 64 = 2 \Rightarrow 8^2 = 64$

5. $\log_7 x = 0 \Rightarrow 7^0 = x$

7. $\ln x = 4 \Rightarrow e^4 = x$

9. $\ln 1 = 0 \Rightarrow e^0 = 1$

11. $3^2 = 9 \Rightarrow \log_3 9 = 2$

13. $4^{-2} = \dfrac{1}{16} \Rightarrow \log_4 \dfrac{1}{16} = -2$

15. $b^x = y \Rightarrow \log_b y = x$

17. $y = e^x \Rightarrow \ln y = x$

19. $100 = 10^2 \Rightarrow \log 100 = 2$

21. $\log_4 16 = 2$ because $4^2 = 16$

23. $\log_3 \dfrac{1}{243} = -5$ because $3^{-5} = \left(\dfrac{1}{3}\right)^5 = \dfrac{1}{243}$

25. $\ln e^3 = 3$ because $e^3 = e^3$

27. $\log \dfrac{1}{100} = -2$ because $10^{-2} = \dfrac{1}{10^2} = \dfrac{1}{100}$

29. $\log_{0.5} 16 = \log_{1/2} 16 = -4$ because $\left(\dfrac{1}{2}\right)^{-4} = 2^4 = 16$

31. $y = \log_4 x$

$x = 4^y$

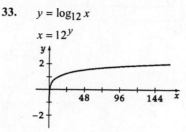

33. $y = \log_{12} x$

$x = 12^y$

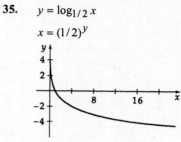

35. $y = \log_{1/2} x$

$x = (1/2)^y$

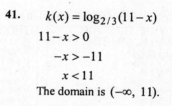

37. $y = \log_{5/2} x$

$x = (5/2)^y$

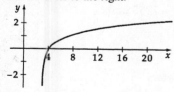

39. $f(x) = \log_5(x - 3)$

$x - 3 > 0$

$x > 3$

The domain is $(3, \infty)$.

41. $k(x) = \log_{2/3}(11 - x)$

$11 - x > 0$

$-x > -11$

$x < 11$

The domain is $(-\infty, 11)$.

43. $P(x) = \ln(x^2 - 4)$

$x^2 - 4 > 0$

$(x + 2)(x - 2) > 0$

The critical values are -2 and 2.
The product is positive.
The domain is $(-\infty,\ -2) \cup (2, \infty)$.

45. $h(x) = \ln\left(\dfrac{x^2}{x-4}\right)$

$\dfrac{x^2}{x-4} > 0$

The critical values are 0 and 4.
The quotient is positive.
$x > 4$
The domain is $(4, \infty)$.

47. $x^3 - x > 0$

$x(x^2 - 1) > 0$

$x(x + 1)(x - 1) > 0$

Critical values are 0, -1 and 1.
Product is positive.
$-1 < x < 0$ or $x > 1$
$(-1, 0) \cup (1, \infty)$

49. Shift 3 units to the right.

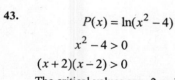

51. Shift 2 units up.

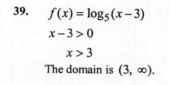

53. Shift 3 units up.

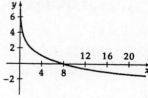

55. Shift 4 units to the right and 1 unit up

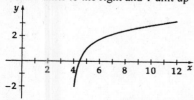

57. The graph of $f(x) = \log_5(x-2)$ is the graph of $y = \log_5 x$ shifted 2 units to the right.

The graph of $g(x) = 2 + \log_5 x$ is the graph of $y = \log_5 x$ shifted 2 units up.

The graph of $h(x) = \log_5(-x)$ is the graph of $y = \log_5 x$ reflected across the y-axis.

The graph of $k(x) = -\log_5(x+3)$ is the graph of $y = \log_5 x$ reflected across the x-axis and shifted left 3 units.

   a. $k(x)$ **b.** $f(x)$ **c.** $g(x)$ **d.** $h(x)$

59.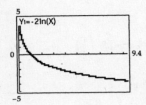

61.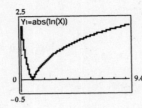

63.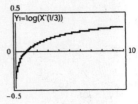

65.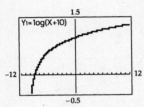

67.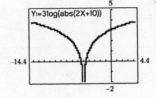

69. **a.** $r(t) = 0.69607 + 0.60781\ln t \Rightarrow r(9) = 0.69607 + 0.60781\ln 9 \approx 2.0\%$

    b.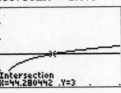

    45 months

71. $N(x) = 2750 + 180\ln\left(\dfrac{x}{1000} + 1\right)$

    a.
$$N(20,000) = 2750 + 180\ln\left(\frac{20,000}{1000} + 1\right) = 2750 + 180\ln(21) \approx 3298 \text{ units}$$

$$N(40,000) = 2750 + 180\ln\left(\frac{40,000}{1000} + 1\right) = 2750 + 180\ln(41) \approx 3418 \text{ units}$$

$$N(60,000) = 2750 + 180\ln\left(\frac{60,000}{1000} + 1\right) = 2750 + 180\ln(61) \approx 3490 \text{ units}$$

    b.
$$N(0) = 2750 + 180\ln\left(\frac{0}{1000} + 1\right) = 2750 + 180\ln(1) = 2750 + 180(0) = 2750 + 0 = 2750 \text{ units}$$

73. $BSA = 0.0003207 \cdot H^{0.3} \cdot W^{(0.7285 - 0.0188\log W)}$

$BSA = 0.0003207 \cdot (185.42)^{0.3} \cdot (81,646.6)^{(0.7285 - 0.0188\log 81,646.6)} \approx 2.05$ square meters

75. $N = \text{int}(x\log b) + 1$

    a. $N = \text{int}(10\log 2) + 1 = 3 + 1 = 4$ digits

    b. $N = \text{int}(200\log 3) + 1 = 95 + 1 = 96$ digits

    c. $N = \text{int}(4005\log 7) + 1 = 3384 + 1 = 3385$ digits

    d. $N = \text{int}(13466917\log 2) + 1 = 4,053,945 + 1 = 4,053,946$ digits

•••

77. $f(x)$ and $g(x)$ are inverse functions

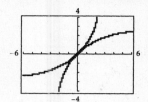

79.   The domain of the inverse is the range of the function.
Range of f: $\{y \mid -1 < y \le 1\}$.
The domain of the function is the range of the inverse.
Range of g: all real numbers.

•••

81. $\log 3 + \log 2 \approx 0.77815$
$\log 6 \approx 0.77815$

82. $\ln 8 - \ln 3 \approx 0.98083$
$\ln\left(\frac{8}{3}\right) \approx 0.98083$

83. $3 \log 4 \approx 1.80618$
$\log(4^3) \approx 1.80618$

84. $2 \ln 5 \approx 3.21888$
$\ln(5^2) \approx 3.21888$

85. $\ln 5 \approx 1.60944$
$\dfrac{\log 5}{\log e} \approx 1.60944$

86. $\log 8 \approx 0.90309$
$\dfrac{\ln 8}{\ln 10} \approx 0.90309$

Section 4.4

1. $\log_b(xyz) = \log_b x + \log_b y + \log_b z$

3. $\ln \dfrac{x}{z^4} = \ln x - \ln z^4$
$= \ln x - 4 \ln z$

5. $\log_2 \dfrac{\sqrt{x}}{y^3} = \log_2 \sqrt{x} - \log_2 y^3 = \log_2 x^{1/2} - \log_2 y^3 = \frac{1}{2}\log_2 x - 3\log_2 y$

7. $\log_7 \dfrac{\sqrt{xz}}{y^2} = \log_7 \dfrac{(xz)^{1/2}}{y^2} = \log_7 \dfrac{x^{1/2}z^{1/2}}{y^2} = \log_7 x^{1/2} + \log_7 z^{1/2} - \log_7 y^2 = \frac{1}{2}\log_7 x + \frac{1}{2}\log_7 z - 2\log_7 y$

9. $\log(x+5) + 2\log x = \log(x+5) + \log x^2 = \log[x^2(x+5)]$

11. $\ln(x^2 - y^2) - \ln(x-y) = \ln \dfrac{x^2 - y^2}{x-y} = \ln \dfrac{(x+y)(x-y)}{x-y} = \ln(x+y)$

13. $3\log x + \frac{1}{3}\log y + \log(x+1) = \log x^3 + \log y^{1/3} + \log(x+1) = \log x^3 + \log \sqrt[3]{y} + \log(x+1) = \log\left[x^3 \cdot \sqrt[3]{y}(x+1)\right]$

15. $\log_7 20 = \dfrac{\log 20}{\log 7} \approx 1.5395$

17. $\log_{11} 8 = \dfrac{\log 8}{\log 11} \approx 0.8672$

19. $\log_6 \frac{1}{3} = \dfrac{\log \frac{1}{3}}{\log 6} \approx -0.6131$

21.
$$\log_9 \sqrt{17} = \frac{\log \sqrt{17}}{\log 9} \approx 0.6447$$

23.
$$f(x) = \log_4 x = \frac{\log x}{\log 4}$$

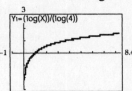

25.
$$g(x) = \log_8 (x-3) = \frac{\log(x-3)}{\log 8}$$

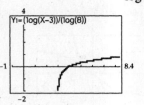

27.
$$h(x) = \log_3 (x-3)^2$$
$$= \frac{\log(x-3)^2}{\log 3}$$
$$= \frac{2\log(x-3)}{\log 3}$$

29.
$$F(x) = -\log_5 |x-2| = -\frac{\log|x-2|}{\log 5}$$

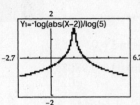

31. False. $\log 10 + \log 10 = 1 + 1 = 2$
but $\log(10+10) = \log 20 \neq 2$.

33. True.

35. False.
$\log 100 - \log 10 = 2 - 1 = 1$
but $\log(100-10) = \log 90 \neq 1$

37. False. $\dfrac{\log 100}{\log 10} = \dfrac{2}{1} = 2$
but $\log 100 - \log 10 = 2 - 1$
$= 1$

39. False. $(\log 10)^2 = 1^2 = 1$ but $2\log 10 = 2(1) = 2$

41.
$$\log_3 5 \cdot \log_5 7 \cdot \log_7 9 = \frac{\log 5}{\log 3} \cdot \frac{\log 7}{\log 5} \cdot \frac{\log 9}{\log 7} = \frac{\log 5}{\log 3} \cdot \frac{\log 7}{\log 5} \cdot \frac{\log 9}{\log 7} = \frac{\log 9}{\log 3} = \frac{\log 3^2}{\log 3} = \frac{2\log 3}{\log 3} = \frac{2\log 3}{\log 3} = 2$$

43.
$\ln 500^{501} = 501 \ln 500 \approx 3113.52$
$\ln 506^{500} = 500 \ln 506 \approx 3113.27$
$\ln 500^{501}$ is larger.

45.
$$S_n = S_0 \cdot 10^{\frac{n}{N}(\log S_f - \log S_o)}$$
$$S_1 = 1{,}000{,}000 \cdot 10^{\frac{1}{5}(\log 500{,}000 - \log 1{,}000{,}000)}$$
$$= 870{,}551$$
$$S_2 = 1{,}000{,}000 \cdot 10^{\frac{2}{5}(\log 500{,}000 - \log 1{,}000{,}000)}$$
$$= 757{,}858$$
$$S_3 = 1{,}000{,}000 \cdot 10^{\frac{3}{5}(\log 500{,}000 - \log 1{,}000{,}000)}$$
$$= 659{,}754$$
$$S_4 = 1{,}000{,}000 \cdot 10^{\frac{4}{5}(\log 500{,}000 - \log 1{,}000{,}000)}$$
$$= 574{,}349$$
$$S_5 = 1{,}000{,}000 \cdot 10^{\frac{5}{5}(\log 500{,}000 - \log 1{,}000{,}000)}$$
$$= 500{,}000$$
The scales are 1:870,551; 1:757,858; 1:659,754; 1:574,349; 1:500,000.

47.
$$pH = -\log[H^+]$$
$$pH = -\log[3.97 \times 10^{-11}]$$
$$pH = 10.4$$
10.4 > 7; milk of magnesia is a base

49.
$$pH = -\log[H^+]$$
$$9.5 = -\log[H^+]$$
$$-9.5 = \log[H^+]$$
$$10^{-9.5} = 10^{\log[H^+]}$$
$$[H^+] = 3.16 \times 10^{-10} \text{ mole per liter}$$

51.
$$dB(I) = 10\log\left(\frac{I}{I_0}\right)$$

a.
$$dB(1.58 \times 10^8 \cdot I_0) = 10\log\left(\frac{1.58 \times 10^8 \cdot I_0}{I_0}\right)$$
$$= 10\log(1.58 \times 10^8)$$
$$\approx 82.0 \text{ decibels}$$

b.
$$dB(10,800 \cdot I_0) = 10\log\left(\frac{10,800 \cdot I_0}{I_0}\right)$$
$$= 10\log(10,800)$$
$$\approx 40.3 \text{ decibels}$$

c.
$$dB(3.16 \times 10^{11} \cdot I_0) = 10\log\left(\frac{3.16 \times 10^{11} \cdot I_0}{I_0}\right)$$
$$= 10\log(3.16 \times 10^{11})$$
$$\approx 115.0 \text{ decibels}$$

d.
$$dB(1.58 \times 10^{15} \cdot I_0) = 10\log\left(\frac{1.58 \times 10^{15} \cdot I_0}{I_0}\right)$$
$$= 10\log(1.58 \times 10^{15})$$
$$\approx 152.0 \text{ decibels}$$

53.
$$dB(I) = 10\log\left(\frac{I}{I_0}\right)$$
$$120 = 10\log\left(\frac{I_{120}}{I_0}\right)$$
$$12 = \log\left(\frac{I_{120}}{I_0}\right)$$
$$10^{12} = \frac{I_{120}}{I_0}$$
$$10^{12} \cdot I_0 = I_{120}$$

$$110 = 10\log\left(\frac{I_{110}}{I_0}\right)$$
$$11 = \log\left(\frac{I_{110}}{I_0}\right)$$
$$10^{11} = \frac{I_{110}}{I_0}$$
$$10^{11} \cdot I_0 = I_{110}$$

$$\frac{I_{120}}{I_{110}} = \frac{10^{12} \cdot I_0}{10^{11} \cdot I_0}$$
$$= \frac{10^{12}}{10^{11}} = 10^{12-11} = 10^1$$
$$= 10 \text{ times more intense}$$

55.
$$M = \log\left(\frac{100,000I_0}{I_0}\right) = \log 100,000 = \log 10^5 = 5$$

57.
$$\log\left(\frac{I}{I_0}\right) = M$$
$$\log\left(\frac{I}{I_0}\right) = 6.5$$
$$\frac{I}{I_0} = 10^{6.5}$$
$$I = 10^{6.5}I_0$$
$$I \approx 3,162,277.7I_0$$

59.

$$M = \log\left(\frac{I}{I_0}\right)$$

$$M_5 = \log\left(\frac{I_5}{I_0}\right) \Rightarrow 5 = \log\left(\frac{I_5}{I_0}\right) \Rightarrow 10^5 = \frac{I_5}{I_0} \Rightarrow 10^5 I_0 = I_5$$

$$M_3 = \log\left(\frac{I_3}{I_0}\right) \Rightarrow 3 = \log\left(\frac{I_3}{I_0}\right) \Rightarrow 10^3 = \frac{I_3}{I_0} \Rightarrow 10^3 I_0 = I_3$$

$$\frac{I_5}{I_3} = \frac{10^5 I_0}{10^3 I_0} = \frac{10^5}{10^3} = 10^{5-3} = 10^2 = 100 \text{ to } 1 \qquad \bullet \text{ short cut: begin with this line}$$

61.

$$\frac{10^{8.9}}{10^{7.1}} = \frac{10^{8.9-7.1}}{1} = 10^{1.8} \text{ to } 1 \approx 63 \text{ to } 1$$

63.

$$M = \log A + 3\log 8t - 2.92$$
$$= \log 18 + 3\log[8(31)] - 2.92 \approx 5.5$$

65. a. $M \approx 6$ **b.** $M \approx 4$

c. When $t = 40$, $M = \log A + 3\log 8t - 2.92 = \log 50 + 3\log[8(40)] - 2.92 \approx 6.3$

When $t = 30$, $M = \log A + 3\log 8t - 2.92 = \log 1 + 3\log[8(30)] - 2.92 \approx 4.2$

The results from parts **a.** and **b.** are close to the magnitudes of 6.3 and 4.2 produced by the Amplitude-Time-Difference Formula.

Prepare for Section 4.5

66. $3^6 = 729 \Rightarrow \log_3 729 = 6$

67. $\log_5 625 = 4 \Rightarrow 5^4 = 625$

68. $a^{x+2} = b \Rightarrow \log_a b = x + 2$

69.

$$4a = 7bx + 2cx$$
$$7bx + 2cx = 4a$$
$$x(7b + 2c) = 4a$$
$$x = \frac{4a}{7b + 2c}$$

70.

$$165 = \frac{300}{1 + 12x}$$
$$165(1 + 12x) = 300$$
$$165 + 1980x = 300$$
$$1980x = 135$$
$$x = \frac{135}{1980} = \frac{3}{44}$$

71.

$$A = \frac{100 + x}{100 - x}$$
$$A(100 - x) = 100 + x$$
$$100A - Ax = 100 + x$$
$$100A - 100 = Ax + x$$
$$100(A - 1) = x(A + 1)$$
$$x = \frac{100(A - 1)}{A + 1}$$

Section 4.5

1.

$$2^x = 64$$
$$2^x = 2^6$$
$$x = 6$$

3.

$$49^x = \frac{1}{343}$$
$$7^{2x} = 7^{-3}$$
$$2x = -3$$
$$x = -\frac{3}{2}$$

5.

$$2^{5x+3} = \frac{1}{8}$$
$$2^{5x+3} = 2^{-3}$$
$$5x + 3 = -3$$
$$5x = -6$$
$$x = -\frac{6}{5}$$

7.

$$\left(\frac{2}{5}\right)^x = \frac{8}{125}$$
$$\left(\frac{2}{5}\right)^x = \left(\frac{2}{5}\right)^3$$
$$x = 3$$

9.
$$5^x = 70$$
$$\log(5^x) = \log 70$$
$$x \log 5 = \log 70$$
$$x = \frac{\log 70}{\log 5}$$

11.
$$3^{-x} = 120$$
$$\log(3^{-x}) = \log 120$$
$$-x \log 3 = \log 120$$
$$-x = \frac{\log 120}{\log 3}$$
$$x = -\frac{\log 120}{\log 3}$$

13.
$$10^{2x+3} = 315$$
$$\log 10^{2x+3} = \log 315$$
$$(2x+3) \log 10 = \log 315$$
$$2x+3 = \log 315$$
$$x = \frac{\log 315 - 3}{2}$$

15.
$$e^x = 10$$
$$\ln e^x = \ln 10$$
$$x = \ln 10$$

17.
$$2^{1-x} = 3^{x+1}$$
$$\log 2^{1-x} = \log 3^{x+1}$$
$$(1-x) \log 2 = (x+1) \log 3$$
$$\log 2 - x \log 2 = x \log 3 + \log 3$$
$$\log 2 - x \log 2 - x \log 3 = \log 3$$
$$-x \log 2 - x \log 3 = \log 3 - \log 2$$
$$-x(\log 2 + \log 3) = \log 3 - \log 2$$
$$x = -\frac{(\log 3 - \log 2)}{(\log 2 + \log 3)}$$
$$x = \frac{\log 2 - \log 3}{\log 2 + \log 3} \text{ or } \frac{\log 2 - \log 3}{\log 6}$$

19.
$$2^{2x-3} = 5^{-x-1}$$
$$\log 2^{2x-3} = \log 5^{-x-1}$$
$$(2x-3) \log 2 = (-x-1) \log 5$$
$$2x \log 2 - 3 \log 2 = -x \log 5 - \log 5$$
$$2x \log 2 + x \log 5 - 3 \log 2 = -\log 5$$
$$2x \log 2 + x \log 5 = 3 \log 2 - \log 5$$
$$x(2 \log 2 + \log 5) = 3 \log 2 - \log 5$$
$$x = \frac{3 \log 2 - \log 5}{2 \log 2 + \log 5}$$

21.
$$\log(4x - 18) = 1$$
$$4x - 18 = 10^1$$
$$4x - 18 = 10$$
$$4x = 28$$
$$x = 7$$

23.
$$\ln(x^2 - 12) = \ln x$$
$$x^2 - 12 = x$$
$$x^2 - x - 12 = 0$$
$$(x-4)(x+3) = 0$$
$$x = 4 \quad \text{or} \quad x = -3 \text{ (No; not in domain.)}$$
$$x = 4$$

25.
$$\log_2 + \log_2(x-4) = 2$$
$$\log_2 x(x-4) = 2$$
$$\log_2(x^2 - 4x) = 2$$
$$2^2 = x^2 - 4x$$
$$0 = x^2 - 4x - 4$$
$$x = \frac{4 \pm \sqrt{16 - 4(1)(-4)}}{2}$$
$$x = \frac{4 \pm 4\sqrt{2}^2}{2}$$
$$x = 2 \pm 2\sqrt{2}$$

$2 - 2\sqrt{2}$ is not a solution because the logarithm of a negative number is not defined. The solution is $x = 2 + 2\sqrt{2}$.

27. $\log_3 x + \log 3(x+6) = 3$

$\log_3 x(x+6) = 3$

$3^3 = x(x+6)$

$27 = x^2 + 6x$

$0 = x^2 + 6x - 27$

$0 = (x+9)(x-3)$

$x = 3$

$x = -9$

$\log_3(-9)$ is not defined. The solution is $x = 3$.

29. $\ln(1-x) + \ln(3-x) = \ln 8$

$\ln[(1-x)(3-x)] = \ln 8$

$(1-x)(3-x) = 8$

$3 - 4x + x^2 = 8$

$x^2 - 4x - 5 = 0$

$(x+1)(x-5) = 0$

$x = -1$ or $x = 5$ (No; not in domain.)

The solution is $x = -1$.

31. $\log\sqrt{x^3 - 17} = \dfrac{1}{2}$

$\dfrac{1}{2}\log\left(x^3 - 17\right) = \dfrac{1}{2}$

$10^1 = x^3 - 17$

$27 = x^3$

$\sqrt[3]{27} = \sqrt[3]{x^3}$

$3 = x$

The solution is $x = 3$.

33. $\log(\log x) = 1$

$10^1 = \log x$

$10^{10} = x$

35. $\ln(e^{3x}) = 6$

$3x \ln e = 6$

$3x(1) = 6$

$3x = 6$

$x = 2$

37. $e^{\ln(x-1)} = 4$

$\ln e^{\ln(x-1)} = \ln 4$

$\ln(x-1)\ln e = \ln 4$

$\ln(x-1)(1) = \ln 4$

$(x-1) = 4$

$x = 5$

39. $\dfrac{10^x - 10^{-x}}{2} = 20$

$10^x\left(10^x - 10^{-x}\right) = 40\left(10^x\right)$

$10^{2x} - 1 = 40\left(10^x\right)$

$10^{2x} - 40(10)^x - 1 = 0$

Let $u = 10^x$.

$u^2 - 40u - 1 = 0$

$u = \dfrac{40 \pm \sqrt{40^2 - 4(1)(-1)}}{2}$

$= \dfrac{40 \pm \sqrt{1600 + 4}}{2}$

$= \dfrac{40 \pm \sqrt{1604}}{2}$

$= \dfrac{40 \pm 2\sqrt{401}}{2}$

$= 20 \pm \sqrt{401}$

$10^x = 20 + \sqrt{401}$

$\log 10^x = \log\left(20 + \sqrt{401}\right)$

$x = \log\left(20 + \sqrt{401}\right)$

41.

$$\frac{10^x + 10^{-x}}{10^x - 10^{-x}} = 5$$

$$10^x + 10^{-x} = 5\left(10^x - 10^{-x}\right)$$

$$10^x\left(10^x + 10^{-x}\right) = 5\left(10^x - 10^{-x}\right)10^x$$

$$10^{2x} + 1 = 5\left(10^{2x} - 1\right)$$

$$4\left(10^{2x}\right) = 6$$

$$2\left(10^{2x}\right) = 3$$

$$\left(10^x\right)^2 = \frac{3}{2}$$

$$10^x = \sqrt{\frac{3}{2}}$$

$$x \log 10 = \log\sqrt{\frac{3}{2}}$$

$$x = \log\sqrt{\frac{3}{2}}$$

$$x = \frac{1}{2}\log\left(\frac{3}{2}\right)$$

43.

$$\frac{e^x + e^{-x}}{2} = 15$$

$$e^x\left(e^x + e^{-x}\right) = (30)e^x$$

$$e^{2x} + 1 = e^x(30)$$

$$e^{2x} - 30e^x + 1 = 0$$

Let $u = e^x$.

$$u^2 - 30u + 1 = 0$$

$$u = \frac{30 \pm \sqrt{900 - 4}}{2}$$

$$u = \frac{30 \pm \sqrt{896}}{2}$$

$$u = \frac{30 \pm 8\sqrt{14}}{2}$$

$$u = 15 \pm 4\sqrt{14}$$

$$e^x = 15 \pm 4\sqrt{14}$$

$$x \ln e = \ln\left(15 \pm 4\sqrt{14}\right)$$

$$x = \ln\left(15 \pm 4\sqrt{14}\right)$$

45.

$$\frac{1}{e^x - e^{-x}} = 4$$

$$1 = 4(e^x - e^{-x})$$

$$1(e^x) = 4(e^x)(e^x - e^{-x})$$

$$e^x = 4(e^{2x} - 1)$$

$$e^x = 4e^{2x} - 4$$

$$0 = 4e^{2x} - e^x - 4$$

Let $u = e^x$.

$$0 = 4u^2 - u - 4$$

$$u = \frac{1 \pm \sqrt{1 - 4(4)(-4)}}{8}$$

$$u = \frac{1 \pm \sqrt{65}}{8}$$

$$e^x = \frac{1 + \sqrt{65}}{8}$$

$$x \ln e = \ln\left(\frac{1 + \sqrt{65}}{8}\right)$$

$$x = \ln(1 + \sqrt{65}) - \ln 8$$

47.

$$2^{-x+3} = x + 1$$

Graph $f = 2^{-x+3} - (x + 1)$.
Its x-intercept is the solution.

$$x \approx 1.61$$

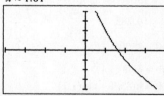

Xmin = −4, Xmax = 4, Xscl = 1,
Ymin = −4, Ymax = 4, Yscl = 1

49. $e^{3-2x} - 2x = 1$

Graph $f = e^{3-2x} - 2x - 1$.

Its x-intercept is the solution.

$x \approx 0.96$

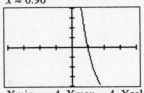

Xmin = –4, Xmax = 4, Xscl = 1,

Ymin = –4, Ymax = 4, Yscl = 1

51. $3 \log_2(x-1) = -x + 3$

Graph $f = \dfrac{3 \log(x-1)}{\log 2} + x - 3$.

Its x-intercept is the solution.

$x \approx 2.20$

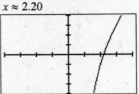

Xmin = –4, Xmax = 4, Xscl = 1,

Ymin = –4, Ymax = 4, Yscl = 1

53. $\ln(2x+4) + \dfrac{1}{2}x = -3$

Graph $f = \ln(2x+4) + \dfrac{1}{2}x + 3$.

Its x-intercept is the solution.

$x \approx -1.93$

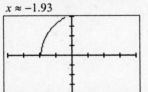

Xmin = –4, Xmax = 4, Xscl = 1,

Ymin = –4, Ymax = 4, Yscl = 1

55. $2^{x+1} = x^2 - 1$

Graph $f = 2^{x+1} - x^2 + 1$.

Its x-intercept is the solution.

$x \approx -1.34$

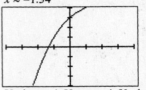

Xmin = –4, Xmax = 4, Xscl = 1,

Ymin = –4, Ymax = 4, Yscl = 1

57. **a.** $P(0) = 8500(1.1)^0 = 8500(1) = 8500$

$P(2) = 8500(1.1)^2 = 10,285$

b.
$$15,000 = 8500(1.1)^t$$
$$\ln 15,000 = 8500(1.1)^t$$
$$\ln 51,000 = \ln 8500 + t \ln(1.1)$$
$$\frac{\ln 15,000 - \ln 8500}{\ln(1.1)} = t$$
$$6 \approx t$$

The population will reach 15,000 in 6 years.

59. **a.** $T(10) = 36 + 43e^{-0.058(10)} = 36 + 43e^{-0.58}$

$T \approx 60°F$

b.
$$45 = 36 + 43e^{-0.058t}$$
$$\ln(45 - 36) = \ln 43 - 0.058t \ln e$$
$$\frac{\ln(45 - 36) - \ln 43}{-0.058} = t$$
$$t \approx 27 \text{ minutes}$$

61. **a.**

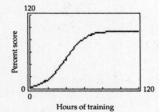

b. 48 hours

c. $P = 100$

d. As the number of hours of training increases, the test scores approach 100%.

63. **a.**

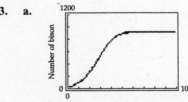

b. in 27 years or 2026

c. $B = 1000$

d. As the number of years increases, the bison population approaches but never exceeds 1000.

65. **a.**

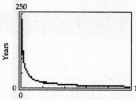

b.   When $r = 3\%$, or 0.03, $T \approx 78$ years

c.   When $T = 100$, $r \approx 0.019$, or 1.9%

67. **a.**

$$t = 2.43 \ln \frac{150 + v}{150 - v}$$

$$5 = 2.43 \ln \frac{150 + v}{150 - v}$$

$$\frac{5}{2.43} = \ln \frac{150 + v}{150 - v}$$

$$e^{5/2.43} = \frac{150 + v}{150 - v}$$

$$150e^{5/2.43} - ve^{5/2.43} = 150 + v$$

$$150e^{5/2.43} - 150 = ve^{5/2.43} + v$$

$$150(e^{5/2.43} - 1) = v(e^{5/2.43} + 1)$$

$$v = \frac{150(e^{5/2.43} - 1)}{e^{5/2.43} + 1}$$

$$v \approx 116 \text{ ft/sec}$$

b.   The vertical asymptote occurs when the denominator of $\frac{150 + v}{150 - v}$ is zero, or when $v = 150$.

c.   The velocity of the package approaches, but never reaches or exceeds 150 feet per second.

71. **a.**

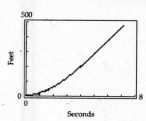

b.   When $s = 100$, $t \approx 2.6$ seconds.

69. **a.**

$$v = 100 \left(\frac{e^{0.64t} - 1}{e^{0.64t} + 1} \right)$$

$$50 = 100 \left(\frac{e^{0.64t} - 1}{e^{0.64t} + 1} \right)$$

$$\frac{50}{100} = \frac{e^{0.64t} - 1}{e^{0.64t} + 1}$$

$$0.5 = \frac{e^{0.64t} - 1}{e^{0.64t} + 1}$$

$$0.5(e^{0.64t} + 1) = e^{0.64t} - 1$$

$$0.5e^{1.64t} + 0.5 = e^{0.64t} - 1$$

$$0.5e^{0.64t} - e^{0.64t} = -1.5$$

$$-0.5e^{0.64t} = -1.5$$

$$e^{0.64t} = 3$$

$$0.64t = \ln 3$$

$$t = \frac{\ln 3}{0.64}$$

$$t \approx 1.72$$

In approximately 1.72 seconds, the velocity will be 50 feet per second.

b.   The horizontal asymptote is the value of $100 \left[\frac{e^{0.64t} - 1}{e^{0.64t} + 1} \right]$ as $t \to \infty$. Therefore, the horizontal asymptote is $v = 100$ feet per second.

c.   The object cannot fall faster than 100 feet per second.

73.

Graph $V = 400,000 - 150,000(1.005)^x$ and $V = 100,000$.

They intersect when $x \approx 138.97$.

After 138 withdrawals, the account has $101,456.39.

After 139 withdrawals, the account has $99,963.67.

The designer can make at most 138 withdrawals and still have $100,000.

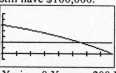

$X\min = 0, X\max = 200, X\text{scl} = 25$
$Y\min = -50000, Y\max = 350000, Y\text{scl} = 50000$

75. The second step because $\log 0.5 < 0$. Thus the inequality sign must be reversed.

77. $\log(x + y) = \log x + \log y$

$\log(x + y) = \log xy$

Therefore $x + y = xy$

$$x - xy = -y$$
$$x(1 - y) = -y$$
$$x = \frac{-y}{1 - y}$$
$$x = \frac{y}{y - 1}$$

79. Since $e^{0.336} \approx 1.4$,

$F(x) = (1.4)^x \approx (e^{0.336})^x = e^{0.336x} = G(x)$

81.
$$A = 1000\left(1 + \frac{0.1}{12}\right)^{12(2)} = 1220.39$$

82.
$$A = 600\left(1 + \frac{0.04}{4}\right)^{4(8)} = 824.96$$

83.
$$0.5 = e^{14k}$$
$$\ln 0.5 = \ln e^{14k}$$
$$\ln 0.5 = 14k$$
$$\frac{\ln 0.5}{14} = k$$
$$-0.0495 \approx k$$

84.
$$0.85 = 0.5^{t/5730}$$
$$\ln 0.85 = \ln 0.5^{t/5730}$$
$$\ln 0.85 = \frac{t}{5730}\ln 0.5$$
$$\frac{5730\ln 0.85}{\ln 0.5} = t$$
$$1340 \approx t$$

85.
$$6 = \frac{70}{5 + 9e^{-12k}}$$
$$6(5 + 9e^{-12k}) = 70$$
$$30 + 54e^{-12k} = 70$$
$$54e^{-12k} = 40$$
$$e^{-12k} = \frac{20}{27}$$
$$\ln e^{-12k} = \ln\frac{20}{27}$$
$$-12k = \ln\frac{20}{27}$$
$$k = -\frac{1}{12}\ln\frac{20}{27}$$
$$k \approx 0.025$$

86.
$$2,000,000 = \frac{3^{n+1} - 3}{2}$$
$$4,000,000 = 3^{n+1} - 3$$
$$3,999,997 = 3^{n+1}$$
$$\ln 3,999,997 = \ln 3^{n+1}$$
$$\ln 3,999,997 = (n+1)\ln 3$$
$$\frac{\ln 3,999,997}{\ln 3} = n+1$$
$$\frac{\ln 3,999,997}{\ln 3} - 1 = n$$
$$12.8 \approx n$$

Section 4.6

1. **a.** $P = 8000$, $r = 0.05$, $t = 4$, $n = 1$

$$B = 8000\left(1 + \frac{0.05}{1}\right)^4 \approx \$9724.05$$

b. $t = 7$, $B = 8000\left(1 + \frac{0.05}{1}\right)^7 \approx \$11,256.80$

3. **a.** $P = 38,000$, $r = 0.065$, $t = 4$, $n = 1$

$$B = 38,000\left(1 + \frac{0.065}{1}\right)^4 \approx \$48,885.72$$

b. $n = 365$, $B = 38,000\left(1 + \frac{0.065}{365}\right)^{4(365)} \approx \$49,282.20$

c. $n = 8760$, $B = 38,000\left(1 + \frac{0.065}{8760}\right)^{4(8760)} \approx \$49,283.30$

5. $P = 15,000$, $r = 0.1$, $t = 5$

$B = 15,000e^{5(0.1)} \approx \$24,730.82$

7. $t = \dfrac{\ln 2}{r}$ $r = 0.0784$

$t = \dfrac{\ln 2}{0.0784}$

$t \approx 8.8$ years

9.
$B = Pe^{rt}$ Let $B = 3P$

$3P = Pe^{rt}$

$3 = e^{rt}$

$\ln 3 = rt \ln e$

$t = \dfrac{\ln 3}{r}$

11. $t = \dfrac{\ln 3}{r}$ $r = 0.076$

$t = \dfrac{\ln 3}{0.076}$

$t \approx 14$ years

13. **a.** $t = 0$ hours, $N(0) = 2200(2)^0 = 2200$ bacteria

b. $t = 3$ hours, $N(3) = 2200(2)^3 = 17,600$ bacteria

15. **a.**
$$N(t) = N_0 e^{kt} \text{ where } N_0 = 24600$$
$$N(5) = 22,600e^{k(5)}$$
$$24,200 = 22,600e^{5k}$$
$$\frac{24,200}{22,600} = e^{5k}$$
$$\ln\left(\frac{24,200}{22,600}\right) = \ln\left(e^{5k}\right)$$
$$\ln\left(\frac{24,200}{22,600}\right) = 5k$$
$$\frac{1}{5}\left[\ln\frac{24,200}{22,600}\right] = k$$
$$0.01368 \approx k$$
$$N(t) = 22,600e^{0.01368t}$$

b. $t = 15$, $N(15) = 22,600e^{0.01368(15)}$
$$= 22,600e^{0.2052}$$
$$\approx 27,700$$

17. **a.** $P = 10,130(1.005)^t$ where $t = 12$

$= 10.130(1.005)^{12}$

$= 110.130(1.061677812)$

$= 10,754.79623$ thousand

$P \approx 10,775,000$

b.
$$13,000 = 10,130(1.005)^t$$
$$\frac{13,000}{10,130} = 1.005^t$$
$$\log\left(\frac{13,000}{10,130}\right) = \log 1.005^t$$
$$\log\left(\frac{13,000}{10,130}\right) = t \log 1.005$$
$$\frac{\log\left(\frac{13,000}{10,130}\right)}{\log 1.005} = t \approx 50$$
in 50 years, or in 2042

19. **a.**

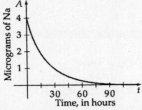

b. $A(5) = 4e^{-0.23} \approx 3.18$ micrograms

c. Since $A = 4$ micrograms are present when $t = 0$, find the time t at which half remains—that is when $A = 2$.

$$2 = 4e^{-0.046t}$$
$$\frac{1}{2} = e^{-0.046t}$$
$$\ln\left(\frac{1}{2}\right) = -0.046t$$
$$\frac{\ln\left(\frac{1}{2}\right)}{-0.046} = t$$
$$15.07 \approx t$$

The half-life of sodium-24 is about 15.07 hours.

d.

$$1 = 4e^{-0.046t}$$
$$\frac{1}{4} = e^{-0.046t}$$
$$\ln\left(\frac{1}{4}\right) = -0.046t$$
$$\frac{\ln\left(\frac{1}{4}\right)}{-0.046t} = t$$
$$30.14 \approx t$$

The amount of sodium-24 will be 1 microgram after 30.14 hours.

21.

$$N(t) = N_0 (0.5)^{t/5730}$$
$$N(t) = 0.45N_0$$
$$0.45N_0 = N_0 (0.5)^{t/5730}$$
$$\ln(0.45) = \frac{t}{5730} \ln 0.5$$
$$5730 \frac{\ln 0.45}{\ln 0.5} = t$$
$$6601 \approx t$$

The bone is about 6601 years old.

23.

$$N(t) = N_0 (0.5)^{t/5730}$$
$$N(t) = 0.75N_0$$
$$0.75N_0 = N_0 (0.5)^{t/5730}$$
$$\ln 0.75 = \frac{t}{5730} \ln 0.5$$
$$5730 \frac{\ln 0.75}{\ln 0.5} = t$$
$$2378 \approx t$$

The Rhind papyrus is about 2378 years old.

25. **a.** $A = 34°F, T_0 = 75°F, T_t = 65°F, t = 5$. Find k.

$$65 = 34 + (75 - 34)e^{-5k}$$
$$31 = 41e^{-5k}$$
$$\frac{31}{41} = e^{-5k}$$
$$\ln\left(\frac{31}{41}\right) = -5k$$
$$k = -\frac{1}{5}\ln\left(\frac{31}{41}\right)$$
$$k \approx 0.056$$

b. $A = 34°F, k = 0.056, T_0 = 75°F, t = 30$

$$T_t = 34 + (75 - 34)e^{-30(0.056)}$$
$$T_t = 34 + (41)e^{-1.68}$$
$$T_t \approx 42°F$$

c. $T_t = 36°F, k = 0.056, T_t = 75°F, A = 34°F$

$$36 = 34 + (75 - 34)e^{-0.056t}$$
$$2 = 41e^{-0.056t}$$
$$t \approx 54 \text{ minutes}$$

27. **a.** 10% of 80,000 is 8000.

$$8000 = 80,000\left(1 - e^{-0.0005t}\right)$$
$$0.1 = 1 - e^{-0.0005t}$$
$$-0.9 = -e^{-0.0005t}$$
$$0.9 = e^{-0.0005t}$$
$$\ln 0.9 = -0.0005t \ln e$$
$$\ln 0.9 = -0.0005t$$
$$\frac{\ln 0.9}{-0.0005} = t$$
$$211 \approx t$$

b. 50% of 80,000 is 40,000.

$$40,000 = 80,000\left(1 - e^{-0.0005t}\right)$$
$$0.5 = 1 - e^{-0.0005t}$$
$$-0.5 = -e^{-0.0005t}$$
$$0.5 = e^{-0.0005t}$$
$$\ln(0.5) = \ln\left(e^{-0.0005t}\right)$$
$$\ln(0.5) = -0.0005t$$
$$\frac{\ln(0.5)}{-0.0005} = t$$
$$1386 \approx t$$

29. $V(t) = V_0(1-r)^t$

$0.5V_0 = V_0(1-0.20)^t$

$0.5 = (1-0.20)^t$

$0.5 = 0.8^t$

$\ln 0.5 = \ln 0.8^t$

$\ln 0.5 = t \ln 0.8$

$\dfrac{\ln 0.5}{\ln 0.8} = t$

$3.1 \text{ years} \approx t$

31. **a.**

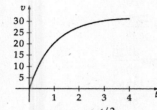

b. $20 = 64(1 - e^{-t/2})$

$0.625 = 1 - e^{-t/2}$

$e^{-t/2} = 0.375$

$-t/2 = \ln 0.375$

$t \approx 0.98 \text{ seconds}$

c. The horizontal asymptote is $v = 32$.

d. As time increases, the object's velocity approaches but never exceeds 32 ft/sec.

33. **a.**

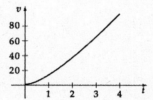

b. The graphs of $s = 32t + 32(e^{-t} - 1)$ and $s = 50$ intersect when $t \approx 2.5$ seconds.

c. The slope m of the secant line containing $(1, s(1))$ and $(2, s(2))$ is $m = \dfrac{s(2) - s(1)}{2 - 1} \approx 24.56$ ft/sec

d. The average speed of the object was 24.56 feet per second between $t = 1$ and $t = 2$.

35. **a.** 1900
  b. 0.16
  c. $P(0) = \dfrac{1900}{1 + 8.5e^{-0.16(0)}} = 200$

37. **a.** 157,500
  b. 0.04
  c. $P(0) = \dfrac{157,500}{1 + 2.5e^{-0.04(0)}} = 45,000$

39. **a.** 2400

b. 0.12

c. $P(0) = \dfrac{2400}{1 + 7e^{-0.12(0)}} = 300$

41.

$a = \dfrac{c - P_0}{P_0} = \dfrac{5500 - 400}{400} = 12.75$

$P(t) = \dfrac{c}{1 + ae^{-bt}}$

$P(2) = \dfrac{5500}{1 + 12.75e^{-b(2)}}$

$780 = \dfrac{5500}{1 + 12.75e^{-2b}}$

$780(1 + 12.75e^{-2b}) = 5500$

$780 + 9945e^{-2b} = 5500$

$9945e^{-2b} = 4720$

$e^{-2b} = \dfrac{4720}{9945}$

$\ln e^{-2b} = \ln \dfrac{4720}{9945}$

$-2b = \ln \dfrac{4720}{9945}$

$b = -\dfrac{1}{2} \ln \dfrac{4720}{9945}$

$b \approx 0.37263$

$P(t) = \dfrac{5500}{1 + 12.75e^{-0.37263t}}$

43.

$a = \dfrac{c - P_0}{P_0} = \dfrac{100 - 18}{18} = 4.55556$

$P(t) = \dfrac{c}{1 + ae^{-bt}}$

$P(3) = \dfrac{100}{1 + 4.55556e^{-b(3)}}$

$30 = \dfrac{100}{1 + 4.55556e^{-3b}}$

$30(1 + 4.55556e^{-3b}) = 100$

$30 + 136.67e^{-3b} = 100$

$136.67e^{-3b} = 70$

$e^{-3b} = \dfrac{70}{136.67}$

$\ln e^{-3b} = \ln \dfrac{70}{136.67}$

$-3b = \ln \dfrac{70}{136.67}$

$b = -\dfrac{1}{3} \ln \dfrac{70}{136.67}$

$b \approx 0.22302$

$P(t) = \dfrac{100}{1 + 4.55556e^{-0.22302t}}$

45. **a.** $R(t) = \dfrac{625,000}{1 + 3.1e^{-0.045t}}$

$R(1) = \dfrac{625,000}{1 + 3.1e^{-0.045(1)}} \approx \$158,000$

$R(2) = \dfrac{625,000}{1 + 3.1e^{-0.045(2)}} \approx \$163,000$

b. $R(t) = \dfrac{625,000}{1 + 3.1e^{-0.045t}}$, as $t \to \infty$, $R(t) \to \$625,000$

47. **a.**
$$a=\frac{c-P_0}{P_0}=\frac{1600-312}{312}=4.12821$$

$$P(t)=\frac{c}{1+ae^{-bt}}$$

$$P(6)=\frac{1600}{1+4.12821e^{-b(6)}}$$

$$416=\frac{1600}{1+4.12821e^{-6b}}$$

$$416(1+4.12821e^{-6b})=1600$$

$$416+1717.34e^{-6b}=1600$$

$$1717.34e^{-6b}=1184$$

$$e^{-6b}=\frac{1184}{1717.34}$$

$$\ln e^{-6b}=\ln\frac{1184}{1717.34}$$

$$-6b=\ln\frac{1184}{1717.34}$$

$$b=-\frac{1}{6}\ln\frac{1184}{1717.34}$$

$$b\approx0.06198$$

$$P(t)=\frac{1600}{1+4.12821e^{-0.06198t}}$$

b.
$$P(10)=\frac{1600}{1+4.12821e^{-0.06198(10)}}\approx497\text{ wolves}$$

49. **a.**
$$a=\frac{c-P_0}{P_0}=\frac{8500-1500}{1500}=4.66667$$

$$P(t)=\frac{c}{1+ae^{-bt}}$$

$$P(2)=\frac{8500}{1+4.66667e^{-b(2)}}$$

$$1900=\frac{8500}{1+4.66667e^{-2b}}$$

$$1900(1+4.66667e^{-2b})=8500$$

$$1900+8866.673e^{-2b}=8500$$

$$8866.673e^{-2b}=6600$$

$$e^{-2b}=\frac{6600}{8866.673}$$

$$\ln e^{-2b}=\ln\frac{6600}{8866.673}$$

$$-2b=\ln\frac{6600}{8866.673}$$

$$b=-\frac{1}{2}\ln\frac{6600}{8866.673}$$

$$b\approx0.14761$$

$$P(t)=\frac{8500}{1+4.66667e^{-0.14761t}}$$

b.
$$4000=\frac{8500}{1+4.66667e^{-0.14761t}}$$

$$4000(1+4.66667e^{-0.14761t})=8500$$

$$1+4.66667e^{-0.14761t}=2.125$$

$$4.66667e^{-0.14761t}=1.125$$

$$e^{-0.14761t}=\frac{1.125}{4.66667}$$

$$\ln e^{-0.14761t}=\ln\frac{1.125}{4.66667}$$

$$-0.14761t=\ln\frac{1.125}{4.66667}$$

$$t=-\frac{1}{0.14761}\ln\frac{1.125}{4.66667}$$

$$t\approx9.6$$

The population will exceed 4000 in 2010.

51.

Xmin = 0, Xmax = 80, Xscl = 10,
Ymin = −10, Ymax = 110, Yscl = 15

When $P=75\%$, $t\approx45$ hours.

● ●

53.

a. $A(1) = 0.5^{1/2}$

≈ 0.71 gram

b. $A(4) = 0.5^{4/2} + 0.5^{(4-3)/2}$

$= 0.5^2 + 0.5^{1/2}$

≈ 0.96 gram

c. $A(9) = 0.5^{9/2} + 0.5^{(9-3)/2} + 0.5^{(9-6)/2}$

$= 0.5^{4.5} + 0.5^3 + 0.5^{1.5}$

≈ 0.52 gram

55.

a. $P(0) = \dfrac{4.1^0 e^{-4.1}}{0!} = \dfrac{1 \cdot e^{-4.1}}{1} \approx 0.017 = 1.7\%$

b. $P(2) = \dfrac{4.1^2 e^{-4.1}}{2!} = \dfrac{16.81 e^{-4.1}}{2} \approx 0.139 = 13.9\%$

c. $P(3) = \dfrac{4.1^3 e^{-4.1}}{3!} = \dfrac{68.921 e^{-4.1}}{6} \approx 0.190 = 19.0\%$

d. $P(4) = \dfrac{4.1^4 e^{-4.1}}{4!} = \dfrac{282.5761 e^{-4.1}}{24} \approx 0.195 = 19.5\%$

e. $P(9) = \dfrac{4.1^9 e^{-4.1}}{9!} = \dfrac{327381.9344 e^{-4.1}}{362880} \approx 0.015 = 1.5\%$

As $x \to \infty$, $P \to 0$.

57.

$\dfrac{3^8 2^{12} 8! 12!}{2 \cdot 3 \cdot 2} = 3^7 2^{10} 8! 12!$

$\text{time} = \left(\dfrac{3^7 2^{10} 8! 12! \text{ arrangements}}{1} \right) \left(\dfrac{1 \text{ second}}{\text{arrangement}} \right) \left(\dfrac{1 \text{ minute}}{60 \text{ seconds}} \right) \left(\dfrac{1 \text{ hour}}{60 \text{ minutes}} \right) \left(\dfrac{1 \text{ day}}{24 \text{ hours}} \right) \left(\dfrac{1 \text{ year}}{365 \text{ days}} \right) \left(\dfrac{1 \text{ century}}{100 \text{ years}} \right)$

$= 3^7 2^{10} 8! 12! \left(\dfrac{1}{60^2 \cdot 24 \cdot 365 \cdot 100} \right)$

$= \dfrac{(2187)(1024)(40320)(479001600)}{(3600)(24)(365)(100)}$

$= 13,715,120,270 \text{ centuries}$

● ●

59. decreasing

60. decreasing

61. $P(0) = \dfrac{108}{1 + 2e^{-0.1(0)}} = \dfrac{108}{1+2} = 36$

62. $N(0) = 840 e^{1.05(0)} = 840$

63.

$10 = \dfrac{20}{1 + 2.2e^{-0.05t}}$

$10(1 + 2.2e^{-0.05t}) = 20$

$10 + 22e^{-0.05t} = 20$

$e^{-0.05t} = \dfrac{10}{22}$

$\ln e^{-0.05t} = \ln \dfrac{10}{22}$

$-0.05t = \ln \dfrac{10}{22}$

$t = -20 \ln \dfrac{10}{22}$

$t \approx 15.8$

64. $P(t) = \dfrac{55}{1 + 3e^{-0.08t}}$

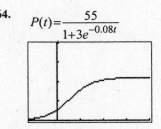

There is a horizontal asymptote at $P = 0$ and $P = 55$.

Section 4.7

1.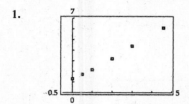

increasing exponential function

3.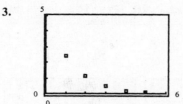

decreasing exponential function;
decreasing logarithmic function

5.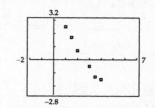

decreasing logarithmic function;
decreasing exponential function

7.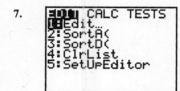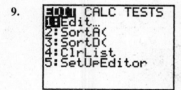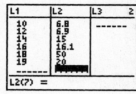

$y \approx 0.99628(1.20052)^x$; $r \approx 0.85705$

9.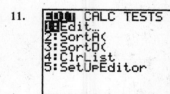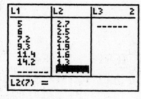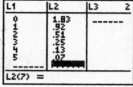

$y \approx 1.81505(0.51979)^x$; $r \approx -0.99978$

11.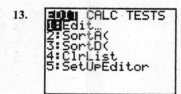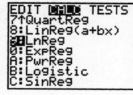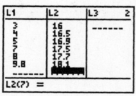

$y \approx 4.89060 - 1.35073 \ln x$; $r \approx -0.99921$

13.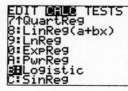

$y \approx 14.05858 + 1.76393 \ln x$; $r \approx 0.99983$

15.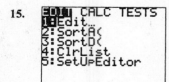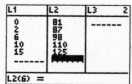

$$y \approx \frac{235.58598}{1 + 1.90188 e^{-0.05101x}}$$

17.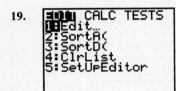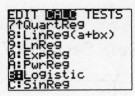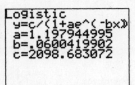

$$y \approx \frac{2098.68307}{1+1.19794e^{-0.06004x}}$$

19.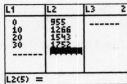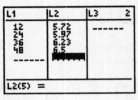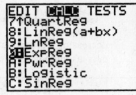

a. $y = 5.48184(1.00356)^x$; $y = 5.48184(1.00356)^{60} \approx 6.78\%$

b. $7 = 5.48184(1.00356)^x \Rightarrow \dfrac{7}{5.48184} = (1.00356)^x \Rightarrow \ln\dfrac{7}{5.48184} = \ln(1.00356)^x$

$$\Rightarrow \ln 7 - \ln 5.48184 = x\ln 1.00356 \Rightarrow \frac{\ln 7 - \ln 5.48184}{\ln 1.00356} = x$$

$$\Rightarrow x \approx 69 \text{ months}$$

21.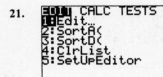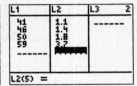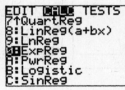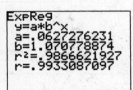

a. Exponential: $T \approx 0.06273(1.07078)^F$

b. $T \approx 0.06273(1.07078)^{65} \approx 5.3$ hours

23.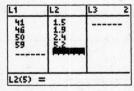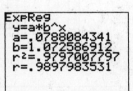

a. $T \approx 0.7881(1.07259)^F$

b. $T \approx 0.07881(1.07259)^{65} \approx 7.5$ hours

$7.5 - 5.3 = 2.2$ hours.

25.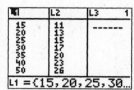

a. $N(t) \approx 1500.093(1.940)^t$

b.
$$1,000,000 \approx 1500.093(1.940)^t \Rightarrow \frac{1,000,000}{1500.093} \approx (1.940)^t \Rightarrow \ln\frac{1,000,000}{1500.093} \approx \ln(1.940)^t$$
$$\Rightarrow \ln 1,000,000 - \ln 1500.093 \approx x \ln 1.940 \Rightarrow x \approx \frac{\ln 1,000,000 - \ln 1500.093}{\ln 1.940}$$
$$\Rightarrow x \approx 9.8 \text{ years after } 1996 \Rightarrow \text{ in } 2005$$

27.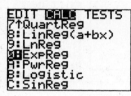

a. $p \approx 7.862(1.026)^y$

b. $p \approx 7.862(1.026)^{60} \approx 36 \text{ cm}$

29.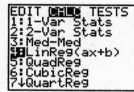

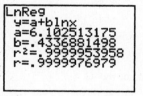 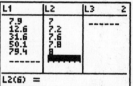

a.   Linear: $\text{pH} \approx 0.01353q + 7.02852$; $r \approx 0.956627$.

Logarithmic: $\text{pH} \approx 6.10251 + 0.43369 \ln q$; $r \approx 0.999998$. The logarithmic model provides the better fit.

b.
$$8.2 \approx 6.10251 + 0.43369 \ln q \Rightarrow 2.09749 \approx 0.43369 \ln q \Rightarrow \frac{2.09749}{0.43369} \approx \ln q \Rightarrow q \approx e^{\frac{2.09749}{0.43369}} \approx 126.0$$

31.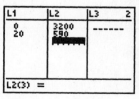

a. $p \approx 3200(0.91894)^t$; $200 \approx 3200(0.91894)^t \Rightarrow \frac{1}{16} \approx (0.91894)^t \Rightarrow \ln\frac{1}{16} \approx \ln(0.91894)^t$
$$\Rightarrow \ln 1 - \ln 16 \approx t \ln 0.91894 \Rightarrow t \approx \frac{-\ln 16}{\ln 0.91894}$$
$$\Rightarrow t \approx 32.8 \text{ years after } 1980 \Rightarrow \text{ in } 2012$$

b.   No. The model fits the data perfectly because there are only two data points.

33.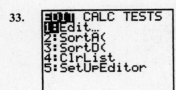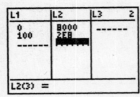

a. $a \approx 8000(1.10657)^t$; $a \approx 8000(1.10657)^{110} \approx 550,500,000$ automobiles

b. $300,000,000 \approx 8000(1.10657)^t \Rightarrow 37500 \approx 1.10657^t \Rightarrow \ln 37500 \approx \ln 1.10657^t$

$\Rightarrow \ln 37500 \approx t \ln 1.10657 \Rightarrow t \approx \dfrac{\ln 37500}{\ln 1.10657}$

$\Rightarrow t \approx 104$ years after 1900 $\Rightarrow$ in 2004.

35.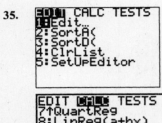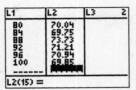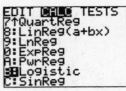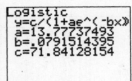

 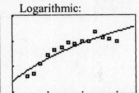

a. Logistic: $y \approx \dfrac{71.84128}{1 + 13.7774e^{-0.07915x}}$

Logarithmic: $y \approx -22.5660 + 20.91276 \ln x$

b. Logistic: Logarithmic:

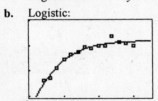

The logistical growth model fits the data better than the logarithmic model.

c. $y \approx \dfrac{71.84128}{1 + 13.7774e^{-0.07915(108)}} \approx 71.65$ ft

37.

a. Linear: $w \approx 10.17227t + 16.45111$; $r \approx 0.95601$. Logarithmic: $w \approx 18.26750 + 31.03499 \ln t$; $r \approx 0.99996$.

b. The logarithmic model provides the better fit.

c. $w \approx 18.26750 + 31.03499 \ln 10 \approx 89.7$ cubic yards

39.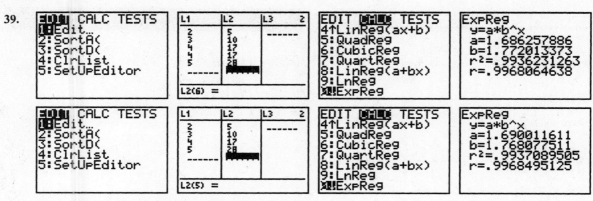

A and B have different exponential regression functions.

41.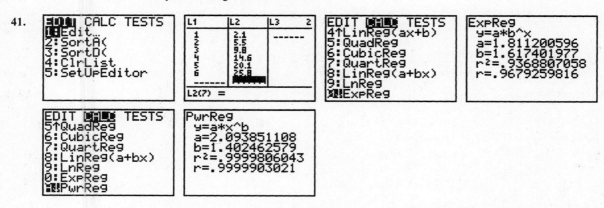

a. Exponential: $y \approx 1.81120(1.61740)^x$; $r \approx 0.96793$. Power: $y \approx 2.09385(x^{1.40246})$; $r \approx 0.99999$.

b. The power regression provides the better fit.

Chapter 4 True/False Exercises

1. False; $f(x) = x^2$ does not have an inverse function.

2. False. Let $f(x) = 2x$ and $g(x) = 3x$. Then $f[g(0)] = f(0) = 0$ and $g[f(0)] = g(0) = 0$, but f and g are not inverses of each other.

3. True   **4.** True   **5.** True

6. False, because f is not defined for negative values of x, and thus $g[f(x)]$ is undefined for negative values of x.

7. False; $h(x)$ is not an increasing function for $0 < b < 1$.   **8.** False; $j(x)$ is not an increasing function for $0 < b < 1$.

9. True   **10.** True

11. True, because $f(-x) = \frac{2^{-x} + 2^{-(-x)}}{2} = \frac{2^{-x} + 2^x}{2} = f(x)$ **12.** True

13. False, $\log x + \log y = \log xy$.   **14.** True   **15.** True   **16.** True

1. $F[G(x)] = F\left(\dfrac{x+5}{2}\right) = 2\left(\dfrac{x+5}{2}\right) - 5 = x + 5 - 5 = x$ [4.1]

$G[F(x)] = G(2x - 5) = \dfrac{2x - 5 + 5}{2} = \dfrac{2x}{2} = x$

Yes, F and G are inverses.

2. $h[k(x)] = h\left(x^2\right) = \sqrt{x^2} = x$ [4.1]

$k[h(x)] = k\left(\sqrt{x}\right) = \left(\sqrt{x}\right)^2 = x$

Yes, h and k are inverses.

3. $l[m(x)] = l\left(\dfrac{3}{x-1}\right) = \dfrac{\frac{3}{x-1} + 3}{\frac{3}{x-1}} = \dfrac{3 + 3(x-1)}{3} = \dfrac{3 + 3x - 3}{3} = \dfrac{3x}{3} = x$ [4.1]

$m[l(x)] = m\left(\dfrac{x+3}{x}\right) = \dfrac{3}{\frac{x+3}{x} - 1} = \dfrac{3x}{x + 3 - x} = \dfrac{3x}{3} = x$

Yes, l and m are inverses.

4. $p[q(x)] = p\left(\dfrac{2x}{x-5}\right) = \dfrac{\frac{2x}{x-5} - 5}{2\left(\frac{2x}{x-5}\right)} = \dfrac{2x - 5(x-5)}{2(2x)} = \dfrac{2x - 5x + 25}{4x} = \dfrac{-3x + 25}{4x} \neq x$ [4.1]

No, p and q are not inverses.

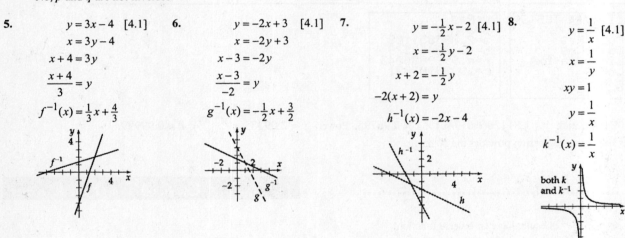

5. $y = 3x - 4$ [4.1]

$x = 3y - 4$

$x + 4 = 3y$

$\dfrac{x+4}{3} = y$

$f^{-1}(x) = \frac{1}{3}x + \frac{4}{3}$

6. $y = -2x + 3$ [4.1]

$x = -2y + 3$

$x - 3 = -2y$

$\dfrac{x-3}{-2} = y$

$g^{-1}(x) = -\frac{1}{2}x + \frac{3}{2}$

7. $y = -\frac{1}{2}x - 2$ [4.1]

$x = -\frac{1}{2}y - 2$

$x + 2 = -\frac{1}{2}y$

$-2(x + 2) = y$

$h^{-1}(x) = -2x - 4$

8. $y = \dfrac{1}{x}$ [4.1]

$x = \dfrac{1}{y}$

$xy = 1$

$y = \dfrac{1}{x}$

$k^{-1}(x) = \dfrac{1}{x}$

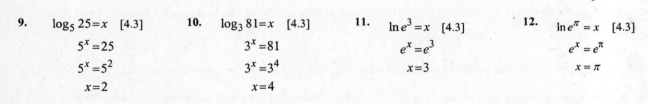

9. $\log_5 25 = x$ [4.3]

$5^x = 25$

$5^x = 5^2$

$x = 2$

10. $\log_3 81 = x$ [4.3]

$3^x = 81$

$3^x = 3^4$

$x = 4$

11. $\ln e^3 = x$ [4.3]

$e^x = e^3$

$x = 3$

12. $\ln e^\pi = x$ [4.3]

$e^x = e^\pi$

$x = \pi$

13. $3^{2x+7} = 27$ [4.5]

$3^{2x+7} = 3^3$

$2x + 7 = 3$

$2x = -4$

$x = -2$

14. $5^{x-4} = 625$ [4.5]

$5^{x-4} = 5^4$

$x - 4 = 4$

$x = 8$

15. $2^x = \dfrac{1}{8}$ [4.5]

$2^x = 2^{-3}$

$x = -3$

16. $27\left(3^x\right) = 3^{-1}$ [4.5]

$27\left(3^x\right) = \dfrac{1}{3}$

$3^x = \dfrac{1}{81}$

$3^x = 3^{-4}$

$x = -4$

17.
$$\log x^2 = 6 \quad [4.5]$$
$$10^6 = x^2$$
$$1,000,000 = x^2$$
$$\pm\sqrt{1,000,000} = x$$
$$\pm 1000 = x$$

18.
$$\frac{1}{2}\log|x| = 5 \qquad [4.5]$$
$$\log|x| = 10$$
$$10^{10} = |x|$$
$$x = \pm 10^{10}$$

19.
$$10^{\log 2x} = 14 \quad [4.5]$$
$$2x = 14$$
$$x = 7$$

20.
$$e^{\ln x^2} = 64 \quad [4.5]$$
$$x^2 = 64$$
$$x = \pm 8$$

21.

22.

23.

24.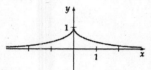

25.

26.

27.

28.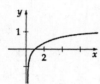

29.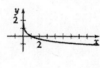

30.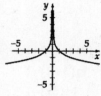

31.

32.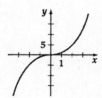

33.
$$\log_4 64 = 3 \quad [4.3]$$
$$4^3 = 64$$

34.
$$\log_{1/2} 8 = -3 \quad [4.3]$$
$$\left(\frac{1}{2}\right)^{-3} = 8$$

35.
$$\log_{\sqrt{2}} 4 = 4 \quad [4.3]$$
$$\left(\sqrt{2}\right)^4 = 4$$

36.
$$\ln 1 = 0 \quad [4.3]$$
$$e^0 = 1$$

37.
$$5^3 = 125 \quad [4.3]$$
$$\log_5 125 = 3$$

38.
$$2^{10} = 1024 \quad [4.3]$$
$$\log_2 1024 = 10$$

39.
$$10^0 = 1 \quad [4.3]$$
$$\log_{10} 1 = 0$$

40.
$$8^{1/2} = 2\sqrt{2} \quad [4.3]$$
$$\log_8 2\sqrt{2} = \frac{1}{2}$$

41.
$$\log_b \frac{x^2 y^3}{z} = 2\log_b x + 3\log_b y - \log_b z \quad [4.4]$$

42.
$$\log_b \frac{\sqrt{x}}{y^2 z} = \frac{1}{2}\log_b x - \left(2\log_b y + \log_b z\right) \quad [4.4]$$
$$= \frac{1}{2}\log_b x - 2\log_b y - \log_b z$$

43.
$$\ln xy^3 = \ln x + 3\ln y \quad [4.4]$$

44.
$$\ln \frac{\sqrt{xy}}{z^4} = \frac{1}{2}\left(\ln x + \ln y\right) - 4\ln z \quad [4.4]$$
$$= \frac{1}{2}\ln x + \frac{1}{2}\ln y - 4\ln z$$

45. $2\log x + \dfrac{1}{3}\log(x+1) = \log\left(x^2\sqrt[3]{x+1}\right)$ [4.4]

46. $5\log x - 2\log(x+5) = \log\dfrac{x^5}{(x+5)^2}$ [4.4]

47. $\dfrac{1}{2}\ln 2xy - 3\ln z = \ln\dfrac{\sqrt{2xy}}{z^3}$ [4.4]

48. $\ln x - (\ln y - \ln z) = \ln\dfrac{x}{y/z} = \ln\dfrac{xz}{y}$ [4.4]

49. $\log_5 101 = \dfrac{\log 101}{\log 5} \approx 2.86754$ [4.4]

50. $\log_3 40 = \dfrac{\log 40}{\log 3} \approx 3.35776$ [4.4]

51. $\log_4 0.85 = \dfrac{\log 0.85}{\log 4} \approx -0.117233$ [4.4]

52. $\log_8 0.3 = \dfrac{\log 0.3}{\log 8} \approx -0.578989$ [4.4]

53.
$$4^x = 30 \quad [4.5]$$
$$\log 4^x = \log 30$$
$$x\log 4 = \log 30$$
$$x = \frac{\log 30}{\log 4}$$

54.
$$5^{x+1} = 41 \quad [4.5]$$
$$(x+1)\log 5 = \log 41$$
$$x+1 = \frac{\log 41}{\log 5}$$
$$x = \frac{\log 41}{\log 5} - 1$$

55.
$$\ln(3x) - \ln(x-1) = \ln 4 \quad [4.5]$$
$$\ln\frac{3x}{x-1} = \ln 4$$
$$\frac{3x}{x-1} = 4$$
$$3x = 4(x-1)$$
$$3x = 4x - 4$$
$$4 = x$$

56.
$$\ln(3x) + \ln 2 = \ln 1 \quad [4.5]$$
$$\ln(3x \cdot 2) = 1$$
$$\ln(6x) = 1$$
$$e^1 = 6x$$
$$\frac{e}{6} = x$$

57.
$$e^{\ln(x+2)} = 6 \quad [4.5]$$
$$(x+2) = 6$$
$$x+2 = 6$$
$$x = 4$$

58.
$$10^{\log(2x+1)} = 31 \quad [4.5]$$
$$2x+1 = 31$$
$$2x = 30$$
$$x = 15$$

59.
$$\frac{4^x + 4^{-x}}{4^x - 4^{-x}} = 2$$
$$4^x\left(4^x + 4^{-x}\right) = 2\left(4^x - 4^{-x}\right)4^x$$
$$4^{2x} + 1 = 2\left(4^{2x} - 1\right)$$
$$4^{2x} + 1 = 2\left(4^{2x} - 1\right)$$
$$4^{2x} - 2\cdot 4^{2x} + 3 = 0$$
$$4^{2x} = 3$$
$$2^x \ln 4 = \ln 3$$
$$x = \frac{\ln 3}{2\ln 4} \quad [4.5]$$

60.
$$\frac{5^x + 5^{-x}}{2} = 8$$
$$5^x\left(5^x + 5^{-x}\right) = 16\left(5^x\right)$$
$$5^{2x} + 1 = 16\left(5^x\right)$$
$$5^{2x} - 16\left(5^x\right) + 1 = 0$$
Let $5^x = u$
$$u^2 - 16u + 1 = 0$$
$$u = \frac{16 \pm \sqrt{16^2 - 4(1)(1)}}{2}$$
$$u = \frac{16 \pm \sqrt{252}}{2}$$
$$u = \frac{16 \pm 6\sqrt{7}}{2}$$
$$u = 8 \pm 3\sqrt{7}$$
$$5^x = 8 \pm 3\sqrt{7}$$
$$x = \frac{\ln\left(8 \pm 3\sqrt{7}\right)}{\ln 5} \quad [4.5]$$

61. $\log(\log x) = 3$ [4.5]

$10^3 = \log x$

$10^{(10^3)} = x$

$10^{1000} = x$

62. $\ln(\ln x) = 2$ [4.5]

$e^2 = \ln x$

$e^{(e^2)} = x$

63. $\log\sqrt{x-5} = 3$ [4.5]

$10^3 = \sqrt{x-5}$

$10^6 = x-5$

$10^6 + 5 = x$

$x = 1,000,005$

64. $\log x + \log(x-15) = 1$

$\log x(x-15) = 1$

$10 = x^2 - 15x$

$0 = x^2 - 15x - 10$

$x = \dfrac{15 \pm \sqrt{15^2 - 4(1)(-10)}}{2}$

$x = \dfrac{15 \pm \sqrt{265}}{2}$

$x = \dfrac{15 + \sqrt{265}}{2}$ [4.5]

65. $\log_4(\log_3 x) = 1$

$4 = \log_3 x$

$3^4 = x$

$81 = x$ [4.5]

66. $\log_7(\log_5 x^2) = 0$

$7^0 = \log_5 x^2$

$1 = \log_5 x^2$

$5 = x^2$

$\pm\sqrt{5} = x$ [4.5]

67. $\log_5 x^3 = \log_5 16x$ [4.5]

$x^3 = 16x$

$x^2 = 16$

$x = 4$

68. $25 = 16^{\log_4 x}$ [4.5]

$25 = 4^{2\log_4 x}$

$25 = 4^{\log_4 x^2}$

$25 = x^2$

$\pm 5 = x$

$5 = x$

69. $m = \log\left(\dfrac{I}{I_0}\right)$ [4.4]

$= \log\left(\dfrac{51,782,000 I_0}{I_0}\right)$

$= \log 51,782,000$

≈ 7.7

70. $M = \log A + 3\log 8t - 2.92$ [4.4]

$= \log 18 + 3\log 8(21) - 2.92$

$= \log 18 + 3\log 168 - 2.92$

≈ 5.0

71. $\log\left(\dfrac{I_1}{I_0}\right) = 7.2$ and $\log\left(\dfrac{I_2}{I_0}\right) = 3.7$ [4.4]

$\dfrac{I_1}{I_0} = 10^{7.2}$ $\dfrac{I_2}{I_0} = 10^{3.7}$

$I_1 = 10^{7.2} I_0$ $I_2 = 10^{3.7} I_0$

$\dfrac{I_1}{I_2} = \dfrac{10^{7.2} I_0}{10^{3.7} I_0} = \dfrac{10^{3.5}}{1} \approx \dfrac{3162}{1}$

3162 to 1

72. $\dfrac{I_1}{I_2} = 600 = 10^x$ [4.4]

$\log 600 = \log 10^x$

$\log 600 = x$

$2.8 \approx x$

73. $pH = -\log\left[H_3O^+\right]$ [4.4]

$= -\log\left[6.28 \times 10^{-5}\right]$

≈ 4.2

74. $5.4 = -\log\left[H_3O^+\right]$ [4.4]

$-5.4 = \log\left[H_3O^+\right]$

$10^{-5.4} = H_3O^+$

$0.00000398 \approx H_3O^+$

$H_3O^+ \approx 3.98 \times 10^{-6}$

75. $P = 16,000, r = 0.08, t = 3$ [4.6]

    a.
$$B = 16,000\left(1 + \frac{0.08}{12}\right)^{36} \approx \$20,323.79$$

    b. $B = 16,000e^{0.08(3)}$

       $B = 16,000e^{0.24} \approx \$20,339.99$

77. $S(n) = P(1-r)^n, P = 12,400, r = 0.29, t = 3$ [4.6]

    $S(n) = 12,400(1 - 0.29)^3 \approx \$4438.10$

76. $P = 19,000, r = 0.06, t = 5$ [4.6]

    a.
$$B = 19,000\left(1 + \frac{0.06}{365}\right)^{1825} \approx \$25,646.69$$

    b. $B = 19,000e^{0.3} \approx \$25,647.32$

78. **a.**
$$N(t) = N_0 e^{-0.12t} \quad [4.6]$$
$$N(10) = N_0 e^{-0.12(10)}$$
$$\frac{N(10)}{N_0} = e^{-1.2}$$
$$= .301$$
$$\frac{N(10)}{N_0} = 30.1\% \text{ healed}$$
$$100\% - 30.1\% = 69.9\% \text{ healed}$$

    b.
$$\frac{N(t)}{N_0} = 0.5$$
$$0.5 = e^{-0.12t}$$
$$\ln 0.5 = -0.12t$$
$$\frac{\ln 0.5}{-0.12} = t$$
$$t \approx 6 \text{ days}$$

    c.
$$\frac{N(t)}{N_0} = 0.1$$
$$0.1 = e^{-0.12t}$$
$$\ln 0.1 = -0.12t$$
$$\frac{\ln 0.1}{-0.12} = t$$
$$t \approx 19 \text{ days}$$

79. $N(0) = 1 \qquad\qquad N(2) = 5$

    $1 = N_0 e^{k(0)} \qquad\quad 5 = e^{2k}$

    $1 = N_0 \qquad\qquad\quad \ln 5 = 2k$

                               $k = \dfrac{\ln 5}{2} \approx 0.8047$

    Thus $N(t) = e^{0.8047t}$ [4.6]

80. $N(0) = N_0 = 2$ and $N(3) = N_0 e^{3k} = 2e^{3k} = 11$

    $e^{3k} = \dfrac{11}{2}$

    $e^{3k} = \dfrac{11}{2}$

    $3k = \ln\left(\dfrac{11}{2}\right)$

    $k = \dfrac{1}{3}\ln\left(\dfrac{11}{2}\right)$

    ≈ 0.5682

    Thus $N(t) = 2e^{0.5682t}$ [4.6]

81. $4 = N(1) = N_0 e^k$ and thus $\dfrac{4}{N_0} = e^k$. Now, we also

have $N(5) = 5 = N_0 e^{5k} = N_0 \left(\dfrac{4}{N_0}\right)^5 = \dfrac{1024}{N_0^4}$.

$N_0 = \sqrt[4]{\dfrac{1024}{5}} \approx 3.783$

Thus $4 = 3.783 e^k$.

$\ln\left(\dfrac{4}{3.783}\right) = k$

$k \approx 0.0558$

Thus $N_0 = 3.783 e^{0.0558t}$. [4.6]

82. $1 = N(0) = N_0$ and $2 = N(-1) = N_0 e^{-k}$.

Since $N_0 = 1$, we have $2 = 1 \cdot e^{-k}$.

$\ln 2 = -k$

$k \approx -0.6931$

Thus $N(t) = e^{-0.6931 t}$. [4.6]

83. **a.** $N(1) = 25{,}200 e^{k(1)} = 26{,}800$ [4.6]

$e^k = \dfrac{26{,}800}{25{,}200}$

$\ln e^k = \ln\left(\dfrac{26{,}800}{25{,}200}\right)$

$k \approx 0.061557893$

$N(t) = 25{,}200 e^{0.061557893\,t}$

b. $N(7) = 25{,}200 e^{0.061557893(7)}$

$= 25{,}200 e^{0.430905251}$

$\approx 38{,}800$

84. $P(t) = 0.5^{\,t/5730} = 0.96$ [4.6]

$\log\left(0.5^{\,t/5730}\right) = \log 0.96$

$\dfrac{t}{5730} \log 0.5 = \log 0.96$

$\dfrac{t}{5730} = \dfrac{\log 0.96}{\log 0.5}$

$t = 5730\left(\dfrac{\log 0.96}{\log 0.5}\right) \approx 340$ years

85. **a.**

linear: $P = -633121t + 7{,}599{,}401$, $\ r \approx -0.93813$

exponential: $P = 64{,}717{,}271\left(0.91674359^t\right)$, $\ r \approx -0.95228$

logarithmic: $P = 29{,}163{,}839 - 6{,}052{,}740 \ln t$, $\ r \approx -0.94256$

b. The exponential equation provides a better fit to the data.

c. $P = 64{,}717{,}271\left(0.91674359^{106}\right) = 1{,}040{,}000$ [4.7]

86. **a.**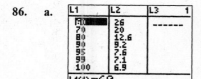

linear: $P = -0.475297t + 53.1037$, $\ r \approx -0.98118$

exponential: $P = 207.544\left(0.966206^t\right)$, $\ r \approx -0.99660$

logarithmic: $P = 181.202 - 38.0586 \ln t$, $\ r \approx -0.99073$

b. The exponential equation provides a better fit to the data.

c. $P = 207.544\left(0.966206^{108}\right) = 5.1$ per 1000 live births [4.7]

87.   **a.**

$$P(t) = \frac{mP_0}{P_0 + (m - P_0)e^{-kt}}$$

$$P(3) = 360 = \frac{1400(210)}{210 + (1400 - 210)e^{-k(3)}}$$

$$360 = \frac{294000}{210 + 1190e^{-3k}}$$

$$360\left(210 + 1190e^{-3k}\right) = 294000$$

$$210 + 1190e^{-3k} = \frac{294000}{360}$$

$$1190e^{-3k} = \frac{29400}{36} - 210$$

$$e^{-3k} = \frac{29400/36 - 210}{1190}$$

$$\ln e^{-3k} = \ln\left(\frac{29400/36 - 210}{1190}\right)$$

$$-3k = \ln\left(\frac{29400/36 - 210}{1190}\right)$$

$$k = -\frac{1}{3}\ln\left(\frac{29400/36 - 210}{1190}\right)$$

$$k \approx 0.2245763649$$

$$P(t) = \frac{294000}{210 + 1190e^{-0.22458t}} = \frac{1400}{1 + \frac{17}{3}e^{-0.22458t}}$$

b.

$$P(13) = \frac{294000}{210 + 1190e^{-0.22458(13)}}$$

$$= \frac{294000}{210 + 1190e^{-2.919492744}}$$

$$\approx 1070 \qquad [4.6]$$

88.   **a.**

$$P(0) = \frac{128}{1 + 5e^{-0.27(0)}} = \frac{128}{1 + 5e^0} = \frac{128}{1 + 5} = \frac{128}{6} = 21\frac{1}{3}$$

b.   As $t \to \infty$, $e^{-0.27t} \to 0$.

$$P(t) \to \frac{128}{1 + 5(0)} = \frac{128}{1} = 128 \quad [4.6]$$

••

Chapter **T**est

1.

$$y = 2x - 3 \quad [4.1]$$

$$x = 2y - 3$$

$$x + 3 = 2y$$

$$\frac{1}{2}x + \frac{3}{2} = y$$

$$f^{-1}(x) = \frac{1}{2}x + \frac{3}{2}$$

2.

$$f(x) = y = \frac{x}{4x - 8} \quad [4.1]$$

$$x = \frac{y}{4y - 8}$$

$$x(4y - 8) = y$$

$$4xy - 8x = y$$

$$4xy - y = 8x$$

$$y(4x - 1) = 8x$$

$$y = \frac{8x}{4x - 1}$$

$$f^{-1}(x) = \frac{8x}{4x - 1}$$

$$4x - 1 \neq 0 \Rightarrow 4x \neq 1 \Rightarrow x \neq \frac{1}{4}$$

Domain of f^{-1}: all real numbers except $\frac{1}{4}$.

Range of f^{-1} = domain of $f \Rightarrow 4x - 8 \neq 0 \Rightarrow x \neq 2$.

Range of f^{-1}: all real numbers except 2.

3. **a.** $\log_b(5x-3)=c$ [4.3]

$b^c = 5x - 3$

b. $3^{x/2} = y$

$\log_3 y = \dfrac{x}{2}$

4. $\log_b \dfrac{z^2}{y^3\sqrt{x}} = \log_b z^2 - \log_b y^3 - \log_b x^{1/2}$ [4.4]

$\qquad\qquad = 2\log_b z - 3\log_b y - \dfrac{1}{2}\log_b x$

5. $\log_{10}(2x+3)-3\log_{10}(x-2)=\log_{10}(2x+3)-\log_{10}(x-2)^3$

$\qquad\qquad\qquad =\log_{10}\dfrac{2x+3}{(x-2)^3}$ [4.4]

6. $\log_4 12 = \dfrac{\log 12}{\log 4}$ [4.4]

$\qquad \approx 1.7925$

7.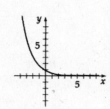

8.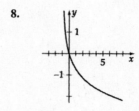

9. $5^x = 22$ [4.5]

$x\log 5 = \log 22$

$x = \dfrac{\log 22}{\log 5}$

$x \approx 1.9206$

10. $4^{5-x} = 7^x$ [4.5]

$\ln 4^{5-x} = \ln 7^x$

$(5-x)\ln 4 = x\ln 7$

$5\ln 4 - x\ln 4 = x\ln 7$

$5\ln 4 = x\ln 7 + x\ln 4$

$5\ln 4 = x(\ln 7 + \ln 4)$

$\dfrac{5\ln 4}{\ln 28} = x$

11. $\log(x+99)-\log(3x-2)=2$ [4.5]

$\log\dfrac{x+99}{3x-2}=2$

$\dfrac{x+99}{3x-2}=10^2$

$x+99=100(3x-2)$

$x+99=300x-200$

$-299x=-299$

$x=1$

12. $\ln(2-x)+\ln(5-x)=\ln(37-x)$

$\ln(2-x)(5-x)=\ln(37-x)$

$(2-x)(5-x)=(37-x)$

$10-7x+x^2=37-x$

$x^2-6x-27=0$

$(x-9)(x+3)=0$

$x=9 \text{ (not in domain) or } x=-3$

$x=-3$ [4.5]

13. **a.** $A = P\left(1+\dfrac{r}{n}\right)^{nt}$ [4.6]

$= 20,000\left(1+\dfrac{0.078}{12}\right)^{12(5)}$

$= 20,000(1.0065)^{60}$

$= \$29,502.36$

b. $A = Pe^{rt}$

$= 20,000e^{0.078(5)}$

$= 20,000e^{0.39}$

$= \$29,539.62$

14. $A = P\left(1+\dfrac{r}{n}\right)^{nt}$ [4.6]

$2P = P\left(1+\dfrac{0.04}{12}\right)^{12t}$

$2 = \left(1+\dfrac{0.04}{12}\right)^{12t}$

$\ln 2 = \ln\left(1+\dfrac{0.04}{12}\right)^{12t}$

$\ln 2 = 12t\ln\left(1+\dfrac{0.04}{12}\right)$

$12t = \dfrac{\ln 2}{\ln\left(1+\dfrac{0.04}{12}\right)}$

$t = \dfrac{1}{12}\cdot\dfrac{\ln 2}{\ln\left(1+\dfrac{0.04}{12}\right)}$

$t \approx 17.36 \text{ years}$

15. **a.**

$$M = \log\left(\frac{I}{I_0}\right) \qquad [4.4]$$

$$= \log\left(\frac{42{,}304{,}000 I_0}{I_0}\right)$$

$$= \log 42{,}304{,}000$$

$$\approx 7.6$$

b.

$$\log\left(\frac{I_1}{I_0}\right) = 6.3 \qquad \text{and} \qquad \log\left(\frac{I_2}{I_0}\right) = 4.5$$

$$\frac{I_1}{I_0} = 10^{6.3} \qquad\qquad \frac{I_2}{I_0} = 10^{4.5}$$

$$I_1 = 10^{6.3} I_0 \qquad\qquad I_2 = 10^{4.5} I_0$$

$$\frac{I_1}{I_2} = \frac{10^{6.3} I_0}{10^{4.5} I_0} = \frac{10^{1.8}}{1} \approx \frac{63}{1}$$

Therefore the ratio is 63 to 1.

17.

$$P(t) = 0.5^{\,t/5730} = 0.92 \quad [4.6]$$

$$\log 0.5^{\,t/5730} = \log 0.92$$

$$\frac{t}{5730}\log 0.5 = \log 0.92$$

$$\frac{t}{5730} = \frac{\log 0.92}{\log 0.5}$$

$$t = 5730\left(\frac{\log 0.92}{\log 0.5}\right)$$

$$t \approx 690 \text{ years}$$

18. **a.**

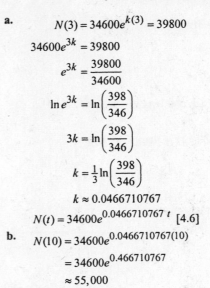

$$y = 1.671991998(2.471878247)^{\,x}$$

b.

$$y = 1.671991998(2.471878247)^{7.8} \quad [4.7]$$

$$\approx 1945$$

16. **a.**

$$N(3) = 34600e^{k(3)} = 39800$$

$$34600e^{3k} = 39800$$

$$e^{3k} = \frac{39800}{34600}$$

$$\ln e^{3k} = \ln\left(\frac{398}{346}\right)$$

$$3k = \ln\left(\frac{398}{346}\right)$$

$$k = \frac{1}{3}\ln\left(\frac{398}{346}\right)$$

$$k \approx 0.0466710767$$

$$N(t) = 34600e^{0.0466710767\,t} \quad [4.6]$$

b.

$$N(10) = 34600e^{0.0466710767(10)}$$

$$= 34600e^{0.466710767}$$

$$\approx 55{,}000$$

19. **a.**

$$R(t) = 1.74830 + 0.78089\ln t$$

$$R(3.5) = 1.74830 + 0.78089\ln 3.5$$

$$\approx 2.73$$

The predicted interest rate for 3.5 years is 2.73%.

b.

$$1.74830 + 0.78089\ln t = 2.5 \qquad [4.7]$$

$$0.78089\ln t = 0.7517$$

$$\ln t = \frac{0.7517}{0.78089}$$

$$e^{\ln t} = e^{0.7517/0.78089}$$

$$t = e^{0.7517/0.78089}$$

$$t \approx 2.6 \text{ years}$$

20. **a.**

$$a = \frac{c - P_0}{P_0} = \frac{1100 - 160}{160} = 5.875$$

$$P(t) = \frac{c}{1 + ae^{-bt}}$$

$$P(1) = \frac{1100}{1 + 5.875e^{-b(1)}}$$

$$190 = \frac{1100}{1 + 5.875e^{-b}}$$

$$190(1 + 5.875e^{-b}) = 1100$$

$$190 + 1116.25e^{-b} = 1100$$

$$1116.25e^{-b} = 910$$

$$e^{-b} = \frac{910}{1116.25}$$

$$\ln e^{-b} = \ln \frac{910}{1116.25}$$

$$-b = \ln \frac{910}{1116.25}$$

$$b = -\ln \frac{910}{1116.25}$$

$$b \approx 0.20429$$

$$P(t) = \frac{1100}{1 + 5.875e^{-0.20429t}} \quad [4.6]$$

b.

$$P(t) = \frac{1100}{1 + 5.875e^{-0.20429(7)}} \approx 457 \text{ raccoons}$$

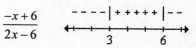

1. $|x - 4| \le 2 \Rightarrow -2 \le x - 4 \le 2 \Rightarrow 2 \le x \le 6$. The solution is [2, 6]. [1.5]

2.

$$\frac{x}{2x - 6} \ge 1 \quad [1.5]$$

$$\frac{x}{2x - 6} - 1 \ge 0$$

$$\frac{x}{2x - 6} - \frac{2x - 6}{2x - 6} \ge 0$$

$$\frac{x - 2x + 6}{2x - 6} \ge 0$$

$$\frac{-x + 6}{2x - 6} \ge 0$$

The critical values are:
$-x + 6 = 0$ or $2x - 6 = 0$
$x = 6$ $\qquad\qquad x = 3$
The intervals are:
$(-\infty, 3), (3, 6),$ and $(6, \infty)$.
The quotient
$\frac{-x + 6}{2x - 6}$ is positive or zero.

$\frac{-x + 6}{2x - 6}$

The denominator $\ne 0 \Rightarrow x \ne 3$.
The solution is $\{x \mid 3 < x \le 6\}$.

3.

$$d = \sqrt{(11 - 5)^2 + (7 - 2)^2} \quad [2.1]$$

$$= \sqrt{6^2 + 5^2} = \sqrt{36 + 25}$$

$$= \sqrt{61} \approx 7.8$$

4. Find the y-value of the vertex of [2.4]
$h(t) = -16t^2 + 44t + 8$.

$$-\frac{b}{2a} = -\frac{44}{2(-16)} = 1.375$$

$$h(1.375) = -16(1.375)^2 + 44(1.375) + 8$$

$$= 38.25 \text{ feet}$$

5.

$f(x) = 2x + 1$ [2.6]

$g(x) = x^2 - 5$

$(g \circ f)(x) = g[f(x)]$

$\qquad = g(2x + 1)$

$\qquad = (2x + 1)^2 - 5$

$\qquad = 4x^2 + 4x + 1 - 5$

$\qquad = 4x^2 + 4x - 4$

6.

$f(x) = 3x - 5$ [4.1]

$x = 3y - 5$

$x + 5 = 3y$

$\frac{1}{3}x + \frac{5}{3} = y$

$f^{-1}(x) = \frac{1}{3}x + \frac{5}{3}$

7.

$L = kwd^2$

$1500 = k(4)(8)^2$

$1500 = 256k$

$\frac{1500}{256} = \frac{375}{64} = k$

$L = \frac{375}{64}wd^2$

$L = \frac{375}{64}(6)(10)^2$

$L \approx 3500$ pounds   [1.6]

8.

$P(x) = x^4 - 3x^3 + x^2 - x - 6$ has three changes of sign. There are three or one positive real zeros.

$P(-x) = x^4 + 3x^3 + x^2 + x - 6$ has one change of sign. There is one negative real zero. [3.3]

9.

$P(x) = x^4 - 5x^3 + x^2 + 15x - 12$ has three or one positive and one negative real zeros. [3.3]

$\frac{p}{q} = \pm 1, \ \pm 2, \ \pm 3, \ \pm 4, \ \pm 6, \ \pm 12$ are the possible rational zeros.

1	1	−5	1	15	−12
		1	−4	−3	12
	1	−4	−3	12	0

4	1	−4	−3	12
		4	0	−12
	1	0	−3	0

$x^2 - 3 = 0 \Rightarrow x^2 = 3 \Rightarrow x = \pm\sqrt{3}$ The zeros are 1, 4, $-\sqrt{3}$, $\sqrt{3}$.

10.

$P(x) = (x - 2)[x - (1 - i)][x - (1 + i)] = (x - 2)[x - 1 + i][x - 1 - i] = (x - 2)[(x - 1) + i][(x - 1) - i]$ [3.4]

$\qquad = (x - 2)[(x - 1)^2 - i^2] = (x - 2)[x^2 - 2x + 1 - (-1)] = (x - 2)[x^2 - 2x + 1 + 1] = (x - 2)(x^2 - 2x + 2)$

$\qquad = x(x^2 - 2x + 2) - 2(x^2 - 2x + 2) = x^3 - 2x^2 + 2x - 2x^2 + 4x - 4 = x^3 - 4x^2 + 6x - 4$

11.

$r(x) = \frac{3x - 5}{x - 4}$ [3.5]

Vertical asymptote:

$x - 4 = 0 \Rightarrow x = 4$

Horizontal asymptote:

$(n = m) \Rightarrow y = \frac{3}{1} \Rightarrow y = 3$

12.

$R(x) = \frac{4}{x^2 + 1}$. The denominator of $R(x)$ will not equal zero for any real value of x. Thus, there are no restrictions on the domain. The domain is all real numbers. $R(x)$ is positive for all values of x. The smallest denominator value is 1, thus the highest $R(x)$ value is 4. The range is $\{y \mid 0 < y \le 4\}$. [3.5]

13.

$f(x) = 0.4^x$ is a decreasing function since $0.4 < 1$. [4.2]

14.

$\log_4 x = y \Rightarrow 4^y = x$ [4.3]

15.

$5^3 = 125 \Rightarrow \log_5 125 = 3$ [4.3]

16.

$M = \log \frac{I}{I_0} = \log \frac{11,650,600 I_0}{I_0} = \log 11,650,600 \approx 7.1$ [4.4]

17.

$2e^x = 15 \Rightarrow e^x = 7.5 \Rightarrow \ln e^x = \ln 7.5 \Rightarrow x = \ln 7.5 \Rightarrow x \approx 2.0149$ [4.5]

18.
$$0.5N_0 = N_0e^{5730k} \Rightarrow 0.5 = e^{5730k} \Rightarrow \ln 0.5 = \ln e^{5730k} \Rightarrow \ln 0.5 = 5730k \Rightarrow k = \frac{\ln 0.5}{5730} \approx -0.000121 \quad [4.6]$$

$$N(t) = N_0e^{-0.000121t} \Rightarrow 0.94N_0 = N_0e^{-0.000121t} \Rightarrow 0.94 = e^{-0.000121t} \Rightarrow \ln 0.94 = \ln e^{-0.000121t}$$

$$\Rightarrow \ln 0.94 = -0.000121t \Rightarrow t = \frac{\ln 0.94}{-0.000121} \approx 510 \text{ years old}$$

19.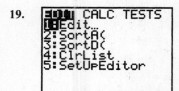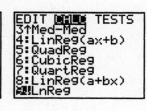

a. $y \approx 84.41319 + 4.88166 \ln x$

b. $y \approx 84.41319 + 4.88166 \ln 21 \approx 99.28$ meters   [4.7]

20.   a.
$$a = \frac{c - P_0}{P_0} = \frac{450 - 160}{160} = \frac{290}{160} = 1.8125 \quad [4.7]$$

$$P(3) = \frac{450}{1 + 1.8125e^{k(3)}} \Rightarrow 205 = \frac{450}{1 + 1.8125e^{3k}} \Rightarrow 205(1 + 1.8125e^{3k}) = 450 \Rightarrow 205 + 371.5625e^{3k} = 450$$

$$\Rightarrow 371.5625e^{3k} = 245 \Rightarrow e^{3k} = \frac{245}{371.5625} \Rightarrow \ln e^{3k} = \ln \frac{245}{371.5625}$$

$$\Rightarrow 3k = \ln 245 - \ln 371.5625 \Rightarrow k = \frac{\ln 245 - \ln 371.5625}{3} \Rightarrow k \approx -0.13882$$

$$P(t) \approx \frac{450}{1 + 1.8125e^{-0.13882t}}$$

b.
$$P(10) \approx \frac{450}{1 + 1.8125e^{-0.13882(10)}} \approx 310 \text{ wolves}$$

Chapter 5
Topics in Analytic Geometry

Section 5.1

1.
$$x^2 = -4y$$
$$4p = -4$$
$$p = -1$$
vertex $= (0,\ 0)$
focus $= (0,\ -1)$
directrix: $y = 1$

3.
$$y^2 = \tfrac{1}{3}x$$
$$4p = \tfrac{1}{3}$$
$$p = \tfrac{1}{12}$$
vertex $= (0,\ 0)$
focus $= \left(\tfrac{1}{12},\ 0\right)$
directrix: $x = -\tfrac{1}{12}$

5.
$$(x-2)^2 = 8(y+3)$$
vertex $= (2,-3)$
$4p = 8 \quad p = 2$
$(h, k+p) = (2, -3+2) = (2, -1)$
focus $= (2, -1)$
$k - p = -3 - 2 = -5$
directrix $: y = -5$

7.
$$(y+4)^2 = -4(x-2)$$
vertex $= (2, -4)$
$4p = -4 \quad p = -1$
$(h+p, k) = (2-1, -4) = (1, -4)$
focus $= (1, -4)$
$h - p = 2 + 1 = 3$
directrix $: x = 3$

9.
$$(y-1)^2 = 2(x+4)$$
vertex $= (-4, 1)$
$4p = 2 \quad p = \dfrac{1}{2}$
$(h+p, k) = \left(-4 + \dfrac{1}{2}, 1\right) = \left(-\dfrac{7}{2}, 1\right)$
focus $= \left(-\dfrac{7}{2}, 1\right)$
$h - p = -4 - \dfrac{1}{2} = -\dfrac{9}{2}$
directrix $: x = -\dfrac{9}{2}$

11.
$$(x-2)^2 = 2(y-2)$$
vertex $= (2,\ 2)$
$4p = 2 \quad p = \dfrac{1}{2}$
$(h, k+p) = \left(2,\ 2 + \dfrac{1}{2}\right) = \left(2,\ \dfrac{5}{2}\right)$
focus $= \left(2,\ \dfrac{5}{2}\right)$
$k - p = 2 - \dfrac{1}{2} = \dfrac{3}{2}$
directrix: $y = \dfrac{3}{2}$

13.
$x^2 + 8x - y + 6 = 0$

$x^2 + 8x = y - 6$

$x^2 + 8x + 16 = y - 6 + 16$

$(x+4)^2 = y + 10$

vertex $= (-4, -10)$

$4p = 1, \ p = \frac{1}{4}$

focus $= \left(-4, \ -\frac{39}{4}\right)$

directrix: $y = -\frac{41}{4}$

15.
$x + y^2 - 3y + 4 = 0$

$y^2 - 3y = -x - 4$

$y^2 - 3y + 9/4 = -x - 4 + 9/4$

$\left(y - \frac{3}{2}\right)^2 = -\left(x + \frac{7}{4}\right)$

vertex $= \left(-\frac{7}{4}, \ \frac{3}{2}\right)$

$4p = -1, \ p = -\frac{1}{4}$

focus $= \left(-2, \ \frac{3}{2}\right)$

directrix: $x = -\frac{3}{2}$

17.
$2x - y^2 - 6y + 1 = 0$

$-y^2 - 6y = -2x - 1$

$y^2 + 6y = 2x + 1$

$y^2 + 6y + 9 = 2x + 1 + 9$

$(y+3)^2 = 2(x+5)$

vertex $= (-5, -3)$

$4p = 2, \ p = \frac{1}{2}$

focus $= \left(-\frac{9}{2}, \ -3\right)$

directrix: $x = -\frac{11}{2}$

17.
$2x - y^2 - 6y + 1 = 0$

$-y^2 - 6y = -2x - 1$

$y^2 + 6y = 2x + 1$

$y^2 + 6y + 9 = 2x + 1 + 9$

$(y+3)^2 = 2(x+5)$

vertex $= (-5, -3)$

$4p = 2, \ p = \frac{1}{2}$

focus $= \left(-\frac{9}{2}, \ -3\right)$

directrix: $x = -\frac{11}{2}$

19.
$x^2 + 3x + 3y - 1 = 0$

$x^2 + 3x = -3y + 1$

$x^2 + 3x + 9/4 = -3y + 1 + 9/4$

$\left(x + \frac{3}{2}\right)^2 = -3\left(y - \frac{13}{12}\right)$

vertex $\left(-\frac{3}{2}, \ \frac{13}{12}\right)$

$4p = -3, \ p = -\frac{3}{4}$

focus $= \left(-\frac{3}{2}, \ \frac{1}{3}\right)$

directrix: $y = \frac{11}{6}$

21.
$2x^2 - 8x - 4y + 3 = 0$

$2(x^2 - 4x) = 4y - 3$

$2(x^2 - 4x + 4) = 4y - 3 + 8$

$2(x-2)^2 = 4y + 5$

$(x-2)^2 = 2y + \frac{5}{2}$

$(x-2)^2 = 2\left(y + \frac{5}{4}\right)$

vertex $= \left(2, \ -\frac{5}{4}\right), \ 4p = 2, \ p = \frac{1}{2}$

focus $= \left(2, \ -\frac{3}{4}\right)$

directrix $y = -\frac{7}{4}$

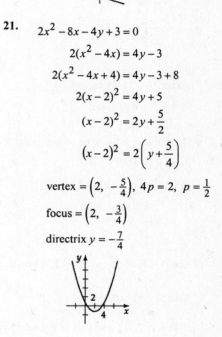

23.
$$2x + 4y^2 + 8y - 5 = 0$$
$$4y^2 + 8y = -2x + 5$$
$$4(y^2 + 2y) = -2x + 5$$
$$4(y^2 + 2y + 1) = -2x + 5 + 4$$
$$4(y + 1)^2 = -2x + 9$$
$$(y + 1)^2 = -\frac{1}{2}x + \frac{9}{4}$$
$$(y + 1)^2 = -\frac{1}{2}\left(x - \frac{9}{2}\right)$$
vertex $= \left(\frac{9}{2}, -1\right)$

$4p = -\frac{1}{2}, \quad p = -\frac{1}{8}$

focus $= \left(\frac{35}{8}, -1\right)$

directrix $x = \frac{37}{8}$

25.
$$(x - 1)^2 = 3\left(y - \frac{1}{9}\right)$$
vertex $= \left(1, \frac{1}{9}\right), \quad 4p = 3, \quad p = \frac{3}{4}$

focus $= \left(1, \frac{31}{36}\right)$

directrix $y = -\frac{23}{36}$

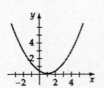

27. vertex $(0, 0)$, focus $(0, -4)$

$$x^2 = 4py$$

$p = -4$ since focus is $(0, p)$

$$x^2 = 4(-4)y$$
$$x^2 = -16y$$

29. vertex $(-1, 2)$, focus $(-1, 3)$

$$(x - h)^2 = 4p(y - k)$$

$h = -1, \quad k = 2.$

The distance p from the vertex to the focus is 1.

$$(x + 1)^2 = 4(1)(y - 2)$$
$$(x + 1)^2 = 4(y - 2)$$

31. focus $(3, -3)$, directrix $y = -5$

The vertex is the midpoint of the line segment joining $(3, -3)$ and the point $(3, -5)$ on the directrix.

$$(h, k) = \left(\frac{3 + 2}{2}, \frac{-3 + (-5)}{2}\right) = (3, -4)$$

The distance p from the vertex to the focus is 1.

$$4p = 4(1) = 4$$
$$(x - h)^2 = 4p(y - k)$$
$$(x - 3)^2 = 4(y + 4)$$

33. vertex $= (-4, 1)$, point: $(-2, 2)$ on the parabola.

Axis of symmetry $x = -4$.

If $P_1 = (-2, 2)$ and axis of symmetry is $x = -4$, then we must

have $(x + 4)^2 = 4p(y - 1)$. Since $(-2, 2)$ is on the curve, we get

$$(-2 + 4)^2 = 4p(2 - 1)$$
$$4 = 4p \Rightarrow p = 1$$

Thus, the equation in standard form is

$$(x + 4)^2 = 4(y - 1)$$

35. Find the vertex.

$$x = -0.325y^2 + 13y + 120$$
$$x - 120 = -0.325y^2 + 13y$$
$$x - 120 = -0.325(y^2 - 40y)$$
$$x - 120 - 130 = -0.325(y^2 - 40y + 400)$$
$$x - 250 = -0.325(y - 20)^2$$
$$-\frac{40}{13}(x - 250) = (y - 20)^2$$

The vertex is $(250, 20)$.

Find the focus.

$$4p = -\frac{40}{13}, \quad p = -\frac{10}{13}$$

The focus is $\left(\frac{3240}{13}, 20\right)$.

37. Place the satellite dish on an xy-coordinate system with its vertex at $(0, -1)$ as shown.

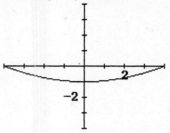

The equation of the parabola is $x^2 = 4p(y+1)$ $-1 \le y \le 0$

Because $(4, 0)$ is a point on this graph, $(4, 0)$ must be a solution of the equation of the parabola. Thus,

$16 = 4p(0+1)$

$16 = 4p$

$4 = p$

Because p is the distance from the vertex to the focus, the focus is on the x-axis 4 feet above the vertex.

39. The focus of the parabola is $(p, 0)$ where $y^2 = 4px$.
Half of 18.75 inches is 9.375 inches.
Therefore, the point $(3.66, 9.375)$ is on the parabola.

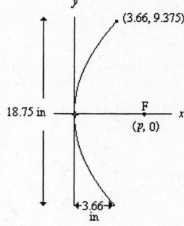

$(9.375)^2 = 4p(3.66)$

$87.890625 = 14.64p$

$\dfrac{87.890625}{14.64} = p$

$p \approx 6.0$ inches

41.

$$S = \frac{\pi r}{6d^2}\left[\left(r^2 + 4d^2\right)^{3/2} - r^3\right]$$

a. $r = 40.5$ feet
$d = 16$ feet

$$S = \frac{\pi(40.5)}{6(16)^2}\left[\left([40.5]^2 + 4[16]^2\right)^{3/2} - (40.5)^3\right]$$

$$= \frac{40.5\pi}{1536}\left[(266.25)^{3/2} - 66430.125\right]$$

$$= \frac{40.5\pi}{1536}[137518.9228 - 66430.125]$$

$$= \frac{40.5\pi}{1536}[71088.79775]$$

$$\approx 5900 \text{ square feet}$$

b. $r = 125$ feet
$d = 52$ feet

$$S = \frac{\pi(125)}{6(52)^2}\left[\left([125]^2 + 4[52]^2\right)^{3/2} - (125)^3\right]$$

$$= \frac{125\pi}{16224}\left[(26441)^{3/2} - 1953125\right]$$

$$= \frac{125\pi}{16224}[4299488.724 - 1953125]$$

$$= \frac{125\pi}{16224}[2346363.724]$$

$$\approx 56,800 \text{ square feet}$$

43. The equation of the mirror is given by

$x^2 = 4py$ $-60 \le x \le 60$

Because p is the distance from the vertex to the focus and the coordinates of the focus are $(0, 600)$, $p = 600$.
Therefore,

$x^2 = 4(600)y$

$x^2 = 2400y$

To determine a, substitute $(60, a)$ into the equation $x^2 = 2400y$ and solve for a.

$x^2 = 2400y$

$60^2 = 2400a$

$3600 = 2400a$

$1.5 = a.$

The concave depth of the mirror is 1.5 inches.

45. $(-0.3660, -0.3660), (1.3660, 1.3660)$

47. $(-1.5616, 3.8769), (2.5616, 12.1231)$

49.
$$x^2 = 4y$$
$$4p = 4$$
$$p = 1$$

focus $= (0, 1)$

Substituting the vertical coordinate of the focus for y to obtain x-coordinates of endpoints (x_1, y_1), (x_2, y_2), we have

$$x^2 = 4(1), \text{ or } x^2 = 4$$
$$x = \pm\sqrt{4}$$
$$x_1 = -2 \quad x_2 = 2$$

Length of latus rectum $= |x_2 - x_1|$
$$= 2 - (-2) = 4.$$

51.
$$(x - h)^2 = 4p(y - k)$$

focus $= (h, k + p)$

Substituting the vertical coordinate of the focus for y to obtain x-coordinates of endpoints (x_1, y_1), (x_2, y_2), we have

$$(x - h)^2 = 4p(k + p - k)$$
$$(x - h)^2 = 4p^2$$
$$x - h = \pm 2p$$
$$x_1 = h - 2p \quad x_2 = h + 2p$$

Solving for $|x_2 - x_1|$, we obtain
$$\Delta x = |x_2 - x_1| = |h + 2p - h + 2p| = 4|p|$$
or $(y - k)^2 = 4p(x - h)$

focus $= (h + p, k)$

Substituting the horizontal coordinate of the focus for x to obtain the y-coordinates of the endpoints (x_1, y_1), (x_2, y_2), we have

$$(y - k)^2 = 4p(h + p - h)$$
$$(y - k)^2 = 4p^2$$
$$y - k = \pm 2p$$
$$y_1 = k - 2p \quad y_2 = k + 2p$$

Solving for $|y_2 - y_1|$, we obtain $\Delta y = |y_2 - y_1|$
$$= |k + 2p - k + 2p|$$
$$= 4|p|$$

Thus, the length of the latus rectum is $4|p|$.

53.

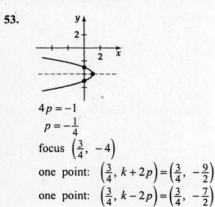

$$4p = -1$$
$$p = -\frac{1}{4}$$

focus $\left(\frac{3}{4}, -4\right)$

one point: $\left(\frac{3}{4}, k + 2p\right) = \left(\frac{3}{4}, -\frac{9}{2}\right)$

one point: $\left(\frac{3}{4}, k - 2p\right) = \left(\frac{3}{4}, -\frac{7}{2}\right)$

55. Graph $y = \frac{7}{4} + \frac{1}{4}x|x|$.

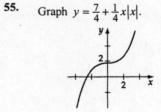

57. By definition, any point on the curve (x, y) will be equidistant from both the focus $(1, 1)$ and the directrix, $(y_2 = -x_2 - 2)$.

If we let d_1 equal the distance from the focus to the point (x, y), we get $d_1 = \sqrt{(x-1)^2 + (y-1)^2}$

To determine the distance d_2 from the point (x, y) to the line $y = -x - 2$, draw a line segment from (x, y) to the directrix so as to meet the directrix at a 90° angle.

Now drop a line segment parallel to the y-axis from (x, y) to the directrix. This segment will meet the directrix at a 45° angle, thus forming a right isosceles triangle with the directrix and the line segment perpendicular to the directrix from (x, y). The length of this segment, which is the hypotenuse of the triangle, is the difference between y and the y-value of the directrix at x, or $-x - 2$. Thus, the

hypotenuse has a length of $y + x + 2$, and since the right triangle is also isosceles, each leg has a length of $\dfrac{y + x + 2}{\sqrt{2}}$.

But since d_2 is the length of the leg drawn from (x, y) to the directrix, $d_2 = \dfrac{y + x + 2}{\sqrt{2}}$.

Thus, $d_1 = \sqrt{(x-1)^2 + (y-1)^2}$ and $d_2 = \dfrac{x + y + 2}{\sqrt{2}}$.

By definition, $d_1 = d_2$. So, by substitution,

$$\sqrt{(x-1)^2 + (y-1)^2} = \frac{x + y + 2}{\sqrt{2}}$$

$$\sqrt{2}\sqrt{(x-1)^2 + (y-1)^2} = x + y + 2$$

$$2\left[(x-1)^2 + (y-1)^2\right] = x^2 + y^2 + 4x + 4y + 2xy + 4$$

$$2\left(x^2 - 2x + 1 + y^2 - 2y + 1\right) = x^2 + y^2 + 4x + 4y + 2xy + 4$$

$$2x^2 - 4x + 2y^2 - 4y + 4 = x^2 + y^2 + 4x + 4y + 2xy + 4$$

$$x^2 + y^2 - 8x - 8y - 2xy = 0$$

•   **P**repare for **S**ection **5.2**

58. midpoint: $\dfrac{x_1 + x_2}{2} \qquad \dfrac{y_1 + y_2}{2}$

$\dfrac{5 + -1}{2} = 2 \qquad \dfrac{1 + 5}{2} = 3$

The midpoint is $(2, 3)$.

length: $\sqrt{(x_2 - x_1)^2 + (y_2 - y_1)^2}$

$\sqrt{(-1 - 5)^2 + (5 - 1)^2} = \sqrt{36 + 16} = \sqrt{52} = 2\sqrt{13}$

The length is $2\sqrt{13}$.

59. $x^2 + 6x - 16 = 0$

$(x + 8)(x - 2) = 0$

$x + 8 = 0 \qquad x - 2 = 0$

$\qquad x = -8 \qquad x = 2$

The solutions are $-8, 2$.

60. $x^2 - 2x = 2$

$x^2 - 2x + 1 = 2 + 1$

$(x - 1)^2 = 3$

$x - 1 = \pm\sqrt{3}$

$x = 1 \pm \sqrt{3}$

61. $x^2 - 8x + 16 = (x - 4)^2$

62. $(x - 2)^2 + y^2 = 4$

$y^2 = 4 - (x - 2)^2$

$y = \pm\sqrt{4 - (x - 2)^2}$

63.

$(x - 2)^2 + (y + 3)^2 = 16$

Center: $(2, -3)$, Radius 4

Section 5.2

1.
$$\frac{x^2}{16} + \frac{y^2}{25} = 1$$

$a^2 = 25 \rightarrow a = 5$
$b^2 = 16 \rightarrow b = 4$
$c = \sqrt{a^2 - b^2}$
$\quad = \sqrt{25 - 16}$
$\quad = \sqrt{9}$
$\quad = 3$

Center $(0, 0)$
Vertices $(0, \pm 5)$
Foci $(0, \pm 3)$

3.
$$\frac{x^2}{9} + \frac{y^2}{4} = 1$$

$a^2 = 9 \rightarrow a = 3$
$b^2 = 4 \rightarrow b = 2$
$c = \sqrt{a^2 - b^2}$
$\quad = \sqrt{9 - 4}$
$\quad = \sqrt{5}$

Center $(0, 0)$
Vertices $(\pm 3, 0)$
Foci $\left(\pm\sqrt{5}, 0\right)$

5.
$$\frac{x^2}{7} + \frac{y^2}{9} = 1$$

$a^2 = 9 \rightarrow a = 3$
$b^2 = 7 \rightarrow b = \sqrt{7}$
$c = \sqrt{a^2 - b^2}$
$\quad = \sqrt{9 - 7}$
$\quad = \sqrt{2}$

Center $(0, 0)$
Vertices $(0, \pm 3)$
Foci $\left(0, \pm\sqrt{2}\right)$

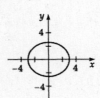

7.
$$\frac{4x^2}{9} + \frac{y^2}{16} = 1$$

Rewrite as
$$\frac{x^2}{9/4} + \frac{y^2}{16} = 1$$

$a^2 = 16 \rightarrow a = 4$
$b^2 = 9/4 \rightarrow b = 3/2$
$c = \sqrt{a^2 - b^2}$
$\quad = \sqrt{16 - 9/4}$
$\quad = \sqrt{55}/2$

Center $(0, 0)$
Vertices $(0, \pm 4)$
Foci $\left(0, \pm \dfrac{\sqrt{55}}{2}\right)$

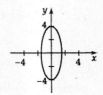

9.
$$\frac{(x-3)^2}{25} + \frac{(y+2)^2}{16} = 1$$

Center $(3, -2)$
Vertices $(3 \pm 5, -2) = (8, -2), (-2, -2)$
Foci $(3 \pm 3, -2) = (6, -2), (0, -2)$

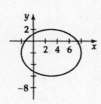

11.
$$\frac{(x+2)^2}{9} + \frac{y^2}{16} = 1$$

Center $(-2, 0)$
Vertices $(-2, 5), (-2, -5)$
Foci $(-2, 4), (-2, -4)$

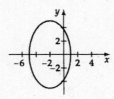

13.
$$\frac{(x-1)^2}{21} + \frac{(y-3)^2}{4} = 1$$
Center $(1, 3)$
Vertices $\left(1 \pm \sqrt{21}, 3\right)$
Foci $\left(1 \pm \sqrt{17}, 3\right)$

15.
$$\frac{9(x-1)^2}{16} + \frac{(y+1)^2}{9} = 1$$
Center $(1, -1)$
Vertices $(1, -1 \pm 3) = (1, 2), (1, -4)$
Foci $\left(1, -1 \pm \frac{\sqrt{65}}{3}\right)$

17.
$$3x^2 + 4y^2 = 12$$
$$\frac{x^2}{4} + \frac{y^2}{3} = 1$$

Center $(0, 0)$
Vertices $(\pm 2, 0)$
Foci $(\pm 1, 0)$

19.
$$25x^2 + 16y^2 = 400$$
$$\frac{x^2}{16} + \frac{y^2}{25} = 1$$

Center $(0, 0)$
Vertices $(0, \pm 5)$
Foci $(0, \pm 3)$

21.
$$64x^2 + 25y^2 = 400$$
$$\frac{x^2}{\frac{25}{4}} + \frac{y^2}{16} = 1$$

Center $(0, 0)$
Vertices $(0, \pm 4)$
Foci $\left(0, \pm \frac{\sqrt{39}}{2}\right)$

23.
$$4x^2 + y^2 - 24x - 8y + 48 = 0$$
$$4\left(x^2 - 6x\right) + \left(y^2 - 8y\right) = -48$$
$$4\left(x^2 - 6x + 9\right) + \left(y^2 - 8y + 16\right) = -48 + 36 + 16$$
$$4(x-3)^3 + (y-4)^2 = 4$$
$$\frac{(x-3)^2}{1} + \frac{(y-4)^2}{4} = 1$$
Center $(3, 4)$
Vertices $(3, 4 \pm 2) = (3, 6), (3, 2)$
Foci $\left(3, 4 \pm \sqrt{3}\right)$

25.
$$5x^2 + 9y^2 - 20x + 54y + 56 = 0$$
$$5\left(x^2 - 4x\right) + 9\left(y^2 + 6y\right) = -56$$
$$5\left(x^2 - 4x + 4\right) + 9\left(y^2 + 6y + 9\right) = -56 + 20 + 81$$
$$5(x-2)^2 + 9(y+3)^2 = 45$$
$$\frac{(x-2)^2}{9} + \frac{(y+3)^2}{5} = 1$$
Center $(2, -3)$
Vertices $(2 \pm 3, -3) = (-1, -3), (5, -3)$
Foci $(2 \pm 2, 3) = (0, -3), (4, -3)$

27.
$$16x^2 + 9y^2 - 64x - 80 = 0$$
$$16(x^2 - 4x) + 9y^2 = 80$$
$$16(x^2 - 4x + 4) + 9y^2 = 80 + 64$$
$$16(x - 2)^2 + 9y^2 = 144$$
$$\frac{(x-2)^2}{9} + \frac{y^2}{16} = 1$$

Center $(2, 0)$
Vertices $(2, \pm 4) = (2, 4), (2, -4)$
Foci $\left(2 \pm \sqrt{7}\right)$

29.
$$25x^2 + 16y^2 + 50x - 32y - 359 = 0$$
$$25(x^2 + 2x) + 16(y^2 - 2y) = 359$$
$$25(x^2 + 2x + 1) + 16(y^2 - 2y + 1) = 359 + 25 + 16$$
$$25(x + 1)^2 + 16(y - 1)^2 = 400$$
$$\frac{(x+1)^2}{16} + \frac{(y-1)^2}{25} = 1$$

Center $(-1, 1)$
Vertices $(-1, 1 \pm 5) = (-1, 6), (-1, -4)$
Foci $(-1, 1 \pm 3) = (-1, 4), (-1, -2)$

31.
$$8x^2 + 25y^2 - 48x + 50y + 47 = 0$$
$$8(x^2 - 6x) + 25(y^2 + 2y) = -47$$
$$8(x^2 - 6x + 9) + 25(y^2 + 2y + 1) = -47 + 72 + 25$$
$$8(x - 3)^2 + 25(y + 1)^2 = 50$$
$$\frac{(x-3)^2}{25/4} + \frac{(y+1)^2}{2} = 1$$

Center: $(3, -1)$

Vertices: $\left(3 \pm \frac{5}{2}, -1\right) = \left(\frac{11}{2}, -1\right), \left(\frac{1}{2}, -1\right)$

Foci: $\left(3 \pm \frac{\sqrt{17}}{2}, -1\right)$

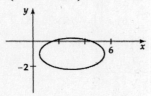

33.
$$2a = 10$$
$$a = 5$$
$$a^2 = 25$$
$$c = 4$$
$$c^2 = a^2 - b^2$$
$$16 = 25 - b^2$$
$$b^2 = 9$$
$$\frac{x^2}{25} + \frac{y^2}{9} = 1$$

35.
$$a = 6$$
$$a^2 = 36$$
$$b = 4$$
$$b^2 = 16$$
$$\frac{x^2}{36} + \frac{y^2}{16} = 1$$

37.
$$2a = 12$$
$$a = 6$$
$$a^2 = 36$$
$$\frac{x^2}{36} + \frac{y^2}{b^2} = 1$$
$$\frac{(2)^2}{36} + \frac{(-3)^2}{b^2} = 1$$
$$\frac{4}{36} + \frac{9}{b^2} = 1$$
$$\frac{9}{b^2} = \frac{8}{9}$$
$$8b^2 = 81$$
$$b^2 = \frac{81}{8}$$
$$\frac{x^2}{36} + \frac{y^2}{81/8} = 1$$

39.
$$c = 3$$
$$2a = 8$$
$$a = 4$$
$$a^2 = 16$$
$$c^2 = a^2 - b^2$$
$$9 = 16 - b^2$$
$$b^2 = 7$$
$$\frac{(x+2)^2}{16} + \frac{(y-4)^2}{7} = 1$$

41.
$$2a = 10$$
$$a = 5$$
$$a^2 = 25$$
Since the center of the ellipse is $(2, 4)$ and the point $(3, 3)$ is on the ellipse, we have
$$\frac{(x-2)^2}{b^2} + \frac{(y-4)^2}{a^2} = 1$$
$$\frac{(3-2)^2}{b^2} + \frac{(3-4)^2}{25} = 1$$
$$\frac{1}{b^2} = 1 - \frac{1}{25}$$
$$b^2 = \frac{25}{24}$$
$$\frac{(x-2)^2}{\frac{25}{24}} + \frac{(y-4)^2}{25} = 1$$

43. center $(5, 1)$
$$c = 3$$
$$2a = 10$$
$$a = 5$$
$$a^2 = 25$$
$$c^2 = a^2 - b^2$$
$$9 = 25 - b^2$$
$$b^2 = 16$$
$$\frac{(x-5)^2}{16} + \frac{(y-1)^2}{25} = 1$$

45.
$$2a = 10$$
$$a = 5$$
$$a^2 = 25$$
$$\frac{c}{a} = \frac{2}{5}$$
$$\frac{c}{5} = \frac{2}{5}$$
$$c = 2$$
$$c^2 = a^2 - b^2$$
$$4 = 25 - b^2$$
$$b^2 = 21$$
$$\frac{x^2}{25} + \frac{y^2}{21} = 1$$

47. center $(0, 0)$
$$c = 4$$
$$\frac{c}{a} = \frac{2}{3}$$
$$\frac{4}{a} = \frac{2}{3}$$
$$a = 6$$
$$c^2 = a^2 - b^2$$
$$16 = 36 - b^2$$
$$b^2 = 20$$
$$\frac{x^2}{20} + \frac{y^2}{36} = 1$$

49. center $(1, 3)$
$$c = 2$$
$$\frac{c}{a} = \frac{2}{5}$$
$$\frac{2}{a} = \frac{2}{5}$$
$$a = 5$$
$$c^2 = a^2 - b^2$$
$$4 = 25 - b^2$$
$$b^2 = 21$$
$$\frac{(x-1)^2}{25} + \frac{(y-3)^2}{21} = 1$$

51.
$$2a = 24$$
$$a = 12$$
$$\frac{c}{a} = \frac{2}{3}$$
$$\frac{c}{12} = \frac{2}{3}$$
$$c = 8$$
$$c^2 = a^2 - b^2$$
$$64 = 144 - b^2$$
$$b^2 = 80$$
$$\frac{x^2}{80} + \frac{y^2}{144} = 1$$

53.
$$484 = 64 + c^2$$
$$c^2 = 420$$
$$c = 20.494$$
$$2c = 40.9878 \approx 41$$
The emitter should be placed 41 cm away.

55. Aphelion $= 2a - $ perihelion
$$934.34 = 2a - 835.14$$
$$a = 884.74 \text{ million miles}$$
Aphelion $= a + c = 934.34$
$$884.74 + c = 934.34$$
$$c = 49.6 \text{ million miles}$$

$$b = \sqrt{a^2 - c^2}$$
$$= \sqrt{884.74^2 - 49.6^2}$$
$$\approx 883.35 \text{ million miles}$$

An equation of the orbit of Saturn is
$$\frac{x^2}{884.74^2} + \frac{y^2}{883.35^2} = 1$$

57. $a = $ semimajor axis $= 50$ feet
$b = $ height $= 30$ feet
$$c^2 = a^2 - b^2$$
$$c^2 = 50^2 - 30^2$$
$$c = \sqrt{1600} = 40$$
The foci are located 40 feet to
the right and to the left of center.

59.
$$2a = 36 \qquad 2b = 9$$
$$a = 18 \qquad b = \frac{9}{2}$$
$$c^2 = a^2 - b^2$$
$$c^2 = 18^2 - \left(\frac{9}{2}\right)^2$$
$$c^2 = 324 - \frac{81}{4}$$
$$c^2 = \frac{1215}{4}$$
$$c = \frac{9\sqrt{15}}{2}$$

Since one focus is at $(0, 0)$, the center
of the ellipse is at $(9\sqrt{15}/2, 0)$
$(17.43, 0)$. The equation of the path of
Halley's Comet in astronomical units is
$$\frac{\left(x - 9\sqrt{15}/2\right)^2}{324} + \frac{y^2}{81/4} = 1$$

61.
$$2a = 16 \Rightarrow a = 8$$
$$2b = 10 \Rightarrow b = 5$$
$$p = \pi\sqrt{2\left(a^2 + b^2\right)}$$
$$= \pi\sqrt{2\left(8^2 + 5^2\right)}$$
$$= \pi\sqrt{2(64 + 25)}$$
$$= \pi\sqrt{2(89)}$$
$$= \pi\sqrt{178} \text{ inches}$$

1 mile $= 5280$ feet $= 5280(12)$ inches $= 63360$ inches

$$\frac{63360 \text{ inches}}{\pi\sqrt{178} \text{ inches per revolution}} \approx 1512 \text{ revolutions}$$

63. a.
$$2a = 615 \Rightarrow a = 307.5$$
$$2b = 510 \Rightarrow b = 255$$
$$\frac{x^2}{307.5^2} + \frac{y^2}{255^2} = 1$$

b.
$$A = \pi a b$$
$$= \pi(307.5)(255)$$
$$= 78412.5\pi$$
$$\approx 246{,}300 \text{ square feet}$$

65. $9y^2 + 36y + 16x^2 - 108 = 0$

$$y = \frac{-36 \pm \sqrt{36^2 - 4(9)(16x^2 - 108)}}{2(9)}$$

$$= \frac{-36 \pm \sqrt{1296 - 36(16x^2 - 108)}}{18}$$

$$= \frac{-36 \pm \sqrt{1296 - 576x^2 + 3888}}{18}$$

$$= \frac{-36 \pm \sqrt{-576x^2 + 5184}}{18}$$

$$= \frac{-36 \pm \sqrt{576(-x^2 + 9)}}{18}$$

$$= \frac{-36 \pm 24\sqrt{(-x^2 + 9)}}{18}$$

$$= \frac{-6 \pm 4\sqrt{(-x^2 + 9)}}{3}$$

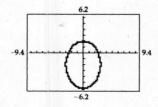

67. $9y^2 - 54y + 16x^2 - 64x + 1 = 0$

$$y = \frac{-(-54) \pm \sqrt{(-54)^2 - 4(9)(16x^2 - 64x + 1)}}{2(9)}$$

$$= \frac{54 \pm \sqrt{2916 - 36(16x^2 - 64x + 1)}}{18}$$

$$= \frac{54 \pm \sqrt{2916 - 576x^2 + 2304x - 36}}{18}$$

$$= \frac{54 \pm \sqrt{-576x^2 + 2304x + 2880}}{18}$$

$$= \frac{54 \pm \sqrt{576(-x^2 + 4x + 5)}}{18}$$

$$= \frac{54 \pm 24\sqrt{-x^2 + 4x + 5}}{18}$$

$$= \frac{9 \pm 4\sqrt{-x^2 + 4x + 5}}{3}$$

69. $9y^2 + 18y + 4x^2 + 24x + 44 = 0$

$$y = \frac{-18 \pm \sqrt{18^2 - 4(9)(4x^2 + 24x + 44)}}{2(9)}$$

$$= \frac{-18 \pm \sqrt{324 - 36(4x^2 + 24x + 44)}}{18}$$

$$= \frac{-18 \pm \sqrt{324 - 144x^2 - 864x - 1584}}{18}$$

$$= \frac{-18 \pm \sqrt{-144x^2 - 864x - 1260}}{18}$$

$$= \frac{-18 \pm \sqrt{36(-4x^2 - 24x - 35)}}{18}$$

$$= \frac{-18 \pm 6\sqrt{-4x^2 - 24x - 35}}{18}$$

$$= \frac{-3 \pm \sqrt{-4x^2 - 24x - 35}}{3}$$

Connecting Concepts

71. The sum of the distances between the two foci and a point on the ellipse is $2a$.

$$2a = \sqrt{\left(\frac{9}{2}-0\right)^2 + (3-3)^2} + \sqrt{\left(\frac{9}{2}-0\right)^2 + (3+3)^2}$$

$$= \sqrt{\left(\frac{9}{2}\right)^2} + \sqrt{\frac{225}{4}}$$

$$= \frac{9}{2} + \frac{15}{2}$$

$$= 12$$

$$a = 6$$
$$c = 3$$
$$c^2 = a^2 - b^2$$
$$9 = 36 - b^2$$
$$b^2 = 27$$

$$\frac{x^2}{36} + \frac{y^2}{27} = 1$$

73. The sum of the distances between the two foci and a point on the ellipse is $2a$.

$$2a = \sqrt{(5-2)^2 + (3+1)^2} + \sqrt{(5-2)^2 + (3-3)^2}$$

$$= \sqrt{25} + \sqrt{3^2}$$

$$= 5 + 3$$

$$= 8$$

$$a = 4$$
$$c = 2$$

$$c^2 = a^2 - b^2$$
$$4 = 16 - b^2$$
$$b^2 = 12$$

$$\frac{(x-1)^2}{16} + \frac{(y-2)^2}{12} = 1$$

75. Center $(1, -1)$

$$c^2 = a^2 - b^2$$
$$c^2 = 16 - 9$$
$$c^2 = 7$$
$$c = \sqrt{7}$$

The latus rectum is on the graph of $y = -1 + \sqrt{7}$, or $y = -1 - \sqrt{7}$

$$\frac{(x-1)^2}{9} + \frac{(y+1)^2}{16} = 1$$

$$\frac{(x-1)^2}{9} + \frac{\left(-1+\sqrt{7}+1\right)^2}{16} = 1 \ \text{ or } \ \frac{(x-1)^2}{9} + \frac{\left(-1-\sqrt{7}+1\right)^2}{16} = 1$$

$$\frac{(x-1)^2}{9} + \frac{7}{16} = 1$$

$$\frac{(x-1)^2}{9} = \frac{9}{16}$$

$$16(x-1)^2 = 81$$

$$(x-1)^2 = \frac{81}{16}$$

$$x - 1 = \pm\sqrt{\frac{81}{16}}$$

$$x - 1 = \pm\frac{9}{4}$$

$$x = \frac{13}{4} \ \text{ and } \ -\frac{5}{4}$$

The x-coordinates of the endpoints of the latus rectum are $\frac{13}{4}$ and $-\frac{5}{4}$.

$$\left|\frac{13}{4} - \left(-\frac{5}{4}\right)\right| = \frac{9}{2}$$

The length of the latus rectum is $\frac{9}{2}$.

77. Let us transform the general equation of an ellipse into an $x'y'$ - coordinate system where the center is at the origin by replacing $(x - h)$ by x' and $(y - k)$ by y'.

We have $\dfrac{x'^2}{a^2} + \dfrac{y'^2}{b^2} = 1$.

Letting $x' = c$ and solving for y' yields

$$\frac{(c)^2}{a^2} + \frac{y'^2}{b^2} = 1$$

$$b^2 c^2 + a^2 y'^2 = a^2 b^2$$

$$a^2 y'^2 = a^2 b^2 - b^2 c^2$$

$$a^2 y'^2 = b^2(a^2 - c^2)$$

But since $c^2 = a^2 - b^2$, $b^2 = a^2 - c^2$, we can substitute to obtain

$$a^2 y'^2 = b^2 (b^2)$$

$$y'^2 = \frac{b^4}{a^2}$$

$$y' = \pm \sqrt{\frac{b^4}{a^2}} = \pm \frac{b^2}{a}$$

The endpoints of the latus rectum, then, are $\left(c, \dfrac{b^2}{a}\right)$ and $\left(c, -\dfrac{b^2}{a}\right)$.

The distance between these points is $\dfrac{2b^2}{a}$.

79.
$$a^2 = 9$$

$$b^2 = 4$$

$$c^2 = a^2 - b^2 = 9 - 4 = 5$$

$$c = \sqrt{5}$$

$$x = \pm \frac{a^2}{c} = \pm \frac{9}{\sqrt{5}} = \pm \frac{9\sqrt{5}}{5}$$

The directrices are $x = \dfrac{9\sqrt{5}}{5}$ and $x = -\dfrac{9\sqrt{5}}{5}$.

81.

The eccentricity is $e = \dfrac{c}{a} = \dfrac{2}{\sqrt{12}} = \dfrac{1}{\sqrt{3}}$. Let $P(x, y)$ be a point on the ellipse $\dfrac{x^2}{12} + \dfrac{y^2}{8} = 1$ and $F(2, 0)$ be a focus.

Then $d(P, F) = \sqrt{(x-2)^2 + y^2}$. The distance from the line $x = 6$ to $P(x, y)$ is $|x - 6|$. Thus, solving the equation of the ellipse for y^2, we have

$$\frac{\sqrt{(x-2)^2 + y^2}}{|x-6|} = \frac{\sqrt{(x-2)^2 + 8\left(1 - \dfrac{x^2}{12}\right)}}{|x-6|}$$

$$= \frac{\sqrt{x^2 - 4x + 4 + 8 - \dfrac{2}{3}x^2}}{|x-6|}$$

$$= \frac{\sqrt{\dfrac{1}{3}x^2 - 4x + 12}}{|x-6|} = \frac{\sqrt{\dfrac{x^2 - 12x + 36}{3}}}{|x-6|}$$

$$= \frac{\sqrt{\dfrac{(x-6)^2}{3}}}{|x-6|} = \frac{\dfrac{|x-6|}{\sqrt{3}}}{|x-6|} = \frac{1}{\sqrt{3}} = e \ \text{(eccentricity)}$$

$$\bullet$$

Prepare for Section 5.3

83.

$\dfrac{4 + -2}{2} = 1$

$\dfrac{-3 + 1}{2} = -1$

Midpoint: $(1, -1)$

$\sqrt{(-2-4)^2 + (1--3)^2} = \sqrt{52} = 2\sqrt{13}$

Distance: $2\sqrt{13}$

84.

$(x-1)(x+3) = 5$

$x^2 + 2x - 3 = 5$

$x^2 + 2x - 8 = 0$

$(x+4)(x-2) = 0$

$x + 4 = 0 \quad x - 2 = 0$

$\quad x = -4 \quad\quad x = 2$

85.

$\dfrac{4}{\sqrt{8}} = \dfrac{4\sqrt{8}}{8} = \dfrac{8\sqrt{2}}{8} = \sqrt{2}$

86.

$4x^2 + 24x = 4(x^2 + 6x)$

$\quad\quad\quad = 4(x^2 + 6x + 9)$

$\quad\quad\quad = 4(x+3)^2$

87.

$\dfrac{x^2}{4} - \dfrac{y^2}{9} = 1$

$-\dfrac{y^2}{9} = 1 - \dfrac{x^2}{4}$

$y^2 = \dfrac{9x^2}{4} - 9$

$y = \pm\sqrt{\dfrac{9x^2}{4} - 9}$

$y = \pm\dfrac{3}{2}\sqrt{x^2 - 4}$

88.

Section 5.3

1. $\dfrac{x^2}{16} - \dfrac{y^2}{25} = 1$

Center $(0, 0)$

Vertices $(\pm 4, 0)$

Foci $\left(\pm\sqrt{41},\, 0\right)$

Asymptotes $y = \pm\dfrac{5}{4}x$

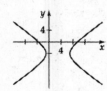

3. $\dfrac{y^2}{4} - \dfrac{x^2}{25} = 1$

Center $(0, 0)$

Vertices $(0,\ \pm 2)$

Foci $\left(0,\ \pm\sqrt{29}\right)$

Asymptotes $y = \pm\dfrac{2}{5}x$

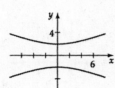

5. $\dfrac{x^2}{7} - \dfrac{y^2}{9} = 1$

Center $(0, 0)$

Vertices $\left(\pm\sqrt{7}, 0\right)$

Foci $(\pm 4, 0)$

Asymptotes $y = \pm\dfrac{3\sqrt{7}}{7}x$

7. $\dfrac{4x^2}{9} - \dfrac{y^2}{16} = 1$

Center $(0, 0)$

Vertices $\left(\pm\dfrac{3}{2}, 0\right)$

Foci $\left(\pm\dfrac{\sqrt{73}}{2},\, 0\right)$

Asymptotes $y = \pm\dfrac{8}{3}x$

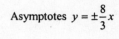
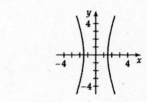

9. $\dfrac{(x-3)^2}{16} - \dfrac{(y+4)^2}{9} = 1$

Center $(3, -4)$

Vertices $(3 \pm 4, -4) = (7, -4),\ (-1, -4)$

Foci $(3 \pm 5, -4) = (8, -4),\ (-2, -4)$

Asymptotes $y + 4 = \pm\dfrac{3}{4}(x-3)$

11. $\dfrac{(y+2)^2}{4} - \dfrac{(x-1)^2}{16} = 1$

Center $(1, -2)$

Vertices $(1,\ -2 \pm 2) = (1, 0),\ (1, -4)$

Foci $\left(1,\ -2 \pm 2\sqrt{5}\right) = \left(1,\ -2 + 2\sqrt{5}\right),\ \left(1,\ -2 - 2\sqrt{5}\right)$

Asymptotes $y + 2 = \pm\dfrac{1}{2}(x-1)$

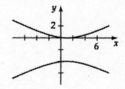

13. $\dfrac{(x+2)^2}{9} - \dfrac{y^2}{25} = 1$

Center $(-2, 0)$

Vertices $(-2 \pm 3, 0) = (1, 0), (-5, 0)$

Foci $\left(-2 \pm \sqrt{34}, 0\right)$

Asymptotes $y = \pm \dfrac{5}{3}(x+2)$

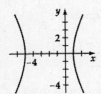

15. $\dfrac{9(x-1)^2}{16} - \dfrac{(y+1)^2}{9} = 1$

$\dfrac{(x-1)^2}{16/9} - \dfrac{(y+1)^2}{9}$

Center $(1, -1)$

Vertices $\left(1 \pm \dfrac{4}{3}, -1\right) = \left(\dfrac{7}{3}, -1\right), \left(-\dfrac{1}{3}, -1\right)$

Foci $\left(1 \pm \dfrac{\sqrt{97}}{3}, -1\right)$

Asymptotes $(y+1) = \pm \dfrac{9}{4}(x-1)$

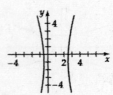

17. $x^2 - y^2 = 9$

$\dfrac{x^2}{9} - \dfrac{y^2}{9} = 1$

Center $(0, 0)$

Vertices $(\pm 3, 0)$

Foci $\left(\pm 3\sqrt{2}, 0\right)$

Asymptotes $y = \pm x$

19. $16y^2 - 9x^2 = 144$

$\dfrac{y^2}{9} - \dfrac{x^2}{16} = 1$

Center $(0, 0)$

Vertices $(0, \pm 3)$

Foci (0 ± 5)

Asymptotes $y = \pm \dfrac{3}{4}x$

21. $9y^2 - 36x^2 = 4$

$\dfrac{y^2}{4/9} - \dfrac{x^2}{1/9} = 1$

Center $(0, 0)$

Vertices $\left(0, \pm \dfrac{2}{3}\right)$

Foci $\left(0, \pm \dfrac{\sqrt{5}}{3}\right)$

Asymptotes $y = \pm 2x$

23.
$$x^2 - y^2 - 6x + 8y = 3$$
$$\left(x^2 - 6x\right) - \left(y^2 - 8y\right) = 3$$
$$\left(x^2 - 6x + 9\right) - \left(y^2 - 8y + 16\right) = 3 + 9 - 16$$
$$(x-3)^2 - (y-4)^2 = -4$$
$$\frac{(y-4)^2}{4} - \frac{(x-3)^2}{4} = 1$$

Center $(3, 4)$
Vertices $(3, 4 \pm 2) = (3, 6), (3, 2)$
Foci $\left(3, 4 \pm 2\sqrt{2}\right) = \left(3, 4 + 2\sqrt{2}\right), \left(3, 4 - 2\sqrt{2}\right)$
Asymptotes $y - 4 = \pm(x - 3)$

25.
$$9x^2 - 4y^2 + 36x - 8y + 68 = 0$$
$$9x^2 + 36x - 4y^2 - 8y = -68$$
$$9\left(x^2 + 4x\right) - 4\left(y^2 + 2y\right) = -68$$
$$9\left(x^2 + 4x + 4\right) - 4\left(y^2 + 2y + 1\right) = -68 + 36 - 4$$
$$9(x+2)^2 - 4(y+1)^2 = -36$$
$$\frac{(y+1)^2}{9} - \frac{(x+2)^2}{4} = 1$$

Center $(-2, -1)$
Vertices $(-2, -1 \pm 3) = (-2, 2), (-2, -4)$
Foci $\left(-2, -1 \pm \sqrt{13}\right) = \left(-2, -1 + \sqrt{13}\right), \left(-2, -1 - \sqrt{13}\right)$
Asymptotes $y + 1 = \pm\dfrac{3}{2}(x + 2)$

27.
$$y = \frac{-6 \pm \sqrt{6^2 - 4(-1)\left(4x^2 + 32x + 39\right)}}{2(-1)}$$
$$= \frac{-6 \pm \sqrt{36 + 4\left(4x^2 + 32x + 39\right)}}{-2}$$
$$= \frac{-6 \pm \sqrt{16x^2 + 128x + 192}}{-2}$$
$$= \frac{-6 \pm \sqrt{16(x^2 + 8x + 12)}}{-2}$$
$$= \frac{-6 \pm 4\sqrt{x^2 + 8x + 12}}{-2}$$
$$= 3 \pm 2\sqrt{x^2 + 8x + 12}$$

29.
$$y = \frac{64 \pm \sqrt{(-64)^2 - 4(-16)\left(9x^2 - 36x + 116\right)}}{2(-16)}$$
$$= \frac{64 \pm \sqrt{4096 + 64(9x^2 - 36x + 116)}}{-32}$$
$$= \frac{64 \pm \sqrt{64(9x^2 - 36x + 116 + 64)}}{-32}$$
$$= \frac{64 \pm 8\sqrt{(9x^2 - 36x + 180)}}{-32}$$
$$= \frac{64 \pm 8\sqrt{9(x^2 - 4x + 20)}}{-32}$$
$$= \frac{64 \pm 24\sqrt{x^2 - 4x + 20}}{-32}$$
$$= \frac{-8 \pm 3\sqrt{x^2 - 4x + 20}}{4}$$

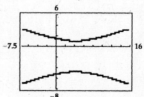

31.

$$y = \frac{18 \pm \sqrt{(-18)^2 - 4(-9)(4x^2 + 8x - 6)}}{2(-9)}$$

$$= \frac{18 \pm \sqrt{324 + 36(4x^2 + 8x - 6)}}{-18}$$

$$= \frac{18 \pm \sqrt{36(4x^2 + 8x - 6 + 9)}}{-18}$$

$$= \frac{18 \pm 6\sqrt{(4x^2 + 8x + 3)}}{-18}$$

$$= \frac{-3 \pm \sqrt{(4x^2 + 8x + 3)}}{3}$$

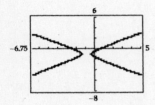

33. vertices $(3, 0)$ and $(-3, 0)$, foci $(4, 0)$ and $(-4, 0)$

Traverse axis is on x-axis. For a standard hyperbola, the vertices are at $(h + a, k)$ and $(h - a, k)$, $h + a = 3$, $h - a = -3$, and $k = 0$..

If $h + a = 3$ and $h - a = -3$, then $h = 0$ and $a = 3$.

The foci are located at $(4, 0)$ and $(-4, 0)$. Thus, $h = 0$ and $c = 4$.

Since $c^2 = a^2 + b^2$, $b^2 = c^2 - a^2$

$b^2 = (4)^2 - (3)^2 = 16 - 9 = 7$

$$\frac{(x - h)^2}{a^2} - \frac{(y - k)^2}{b^2} = 1$$

$$\frac{(x - 0)^2}{(3)^2} - \frac{(y - 0)^2}{7} = 1$$

$$\frac{x^2}{9} - \frac{y^2}{7} = 1$$

35. foci $(0, 5)$ and $(0, -5)$, asymptotes $y = 2x$ and $y = -2x$

Transverse axis is on y-axis. Since foci are at $(h, k + c)$ and $(h, k - c)$, $k + c = 5$, $k - c = -5$, and $h = 0$.

Therefore, $k = 0$ and $c = 5$.

Since one of the asymptotes is $y = \frac{a}{b}x$, $\frac{a}{b} = 2$ and $a = 2b$.

$a^2 + b^2 = c^2$; then substituting $a = 2b$ and $c = 5$ yields $(2b)^2 + b^2 = (5)^2$, or $5b^2 = 25$.

Therefore, $b^2 = 5$ and $b = \sqrt{5}$.
Since $a = 2b$, $a = 2(\sqrt{5}) = 2\sqrt{5}$.

$$\frac{(y - k)^2}{a^2} - \frac{(x - h)^2}{b^2} = 1$$

$$\frac{y^2}{(2\sqrt{5})^2} - \frac{x^2}{5} = 1$$

$$\frac{y^2}{20} - \frac{x^2}{5} = 1$$

37. vertices $(0, 3)$ and $(0, -3)$, point $(2, 4)$

The distance between the two vertices is the length of the transverse axis, which is $2a$.

$$2a = |3 - (-3)| = 6 \text{ or } a = 3.$$

Since the midpoint of the transverse axis is the center of the hyperbola, the center is given by

$\left(\frac{0 + 0}{2}, \frac{3 + (-3)}{2}\right)$, or $(0, 0)$

Since both vertices lie on the y-axis, the transverse axis must be on the y-axis.

Taking the standard form of the hyperbola, we have

$$\frac{y^2}{a^2} - \frac{x^2}{b^2} = 1$$

Substituting the point $(2, 4)$ for x and y, and 3 for a, we have

$$\frac{16}{9} - \frac{4}{b^2} = 1$$

Solving for b^2 yields $b^2 = \frac{36}{7}$.

Therefore, the equation is

$$\frac{y^2}{9} - \frac{x^2}{36/7} = 1$$

39. vertices $(0, 4)$ and $(0, -4)$, asymptotes $y = \frac{1}{2}x$ and $y = -\frac{1}{2}x$.

The length of the transverse axis, or the distance between the vertices, is equal to $2a$.

$2a = 4 - (-4) = 8$, or $a = 4$

The center of the hyperbola, or the midpoint of the line segment joining the vertices, is
$\left(\dfrac{0 + 0}{2}, \dfrac{4 + (-4)}{2} \right)$, or $(0, 0)$

Since both vertices lie on the y-axis, the transverse axis must lie on the y-axis. Therefore, the asymptotes are given by
$y = \frac{a}{b}x$ and $y = -\frac{a}{b}x$. One asymptote is $y = \frac{1}{2}x$. Thus $\frac{a}{b} = \frac{1}{2}$ or $b = 2a$.
Since $b = 2a$ and $a = 4$, $b = 2(4) = 8$.

Thus, the equation is
$\dfrac{y^2}{4^2} - \dfrac{x^2}{8^2} = 1$ or $\dfrac{y^2}{16} - \dfrac{x^2}{64} = 1$

41. vertices $(6, 3)$ and $(2, 3)$, foci $(7, 3)$ and $(1, 3)$
Length of transverse axis = distance between vertices
$$2a = |6 - 2|$$
$$a = 2$$

The center of the hyperbola (h, k) is the midpoint of the line segment joining the vertices, or the point $\left(\dfrac{6 + 2}{2}, \dfrac{3 + 3}{2} \right)$.

Thus, $h = \dfrac{6 + 2}{2}$, or 4, and $k = \dfrac{3 + 3}{3}$, or 3.

Since both vertices lie on the horizontal line $y = 3$, the transverse axis is parallel to the x-axis. The location of the foci is given by $(h + c, k)$ and $(h - c, k)$, or specifically $(7, 3)$ and $(1, 3)$. Thus $h + c = 7$, $h - c = 1$, and $k = 3$. Solving for h and c simultaneously yields $h = 4$ and $c = 3$.

Since $c^2 = a^2 + b^2$, $b^2 = c^2 - a^2$.

Substituting, we have $b^2 = 3^2 - 2^2 = 9 - 4 = 5$.

Substituting $a = 2, b^2 = 5, h = 4$, and $k = 3$ in the standard equation $\dfrac{(x - h)^2}{a^2} - \dfrac{(y - k)^2}{b^2} = 1$ yields $\dfrac{(x - 4)^2}{4} - \dfrac{(y - 3)^2}{5} = 1$.

43. foci $(1, -2)$ and $(7, -2)$, slope of an asymptote $= \frac{5}{4}$

Both foci lie on the horizontal line $y = -2$; therefore, the transverse axis is parallel to the x-axis.

The foci are given by $(h + c, k)$ and $(h - c, k)$.

Thus, $h - c = 1, h + c = 7$, and $k = -2$. Solving simultaneously for h and c yields $h = 4$ and $c = 3$.

Since $y - k = \frac{b}{a}(x - h)$ is the equation for an asymptote, and the slope of an asymptote is given as $\frac{5}{4}, \frac{b}{a} = \frac{5}{4}, b = \frac{5a}{4}$, and $b^2 = \frac{25a^2}{16}$.

Because $a^2 + b^2 = c^2$, substituting $c = 3$ and $b^2 = \dfrac{25a^2}{16}$ yields $a^2 = \dfrac{144}{41}$.

Therefore, $b^2 = \dfrac{3600}{656} = \dfrac{225}{41}$.

Substituting in the standard equation for a hyperbola yields $\dfrac{(x - 4)^2}{144/41} - \dfrac{(y + 2)^2}{225/41} = 1$

45. Because the transverse axis is parallel to the y-axis and the center is (7, 2), the equation of the hyperbola is

$$\frac{(y-2)^2}{a^2} - \frac{(x-7)^2}{b^2} = 1$$

Because (9, 4) is a point on the hyperbola,

$$\frac{(4-2)^2}{a^2} - \frac{(9-7)^2}{b^2} = 1$$

The slope of the asymptote is $\frac{1}{2}$. Therefore $\frac{1}{2} = \frac{a}{b}$ or $b = 2a$.

Substituting, we have

$$\frac{4}{a^2} - \frac{4}{4a^2} = 1$$

$$\frac{4}{a^2} - \frac{1}{a^2} = 1, \text{ or } a^2 = 3$$

Since $b = 2a$, $b^2 = 4a^2$, or $b^2 = 12$. The equation is $\dfrac{(y-2)^2}{3} - \dfrac{(x-7)^2}{12} = 1$.

47. vertices (1, 6) and (1, 8), eccentricity = 2

Length of transverse axis = distance between vertices

$$2a = |6 - 8| = 2$$

$$a = 1 \text{ and } a^2 = 1$$

Center (midpoint of transverse axis) is $\left(\dfrac{1+1}{2}, \dfrac{6+8}{2}\right)$, or $(1, 7)$.

Therefore, $h = 1$ and $k = 7$.

Since both vertices lie on the vertical line $x = 1$, the transverse axis is parallel to the y-axis.

Since $e = \frac{c}{a}$, $c = ae = (1)(2) = 2$.

Because $b^2 = c^2 - a^2$, $b^2 = (2)^2 - (1)^2 = 4 - 1 = 3$.

Substituting h, k, a^2, and b^2 into the standard equation yields $\dfrac{(y-7)^2}{1} - \dfrac{(x-1)^2}{3} = 1$

49. foci (4, 0) and $(-4, 0)$, eccentricity = 2

Center (midpoint of line segment joining foci) is $\left(\dfrac{4+(-4)}{2}, \dfrac{0+0}{2}\right)$, or $(0, 0)$

Thus, $h = 0$ and $k = 0$.

Since both foci lie on the horizontal line $y = 0$, the transverse axis is parallel to the x-axis. The locations of the foci are given by $(h + c, k)$ and $(h - c, k)$, or specifically $(4, 0)$ and $(-4, 0)$

Since $h = 0$, $c = 4$.

Because $e = \dfrac{c}{a}$, $a = \dfrac{c}{e} = \dfrac{4}{2} = 2$ and $a^2 = 4$.

Because $b^2 = c^2 - a^2$, $b^2 = 4^2 - 2^2 = 16 - 4 = 12$.

Substituting h, k, a^2 and b^2 into the standard formula for a hyperbola yields $\dfrac{x^2}{4} - \dfrac{y^2}{12} = 1$

51. conjugate axis length = 4, center (4, 1), eccentricity = $\frac{4}{3}$

$2b$ = conjugate axis length = 4

$b = 2$ and $b^2 = 4$

Since

$e = \dfrac{c}{a} = \dfrac{4}{3}$, $c = \dfrac{4a}{3}$ and $c^2 = \dfrac{16a^2}{9}$. Since $a^2 + b^2 = c^2$, substituting $b^2 = 4$ and $c^2 = \dfrac{16a^2}{9}$ and solving for a^2 yields $a^2 = \dfrac{36}{7}$.

Substituting into the two standard equations of a hyperbola yields $\dfrac{(x-4)^2}{36/7} - \dfrac{(y-1)^2}{4} = 1$ and $\dfrac{(y-1)^2}{36/7} - \dfrac{(x-4)^2}{4} = 1$

53. **a.** Because the transmitters are 250 miles apart,

$2c = 250$ and $c = 125$.

$2a$ = rate × time

$2a = 0.186 \times 500 = 93$

Thus, $a = 46.5$ miles.

$b = \sqrt{c^2 - a^2} = \sqrt{125^2 - 46.5^2} = \sqrt{13,462.75}$ miles

The ship is located on the hyperbola given by

$\dfrac{x^2}{2,162.25} - \dfrac{y^2}{13,462.75} = 1$

b. $x = 100$

$\dfrac{10,000}{2,162.25} - \dfrac{y^2}{13,462.75} = 1$

$\dfrac{-y^2}{13,462.75} \approx -3.6248121$

$y^2 \approx 48,799.939$

$y \approx 221$

The ship is 221 miles from the coastline.

55. When the wave hits Earth, $z = 0$.

$y^2 = x^2 + (z - 10,000)^2$

$y = x^2 + (0 - 10,000)^2$

$y - x^2 = 10,000^2$

It is a hyperbola.

57.
$$4x^2 + 9y^2 - 16x - 36y + 16 = 0$$
$$4\left(x^2 - 4x\right) + 9\left(y^2 - 4y\right) = -16$$
$$4\left(x^2 - 4x + 4\right) + 9\left(y^2 - 4y + 4\right) = -16 + 16 + 36$$
$$4(x-2)^2 + 9(y-2)^2 = 36$$
$$\frac{(x-2)^2}{9} + \frac{(y-2)^2}{4} = 1$$

ellipse

center (2, 2)

vertices $(2 \pm 3, 2) = (5, 2), (-1, 2)$

foci $\left(2 \pm \sqrt{5}, 2\right) = \left(2 + \sqrt{5}, 2\right), \left(2 - \sqrt{5}, 2\right)$

59.
$$5x - 4y^2 + 24y - 11 = 0$$
$$-4\left(y^2 - 6y\right) = -5x + 11$$
$$-4\left(y^2 - 6y + 9\right) = -5x + 11 - 36$$
$$-4(y-3)^2 = -5(x - 25)$$
$$-4(y-3)^2 = -5(x + 5)$$
$$(y-3)^2 = \frac{5}{4}(x + 5)$$

parabola

vertex $(-5, 3)$

focus $\left(-5 + \dfrac{5}{16}, 3\right) = \left(-\dfrac{75}{16}, 3\right)$

directrix $x = -5 - \dfrac{5}{16}$, or $x = \dfrac{-85}{16}$

61.
$$x^2 + 2y - 8x = 0$$
$$x^2 - 8x = -2y$$
$$x^2 - 8x + 16 = -2y + 16$$
$$(x-4)^2 = -2(y-8)$$

parabola

vertex $(4, 8)$

foci $\left(4, 8 - \frac{1}{2}\right) = \left(4, \frac{15}{2}\right)$

directrix $y = 8 + \frac{1}{2}$, or $y = \frac{17}{2}$

63.
$$25x^2 + 9y^2 - 50x - 72y - 56 = 0$$
$$25\left(x^2 - 2x\right) + 9\left(y^2 - 8y\right) = 56$$
$$25\left(x^2 - 2x + 1\right) + 9\left(y^2 - 8y + 16\right) = 56 + 25 + 144$$
$$25(x-1)^2 + 9(y-4)^2 = 225$$
$$\frac{(x-1)^2}{9} + \frac{(y-4)^2}{25} = 1$$

ellipse

center $(1, 4)$

vertices $(1, 4 \pm 5) = (1, 9), (1, -1)$

foci $(1, 4 \pm 4) = (1, 8), (1, 0)$

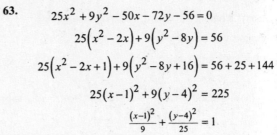

....

65.   foci $F_1(2, 0)$, $F_2(-2, 0)$ passing through $P_1(2, 3)$

$$d(P_1, F_2) - d(P_1, F_1) = \sqrt{(2+2)^2 + 3^2} - \sqrt{(2-2)^2 + 3^2} = 5 - 3 = 2$$

Let $P(x, y)$ be any point on the hyperbola. Since the difference between F_1P and F_2P is the same as the difference between F_1P_1 and

F_2P_1, we have

$$\sqrt{(x-2)^2 + y^2} - \sqrt{(x+2)^2 + y^2} = 2$$
$$\sqrt{(x-2)^2 + y^2} = 2 + \sqrt{(x+2)^2 + y^2}$$
$$x^2 - 4x + 4 + y^2 = 4 + 4\sqrt{(x+2)^2 + y^2} + x^2 + 4x + 4 + y^2$$
$$-8x - 4 = 4\sqrt{(x+2)^2 + y^2}$$
$$-2x - 1 = \sqrt{(x+2)^2 + y^2}$$
$$4x^2 + 4x + 1 = x^2 + 4x + 4 + y^2$$
$$3x^2 - y^2 = 3$$
$$\frac{x^2}{1} - \frac{y^2}{3} = 1$$

67.

foci $(0, 4)$ and $(0, -4)$, point $\left(\dfrac{7}{3}, 4\right)$

Difference in distances from (x, y) to foci = difference of distances from $\left(\dfrac{7}{3}, 4\right)$ to foci

$$\sqrt{(x-0)^2 + (y-4)^2} - \sqrt{(x-0)^2 + (y+4)^2} = \sqrt{\left(\dfrac{7}{3}-0\right)^2 + (4-4)^2} - \sqrt{\left(\dfrac{7}{3}-0\right)^2 + (4+4)^2}$$

$$\sqrt{x^2 + y^2 - 8y + 16} - \sqrt{x^2 + y^2 + 8y + 16} = \dfrac{7}{3} - \dfrac{25}{3} = -6$$

$$\sqrt{x^2 + y^2 - 8y + 16} = \sqrt{x^2 + y^2 + 8y + 16} - 6$$

$$x^2 + y^2 - 8y + 16 = x^2 + y^2 + 8y + 16 - 12\sqrt{x^2 + y^2 + 8y + 16} + 36$$

$$-16y - 36 = -12\sqrt{x^2 + y^2 + 8y + 16}$$

$$4y + 9 = 3\sqrt{x^2 + y^2 + 8y + 16}$$

$$16y^2 + 72y + 81 = 9x^2 + 9y^2 + 72y + 144$$

$$7y^2 - 9x^2 = 63$$

$$\dfrac{y^2}{9} - \dfrac{x^2}{7} = 1$$

69.

$$\dfrac{x^2}{16} - \dfrac{y^2}{25} = 1$$

$$a^2 = 16$$

$$b^2 = 25$$

$$c^2 = a^2 + b^2 = 16 + 25 = 41$$

$$c = \sqrt{41}$$

$$\dfrac{a^2}{c} = \dfrac{16}{\sqrt{41}} = \dfrac{16\sqrt{41}}{41}.$$

Thus, the directrices are $x = \pm\dfrac{16\sqrt{41}}{41}$.

71. $\dfrac{x^2}{9} - \dfrac{y^2}{16} = 1$, focus $(5, 0)$, directrix $x = \dfrac{9}{5}$

Solving for y^2 gives us

$16x^2 - 9y^2 = 144$

$\qquad 9y^2 = 16x^2 - 144$

$\qquad y^2 = \dfrac{16}{9}x^2 - 16$

Let $k = \dfrac{\text{distance from } P(x,\, y) \text{ to focus } (5,\, 0)}{\text{distance from } P(x,\, y) \text{ to directrix } (x = 9/5)}$

$k = \dfrac{\sqrt{(x-5)^2 + (y-0)^2}}{|x - 9/5|} = \dfrac{\sqrt{x^2 - 10x + 25 + y^2}}{|x - 9/5|}$

But since $P(x,\, y)$ lies on the curve, $y^2 = \dfrac{16}{9}x^2 - 16$.

Substituting gives us $k = \dfrac{\sqrt{x^2 - 10x + 25 + 16x^2/9 - 16}}{|x - 9/5|} = \dfrac{\sqrt{\dfrac{25x^2}{9} - \dfrac{90x}{9} + \dfrac{81}{9}}}{|x - 9/5|} = \dfrac{\sqrt{25x^2 - 90x + 81}}{3|x - 9/5|}$.

Solving for k^2 yields

$k^2 = \dfrac{25\left(x^2 - \dfrac{18}{5} + \dfrac{81}{25}\right)}{9\left(x^2 - \dfrac{18}{5} + \dfrac{81}{25}\right)} = \dfrac{25}{9}$

$k = \pm\sqrt{\dfrac{25}{9}} = \pm\dfrac{5}{3}$

But since $k = \dfrac{\text{distance from } P \text{ to focus}}{\text{distance from } P \text{ to directrix}}$, and the ratio of two distances must be positive, $k = \dfrac{5}{3}$.

$a^2 = 9$

$b^2 = 16$

$c^2 = a^2 + b^2 = 9 + 16 = 25$

$\quad c = 5 \text{ and } a = 3$

Since $e = \dfrac{c}{a} = \dfrac{5}{3}$ and $k = \dfrac{5}{3}$, $e = k$.

73.

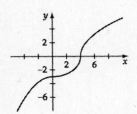

Chapter 5 True/False Exercises

1. False, a parabola has no asymptotes.   **2.** True

3. False. By keeping the foci fixed and varying the asymptotes, we can make the conjugate axis any size needed

4. False. $\dfrac{x^2}{25} + \dfrac{y^2}{9} = 1$ and $\dfrac{x^2}{36} + \dfrac{y^2}{20} = 1$ have the same c's but different a's.

5. False, parabolas have no asymptotes.

6. True

7. False, a parabola can be a function.

8. True

9. True

1. $x^2 - y^2 = 4$ [5.3]

$$\frac{x^2}{4} - \frac{y^2}{4} = 1$$

hyperbola
center $(0, 0)$
vertex $(\pm 2, 0)$
foci $\left(\pm 2\sqrt{2}, 0\right)$
asymptotes $y = \pm x$

2. $y^2 = 16x$ [5.1]

parabola
vertex $(0, 0)$
focus $(4, 0)$
directrix $x = -4$

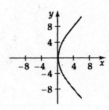

3. $x^2 + 4y^2 - 6x + 8y - 3 = 0$ [5.2]

$$x^2 - 6x + 4\left(y^2 + 2y\right) = 3$$
$$\left(x^2 - 6x + 9\right) + 4\left(y^2 + 2y + 1\right) = 3 + 9 + 4$$
$$(x-3)^2 + 4(y+1)^2 = 16$$
$$\frac{(x-3)^2}{16} + \frac{(y+1)^2}{4} = 1$$

ellipse
center $(3, -1)$
vertices $(3 \pm 4, -1) = (7, -1), (-1, -1)$
foci $\left(3 \pm 2\sqrt{3}, -1\right) = \left(3 + 2\sqrt{3}, -1\right), \left(3 - 2\sqrt{3}, -1\right)$

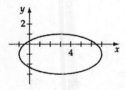

4. $3x^2 - 4y^2 + 12x - 24y - 36 = 0$ [5.3]

$$3\left(x^2 + 4x\right) - 4\left(y^2 + 6y\right) = 36$$
$$3\left(x^2 + 4x + 4\right) - 4\left(y^2 + 6y + 9\right) = 36 + 12 - 36$$
$$3(x+2)^2 - 4(y+3)^2 = 12$$
$$\frac{(x+2)^2}{4} - \frac{(y+3)^2}{3} = 1$$

hyperbola
center $(-2, -3)$
vertices $(-2 \pm 2, -3) = (0, -3), (-4, -3)$
foci $\left(-2 \pm \sqrt{7}, -3\right) = \left(-2 + \sqrt{7}, -3\right), \left(-2 - \sqrt{7}, -3\right)$
asymptotes $(y+3) = \pm \frac{\sqrt{3}}{2}(x+2)$

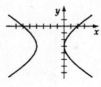

5.
$$3x - 4y^2 + 8y + 2 = 0 \qquad [5.1]$$
$$-4\left(y^2 - 2y\right) = -3x - 2$$
$$-4\left(y^2 - 2y + 1\right) = -3x - 2 - 4$$
$$-4(y - 1)^2 = -3(x + 2)$$
$$(y - 1)^2 = \frac{3}{4}(x + 2)$$

parabola
vertex $(-2, 1)$

focus $\left(-2 + \dfrac{3}{16}, 1\right) = \left(-\dfrac{29}{16}, 1\right)$

directrix $x = -2 - \dfrac{3}{16}$ or $x = -\dfrac{35}{16}$

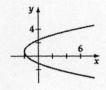

6.
$$3x + 2y^2 - 4y - 7 = 0 \qquad [5.1]$$
$$2\left(y^2 - 2y\right) = -3x + 7$$
$$2\left(y^2 - 2y + 1\right) = -3x + 7 + 2$$
$$2(y - 1)^2 = -3(x - 3)$$
$$(y - 1)^2 = -\frac{3}{2}(x - 3)$$

parabola
vertex $(3, 1)$

focus $\left(3 - \dfrac{3}{8}, 1\right) = \left(\dfrac{21}{8}, 1\right)$

directrix $x = 3 + \dfrac{3}{8}$ or $x = \dfrac{27}{8}$

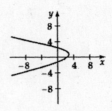

7.
$$9x^2 + 4y^2 + 36x - 8y + 4 = 0 \quad [5.2]$$
$$9\left(x^2 + 4x\right) + 4\left(y^2 - 2y\right) = -4$$
$$9\left(x^2 + 4x + 4\right) + 4\left(y^2 - 2x + 1\right) = -4 + 36 + 4$$
$$9(x + 2)^2 + 4(y - 1)^2 = 36$$
$$\frac{(x + 2)^2}{4} + \frac{(y - 1)^2}{9} = 1$$

ellipse
center $(-2, 1)$
vertices $(-2, 1 \pm 3) = (-2, 4), (-2, -2)$
foci $\left(-2, 1 \pm \sqrt{5}\right) = \left(-2, 1 + \sqrt{5}\right), \left(-2, 1 - \sqrt{5}\right)$

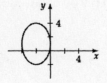

8.
$$11x^2 - 25y^2 - 44x - 50y - 256 = 0 \qquad [5.3]$$
$$11\left(x^2 - 4x\right) - 25\left(y^2 + 2y\right) = 256$$
$$11\left(x^2 - 4x + 4\right) - 25\left(y^2 + 2y + 1\right) = 256 + 44 - 25$$
$$11(x - 2)^2 - 25(y + 1)^2 = 275$$
$$\frac{(x - 2)^2}{25} - \frac{(y + 1)^2}{11} = 1$$

hyperbola
center $(2, -1)$

vertices $(2 \pm 5, -1) = (7, -1), (-3, -1)$

foci $(2 \pm 6, -1) = (8, -1), (-4, -1)$

asymptotes $(y + 1) = \pm\dfrac{\sqrt{11}}{5}(x - 2)$

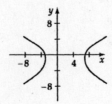

9.
$$4x^2 - 9y^2 - 8x + 12y - 144 = 0 \qquad [5.3]$$
$$4\left(x^2 - 2x\right) - 9\left(y^2 - \frac{4}{3}y\right) = 144$$
$$4\left(x^2 - 2x + 1\right) - 9\left(y^2 - \frac{4}{3}y + \frac{4}{9}\right) = 144 + 4 - 4$$
$$4(x-1)^2 - 9\left(y - \frac{2}{3}\right)^2 = 144$$
$$\frac{(x-1)^2}{36} - \frac{(y-2/3)^2}{16} = 1$$

hyperbola

center $\left(1, \dfrac{2}{3}\right)$

vertices $\left(1 \pm 6, \dfrac{2}{3}\right) = \left(7, \dfrac{2}{3}\right), \left(-5, \dfrac{2}{3}\right)$

foci $\left(1 \pm 2\sqrt{13}, \dfrac{2}{3}\right) = \left(1 + 2\sqrt{13}, \dfrac{2}{3}\right), \left(1 - 2\sqrt{13}, \dfrac{2}{3}\right)$

asymptotes $y - \dfrac{2}{3} = \pm\dfrac{2}{3}(x-1)$

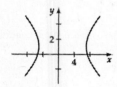

10.
$$9x^2 + 16y^2 + 36x - 16y - 104 = 0 \qquad [5.2]$$
$$9\left(x^2 + 4x\right) + 16\left(y^2 - y\right) = 104$$
$$9\left(x^2 + 4x + 4\right) + 16\left(y^2 - y + \frac{1}{4}\right) = 104 + 36 + 4$$
$$9(x+2)^2 + 16\left(y - \frac{1}{2}\right)^2 = 144$$
$$\frac{(x+2)^2}{16} + \frac{\left(y - \frac{1}{2}\right)^2}{9} = 1$$

ellipse

center $\left(-2, \dfrac{1}{2}\right)$

vertices $\left(-2 \pm 4, \dfrac{1}{2}\right) = \left(2, \dfrac{1}{2}\right), \left(-6, \dfrac{1}{2}\right)$

foci $\left(-2 \pm \sqrt{7}, \dfrac{1}{2}\right) = \left(-2 + \sqrt{7}, \dfrac{1}{2}\right), \left(-2 - \sqrt{7}, \dfrac{1}{2}\right)$

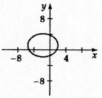

11.
$$4x^2 + 28x + 32y + 81 = 0 \qquad [5.1]$$
$$4\left(x^2 + 7x\right) = -32y - 81$$
$$4\left(x^2 + 7x + \frac{49}{4}\right) = -32y - 81 + 49$$
$$4\left(x + \frac{7}{2}\right)^2 = -32(y+1)$$
$$\left(x + \frac{7}{x}\right)^2 = -8(y+1)$$

parabola

vertex $\left(-\dfrac{7}{2}, -1\right)$ $\qquad 4p = -8, p = -2$

focus $\left(-\dfrac{7}{2}, -3\right)$

directrix $y = 1$

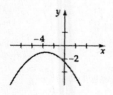

12.
$$x^2 - 6x - 9y + 27 = 0 \qquad [5.1]$$
$$x^2 - 6x = 9y - 27$$
$$x^2 - 6x + 9 = 9y - 27 + 9$$
$$(x-3)^2 = 9(y-2)$$

parabola
vertex $(3, 2)$

focus $\left(3, 2 + \dfrac{9}{4}\right) = \left(3, \dfrac{17}{4}\right)$

directrix $y = 3 - \dfrac{9}{4}$ or $y = -\dfrac{1}{4}$

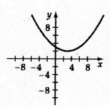

13. $2a = |7 - (-3)| = 10$ [5.2]

$a = 5$

$a^2 = 25$

$2b = 8$

$b = 4$

$b^2 = 16$

Center (2, 3)

$$\frac{(x-2)^2}{25} + \frac{(y-3)^2}{16} = 1$$

14. $2a = |4 - (-2)| = 6$ [5.3]

$a = 3$

$a^2 = 9$

$e = \frac{c}{a} = \frac{4}{3}$

$\frac{c}{3} = \frac{4}{3}$

$c = 4$

$c^2 = a^2 + b^2$

$16 = 9 + b^2$

$b^2 = 7$

center (1, 1)

$$\frac{(x-1)^2}{9} - \frac{(y-1)^2}{7} = 1$$

15. center $(-2, 2), c = 3$ [5.3]

$2a = 4$

$a = 2$

$a^2 = 4$

$c^2 = a^2 + b^2$

$9 = 4 + b^2$

$b^2 = 5$

$$\frac{(x+2)^2}{4} - \frac{(y-2)^2}{5} = 1$$

16. $(h, k) = \left(\frac{6+2}{2}, \frac{-3-3}{2} \right) = (4, -3)$ [5.1]

$p = 2 - 4 = -2$

$4p = -8$

$(y + 3)^2 = -8(x - 4)$

17.

$(x-h)^2 = 4p(y-k)$ $(y-k)^2 = 4p(x-h)$ [5.1]

$(3-0)^2 = 4p(4+2)$ $(4+2)^2 = 4p(3-0)$

$9 = 4p(6)$ $36 = 4p(3)$

$p = \frac{3}{8}$ $p = 3$

Thus, there are two parabolas that satisfy the given conditions:

$$x^2 = \frac{3}{2}(y + 2) \quad \text{or} \quad (y + 2)^2 = 12x$$

18. center $(-2, -1)$ [5.2]

$c = 2$

$e = \frac{c}{a} = \frac{2}{3}$

$\frac{2}{a} = \frac{2}{3}$

$a = 3$

$c^2 = a^2 - b^2$

$4 = 9 - b^2$

$b^2 = 5$

$$\frac{(x+2)^2}{9} + \frac{(y+1)^2}{5} = 1$$

19. $a = 6$ and the transverse axis   [5.2]
is on the x-axis.

$\pm \frac{b}{a} = \pm \frac{1}{9}$

$\frac{b}{6} = \frac{1}{9}$

$b = \frac{2}{3}$

$$\frac{x^2}{36} - \frac{y^2}{4/9} = 1$$

20. $(x-h)^2 = 4p(y-k)$ [5.1]

$(1-h)^2 = 4p(0-k)$

$(2-h)^2 = 4p(1-k)$

$(0-h)^2 = 4p(1-k)$

In the last two equations, by substitution:

$(2-h)^2 = (0-h)^2$

$4 - 4h + h^2 = h^2$

$4 - 4h = 0$

$4h = 4$

$h = 1$

Thus:

$(1-1)^2 = 4p(0-k)$

$0 = -4pk$

$k = 0$

$(2-1)^2 = 4p(1-k)$

$1 = 4p(1)$

$p = \frac{1}{4}$

The equation is $(x-1)^2 = y$

21. focus $(-2, 3)$, directrix $x = 2$ [5.1]

The vertex is the midpoint of the line segment joining $(-2, 3)$, and $(2, 3)$ on the directrix.

$$(h, k) = \left(\frac{-2+2}{2}, \frac{3+3}{2}\right) = (0, 3)$$

The directed distance p from the vertex to the focus is -2.

$$4p = 4(-2) = -8$$
$$(y - k)^2 = 4p(x - h)$$
$$(y - 3)^2 = -8x$$

22. focus $(-1, 2)$, directrix $y = 1$ [5.1]

The vertex is the midpoint of the line segment joining $(-1, 2)$, and $(1, 1)$ on the directrix.

$$(h, k) = \left(\frac{-1 + (-1)}{2}, \frac{2+1}{2}\right) = \left(-1, \frac{3}{2}\right)$$

The directed distance p from the vertex to the focus is $\frac{1}{2}$.

$$4p = 4\left(\frac{1}{2}\right) = 2$$
$$(x - h)^2 = 4p(y - k)$$
$$(x + 1)^2 = 2\left(y - \frac{3}{2}\right)$$

23. foci $(-3, 1)$ and $(5, 1)$, length of major axis 10   [5.2]

The center of the ellipse is the midpoint of the line segment joining the foci.

$$(h, k) = \left(\frac{-3+5}{2}, \frac{1+1}{2}\right) = (1, 1)$$
$$2a = 10$$
$$a = 5$$
$$a^2 = 25$$
$$c = 4$$
$$c^2 = a^2 - b^2$$
$$16 = 25 - b^2$$
$$b^2 = 9$$

$$\frac{(x-1)^2}{25} + \frac{(y-1)^2}{9} = 1$$

24. foci $(3, 5)$ and $(3, -1)$, length of major axis 8   [5.2]

The center of the ellipse is the midpoint of the line segment joining the foci.

$$(h, k) = \left(\frac{3+3}{2}, \frac{5 + (-1)}{2}\right) = (3, 2)$$
$$2a = 8$$
$$a = 4$$
$$a^2 = 16$$
$$c = 3$$
$$c^2 = a^2 - b^2$$
$$9 = 16 - b^2$$
$$b^2 = 7$$

$$\frac{(x-3)^2}{7} + \frac{(y-2)^2}{16} = 1$$

Chapter Test

1.
$$y = \frac{1}{8}x^2 \quad [5.1]$$
$$x^2 = 8y$$
$$4p = 8$$
$$p = 2$$

vertex: $(0, 0)$
focus: $(0, 2)$
directrix: $y = -2$

2.
$$x^2 + 4x - 12y + 16 = 0 \quad [5.1]$$
$$x^2 + 4x + 4 = 12y - 12$$
$$(x + 2)^2 = 12(y - 1)$$
$$4p = 12$$
$$p = 3$$

vertex: $(-2, 1)$
focus: $(-2, 4)$
directrix: $y = -2$

3. $(h, k) = \left(\dfrac{-1+3}{2}, \dfrac{-2-2}{2}\right) = (1, -2)$ [5.1]

$p = -2$

$4p = -8$

$(y-k)^2 = 4p(x-h)$

$(y+2)^2 = -8(x-1)$

4.

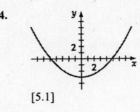

[5.1]

5. $a^2 = 64 \qquad b^2 = 9, \qquad\qquad c^2 = 55$

$a = 8 \qquad\quad b = 3 \qquad\qquad c = \sqrt{55}$

vertices: $(0, 8), (0, -8)$

foci: $\left(0, \sqrt{55}\right), \left(0, -\sqrt{55}\right)$ [5.2]

6.

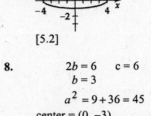

[5.2]

7. $25x^2 + 150x + 9y^2 + 18y + 9 = 0$

$25\left(x^2 - 6x + 9\right) + 9\left(y^2 + 2y + 1\right) = -9 + 255 + 9$

$25(x-3)^2 + 9(y-1)^2 = 225$

$\left(\dfrac{x-3}{9}\right)^2 + \dfrac{(y+1)^2}{25} = 1$

$a = 5 \quad b = 3 \quad c = 4$

vertices: $(3, 4), (3, -6)$

foci: $(3, 3), (3, -5)$ [5.2]

8. $2b = 6 \qquad c = 6$

$b = 3$

$a^2 = 9 + 36 = 45$

center $= (0, -3)$

$\dfrac{x^2}{45} + \dfrac{(y+3)^2}{9} = 1$ [5.2]

9. $9x^2 + 25y^2 = 81$ [5.2]

$\dfrac{9x^2}{81} + \dfrac{25y^2}{81} = 1$

$\dfrac{x^2}{9} + \dfrac{y^2}{18/25} = 1$

$c^2 = a^2 - b^2 = 9 - \dfrac{81}{25} = \dfrac{225 - 81}{25} = \dfrac{144}{25}$

$c = \dfrac{12}{5}$

$e = \dfrac{c}{a} = \dfrac{12/5}{3} = \dfrac{4}{5}$

10.

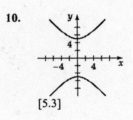

[5.3]

11. $\dfrac{x^2}{36} - \dfrac{y^2}{64} = 1$

vertices: $(6, 0), (-6, 0)$

asymptotes: $y = \pm\dfrac{4}{3}x$

foci: $(10, 0), (-10, 0)$ [5.3]

12. $\dfrac{(y+1)^2}{4} - \dfrac{(x+3)^2}{16} = 1$

[5.3]

13. $\dfrac{(y-4)^2}{36} - \dfrac{(x+5)^2}{9} = 1$

vertices: $(-5,\ 4 \pm 6) = (-5,\ 10),\ (-5,\ -2)$

$c^2 = 36 + 9 = 45$

$c = 3\sqrt{5}$

foci: $\left(-5, 4 \pm 3\sqrt{5}\right)$ [5.3]

14. vertices $(-2,-3), (-6,-3)$

$a = \dfrac{\left|-6 - (-2)\right|}{2} = 2 \qquad c = \sqrt{34}$

$c^2 = a^2 + b^2$

$\left(\sqrt{34}\right)^2 = 4 + b^2$

$30 = b^2$

center: $(-4,\ -3)$

$\dfrac{(x+4)^2}{4} - \dfrac{(y+3)^2}{30} = 1$ [5.3]

15. $(y-4)^2 = -16(x-2)$ [5.1]

••

1. $x^4 - 2x^2 - 8 = 0$ [1.4]

Let $u = x^2$.

$u^2 - 2u - 8 = 0$

$(u-4)(u+2) = 0$

$u = 4$ or $u = -2$

$x^2 = 4 \qquad\quad x^2 = -2$

$x = \pm 2 \qquad\quad x = \pm i\sqrt{2}$

The solutions are $2,\ -2,\ i\sqrt{2},\ -i\sqrt{2}$.

2. $\dfrac{2}{x-1} - \dfrac{3}{x+2} = \dfrac{2(x+2) - 3(x-1)}{(x-1)(x+2)}$ [P.5]

$= \dfrac{2x + 4 - 3x + 3}{(x-1)(x+2)}$

$= \dfrac{-x + 7}{(x-1)(x+2)}$

3. $\dfrac{f(2+h) - f(2)}{h} = \dfrac{\left[1 - (2+h)^2\right] - \left[1 - (2)^2\right]}{h}$ [2.6]

$= \dfrac{1 - 4 - 4h - (h)^2 - 1 + 4}{h}$

$= \dfrac{-4h - h^2}{h}$

$= -4 - h$

4. $(f \circ g)(x) = f[g(x)]$ [2.6]

$= f[2 - x^2]$

$= 3(2 - x^2) + 2$

$= 6 - 3x^2 + 2$

$= -3x^2 + 8$

$(f \circ g)(-3) = -3(-3)^2 + 8$

$= -27 + 8$

$= -19$

5. By the Linear Factor Theorem, since the polynomial is of degree 6, there are 6 complex number solutions to

$x^6 + 2x^4 - 3x^3 - x^2 + 5x - 7 = 0$.

[3.4]

6. $m = \dfrac{2 - (-4)}{-3 - 1} = \dfrac{6}{-4} = -\dfrac{3}{2}$ [2.3]

$y - (-4) = -\dfrac{3}{2}(x - 1)$

$y + 4 = -\dfrac{3}{2}x + \dfrac{3}{2}$

$y = -\dfrac{3}{2}x - \dfrac{5}{2}$

7. $x = -3, y = 2$ [3.5]

8. $d = \sqrt{(-5 - (-3))^2 + (4 - (-1))^2}$

$= \sqrt{(-2)^2 + (5)^2}$

$= \sqrt{4 + 25}$

$= \sqrt{29}$

[2.1]

9.

[4.2]

10. $\log_2(x+3) - \log_2(x) = 2$ [4.5]

$\log_2 \dfrac{(x+3)}{x} = 2$

$2^2 = \dfrac{(x+3)}{x}$

$4x = x + 3$

$3x = 3$

$x = 1$

11.

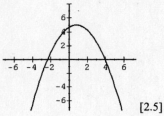

[2.5]

12. $f(x) = 2x - 8$ [4.1]
$x = 2y - 8$
$x + 8 = 2y$
$\frac{1}{2}x + 4 = y$
$f^{-1}(x) = \frac{1}{2}x + 4$

13.

$$\begin{array}{r|rrrrr} 2i & 1 & 1 & -8 & 4 & -48 \\ & & 2i & -4+2i & -4-24i & 48 \\ \hline & 1 & 1+2i & -12+2i & -24i & 0 \end{array}$$

$$\begin{array}{r|rrrr} -2i & 1 & 1+2i & -12+2i & -24i \\ & & -2i & -2i & 24i \\ \hline & 1 & 1 & -12 & 0 \end{array}$$

$x^2 + x - 12 = (x-3)(x+4) = 0$
$x = 3,\ x = -4$
The remaining zeros are $-2i$ and -4. [3.4]

14. odd [2.5]

15. Not symmetric with respect to [2.5]
either axis.
Symmetric to the origin since
$(-x) = (-y)^3 - (-y)$ simplifies to
$-x = -y^3 + y$, which is equivalent
to the original equation $x = y^3 - y$.

16. $3^x = 5$ [4.5]
$\log(3^x) = \log 5$
$x \log 3 = \log 5$
$x = \dfrac{\log 5}{\log 3} \approx 1.465$

17. $x^2 + 3x - 4 < 0$ [1.5]
$(x-1)(x+4) < 0$
The product $(x-1)(x+4)$ is negative.
$x - 1 = 0 \Rightarrow x = 1$ is a critical value.
$x + 4 = 0 \Rightarrow x = -4$ is a critical value.

$(x-1)(x+4)$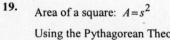

$(-4, 1)$

18. $G(x) = \dfrac{x}{x^2 - 4}$ [2.2]
$x^2 - 4 = (x-2)(x+2)$
Domain is $\{x \mid x \neq -2,\ x \neq 2\}$.

19. Area of a square: $A = s^2$

Using the Pythagorean Theorem and solving for s^2: $s^2 + s^2 = d^2$
$2s^2 = d^2$
$s^2 = \dfrac{d^2}{2}$

$A(d) = \dfrac{d^2}{2}$ [2.2]

20.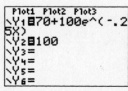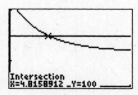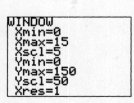

4.8 s [4.2]

Chapter 6
Systems of Equations

Section 6.1

1. $\begin{cases} 2x - 3y = 16 \\ x = 2 \end{cases}$

$2(2) - 3y = 16$
$-3y = 12$
$y = -4$

The solution is $(2, -4)$.

3. $\begin{cases} 3x + 4y = 18 \\ y = -2x + 3 \end{cases}$

$3x + 4(-2x + 3) = 18$
$3x - 8x + 12 = 18$
$-5x = 6$
$x = -\dfrac{6}{5}$

$y = -2\left(-\dfrac{6}{5}\right) + 3$

$y = \dfrac{27}{5}$

The solution is $\left(-\dfrac{6}{5}, \dfrac{27}{5}\right)$.

5. $\begin{cases} -2x + 3y = 6 \\ x = 2y - 5 \end{cases}$

$-2(2y - 5) + 3y = 6$
$-4y + 10 + 3y = 6$
$-y = -4$
$y = 4$

$x = 2(4) - 5$
$x = 3$

The solution is $(3, 4)$.

7. $\begin{cases} 6x + 5y = 1 & (1) \\ x - 3y = 4 & (2) \end{cases}$

Solve (2) for x: $x = 3y + 4$

$6(3y + 4) + 5y = 1$
$18y + 24 + 5y = 1$
$23y = -23$
$y = -1$
$x = 3(-1) + 4$
$x = 1$

The solution is $(1, -1)$.

9. $\begin{cases} 7x + 6y = -3 & (1) \\ y = \dfrac{2}{3}x - 6 & (2) \end{cases}$

$7x + 6\left(\dfrac{2}{3}x - 6\right) = -3$
$7x + 4x - 36 = -3$
$11x = 33$
$x = 3$
$y = \dfrac{2}{3}(3) - 6$
$y = -4$

The solution is $(3, -4)$.

11. $\begin{cases} y = 4x - 3 \\ y = 3x - 1 \end{cases}$

$4x - 3 = 3x - 1$
$x = 2$

$y = 4(2) - 3$
$y = 5$

The solution is $(2, 5)$.

13. $\begin{cases} y = 5x + 4 \\ x = -3y - 4 \end{cases}$

$y = 5(-3y - 4) + 4$

$y = -15y - 20 + 4$

$16y = -16$

$y = -1$

$x = -3(-1) - 4$

$x = -1$

The solution is $(-1, -1)$.

15. $\begin{cases} 3x - 4y = 2 & (1) \\ 4x + 3y = 14 & (2) \end{cases}$

Solve (1) for x and substitute into (2).

$3x = 4y + 2$

$x = \dfrac{4y + 2}{3}$

$4\left(\dfrac{4y + 2}{3}\right) + 3y = 14$

$16y + 8 + 9y = 42$

$25y = 34$

$y = \dfrac{34}{25}$

$x = \dfrac{4}{3}\left(\dfrac{34}{25}\right) + \dfrac{2}{3}$

$x = \dfrac{62}{25}$

The solution is $\left(\dfrac{62}{25}, \dfrac{34}{25}\right)$.

17. $\begin{cases} 3x - 3y = 5 & (1) \\ 4x - 4y = 9 & (2) \end{cases}$

Solve (1) for x and substitute into (2).

$3x - 3y = 5$

$x = \dfrac{3y + 5}{3}$

$4\left(\dfrac{3y + 5}{3}\right) - 4y = 9$

$12y + 20 - 12y = 27$

$20 = 27$

The system of equations is inconsistent and has no solution.

19. $\begin{cases} 4x + 3y = 6 \\ y = -\dfrac{4}{3}x + 2 \end{cases}$

$4x + 3\left(-\dfrac{4}{3}x + 2\right) = 6$

$4x - 4x + 6 = 6$

$0 = 0$

The system of equations is dependent.

Let $x = c$ and $y = -\dfrac{4}{3}c + 2$.

The solutions are $\left(c, \ -\dfrac{4}{3}c + 2\right)$.

21. $\begin{cases} 3x - y = 10 & (1) \\ 4x + 3y = -4 & (2) \end{cases}$

$9x - 3y = 30$ 3 times (1)

$\underline{4x + 3y = -4}$ (2)

$13x = 26$

$x = 2$

$3(2) - y = 10$

$6 - y = 10$

$y = -4$

The solution is $(2, -4)$.

23. $\begin{cases} 4x + 7y = 21 & (1) \\ 5x - 4y = -12 & (2) \end{cases}$

$20x + 35y = 105$ 5 times (1)

$\underline{-20x + 16y = 48}$ -4 times (2)

$51y = 153$

$y = 3$

$4x + 7(3) = 21$

$x = 0$

The solution is $(0, 3)$.

25. $\begin{cases} 5x - 3y = 0 & (1) \\ 10x - 6y = 0 & (2) \end{cases}$

$-10x + 6y = 0$ -2 times (1)

$\underline{10x - 6y = 0}$ (2)

$0 = 0$

$5x - 3c = 0$

$x = \dfrac{3c}{5}$

The solution is $\left(\dfrac{3c}{5}, c\right)$.

27. $\begin{cases} 6x + 6y = 1 & (1) \\ 4x + 9y = 4 & (2) \end{cases}$

$12x + 12y = 2$ 2 times (1)

$\underline{-12x - 27y = -12}$ -3 times (2)

$-15y = -10$

$y = \dfrac{2}{3}$

$6x + 6\left(\dfrac{2}{3}\right) = 1$

$6x = -3$

$x = -\dfrac{1}{2}$

The solution is $\left(-\dfrac{1}{2}, \dfrac{2}{3}\right)$.

29. $\begin{cases} 3x + 6y = 11 & (1) \\ 2x + 4y = 9 & (2) \end{cases}$

$6x + 12y = 22$ 2 times (1)

$\underline{-6x - 12y = -27}$ -3 times (2)

$0 = -5$

The system of equations is inconsistent and has no solution.

31. $\begin{cases} \dfrac{5}{6}x - \dfrac{1}{3}y = -6 & (1) \\ \dfrac{1}{6}x + \dfrac{2}{3}y = 1 & (2) \end{cases}$

$\dfrac{5}{3}x - \dfrac{2}{3}y = -12 \qquad 2 \text{ times } (1)$

$\dfrac{1}{6}x + \dfrac{2}{3}y = 1 \qquad (2)$

$\dfrac{11}{6}x = -11$

$x = -6$

$\dfrac{1}{6}x + \dfrac{2}{3}y = 1$

$\dfrac{1}{6}(-6) + \dfrac{2}{3}y = 1$

$\dfrac{2}{3}y = 2$

$y = 3$

The solution is $(-6, 3)$.

33. $\begin{cases} \dfrac{3}{4}x + \dfrac{1}{3}y = 1 \\ \dfrac{1}{2}x + \dfrac{2}{3}y = 0 \end{cases}$

$\begin{cases} 9x + 4y = 12 & (1) \\ 3x + 4y = 0 & (2) \end{cases}$

$9x + 4y = 12 \qquad (1)$

$-3x - 4y = 0 \qquad -1 \text{ times } (2)$

$6x = 12$

$x = 2$

$3(2) + 4y = 0$

$4y = -6$

$y = -\dfrac{3}{2}$

The solution is $\left(2, -\dfrac{3}{2}\right)$.

35. $\begin{cases} 2\sqrt{3}x - 3y = 3 & (1) \\ 3\sqrt{3}x + 2y = 24 & (2) \end{cases}$

$6\sqrt{3}x - 9y = 9 \qquad 3 \text{ times } (1)$

$-6\sqrt{3}x - 4y = -48 \qquad -2 \text{ times } (2)$

$-13y = -39$

$y = 3$

$2\sqrt{3}x - 3(3) = 3$

$2\sqrt{3}x = 12$

$\sqrt{3}x = 6$

$x = 2\sqrt{3}$

The solution is $\left(2\sqrt{3}, \ 3\right)$.

37. $\begin{cases} 3\pi x - 4y = 6 & (1) \\ 2\pi x + 3y = 5 & (2) \end{cases}$

$6\pi x - 8y = 12 \qquad 2 \text{ times } (1)$

$-6\pi x - 9y = -15 \qquad -3 \text{ times } (2)$

$-17y = -3$

$y = \dfrac{3}{17}$

$9\pi x - 12y = 18 \qquad 3 \text{ times } (1)$

$8\pi x + 12y = 20 \qquad 4 \text{ times } (2)$

$17\pi x = 38$

$x = \dfrac{38}{17\pi}$

The solution is $\left(\dfrac{38}{17\pi}, \ \dfrac{3}{17}\right)$.

39.
$$\begin{cases} 3\sqrt{2}x - 4\sqrt{3}y = -6 & (1) \\ 2\sqrt{2}x + 3\sqrt{3}y = 13 & (2) \end{cases}$$

$6\sqrt{2}x - 8\sqrt{3}y = -12$ 2 times (1)

$-6\sqrt{2}x - 9\sqrt{3}y = -39$ -3 times (2)

$\overline{\qquad\quad -17\sqrt{3}y = -51}$

$$y = \frac{3}{\sqrt{3}}$$

$$y = \sqrt{3}$$

$9\sqrt{2}x - 12\sqrt{3}y = -18$

$8\sqrt{2}x + 12\sqrt{3}y = 52$

$\overline{17\sqrt{2}x \qquad\quad = 34}$

$$x = \frac{2}{\sqrt{2}}$$

$$x = \sqrt{2}$$

The solution is $\left(\sqrt{2}, \sqrt{3}\right)$.

41. Solve the system by substitution.

$$20p - 2000 = -4p + 1000$$
$$24p = 3000$$
$$p = 125$$

The solution is $125.

43. Rate of plane with the wind: $r + w$
Rate of plane against the wind: $r - w$
$$r \cdot t = d$$
$$\begin{cases} (r + w) \cdot 3 = 450 \\ (r - w) \cdot 5 = 450 \end{cases}$$

$r + w = 150$

$\underline{r - w = 90}$

$2r \qquad = 240$

$r = 120$

$120 + w = 150$

$w = 30$

Rate of plane = 120 mph.
Rate of wind = 30mph.

45. Rate of boat with the current: $r + w$
Rate of boat against the wind: $r - w$
$$r \cdot t = d$$
$$\begin{cases} (r + w) \cdot 4 = 120 \\ (r - w) \cdot 6 = 120 \end{cases}$$

$r + w = 30$

$\underline{r - w = 20}$

$2r \qquad = 50$

$r = 25$

$25 + w = 30$

$w = 5$

Rate of boat = 25 mph.
Rate of current = 5 mph.

47. $x =$ cost per kilogram of iron alloy
$y =$ cost per kilogram of lead alloy

$$\begin{cases} 30x + 45y = 1080 & (1) \\ 15x + 12y = 372 & (2) \end{cases}$$

$$\begin{cases} 30x + 45y = 1080 & (1) \\ -30x - 24y = -744 & -2 \text{ times (2)} \end{cases}$$

$21y = 336$

$y = 16$

$15x + 12(16) = 372$

$15x = 180$

$x = 12$

Cost of iron alloy: $12 per kilogram
Cost of lead alloy: $16 per kilogram

49. $x =$ amount of 40% gold
$y =$ amount of 60% gold

$$\begin{cases} x + y = 20 & (1) \\ 0.40x + 0.60y = (0.52)(20) & (2) \end{cases}$$

$-0.40x - 0.40y = -8$ -0.40 times (1)

$\underline{0.40 + 0.60y = 10.4}$ (2)

$0.20y = 2.4$

$y = 12$

$x + 12 = 20$

$x = 8$

Amount of 40% gold: 8 g
Amount of 60% gold: 12 g

51. Sketch a graph to visualize the right triangle.

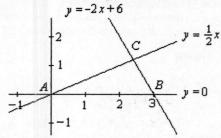

To find the coordinates of point A, solve the system
$$\begin{cases} y = 0 \\ y = \frac{1}{2}x \end{cases}$$

By substitution, $\frac{1}{2}x = 0$
$$x = 0 \quad \text{Thus } A \text{ is } (0, 0).$$

To find the coordinates of point B, solve the system
$$\begin{cases} y = 0 \\ y = -2x + 6 \end{cases}$$

By substitution, $-2x + 6 = 0$
$$-2x = -6$$
$$x = 3 \quad \text{Thus } B \text{ is } (3, 0).$$

To find the coordinates of the point C, solve the system
$$\begin{cases} y = -2x + 6 & (1) \\ y = \frac{1}{2}x & (2) \end{cases}$$

By substitution, $\frac{1}{2}x = -2x + 6$
$$\frac{5}{2}x = 6$$
$$x = \frac{12}{5}$$

Substituting $\frac{12}{5}$ for x in Equation (2), we have
$$y = \frac{1}{2}\left(\frac{12}{5}\right) = \frac{6}{5}. \quad \text{Thus } C \text{ is } \left(\frac{12}{5}, \frac{6}{5}\right).$$

From the graph, $\angle C$ is the right angle.

Use the distance formula to find AC and BC.

$$AC = \sqrt{\left(\frac{12}{5} - 0\right)^2 + \left(\frac{6}{5} - 0\right)^2}$$
$$= \sqrt{\frac{144}{25} + \frac{36}{25}} = \sqrt{\frac{180}{25}} = \frac{6}{5}\sqrt{5}$$

$$BC = \sqrt{\left(3 - \frac{12}{5}\right)^2 + \left(0 - \frac{6}{5}\right)^2}$$
$$= \sqrt{\left(\frac{3}{5}\right)^2 + \left(-\frac{6}{5}\right)^2} = \sqrt{\frac{45}{25}} = \frac{3}{5}\sqrt{5}$$

Area $= \frac{1}{2}$ (base)(height)
$$= \frac{1}{2}\left(\frac{6}{5}\sqrt{5}\right)\left(\frac{3}{5}\sqrt{5}\right)$$
$$= \frac{9}{25}(5)$$
$$= \frac{9}{5} \text{ square units}$$

53.
$$5Z7$$
$$+\ \underline{256}$$
$$XY3$$

Case 1: $Z + 5 + 1 \leq 9$
$$\begin{cases} Z + 5 + 1 = Y \\ 5 + 2 = X \end{cases}$$
$$\begin{cases} Z + 6 = Y \\ 7 = X \end{cases}$$
$$X + Y = 7 + Z + 6$$
$$X + Y = Z + 13$$

Case 2: $Z + 5 + 1 > 9$
$$\begin{cases} Z + 5 + 1 = 10 + Y \\ 5 + 2 + 1 = X \end{cases}$$
$$\begin{cases} Z - 4 = Y \\ 8 = X \end{cases}$$
$$X + Y = 8 + Z - 4$$
$$X + Y = Z + 4$$

$XY3$ is divisible by $3 \Rightarrow X + Y$ is divisible by 3.

If $Z + 13$ is divisible by 3, then $Z = 2, 5,$ or 8.
If $Z + 4$ is divisible by 3, then $Z = 2, 5,$ or 8.

In both cases, the largest digit Z can be is 8.

55.

$14=c-b$
$126=c+b$

$140=2c$
$70=c, b=56$

$294=c-b$
$6=c+b$

$300=2c$
$150=c, b=144$

$18=c-b$
$98=c+b$

$116=2c$
$58=c, b=40$

$2=c-b$
$882=c+b$

$884=2c$
$442=c, b=440$

The Pythagorean triples are: 42, 56, 70; 42, 40, 58; 42, 144, 150; 42, 440, 442.

57. x = people who like lip balm but do not like skin cream
y = people who like lip balm and skin cream
z = people who do not like lip balm but do like skin cream
w = people who do not like lip balm nor skin cream

$x+y+z+w=100$
$0.80(y+z)=y$
$0.50(x+w)=w$
$x+y=77$

Rewrite the system by solving eq (2) for z, eq (3) for w, and eq (4) for x.

$x+y+z+w=100$
$z=0.25y$
$w=x$
$x=-y+77$

Substitute the values from equations (2), (3), and (4) into equation (1) and solve for y.

$(-y+77)+y+0.25y+(-y+77)=100$
$-0.75y+154=100$
$-0.75y=-54$
$y=72$

$z = 0.25(72) = 18$
$x = -72 + 77 = 5$
$w = 5$

Find the number of people who like skin cream $(y + z)$
$y+z=72+18=90$

90 people liked the skin cream.

59.
$$\begin{cases} T=0.25I-3190 \\ T=0.20I \end{cases}$$

$0.25I-3190=0.20I$
$0.05I=3190$
$I=63,800$
$T = 0.20(63,800) = 12,760$

The solution is (63,800, 12,760). This point indicates that a person with an adjusted gross income of \$63,800 would pay the same tax using either tax method.

61. x = amount invested in 6% bond
y = amount invested in 6.5% bond

$$\begin{cases} x + y = 25,000 & (1) \\ 0.06x + 0.065y = 1,555 & (2) \end{cases}$$

$-0.06x - 0.06y = -1500 \qquad -0.06$ times (1)
$\underline{0.06x + 0.065y = 1555}$

$0.005y = 55$
$y = 11,000$
$x + 11,000 = 25,000$
$x = 14,000$

Amount invested at 6%: \$14,000
Amount invested at 6.5%: \$11,000

63.
$$(3 + 2i)x + (4 - 3i)y = 2 - 16i$$
$$3x + 2xi + 4y - 3yi = 2 - 16i$$
$$(3x + 4y) + (2x - 3y)i = 2 - 16i$$
$$\begin{cases} 2x + 4y = 2 & (1) \\ 2x - 3y = -16 & (2) \end{cases}$$
$$\begin{array}{ll} 9x + 12y = 6 & 3 \text{ times } (1) \\ \underline{8x - 12y = -64} & 4 \text{ times } (2) \\ 17x \quad\quad = -58 \end{array}$$
$$x = -\frac{58}{17}$$
$$3x + 4y = 2$$
$$4y = 2 - 3\left(-\frac{58}{17}\right)$$
$$4y = \frac{208}{17}$$
$$y = \frac{52}{17}$$

65.
$$(2 + 6i)x + (4 - 5i)y = -8 - 7i$$
$$2x + 6xi + 4y - 5yi = -8 - 7i$$
$$(2x + 4y) + (6x - 5y)i = -8 - 7i$$
$$\begin{cases} 2x + 4y = -8 & (1) \\ 6x - 5y = -7 & (2) \end{cases}$$
$$\begin{array}{ll} -6x - 12y = 24 & -3 \text{ times } (1) \\ \underline{6x - 5y = -7} & (2) \\ -17y = 17 \\ y = -1 \end{array}$$
$$2x + 4(-1) = -8$$
$$2x = -4$$
$$x = -2$$

67.
$$(5 - 2i)x + (-3 - 4i)y = 12 - 35i$$
$$5x - 2xi - 3y - 4yi = 12 - 35i$$
$$\begin{cases} 5x - 3y = 12 & (1) \\ -2x - 4y = -35 & (2) \end{cases}$$
$$\begin{array}{ll} 10x - 6y = 24 & 2 \text{ times } (1) \\ \underline{-10x - 20y = -175} & 5 \text{ times } (2) \\ -26 = -151 \end{array}$$
$$y = \frac{151}{26}$$
$$\begin{array}{ll} 20x - 12y = 48 & 4 \text{ times } (1) \\ \underline{6x + 12y = 105} & -3 \text{ times } (2) \\ 26x \quad\quad = 153 \end{array}$$
$$x = \frac{153}{26}$$

69.
$$\begin{cases} 4x + 3y = 11 + 6i & (1) \\ 3x - 5y = 1 + 19i & (2) \end{cases}$$
$$\begin{array}{ll} 20x + 15y = 55 + 30i & 5 \text{ times } (1) \\ \underline{9x - 15y = 3 + 57i} & 3 \text{ times } (2) \\ 29x \quad\quad = 58 + 87i \\ x = 2 + 3i \end{array}$$
$$\begin{array}{ll} 12x + 9y = 33 + 18i & 3 \text{ times } (1) \\ \underline{-12x + 20y = -4 - 76i} & -4 \text{ times } (2) \\ 29y = 29 - 58i \\ y = 1 - 2i \end{array}$$

71.
$$\begin{cases} 5x - 4y = 15 - 41i & (1) \\ 3x + 5y = 9 + 5i & (2) \end{cases}$$
$$\begin{array}{ll} 25x - 20y = 75 - 205i & 5 \text{ times } (1) \\ \underline{12x + 20y = 36 + 20i} & 4 \text{ times } (2) \\ 37x \quad\quad = 111 - 185i \\ x = 3 - 5i \end{array}$$
$$5(3 - 5i) - 4y = 15 - 41i$$
$$15 - 25i - 4y = 15 - 41i$$
$$-4y = -16i$$
$$y = 4i$$

72. $2x-5y=15$
$-5y=-2x+15$
$y=\dfrac{2}{5}x-3$

73. $x=2c+1$
$y=-c+3$
$z=2x+5y-4$
$z=2(2c+1)+5(-c+3)-4$
$=4c+2-5c+15-4$
$=-c+13$

74. $\begin{cases} 5x-2y=10 \\ 2y=8 \end{cases}$

$y=4$

$5x-2(4)=10$
$5x=18$
$x=\dfrac{18}{5}$

The solution is $\left(\dfrac{18}{5}, 4\right)$.

75. $\begin{cases} 3x-y=11 & (1) \\ 2x+3y=-11 & (2) \end{cases}$

Solve (1) for y: $y=3x-11$

$2x+3(3x-11)=-11$
$2x+9x-33=-11$
$11x=22$
$x=2$
$y=3(2)-11$
$y=-5$

The solution is $(2, -5)$.

76. $\begin{cases} y=3x-4 \\ y=4x-2 \end{cases}$

$3x-4=4x-2$
$x=-2$

$y=3(-2)-4$
$y=-10$

The solution is $(-2, -10)$.

77. $\begin{cases} 4x+y=9 & (1) \\ -8x-2y=-18 & (2) \end{cases}$

Solve (1) for y: $y=-4x+9$

$-8x-2(-4x+9)=-18$
$-8x+8x-18=-18$
$0=0$
The system of equations is dependent.
Let $x=c$ and $y=-4c+9$.
The solutions are $\left(c, -4c+9\right)$.

Section 6.2

1.
$$\begin{cases} 2x - y + z = 8 & (1) \\ 2y - 3z = -11 & (2) \\ 3y + 2z = 3 & (3) \end{cases}$$

$$\begin{array}{ll} 6y - 9z = -33 & \text{3 times (2)} \\ \underline{-6y - 4z = -6} & \text{- 2 times (3)} \\ -13z = -39 \\ z = 3 & (4) \end{array}$$

$$\begin{cases} 2x - y + z = 8 \\ 2y - 3z = -11 \\ z = 3 \quad (4) \end{cases}$$

$$2y - 3(3) = -11$$
$$y = -1$$

$$2x - (-1) + 3 = 8$$
$$x = 2$$

The solution is $(2, -1, 3)$.

3.
$$\begin{cases} x + 3y - 2z = 8 & (1) \\ 2x - y + z = 1 & (2) \\ 3x + 2y - 3z = 15 & (3) \end{cases}$$

$$\begin{array}{ll} -2x - 6y + 4z = -6 & \text{- 2 times (1)} \\ \underline{2x - y + z = 1} & (2) \\ -7y + 5z = -15 & (4) \\ -3x - 9y + 6z = -24 & \text{- 3 times (1)} \\ \underline{3x + 2y - 3z = 15} & (3) \\ -7y + 3z = -9 & (5) \end{array}$$

$$\begin{cases} x + 3y - 2z = 8 \\ -7y + 5z = -15 & (4) \\ -7y + 3z = -9 & (5) \end{cases}$$

$$\begin{array}{ll} -7y + 5z = -15 & (4) \\ \underline{7y - 3z = 9} & \text{-1 times (5)} \\ 2z = -6 \\ z = -3 & (6) \end{array}$$

$$\begin{cases} x + 3y - 2z = 8 \\ -7y + 5z = -15 \\ z = -3 & (6) \end{cases}$$

$$-7y + 5(-3) = -15 \qquad x + 3(0) - 2(3) = 8$$
$$y = 0 \qquad\qquad x = 2$$

The solution is $(2, 0, -3)$.

5. $\begin{cases} 3x+4y-z=-7 & (1) \\ x-5y+2z=19 & (2) \\ 5x+y-2z=5 & (3) \end{cases}$

$$\begin{array}{ll} 3x+4y-z=-7 & (1) \\ -3x+15y-6z=-57 & -3 \text{ times } (2) \\ \hline 19y-7z=-64 & (4) \end{array}$$

$$\begin{array}{ll} -5x+25y-10z=-95 & -5 \text{ times } (2) \\ 5x+y-2z=5 & (3) \\ \hline 26y-12z=-90 & (5) \end{array}$$

$\begin{cases} 3x+4y-z=-7 \\ 19y-7z=-64 & (4) \\ 26y-12z=-90 & (5) \end{cases}$

$$\begin{array}{ll} 494y-182z=-1664 & 26 \text{ times } (4) \\ -494y+228z=1710 & -19 \text{ times } (3) \\ \hline 46z=46 \\ z=1 & (6) \end{array}$$

$\begin{cases} 3x+4y-z=-7 \\ 19y-7z=-64 \\ z=1 & (6) \end{cases}$

$$19y-7(1)=-64$$
$$y=-3$$

$$3x+4(-3)-1=-7$$
$$x=2$$

The solution is $(2,\ -3,\ 1)$.

7. $\begin{cases} 2x-5y+3z=-18 & (1) \\ 3x+2y-z=-12 & (2) \\ x-3y-4z=-4 & (3) \end{cases}$

$$\begin{array}{ll} 3x+2y-z=-12 & (2) \\ -3x+9y+12z=12 & -2 \text{ times } (3) \\ \hline 11y+11z=0 \\ y+z=0 & (4) \end{array}$$

$$\begin{array}{ll} 2x-5y+3z=-18 & (1) \\ -2x+6y+8z=8 & -2 \text{ times } (3) \\ \hline y+11z=-10 & (2) \end{array}$$

$\begin{cases} 2x-5y+3z=-18 \\ y+z=0 & (4) \\ y+11z=-10 & (5) \end{cases}$

$$\begin{array}{ll} y+z=0 & (4) \\ -y-11z=10 & -1 \text{ times } (5) \\ \hline -10z=10 \\ z=-1 & (6) \end{array}$$

$\begin{cases} 2x-5y+3z=-18 \\ y+z=0 \\ z=-1 & (6) \end{cases}$

$$y-1=0$$
$$y=1$$

$$2x-5(1)+3(-1)=-18$$
$$x=-5$$

The solution is $(-5,\ 1,\ -1)$.

9. $\begin{cases} x + 2y - 3z = -7 & (1) \\ 2x - y + 4z = 11 & (2) \\ 4x + 3y - 4z = -3 & (3) \end{cases}$

$$\begin{array}{ll} -2x - 4y + 6z = 14 & -2 \text{ times } (1) \\ \underline{2x - y + 4z = 11} & (2) \\ -5y + 10z = 25 & (4) \end{array}$$

$$\begin{array}{ll} -4x - 8y + 12z = 28 & -4 \text{ times } (1) \\ \underline{4x + 3y - 4z = -3} & (3) \\ -5y + 8z = 25 & (5) \end{array}$$

$\begin{cases} x + 2y - 3z = -7 \\ -y + 2z = 5 & (4) \\ -5y + 8z = 25 & (5) \end{cases}$

$$\begin{array}{ll} 5y - 10z = -25 & -1 \text{ times } (4) \\ \underline{-5y + 8z = 25} & (5) \\ -2z = 0 \\ z = 0 & (6) \end{array}$$

$\begin{cases} x + 2y - 3z = -7 \\ -y + 2z = 5 \\ z = 0 & (6) \end{cases}$

$$-y + 2(0) = 5$$
$$y = -5$$

$$x + 2(-5) - 3(0) = -7$$
$$x = 3$$

The solution is $(3, -5, 0)$.

11. $\begin{cases} 2x - 5y + 2z = -4 & (1) \\ 3x + 2y + 3z = 13 & (2) \\ 5x - 3y - 4z = -18 & (3) \end{cases}$

$$\begin{array}{ll} 6x - 15y + 6z = -12 & 3 \text{ times } (1) \\ \underline{-6x - 4y - 6z = -26} & -2 \text{ times } (2) \\ -19y = -38 \\ y = 2 & (4) \end{array}$$

$$\begin{array}{ll} 10x - 25y + 10z = -20 & 5 \text{ times } (1) \\ \underline{-10x + 6y + 8z = 36} & -2 \text{ times } (3) \\ -19y + 18z = 16 & (5) \end{array}$$

$\begin{cases} 2x - 5y + 2z = -4 \\ y = 2 & (4) \\ -19y + 18z = 16 & (5) \end{cases}$

$$\begin{array}{ll} 19y = 38 & 19 \text{ times } (4) \\ \underline{-19y - 18z = 16} & (5) \\ 18z = 54 \\ z = 3 & (6) \end{array}$$

$\begin{cases} 2x - 5y + 2z = -4 \\ y = 2 \\ z = 3 & (6) \end{cases}$

$$2x - 5(2) + 2(3) = -4$$
$$x = 0$$

The solution is $(0, 2, 3)$.

13.
$$\begin{cases} 2x+y-z=-2 & (1) \\ 3x+2y+3z=21 & (2) \\ 7x+4y+z=17 & (3) \end{cases}$$

$$\begin{array}{ll} 6x+3y-3z=-6 & 3 \text{ times}(1) \\ \underline{-6x-4y-6z=-42} & -2 \text{ times}(2) \\ \quad -y-9z=-48 & (4) \end{array}$$

$$\begin{array}{ll} 14x+7y-7z=-14 & 7 \text{ times}(1) \\ \underline{-14x-8y-2z=-34} & -2 \text{ times}(3) \\ \quad -y-9z=-48 & (5) \end{array}$$

$$\begin{cases} 2x+y-z=-2 & \\ \quad -y-9z=-48 & (4) \\ \quad -y-9z=-48 & (5) \end{cases}$$

$$\begin{array}{ll} -y-9z=-48 & (4) \\ \underline{y+9z=48} & -1 \text{ times}(5) \\ \quad 0=0 & (6) \end{array}$$

$$\begin{cases} 2x+y-z=-2 & \\ \quad -y-9z=-48 & \\ \quad\quad 0=0 & (6) \end{cases}$$

The system of equations is dependent.

Let $z=c$. $-y-9c=-48$

$\qquad\qquad\qquad\qquad y=48-9c$

$2x+(48-9c)-c=-2$

$\qquad\qquad x=5c-25$

The solution is $(5c-25,\ 48-9c,\ c)$.

15.
$$\begin{cases} 3x-2y+3z=11 & (1) \\ 2x+3y+z=3 & (2) \\ 5x+14y-z=1 & (3) \end{cases}$$

$$\begin{array}{ll} 6x-4y+6z=22 & 2 \text{ times}(1) \\ \underline{-6x-9y-3z=-9} & -3 \text{ times}(2) \\ \quad 13y+3z=13 & (4) \end{array}$$

$$\begin{array}{ll} 15x-10y+15z=55 & 5 \text{ times}(1) \\ \underline{-15x-42y+3z=-3} & -3 \text{ times}(3) \\ \quad -52y+18z=52 & \\ \quad -26y+9z=26 & (5) \end{array}$$

$$\begin{cases} 3x-2y+3z=11 & \\ \quad -13y+3z=13 & (4) \\ \quad -26y+9z=26 & (5) \end{cases}$$

$$\begin{array}{ll} 26y-6z=-26 & -2 \text{ times}(4) \\ \underline{-26y+9z=26} & (5) \\ \quad z=0 & (6) \end{array}$$

$$\begin{cases} 3x-2y+3z=11 & \\ \quad -13y+3z=13 & \\ \quad\quad z=0 & (6) \end{cases}$$

$-31y+3(0)=13\qquad\qquad 3x-2(-1)+3(0)=11$

$\qquad y=-1\qquad\qquad\qquad\qquad\quad x=3$

The solution is $(3,\ -1,\ 0)$.

17.
$$\begin{cases} 2x-3y+6z=3 & (1) \\ x+2y-4z=5 & (2) \\ 3x+4y-8z=7 & (3) \end{cases}$$

$$\begin{array}{ll} 2x-3y+6z=3 & (1) \\ \underline{-2x-4y+8z=-10} & -2\text{ times (2)} \\ -7y+14z=-7 & \\ -y+2z=-1 & (4) \end{array}$$

$$\begin{array}{ll} -3x-6y+12z=-15 & -3\text{ times (2)} \\ \underline{3x+4y-8z=7} & (3) \\ -2y+4z=-8 & \\ -y+2z=-4 & (5) \end{array}$$

$$\begin{cases} 2x-3y+6z=3 & \\ -y+2z=-1 & (4) \\ -y+2z=-4 & (5) \end{cases}$$

$$\begin{array}{ll} -y+2z=-1 & (4) \\ \underline{y-2z=4} & -1\text{ times (5)} \\ 0=3 & (6) \end{array}$$

$$\begin{cases} 2x-3y+6z=3 & \\ -y+2z=-1 & \\ 0=3 & (6) \end{cases}$$

The system of equations is inconsistent and has no solution.

21.
$$\begin{cases} 6x-9y+6z=7 & (1) \\ 4x-6y+4z=9 & (2) \end{cases}$$

$$\begin{array}{ll} 24x-36y+24z=28 & 4\text{ times (1)} \\ \underline{-24x+36y-24z=-54} & -6\text{ times (2)} \\ 0=-26 & \end{array}$$

$$\begin{cases} 6x-9y+6z=7 & \\ 0=-26 & (3) \end{cases}$$

The system of equations is inconsistent and has no solution.

19.
$$\begin{cases} 2x-3y+5z=14 & (1) \\ x+4y-3z=-2 & (2) \end{cases}$$

$$\begin{array}{ll} 2x-3y+5z=14 & (1) \\ \underline{-2x-8y+6z=4} & -2\text{ times (2)} \\ -11y+11z=18 & (3) \end{array}$$

$$\begin{cases} 2x-3y+5z=14 & \\ -11y+11z=18 & (3) \end{cases}$$

Let $z=c$. $\qquad -11y+11c=18$

$$y=\frac{18-11c}{-11}$$

$$y=\frac{11c-18}{11}$$

$$2x-3\left(\frac{11c-18}{11}\right)+5c=14$$

$$2x=14-5c+\frac{33c-54}{11}$$

$$2x=\frac{154-55c+33c-54}{11}$$

$$x=\frac{50-11c}{11}$$

The solution is $\left(\dfrac{50-11c}{11},\ \dfrac{11c-18}{11},\ c\right)$.

23.
$$\begin{cases} 5x+3y+2z=10 & (1) \\ 3x-4y-4z=-5 & (2) \end{cases}$$

$$\begin{array}{ll} 15x+9y+6z=30 & 3\text{ times (1)} \\ \underline{-15x+20y+20z=25} & -5\text{ times (2)} \\ 29y+26z=55 & (3) \end{array}$$

$$\begin{cases} 5x+3y+2z=10 & \\ 29y+26z=55 & (3) \end{cases}$$

Let $z=c$. $\qquad 29y+26c=55$

$$y=\frac{55-26c}{29}$$

$$5x+3\left(\frac{55-26c}{29}\right)+2c=10$$

$$5x=10-2c-\frac{165-78c}{29}$$

$$5x=\frac{290-58c-165+78c}{29}$$

$$x=\frac{25+4c}{29}$$

The solution is $\left(\dfrac{25+4c}{29},\ \dfrac{55-26c}{29},\ c\right)$.

25. $\begin{cases} x+3y-4z=0 & (1) \\ 2x+7y+z=0 & (2) \\ 3x-5y-2z=0 & (3) \end{cases}$

$\begin{array}{ll} -2x-6y+8z=0 & -2 \text{ times } (1) \\ \underline{2x+7y+z=0} & (2) \\ y+9z=0 & (4) \end{array}$

$\begin{array}{ll} -3x-9y+12z=0 & -3 \text{ times } (1) \\ \underline{3x-5y-2z=0} & (3) \\ -14y+10z=0 \\ -7y+5z=0 & (5) \end{array}$

$\begin{cases} x+3y-4z=0 \\ y+9z=0 & (4) \\ -7y+5z=0 & (5) \end{cases}$

$\begin{array}{ll} 7y+63z=0 & 7 \text{ times } (4) \\ \underline{-7y+5z=0} & (5) \\ 68z=0 \\ z=0 & (6) \end{array}$

$\begin{cases} x+3y-4z=0 \\ y+9z=0 \\ z=0 & (6) \end{cases}$

$\begin{array}{ll} y+9(0)=0 & x+3(0)-4(0)=0 \\ y=0 & x=0 \end{array}$

The solution is (0, 0, 0).

27. $\begin{cases} 2x-3y+z=0 & (1) \\ 2x+4y-3z=0 & (2) \\ 6x-2y-z=0 & (3) \end{cases}$

$\begin{array}{ll} -2x+3y-z=0 & -1 \text{ times } (1) \\ \underline{2x+4y-3z=0} & (2) \\ 7y-4z=0 & (4) \end{array}$

$\begin{array}{ll} -6x+9y-3z=0 & -3 \text{ times } (1) \\ \underline{6x-2y-z=0} & (3) \\ 7y-4z=0 & (5) \end{array}$

$\begin{cases} 2x-3y+z=0 \\ 7y-4z=0 & (4) \\ 7y-4z=0 & (5) \end{cases}$

$\begin{array}{ll} -7y+4z=0 & -1 \text{ times } (4) \\ \underline{7y-4z=0} & (5) \\ 0=0 \end{array}$

$\begin{cases} 2x-3y+z=0 \\ 7y-4z=0 \\ 0=0 \end{cases}$

Let $z=c$. Then $7y=4c$ or $y=\dfrac{4}{7}c$. Substitute for y and z in Eq. (1) and solve for x.

$$2x-3\left(\frac{4}{7}c\right)+c=0$$

$$2x=\frac{5}{7}c$$

$$x=\frac{5}{14}c$$

The solution is $\left(\dfrac{5}{14}c,\ \dfrac{4}{7}c,\ c\right)$.

29. $\begin{cases} 3x-5y+3z=0 & (1) \\ 2x-3y+4z=0 & (2) \\ 7x-11y+11z=0 & (3) \end{cases}$

$\begin{array}{ll} -6x+10y-6z=0 & -2 \text{ times} (1) \\ \underline{6x-9y+12z=0} & 3 \text{ times} (2) \\ y+6z=0 & (4) \end{array}$

$\begin{array}{ll} -21x+35y-21z=0 & -7 \text{ times} (1) \\ \underline{21x-33y+33z=0} & 3 \text{ times} (3) \\ 2y+12z=0 & (5) \end{array}$

$\begin{cases} 3x-5y+3z=0 & (1) \\ y+6z=0 & (4) \\ 2y+12z=0 & (5) \end{cases}$

$\begin{array}{ll} -2y-12z=0 & -2 \text{ times} (4) \\ \underline{2y+12z=0} & (5) \\ 0=0 & (6) \end{array}$

$\begin{cases} 3x-5y+3z=0 & (1) \\ y+6z=0 & (4) \\ 0=0 & (6) \end{cases}$

From Eq. (4), $y=-6z$. Substitute into Eq. (1).

$\begin{aligned} 3x-5(-6z)+3z&=0 \\ 3x&=-33z \\ x&=-11z \end{aligned}$

Let z be any real number c, then the solutions are $(-11c, -6c, c)$.

31. $\begin{cases} 4x-7y-2z=0 & (1) \\ 2x+4y+3z=0 & (2) \\ 3x-2y-5z=0 & (3) \end{cases}$

$\begin{array}{ll} 4x-7y-2z=0 & (1) \\ \underline{-4x-8y-6z=0} & -2 \text{ times} (2) \\ -15y-8z=0 & (4) \end{array}$

$\begin{array}{ll} 6x+12y+9z=0 & 3 \text{ times} (2) \\ \underline{-6x+4y+10z=0} & -2 \text{ times} (3) \\ 16y+19z=0 & (5) \end{array}$

$\begin{cases} 4x-7y-2z=0 \\ -15y-8z=0 & (4) \\ 16y+19z=0 & (5) \end{cases}$

$\begin{array}{ll} -240y-128z=0 & 16 \text{ times} (4) \\ \underline{240y+285z=0} & 15 \text{ times} (5) \\ 157z=0 \\ z=0 & (6) \end{array}$

$\begin{cases} 4x-7y-2z=0 \\ -15y-8z=0 \\ z=0 & (6) \end{cases}$

$z=0$, $y=0$, $x=0$. The solution is $(0, 0, 0)$.

33.

$$y = ax^2 + bx + c$$
$$3 = a(2)^2 + b(2) + c$$
$$7 = a(-2)^2 + b(-2) + c$$
$$-2 = a(1)^2 + b(1) + c$$

$$\begin{cases} 4a + 2b + c = 3 & (1) \\ 4a - 2b + c = 7 & (2) \\ a + b + c = -2 & (3) \end{cases}$$

$$\begin{array}{ll} 4a + 2b + c = 3 & (1) \\ \underline{-4a + 2b - c = -7} & -1 \text{ times } (2) \\ \qquad\quad 4b = -4 & (4) \end{array}$$

$$\begin{array}{ll} 4a + 2b + c = 3 & (1) \\ \underline{-4a - 4b - 4c = 8} & -4 \text{ times } (3) \\ \quad -2b - 3c = 11 & (5) \end{array}$$

$$\begin{cases} 4a + 2b + c = 3 \\ \quad 4b \quad\;\; = -4 & (4) \\ \; -2b - 3c = 11 & (5) \end{cases}$$

From $(4): 4b = -4$
$$\qquad\qquad\;\; b = -1$$

From $(5): -2(-1) - 3c = 11$
$$\qquad\qquad\qquad\qquad c = -3$$

From $(1): 4a + 2(-1) - 3 = 3$
$$\qquad\qquad\qquad\quad a = 2$$

The equation whose graph passes through the three points is
$y = 2x^2 - x - 3$.

35.

$$x^2 + y^2 + ax + by + c = 0$$
$$5^2 + 3^2 + a(5) + b(3) + c = 0$$
$$(-1)^2 + (-5)^2 + a(-1) + b(-5) + c = 0$$
$$(-2)^2 + 2^2 + a(-2) + b(2) + c = 0$$

$$\begin{cases} 5a + 3b + c = -34 & (1) \\ -a - 5b + c = -26 & (2) \\ -2a + 2b + c = -8 & (3) \end{cases}$$

$$\begin{array}{ll} 5a + 3b + c = -34 & (1) \\ \underline{a + 5b - c = 26} & -1 \text{ times } (2) \\ 6a + 8b = -8 & \\ 3a + 4b = -4 & (4) \end{array}$$

$$\begin{array}{ll} 5a + 3b + c = -34 & (1) \\ \underline{2a - 2b - c = 8} & -1 \text{ times } (3) \\ 7a + b = -26 & (5) \end{array}$$

$$\begin{cases} 5a + 3b + c = -34 \\ 3a + 4b = 4 & (4) \\ 7a + b = -26 & (5) \end{cases}$$

$$\begin{array}{ll} 3a + 4b = -4 & (4) \\ \underline{-28a - 4b = 104} & -4 \text{ times } (5) \\ -25a \quad\;\; = 100 & \\ \qquad\; a = -4 & (6) \end{array}$$

$$\begin{cases} 5a + 3b + c = -34 \\ 3a + 4b \quad\;\; = -4 \\ a \qquad\qquad = -4 & (6) \end{cases}$$

$$3(-4) + 4b = -4 \qquad 5(-4) + 3(2) + c = -34$$
$$\qquad\quad b = 2 \qquad\qquad\qquad\qquad c = -20$$

The equation whose graph passes through the three points is
$x^2 + y^2 - 4x + 2y - 20 = 0$.

37.

$$x^2 + y^2 + ax + by + c = 0$$
$$(-2)^2 + 10^2 + a(-2) + b(10) + c = 0$$
$$(-12)^2 + (-14)^2 + a(-12) + b(-14) + c = 0$$
$$5^2 + 3^2 + a(5) + b(3) + c = 0$$

$$\begin{cases} -2a + 10b + c = -104 & (1) \\ -12a - 14b + c = -340 & (2) \\ 5a + 3b + c = -34 & (3) \end{cases}$$

$$\begin{aligned} -2a + 10b + c &= -104 \quad (1) \\ \underline{12a + 14b - c = 340} &\quad -1 \text{ times } (2) \\ 10a + 24b &= 236 \\ 5a + 12b &= 118 \quad (4) \end{aligned}$$

$$\begin{aligned} -2a + 10b + c &= -104 \quad (1) \\ \underline{-5a - 3b - c = 34} &\quad -1 \text{ times } (3) \\ -7a + 7b &= -70 \\ -a + b &= -10 \quad (5) \end{aligned}$$

$$\begin{cases} -2a + 10b + c = -104 & (1) \\ 5a + 12b = 118 & (4) \\ -a + b = -10 & (5) \end{cases}$$

$$\begin{aligned} 5a + 12b &= 118 \quad (4) \\ \underline{-5a + 5b = -50} &\quad 5 \text{ times } (5) \\ 17b &= 68 \\ b &= 4 \quad (6) \end{aligned}$$

$$\begin{cases} -2a + 10b + c = -104 \\ 5a + 12b = 118 \\ b = 4 \quad (6) \end{cases}$$

$$5a + 12(4) = 118 \qquad -2(14) + 10(4) + c = -104$$
$$a = 14 \qquad\qquad\qquad c = -116$$

The equation whose graph passes through the three points is $x^2 + y^2 + 14x + 4y - 116 = 0$.

$$(x^2 + 14x + 49) + (y^2 + 4y + 4) = 116 + 49 + 4$$
$$(x + 7)^2 + (y + 2)^2 = 169$$

The center is $(-7, -2)$ and radius is 13.

39. For intersection A, $275 + 225 = x_1 + x_2$
$$x_1 + x_2 = 500$$
For intersection B, $x_2 + 90 = x_3 + 150$
$$x_2 - x_3 = 60$$
For intersection C, $x_1 + x_3 = 240 + 200$
$$x_1 + x_3 = 440$$

$$\begin{cases} x_1 + x_2 = 500 & (1) \\ x_2 - x_3 = 60 & (2) \\ x_1 + x_3 = 440 & (3) \end{cases}$$

Add equations (1) and (3)
$$x_1 = x_2 - 500$$
$$x_3 = -x_2 + 990$$

Because $x_1 \geq 0$ and $x_3 \geq 0$, $x_2 \geq 500$. The minimum number of cars traveling between A and C is 500.

41. For intersection A, $256 + x_4 = 389 + x_1$
$$x_1 - x_4 = -133$$
For intersection B, $437 + x_1 = x_2 + 300$
$$x_1 - x_2 = -137$$
For intersection C, $298 + x_3 = 249 + x_4$
$$x_3 - x_4 = -49$$
For intersection D, $314 + x_2 = 367 + x_3$
$$x_2 - x_3 = 53$$

$$\begin{cases} x_1 - x_4 = -133 & (1) \\ x_1 - x_2 = -137 & (2) \\ x_3 - x_4 = -49 & (3) \\ x_2 - x_3 = 53 & (4) \end{cases}$$

The equations are dependent. Solving the system gives
$$x_1 = x_4 - 133$$
$$x_2 = x_4 + 4$$
$$x_3 = x_4 - 49$$

Because $125 \le x_1 \le 175$, then

$125 \le x_4 - 133 \le 175$ and $258 \le x_2 - 4 \le 308$ and $258 \le x_3 + 49 \le 308$

$258 \le x_4 \le 308$ $262 \le x_2 \le 312$ $209 \le x_3 \le 259$

The flow between C and A is 258 to 308 cars per hour
The flow between B and D is 262 to 312 cars per hour.
The flow between D and C is 209 to 259 cars per hour.

43. $w_1 d_1 + w_2 d_2 = w_3 d_3$ and $w_1 = 2$, $w_2 = 6$, $w_3 = 9$
$$2d_1 + 6d_2 = 9d_3 \quad (1)$$
From the words in the exercise,
$$d_1 + d_3 = 13 \qquad (2)$$
$$d_2 = \tfrac{1}{3} d_1 \quad (3)$$

$$\begin{array}{ll} 2d_1 + 6d_2 - 9d_3 = 0 & (1) \\ \underline{2d_1 - 6d_2 \qquad\quad = 0} & \text{6 times (3)} \\ 4d_1 \qquad\; - 9d_3 = 0 & (4) \end{array}$$

$$\begin{array}{ll} 4d_1 - 9d_3 = 0 & (4) \\ \underline{9d_1 + 9d_3 = 0} & \text{9 times (2)} \\ 13d_1 \qquad\; = 117 & (5) \\ \quad d_1 = 9 & \end{array}$$

Substitute into equation (3) and (2)
$$d_2 = \tfrac{1}{3}(9) = 3$$
$$9 + d_3 = 13$$
$$d_3 = 4$$

The positions are: $d_1 = 9$ in., $d_2 = 3$ in., and $d_3 = 4$ in.

45. $\begin{cases} 2x + y - 3z + 2w = -1 & (1) \\ 2y - 5z - 3w = 9 & (2) \\ 3y - 8z + w = -4 & (3) \\ 2y - 2z + 3w = -3 & (4) \end{cases}$

$\begin{array}{ll} 6y - 15z - 9w = 27 & \text{3 times (2)} \\ \underline{-6y + 16z - 2w = 8} & -\text{2 times (3)} \\ \quad z - 11w = 35 & (5) \end{array}$

$\begin{array}{ll} 2y - 5z - 3w = 9 & (2) \\ \underline{-2y + 2z - 3w = 8} & -\text{1 times (4)} \\ \quad -3z - 6w = 12 \\ \quad z + 2w = -4 & (6) \end{array}$

$\begin{cases} 2x + y - 3z + 2w = -1 \\ 2y - 5z - 3w = 9 \\ z - 11w = 35 & (5) \\ z + 2w = -4 & (6) \end{cases}$

$\begin{array}{ll} z - 11w = 35 & (5) \\ \underline{-z - 2w = 4} & -\text{1 times (6)} \\ \quad -13w = 39 \\ \quad w = -3 & (7) \end{array}$

$\begin{cases} 2x + y - 3z + 2w = -1 \\ 2y - 5z - 3w = 9 \\ z - 11w = 35 \\ w = -3 & (7) \end{cases}$

$z - 11(-3) = 35$
$z = 2$

$2y - 5(2) - 3(-3) = 9$
$2y = 10$
$y = 5$

$2x + 5 - 3(2) + 2(-3) = -1$
$2x = 6$
$x = 3$

The solution is $(3, 5, 2, -3)$.

47. $\begin{cases} x - 3y + 2z - w = 2 & (1) \\ 2x - 5y - 3z + 2w = 21 & (2) \\ 3x - 8y - 2z - 3w = 12 & (3) \\ -2x + 8y + z + 2w = -13 & (4) \end{cases}$

$\begin{array}{ll} -2x + 6y - 4z + 2w = -4 & -\text{2 times (1)} \\ \underline{2x - 5y - 3z + 2w = 21} & (2) \\ \quad y - 7z + 4w = 17 & (5) \end{array}$

$\begin{array}{ll} -3x + 9y - 6z + 3w = -6 & -\text{3 times (1)} \\ \underline{3x - 8y - 2z - 3w = 12} & (3) \\ \quad y - 8z \qquad = 6 & (6) \end{array}$

$\begin{array}{ll} 2x - 5y - 3z + 2w = 21 & (2) \\ \underline{-2x + 8y + z + 2w = -13} & (4) \\ \quad 3y - 2z + 4w = 8 & (7) \end{array}$

$\begin{cases} x - 3y + 2z - w = 2 \\ y - 7z + 4w = 17 & (5) \\ y - 8z \qquad = 6 & (6) \\ 3y - 2z + 4w = 8 & (7) \end{cases}$

$\begin{array}{ll} y - 7z + 4w = 17 & (5) \\ \underline{-3y + 2z - 4w = -8} & -\text{1 times (7)} \\ \quad -2y - 5z \quad = 9 & (8) \end{array}$

$\begin{cases} x - 3y + 2z - w = 2 \\ y - 7z + 4w = 17 \\ y - 8z \qquad = 6 & (6) \\ -2y - 5z \quad = 9 & (8) \end{cases}$

$\begin{array}{ll} 2y - 16z = 12 & \text{2 times (6)} \\ \underline{-2y - 5z = 9} & (8) \\ \quad -21z = 21 \\ \quad z = -1 & (9) \end{array}$

$\begin{cases} x - 3y + 2z - w = 2 \\ y - 7z + 4w = 17 \\ y - 8z \qquad = 6 \\ z \qquad = -1 & (9) \end{cases}$

$y - 8(-1) = 6$
$y = -2$

$(-2) - 7(-1) + 4w = 17$
$4w = 12$
$w = 3$

$x - 3(-2) + 2(-1) - 3 = 2$
$x = 1$

The solution is $(1, -2, -1, 3)$.

49.
$$\begin{cases} x + 2y - 2z + 3w = 2 & (1) \\ 2x + 5y + 2z + 4w = 9 & (2) \\ 4x + 9y - 2z + 10w = 13 & (3) \\ -x - y + 8z - 5w = 3 & (4) \end{cases}$$

$$\begin{array}{ll} -2x - 4y + 4z - 6w = -4 & -2 \text{ times (1)} \\ \underline{2x + 5y + 2z + 4w = 9} & (2) \\ y + 6z - 2w = 5 & (5) \end{array}$$

$$\begin{array}{ll} -4x - 8y + 8z - 12w = -8 & -4 \text{ times (1)} \\ \underline{4x + 9y - 2z + 10w = 13} & (3) \\ y + 6z - 2w = 5 & (6) \end{array}$$

$$\begin{array}{ll} x + 2y - 2z + 3w = 2 & (1) \\ \underline{-x - y + 8z - 5w = 3} & (4) \\ y + 6z - 2w = 5 & (7) \end{array}$$

$$\begin{cases} x + 2y - 2z + 3w = 2 \\ y + 6z - 2w = 5 & (5) \\ y + 6z - 2w = 5 & (6) \\ y + 6z - 2w = 5 & (7) \end{cases}$$

$$\begin{cases} x + 2y - 2z + 3w = 2 \\ y + 6z - 2w = 5 \\ 0 = 0 \\ 0 = 0 \end{cases}$$

Let $z = a, w = b$.

$$y + 6a - 2b = 5$$
$$y = -6a + 2b + 5$$

$$x + 2(-6a + 2b + 5) - 2a + 3b = 2$$
$$x - 12a + 4b + 10 - 2a + 3b = 2$$
$$x = 14a - 7b - 8$$

The solutions are $(14a - 7b - 8, \ -6a + 2b + 5, \ a, \ b)$.

51.
$$\begin{cases} x - 3y - 2z = A^2 & (1) \\ 2x - 5y + Az = 9 & (2) \\ 2x - 8y + z = 18 & (3) \end{cases}$$

Multiply Eq. (1) by -2 and add to Eq. (2). Now multiply Eq. (1) by -2 and add to Eq. (3). The resulting system is

$$\begin{cases} x - 3y - 2z = A^2 & (4) \\ y + (4 + A)z = -2A^2 + 9 & (5) \\ -2y + 5z = -2A^2 + 18 & (6) \end{cases}$$

Multiply Eq. (5) by 2 and add to Eq. (6). We now have

$$\begin{cases} x - 3y - 2z = A^2 \\ y + (4 + A)z = -2A^2 + 9 \\ (2A + 13)z = -6A^2 + 36 & (7) \end{cases}$$

For Exercise 51, the system of equations has no solution when $2A + 13 = 0$ or $A = -\dfrac{13}{2}$.

53-55.

$$\begin{cases} x+2y+z=A^2 & (1) \\ -2x-3y+Az=1 & (2) \\ 7x+12y+A^2z=4A^2-3 & (3) \end{cases}$$

Multiply Eq. (1) by 2 and add to Eq. (2). Then multiply Eq. (1) by -7 and add to Eq. (3). The resulting system is

$$\begin{cases} x+2y+z=A^2 & (4) \\ y+(A+2)z=2A^2+1 & (5) \\ -2y+(A^2-7)z=-3A^2-3 & (6) \end{cases}$$

Multiply Eq. (5) by 2 and add to Eq. (6).

$$\begin{cases} x+2y+z=A^2 \\ y+(A+2)z=2A^2+1 \\ (A^2+2A-3)z=A^2-1 & (7) \end{cases}$$

In Exercise 53, the system of equations will have a unique solution when $(A^2+2A-3) \neq 0$ in Eq. (7). That is, $(A+3)(A-1) \neq 0$, or $A \neq -3$, $A \neq 1$

In Exercise 55, the system of equations will have no solution when $A^2+2A-3=0$ and $A^2-1 \neq 0$. This occurs when $A=-3$.

57. $z = ax + by + c$

$$\begin{cases} a-b+c=5 & (1) \\ 2a-2b+c=9 & (2) \\ -3a-b+c=-1 & (3) \end{cases}$$

$$\begin{array}{ll} 3a-3b+3c=15 & 3 \text{ times } (1) \\ \underline{-3a-b+c=-1} & (3) \\ -4b+4c=14 \end{array}$$

$$\begin{array}{ll} -2a+2b-2c=-10 & -2 \text{ times } (1) \\ \underline{2a-2b+c=9} & (2) \\ -c=-1 \\ c=1 \end{array}$$

$$-4b+4(1)=14$$
$$b=-\frac{5}{2}$$
$$a-\left(-\frac{5}{2}\right)+1=5$$
$$a=\frac{3}{2}$$

Thus the equation of the plane is $z=\frac{3}{2}x-\frac{5}{2}y+1$ or $3x-5y-2z=-2$.

Prepare for Section 6.3

58.
$$x^2+2x-2=0$$
$$x^2+2x+1=2+1$$
$$(x+1)^2=3$$
$$x+1=\pm\sqrt{3}$$
$$x=-1\pm\sqrt{3}$$

59.
$$\begin{cases} x+4y=-11 & (1) \\ 3x-2y=9 & (2) \end{cases}$$

Solve equation (1) for x: $x=-4y-11$

$$3(-4y-11)-2y=9$$
$$-12y-33-2y=9$$
$$-14y=42$$
$$y=-3$$
$$x=-4(-3)-11$$
$$x=1$$

The solution is $(1,-3)$.

60. parabola

61. hyperbola

62. 2

63. 4

Section 6.3

1. $\begin{cases} y = x^2 - x & (1) \\ y = 2x - 2 & (2) \end{cases}$

Set the expressions for y equal to each other.

$$x^2 - x = 2x - 2$$
$$x^2 - 3x + 2 = 0$$
$$(x - 2)(x - 1) = 0$$
$$x - 2 = 0 \qquad x - 1 = 0$$
$$x = 2 \qquad\quad x = 1$$

When $x = 2$, $y = 2^2 - 2 = 2$ (From Eq. (1))

When $x = 1$, $y = 1^2 - 1 = 0$

The solutions are $(1, 0)$ and $(2, 2)$.

3. $\begin{cases} y = 2x^2 - 3x - 3 & (1) \\ y = x - 4 & (2) \end{cases}$

Set the expressions for y equal to each other.

$$2x^2 - 3x - 3 = x - 4$$
$$2x^2 - 4x + 1 = 0$$
$$x = \frac{4 \pm \sqrt{16 - 4(2)(1)}}{2 \cdot 2} \text{ (Quadratic Formula)}$$
$$= \frac{4 \pm \sqrt{8}}{4} = \frac{4 \pm 2\sqrt{2}}{4} = \frac{2 \pm \sqrt{2}}{2}$$

Substitute for x in (1) and solve for y.

When $x = \dfrac{2 + \sqrt{2}}{2}$, $y = \dfrac{2 + \sqrt{2}}{2} - 4 = \dfrac{-6 + \sqrt{2}}{2}$.

When $x = \dfrac{2 - \sqrt{2}}{2}$, $y = \dfrac{2 - \sqrt{2}}{2} - 4 = \dfrac{-6 - \sqrt{2}}{2}$.

The solutions are

$$\left(\frac{2 + \sqrt{2}}{2}, \frac{-6 + \sqrt{2}}{2} \right) \text{ and } \left(\frac{2 - \sqrt{2}}{2}, \frac{-6 - \sqrt{2}}{2} \right).$$

5. $\begin{cases} y = x^2 - 2x + 3 & (1) \\ y = x^2 - x - 2 & (2) \end{cases}$

Set the expressions for y equal to each other.

$$x^2 - 2x + 3 = x^2 - x - 2$$
$$-x = -5$$
$$x = 5$$

Substitute for x in Eq. (1).

$$y = 5^2 - 2(5) + 3$$
$$y = 18$$

The solution is $(5, 18)$.

7. $\begin{cases} x + y = 10 & (1) \\ xy = 24 & (2) \end{cases}$

Substitute y from Eq. (1) into Eq. (2).

$$x(10 - x) = 24$$
$$10x - x^2 = 24$$
$$0 = x^2 - 10x + 24$$
$$0 = (x - 4)(x - 6)$$
$$x = 4 \text{ or } x = 6$$

Substitute for x in Eq. (1).

$$4 + y = 10 \qquad\qquad 6 + y = 10$$
$$y = 6 \qquad\qquad\qquad y = 4$$

The solutions are $(4, 6)$ and $(6, 4)$.

9. $\begin{cases} 2x - y = 1 & (1) \\ xy = 6 & (2) \end{cases}$

Solve Eq. (1) for y.

$y = 2x - 1$ (3)

Substitute into Eq. (2).

$x(2x - 1) = 6$

$2x^2 - x = 6$

$2x^2 - x - 6 = 0$

$(2x + 3)(x - 2) = 0$

$2x + 3 = 0,$ or $x - 2 = 0$

$x = -\dfrac{3}{2} \qquad x = 2$

Substitute for x in Eq. (3).

When $x = -\dfrac{3}{2},\ y = 2\left(-\dfrac{3}{2}\right) - 1 = -4.$

When $x = 2,\ y = 2(2) - 1 = 3$.

The solutions are $(-3/2, -4)$ and $(2, 3)$.

11. $\begin{cases} 3x^2 - 2y^2 = 1 & (1) \\ y = 4x - 3 & (2) \end{cases}$

Substitute y from Eq. (2) into Eq. (1).

$3x^2 - 2(4x - 3)^2 = 1$

$3x^2 - 32x^2 + 48x - 18 = 1$

$29x^2 - 48x + 19 = 0$

$(29x - 19)(x - 1) = 0$

$x = \dfrac{19}{29}$ or $x = 1$

Substitute for x in Eq. (2).

$y = 4\left(\dfrac{19}{29}\right) - 3 \qquad\quad y = 4(1) - 3$

$\qquad\qquad\qquad\qquad\qquad\quad y = 1$

$y = \dfrac{76}{29} - \dfrac{87}{29}$

$y = -\dfrac{11}{29}$

The solutions are $(19/29, -11/29)$ and $(1, 1)$.

13. $\begin{cases} y = x^3 + 4x^2 - 3x - 5 & (1) \\ y = 2x^2 - 2x - 3 & (2) \end{cases}$

Set the expressions for y equal to each other.

$x^3 + 4x^2 - 3x - 5 = 2x^2 - 2x - 3$

$x^3 + 2x^2 - x - 2 = 0$

$x^2(x + 2) - (x + 2) = 0$

$(x + 2)(x^2 - 1) = 0$

$(x + 2)(x - 1)(x + 1) = 0$

$x = -2,\ x = 1,$ or $x = -1$

Substitute for x in Eq. (2).

$y = 2(-2)^2 - 2(-2) - 3$

$y = 9$

$y = 2(1)^2 - 2(1) - 3$

$y = -3$

$y = 2(-1)^2 - 2(-1) - 3$

$y = 1$

The solutions are $(-2, 9),\ (1, -3)$ and $(-1, 1)$.

15. $\begin{cases} 2x^2 + y^2 = 9 & (1) \\ x^2 - y^2 = 3 & (2) \end{cases}$

$2x^2 + y^2 = 9$

$\underline{x^2 - y^2 = 3}$

$ 3x^2 = 12$ Add the equations.

$x^2 = 4$

$x = \pm 2$

When $x = -2,\ (-2)^2 - y^2 = 3$ From Eq. (2)

$4 - y^2 = 3$

$-y^2 = -1$

$y^2 = 1$

$y = \pm 1$

When $x = 2,\ (2)^2 - y^2 = 3$

$4 - y^2 = 3$

$-y^2 = -1$

$y^2 = 1$

$y = \pm 1$

The solutions are $(-2, 1),\ (-2, -1),\ (2, 1)$ and $(2, -1)$.

17.
$$\begin{cases} x^2 - 2y^2 = 8 & (1) \\ x^2 + 3y^2 = 28 & (2) \end{cases}$$

Use the elimination method to eliminate x^2.

$$x^2 - 2y^2 = 8$$
$$\underline{-x^2 - 3y^2 = -28}$$
$$-5y^2 = -20$$
$$y^2 = 4$$
$$y = \pm 2$$

Substitute for y in Eq. (1).

$$x^2 - 2(2)^2 = 8 \qquad x^2 - 2(-2)^2 = 8$$
$$x^2 = 16 \qquad\qquad x^2 = 16$$
$$x = \pm 4 \qquad\qquad x = \pm 4$$

The solutions are (4, 2), (–4, 2), (4, –2) and (–4, –2).

19.
$$\begin{cases} 2x^2 + 4y^2 = 5 & (1) \\ 3x^2 + 8y^2 = 14 & (2) \end{cases}$$

Use the elimination method to eliminate y^2.

$$-4x^2 - 8y^2 = -10 \quad -2 \text{ times (1)}$$
$$\underline{3x^2 + 8y^2 = 14}$$
$$-x^2 \qquad\quad = 4$$
$$x^2 = -4$$

$x^2 = -4$ has no real number solutions. The graphs of the equations do not intersect.

21.
$$\begin{cases} x^2 - 2x + y^2 = 1 & (1) \\ 2x + y = 5 & (2) \end{cases}$$

Substitute y from Eq. (2) into Eq. (1).

$$x^2 - 2x + (5 - 2x)^2 = 1$$
$$x^2 - 2x + 25 - 20x + 4x^2 = 1$$
$$5x^2 - 22x + 24 = 0$$
$$(5x - 12)(x - 2) = 0$$

$$x = \frac{12}{5} \text{ or } x = 2$$

Substitute for x in Eq. (2).

$$2\left(\frac{12}{5}\right) + y = 5 \qquad 2(2) + y = 5$$
$$y = \frac{1}{5} \qquad\qquad y = 1$$

The solutions are (12/5, 1/5) and (2, 1).

23.
$$\begin{cases} (x-3)^2 + (y+1)^2 = 5 & (1) \\ x - 3y = 7 & (2) \\ x = 3y + 7 \end{cases}$$

Substitute x from Eq. (2) into Eq. (1).

$$(3y + 4)^2 + (y + 1)^2 = 5$$
$$9y^2 + 24y + 16 + y^2 + 2y + 1 = 5$$
$$10y^2 + 26y + 12 = 0$$
$$5y^2 + 13y + 6 = 0$$
$$(5y + 3)(y + 2) = 0$$

$$y = -\frac{3}{5} \text{ or } y = -2$$

Substitute for y in Eq. (3).

$$x = 3\left(-\frac{3}{5}\right) + 7 \qquad x = 3(-2) + 7$$
$$x = \frac{26}{5} \qquad\qquad\quad x = 1$$

The solutions are (26/5, –3/5) and (1, –2).

25. $\begin{cases} x^2 - 3x + y^2 = 4 & (1) \\ \qquad\quad 3x + y = 11 & (2) \end{cases}$

Substitute y from Eq. (2) into Eq. (1).

$$x^2 - 3x + (11 - 3x)^2 = 4$$
$$x^2 - 3x + 121 - 66x + 9x^2 = 4$$
$$10x^2 - 69x + 117 = 0$$
$$(10x - 29)(x - 3) = 0$$
$$x = \frac{39}{10} \text{ or } x = 3$$

Substitute for x in Eq. (2).

$$3\left(\frac{39}{10}\right) + y = 11 \qquad\qquad 3(3) + y = 11$$
$$\qquad\qquad\qquad\qquad\qquad\qquad y = 2$$
$$y = -\frac{7}{10}$$

The solutions are (39/10, −7/10) and (3, 2).

27. $\begin{cases} (x-1)^2 + (y+2)^2 = 14 & (1) \\ (x+2)^2 + (y-1)^2 = 2 & (2) \end{cases}$

Expand the binomials and then subtract.

$$x^2 - 2x + 1 + y^2 + 4y + 4 = 14$$
$$\underline{x^2 + 4x + 4 + y^2 - 2y + 1 = 2}$$
$$-6x - 3 \qquad + 6y + 3 = 12$$
$$-6x \qquad\qquad + 6y = 12$$
$$\qquad\qquad\qquad\quad y = x + 2$$

Substitute for y in Eq. (2).

$$(x+2)^2 + (x+2-1)^2 = 2$$
$$x^2 + 4x + 4 + x^2 + 2x + 1 = 2$$
$$2x^2 + 6x + 3 = 0$$

$$x = \frac{-6 \pm \sqrt{36 - 4 \cdot 2 \cdot 3}}{4}$$
$$= \frac{-6 \pm \sqrt{12}}{4} = \frac{-3 \pm \sqrt{3}}{2}$$

Substitute for x in $y = x + 2$.

$$y = \frac{-3 + \sqrt{3}}{2} + 2 \qquad\qquad y = \frac{-3 - \sqrt{3}}{2} + 2$$
$$y = \frac{1 + \sqrt{3}}{2} \qquad\qquad\qquad y = \frac{1 - \sqrt{3}}{2}$$

The solutions are
$$\left(\frac{-3 + \sqrt{3}}{2}, \frac{1 + \sqrt{3}}{2}\right) \text{ and } \left(\frac{-3 - \sqrt{3}}{2}, \frac{1 - \sqrt{3}}{2}\right).$$

29. $\begin{cases} (x+3)^2 + (y-2)^2 = 20 & (1) \\ (x-2)^2 + (y-3)^2 = 2 & (2) \end{cases}$

Expand the binomials and then subtract.

$$x^2 + 6x + 9 + y^2 - 4y + 4 = 20$$
$$\underline{x^2 - 4x + 4 + y^2 - 6y + 9 = 2}$$
$$10x + 5 \quad\;\; + 2y - 5 = 18$$
$$10x \quad\;\;\;\; + 2y \quad\; = 18$$
$$y = -5x + 9$$

Substitute for y in Eq. (2): $y - 3 = -5x + 6$.

$$(x-2)^2 + (-5x+6)^2 = 2$$
$$x^2 - 4x + 4 + 25x^2 - 60x + 36 = 2$$
$$26x^2 - 64x + 38 = 0$$
$$13x^2 - 32x + 19 = 0$$
$$(13x - 19)(x - 1) = 0$$

$$x = \frac{19}{13} \text{ or } x = 1$$

Substitute for x in $y = -5x + 9$.

$$y = -5\left(\frac{19}{13}\right) + 9 \qquad\qquad y = -5(1) + 9$$
$$\qquad\qquad\qquad\qquad\qquad\qquad\;\; y = 4$$
$$y = \frac{22}{13}$$

The solutions are (19/13, 22/13) and (1, 4).

31. $\begin{cases} (x-1)^2 + (y+1)^2 = 2 & (1) \\ (x+2)^2 + (y-3)^2 = 3 & (2) \end{cases}$

Expand the binomials and then subtract.

$$x^2 - 2x + 1 + y^2 + 2y + 1 = 2$$
$$\underline{x^2 + 4x + 4 + y^2 - 6y + 9 = 3}$$
$$-6x - 3 \quad\;\; + 8y - 8 = -1$$
$$-6x \quad\;\;\;\; + 8y \quad\; = 10$$
$$y = \frac{3x + 5}{4}$$

Substitute for y in Eq. (1): $y + 1 = \dfrac{3x+9}{4}$.

$$(x-1)^2 + \left(\frac{3x+9}{4}\right)^2 = 2$$
$$x^2 - 2x + 1 + \frac{9x^2 + 54x + 81}{16} = 2$$
$$16x^2 - 32x + 16 + 9x^2 + 54x + 81 = 32$$
$$25x^2 + 22x + 65 = 0$$
$$x = \frac{-22 \pm \sqrt{22^2 - 4(25)(65)}}{2(25)}$$
$$x = \frac{-22 \pm \sqrt{-6016}}{50}$$

x is not a real number. There are no real solutions. The curves do not intersect.

33. $\begin{cases} x^2 = y & (1) \\ 18x - 22 = 3y + 5 & (2) \end{cases}$

Substitute for y in Eq. (2).

$$18x - 22 = 3\left(x^2\right) + 5$$
$$0 = 3x^2 - 18x + 27$$
$$0 = 3(x^2 - 6x + 9)$$
$$0 = 3(x - 3)^2$$

$x = 3$

$y = 3^2 = 9$

$P = x^2 + 3y + 5 + y + 18x - 22$
$\quad = 3^2 + 3(9) + 5 + 9 + 18(3) - 22$
$\quad = 82$ units

35. $\begin{cases} x^2 + y^2 = r^2 & (1) \\ \quad\quad y = 2x + 1 & (2) \end{cases}$

Substitute for y in Eq. (1)

$$x^2 + (2x + 1)^2 = r^2$$
$$x^2 + 4x^2 + 4x + 1 = r^2$$
$$5x^2 + 4x + 1 = r^2$$

Minimize r^2 by completing the square.

$$r^2 = 5x^2 + 4x + 1 = 5\left(x^2 + \frac{4}{5}x + \frac{4}{25}\right) + 1 - \frac{4}{5}$$
$$= 5\left(x + \frac{2}{5}\right)^2 + \frac{1}{5}$$

Thus $\left(-\frac{2}{5}, \frac{1}{5}\right)$ is the point on both $x^2 + y^2 = r^2$ and

$y = 2x + 1$ for which $x^2 + y^2 = r^2$ has the smallest radius.

Substitute for x in $r^2 = 5x^2 + 4x + 1$

$$r^2 = 5\left(-\frac{2}{5}\right)^2 + 4\left(-\frac{2}{5}\right) + 1 = \frac{1}{5}.$$
$$r = \sqrt{\frac{1}{5}} \text{ or } \frac{\sqrt{5}}{5} \text{ is the minimum radius.}$$

Therefore $r \geq \frac{\sqrt{5}}{5}$.

37. $\begin{cases} x = \dfrac{p^2}{5} - 20 \\ x = \dfrac{17{,}710}{p+1} \end{cases}$

Use a graphing calculator and INTERSECTION.

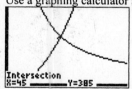

on [0, 100] by [0, 600]
The graphs intersect at (45, 385).

The solution is $45.

39. $\begin{cases} y = 2^x \\ y = x + 1 \end{cases}$

Using a graphing calculator, graph the two equations on the same coordinate grid. Using the ZOOM feature, estimate the coordinates of the points where the graphs intersect. These coordinates are the solutions of the system of equations. For this system of equations, the solutions are (0, 1) and (1, 2).

41. $\begin{cases} y = e^{-x} \\ y = x^2 \end{cases}$

Using a graphing calculator, graph the two equations on the same coordinate grid. Using the ZOOM feature, estimate the coordinates of the points where the graphs intersect. These coordinates are the solutions of the system of equations. For this system of equations, the solution is approximately (0.7035, 0.4949).

43. $\begin{cases} y = \sqrt{x} \\ y = \dfrac{1}{x-1} \end{cases}$

Using a graphing calculator, graph the two equations on the same coordinate grid. Using the ZOOM feature, estimate the coordinates of the points where the graphs intersect. These coordinates are the solutions of the system of equations. For this system of equations, the solution is approximately (1.7549, 1.3247).

45.
$$\begin{cases} y = |x| \\ y = 2^{-x^2} \end{cases}$$

Using a graphing calculator, graph the two equations on the same coordinate grid. Using the ZOOM feature, estimate the coordinates of the points where the graphs intersect. These coordinates are the solutions of the system of equations. For this system of equations, the solutions are $(-0.7071, 0.7071)$ and $(0.7071, 0.7071)$.

•••

47.
$$\begin{cases} y = x^2 + 4 \\ x = y^2 - 24 \end{cases}$$

Solve by substitution.
$$x = (x^2 + 4)^2 - 24$$
$$x = x^4 + 8x^2 + 16 - 24$$

$$0 = x^4 + 8x^2 - x - 8$$
$$0 = (x-1)(x^3 + x^2 + 9x + 8)$$

$x^3 + x^2 + 9x + 8$ is not factorable over the rational numbers because the Rational Zero Theorem implies the only rational; zeros are ± 1, ± 2, ± 4, ± 8. Thus, the only rational ordered-pair solution is $(1, 5)$.

49.
$$x^2 - 3xy + y^2 = 5$$
$$x^2 - xy - 2y^2 = 0$$
Factor the second equation.

$$(x - 2y)(x + y) = 0$$

Thus $x = 2y$ or $x = -y$. Substituting each expression into the first equation, we have
$$(2y)^2 - 3(2y)y + y^2 = 5$$
$$4y^2 - 6y^2 + y^2 = 5$$
$$-y^2 = 5$$
$$y^2 = -5$$

There are no rational solutions.

$$(-y)^2 - 3(-y)y + y^2 = 5$$
$$y^2 + 3y^2 + y^2 = 5$$
$$5y^2 = 5$$
$$y^2 = 1 \Rightarrow y = \pm 1$$

Substituting into $x = -y$, we have $x = -1$ or $x = 1$. The rational ordered-pair solutions are $(-1, 1)$ and $(1, -1)$.

51. $\begin{cases} 2x^2 - 4xy - y^2 = 6 \\ 4x^2 - 3xy - y^2 = 6 \end{cases}$

Subtract the two equations.

$-2x^2 - xy = 0$

$-x(2x + y) = 0$

$x = 0$ or $y = -2x$

Substituting $x = 0$ into the first equation gives $-y^2 = 6$ or $y^2 = -6$. There are no rational solutions.

Substituting $y = -2x$ into the first equation gives

$2x^2 + 8x^2 - 4x^2 = 6$

$6x^2 = 6$

$x^2 = 1$

$x = \pm 1$

The rational ordered-pair solutions are $(1, -2)$ and $(-1, 2)$.

53. Substitute $y = mx$ into $\dfrac{x^2}{a^2} - \dfrac{y^2}{b^2} = 1$.

$$\frac{x^2}{a^2} - \frac{m^2 x^2}{b^2} = 1$$

$$x^2\left(\frac{1}{a^2} - \frac{m^2}{b^2}\right) = 1$$

$$x^2 = \frac{1}{\left(\dfrac{1}{a^2} - \dfrac{m^2}{b^2}\right)}$$

Since $x^2 \geq 0$, $\left(\dfrac{1}{a^2} - \dfrac{m^2}{b^2}\right)$ must be positive.

Thus $\dfrac{1}{a^2} - \dfrac{m^2}{b^2} > 0$

$$-\frac{m^2}{b^2} > -\frac{1}{a^2}$$

$$m^2 < \frac{b^2}{a^2}$$

Thus, $|m| < \left|\dfrac{b}{a}\right|$.

• •

Prepare for Section 6.4

54. $x^4 + 14x^2 + 49 = (x^2 + 7)^2$

55. $\dfrac{5}{x-1} + \dfrac{1}{x+2} = \dfrac{x+2}{x+2} \cdot \dfrac{5}{x-1} + \dfrac{x-1}{x-1} \cdot \dfrac{1}{x+2}$

$= \dfrac{5x+10}{(x-1)(x+2)} + \dfrac{x-1}{(x-1)(x+2)}$

$= \dfrac{6x+9}{(x-1)(x+2)}$

56. $\dfrac{7}{x} - \dfrac{6}{x-1} + \dfrac{10}{(x-1)^2} = \dfrac{(x-1)^2}{(x-1)^2} \cdot \dfrac{7}{x} - \dfrac{x(x-1)}{x(x-1)} \cdot \dfrac{6}{x-1} + \dfrac{x}{x} \cdot \dfrac{10}{(x-1)^2}$

$= \dfrac{7x^2 - 14x + 7}{x(x-1)^2} - \dfrac{6x^2 - 6x}{x(x-1)^2} + \dfrac{10x}{x(x-1)^2}$

$= \dfrac{x^2 + 2x + 7}{x(x-1)^2}$

57. $\begin{cases} 1 = A + B & (1) \\ 11 = -5A + 3B & (2) \end{cases}$

Solve equation (1) for A and substitute into equation (2).

$11 = -5(1 - B) + 3B$

$11 = -5 + 8B$

$16 = 8B$

$2 = B$

$A = 1 - 2$

$= -1$

The solution is $(-1, 2)$.

58.
$$\begin{cases} 0=A+B & (1) \\ 3=-2B+C & (2) \\ 16=7A-2C & (3) \end{cases}$$

Solve equation (1) for A and substitute into equation (3).
$$16=-7B-2C \quad (4)$$

Multiply equation (2) by 2 and add to equation (4).
$$6=-4B+2C$$
$$\underline{16=-7B-2C}$$
$$22=-11B$$
$$-2=B$$

$$A=2$$

$$C=2B+3$$
$$=2(-2)+3$$
$$=-1$$

The solution is $(2,-2,-1)$.

59.
$$\frac{x^3-4x^2-19x-35}{x^2-7x}$$
Use long division.

$$\begin{array}{r} x+3 \\ x^2-7x\overline{)x^3-4x^2-19x-35} \\ \underline{x^3-7x^2} \\ 3x^2-19x \\ \underline{3x^2-21x} \\ 2x-35 \end{array}$$

$$\frac{x^3-4x^2-19x-35}{x^2-7x}=x+3+\frac{2x-35}{x^2-7x}$$

Section 6.4

1.
$$\frac{x+15}{x(x-5)}=\frac{A}{x}+\frac{B}{x-5}$$

$$x+15=A(x-5)+Bx$$
$$x+15=(A+B)x-5A$$
$$\begin{cases} 1=A+B \\ 15=-5A \end{cases} \quad A=-3 \quad \begin{array}{l} -3+B=1 \\ B=4 \end{array}$$

3.
$$\frac{1}{(2x+3)(x-1)}=\frac{A}{2x+3}+\frac{B}{x-1}$$

$$1=A(x-1)+B(2x+3)$$
$$1=Ax-A+2Bx+3B$$
$$1=(A+2B)x+(-A+3B)$$
$$0=A+2B$$
$$\underline{1=-A+3B}$$
$$1=\quad 5B$$

$$B=\frac{1}{5} \qquad 0=A+2\left(\frac{1}{5}\right)$$

$$A=-\frac{2}{5}$$

5.
$$\frac{x+9}{x(x-3)^2}=\frac{A}{x}+\frac{B}{x-3}+\frac{C}{(x-3)^2}$$

$$x+9=A(x-3)^2+Bx(x-3)+Cx$$
$$x+9=Ax^2-6Ax+9A+Bx^2-3Bx+Cx$$
$$x+9=(A+B)x^2+(-6A-3B+C)x+9A$$

$$\begin{cases} 0=A+B \\ 1=-6A-3B+C \\ 9=9A \end{cases}$$

$$\begin{array}{llll} A=1 & A+B=0 & & -6A-3B+C=1 \\ & 1+B=0 & & -6(1)-3(-1)+C=1 \\ & B=-1 & & C=4 \end{array}$$

7.
$$\frac{4x^2+3}{(x-1)(x^2+x+5)}=\frac{A}{x-1}+\frac{Bx+C}{x^2+x+5}$$

$$4x^2+3=A(x^2+x+5)+(Bx+C)(x-1)$$
$$4x^2+3=Ax^2+Ax+5A+Bx^2-Bx+Cx-C$$
$$4x^2+3=(A+B)x^2+(A-B+C)x+(5A-C)$$

$$\begin{cases} 4=A+B & (1) \\ 0=A-B+C & (2) \\ 3=5A-C & (3) \end{cases}$$

From (3), $C=5A-3$. From (1), $B=4-A$.
Substitute C and B into Eq. (2).

$$\begin{array}{lll} 0=A-(4-A)+5A-3 & C=5(1)-3 & B=4-1 \\ 0=A-4+A+5A-3 & C=2 & B=3 \\ 7=7A & & \\ 1=A & & \end{array}$$

9.

$$\frac{x^3 + 2x}{(x^2+1)^2} = \frac{Ax+B}{x^2+1} + \frac{Cx+D}{(x^2+1)^2}$$

$$x^3 + 2x = (Ax+B)(x^2+1) + (Cx+D)$$

$$x^3 + 2x = Ax^3 + Ax + Bx^2 + B + Cx + D$$

$$x^3 + 2x = Ax^3 + Bx^2 + (A+C)x + (B+D)$$

$$\begin{cases} 1 = A \\ 0 = B \\ 2 = A + C \\ 0 = B + D \end{cases} \qquad A = 1 \qquad B = 0 \qquad \begin{matrix} 1 + C = 2 \\ C = 1 \end{matrix} \qquad \begin{matrix} 0 + D = 0 \\ D = 0 \end{matrix}$$

11.

$$\frac{8x+12}{x(x+4)} = \frac{A}{x} + \frac{B}{x+4}$$

$$8x + 12 = A(x+4) + Bx$$

$$8x + 12 = Ax + 4A + Bx$$

$$8x + 12 = (A+B)x + 4A$$

$$\begin{cases} 8 = A + B \\ 12 = 4A \end{cases} \qquad \begin{matrix} A = 3 & 3 + B = 8 \\ & B = 5 \end{matrix}$$

$$\frac{8x+12}{x(x+4)} = \frac{3}{x} + \frac{5}{x+4}$$

13.

$$\frac{3x+50}{x^2 - 7x - 18} = \frac{3x+50}{(x-9)(x+2)}$$

$$= \frac{A}{x-9} + \frac{B}{x+2}$$

$$3x + 50 = A(x+2) + B(x-9)$$

$$3x + 50 = Ax + 2A + Bx - 9B$$

$$3x + 50 = (A+B)x + (2A - 9B)$$

$$\begin{cases} 3 = A + B \\ 50 = 2A - 9B \end{cases}$$

$$\begin{matrix} -2A - 2B = -6 & \qquad 3 = A + (-4) \\ \underline{2A - 9B = 50} & \qquad 7 = A \\ -11B = 44 & \\ B = -4 & \end{matrix}$$

$$\frac{3x+50}{x^2 - 7x - 18} = \frac{7}{x-9} + \frac{-4}{x+2}$$

15.

$$\frac{16x+34}{4x^2 + 16x + 15} = \frac{16x+34}{(2x+3)(2x+5)}$$

$$= \frac{A}{2x+3} + \frac{B}{2x+5}$$

$$16x + 34 = A(2x+5) + B(2x+3)$$

$$16x + 34 = 2Ax + 5A + 2Bx + 3B$$

$$16x + 34 = (2A+2B)x + (5A+3B)$$

$$\begin{cases} 16 = 2A + 2B & (1) \\ 34 = 5A + 3B & (2) \end{cases}$$

$$\begin{matrix} 6A + 6B = 48 & 3 \text{ times } (1) \\ \underline{-10A - 6B = -68} & -2 \text{ times } (2) \\ -4A \quad = -20 & \\ A = 5 & \end{matrix}$$

$$2(5) + 2B = 16$$

$$B = 3$$

$$\frac{16x+34}{4x^2 + 16x + 15} = \frac{5}{2x+3} + \frac{3}{2x+5}$$

17.

$$\frac{x-5}{(3x+5)(x-2)} = \frac{A}{3x+5} + \frac{B}{x-2}$$

$$x - 5 = A(x-2) + B(3x+5)$$

$$x - 5 = Ax - 2A + 3Bx + 5B$$

$$x - 5 = (A+3B)x + (-2A+5B)$$

$$\begin{cases} 1 = A + 3B & (1) \\ -5 = -2A + 5B & (2) \end{cases}$$

$$\begin{matrix} 2A + 6B = 2 & 2 \text{ times } (1) \\ \underline{-2A + 5B = -5} & (2) \\ 11B = -3 & \qquad A + 3\left(-\dfrac{3}{11}\right) = 1 \\ B = -\dfrac{3}{11} & \qquad A = \dfrac{20}{11} \end{matrix}$$

$$\frac{x-5}{(3x+5)(x-2)} = \frac{20}{11(3x+5)} + \frac{-3}{11(x-2)}$$

19.

$$\begin{array}{r} x+3 \\ x^2-4{\overline{\smash{\big)}\,x^3+3x^2-4x-8}} \end{array}$$

$$\begin{array}{r} x^3 \qquad -4x \\ \hline 3x^2 \qquad -8 \end{array}$$

$$\begin{array}{r} 3x^2 \qquad -12 \\ \hline 4 \end{array}$$

$$\frac{x^3+3x^2-4x-8}{x^2-4}=x+3+\frac{4}{(x-2)(x+2)}$$

$$\frac{4}{(x-2)(x+2)}=\frac{A}{x-2}+\frac{B}{x+2}$$

$$4=A(x+20+B(x-2)$$

$$4=Ax+2A+Bx-2B$$

$$4=(A+B)x+(2A-2B)$$

$$\begin{cases} 0=A+B & (1) \\ 4=2A-2B & (2) \end{cases}$$

$$2A+2B=0 \quad 2\text{ times }(1)$$

$$\underline{2A-2B=4 \quad (2)}$$

$$4A \quad\ \ =4 \qquad\qquad 1+B=0$$

$$\ \ A=1 \qquad\qquad\quad\ B=-1$$

$$\frac{x^3+3x^2-4x-8}{x^2-4}=x+3+\frac{1}{x-2}+\frac{-1}{x+2}$$

21.

$$\frac{3x^2+49}{x(x+7)^2}=\frac{A}{x}+\frac{B}{x+7}+\frac{C}{(x+7)^2}$$

$$3x^2+49=A(x+7)^2+Bx(x+7)+Cx$$

$$3x^2+49=Ax^2+14Ax+49A+Bx^2+7Bx+Cx$$

$$3x^2+49=(A+B)x^2+(14A+7B+C)x+49A$$

$$\begin{cases} 3=A+B & A=1 \quad 1+B=3 \quad 14(1)+7(2)+C=0 \\ 0=14A+7B+C & \qquad\ \ B=2 \qquad\qquad\qquad\ C=-28 \\ 49=49A \end{cases}$$

$$\frac{3x^2+49}{x(x+7)^2}=\frac{1}{x}+\frac{2}{x+7}+\frac{-28}{(x+7)^2}$$

23.

$$\frac{5x^2-7x+2}{x^3-3x^2+x}=\frac{5x^2-7x+2}{x(x^2-3x+1)}=\frac{A}{x}+\frac{Bx+C}{x^2-3x+1}$$

$$5x^2-7x+2=A(x^2-3x+1)+(Bx+C)x$$

$$5x^2-7x+2=Ax^2-3Ax+A+Bx^2+Cx$$

$$5x^2-7x+2=(A+B)x^2+(-3A+C)x+A$$

$$\begin{cases} 5=A+B & A=2 \quad 2+B=5 \quad -3(2)+C=-7 \\ -7=-3A+C & \qquad\ \ B=3 \qquad\quad\ C=-1 \\ 2=A \end{cases}$$

$$\frac{5x^2-7x+2}{x^3-3x^2+x}=\frac{2}{x}+\frac{3x-1}{x^2-3x+1}$$

25.

$$\frac{2x^3+9x^2+26x+41}{(x+3)^2(x^2+1)}=\frac{A}{x+3}+\frac{B}{(x+3)^2}+\frac{Cx+D}{x^2+1}$$

$$2x^3+9x^2+26x+41=A(x+3)(x^2+1)+B(x^2+1)+(Cx+D)(x+3)^2$$

$$2x^3+9x^2+26x+41=Ax^3+Ax+3Ax^2+3A+Bx^2+B+Cx^3+6Cx^2+9Cx+Dx^2+6Dx+9D$$

$$2x^3+9x^2+26x+41=(A+C)x^3+(3A+B+6C+D)x^2+(A+9C+6D)x+(3A+B+9D)$$

$$\begin{cases} 2=A+C & (1) \\ 9=3A+B+6C+D & (2) \\ 26=A+9C+6D & (3) \\ 41=3A+B+9D & (4) \end{cases}$$

$$3A+B+6C+D=9 \qquad (3)$$

$$\underline{-3A-B\quad -9D=-41} \qquad -1\text{ times }(4)$$

$$6C-8D=-32 \quad (5)$$

$$A+9C+6D=26 \quad (3)$$

$$\underline{-A-C\qquad =-2} \qquad -1\text{ times }(1)$$

$$8C+6D=24 \quad (6)$$

$$\begin{cases} 2=A+C \\ 9=3A+B+6C+D \\ 24=8C+6D & (6) \\ -32=6C-8D & (5) \end{cases}$$

$$64C+48D=192 \qquad 8\text{ times }(6)$$

$$\underline{36C-48D=-192} \qquad 6\text{ times }(5)$$

$$100C\qquad =0$$

$$C=0 \qquad \begin{array}{l} A+0=2 \\ A=2 \end{array} \qquad \begin{array}{l} 8(0)+6D=24 \\ D=4 \end{array} \qquad \begin{array}{l} 3(2)+B+9(4)=41 \\ B=-1 \end{array}$$

$$\frac{2x^3+9x^2+26x+41}{(x+3)^2(x^2+1)}=\frac{2}{x+3}+\frac{-1}{(x+3)^2}+\frac{4}{x^2+1}$$

27.

$$\frac{3x-7}{(x-4)^2}=\frac{A}{x-4}+\frac{B}{(x-4)^2}$$

$$3x-7=A(x-4)+B$$

$$3x-7=Ax-4A+B$$

$$3x-7=Ax+(-4A+B)$$

$$\begin{cases} 3=A \\ -7=-4A+B \end{cases} \qquad \begin{array}{l} B-4(3)=-7 \\ B=5 \end{array}$$

$$\frac{3x-7}{(x-4)^2}=\frac{3}{x-4}+\frac{5}{(x-4)^2}$$

29.

$$\frac{3x^3-x^2+34x-10}{(x^2+10)^2}=\frac{Ax+B}{x^2+10}+\frac{Cx+D}{(x^2+10)^2}$$

$$3x^3-x^2+34x-10=(Ax+B)(x^2+10)+Cx+D$$

$$3x^3-x^2+34x-10=Ax^3+Bx^2+10Ax+10B+Cx+D$$

$$3x^3-x^2+34x-10=Ax^3+Bx^2+(10A+C)x+(10B+D)$$

$$\begin{cases} 3=A \\ -1=B \\ 34=1-A+C \\ -10=10B+D \end{cases} \qquad \begin{array}{l} 10(3)+C=34 \\ C=4 \end{array} \qquad \begin{array}{l} 10(-1)+D=-10 \\ D=0 \end{array}$$

$$\frac{3x^3-x^2+34x-10}{(x^2+10)^2}=\frac{3x-1}{x^2+10}+\frac{4x}{(x^2+10)^2}$$

31.

$$\frac{1}{k^2 - x^2} = \frac{1}{(k-x)(k+x)} = \frac{A}{k-x} + \frac{B}{k+x}$$

$$1 = A(k+x) + B(k-x)$$
$$1 = Ak + Ax + Bk - Bx$$
$$1 = (A-B)x + (Ak+Bk)$$

$$\begin{cases} 0 = A - B & (1) \\ 1 = Ak + Bk & (2) \end{cases}$$

$$Ak + Bk = 1 \qquad (2)$$
$$\underline{Ak - Bk = 0} \qquad k \text{ times } (1)$$
$$2Ak \qquad = 1$$

$$A = \frac{1}{2k}$$

$$\frac{1}{2k} - B = 0$$

$$B = \frac{1}{2k}$$

$$\frac{1}{k^2 - x^2} = \frac{1}{2k(k-x)} + \frac{1}{2k(k+x)}$$

33.

$$\begin{array}{r} x \\ x^2 - x \overline{\smash{\big)}\, x^3 - x^2 - x - 1} \\ \underline{x^3 - x^2 } \\ -x - 1 \end{array}$$

$$\frac{x^3 - x^2 - x - 1}{x^2 - x} = x + \frac{-x-1}{x^2 - x}$$

$$\frac{-x-1}{x(x-1)} = \frac{A}{x} + \frac{B}{x-1}$$

$$-x - 1 = Ax - A + Bx$$
$$-x - 1 = (A+B)x - A$$

$$\begin{cases} -1 = A + B \\ -1 = -A \end{cases} \qquad A = 1 \qquad \begin{array}{c} 1 + B = -1 \\ B = -2 \end{array}$$

$$\frac{x^3 - x^2 - x - 1}{x^2 - x} = x + \frac{1}{x} + \frac{-2}{x-1}$$

35.

$$\begin{array}{r} 2x - 2 \\ x^2 - x - 1 \overline{\smash{\big)}\, 2x^3 - 4x^2 + 5} \\ \underline{2x^3 - 2x^2 - 2x } \\ -2x^2 + 2x + 5 \\ \underline{-2x^2 + 2x + 2} \\ 3 \end{array}$$

$$\frac{2x^3 - 4x^2 + 5}{x^2 - x - 1} = 2x - 2 + \frac{3}{x^2 - x - 1}$$

•••

37.

$$\frac{x^2 - 1}{(x-1)(x+2)(x-3)} = \frac{(x-1)(x+1)}{(x-1)(x+2)(x-3)}$$

$$= \frac{x+1}{(x+2)(x-3)} = \frac{A}{x+2} + \frac{B}{x-3}$$

$$x + 1 = A(x-3) + B(x+2)$$
$$x + 1 = Ax - 3A + Bx + 2B$$
$$x + 1 = (A+B)x + (-3A + 2B)$$

$$\begin{cases} A + B = 1 \\ -3A + 2B = 1 \end{cases}$$

$$3A + 3B = 3$$
$$5B = 4$$

$$B = \frac{4}{5} \qquad A = \frac{1}{5}$$

$$\frac{x^2 - 1}{(x-1)(x+2)(x-3)} = \frac{1}{5(x+2)} + \frac{4}{5(x-3)}$$

39.

$$\frac{-x^4-4x^2+3x-6}{x^4(x-2)}=\frac{A}{x}+\frac{B}{x^2}+\frac{C}{x^3}+\frac{D}{x^4}+\frac{E}{x-2}$$

$$-x^4-4x^2+3x-6=Ax^3(x-2)+Bx^2(x-2)+Cx(x-2)+D(x-2)+Ex^4$$

$$-x^4-4x^2+3x-6=Ax^4-2Ax^3+Bx^3-2Bx^2+Cx^2-2Cx+Dx-2D+Ex^4$$

$$-x^4-4x^2+3x-6=(A+E)x^4+(-2A+B)x^3+(-2B+C)x^2+(-2C+D)x+(-2D)$$

$$\begin{cases}-1=A+E\\0=-2A+B\\-4=-2B+C\\3=-2C+D\\-6=-2D\end{cases}$$

$-2D=-6$	$-2C+3=3$	$-2B+0=-4$	$-2A+2=0$	$1+E=-1$
$D=3$	$C=0$	$B=2$	$A=-2$	$E=-2$

$$\frac{-x^4-4x^2+3x-6}{x^4(x-2)}=\frac{1}{x}+\frac{2}{x^2}+\frac{3}{x^4}+\frac{-2}{x-2}$$

41.

$$\frac{2x^2+3x-1}{(x^3-1)}=\frac{2x^2+3x-1}{(x-1)(x^2+x+1)}=\frac{A}{x-1}+\frac{Bx+C}{x^2+x+1}$$

$$2x^2+3x-1=A(x^2+x+1)+(Bx+C)(x-1)$$

$$2x^2+3x-1=Ax^2+Ax+A+Bx^2-Bx+Cx-C$$

$$2x^2+3x-1=(A+B)x^2+(A-B+C)x+(A-C)$$

$$\begin{cases}2=A+B & (1)\\3=A-B+C & (2)\\-1=A-C & (3)\end{cases}$$

Solve Eq. (1) for B and Eq. (3) for C and substitute into Eq. (2).

$$A+B=2 \qquad\qquad A-C=-1$$
$$B=2-A \qquad\qquad C=A+1$$

$$A-B+C=3$$
$$A-(2-A)+(A+1)=3 \qquad B=2-A \qquad C=A+1$$
$$A-2+A+A+1=3 \qquad B=2-\frac{4}{3} \qquad C=\frac{4}{3}+1$$
$$3A=4$$
$$A=\frac{4}{3} \qquad\qquad B=\frac{2}{3} \qquad C=\frac{7}{3}$$

$$\frac{2x^2+3x-1}{x^3-1}=\frac{4}{3(x-1)}+\frac{2x+7}{3(x^2+x+1)}$$

43.

$$\frac{1}{(b-a)(p(x)+a)}+\frac{1}{(a-b)(p(x)+b)}=\frac{(a-b)(p(x)+b)+(b-a)(p(x)+a)}{(b-a)(a-b)(p(x)+a)(p(x)+b)}$$

$$=\frac{(a-b)p(x)+(a-b)b+(b-a)p(x)+(b-a)a}{(b-a)(a-b)(p(x)+a)(p(x)+b)}$$

$$=\frac{(a-b)p(x)+(a-b)b-(a-b)p(x)-(a-b)a}{(b-a)(a-b)(p(x)+a)(p(x)+b)}$$

$$=\frac{(a-b)b-(a-b)a}{(b-a)(a-b)(p(x)+a)(p(x)+b)}$$

$$=\frac{(a-b)(b-a)}{(b-a)(a-b)(p(x)+a)(p(x)+b)}$$

$$=\frac{1}{(p(x)+a)(p(x)+b)}$$

45.

46.

47.

48.

49.

50.

Section 6.5

1.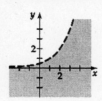

3.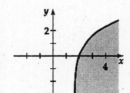

5. $y > \frac{2}{3}x - 2$
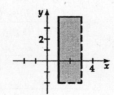

7. $y \le -\frac{4}{3}x + 4$

9. vertex $(0,0)$

11. vertex $(1,-4)$
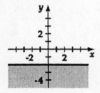

13. center $(2, 1)$, $r = 4$

15. center $(3, -1)$, $a = 3$, $b = 4$
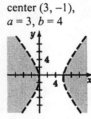

17.
$$4x^2 + 9y^2 - 8x + 18y \ge 23$$
$$4(x^2 - 2x + 1) + 9(y^2 + 2y + 1) \ge 23 + 4 + 9$$
$$4(x-1)^2 + 9(y+1)^2 \ge 36$$
$$\frac{(x-1)^2}{9} + \frac{(y+1)^2}{4} \ge 1$$
center $(1, -1)$, $a = 3$, $b = 2$

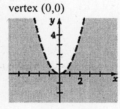

19.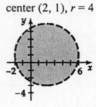

21.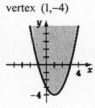

23.

25.

27.

29. The graphs of the two inequalities are shown.

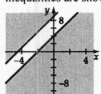

Because the solution sets of the inequalities do not intersect, the system has no solution. Thus, there is no graph of the solution set of the system.

31.

33.

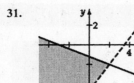

35.

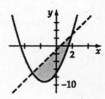

37.

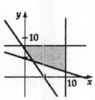

39.

41.

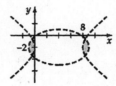

43.

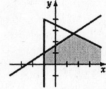

45.

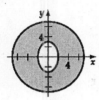

47.

49.

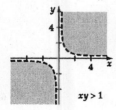

51.

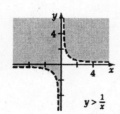

53.

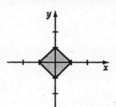

55.

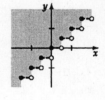

57. If x is a negative number, then the inequality is reversed when multiplying both sides of the inequality by the negative number $\dfrac{1}{x}$.

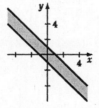

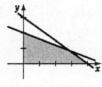

•••

59.

60.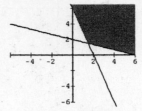

61.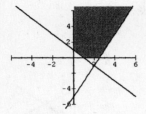

62.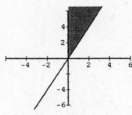

63. $\begin{cases} 3x+y=6 & (1) \\ x+y=4 & (2) \end{cases}$

Solve equation (1) for y and substitute into equation (2).
$x+(-3x+6)=4$
$\quad -2x+6=4$
$\qquad -2x=-2$
$\qquad\quad x=1$
$y=-3(1)+6$
$\ =3$

The solution is $(1, 3)$.

64. $\begin{cases} 300x+100y=900 & (1) \\ 400x+300y=2200 & (2) \end{cases}$

$\begin{array}{ll} -900x-300y=-2700 & -3 \text{ times (1)} \\ \underline{400x+300y=2200} & (2) \\ -500x \qquad\quad =-500 \\ x=1 \end{array}$

$300(1)+100y=900$
$\qquad\quad 100y=600$
$\qquad\qquad y=6$

The solution is $(1, 6)$.

Section 6.6

1. $C=4x+2y$

$\begin{cases} x+y \geq 7 \\ 4x+3y \geq 24 \\ \\ x \leq 10, \ y \leq 10 \\ x \geq 0, \quad y \geq 0 \end{cases}$

$C=4x+2y$	
$(0, 10)$	20
$(0, 8)$	16
$(3, 4)$	20
$(7, 0)$	28
$(10, 0)$	40
$(10, 10)$	60

minimum (at $(0,8)$)

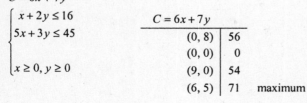

The minimum is 16 at $(0, 8)$.

3. $C=6x+7y$

$\begin{cases} x+2y \leq 16 \\ 5x+3y \leq 45 \\ \\ x \geq 0, y \geq 0 \end{cases}$

$C=6x+7y$	
$(0, 8)$	56
$(0, 0)$	0
$(9, 0)$	54
$(6, 5)$	71

maximum (at $(6,5)$)

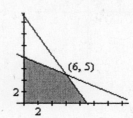

The maximum is 71 at $(6, 5)$.

---

5. $C = 5x + 6y$

$$\begin{cases} 4x - 3y \le 2 \\ 2x + 3y \ge 10 \\ \\ x \ge 0, y \ge 0 \end{cases}$$

$C = 5x + 6y$		
$\left(0, \frac{10}{3}\right)$	20	minimum
$(2, 2)$	22	

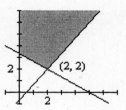

The minimum is 20 at (0, 10/3)

7. $C = x + 6y$

$$\begin{cases} 5x + 8y \le 120 \\ 7x + 16y \le 192 \\ \\ x \ge 0, \ y \ge 0 \end{cases}$$

$C = x + 6y$		
$(0, 12)$	72	maximum
$(0, 0)$	0	
$(24, 0)$	24	
$(16, 5)$	46	

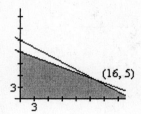

The maximum is 72 at (0, 12).

9. $C = 4x + y$

$$\begin{cases} 3x + 5y \ge 120 \\ x + y \ge 32 \\ \\ x \ge 0, \ y \ge 0 \end{cases}$$

$C = 4x + y$		
$(40, 0)$	160	
$(0, 32)$	32	minimum
$(20, 12)$	92	

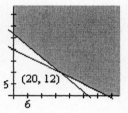

The minimum is 32 at (0, 32).

11. $C = 2x + 7y$

$$\begin{cases} x + y \le 10 \\ x + 2y \le 16 \\ 2x + y \le 16 \\ \\ x \ge 0, y \ge 0 \end{cases}$$

$C = 2x + 7y$		
$(0, 8)$	56	maximum
$(0, 0)$	0	
$(8, 0)$	16	
$(6, 4)$	40	
$(4, 6)$	50	

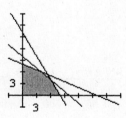

The maximum is 56 at (0, 8).

13. $C = 3x + 2y$

$$\begin{cases} 3x + y \ge 12 \\ 2x + 7y \ge 21 \\ x + y \ge 8 \\ \\ x \ge 0, y \ge 0 \end{cases}$$

$C = 3x + 2y$		
$(0, 12)$	24	
$(2, 6)$	18	minimum
$(7, 1)$	23	
$(10.5, 0)$	31.5	

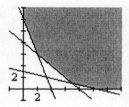

The minimum is 18 at (2, 6).

15. $C = 3x + 4y$

$$\begin{cases} 2x + y \le 10 \\ 2x + 3y \le 18 \\ x - y \le 2 \\ \\ x \ge 0, \, y \ge 0 \end{cases}$$

$C = 3x + 4y$	
(0, 6)	24
(3, 4)	25 maximum
(4, 2)	20
(2, 0)	6
(0, 0)	0

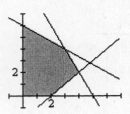

The maximum is 25 at (3, 4).

17. $C = 3x + 2y$

$$\begin{cases} x + 2y \ge 8 \\ 3x + y \ge 9 \\ x + 4y \ge 12 \\ \\ x \ge 0, \, y \ge 0 \end{cases}$$

$C = 3x + 2y$	
(0, 9)	18
(2, 3)	12 maximum
(4, 2)	16
(12, 0)	36

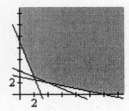

The minimum is 12 at (2, 3).

19. $C = 6x + 7y$

$$\begin{cases} x + 2y \le 900 \\ x + y \le 500 \\ 3x + 2y \le 1200 \\ \\ x \ge 0, \, y \ge 0 \end{cases}$$

$C = 6x + 7y$	
(0, 450)	3150
(100, 400)	3400 maximum
(200, 300)	3300
(400, 0)	2400
(0, 0)	0

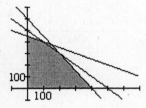

The maximum is 3400 at (100, 400).

21. $W =$ acres of wheat to plant
$B =$ acres of barley to plant

$P = 50W + 70B$

Constraints:

$$\begin{cases} 4W + 3B \le 200 \\ W + 2B \le 100 \\ \\ W \ge 0, \ B \ge 0 \end{cases}$$

$50W + 70B = P$	
(0, 50)	3500
(20, 40)	3800 maximum
(50, 0)	2500
(0, 0)	0

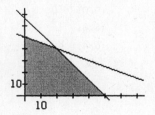

The maximum profit is achieved by planting 20 acres of wheat and 40 acres of barley.

23. S = Number of Starter sets
P = Number of Pro sets

Profit $= 35S + 55P$

Constraints:

$$\begin{cases} 4S + 6P \le 108 \\ S + P \le 24 \\ \\ S \ge 0, \ P \ge 0 \end{cases}$$

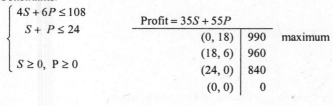

Profit $= 35S + 55P$		
(0, 18)	990	maximum
(18, 6)	960	
(24, 0)	840	
(0, 0)	0	

To maximize profit, produce zero starter sets and 18 pro sets.

· ·

25. A = ounces of food group A
B = ounces of food group B

Cost $= 40A + 10B$

Constraints:

$$\begin{cases} 3A + B \ge 24 \\ A + B \ge 16 \\ A + 3B \ge 30 \\ \\ A \ge 0, B \ge 0 \end{cases}$$

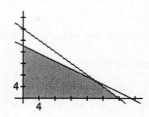

Cost $= 40A + 10B$		
(0, 24)	240	minimum
(4, 12)	280	
(9, 7)	430	
(30, 0)	120	
	0	

To minimize cost, use 24 ounces of food group B and zero ounces of food group A. The minimum cost is $240.

27. x = number of 4-cylinder engines
y = number of 6-cylinder engines

Profit $= 150x + 250y$

Constraints:

$$\begin{cases} x + y \le 9 \\ 5x + 10y \le 80 \\ 3x + 2y \le 24 \\ \\ x \ge 0, y \ge 0 \end{cases}$$

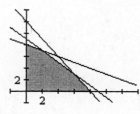

$150x + 250y = $ Profit		
(0, 8)	2000	
(2, 7)	2050	maximum
(6, 3)	1650	
(8, 0)	1200	
(0, 0)	0	

To achieve the maximum profit of $2050, produce two 4-cylinder engines and seven 6-cylinder engines.

1. False, $\begin{cases} x+y=1 \\ x+y=2 \end{cases}$ has no solution.

2. True

3. False, a homogeneous system is one where the constant term in each equation is zero.

4. True, assuming the planes intersect.

5. True

6. False, $\begin{cases} x+y=2 \\ x+2y=3 \end{cases}$ and $\begin{cases} 2x+3y=5 \\ 2x-2y=0 \end{cases}$ are two systems with the same solution but no common equations.

7. True

8. True

9. False, it is inconsistent.

10. False, since $(-1, 1)$ satisfies the first equation but not the second equation and $(-2, -1)$ satisfies the second equation but not the first equation.

1. $\begin{cases} 2x-4y=-3 \quad (1) \\ 3x+8y=-12 \quad (2) \end{cases}$

$4x-8y=-6 \quad$ 2 times (1)

$\underline{3x+8y=-12 \quad (2)}$

$7x=-18$

$x=-\frac{18}{7} \quad 2\left(-\frac{18}{7}\right)-4y=-3$

$y=-\frac{15}{28}$

The solution is $\left(-\frac{18}{7}, -\frac{15}{28}\right)$. [6.1]

2. $\begin{cases} 4x-3y=15 \\ 2x=5y=-12 \end{cases}$

$4x-3y=15 \quad (1)$

$\underline{-4x-10y=24 \quad -2 \text{ times (2)}}$

$-13y=39$

$y=-3 \quad 4x-3(-3)=15$

$x=\frac{3}{2}$

The solution is $\left(\frac{3}{2}, -3\right)$. [6.1]

3. $\begin{cases} 3x-4y=-5 \quad (1) \\ y=\frac{2}{3}x+1 \quad (2) \end{cases}$

Substitute y from Eq. (2) into Eq. (1).

$3x-4\left(\frac{2}{3}x+1\right)=-5$

$3x-\frac{8}{3}x-4=-5$

$\frac{1}{3}x=-1$

$x=-3$

$y=\frac{2}{3}(-3)+1$

$y=-1$

The solution is $(-3, -1)$. [6.1]

4. $\begin{cases} 7x+2y=-14 \quad (1) \\ y=-\frac{5}{2}x-3 \quad (2) \end{cases}$

Substitute y from Eq. (2) into Eq. (1).

$7x+2\left(-\frac{5}{2}x-3\right)=-14$

$7x-5x-6=-14$

$2x=-8$

$x=-4$

$y=-\frac{5}{2}(-4)-3$

$y=7$

The solution is $(-4, 7)$. [6.1]

5. $\begin{cases} y=2x-5 \quad (1) \\ x=4y-1 \quad (2) \end{cases}$

Substitute x from Eq. (2) into Eq. (1).

$y=2(4y-1)-5$

$y=8y-2-5$

$-7y=-7 \quad x=4(1)-1$

$y=1 \quad x=3$

The solution is $(3, 1)$. [6.1]

6. $\begin{cases} y=3x+4 \quad (1) \\ x=4y-5 \quad (2) \end{cases}$

Substitute x from Eq. (2) into Eq. (1).

$y=3(4y-5)+4 \quad x=4(1)-5$

$y=12y-15+4 \quad x=-1$

$-11y=-11$

$y=1$

The solution is $(-1, 1)$. [6.1]

7. $\begin{cases} 6x + 9y = 15 \quad (1) \\ 10x + 15y = 25 \quad (2) \end{cases}$

$2x + 3y = 5 \quad \dfrac{1}{3} \text{ times (1)}$

$\dfrac{2x + 3y = 5}{0 = 0} \quad \dfrac{1}{5} \text{ times (2)}$

Let $y = c$. $\qquad 2x + 3c = 5$

$$x = \frac{5 - 3c}{2}$$

The ordered-pair solutions are $\left(\dfrac{5 - 3c}{2}, c \right)$. [6.1]

8. $\begin{array}{lr} 4x - 8y = \quad 9 & (1) \\ -4x + 8y = -10 & -2 \text{ times (2)} \\ \hline 0 = -1 \end{array}$

The system of equations is inconsistent.
The system has no solution. [6.1]

9. $\begin{cases} 2x - 3y + z = -9 \quad (1) \\ 2x + 5y - 2z = 18 \quad (2) \\ 4x - y + 3z = -4 \quad (3) \end{cases}$

$\begin{array}{lr} 2x - 3y + z = -9 & (1) \\ -2x - 5y + 2z = -18 & -1 \text{ times (2)} \\ \hline -8y + 3z = -27 & (4) \end{array}$

$\begin{array}{lr} -4x + 6y - 2z = 18 & -2 \text{ times (1)} \\ 4x - y + 3z = -4 & (3) \\ \hline 5y + z = 14 & (5) \end{array}$

$\begin{cases} 2x - 3y + z = -9 \\ -8y + 3z = -27 \quad (4) \\ 5y + z = 14 \quad (5) \end{cases}$

$\begin{array}{lr} -8y + 3z = -27 & (4) \\ -15y - 3z = -42 & -3 \text{ times (5)} \\ \hline -23y = -69 \\ y = 3 & (6) \end{array}$

$\begin{cases} 2x - 3y + z = -9 \\ -8y + 3z = -27 \\ y = 3 \quad (6) \end{cases}$

$\begin{array}{ll} -8(3) + 3z = -27 & 2x - 3(3) - 1 = 9 \\ 3z = -3 & 2x = 1 \\ z = -1 & x = 1 \end{array}$

The ordered-triple solution is $\left(\dfrac{1}{2}, 3, -1 \right)$. [6.2]

10. $\begin{cases} x - 3y + 5z = 1 \quad (1) \\ 2x + 3y - 5z = 15 \quad (2) \\ 3x + 6y + 5z = 15 \quad (3) \end{cases}$

$\begin{array}{lr} -2x + 6y - 10z = -2 & -2 \text{ times (1)} \\ 2x + 3y - 5z = 15 & (2) \\ \hline 9y - 15z = 13 & (4) \end{array}$

$\begin{array}{lr} -3x + 9y - 15z = -3 & -3 \text{ times (1)} \\ 3x + 6y + 5z = 15 & (3) \\ \hline 15y - 10z = 12 & (5) \end{array}$

$\begin{cases} x - 3y + 5z = 1 \\ 9y - 15z = 13 \quad (4) \\ 15y - 10z = 12 \quad (5) \end{cases}$

$\begin{array}{lr} 18y - 30z = 26 & 2 \text{ times (4)} \\ -45y + 30z = -36 & -3 \text{ times (5)} \\ \hline -27y = -10 \\ y = \dfrac{10}{27} & (6) \end{array}$

$\begin{cases} x - 3y + 5z = 1 \\ 9y - 15z = 13 \\ y = \dfrac{10}{27} \quad (6) \end{cases}$

$-15z = 13 - 9y \qquad\qquad x = 3y - 5z + 1$

$-15z = 13 - 9\left(\dfrac{10}{27} \right) \qquad x = 3\left(\dfrac{10}{27} \right) - 5\left(-\dfrac{29}{45} \right) + 1$

$-15z = \dfrac{29}{3} \qquad\qquad\qquad x = \dfrac{16}{3}$

$z = -\dfrac{29}{45}$

The solution is $\left(\dfrac{16}{3}, \dfrac{10}{27}, -\dfrac{29}{45} \right)$. [6.2]

11. $\begin{cases} x+3y-5z=-12 & (1) \\ 3x-2y+\ z=\ 7 & (2) \\ 5x+4y-9z=-17 & (3) \end{cases}$

$\begin{array}{ll} -3x-9y+15z=36 & -3 \text{ times } (1) \\ \underline{3x-2y+\ \ z=\ 7} & (2) \\ -11y+16z=43 & (4) \end{array}$

$\begin{array}{ll} -5x-15y+25z=\ 60 & -5 \text{ times } (1) \\ \underline{5x+\ 4y-\ 9z=-17} & (3) \\ -11y+16z=\ 43 & (5) \end{array}$

$\begin{cases} x+\ \ 3y-\ 5z=-12 & \\ -11y+16z=\ 43 & (4) \\ -11y+16z=\ 43 & (5) \end{cases}$

$\begin{cases} x+\ \ 3y-\ 5z=-12 & \\ -11y+16z=\ 43 & \\ 0=\ \ 0 & (6) \end{cases}$

The system of equations is dependent.

Let $z=c$.
$-11y+16c=43$
$$y=\frac{16c-43}{11}$$
$$x+3\left(\frac{16c-43}{11}\right)-5c=-12$$
$$x=\frac{7c-3}{11}$$

The solution is $\left(\dfrac{7c-3}{11}, \dfrac{16c-43}{11}, c\right)$. [6.2]

12. $\begin{cases} 2x-\ y+2z=\ 5 & (1) \\ x+3y-3z=\ 2 & (2) \\ 5x-9y+8z=13 & (3) \end{cases}$

$\begin{array}{ll} 2x-\ y+2z=\ 5 & (1) \\ \underline{-2x-6y+6z=-4} & -2 \text{ times } (2) \\ -7y+8z=\ 1 & (4) \end{array}$

$\begin{array}{ll} -5x-15y+15z=-10 & -5 \text{ times } (2) \\ \underline{5x-\ 9y+\ 8z=\ 13} & (3) \\ -24y+23z=\ 3 & (5) \end{array}$

$\begin{cases} 2x-\ y+\ 2z=5 & \\ -7y+\ 8z=1 & (4) \\ -24y+23z=3 & (5) \end{cases}$

$\begin{array}{ll} -168y+192z=\ 24 & 24 \text{ times } (4) \\ \underline{168y-161z=-21} & -7 \text{ times } (2) \\ 31z=\ \ 3 & \end{array}$
$$z=\frac{3}{31} \quad (6)$$

$\begin{cases} 2x-\ y+2z=\ 5 & \\ -7y+8z=\ 1 & \\ z=\dfrac{3}{31} & (6) \end{cases}$

$$-7y+8\left(\frac{3}{31}\right)=1$$
$$-7y=\frac{31}{31}-\frac{24}{31}$$
$$y=-\frac{1}{31}$$

$$2x-\left(-\frac{1}{31}\right)+2\left(\frac{3}{31}\right)=5$$
$$2x=-\frac{1}{31}-\frac{6}{31}+\frac{155}{31}$$
$$2x=\frac{148}{31}$$
$$x=\frac{74}{31}$$

The solution is $\left(\dfrac{74}{31}, -\dfrac{1}{31}, \dfrac{3}{31}\right)$. [6.2]

13.
$$\begin{cases} 3x + 4y - 6z = 10 & (1) \\ 2x + 2y - 3z = 6 & (2) \\ x - 6y + 9z = -4 & (3) \end{cases}$$

Rearrange the equations so that the equation with the 1 as the coefficient of x is in the first row.

$$\begin{cases} x - 6y + 9z = -4 & (3) \\ 2x + 2y - 3z = 6 & (2) \\ 3x + 4y - 6z = 10 & (1) \end{cases}$$

$$\begin{array}{rl} -2x + 12y - 18z = 8 & -2 \text{ times } (3) \\ \underline{2x + 2y - 3z = 6} & (2) \\ 14y - 21z = 14 & \\ 2y - 3z = 2 & (4) \end{array}$$

$$\begin{array}{rl} -3x + 18y - 27z = 12 & -3 \text{ times } (3) \\ \underline{3x + 4y - 6z = 10} & (1) \\ 22y - 33z = 22 & \\ 2y - 3z = 2 & (5) \end{array}$$

$$\begin{array}{rl} x - 6y + 9z = -4 & (3) \\ 2y - 3z = 2 & (4) \\ 2y - 3z = 2 & (5) \end{array}$$

$$\begin{cases} x - 6y + 9z = -4 \\ 2y - 3z = 2 \\ 0 = 0 \end{cases}$$

The system of equations is dependent.

Let $z = c$.
$$2y - 3c = 2$$
$$y = \frac{3c + 2}{2}$$
$$x - 6\left(\frac{3c + 2}{2}\right) + 9c = -4$$
$$x - 9c - 6 + 9c = -4$$
$$x = 2$$

The solution is $\left(2, \dfrac{3c + 2}{2}, c\right)$. [6.2]

14.
$$\begin{cases} x - 6y + 4z = 6 & (1) \\ 4x + 3y - 4z = 1 & (2) \\ 5x - 9y + 8z = 13 & (3) \end{cases}$$

$$\begin{array}{rl} x - 6y + 4z = 6 & (1) \\ \underline{4x + 3y - 4z = 1} & (2) \\ 5x - 3y = 7 & (4) \end{array}$$

$$\begin{array}{rl} 8x + 6y - 8z = 2 & 2 \text{ times } (2) \\ \underline{5x - 9y + 8z = 13} & (3) \\ 13x - 3y = 15 & (5) \end{array}$$

$$\begin{cases} x - 6y + 4z = 6 \\ 5x - 3y = 7 & (4) \\ 13x - 3y = 15 & (5) \end{cases}$$

$$\begin{array}{rl} 5x - 3y = 7 & (4) \\ \underline{-13x + 3y = -15} & -1 \text{ times } (5) \\ -8x = -8 & \\ x = 1 & (6) \end{array}$$

$$\begin{cases} x - 6y + 4z = 6 \\ 5x - 3y = 7 \\ x = 1 & (6) \end{cases}$$

$$\begin{array}{ll} 5(1) - 3y = 7 & 1 - 6\left(-\dfrac{2}{3}\right) + 4z = 6 \\ y = -\dfrac{2}{3} & 4z = 1 \\ & z = \dfrac{1}{4} \end{array}$$

The solution is $\left(1, -\dfrac{2}{3}, \dfrac{1}{4}\right)$. [6.2]

15. $\begin{cases} 2x + 3y - 2z = 0 & (1) \\ 3x - y - 4z = 0 & (2) \\ 5x + 13y - 4z = 0 & (3) \end{cases}$

$\begin{array}{l} 6x + 9y - 6z = 0 \quad 3 \text{ times (1)} \\ \underline{-6x + 2y + 8z = 0 \quad -2 \text{ times (2)}} \\ 11y + 2z = 0 \quad (4) \end{array}$

$\begin{array}{l} 15x - 5y - 20z = 0 \quad 5 \text{ times (2)} \\ \underline{-15x - 39y + 12z = 0 \quad -3 \text{ times (3)}} \\ -44y - 8z = 0 \\ 11y + 2z = 0 \quad (5) \end{array}$

$\begin{cases} 2x + 3y - 2z = 0 & (1) \\ 11y + 2z = 0 & (4) \\ 11y + 2z = 0 & (5) \end{cases}$

$\begin{cases} 2x + 3y - 2z = 0 \\ 11y + 2z = 0 \\ 0 = 0 \end{cases}$

Let $z = c$ $11y + 2c = 0$

$$y = -\frac{2}{11}c$$

$$2x + 3\left(-\frac{2c}{11}\right) - 2c = 0$$

$$2x = \frac{28c}{11}$$

$$x = \frac{14c}{11}$$

The solution is $\left(\frac{14}{11}c, \ -\frac{2}{11}c, \ c\right)$. [6.2]

17. $\begin{cases} x - 2y + z = 1 & (1) \\ 3x + 2y - 3z = 1 & (2) \end{cases}$

$\begin{array}{l} -3x + 6y - 3z = -3 \quad -3 \text{ times (1)} \\ \underline{3x + 2y - 3z = 1 \quad\quad (2)} \\ 8y - 6z = -2 \\ 4y - 3z = -1 \quad (3) \end{array}$

$\begin{cases} x - 2y + z = 1 \\ 4y - 3z = -1 \quad (3) \end{cases}$

Let $z = c$. $4y - 3c = -1$

$$y = \frac{3c - 1}{4}$$

$$x - 2\left(\frac{3c - 1}{4}\right) + c = 1$$

$$x = \frac{c + 1}{2}$$

The solution is $\left(\frac{c + 1}{2}, \ \frac{3c - 1}{4}, \ c\right)$. [6.2]

16. $\begin{cases} 3x - 5y + z = 0 & (1) \\ x + 4y - 3z = 0 & (2) \\ 2x + y - 2z = 0 & (3) \end{cases}$

$\begin{array}{l} 3x - 5y + z = 0 \quad (1) \\ \underline{-3x - 12y + 9z = 0 \quad -3 \text{ times (2)}} \\ -17y + 10z = 0 \quad (4) \end{array}$

$\begin{array}{l} -2x - 8y + 6z = 0 \quad -2 \text{ times (2)} \\ \underline{2x + y - 2z = 0 \quad\quad (3)} \\ -7y + 4z = 0 \quad (5) \end{array}$

$\begin{cases} 3x - 5y + z = 0 \\ -17y + 10z = 0 & (4) \\ -7y + 4z = 0 & (5) \end{cases}$

$\begin{array}{l} -34y + 20z = 0 \quad 2 \text{ times (4)} \\ \underline{35y - 20z = 0 \quad -5 \text{ times (5)}} \\ y = 0 \quad (6) \end{array}$

$\begin{cases} 3x - 5y + z = 0 \\ -17y + 10z = 0 \\ y = 0 & (6) \end{cases}$

$x = 0$, $y = 0$, $z = 0$. The solution is $(0, 0, 0)$. [6.2]

18. $\begin{cases} 2x - 3y + z = 1 & (1) \\ 4x + 2y + 3z = 21 & (2) \end{cases}$

$\begin{array}{l} -4x + 6y - 2z = -2 \quad -2 \text{ times (1)} \\ \underline{4x + 2y + 3z = 21 \quad\quad (2)} \\ 8y + z = 19 \quad (3) \end{array}$

$\begin{cases} 2x - 3y + z = 1 \\ 8y + z = 19 & (3) \end{cases}$

Let $z = c$. $8y = 19 - c$

$$y = \frac{19 - c}{8}$$

$$2x - 3\left(\frac{19 - c}{8}\right) + c = 1$$

$$2x = \frac{65 - 11c}{8}$$

$$x = \frac{65 - 11c}{16}$$

The solution is $\left(\frac{65 - 11c}{16}, \ \frac{19 - c}{8}, \ c\right)$. [6.2]

19.
$$\begin{cases} y = x^2 - 2x - 3 \\ y = 2x - 7 \end{cases}$$

$$x^2 - 2x - 3 = 2x - 7$$
$$x^2 - 4x + 4 = 0$$
$$(x - 2)(x - 2) = 0$$
$$x = 2$$

$$y = 2(2) - 7$$
$$y = -3$$

The solution is $(2, -3)$. [6.3]

20.
$$\begin{cases} y = 2x^2 + x \\ y = 2x + 1 \end{cases}$$

$$2x^2 + x = 2x + 1$$
$$2x^2 - x - 1 = 0$$
$$(2x + 1)(x - 1) = 0$$

$$x = -\frac{1}{2} \qquad x = 1$$
$$y = 2\left(-\frac{1}{2}\right) + 1 \qquad y = 2(1) + 1$$
$$y = 0 \qquad y = 3$$

The solutions are $\left(-\frac{1}{2}, 0\right)$ and $(1, 3)$. [6.3]

21.
$$\begin{cases} y = 3x^2 - x + 1 \\ y = x^2 + 2x - 1 \end{cases}$$

$$3x^2 - x + 1 = x^2 + 2x - 1$$
$$2x^2 - 3x + 2 = 0$$
$$x = \frac{-(-3) \pm \sqrt{(-3)^2 - 4(2)(2)}}{2(2)}$$

$$x = \frac{3 \pm \sqrt{9 - 16}}{4} = \frac{3 \pm \sqrt{-7}}{4}$$

x has no real number solution. The system of equations is inconsistent. The graphs of the equations do not intersect. No real solution. [6.3]

22.
$$\begin{cases} y = 4x^2 - 2x - 3 \\ y = 2x^2 + 3x - 6 \end{cases}$$

$$4x^2 - 2x - 3 = 2x^2 + 3x - 6$$
$$2x^2 - 5x + 3 = 0$$
$$(2x - 3)(x - 1) = 0$$
$$x = \frac{3}{2} \quad \text{or} \quad x = 1$$
$$y = 2\left(\frac{3}{2}\right)^2 + 3\left(\frac{3}{2}\right) - 6$$
$$y = 3$$

$$y = 2(1)^2 + 3(1) - 6$$
$$y = -1$$

The solutions are $\left(\frac{3}{2}, 3\right)$ and $(1, -1)$. [6.3]

23.
$$(x + 1)^2 + (y - 2)^2 = 4 \quad (1)$$
$$2x + y = 4 \quad (2)$$

From Eq. (2), $y = -2x + 4$.
Substitute y in Eq. (1).

$$(x + 1)^2 + (-2x + 4 - 2)^2 = 4$$
$$(x + 1)^2 + (-2x + 2)^2 = 4$$
$$x^2 + 2x + 1 + 4x^2 - 8x + 4 = 4$$
$$5x^2 - 6x + 1 = 0$$
$$(5x - 1)(x - 1) = 0$$

$$x = \frac{1}{5} \text{ or } x = 1$$

$$y = -2\left(\frac{1}{5}\right) + 4 \qquad y = -2(1) + 4$$
$$y = \frac{18}{5} \qquad\qquad y = 2$$

The solutions are $\left(\frac{1}{5}, \frac{18}{5}\right)$ and $(1, 2)$. [6.3]

24.
$$\begin{cases} (x - 1)^2 + (y + 1)^2 = 5 \\ y = 2x - 3 \end{cases}$$

$$(x - 1)^2 + (2x - 3 + 1)^2 = 5$$
$$(x - 1)^2 + (2x - 2)^2 = 5$$
$$x^2 - 2x + 1 + 4x^2 - 8x + 4 = 5$$
$$5x^2 - 10x = 0$$
$$5x(x - 2) = 0$$

$$x = 0 \quad \text{or} \quad x = 2$$
$$y = 2(0) - 3 \qquad y = 2(2) - 3$$
$$y = -3 \qquad\qquad y = 1$$

The solutions are $(0, -3)$ and $(2, 1)$. [6.3]

25. $\begin{cases} (x-2)^2 + (y+2)^2 = 4 \quad (1) \\ (x+2)^2 + (y+1)^2 = 17 \quad (2) \end{cases}$

Expand the binomials. Then subtract.

$$x^2 - 4x + 4 + y^2 + 4y + 4 = \quad 4$$
$$\underline{x^2 + 4x + 4 + y^2 + 2y + 1 = \quad 17}$$
$$-8x \qquad + 2y + 3 = -13$$
$$-8x \qquad + 2y \quad = -16$$
$$y = 4x - 8$$

Substitute y into Eq. (1).

$$(x-2)^2 + (4x - 8 + 2)^2 = 4$$
$$(x-2)^2 + (4x - 6)^2 = 4$$
$$x^2 - 4x + 4 + 16x^2 - 48x + 36 = 4$$
$$17x^2 - 52x + 36 = 0$$
$$(x-2)(17x - 18) = 0$$

$$x = 2 \text{ or } x = \frac{18}{17}$$

$$y = 4(2) - 8 \qquad y = 4\left(\frac{18}{17}\right) - 8$$

$$y = 0 \qquad\qquad y = -\frac{64}{17}$$

The solutions are $(2, 0)$ and $\left(\dfrac{18}{17}, \ -\dfrac{64}{17}\right)$. [6.3]

26. $\begin{cases} (x+1)^2 + (y-2)^2 = \quad 1 \quad (1) \\ (x-2)^2 + (y+2)^2 = 20 \quad (2) \end{cases}$

Expand the binomials. Then subtract.

$$x^2 + 2x + 1 + y^2 - 4y + 4 = \quad 1$$
$$\underline{x^2 - 4x + 4 + y^2 + 4y + 4 = 20}$$
$$6x - 3 \qquad - 8y \quad = -19$$
$$6x \qquad\quad - 8y \quad = -16$$
$$y = \frac{3x + 8}{4}$$

$$(x+1)^2 + \left(\frac{3x+8}{4} - 2\right)^2 = 1$$

$$(x+1)^2 + \left(\frac{3x}{4}\right)^2 = 1$$

$$x^2 + 2x + 1 + \frac{9x^2}{16} = 1$$

$$16x^2 + 32x + 16 + 9x^2 = 16$$

$$25x^2 + 32x = 0$$

$$x(25x + 32) = 0$$

$$x = 0 \quad \text{ or } \quad x = -\frac{32}{25}$$

$$y = \frac{3}{4}(0) + 2 \qquad y = \frac{3}{4}\left(-\frac{32}{25}\right) + 2$$

$$y = 2 \qquad\qquad y = \frac{26}{25}$$

The solutions are $(0, 2)$ and $\left(-\dfrac{32}{25}, \ \dfrac{26}{25}\right)$. [6.3]

27.
$$\begin{cases} x^2 - 3xy + y^2 = -1 & (1) \\ 3x^2 - 5xy - 2y^2 = 0 & (2) \end{cases}$$

Factor Eq. (2).

$$(3x + y)(x - 2y) = 0$$

$$x = \frac{-y}{3} \text{ or } x = 2y$$

$x = -\dfrac{y}{3}$ implies $y = -3x$. Substitute for y in Eq. (1).

$$x^2 - 3x(-3x) + (-3x)^2 = -1$$
$$x^2 + 9x^2 + 9x^2 = -1$$
$$19x^2 = -1$$
$$x^2 = -\frac{1}{19}$$

This equation yields no real solutions. Substituting $x = 2y$ in Eq. (1) yields

$$(2y)^2 - 3(2y)y + y^2 = -1$$
$$4y^2 - 6y^2 + y^2 = -1$$
$$-y^2 = -1$$
$$y^2 = 1$$
$$y = \pm 1$$

The solutions are $(2, 1)$ and $(-2, -1)$. [6.3]

28.
$$\begin{cases} 2x^2 + 2xy - y^2 = -1 & (1) \\ 6x^2 + xy - y^2 = 0 & (2) \end{cases}$$

Factor Eq. (2).

$$(3x - y)(2x + y) = 0$$

$$y = 3x \qquad y = -2x$$

$$2x^2 + 2x(3x) - (3x)^2 = -1 \qquad\qquad 2x^2 + 2x(-2x) - (-2x)^2 = -1$$
$$2x^2 + 6x^2 - 9x^2 = -1 \qquad\qquad\quad 2x^2 - 4x^2 - 4x^2 = -1$$
$$x^2 = 1 \qquad\qquad\qquad\qquad\qquad x^2 = \frac{1}{6}$$
$$x = \pm 1 \qquad\qquad\qquad\qquad\qquad x = \pm \frac{\sqrt{6}}{6}$$

$$y = 3(1) \quad y = 3(-1) \qquad y = -2\left(\frac{\sqrt{6}}{6}\right) \qquad y = -2\left(-\frac{\sqrt{6}}{6}\right)$$
$$y = 3 \qquad y = -3 \qquad\qquad y = -\frac{\sqrt{6}}{3} \qquad\qquad y = \frac{\sqrt{6}}{3}$$

The solutions are $(1, 3)$, $(-1, -3)$, $\left(\dfrac{\sqrt{6}}{6}, -\dfrac{\sqrt{6}}{3}\right)$ and $\left(-\dfrac{\sqrt{6}}{6}, \dfrac{\sqrt{6}}{3}\right)$. [6.3]

29.

$$\begin{cases} 2x^2 - 5xy + 2y^2 = 56 & (1) \\ 14x^2 - 3xy - 2y^2 = 56 & (2) \end{cases}$$

Subtract Eq. (1) From Eq. (2)

$$12x^2 + 2xy - 4y^2 = 0$$

Factor $2(3x + 2y)(2x - y) = 0$. Thus

$$3x + 2y = 0 \qquad 2x - y = 0$$
$$y = -\frac{3}{2} \quad \text{or} \quad y = 2x$$

Substituting $y = -\frac{3}{2}x$ into Eq. (1), we have

$$2x^2 - 5x\left(-\frac{3}{2}x\right) + 2\left(-\frac{3}{2}x\right)^2 = 56$$
$$2x^2 + \frac{15}{2}x^2 + \frac{9}{2}x^2 = 56$$
$$14x^2 = 56$$
$$x^2 = 4$$
$$x = \pm 2$$

When $x = 2, y = -\frac{3}{2}(2) = -3$;

When $x = -2, y = -\frac{3}{2}(-2) = 3$.

Two solutions are $(2, -3)$ and $(-2, 3)$. Substituting $y = 2x$ into Eq. (1) yields $0 = 56$. Thus the only solutions of the system are $(2, -3)$, and $(-2, 3)$. [6.3]

30.

$$\begin{cases} 2x^2 + 7xy + 6y^2 = 1 & (1) \\ 6x^2 + 7xy + 2y^2 = 1 & (2) \end{cases}$$

Subtract Eq. (2) from Eq. (1)

$$-4x^2 + 4y^2 = 0$$
$$-x^2 + y^2 = 0$$
$$y = x \quad \text{or} \quad y = -x$$

When $y = x$, we have, from Eq. (1),

$$2x^2 + 7x^2 + 6x^2 = 1$$
$$15x^2 = 1$$
$$x^2 = \frac{1}{15}$$
$$x = \pm \frac{\sqrt{15}}{15}$$

Since $y = x, y = \pm \frac{\sqrt{15}}{15}$. The solutions are

$$\left(\frac{\sqrt{15}}{15}, \frac{\sqrt{15}}{15}\right), \left(-\frac{\sqrt{15}}{15}, -\frac{\sqrt{15}}{15}\right).$$

When $y = -x$, we have, from Eq. (1)
$$2x^2 - 7x^2 + 6x^2 = 1$$
$$x^2 = 1$$
$$x = \pm 1$$

Since $y = -x, y = \pm 1$.

The solutions are $(1, -1), (-1, 1)$.
The solutions of the system of equations are
$$\left(\frac{\sqrt{15}}{15}, \frac{\sqrt{15}}{15}\right), \left(-\frac{\sqrt{15}}{15}, -\frac{\sqrt{15}}{15}\right), (1, -1), (-1, 1). \quad [6.3]$$

31.

$$\frac{7x - 5}{x^2 - x - 2} = \frac{7x - 5}{(x - 2)(x + 1)} = \frac{A}{x - 2} + \frac{B}{x + 2}$$

$$7x - 5 = A(x + 1) + B(x - 2)$$
$$7x - 5 = Ax + A + Bx - 2b$$
$$7x - 5 = (A + B)x + (A - 2B)$$

$$\begin{cases} 7 = A + B \\ -5 = A - 2B \end{cases}$$

$$7 = \quad A + B$$
$$\underline{5 = -A + 2B}$$
$$12 = \quad\quad 3B \qquad A + 4 = 7$$
$$4 = B \qquad\quad A \quad = 3$$

$$\frac{7x - 5}{x^2 - x - 2} = \frac{3}{x - 2} + \frac{4}{x + 1} \quad [6.4]$$

32.

$$\frac{x + 1}{(x - 1)^2} = \frac{A}{x - 1} + \frac{B}{(x - 1)^2}$$

$$x + 1 = A(x - 1) + B$$
$$x + 1 = Ax - A + B$$

$$1 = A$$
$$1 = -A + B \qquad -1 + B = 1$$
$$B = 2$$

$$\frac{x + 1}{(x - 2)^2} = \frac{1}{x - 1} + \frac{2}{(x - 1)^2} \quad [6.4]$$

33.

$$\frac{2x-2}{\left(x^2+1\right)\left(x+2\right)} = \frac{Ax+B}{x^2+1} + \frac{C}{x+2}$$

$$2x-2 = (Ax+B)(x+2) + C\left(x^2+1\right)$$

$$2x-2 = Ax^2 + 2Ax + Bx + 2B + Cx^2 + C$$

$$2x-2 = (A+C)x^2 + (2A+B)x + (2B+C)$$

$$\begin{cases} 0 = A+C & (1) \\ 2 = 2A+B & (2) \\ -2 = 2B+C & (3) \end{cases}$$

$$\begin{cases} 0 = A+C \\ 2 = 2A+B \\ 2 = A-2B & (4) \end{cases}$$

$$\begin{aligned} 0 &= A && + C & (1) \\ \underline{2} &= && -2B-C & -1 \text{ times } (3) \\ 2 &= A-2B && & (4) \end{aligned}$$

$$\begin{aligned} 4 &= 4A + 2B & 2 \text{ times } (2) \\ \underline{2} &= A - 2B & (4) \\ 6 &= 5A & (5) \end{aligned}$$

$$\frac{6}{5} = A$$

$$A = \frac{6}{5} \qquad 2\left(\frac{6}{5}\right) + B = 2 \qquad \frac{6}{5} + C = 0$$

$$\qquad\qquad B = -\frac{2}{5} \qquad\qquad C = -\frac{6}{5}$$

$$\frac{2x-2}{\left(x^2+1\right)(x-2)} = \frac{6x-2}{5\left(x^2+1\right)} + \frac{-6}{5(x+2)} \quad [6.4]$$

34.

$$\frac{5x^2-10x+9}{(x-2)^2(x+1)} = \frac{A}{x-2} + \frac{B}{(x-2)^2} + \frac{C}{x+1}$$

$$5x^2-10x+9 = A(x-2)(x+1) + B(x+1) + C(x-2)^2$$

$$5x^2-10x+9 = Ax^2 - Ax - 2A + Bx + B + Cx^2 - 4Cx + 4C$$

$$5x^2-10x+9 = (A+C)x^2 + (-A+B-4C)x + (-2A+B+4C)$$

$$\begin{cases} 5 = A+C & (1) \\ -10 = -A+B-4C & (2) \\ 9 = -2A+B+4C & (3) \end{cases}$$

$$\begin{aligned} -10 &= -A+B-4C & (2) \\ \underline{-9} &= 2A-B-4C & -1 \text{ times } (3) \\ -19 &= A \qquad -8C & (4) \end{aligned}$$

$$\begin{cases} 5 = A+C \\ -19 = A-8C & (4) \\ 9 = -2A+B+4C \end{cases}$$

$$\begin{aligned} 5 &= A+C & (1) \\ \underline{19} &= -A-8C & -1 \text{ times } (4) \\ 24 &= \qquad 9C \end{aligned}$$

$$\frac{8}{3} = C \qquad (5)$$

$$\begin{cases} 5 = A+C \\ \dfrac{8}{3} = C & (5) \\ 9 = -2A+B+4C \end{cases}$$

$$A + \frac{8}{3} = 5 \qquad -2\left(\frac{7}{3}\right) + B + 4\left(\frac{8}{3}\right) = 9$$

$$A = \frac{7}{3} \qquad\qquad B = 9 + \frac{14}{3} - \frac{32}{3}$$

$$\qquad\qquad\qquad\qquad B = 3$$

$$\frac{5x^2-10x+9}{(x-2)^2(x+1)} = \frac{7}{3(x-2)} + \frac{3}{(x-2)^2} + \frac{8}{3(x+1)} \quad [6.4]$$

35.

$$\frac{11x^2 - x - 2}{x^3 - x} = \frac{11x^2 - x - 2}{x(x-1)(x+1)} = \frac{A}{x} + \frac{B}{x-1} + \frac{C}{x+1}$$

$$11x^2 - x - 2 = A(x-1)(x+1) + Bx(x+1) + Cx(x-1)$$

$$11x^2 - x - 2 = Ax^2 - A + Bx^2 + Bx + Cx^2 - Cx$$

$$11x^2 - x - 2 = (A+B+C)x^2 + (B-C)x + (-A)$$

$$\begin{cases} 11 = A+B+C & (1) \\ -1 = B-C & (2) \\ -2 = -A & (3) \end{cases}$$

$$\begin{cases} 11 = A+B+C & (1) \\ -1 = B-C & (2) \\ 2 = -A & (4) \end{cases}$$

$B + C = 9$ from (1) with $A = 2$

$\underline{B - C = -1 \quad (2)}$

$2B \quad\;\; = 8$

$\quad\; B = 4$

$4 - C = -1$

$\quad\; C = 5$

$$\frac{11x^2 - x - 2}{x^3 - x} = \frac{2}{x} + \frac{4}{x-1} + \frac{5}{x+1} \quad [6.4]$$

36.

$$\frac{x^4 + x^3 + 4x^2 + x + 3}{(x^2+1)^2} = \frac{x^4 + x^3 + 4x^2 + x + 3}{x^4 + 2x^2 + 1}$$

$$= 1 + \frac{x^3 + 2x^2 + x + 2}{(x^2+1)^2}$$

$$= 1 + \frac{x^2(x+2) + 1(x+2)}{(x^2+1)^2}$$

$$= 1 + \frac{(x^2+1)(x+2)}{(x^2+1)^2}$$

$$= 1 + \frac{x+2}{x^2+1} \qquad [6.4]$$

37.

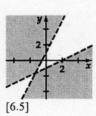

[6.5]

38.

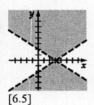

[6.5]

39.

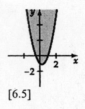

[6.5]

40. vertex $\left(\dfrac{5}{2},\ -\dfrac{49}{4}\right)$

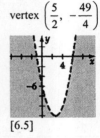

[6.5]

41.

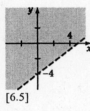

[6.5]

42. center $(-3,\ -1)$, $r = 3$

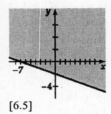

[6.5]

43.

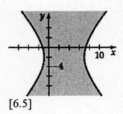

[6.5]

44.

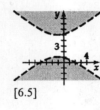

[6.5]

45.

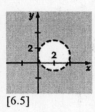

[6.5]

46.

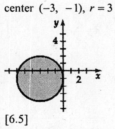

[6.5]

47.

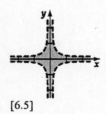

[6.5]

48.

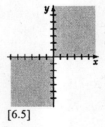

[6.5]

49.

[6.5]

50.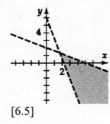

[6.5]

51.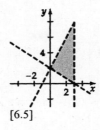

[6.5]

52.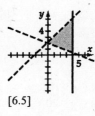

[6.5]

53.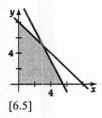

[6.5]

54.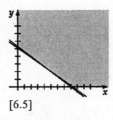

[6.5]

55.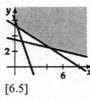

[6.5]

56.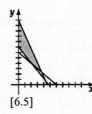

[6.5]

57.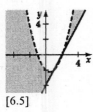

[6.5]

58.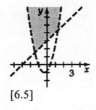

[6.5]

59.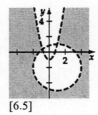

[6.5]

60.

[6.5]

61. $P = 2x + 2y$ [6.6]

$$\begin{cases} x + 2y \le 14 \\ 5x + 2y \le 30 \\ x \le 0, y \le 0 \end{cases}$$

$P = 2x + 2y$	
(0, 7)	14
(6, 0)	12
(4, 5)	18 maximum
(0, 0)	0

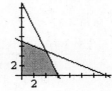

The maximum is 18 at (4, 5).

62. $P = 4x + 5y$ [6.6]

$$\begin{cases} 2x + 3y \le 24 \\ 4x + 3y \le 36 \\ \\ x \ge 0, \ y \ge 0 \end{cases}$$

$4x + 5y = P$	
(0, 8)	40
(6, 4)	44 maximum
(9, 0)	36
(0, 0)	0

The maximum is 44 at (6, 4).

63. $P = 4x + y$ [6.6]

$$\begin{cases} 5x + 2y \ge 16 \\ x + 2y \ge 8 \\ \\ 0 \le x \le 20 \\ 0 \le y \le 20 \end{cases}$$

$P = 4x + y$		
(0, 8)	8	minimum
(2, 3)	11	
(8, 0)	32	
(20, 0)	80	
(20, 20)	100	
(0, 20)	20	

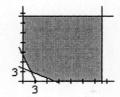

The minimum is 8 at (0, 8).

64. $P = 2x + 7y$ [6.6]

$$\begin{cases} 4x + 3y \geq 24 \\ 4x + 7y \geq 40 \\ 0 \leq x \leq 10 \\ 0 \leq y \leq 20 \end{cases}$$

$P = 2x + 7y$	
(0, 8)	56
(0, 10)	70
(3, 4)	34
(10, 0)	20 minimun
(10, 10)	90

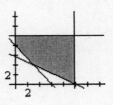

The minimum is 20 at (10, 0).

65. $P = 6x + 3y$ [6.6]

$$\begin{cases} 5x + 2y \geq 20 \\ x + y \geq 7 \\ x + 2y \geq 10 \\ 0 \leq x \leq 15, \; 0 \leq y \leq 10 \end{cases}$$

$6x + 3y = P$	
(0, 10)	30
(2, 5)	27 minimum
(4, 3)	33
(10, 0)	60
(0, 15)	45
(15, 15)	13 5
(15, 0)	90

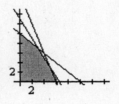

The minimum is 27 at (2, 5).

66. $P = 5x + 4y$ [6.6]

$$\begin{cases} x + y \leq 10 \\ 2x + y \leq 13 \\ 3x + y \leq 18 \\ x \geq 0, \quad y \geq 0 \end{cases}$$

$5x + 4y = P$	
(0, 10)	40
(3, 7)	43 maximum
(5, 3)	37
(6, 0)	30
(0, 0)	0

The maximum is 43 at (3, 7).

67.

$$y = ax^2 + bx + c$$

$$0 = a(1)^2 + b(1) + c$$
$$5 = a(-1)^2 + b(-1) + c$$
$$3 = a(2)^2 + b(2) + c$$

$$\begin{cases} a + b + c = 0 & (1) \\ a - b + c = 5 & (2) \\ 4a + 2b + c = 3 & (3) \end{cases}$$

$$\begin{array}{ll} a + b + c = 0 & (1) \\ \underline{-a + b - c = -5} & -1 \text{ times } (2) \\ 2b = -5 & (4) \end{array}$$

$$\begin{array}{ll} a - b + c = 5 & (2) \\ \underline{-4a - 2b - c = -3} & -1 \text{ times } (3) \\ -3a - 3b = 2 & (5) \end{array}$$

$$\begin{cases} a + b + c = 0 \\ 2b = -5 & (4) \\ -3a - 3b = 2 & (5) \end{cases}$$

$$2b = -5 \qquad -3a - 3\left(-\dfrac{5}{2}\right) = 2 \qquad \dfrac{11}{6} - \dfrac{5}{2} + c = 0$$
$$b = -\dfrac{5}{2} \qquad\qquad a = \dfrac{11}{6} \qquad\qquad c = \dfrac{2}{3}$$

The equation of the graph that passes through the three points is

$$y = \dfrac{11}{6}x^2 - \dfrac{5}{2}x + \dfrac{2}{3}. \quad [6.2]$$

68.

$$x^2 + y^2 + ax + by + c = 0$$

$$4^2 + 2^2 + 4a + 2b + c = 0$$
$$0^2 + 1^2 + 0a + 1b + c = 0$$
$$3^2 + (-1)^2 + 3a + (-1)b + c = 0$$

$$\begin{cases} 4a + 2b + c = -20 & (1) \\ b + c = -1 & (2) \\ 3a - b + c = -10 & (3) \end{cases}$$

$$\begin{array}{ll} -12a - 6b + 3c = 60 & -3 \text{ times } (1) \\ \underline{12a - 4b + 4c = -40} & 4 \text{ times } (3) \\ -10b + c = 20 & (4) \end{array}$$

$$\begin{cases} 4a + 2b + c = -20 \\ b + c = -1 \\ -10b + c = 20 & (4) \end{cases}$$

$$\begin{array}{ll} b + c = -1 & (2) \\ \underline{10b - c = -20} & -1 \text{ times } (4) \\ 11b = -21 & (5) \\ b = -\dfrac{21}{11} \end{array}$$

$$\begin{cases} 4a + 2b + c = -20 \\ b + c = -1 \\ 11b = -21 & (5) \end{cases}$$

$$-\dfrac{21}{11} + c = -1 \qquad 4a + 2\left(-\dfrac{21}{11}\right) + \left(\dfrac{10}{11}\right) = -20$$
$$c = \dfrac{10}{11} \qquad\qquad 4a = -\dfrac{188}{11}$$
$$\qquad\qquad a = -\dfrac{47}{11}$$

The equation of the circle that passes through the three points is

$$x^2 + y^2 - \dfrac{47}{11}x - \dfrac{21}{11}y + \dfrac{10}{11} = 0. \quad [6.2]$$

69.
$$x = ax + by + c$$
$$2 = 2a + b + c$$
$$0 = 3a + b + c$$
$$-2 = -2a - 3b + c$$

$$\begin{cases} 2a + b + c = 2 & (1) \\ 3a + b + c = 0 & (2) \\ -2a - 3b + c = -2 & (3) \end{cases}$$

$$\begin{aligned} 6a + 3b + 3c &= 6 & \text{3 times (1)} \\ \underline{-6a - 2b - 2c} &= 0 & \text{- 2 times (2)} \\ b + c &= 6 & (4) \end{aligned}$$

$$\begin{aligned} 2a + b + c &= 2 & (1) \\ \underline{-2a - 3b + c} &= -2 & (3) \\ -2b + 2c &= 0 \\ -b + c &= 0 & (5) \end{aligned}$$

$$\begin{cases} 2a + b + c = 2 \\ b + c = 6 & (4) \\ -b + c = 0 & (5) \end{cases}$$

$$\begin{aligned} b + c &= 6 & (4) \\ \underline{-b + c} &= 0 & (5) \\ 2c &= 6 \\ c &= 3 & (6) \end{aligned}$$

$$\begin{cases} 2a + b + c = 2 \\ b + c = 6 \\ c = 3 & (6) \end{cases}$$

$$\begin{array}{ll} b + 3 = 6 & 2a + 3 + 3 = 2 \\ \quad b = 3 & \qquad 2a = -4 \\ & \qquad \; a = -2 \end{array}$$

The equation of the graph that passes through the three points
is $z = -2x + 3y + 3$. [6.2]

70. $x =$ amount of 20% acid

$$0.20x + 0.10(10) = 0.16(x + 10)$$
$$0.20x + 1 = 0.16x + 1.6$$
$$0.04x = 0.6$$
$$x = 15 \text{ liters}$$

[6.1]

---

71. Rate flying with the wind: $r + w$
Rate flying against the wind: $r - w$

$$\begin{cases} 855 = (r + w)5 \\ 575 = (r - w)5 \end{cases} \quad \begin{array}{l} 171 = r + w \\ \underline{115 = r - w} \end{array}$$

$$171 = 143 + w \qquad 286 = 2r$$
$$28 = w \qquad\qquad 143 = r$$

Rate of the wind is 28 mph.
Rate of the plane in calm air is 143 mph.
[6.1]

72. $x = $ number of nickels
$y = $ number of dimes
$z = $ number of quarters

$$\begin{cases} x + y + z = 10 & (1) \\ 5x + 10y + 25z = 125 & (2) \end{cases}$$
$$\begin{cases} x + y + z = 10 \\ y + 4z = 15 \end{cases}$$
$$\begin{array}{l} -5x - 5y - 5z = -50 \quad -5 \text{ times } (1) \\ \underline{5x + 10y + 25z = 125} \\ \qquad\quad 5y + 20z = 75 \\ \qquad\quad y + 4z = 15 \end{array}$$

Solving the last equation for y, we have
$y = -4z + 15$. Substitute this into Eq. (1) and
solve for x.

$$x + (-4z + 15) + z = 10$$
$$x - 3z + 15 = 10$$
$$x = 3x - 5$$

Since x, y, and z must all be positive integers, from
$x = 3z - 5$, we have $x \geq 2$. For $y = -4x + 15$, $x \leq 3$.
Thus $z = 2$ or $z = 3$.

When $z = 2$, $x = 1$, $y = 7$, there could be 1 nickel, 7 dimes
and 2 quarters.

When $z = 3$, $x = 4$, $y = 3$, there could be 4 nickels, 3 dimes
and 3 quarters. [6.2]

73. Given (a, b, c) with $ab = c$, $ac = b$. [6.2]
If $ab = c$, then $b \cdot (ab) = a$ and $b^2 = 1$, $b = \pm 1$, or $a = 0$.
If $bc = a$, then $bc \cdot c = b$ and $c^2 = 1$, $c = \pm 1$, or $b = 0$
If $ac = b$, then $a \cdot ac = c$ and $a^2 = 1$, $a \pm 1$, or $c = 0$
The ordered triples are $(1, 1, 1)$, $(1, -1, -1)$, $(-1, -1, 1)$, $(-1, 1, -1)$, $(0, 0, 0)$.

1. $$\begin{cases} 3x + 2y = -5 & (1) \\ 2x - 5y = -16 & (2) \end{cases}$$

$$\begin{array}{l} 15x + 10y = -25 \quad 5 \text{ times } (1) \\ \underline{4x - 10y = -32} \quad 2 \text{ times } (2) \\ \qquad 19x = -57 \\ \qquad\quad x = -3 \end{array}$$

$$3(-3) + 2y = -5$$
$$2y = 4$$
$$y = 2$$

The solution is $(-3, 2)$. [6.1]

2. $$\begin{cases} x - \dfrac{1}{2}y = 3 & (1) \\ 2x - y = 6 & (2) \end{cases}$$

$$\begin{array}{l} -2x + y = -6 \quad -2 \text{ times } (1) \\ \underline{2x - y = -6} \\ \qquad 0 = 0 \end{array}$$

The system of equations is dependent.

Let $y = c$.
$2x - c = 6$
$$x = \frac{6 + c}{2}$$

The solution is $\left(\dfrac{6 + c}{2}, c \right)$. [6.1]

3.
$$\begin{cases} x+3y-\ z=8 & (1) \\ 2x-7y+2z=1 & (2) \\ 4x-\ y+3z=13 & (3) \end{cases}$$

$$\begin{array}{ll} -2x-6y+2z=-16 & -2\text{ times }(1) \\ \underline{2x-7y+2z=\quad 1} & (2) \\ -13y+4z=-15 & (4) \end{array}$$

$$\begin{array}{ll} -4x-12y+4z=-32 & -4\text{ times }(1) \\ \underline{4x-\ y+3z=\quad 13} & (3) \\ -13y+7z=-19 & (5) \end{array}$$

$$\begin{cases} x+3y-\ z=\quad 8 \\ -13y+4z=-15 & (4) \\ -13y+7z=\quad 19 & (5) \end{cases}$$

$$\begin{array}{ll} -13y+4z=-15 & (4) \\ \underline{13y-7z=\quad 19} & -1\text{ times }(5) \\ -3z=\quad 4 \end{array}$$

$$z=-\frac{4}{3} \qquad (6)$$

$$\begin{cases} x+3y-\ z=\quad 8 \\ -13y+4z=-15 \\ \qquad z=\ -\frac{4}{3} \end{cases}$$

$$-13y+4\left(-\frac{4}{3}\right)=-15 \qquad\qquad x+3\left(\frac{29}{39}\right)-\left(-\frac{4}{3}\right)=8$$
$$y=\frac{29}{39} \qquad\qquad\qquad\qquad x=\frac{173}{39}$$

The solution is $\left(\frac{173}{39},\ \frac{29}{39},\ -\frac{4}{3}\right)$. [6.2]

4.
$$\begin{cases} 3x-2y+\ z=2 & (1) \\ x+2y-2z=1 & (2) \\ 4x\qquad -z=3 & (3) \end{cases}$$

$$\begin{array}{ll} 3x-2y+\ z=\quad 2 & (1) \\ \underline{-3x-6y+6z=-3} & -3\text{ times }(2) \\ -8y+7z=-1 & (5) \end{array}$$

$$\begin{array}{ll} -4x-8y+\ 8z=-4 & -4\text{ times }(2) \\ \underline{4x\qquad -\ z=-3} & (3) \\ -8y+7z=-1 & (5) \end{array}$$

$$\begin{cases} 3x-2y+\ z=\quad 2 \\ -8y+7z=-1 & (4) \\ -8y+7z=-1 & (5) \end{cases}$$

$$\begin{array}{ll} 8y-7z=\quad 1 & -1\text{ times }(4) \\ \underline{-8y+7z=-1} & (5) \\ 0=0 & (6) \end{array}$$

$$\begin{cases} 3x-2y+\ z=\quad 2 \\ -8y+7z=-1 \\ \qquad\quad 0=0 & (6) \end{cases}$$

The system of equations is dependent.

Let $z=c.$ $\qquad -8y+7(c)=-1 \qquad\quad 4x-c=3$
$$y=\frac{7c+1}{8} \qquad\qquad x=\frac{c+3}{4}$$

The solution is $\left(\dfrac{c+3}{4},\ \dfrac{7c+1}{8},\ c\right)$.

[6.2]

5.
$$\begin{cases} 2x - 3y + z = -1 & (1) \\ x + 5y - 2z = 5 & (2) \end{cases}$$

$$\begin{array}{r} 2x - 3y + z = -1 \quad (1) \\ -2x - 10y + 4z = -10 \quad -2 \text{ times (2)} \\ \hline -13y + 5z = -11 \quad (3) \end{array}$$

$$\begin{cases} 2x - 3y + z = -1 \\ -13y + 5z = -11 & (3) \end{cases}$$

The system of equations is dependent.

Let $z = c$. $-8y + 7(c) = -1$ $4x - c = 3$

$$y = \frac{7c+1}{8} \qquad x = \frac{c+3}{4}$$

The solution is $\left(\dfrac{c+10}{13}, \dfrac{5c+11}{13}, c \right)$. [6.2]

6.
$$\begin{cases} 4x + 2y + z = 0 & (1) \\ x - 3y - 2z = 0 & (2) \\ 3x + 5y + 3z = 0 & (3) \end{cases}$$

$$\begin{array}{r} 4x + 2y + z = 0 \quad (1) \\ -4x + 12y + 8z = 0 \quad -4 \text{ times (2)} \\ \hline 14y + 9z = 0 \quad (4) \end{array}$$

$$\begin{array}{r} -3x + 9y + 6z = 0 \quad -3 \text{ times (2)} \\ 3x + 5y + 3z = 0 \quad (3) \\ \hline 14y + 9z = 0 \quad (5) \end{array}$$

$$\begin{cases} 4x + 2y + z = 0 \\ 14y + 9z = 0 & (4) \\ 14y + 9z = 0 & (5) \end{cases}$$

$$\begin{array}{r} 14y + 9z = 0 \\ -14y - 9z = 0 \quad -1 \text{ times (5)} \\ \hline 0 = 0 \quad (6) \end{array}$$

$$\begin{cases} 4x + 2y + z = 0 \\ 14y + 9z = 0 \\ 0 = 0 \end{cases}$$

The system of equations is dependent.

Let $z = c$. $14y + 9c = 0$ $x - 3\left(-\dfrac{9c}{14}\right) - 2c = 0$

$$y = -\frac{9c}{14} \qquad x = \frac{c}{14}$$

The solution is $\left(\dfrac{c}{14}, -\dfrac{9c}{14}, c \right)$. [6.2]

7.
$$\begin{cases} y = x + 3 & (1) \\ y = x^2 + x - 1 & (2) \end{cases}$$

Set the expressions equal to each other.

$$x^2 + x - 1 = x + 3$$
$$x^2 = 4$$
$$x = \pm 2$$

Substitute for x in Eq. (1).

$y = 2 + 3$ $y = -2 + 3$
$y = 5$ $y = 1$

The solutions are (2, 5) and (−2, 1). [6.3]

8.
$$\begin{cases} y = x^2 - x - 3 & (1) \\ y = 2x^2 + 2x - 1 & (2) \end{cases}$$

Set the expressions equal to each other.

$$x^2 + 2x - 1 = x^2 - x - 3$$
$$x^2 + 3x + 2 = 0$$
$$(x + 2)(x + 1) = 0$$

Substitute for x in Eq. (1).

$y = (-2)^2 - (-2) - 3$ $y = (-1)^2 - (-1) - 3$
$y = 3$ $y = -1$

The solutions are (−2, 3) and (−1, −1). [6.3]

9.
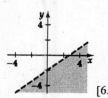

[6.5]

10.
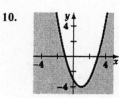

[6.5]

11.
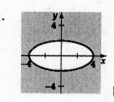

[6.5]

12.

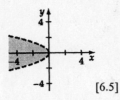

[6.5]

13.

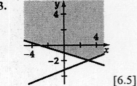

[6.5]

14. No solution. The solution set is empty.
[6.5]

15.

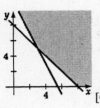

[6.5]

16.

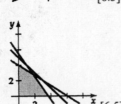

[6.5]

17.
$$\frac{3x-5}{x^2-3x-4} = \frac{3x-5}{(x-4)(x+1)}$$

$$= \frac{A}{x-4} + \frac{B}{x+1}$$

$3x-5 = A(x+1) + B(x-4)$

$3x-5 = Ax + A + Bx - 4B$

$$\begin{cases} 3 = A+B \\ -5 = A-4B \end{cases}$$

$3 = A+B$

$\underline{5 = -A+4B}$

$8 = 5B \qquad 3 = A + \dfrac{8}{5}$

$\dfrac{8}{5} = B \qquad \dfrac{7}{5} = A$

$$\frac{3x-5}{(x-4)(x+1)} = \frac{7}{5(x-4)} + \frac{8}{5(x+1)} \quad [6.4]$$

18.
$$\frac{2x+1}{x(x^2+1)} = \frac{A}{x} + \frac{Bx+C}{x^2+1}$$

$2x+1 = A(x^2+1) + (Bx+C)x$

$2x+1 = Ax^2 + A + Bx^2 + Cx$

$$\begin{cases} 0 = A+B \\ 2 = C \\ 1 = A \end{cases} \qquad \begin{matrix} 0 = 1+B \\ -1 = B \end{matrix}$$

$$\frac{2x+1}{x(x^2+1)} = \frac{1}{x} + \frac{-x+2}{x^2+1} \quad [6.4]$$

19. x = Acres of oats
y = Acres of barley
Constraints

$$\begin{cases} x + \ y \le 160 \\ 15x + 13y \le 2200 \\ 15x + 20y \le 2600 \\ x \le 0, \quad y \ge 0 \end{cases}$$

maximize
$p = 120x + 150y$

$(0, 130)$	$19,500
$\left(\dfrac{680}{7}, \dfrac{400}{7}\right)$	$20,228.57
$\left(146\dfrac{2}{3}, 0\right)$	$17,600
$(0, 0)$	0

maximum

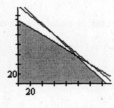

To maximize profit, $\dfrac{680}{7}$ acres of oats and $\dfrac{400}{7}$ acres of barley must be planted.

[6.6]

20.

$$x^2 + y^2 + ax + by + c = 0$$

$$3^2 + 5^2 + 3a + 5b + c = 0$$

$$(-3)^2 + (-3)^2 - 3a - 3b + c = 0$$

$$4^2 + 4^2 + 4a + 4b + c = 0$$

$$\begin{cases} 3a + 5b + c = -34 & (1) \\ -3a - 3b + c = -18 & (2) \\ 4a + 4b + c = -32 & (3) \end{cases}$$

$$\begin{aligned} 3a + 5b + c &= -34 \quad (1) \\ \underline{-3a - 3b + c} &= -18 \quad (2) \\ 2b + 2c &= -52 \\ b + c &= -26 \quad (4) \end{aligned}$$

$$\begin{aligned} -12a - 12b + 4c &= -72 \quad 4 \text{ times } (2) \\ \underline{12a + 12b + 3c} &= -96 \quad 3 \text{ times } (3) \\ 7c &= -168 \\ c &= -24 \quad (5) \end{aligned}$$

$$\begin{cases} 3a + 5b + c = -34 \\ b + c = -26 & (4) \\ c = -24 & (5) \end{cases}$$

$$c = -24 \qquad b + (-24) = -26 \qquad 3a + 5(-2) - 24 = -34$$
$$b = -2 \qquad\qquad a = 0$$

The equation of the circle is $x^2 + y^2 - 2y - 24 = 0$. [6.2]

••

Cumulative Review

1.

$$m = \frac{-\frac{1}{3} - 2}{4 - \left(-\frac{1}{2}\right)} = \frac{-\frac{7}{3}}{\frac{9}{2}} = -\frac{7}{3} \cdot \frac{2}{9} = -\frac{14}{27} \quad [2.3]$$

2.

$$\begin{aligned} f(x) &= -x^2 + 2x - 4 \qquad [2.4] \\ &= -(x^2 - 2x) + 4 \\ &= -(x^2 - 2x + 1) + 4 - 1 \\ &= -(x - 1)^2 + 3 \end{aligned}$$

Vertex $(1, -3)$, parabola opens down.
Range: $\{y \mid y \le -3\}$

3.

$$\begin{aligned} 3(-2)^4 - 4(-2)^3 &+ 2(-2)^2 - (-2) + 1 \quad [P.1] \\ &= 3(16) - 4(-8) + 2(4) + 2 + 1 \\ &= 48 + 32 + 8 + 2 + 1 \\ &= 91 \end{aligned}$$

4.

$$\begin{aligned} \log_6(x-5) + 3\log_6(2x) &= \log_6(x-5) + \log_6(2x)^3 \quad [4.4] \\ &= \log_6(x-5)(2x)^3 \\ &= \log[8x^3(x-5)] \end{aligned}$$

5. Vertex $= (4, 2)$, point $(-1, 1)$, axis of symmetry $x = 4$

$$\begin{aligned} (x-4)^2 &= 4p(y-2) \\ (-1-4)^2 &= 4p(1-2) \\ 25 &= 4p(-1) \\ p &= -\frac{25}{4} \\ (x-4)^2 &= 4\left(-\frac{25}{4}\right)(y-2) \\ (x-4)^2 &= -25(y-2) \qquad [5.1] \end{aligned}$$

6.

$$\frac{1}{F} = \frac{1}{d_0} + \frac{1}{d_1} \quad [1.2]$$

$$\frac{1}{F} - \frac{1}{d_1} = \frac{1}{d_0}$$

$$\frac{d_1 - F}{Fd_1} = \frac{1}{d_0}$$

$$d_0 = \frac{Fd_1}{d_1 - F}$$

7.
$$m = \frac{-1-2}{2-(-4)} = \frac{-3}{6} = -\frac{1}{2} \quad [2.2]$$

$$y - (-1) = -\frac{1}{2}(x-2)$$

$$y + 1 = -\frac{1}{2}x + 1$$

$$y = -\frac{1}{2}x$$

8.   even [2.5]

9.
$$\log x - \log(2x-3) = 2 \qquad [4.5]$$

$$\log\frac{x}{2x-3} = 2$$

$$\frac{x}{2x-3} = 10^2$$

$$x = 100(2x-3)$$

$$x = 200x - 300$$

$$-199x = -300$$

$$x = \frac{300}{199}$$

10.   vertices (2, 2) and (10, 2), eccentricity = 3   [5.3]
Length of transverse axis = distance between vertices
$$2a = |10 - 2| = 8$$
$$a = 4 \text{ and } a^2 = 16$$

Center (midpoint of transverse axis) is $\left(\dfrac{2+10}{2}, \dfrac{2+2}{2}\right) = (6,2)$

Therefore, $h = 6$ and $k = 2$.
Since both vertices lie on the horizontal line $x = 2$, the
transverse axis is parallel to the x-axis.

Since $e = \dfrac{c}{a}, c = ae = (4)(3) = 12$

Because $b^2 = c^2 - a^2, b^2 = 144 - 16 = 128$

Substituting h, k, a^2, b^2 into the standard equation yields

$$\frac{(x-6)^2}{16} - \frac{(y-2)^2}{128} = 1.$$

11.
$$g\left(-\frac{1}{2}\right) = \frac{-\frac{1}{2} - 2}{-\frac{1}{2}} = \frac{-\frac{5}{2}}{-\frac{1}{2}} = 5 \quad [2.2]$$

12.
$$f(-2) \cdot g(-2) = [(-2)^2 - 1][(-2)^2 - 4(-2) - 2] \quad [2.6]$$
$$= [4-1][4+8-2]$$
$$= [3][10]$$
$$= 30$$

13. $\log_{0.25} 0.015625 = 3$ [4.3]

14.

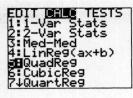

$$y = x^2 + 0.4x - 0.8$$

15.
$$(x+2)(x-3i)(x+3i) = (x+2)(x^2+9) \qquad [3.4]$$
$$= x^3 + 2x^2 + 9x + 18$$

16.
$$Q(r) = \frac{2}{1-r} \quad [4.1]$$

$$r = \frac{2}{1-Q}$$

$$r(1-Q) = 2$$

$$r - rQ = 2$$

$$-rQ = 2 - r$$

$$Q = \frac{2-r}{-r}$$

$$Q^{-1}(r) = \frac{r-2}{r}$$

17.

$$x^2 - x - 1 \overline{)\,2x^3 - x^2 \quad - 2}$$

$$\begin{array}{r} 2x+1 \\ \underline{2x^3 - 2x^2} \\ x^2 \quad - 2 \\ \underline{x^2 - x - 1} \\ x + 1 \end{array}$$

$$H(x) = \frac{2x^3 - x^2 - 2}{x^2 - x - 1} = 2x + 1 + \frac{x+1}{x^2 - x - 1}$$

Slant asymptote: $y = 2x + 1$ p3.5]

18.

$$\begin{aligned} g[f(1)] &= g[2^1] \quad [4.2] \\ &= g[2] \\ &= 3^{2(2)} \\ &= 3^4 \\ &= 81 \end{aligned}$$

19.

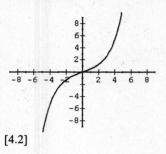

[4.2]

20.

$$t = \frac{\ln 2}{r} \qquad r = 0.065$$

$$t = \frac{\ln 2}{0.065}$$

$t \approx 11$ years

[4.6]

Chapter 7
Matrices

1. $\begin{bmatrix} 2 & -3 & 1 & | & 1 \\ 3 & -2 & 3 & | & 0 \\ 1 & 0 & 5 & | & 4 \end{bmatrix}$, $\begin{bmatrix} 2 & -3 & 1 \\ 3 & -2 & 3 \\ 1 & 0 & 5 \end{bmatrix}$, $\begin{bmatrix} 1 \\ 0 \\ 4 \end{bmatrix}$

3. $\begin{bmatrix} 2 & -3 & -4 & 1 & | & 2 \\ 0 & 2 & 1 & 0 & | & 2 \\ 1 & -1 & 2 & 0 & | & 4 \\ 3 & -3 & -2 & 0 & | & 1 \end{bmatrix}$, $\begin{bmatrix} 2 & -3 & -4 & 1 \\ 0 & 2 & 1 & 0 \\ 1 & -1 & 2 & 0 \\ 3 & -3 & -2 & 0 \end{bmatrix}$, $\begin{bmatrix} 2 \\ 2 \\ 4 \\ 1 \end{bmatrix}$

5. $\begin{bmatrix} 2 & -1 & 3 & -2 \\ 1 & -1 & 2 & 2 \\ 3 & 2 & -1 & 3 \end{bmatrix}$ $\xrightarrow{R_1 \longleftrightarrow R_2}$ $\begin{bmatrix} 1 & -1 & 2 & 2 \\ 2 & -1 & 3 & -2 \\ 3 & 2 & -1 & 3 \end{bmatrix}$ $\xrightarrow[\;-3R_1+R_3\;]{-2R_1+R_2}$ $\begin{bmatrix} 1 & -1 & 2 & 2 \\ 2 & -1 & -1 & -6 \\ 0 & 5 & -7 & -3 \end{bmatrix}$ $\xrightarrow{-5R_2+R_3}$ $\begin{bmatrix} 1 & -1 & 2 & 2 \\ 0 & 1 & -1 & -6 \\ 0 & 0 & -2 & 27 \end{bmatrix}$

$\xrightarrow{(-1/2)R_3}$ $\begin{bmatrix} 1 & -1 & 2 & 2 \\ 0 & 1 & -1 & -6 \\ 0 & 0 & 1 & -27/2 \end{bmatrix}$

7. $\begin{bmatrix} 4 & -5 & -1 & 2 \\ 3 & -4 & 1 & -2 \\ 1 & -2 & -1 & 3 \end{bmatrix}$ $\xrightarrow{R_1 \longleftrightarrow R_3}$ $\begin{bmatrix} 1 & -2 & -1 & 3 \\ 3 & -2 & 1 & -2 \\ 4 & -5 & -1 & 2 \end{bmatrix}$ $\xrightarrow[\;-4R_1+R_3\;]{-3R_1+R_2}$ $\begin{bmatrix} 1 & -2 & -1 & 3 \\ 0 & 2 & 4 & -11 \\ 0 & 3 & 3 & -10 \end{bmatrix}$ $\xrightarrow{\frac{1}{2}R_2}$ $\begin{bmatrix} 1 & -2 & -1 & 3 \\ 0 & 1 & 2 & -11/2 \\ 0 & 3 & 3 & -10 \end{bmatrix}$

$\xrightarrow{-3R_2+R_3}$ $\begin{bmatrix} 1 & -2 & -1 & 3 \\ 0 & 1 & 2 & -11/2 \\ 0 & 0 & -3 & 13/2 \end{bmatrix}$ $\xrightarrow{-\frac{1}{3}R_3}$ $\begin{bmatrix} 1 & -2 & -1 & 3 \\ 0 & 1 & 2 & -11/2 \\ 0 & 0 & 1 & -13/6 \end{bmatrix}$

9. $\begin{bmatrix} 1 & -2 & 3 & -4 \\ 3 & -6 & 10 & -14 \\ 5 & -8 & 19 & -21 \\ 2 & -4 & 7 & -10 \end{bmatrix}$ $\xrightarrow[\substack{-5R_1+R_3 \\ -2R_1+R_4}]{-3R_1+R_2}$ $\begin{bmatrix} 1 & -2 & 3 & -4 \\ 0 & 0 & 1 & -2 \\ 0 & 2 & 4 & -1 \\ 0 & 0 & 1 & -2 \end{bmatrix}$ $\xrightarrow{R_2 \longleftrightarrow R_3}$ $\begin{bmatrix} 1 & -2 & 3 & -4 \\ 0 & 2 & 4 & -1 \\ 0 & 0 & 1 & -2 \\ 0 & 0 & 1 & -2 \end{bmatrix}$ $\xrightarrow{(1/2)R_2}$ $\begin{bmatrix} 1 & -2 & 3 & -4 \\ 0 & 1 & 2 & -1/2 \\ 0 & 0 & 1 & -2 \\ 0 & 0 & 1 & -2 \end{bmatrix}$

$\xrightarrow{-R_3+R_4}$ $\begin{bmatrix} 1 & -2 & 3 & -4 \\ 0 & 1 & 2 & -1/2 \\ 0 & 0 & 1 & -2 \\ 0 & 0 & 0 & 0 \end{bmatrix}$

11. $\begin{bmatrix} 1 & -3 & 4 & 2 & 1 \\ 2 & -3 & 5 & -2 & -1 \\ -1 & 2 & -3 & 1 & 3 \end{bmatrix}$ $\xrightarrow[\;R_1+R_3\;]{-2R_1+R_2}$ $\begin{bmatrix} 1 & -3 & 4 & 2 & 1 \\ 0 & 3 & -3 & -6 & -3 \\ 0 & -1 & 1 & 3 & 4 \end{bmatrix}$ $\xrightarrow{(1/3)R_2}$ $\begin{bmatrix} 1 & -3 & 4 & 2 & 1 \\ 0 & 1 & -1 & -2 & -1 \\ 0 & -1 & 1 & 3 & 4 \end{bmatrix}$

$\xrightarrow{R_2+R_3}$ $\begin{bmatrix} 1 & -3 & 4 & 2 & 1 \\ 0 & 1 & -1 & -2 & -1 \\ 0 & 0 & 0 & 1 & 3 \end{bmatrix}$

13.

$$\begin{bmatrix} 1 & 2 & -2 & | & -2 \\ 5 & 9 & -4 & | & -3 \\ 3 & 4 & -5 & | & -3 \end{bmatrix} \xrightarrow{\substack{-5R_1+R_2 \\ -3R_1+R_3}} \begin{bmatrix} 1 & 2 & -2 & | & -2 \\ 0 & -1 & 6 & | & 7 \\ 0 & -2 & 1 & | & 3 \end{bmatrix} \xrightarrow{-1R_2} \begin{bmatrix} 1 & 2 & -2 & | & 2 \\ 0 & 1 & -6 & | & -7 \\ 0 & -2 & 1 & | & 3 \end{bmatrix} \xrightarrow{2R_2+R_3} \begin{bmatrix} 1 & 2 & -2 & | & -2 \\ 0 & 1 & -6 & | & -7 \\ 0 & 0 & -11 & | & -11 \end{bmatrix}$$

$$\xrightarrow{(-1/11)R_3} \begin{bmatrix} 1 & 2 & -2 & | & -2 \\ 0 & 1 & -6 & | & -7 \\ 0 & 0 & 1 & | & 1 \end{bmatrix}$$

$$\begin{cases} x + 2y - 2z = -2 \\ \quad\; y - 6z = -7 \\ \qquad\quad z = 1 \end{cases} \quad \begin{aligned} y - 6(1) &= -7 \\ y &= -1 \end{aligned} \qquad \begin{aligned} x + 2(-1) - 2(1) &= -2 \\ x &= 2 \end{aligned}$$

The solution is $(2, -1, 1)$.

15.

$$\begin{bmatrix} 3 & 7 & -7 & | & -4 \\ 1 & 2 & -3 & | & 0 \\ 5 & 6 & 1 & | & -8 \end{bmatrix} R_1 \longleftrightarrow R_2 \begin{bmatrix} 1 & 2 & -3 & | & 0 \\ 3 & 7 & -7 & | & -4 \\ 5 & 6 & 1 & | & -8 \end{bmatrix} \xrightarrow{\substack{-3R_1+R_2 \\ -5R_1+R_3}} \begin{bmatrix} 1 & 2 & -3 & | & 0 \\ 0 & 1 & 2 & | & -4 \\ 0 & -4 & 16 & | & -8 \end{bmatrix} \xrightarrow{4R_2+R_3} \begin{bmatrix} 1 & 2 & -3 & | & 0 \\ 0 & 1 & 2 & | & -4 \\ 0 & 0 & 24 & | & -24 \end{bmatrix}$$

$$\xrightarrow{\frac{1}{24}R_3} \begin{bmatrix} 1 & 2 & -3 & | & 0 \\ 0 & 1 & 2 & | & -4 \\ 0 & 0 & 1 & | & -1 \end{bmatrix}$$

$$\begin{cases} x + 2y - 3z = 0 \\ \quad\; y + 2z = -4 \\ \qquad\quad z = -1 \end{cases} \quad \begin{aligned} y + 2(-1) &= -4 \\ y &= -2 \end{aligned} \qquad \begin{aligned} x + 2(-2) - 3(-1) &= 0 \\ x &= 1 \end{aligned}$$

The solution is $(1, -2, -1)$.

17.

$$\begin{bmatrix} 1 & 2 & -2 & | & 3 \\ 5 & 8 & -6 & | & 14 \\ 3 & 4 & -2 & | & 8 \end{bmatrix} \xrightarrow{\substack{-5R_1+R_2 \\ -3R_1+R_3}} \begin{bmatrix} 1 & 2 & -2 & | & 3 \\ 0 & -2 & 4 & | & -1 \\ 0 & -2 & 4 & | & -1 \end{bmatrix} \xrightarrow{(1/2)R_2} \begin{bmatrix} 1 & 2 & -2 & | & 3 \\ 0 & 1 & -2 & | & \tfrac{1}{2} \\ 0 & -2 & 4 & | & -1 \end{bmatrix} \xrightarrow{2R_2+R_3} \begin{bmatrix} 1 & 2 & -2 & | & 3 \\ 0 & 1 & -2 & | & \tfrac{1}{2} \\ 0 & 0 & 0 & | & 0 \end{bmatrix}$$

$$\begin{cases} x + 2y - 2z = 3 \\ \quad\; y - 2z = \dfrac{1}{2} \end{cases}$$

$$y = 2z + \frac{1}{2}$$

$$x + 2\left(2z + \frac{1}{2}\right) - 2z = 3$$

$$x = 2 - 2z$$

Let z be any real number c. The solution is $\left(2 - 2c, 2c + \dfrac{1}{2}, c\right)$.

19.

$$\begin{bmatrix} 3 & 2 & -1 & | & 1 \\ 2 & 3 & -1 & | & 1 \\ 1 & -1 & 2 & | & 3 \end{bmatrix} R_1 \longleftrightarrow R_3 \begin{bmatrix} 1 & -1 & 2 & | & 3 \\ 2 & 3 & -1 & | & 1 \\ 3 & 2 & -1 & | & 1 \end{bmatrix} \xrightarrow{\substack{-2R_1+R_2 \\ -3R_1+R_3}} \begin{bmatrix} 1 & -1 & 2 & | & 3 \\ 0 & 5 & -5 & | & -5 \\ 0 & 5 & -7 & | & -8 \end{bmatrix} \xrightarrow{\frac{1}{5}R_2} \begin{bmatrix} 1 & -1 & 2 & | & 3 \\ 0 & 1 & -1 & | & -1 \\ 0 & 5 & -7 & | & -8 \end{bmatrix}$$

$$\xrightarrow{-5R_2+R_3} \begin{bmatrix} 1 & -1 & 2 & | & 3 \\ 0 & 1 & -1 & | & -1 \\ 0 & 0 & -2 & | & -3 \end{bmatrix} \xrightarrow{-\frac{1}{2}R_3} \begin{bmatrix} 1 & -1 & 2 & | & 3 \\ 0 & 1 & -1 & | & -1 \\ 0 & 0 & 1 & | & \tfrac{3}{2} \end{bmatrix}$$

$$\begin{cases} x - y + 2z = 3 \\ \quad\; y - z = -1 \\ \qquad\quad z = \dfrac{3}{2} \end{cases} \quad \begin{aligned} y - \dfrac{3}{2} &= -1 \\ y &= \dfrac{1}{2} \end{aligned} \qquad \begin{aligned} x - \dfrac{1}{2} + 2\left(\dfrac{3}{2}\right) &= 3 \\ x &= \dfrac{1}{2} \end{aligned}$$

The solution is $\left(\dfrac{1}{2}, \dfrac{1}{2}, \dfrac{3}{2}\right)$.

21.

$$\begin{bmatrix} 1 & -3 & 2 & | & 0 \\ 2 & -5 & -2 & | & 0 \\ 4 & -11 & 2 & | & 0 \end{bmatrix} \xrightarrow[\substack{-2R_1+R_2 \\ -4R_1+R_3}]{} \begin{bmatrix} 1 & -3 & 2 & | & 0 \\ 0 & 1 & -6 & | & 0 \\ 0 & 1 & -6 & | & 0 \end{bmatrix} \xrightarrow{-1R_2+R_3} \begin{bmatrix} 1 & -3 & 2 & | & 0 \\ 0 & 1 & -6 & | & 0 \\ 0 & 0 & 0 & | & 0 \end{bmatrix}$$

$$\begin{cases} x - 3y + 2z = 0 \\ y - 6z = 0 \end{cases} \qquad y = 6z \qquad x - 3(6z) + 2z = 0$$
$$x = 16z$$

Let z be any real number c. The solution is $(16c,\, 6c,\, c)$.

23.

$$\begin{bmatrix} 2 & 1 & -3 & | & 4 \\ 3 & 2 & 1 & | & 2 \end{bmatrix} \xrightarrow{-R_1+R_2} \begin{bmatrix} 2 & 1 & -3 & | & 4 \\ 1 & 1 & 4 & | & -2 \end{bmatrix} \xrightarrow{R_1 \longleftrightarrow R_2} \begin{bmatrix} 1 & 1 & 4 & | & -2 \\ 2 & 1 & -3 & | & 4 \end{bmatrix} \xrightarrow{-2R_1+R_2} \begin{bmatrix} 1 & 1 & 4 & | & -2 \\ 0 & -1 & -11 & | & 8 \end{bmatrix}$$

$$\xrightarrow{-1R_2} \begin{bmatrix} 1 & 1 & 4 & | & -2 \\ 0 & 1 & 11 & | & -8 \end{bmatrix}$$

$$\begin{cases} x + y + 4z = -2 \\ y + 11z = -8 \end{cases} \qquad y = -11z - 8 \qquad x + (-11z - 8) + 4z = -2$$
$$x = 7z + 6$$

Let z be any real number c. The solution is $(7c + 6,\, -11c - 8,\, c)$.

25.

$$\begin{bmatrix} 2 & 2 & -4 & | & 4 \\ 2 & 3 & -5 & | & 4 \\ 4 & 5 & -9 & | & 8 \end{bmatrix} \xrightarrow{(1/2)R_1} \begin{bmatrix} 1 & 1 & -2 & | & 2 \\ 2 & 3 & -5 & | & 4 \\ 4 & 5 & -9 & | & 8 \end{bmatrix} \xrightarrow[\substack{-2R_1+R_2 \\ -4R_1+R_3}]{} \begin{bmatrix} 1 & 1 & -2 & | & 2 \\ 0 & 1 & -1 & | & 0 \\ 0 & 1 & -1 & | & 0 \end{bmatrix} \xrightarrow{-1R_2+R_3} \begin{bmatrix} 1 & 1 & -2 & | & 2 \\ 0 & 1 & -1 & | & 0 \\ 0 & 0 & 0 & | & 0 \end{bmatrix}$$

$$\begin{cases} x + y - 2z = 2 \\ y - z = 0 \end{cases} \qquad y = z \qquad x + z - 2z = 2$$
$$x = z + 2$$

Let z be any real number c. The solution is $(c + 2,\, c,\, c)$.

27.

$$\begin{bmatrix} 1 & 3 & 4 & | & 11 \\ 2 & 3 & 2 & | & 7 \\ 4 & 9 & 10 & | & 20 \\ 3 & -2 & 1 & | & 1 \end{bmatrix} \xrightarrow[\substack{-2R_1+R_2 \\ -4R_1+R_3 \\ -3R_1+R_4}]{} \begin{bmatrix} 1 & 3 & 4 & | & 11 \\ 0 & -3 & -6 & | & -15 \\ 0 & -3 & -6 & | & -24 \\ 0 & -11 & -11 & | & -32 \end{bmatrix} \xrightarrow{(-1/3)R_2} \begin{bmatrix} 1 & 3 & 4 & | & 11 \\ 0 & 1 & 2 & | & 5 \\ 0 & -3 & -6 & | & -24 \\ 0 & -11 & -11 & | & -32 \end{bmatrix} \xrightarrow{3R_2+R_3} \begin{bmatrix} 1 & 3 & 4 & | & 11 \\ 0 & 1 & 2 & | & 5 \\ 0 & 0 & 0 & | & -9 \\ 0 & -11 & -11 & | & -32 \end{bmatrix}$$

$$\xrightarrow{R_3 \longleftrightarrow R_4} \begin{bmatrix} 1 & 3 & 4 & | & 11 \\ 0 & 1 & 2 & | & 5 \\ 0 & -11 & -11 & | & -32 \\ 0 & 0 & 0 & | & -9 \end{bmatrix} \xrightarrow{(-1/11)R_3} \begin{bmatrix} 1 & 3 & 4 & | & 11 \\ 0 & 1 & 2 & | & 5 \\ 0 & 1 & 1 & | & \frac{32}{11} \\ 0 & 0 & 0 & | & -9 \end{bmatrix} \xrightarrow{-R_2+R_3} \begin{bmatrix} 1 & 3 & 4 & | & 11 \\ 0 & 1 & 2 & | & 5 \\ 0 & 0 & -1 & | & -\frac{23}{11} \\ 0 & 0 & 0 & | & -9 \end{bmatrix} \xrightarrow{-1R_3} \begin{bmatrix} 1 & 3 & 4 & | & 11 \\ 0 & 1 & 2 & | & 5 \\ 0 & 0 & 1 & | & \frac{23}{11} \\ 0 & 0 & 0 & | & -9 \end{bmatrix}$$

$$\begin{cases} x + 3y + 4z = 11 \\ y + 2z = 5 \\ z = \frac{23}{11} \\ 0z = -9 \end{cases}$$

Because $0z = -9$ has no solutions, the system of equations has no solution.

29.

$$\begin{bmatrix} 1 & 2 & -3 & 1 & | & -7 \\ 3 & 5 & -8 & 5 & | & -8 \\ 2 & 3 & -7 & 3 & | & -11 \\ 4 & 8 & -10 & 7 & | & -10 \end{bmatrix} \xrightarrow[\substack{-3R_1+R_2 \\ -2R_1+R_3 \\ -4R_1+R_4}]{} \begin{bmatrix} 1 & 2 & -3 & 1 & | & -7 \\ 0 & -1 & 1 & 2 & | & 13 \\ 0 & -1 & -1 & 1 & | & 3 \\ 0 & 0 & 2 & 3 & | & 18 \end{bmatrix} \xrightarrow{-1R_2} \begin{bmatrix} 1 & 2 & -3 & 1 & | & -7 \\ 0 & 1 & -1 & -2 & | & -13 \\ 0 & -1 & -1 & 1 & | & 3 \\ 0 & 0 & 2 & 3 & | & 18 \end{bmatrix}$$

$$\xrightarrow{R_2+R_3} \begin{bmatrix} 1 & 2 & -3 & 1 & | & -7 \\ 0 & 1 & -1 & -2 & | & -13 \\ 0 & 0 & -2 & -1 & | & -10 \\ 0 & 0 & 2 & 3 & | & 18 \end{bmatrix} \xrightarrow{(-1/2)R_3} \begin{bmatrix} 1 & 2 & -3 & 1 & | & -7 \\ 0 & 1 & -1 & -2 & | & -13 \\ 0 & 0 & 1 & \frac{1}{2} & | & 5 \\ 0 & 0 & 2 & 3 & | & 18 \end{bmatrix} \xrightarrow{-2R_3+R_4} \begin{bmatrix} 1 & 2 & -3 & 1 & | & -7 \\ 0 & 1 & -1 & -2 & | & -13 \\ 0 & 0 & 1 & \frac{1}{2} & | & 5 \\ 0 & 0 & 0 & 2 & | & 8 \end{bmatrix}$$

$$\begin{cases} t + 2u - 3v + w = -7 \\ u - v - 2w = -13 \\ v + \frac{1}{2}w = 5 \\ 2w = 8 \end{cases}$$

$$v + \frac{1}{2}(4) = 5 \qquad u - 3 - 2(4) = -13 \qquad t + 2(-2) - 3(3) + 4 = -7$$
$$v = 3 \qquad u = -2 \qquad t = 2$$

The solution is $(2, -2, 3, 4)$.

31.

$$\begin{bmatrix} 2 & -1 & 3 & 2 & | & 2 \\ 1 & -1 & 2 & 1 & | & 2 \\ 3 & 0 & -2 & -3 & | & 13 \\ 2 & 2 & 0 & -2 & | & 6 \end{bmatrix} \xrightarrow{(1/2)R_1} \begin{bmatrix} 1 & -\frac{1}{2} & \frac{3}{2} & 1 & | & 1 \\ 1 & -1 & 2 & 1 & | & 2 \\ 3 & 0 & -2 & -3 & | & 13 \\ 2 & 2 & 0 & -2 & | & 6 \end{bmatrix} \xrightarrow[\substack{-3R_1+R_3 \\ -2R_1+R_4}]{-1R_1+R_2} \begin{bmatrix} 1 & -\frac{1}{2} & \frac{3}{2} & 1 & | & 1 \\ 0 & -\frac{1}{2} & \frac{1}{2} & 0 & | & 1 \\ 0 & \frac{3}{2} & -\frac{13}{2} & -6 & | & 10 \\ 0 & 3 & -3 & -4 & | & 4 \end{bmatrix}$$

$$\xrightarrow{-2R_2} \begin{bmatrix} 1 & -\frac{1}{2} & \frac{3}{2} & 1 & | & 1 \\ 0 & 1 & -1 & 0 & | & -2 \\ 0 & \frac{3}{2} & -\frac{13}{2} & -6 & | & 10 \\ 0 & 3 & -3 & -4 & | & 4 \end{bmatrix} \xrightarrow[\substack{-3R_2+R_4}]{(-3/2)R_2+R_3} \begin{bmatrix} 1 & -\frac{1}{2} & \frac{3}{2} & 1 & | & 1 \\ 0 & 1 & -1 & 0 & | & -2 \\ 0 & 0 & -5 & -6 & | & 13 \\ 0 & 0 & 0 & -4 & | & 10 \end{bmatrix}$$

$$\xrightarrow{(1/5)R_3} \begin{bmatrix} 1 & -\frac{1}{2} & \frac{3}{2} & 1 & | & 1 \\ 0 & 1 & -1 & 0 & | & -2 \\ 0 & 0 & 1 & \frac{6}{5} & | & -\frac{13}{5} \\ 0 & 0 & 0 & -4 & | & 10 \end{bmatrix} \xrightarrow{(-1/4)R_4} \begin{bmatrix} 1 & -\frac{1}{2} & \frac{3}{2} & 1 & | & 1 \\ 0 & 1 & -1 & 0 & | & -2 \\ 0 & 0 & 1 & \frac{6}{5} & | & -\frac{13}{5} \\ 0 & 0 & 0 & 1 & | & -\frac{5}{2} \end{bmatrix}$$

$$\begin{cases} t - \frac{1}{2}u + \frac{3}{2}v + w = 1 \\ u - v = -2 \\ v + \frac{6}{5}w = -\frac{13}{5} \\ w = -\frac{5}{2} \end{cases}$$

$$v + \frac{6}{5}\left(-\frac{5}{2}\right) = -\frac{13}{5} \qquad u - \frac{2}{5} = -2 \qquad t - \frac{1}{2}\left(-\frac{8}{5}\right) + \frac{3}{2}\left(\frac{2}{5}\right) - \frac{5}{2} = 1$$

$$v = \frac{2}{5} \qquad\qquad u = -\frac{8}{5} \qquad\qquad t = \frac{21}{10}$$

The solution is $\left(\dfrac{21}{10},\ -\dfrac{8}{5},\ \dfrac{2}{5},\ -\dfrac{5}{2}\right)$.

33.

$$\begin{bmatrix} 3 & 10 & 7 & -6 & | & 7 \\ 2 & 8 & 6 & -5 & | & 5 \\ 1 & 4 & 2 & -3 & | & 2 \\ 4 & 14 & 9 & -8 & | & 8 \end{bmatrix} \xrightarrow{R_1 \longleftrightarrow R_3} \begin{bmatrix} 1 & 4 & 2 & -3 & | & 2 \\ 2 & 8 & 6 & -5 & | & 5 \\ 3 & 10 & 7 & -6 & | & 7 \\ 4 & 14 & 9 & -8 & | & 8 \end{bmatrix} \xrightarrow[\substack{-3R_1+R_3 \\ -4R_1+R_4}]{-2R_1+R_2} \begin{bmatrix} 1 & 4 & 2 & -3 & | & 2 \\ 0 & 0 & 2 & 1 & | & 1 \\ 0 & -2 & 1 & 3 & | & 1 \\ 0 & -2 & 1 & 4 & | & 0 \end{bmatrix} \xrightarrow{R_2 \longleftrightarrow R_3} \begin{bmatrix} 1 & 4 & 2 & -3 & | & 2 \\ 0 & -2 & 1 & 3 & | & 1 \\ 0 & 0 & 2 & 1 & | & 1 \\ 0 & -2 & 1 & 4 & | & 0 \end{bmatrix}$$

$$\xrightarrow{(-1/2)R_2} \begin{bmatrix} 1 & 4 & 2 & -3 & | & 2 \\ 0 & 1 & -\frac{1}{2} & -\frac{3}{2} & | & -\frac{1}{2} \\ 0 & 0 & 2 & 1 & | & 1 \\ 0 & -2 & 1 & 4 & | & 0 \end{bmatrix} \xrightarrow{2R_2+R_4} \begin{bmatrix} 1 & 4 & 2 & -3 & | & 2 \\ 0 & 1 & -\frac{1}{2} & -\frac{3}{2} & | & -\frac{1}{2} \\ 0 & 0 & 2 & 1 & | & 1 \\ 0 & 0 & 0 & 1 & | & -1 \end{bmatrix}$$

$$\begin{cases} t + 4u + 2v - 3w = 2 \\ u - \frac{1}{2}v - \frac{3}{2}w = -\frac{1}{2} \\ 2v + w = 1 \\ w = -1 \end{cases}$$

$$2v + (-1) = 1 \qquad u - \frac{1}{2}(1) - \frac{3}{2}(-1) = -\frac{1}{2} \qquad t + 4\left(-\frac{3}{2}\right) + 2(1) - 3(-1) = 2$$

$$v = 1 \qquad\qquad u = -\frac{3}{2} \qquad\qquad t = 3$$

The solution is $\left(3, -\dfrac{3}{2}, 1, -1\right)$.

35.

$$\begin{bmatrix} 1 & -1 & 2 & -3 & | & 9 \\ 4 & 0 & 11 & -10 & | & 46 \\ 3 & -1 & 8 & -6 & | & 27 \end{bmatrix} \xrightarrow[\substack{-3R_1+R_3}]{-4R_1+R_2} \begin{bmatrix} 1 & -1 & 2 & -3 & | & 9 \\ 0 & 4 & 3 & 2 & | & 10 \\ 0 & 2 & 2 & 3 & | & 0 \end{bmatrix} \xrightarrow{R_2 \longleftrightarrow R_3} \begin{bmatrix} 1 & -1 & 2 & -3 & | & 9 \\ 0 & 2 & 2 & 3 & | & 0 \\ 0 & 4 & 3 & 2 & | & 10 \end{bmatrix}$$

$$\xrightarrow{-2R_2+R_3} \begin{bmatrix} 1 & -1 & 2 & -3 & | & 9 \\ 0 & 2 & 2 & 3 & | & 0 \\ 0 & 0 & -1 & -4 & | & 10 \end{bmatrix}$$

$$\begin{cases} t - u + 2v - 3w = 9 \\ 2u + 2v + 3w = 0 \\ -v - 4w = 10 \end{cases} \qquad v = -4w - 10$$

$$2u + 2(-4w - 10) + 3w = 0$$

$$u = \frac{5}{2}w + 10$$

$$t - \left(\frac{5}{2}w + 10\right) + 2(-4w - 10) - 3w = 9$$

$$t = \frac{27}{2}w + 39$$

Let w be any real number c. The solution is $\left(\dfrac{27}{2}c + 39, \dfrac{5}{2}c + 10. - 4c - 10, c\right)$.

37.

$$\begin{bmatrix} 3 & -4 & 1 & 0 & | & 2 \\ 1 & 1 & -2 & 3 & | & 1 \end{bmatrix} \xrightarrow{(1/3)R_1} \begin{bmatrix} 1 & -\frac{4}{3} & \frac{1}{3} & 0 & | & \frac{2}{3} \\ 1 & 1 & -2 & 3 & | & 1 \end{bmatrix} \xrightarrow{-R_1 + R_2} \begin{bmatrix} 1 & -\frac{4}{3} & \frac{1}{3} & 0 & | & \frac{2}{3} \\ 1 & \frac{7}{3} & -\frac{7}{3} & 3 & | & \frac{1}{3} \end{bmatrix} \xrightarrow{(3/7)R_2} \begin{bmatrix} 1 & -\frac{4}{3} & \frac{1}{3} & 0 & | & \frac{2}{3} \\ 0 & 1 & -1 & \frac{9}{7} & | & \frac{1}{7} \end{bmatrix}$$

$$\begin{cases} t - \frac{4}{3}u + \frac{1}{3}v = \frac{2}{3} \\ u - v + \frac{9}{7} = \frac{1}{7} \end{cases} \qquad u = v - \frac{9}{7}w + \frac{1}{7} \qquad t - \frac{4}{3}\left(v - \frac{9}{7}w + \frac{1}{7}\right) + \frac{1}{3}v = \frac{2}{3}$$

$$t = v - \frac{12}{7}w + \frac{6}{7}$$

Let v be any real number c_1 and w be any real number c_2. The solution is $\left(c_1 - \frac{12}{7}c_2 + \frac{6}{7}, c_1 - \frac{9}{7}c_2 + \frac{1}{7}, c_1, c_2\right)$

39. Because there are two points, the degree of the interpolating polynomial is at most 1. The form of the polynomial is $p(x) = a_1 x + a_0$
Use this polynomial and the given points to find the system of equations.

$$p(-2) = a_1(-2) + a_0 = -7$$
$$p(1) = a_1(1) + a_0 = -1$$

The system of equations and the associated augmented matrix are $\begin{cases} -2a_1 + a_0 = -7 \\ a_1 + a_0 = -1 \end{cases}$ $\begin{bmatrix} -2 & 1 & | & -7 \\ 1 & 1 & | & -1 \end{bmatrix}$

The ref (row echelon form) feature of a graphing calculator can be used to rewrite the augmented matrix in echelon form. Consider using the function of your calculator that converts a decimal to a fraction.

The augmented matrix in echelon form and resulting system of equations are $\begin{bmatrix} 1 & -1/2 & | & 7/2 \\ 0 & 1 & | & -3 \end{bmatrix}$ $\begin{cases} a_1 - \frac{1}{2}a_0 = \frac{7}{2} \\ a_0 = -3 \end{cases}$

Solving by back substitution yields $a_0 = -3$ and $a_1 = 2$.
The interpolating polynomial is $p(x) = 2x - 3$.

41. Because there are three points, the degree of the interpolating polynomial is at most 2.
The form of the polynomial is $p(x) = a_2 x^2 + a_1 x + a_0$.
Use this polynomial and the given points to find the system of equations.

$$p(-1) = a_2(-1)^2 + a_1(-1) + a_0 = 6$$
$$p(1) = a_2(1)^2 + a_1(1) + a_0 = 2$$
$$p(2) = a_2(2)^2 + a_1(2) + a_0 = 3$$

The system of equations and the associated augmented matrix are $\begin{cases} a_2 - a_1 + a_0 = 6 \\ a_2 + a_1 + a_0 = 2 \\ 4a_2 + 2a_1 + a_0 = 3 \end{cases}$ $\begin{bmatrix} 1 & -1 & 1 & | & 6 \\ 1 & 1 & 1 & | & 2 \\ 4 & 2 & 1 & | & 3 \end{bmatrix}$

The ref (row echelon form) feature of a graphing calculator can be used to rewrite the augmented matrix in echelon form. Consider using the function of your calculator that converts a decimal to a fraction.

The augmented matrix in echelon form and resulting system of equations are $\begin{bmatrix} 1 & 1/2 & 1/4 & | & 3/4 \\ 0 & 1 & -1/2 & | & -7/2 \\ 0 & 0 & 1 & | & 3 \end{bmatrix}$ $\begin{cases} a_2 + \frac{1}{2}a_1 + \frac{1}{4}a_0 = \frac{3}{4} \\ a_1 - \frac{1}{2}a_0 = -\frac{7}{2} \\ a_0 = 3 \end{cases}$

Solving by back substitution yields $a_0 = 3$, $a_1 = -2$, and $a_2 = 1$.

The interpolating polynomial is $p(x) = x^2 - 2x + 3$.

43. Because there are four points, the degree of the interpolating polynomial is at most 3.

The form of the polynomial is $p(x) = a_3 x^3 + a_2 x^2 + a_1 x + a_0$.

Use this polynomial and the given points to find the system of equations.

$$p(-2) = a_3(-2)^3 + a_2(-2)^2 + a_1(-2) + a_0 = -12$$

$$p(0) = a_3(0)^3 + a_2(0)^2 + a_1(0) + a_0 = 2$$

$$p(1) = a_3(1)^3 + a_2(1)^2 + a_1(1) + a_0 = 0$$

$$p(3) = a_3(3)^3 + a_2(3)^2 + a_1(3) + a_0 = 8$$

The system of equations and the associated augmented matrix are
$$\begin{cases} -8a_3 + 4a_2 - 2a_1 + a_0 = -12 \\ a_0 = 2 \\ a_3 + a_2 + a_1 + a_0 = 0 \\ 27a_3 + 9a_2 + 3a_1 + a_0 = 8 \end{cases} \qquad \begin{bmatrix} -8 & 4 & -2 & 1 & | & -12 \\ 0 & 0 & 0 & 1 & | & 2 \\ 1 & 1 & 1 & 1 & | & 0 \\ 27 & 9 & 3 & 1 & | & 8 \end{bmatrix}$$

The ref (row echelon form) feature of a graphing calculator can be used to rewrite the augmented matrix in echelon form. Consider using the function of your calculator that converts a decimal to a fraction.

The augmented matrix in echelon form and resulting system of equations are

$$\begin{bmatrix} 1 & 1/3 & 1/9 & 1/27 & | & 8/27 \\ 0 & 1 & -1/6 & 7/36 & | & -13/9 \\ 0 & 0 & 1 & 5/6 & | & 2/3 \\ 0 & 0 & 0 & 1 & | & 2 \end{bmatrix} \qquad \begin{cases} a_3 + \dfrac{1}{3}a_2 + \dfrac{1}{9}a_1 + \dfrac{1}{27}a_0 = \dfrac{8}{27} \\ a_2 - \dfrac{1}{6}a_1 + \dfrac{7}{36}a_0 = -\dfrac{13}{9} \\ a_1 + \dfrac{5}{6}a_0 = \dfrac{2}{3} \\ a_0 = 2 \end{cases}$$

Solving by back substitution yields $a_0 = 2$, $a_1 = -1$, $a_2 = -2$ and $a_3 = 1$.

The interpolating polynomial is $p(x) = x^3 - 2x^2 - x + 2$.

45. Because there are three points, the degree of the interpolating polynomial is at most 2.

The form of the polynomial is $p(x) = a_2 x^2 + a_1 x + a_0$.

Use this polynomial and the given points to find the system of equations.

$$p(-1) = a_2(-1)^2 + a_1(-1) + a_0 = 3$$

$$p(1) = a_2(1)^2 + a_1(1) + a_0 = 7$$

$$p(2) = a_2(2)^2 + a_1(2) + a_0 = 9$$

The system of equations and the associated augmented matrix are
$$\begin{cases} a_2 - a_1 + a_0 = 3 \\ a_2 + a_1 + a_0 = 7 \\ 4a_2 + 2a_1 + a_0 = 9 \end{cases} \qquad \begin{bmatrix} 1 & -1 & 1 & | & 3 \\ 1 & 1 & 1 & | & 7 \\ 4 & 2 & 1 & | & 9 \end{bmatrix}$$

The ref (row echelon form) feature of a graphing calculator can be used to rewrite the augmented matrix in echelon form. Consider using the function of your calculator that converts a decimal to a fraction.

The augmented matrix in echelon form and resulting system of equations are
$$\begin{bmatrix} 1 & 1/2 & 1/4 & | & 9/4 \\ 0 & 1 & -1/2 & | & -1/2 \\ 0 & 0 & 1 & | & 5 \end{bmatrix} \qquad \begin{cases} a_2 + \dfrac{1}{2}a_1 + \dfrac{1}{4}a_0 = \dfrac{9}{4} \\ a_1 - \dfrac{1}{2}a_0 = -\dfrac{1}{2} \\ a_0 = 5 \end{cases}$$

Solving by back substitution yields $a_0 = 5$, $a_1 = 2$, and $a_2 = 0$.

The interpolating polynomial is $p(x) = 2x + 5$.

47. The form of the polynomial is: $z = ax + by + c$.

Use this polynomial and the given points to find the system of equations.

$$-4 = a(-1) + b(0) + c$$
$$5 = a(2) + b(1) + c$$
$$-1 = a(-1) + b(1) + c$$

The system of equations and the associated augmented matrix are
$\begin{cases} -a \quad +c = -4 \\ 2a + b + c = 5 \\ -a + b + c = -1 \end{cases}$
$\begin{bmatrix} -1 & 0 & 1 & | & -4 \\ 2 & 1 & 1 & | & 5 \\ -1 & 1 & 1 & | & -1 \end{bmatrix}$

The **ref** (row echelon form) feature of a graphing calculator can be used to rewrite the augmented matrix in echelon form. Consider using the function of your calculator that converts a decimal to a fraction.

The augmented matrix in echelon form and resulting system of equations are
$\begin{bmatrix} 1 & 1/2 & 1/2 & | & 5/2 \\ 0 & 1 & 1 & | & 1 \\ 0 & 0 & 1 & | & -2 \end{bmatrix}$
$\begin{cases} a + \frac{1}{2}b + \frac{1}{2}c = \frac{5}{2} \\ b + c = 1 \\ c = -2 \end{cases}$

Solving by back substitution yields $a = 2$, $b = 3$, and $c = -2$.

The interpolating polynomial is $z = 2x + 3y - 2$.

49. The form of the polynomial is: $x^2 + y^2 + ax + by = c$

Use this polynomial and the given points to find the system of equations.

$$(2)^2 + (6)^2 + a(2) + b(6) = c$$
$$(-4)^2 + (-2)^2 + a(-4) + b(-2) = c$$
$$(3)^2 + (-1)^2 + a(3) + b(-1) = c$$

The system of equations and the associated augmented matrix are
$\begin{cases} 2a + 6b - c = -40 \\ -4a - 2b - c = -20 \\ 3a - b - c = -10 \end{cases}$
$\begin{bmatrix} 2 & 6 & -1 & | & -40 \\ -4 & -2 & -1 & | & -20 \\ 3 & -1 & -1 & | & -10 \end{bmatrix}$

The **ref** (row echelon form) feature of a graphing calculator can be used to rewrite the augmented matrix in echelon form. Consider using the function of your calculator that converts a decimal to a fraction.

The augmented matrix in echelon form and resulting system of equations are
$\begin{bmatrix} 1 & 1/2 & 1/4 & | & 5 \\ 0 & 1 & -3/10 & | & -10 \\ 0 & 0 & 1 & | & 20 \end{bmatrix}$
$\begin{cases} a - \frac{1}{2}b + \frac{1}{4}c = 5 \\ b - \frac{3}{10}c = -10 \\ c = 20 \end{cases}$

Solving by back substitution yields $a = 2$, $b = -4$, and $c = 20$.

The interpolating polynomial is $x^2 + y^2 + 2x - 4y = 20$.

51. Using a calculator,

$\begin{bmatrix} 1 & 2 & -1 & 2 & 3 & | & 11 \\ 1 & -1 & 2 & -1 & 2 & | & 0 \\ 2 & 1 & -1 & 2 & -1 & | & 4 \\ 3 & 2 & -1 & 1 & -2 & | & 2 \\ 2 & 1 & -1 & -2 & 1 & | & 4 \end{bmatrix} \longrightarrow \begin{bmatrix} 1 & 2 & -1 & 2 & 3 & | & 11 \\ 0 & 1 & -1 & 1 & \frac{1}{3} & | & \frac{11}{3} \\ 0 & 0 & 1 & -\frac{1}{2} & 3 & | & \frac{7}{2} \\ 0 & 0 & 0 & 1 & \frac{11}{6} & | & \frac{14}{3} \\ 0 & 0 & 0 & 0 & 1 & | & 2 \end{bmatrix}$

$\begin{cases} x_1 + 2x_2 - x_3 + 2x_4 + 3x_5 = 11 \\ x_2 - x_3 + x_4 + \frac{1}{3}x_5 = \frac{11}{3} \\ x_3 - \frac{1}{2}x_4 + 3x_5 = \frac{7}{2} \\ x_4 + \frac{11}{6}x_5 = \frac{14}{3} \\ x_5 = 2 \end{cases}$

The solution is $(1, 0, -2, 1, 2)$.

53. Using a calculator,

$$\begin{bmatrix} 1 & 2 & -3 & -1 & 2 & | & -10 \\ -1 & -3 & 1 & 1 & -1 & | & 4 \\ 2 & 3 & -5 & 2 & 3 & | & -20 \\ 3 & 4 & -7 & 3 & -2 & | & -16 \\ 2 & 1 & -6 & 4 & -3 & | & -12 \end{bmatrix} \longrightarrow \begin{bmatrix} 1 & 2 & -3 & -1 & 2 & | & -10 \\ 0 & 1 & 2 & 0 & -1 & | & 6 \\ 0 & 0 & 1 & \frac{4}{3} & -\frac{2}{3} & | & 2 \\ 0 & 0 & 0 & 1 & 3 & | & -7 \\ 0 & 0 & 0 & 0 & 0 & | & 0 \end{bmatrix}$$

$$\begin{cases} x_1 + 2x_2 - 3x_3 - x_4 + 2x_5 = -10 \\ x_2 + 2x_3 - x_5 = 6 \\ x_3 + \frac{4}{3}x_4 - \frac{2}{3}x_5 = 2 \\ x_4 + 3x_5 = -7 \end{cases}$$

$$x_4 = -3x_5 - 7$$

$$x_3 + \frac{4}{3}(-3x_5 - 7) - \frac{2}{3}x_5 = 2$$

$$x_3 = \frac{14}{3}x_5 + \frac{34}{3}$$

$$x_2 + 2\left(\frac{14}{3}x_5 + \frac{34}{3}\right) - x_5 = 6$$

$$x_2 = -\frac{25}{3}x_5 - \frac{50}{3}$$

$$x_1 + 2\left(-\frac{25}{3}x_5 - \frac{50}{3}\right) - 3\left(\frac{14}{3}x_5 + \frac{34}{3}\right) - (-3x_5 - 7) + 2x_5 = -10$$

$$x_1 = \frac{77}{3}x_5 + \frac{151}{3}$$

Let x_5 be any real number c. The solution is $\left(\frac{77}{3}c + \frac{151}{3}, \ -\frac{25}{3}c - \frac{50}{3}, \ \frac{14}{3}c + \frac{34}{3}, \ -3c - 7, \ c\right)$.

••• **Connecting Concepts**

55.

$$\begin{bmatrix} 1 & 3 & -a^2 & | & a^2 \\ 3 & 4 & 2 & | & 3 \\ 2 & 3 & a & | & 2 \end{bmatrix} \xrightarrow[\ -2R_1 + R_3\ ]{-3R_1 + R_2} \begin{bmatrix} 1 & 3 & -a^2 & | & a^2 \\ 0 & -5 & 3a^2 + 2 & | & -3a^2 + 3 \\ 0 & -3 & 2a^2 + a & | & -2a^2 + 2 \end{bmatrix} \xrightarrow[\ 5R_3\ ]{-3R_2} \begin{bmatrix} 1 & 3 & -a^2 & | & a^2 \\ 0 & 15 & -9a^2 - 6 & | & 9a^2 - 9 \\ 0 & -15 & 10a^2 + 5a & | & -10a^2 + 10 \end{bmatrix}$$

$$\xrightarrow{R_2 + R_3} \begin{bmatrix} 1 & 3 & -a^2 & | & a^2 \\ 0 & 15 & -9a^2 - 6 & | & 9a^2 - 9 \\ 0 & 0 & a^2 + 5a - 6 & | & -a^2 + 1 \end{bmatrix}$$

$$\begin{cases} x + 3y - a^2 z = a^2 \\ 15y - (9a^2 + 6)z = 9a^2 - 9 \\ (a^2 + 5a - 6)z = -a^2 + 1 \end{cases}$$

For the system of equations to have a unique solution, $a^2 + 5a - 6$ cannot be zero. Thus $a^2 + 5a - 6 \neq 0$, or $a \neq 1$ and $a \neq -6$. The system of equations has a unique solution for all values of a except 1 and -6.

57. See the solution to exercise 55. For the system of equations to have no solution, $a^2 + 5a - 6$ must be zero and $-a^2 + 1$ must not equal zero. Thus

$$a^2 + 5a - 6 = 0 \qquad \text{and} \qquad -a^2 + 1 \neq 0$$

$$(a + 6)(a - 1) = 0 \qquad a^2 \neq 1$$

$$a = -6 \ \text{ or } \ a = 1 \qquad a \neq 1 \ \text{ or } \ a \neq -1$$

The system of equations will have no solution when $a = -6$.

59. Substitute the three given points into the equation $z = ax + by + c$.

$$\begin{cases} -4 = -a \quad + c \\ 5 = 2a + b + c \\ -1 = -a + b + c \end{cases}$$

$$\begin{bmatrix} -1 & 0 & 1 & | & -4 \\ 2 & 1 & 1 & | & 5 \\ -1 & 1 & 1 & | & -1 \end{bmatrix} \xrightarrow{-1R_1} \begin{bmatrix} 1 & 0 & -1 & | & 4 \\ 2 & 1 & 1 & | & 5 \\ -1 & 1 & 1 & | & -1 \end{bmatrix} \xrightarrow[R_1 + R_3]{-2R_1 + R_2} \begin{bmatrix} 1 & 0 & -1 & | & 4 \\ 0 & 1 & 3 & | & -3 \\ 0 & 1 & 0 & | & 3 \end{bmatrix} \xrightarrow{-R_2 + R_3} \begin{bmatrix} 1 & 0 & -1 & | & 4 \\ 0 & 1 & 3 & | & -3 \\ 0 & 0 & -3 & | & 6 \end{bmatrix}$$

$$\xrightarrow{(-1/3)R_3} \begin{bmatrix} 1 & 0 & -1 & | & 4 \\ 0 & 1 & 3 & | & -3 \\ 0 & 0 & 1 & | & -2 \end{bmatrix}$$

$$\begin{cases} a - c = 4 \\ b + 3c = -3 \\ c = -2 \end{cases}$$

$b + 3(-2) = -3$

$\quad\quad b = 3$

$a - (-2) = 4$

$\quad\quad a = 2$

The equation of the plane is $z = 2x + 3y - 2$.

•••

Prepare for Section 7.2

60. $-c$

61. 1

62. No

63. $z = 5, b = -1$

64. 3×1

65. $\begin{cases} 3x - 5y = 16 \\ 2x + 7y = -10 \end{cases}$

Section 7.2

1. **a.** $A + B = \begin{bmatrix} 2 & -1 \\ 3 & 3 \end{bmatrix} + \begin{bmatrix} -1 & 3 \\ 2 & 1 \end{bmatrix} = \begin{bmatrix} 1 & 2 \\ 5 & 4 \end{bmatrix}$

 b. $A - B = \begin{bmatrix} 2 & -1 \\ 3 & 3 \end{bmatrix} - \begin{bmatrix} -1 & 3 \\ 2 & 1 \end{bmatrix} = \begin{bmatrix} 3 & -4 \\ 1 & 2 \end{bmatrix}$

 c. $2B = 2\begin{bmatrix} -1 & 3 \\ 2 & 1 \end{bmatrix} = \begin{bmatrix} -2 & 6 \\ 4 & 2 \end{bmatrix}$

 d. $2A - 3B = 2\begin{bmatrix} 2 & -1 \\ 3 & 3 \end{bmatrix} - 3\begin{bmatrix} -1 & 3 \\ 2 & 1 \end{bmatrix} = \begin{bmatrix} 4 & -2 \\ 6 & 6 \end{bmatrix} - \begin{bmatrix} -3 & 9 \\ 6 & 3 \end{bmatrix} = \begin{bmatrix} 7 & -11 \\ 0 & 3 \end{bmatrix}$

3. **a.** $A + B = \begin{bmatrix} 0 & -1 & 3 \\ 1 & 0 & -2 \end{bmatrix} + \begin{bmatrix} -3 & 1 & 2 \\ 2 & 5 & -3 \end{bmatrix} = \begin{bmatrix} -3 & 0 & 5 \\ 3 & 5 & -5 \end{bmatrix}$

 b. $A - B = \begin{bmatrix} 0 & -1 & 3 \\ 1 & 0 & -2 \end{bmatrix} - \begin{bmatrix} -3 & 1 & 2 \\ 2 & 5 & -3 \end{bmatrix} = \begin{bmatrix} 3 & -2 & 1 \\ -1 & -5 & 1 \end{bmatrix}$

 c. $2B = 2\begin{bmatrix} -3 & 1 & 2 \\ 2 & 5 & -3 \end{bmatrix} = \begin{bmatrix} -6 & 2 & 4 \\ 4 & 10 & -6 \end{bmatrix}$

 d. $2A - 3B = 2\begin{bmatrix} 0 & -1 & 3 \\ 1 & 0 & -2 \end{bmatrix} - 3\begin{bmatrix} -3 & 1 & 2 \\ 2 & 5 & -3 \end{bmatrix} = \begin{bmatrix} 0 & -2 & 6 \\ 2 & 0 & -4 \end{bmatrix} - \begin{bmatrix} -9 & 3 & 6 \\ 6 & 15 & -9 \end{bmatrix} = \begin{bmatrix} 9 & -5 & 0 \\ -4 & -15 & 5 \end{bmatrix}$

5. **a.**
$$A+B=\begin{bmatrix}-3 & 4 \\ 2 & -3 \\ -1 & 0\end{bmatrix}+\begin{bmatrix}4 & 1 \\ 1 & -2 \\ 3 & -4\end{bmatrix}=\begin{bmatrix}1 & 5 \\ 3 & -5 \\ 2 & -4\end{bmatrix}$$

b.
$$A-B=\begin{bmatrix}-3 & 4 \\ 2 & -3 \\ -1 & 0\end{bmatrix}-\begin{bmatrix}4 & 1 \\ 1 & -2 \\ 3 & -4\end{bmatrix}=\begin{bmatrix}-7 & 3 \\ 1 & -1 \\ -4 & 4\end{bmatrix}$$

c.
$$2B=2\begin{bmatrix}4 & 1 \\ 1 & -2 \\ 3 & -4\end{bmatrix}=\begin{bmatrix}8 & 2 \\ 2 & -4 \\ 6 & -8\end{bmatrix}$$

d.
$$2A-3B=2\begin{bmatrix}-3 & 4 \\ 2 & -3 \\ -1 & 0\end{bmatrix}-3\begin{bmatrix}4 & 1 \\ 1 & -2 \\ 3 & -4\end{bmatrix}=\begin{bmatrix}-6 & 8 \\ 4 & -6 \\ -2 & 0\end{bmatrix}-\begin{bmatrix}12 & 3 \\ 3 & -6 \\ 9 & -12\end{bmatrix}=\begin{bmatrix}-18 & 5 \\ 1 & 0 \\ -11 & 12\end{bmatrix}$$

7. **a.**
$$A+B=\begin{bmatrix}-2 & 3 & -1 \\ 0 & -1 & 2 \\ -4 & 3 & 3\end{bmatrix}+\begin{bmatrix}1 & -2 & 0 \\ 2 & 3 & -1 \\ 3 & -1 & 2\end{bmatrix}=\begin{bmatrix}-1 & 1 & -1 \\ 2 & 2 & 1 \\ -1 & 2 & 5\end{bmatrix}$$

b.
$$A-B=\begin{bmatrix}-2 & 3 & -1 \\ 0 & -1 & 2 \\ -4 & 3 & 3\end{bmatrix}-\begin{bmatrix}1 & -2 & 0 \\ 2 & 3 & -1 \\ 3 & -1 & 2\end{bmatrix}=\begin{bmatrix}-3 & 5 & -1 \\ -2 & -4 & 3 \\ -7 & 4 & 1\end{bmatrix}$$

c.
$$2B=2\begin{bmatrix}1 & -2 & 0 \\ 2 & 3 & -1 \\ 3 & -1 & 2\end{bmatrix}=\begin{bmatrix}2 & -4 & 0 \\ 4 & 6 & -2 \\ 6 & -2 & 4\end{bmatrix}$$

d.
$$2A-3B=2\begin{bmatrix}-2 & 3 & -1 \\ 0 & -1 & 2 \\ -4 & 3 & 3\end{bmatrix}-3\begin{bmatrix}1 & -2 & 0 \\ 2 & 3 & -1 \\ 3 & -1 & 2\end{bmatrix}=\begin{bmatrix}-4 & 6 & -2 \\ 0 & -2 & 4 \\ -8 & 6 & 6\end{bmatrix}-\begin{bmatrix}3 & -6 & 0 \\ 6 & 9 & -3 \\ 9 & -3 & 6\end{bmatrix}=\begin{bmatrix}-7 & 12 & -2 \\ -6 & -11 & 7 \\ -17 & 9 & 0\end{bmatrix}$$

9.
$$AB=\begin{bmatrix}2 & -3 \\ 1 & 4\end{bmatrix}\begin{bmatrix}-2 & 4 \\ 2 & -3\end{bmatrix}=\begin{bmatrix}(2)(-2)+(-3)(2) & (2)(4)+(-3)(-3) \\ (1)(-2)+(4)(2) & (1)(4)+(4)(-3)\end{bmatrix}=\begin{bmatrix}-10 & 17 \\ 6 & -8\end{bmatrix}$$

$$BA=\begin{bmatrix}-2 & 4 \\ 2 & -3\end{bmatrix}\begin{bmatrix}2 & -3 \\ 1 & 4\end{bmatrix}=\begin{bmatrix}(-2)(2)+(4)(1) & (-2)(-3)+(4)(4) \\ (2)(2)+(-3)(1) & (2)(-3)+(-3)(4)\end{bmatrix}=\begin{bmatrix}0 & 22 \\ 1 & -18\end{bmatrix}$$

11.
$$AB=\begin{bmatrix}3 & -1 \\ 2 & 3\end{bmatrix}\begin{bmatrix}4 & 1 \\ 2 & -3\end{bmatrix}=\begin{bmatrix}(3)(4)+(-1)(2) & (3)(1)+(-1)(-3) \\ (2)(4)+(3)(2) & (2)(1)+(3)(-3)\end{bmatrix}=\begin{bmatrix}10 & 6 \\ 14 & -7\end{bmatrix}$$

$$BA=\begin{bmatrix}4 & 1 \\ 2 & -3\end{bmatrix}\begin{bmatrix}3 & -1 \\ 2 & -3\end{bmatrix}=\begin{bmatrix}(4)(3)+(1)(2) & (4)(-1)+(1)(3) \\ (2)(3)+(-3)(2) & (2)(-1)+(-3)(3)\end{bmatrix}=\begin{bmatrix}14 & -1 \\ 0 & -11\end{bmatrix}$$

13.
$$AB=\begin{bmatrix}2 & -1 \\ 0 & 3 \\ 1 & -2\end{bmatrix}\begin{bmatrix}1 & -2 & 3 \\ 2 & 0 & 1\end{bmatrix}=\begin{bmatrix}(2)(1)+(-1)(2) & (2)(-2)+(-1)(0) & (2)(3)+(-1)(1) \\ (0)(1)+(3)(2) & (0)(-2)+(3)(0) & (0)(3)+(3)(1) \\ (1)(1)+(-2)(2) & (1)(-2)+(-2)(0) & (1)(3)+(-2)(1)\end{bmatrix}=\begin{bmatrix}0 & -4 & 5 \\ 6 & 0 & 3 \\ -3 & -2 & 1\end{bmatrix}$$

$$BA=\begin{bmatrix}1 & -2 & 3 \\ 2 & 0 & 1\end{bmatrix}\begin{bmatrix}2 & -1 \\ 0 & 3 \\ 1 & -2\end{bmatrix}=\begin{bmatrix}(1)(2)+(-2)(0)+(3)(1) & (1)(-1)+(-2)(3)+(-2) \\ (2)(2)+(0)(0)+(1)(1) & (2)(-1)+(0)(3)+(1)(-2)\end{bmatrix}=\begin{bmatrix}5 & -13 \\ 5 & -4\end{bmatrix}$$

15.
$$AB=\begin{bmatrix}2 & -1 & 3 \\ 0 & 2 & -1 \\ 0 & 0 & 2\end{bmatrix}\begin{bmatrix}2 & 0 & 0 \\ 1 & -1 & 0 \\ 2 & -1 & -2\end{bmatrix}=\begin{bmatrix}(2)(2)+(-1)(1)+(3)(2) & (2)(0)+(-1)(-1)+(3)(-1) & (2)(0)+(-1)(0)(3)(-2) \\ (0)(2)+(2)(1)+(-1)(2) & (0)(0)+(2)(-1)+(-1)(-1) & (0)(0)+(2)(0)+(-1)(-2) \\ (0)(2)+(0)(1)+(2)(2) & (0)(0)+(0)(-1)+(2)(-1) & (0)(0)+(0)(0)+(2)(-2)\end{bmatrix}=\begin{bmatrix}9 & -2 & -6 \\ 0 & -1 & 2 \\ 4 & -2 & -4\end{bmatrix}$$

$$BA=\begin{bmatrix}2 & 0 & 0 \\ 1 & -1 & 0 \\ 2 & -1 & -2\end{bmatrix}\begin{bmatrix}2 & -1 & 3 \\ 0 & 2 & -1 \\ 0 & 0 & 2\end{bmatrix}=\begin{bmatrix}(2)(2)+(0)(0)+(0)(0) & (2)(-1)+(0)(2)+(0)(0) & (2)(3)+(0)(-1)+(0)(2) \\ (1)(2)+(-1)(0)+(0)(0) & (1)(-1)+(-1)(2)(-1)+(0)(0) & (1)(3)+(-1)(-1)+(0)(2) \\ (2)(2)+(-1)(0)+(-2)(0) & (2)(-1)+(-1)(2)+(-2)(0) & (2)(3)+(-1)(-1)+(-2)(2)\end{bmatrix}=\begin{bmatrix}4 & -2 & 6 \\ 2 & -3 & 4 \\ 4 & -4 & 3\end{bmatrix}$$

17.
$$AB=\begin{bmatrix}1 & -2 & 3\end{bmatrix}\begin{bmatrix}1 & 0 \\ 2 & -1 \\ 1 & 2\end{bmatrix}=\begin{bmatrix}(1)(1)+(-2)(2)+(3)(1) & (1)(0)+(-2)(-1)+(3)(2)\end{bmatrix}=\begin{bmatrix}0 & 8\end{bmatrix}$$

19. The number of columns of the first matrix is not equal to the number of rows of the second matrix. The product is not possible.

21.
$$AB = \begin{bmatrix} 2 & 3 \\ -4 & -6 \end{bmatrix} \begin{bmatrix} 3 & 6 \\ -2 & -4 \end{bmatrix} = \begin{bmatrix} (2)(3)+(3)(-2) & (2)(6)+(3)(-4) \\ (-4)(3)+(-6)(-2) & (-4)(6)+(-6)(-4) \end{bmatrix} = \begin{bmatrix} 0 & 0 \\ 0 & 0 \end{bmatrix}$$

23. The number of columns of the first matrix is not equal to the number of rows of the second matrix. The product is not possible.

25.
$$3X + A = B$$
$$3X + \begin{bmatrix} -1 & 3 \\ 2 & -1 \\ 3 & 1 \end{bmatrix} = \begin{bmatrix} 0 & -2 \\ 1 & 3 \\ 4 & -3 \end{bmatrix}$$
$$3X = \begin{bmatrix} 0 & -2 \\ 1 & 3 \\ 4 & -3 \end{bmatrix} - \begin{bmatrix} -1 & 3 \\ 2 & -1 \\ 3 & 1 \end{bmatrix}$$
$$3X = \begin{bmatrix} 1 & -5 \\ -1 & 4 \\ 1 & -4 \end{bmatrix}$$
$$X = \begin{bmatrix} \frac{1}{3} & -\frac{5}{3} \\ -\frac{1}{3} & \frac{4}{3} \\ \frac{1}{3} & -\frac{4}{3} \end{bmatrix}$$

27.
$$2X - A = X + B$$
$$2X - \begin{bmatrix} -1 & 3 \\ 2 & -1 \\ 3 & 1 \end{bmatrix} = X + \begin{bmatrix} 0 & -2 \\ 1 & 3 \\ 4 & -3 \end{bmatrix}$$
$$X - \begin{bmatrix} -1 & 3 \\ 2 & -1 \\ 3 & 1 \end{bmatrix} = \begin{bmatrix} 0 & -2 \\ 1 & 3 \\ 4 & -3 \end{bmatrix}$$
$$X = \begin{bmatrix} 0 & -2 \\ 1 & 3 \\ 4 & -3 \end{bmatrix} + \begin{bmatrix} -1 & 3 \\ 2 & -1 \\ 3 & 1 \end{bmatrix}$$
$$X = \begin{bmatrix} -1 & 1 \\ 3 & 2 \\ 7 & -2 \end{bmatrix}$$

29.
$$A^2 = A \cdot A = \begin{bmatrix} 2 & -3 \\ 1 & -1 \end{bmatrix} \begin{bmatrix} 2 & -3 \\ 1 & -1 \end{bmatrix} = \begin{bmatrix} 2(2)+(-3)(1) & 2(-3)+(-3)(-1) \\ 1(2)+(-1)(1) & 1(-3)+(-1)(-1) \end{bmatrix} = \begin{bmatrix} 1 & -3 \\ 1 & -2 \end{bmatrix}$$

31.
$$B^2 = B \cdot B = \begin{bmatrix} 3 & -1 & 0 \\ 2 & -2 & -1 \\ 1 & 0 & 2 \end{bmatrix} \begin{bmatrix} 3 & -1 & 0 \\ 2 & -2 & -1 \\ 1 & 0 & 2 \end{bmatrix} = \begin{bmatrix} 3(3)+(-1)(2)+0(1) & 3(-1)+(-1)(-2)+0(0) & 3(0)+(-1)(-1)+0(2) \\ 2(3)+(-2)(2)+(-1)(1) & 2(-1)+(-2)(-2)+(-1)(0) & 2(0)+(-2)(-1)+(-1)(2) \\ 1(3)+0(2)+2(1) & 1(-1)+0(-2)+2(0) & 1(0)+0(-1)+2(2) \end{bmatrix} = \begin{bmatrix} 7 & -1 & 1 \\ 1 & 2 & 0 \\ 5 & -1 & 4 \end{bmatrix}$$

33.
$$\begin{bmatrix} 3 & -8 \\ 4 & 3 \end{bmatrix} \begin{bmatrix} x \\ y \end{bmatrix} = \begin{bmatrix} 11 \\ 1 \end{bmatrix}$$
$$\begin{cases} 3x - 8y = 11 \\ 4x + 3y = 1 \end{cases}$$

35.
$$\begin{bmatrix} 1 & -3 & -2 \\ 3 & 1 & 0 \\ 2 & -4 & 5 \end{bmatrix} \begin{bmatrix} x \\ y \\ z \end{bmatrix} = \begin{bmatrix} 6 \\ 2 \\ 1 \end{bmatrix}$$
$$\begin{cases} x - 3y - 2z = 6 \\ 3x + y = 2 \\ 2x - 4y + 5z = 1 \end{cases}$$

37.
$$\begin{bmatrix} 2 & -1 & 0 & 2 \\ 4 & 1 & 2 & -3 \\ 6 & 0 & 1 & -2 \\ 5 & 2 & -1 & -4 \end{bmatrix} \begin{bmatrix} x_1 \\ x_2 \\ x_3 \\ x_4 \end{bmatrix} = \begin{bmatrix} 5 \\ 6 \\ 10 \\ 8 \end{bmatrix}$$
$$\begin{cases} 2x_1 - x_2 + 2x_4 = 5 \\ 4x_1 + x_2 + 2x_3 - 3x_4 = 6 \\ 6x_1 + x_3 - 2x_4 = 10 \\ 5x_1 + 2x_2 - x_3 - 4x_4 = 8 \end{cases}$$

39.
   a. 3 × 4. There are three different fish in four different samples.
   b. Fish A was caught in sample number 4.
   c. Fish B. There are more 1's in this row than in any other row.

41.
$$0.98 \begin{bmatrix} 2.0 & 1.4 & 3.0 & 1.4 \\ 0.8 & 1.1 & 2.0 & 0.9 \\ 3.6 & 1.2 & 4.5 & 1.5 \end{bmatrix} = \begin{bmatrix} 0.98(2.0) & 0.98(1.4) & 0.98(3.0) & 0.98(1.4) \\ 0.98(0.8) & 0.98(1.1) & 0.98(2.0) & 0.98(0.9) \\ 0.98(3.6) & 0.98(1.2) & 0.98(4.5) & 0.98(1.5) \end{bmatrix} = \begin{bmatrix} 1.96 & 1.37 & 2.94 & 1.37 \\ 0.78 & 1.08 & 1.96 & 0.88 \\ 3.53 & 1.18 & 4.41 & 1.47 \end{bmatrix}$$

43.
   a.
$$\begin{bmatrix} 44 & 36 \\ 42 & 39 \\ 45 & 36 \end{bmatrix} + \begin{bmatrix} 43 & 38 \\ 43 & 38 \\ 38 & 43 \end{bmatrix} = \begin{bmatrix} 87 & 74 \\ 85 & 77 \\ 83 & 79 \end{bmatrix}$$
   b. The matrix represents the total number of wins and losses for each team.
   c.
$$\begin{bmatrix} 44 & 36 \\ 42 & 39 \\ 45 & 36 \end{bmatrix} - \begin{bmatrix} 43 & 38 \\ 43 & 38 \\ 38 & 43 \end{bmatrix} = \begin{bmatrix} 1 & -2 \\ -1 & 1 \\ 7 & -7 \end{bmatrix}$$
   d. The matrix represents the difference between performance at home and performance away.

45. a.
$$A+T = \begin{bmatrix} -2 & 4 & 2 & -4 \\ 5 & 2 & -2 & 1 \end{bmatrix} + \begin{bmatrix} 2 & 2 & 2 & 2 \\ -1 & -1 & -1 & -1 \end{bmatrix} = \begin{bmatrix} 0 & 6 & 4 & -2 \\ 4 & 1 & -3 & 0 \end{bmatrix}$$

b.

c. A rectangle that has been shifted two units to the right and one unit down.

47. a.
$$R \cdot A = \begin{bmatrix} 0 & -1 \\ 1 & 0 \end{bmatrix} \begin{bmatrix} -2 & 4 & 2 & -4 \\ 5 & 2 & -2 & 1 \end{bmatrix} = \begin{bmatrix} -5 & -2 & 2 & -1 \\ -2 & 4 & 2 & -4 \end{bmatrix}$$

b.

c. The new rectangle is obtained by reflecting the original rectangle first about $y = x$ and then reflecting the result about $x = 0$.

49.
$$A = \begin{bmatrix} 530 & 650 & 815 \\ 190 & 385 & 715 \\ 485 & 600 & 610 \\ 150 & 210 & 305 \end{bmatrix}, \quad B = \begin{bmatrix} 480 & 500 & 675 \\ 175 & 215 & 345 \\ 400 & 350 & 480 \\ 70 & 95 & 280 \end{bmatrix}$$

$$A - B = \begin{bmatrix} 50 & 150 & 140 \\ 15 & 170 & 370 \\ 85 & 250 & 130 \\ 80 & 115 & 25 \end{bmatrix}$$

$A - B$ is number sold of each item during the week.

51.
$$C = \begin{bmatrix} 0.04 & 0.06 & 0.05 \\ 0.04 & 0.04 & 0.04 \\ 0.03 & 0.07 & 0.06 \end{bmatrix}, \quad S = \begin{bmatrix} 500 & 600 \\ 250 & 450 \\ 600 & 750 \end{bmatrix}$$

$$CS = \begin{bmatrix} 0.04 & 0.06 & 0.05 \\ 0.04 & 0.04 & 0.04 \\ 0.03 & 0.07 & 0.06 \end{bmatrix} \begin{bmatrix} 500 & 600 \\ 250 & 450 \\ 600 & 750 \end{bmatrix}$$

$$= \begin{bmatrix} 65 & 88.5 \\ 54 & 72 \\ 68.5 & 94.5 \end{bmatrix}$$

To minimize commissions costs, customer S_1 should use company T_2.

53. a. For 1 year from now, $n = 2$.

$$\begin{bmatrix} 0.55 & 0.45 \end{bmatrix} \begin{bmatrix} 0.989 & 0.011 \\ 0.007 & 0.993 \end{bmatrix}^2 = \begin{bmatrix} 0.5443 & 0.4557 \end{bmatrix}$$

1 year from now 45.6% of the customers will be drinking diet soda.

b. For 3 years from now, $n = 6$.

$$\begin{bmatrix} 0.55 & 0.45 \end{bmatrix} \begin{bmatrix} 0.989 & 0.011 \\ 0.007 & 0.993 \end{bmatrix}^6 = \begin{bmatrix} 0.5334 & 0.4666 \end{bmatrix}$$

3 years from now 46.7% of the customers will be drinking diet soda.

55. a. For 6 months from now, $n = 6$.

$$\begin{bmatrix} 0.88 & 0.12 \end{bmatrix} \begin{bmatrix} 0.992 & 0.008 \\ 0.001 & 0.999 \end{bmatrix}^6 = \begin{bmatrix} 0.8394 & 0.1606 \end{bmatrix}$$

6 months from now 16.1% of the customers will be renting DVD movies.

b. For 18 months from now, $n = 18$.

$$\begin{bmatrix} 0.88 & 0.12 \end{bmatrix} \begin{bmatrix} 0.992 & 0.008 \\ 0.001 & 0.999 \end{bmatrix}^{18} = \begin{bmatrix} 0.76452 & 0.23547 \end{bmatrix}$$

18 months from now 23.5% of the customers will be renting DVD movies.

57. When $n = 11$, $a > 0.5053$.

$$\begin{bmatrix} 0.25 & 0.75 \end{bmatrix} \begin{bmatrix} 0.98 & 0.02 \\ 0.05 & 0.95 \end{bmatrix}^{11} = \begin{bmatrix} 0.5053 & 0.4947 \end{bmatrix}$$

After 11 months, Store A will have 50% of the town's customers.

59. Using A and B as given and a calculator,

$$AB = \begin{bmatrix} 24 & 21 & -12 & 32 & 0 \\ -7 & -8 & 3 & 21 & 20 \\ 32 & 10 & -32 & 1 & 5 \\ 19 & -15 & -17 & 30 & 20 \\ 29 & 9 & -28 & 13 & -6 \end{bmatrix}$$

61. Using A as given and a calculator,

$$A^3 = \begin{bmatrix} 46 & -100 & 36 & 273 & 93 \\ 82 & -93 & 19 & 27 & 97 \\ 73 & -10 & -23 & 109 & 83 \\ 212 & -189 & 52 & 37 & 156 \\ 68 & -22 & 54 & 221 & 58 \end{bmatrix}$$

63. Using A and B as given and a calculator,

$$A^2 + B^2 = \begin{bmatrix} 76 & -8 & -25 & 30 & 6 \\ 14 & 16 & -10 & 14 & 2 \\ 39 & 0 & -45 & 22 & 27 \\ 0 & -4 & 23 & 83 & -16 \\ 56 & -20 & -22 & 7 & 5 \end{bmatrix}$$

Connecting Concepts

65. $3A = 3\begin{bmatrix} 2+3i & 1-2i \\ 1+i & 2-i \end{bmatrix} = \begin{bmatrix} 6+9i & 3-6i \\ 3+3i & 6-3i \end{bmatrix}$

67. $2iB = 2i\begin{bmatrix} 1-i & 2+3i \\ 3+2i & 4-i \end{bmatrix} = \begin{bmatrix} 2+2i & -6+4i \\ -4+6i & 2+8i \end{bmatrix}$

69. $A + B = \begin{bmatrix} 2+3i & 1-2i \\ 1+i & 2-i \end{bmatrix} + \begin{bmatrix} 1-i & 2+3i \\ 3+2i & 4-i \end{bmatrix} = \begin{bmatrix} 3+2i & 3+i \\ 4+3i & 6-2i \end{bmatrix}$

71. $AB = \begin{bmatrix} 2+3i & 1-2i \\ 1+i & 2-i \end{bmatrix}\begin{bmatrix} 1-i & 2+3i \\ 3+2i & 4-i \end{bmatrix} = \begin{bmatrix} (2+3i)(1-i) + (1-2i)(3+2i) & (2+3i)(2+3i) + (1-2i)(4-i) \\ (1+i)(1-i) + (2-i)(3+2i) & (1+i)(2+3i) + (2-i)(4-i) \end{bmatrix} = \begin{bmatrix} 12-3i & -3+3i \\ 10+i & 6-i \end{bmatrix}$

73. $A^2 = A \cdot A = \begin{bmatrix} 2+3i & 1-2i \\ 1+i & 2-i \end{bmatrix}\begin{bmatrix} 2+3i & 1-2i \\ 1+i & 2-i \end{bmatrix}$

$= \begin{bmatrix} (2+3i)(2+3i) + (1-2i)(1+i) & (2+3i)(1-2i) + (1-2i)(2-i) \\ (1+i)(2+3i) + (2-i)(1+i) & (1+i)(1-2i) + (2-i)(2-i) \end{bmatrix}$

$= \begin{bmatrix} -2+11i & 8-6i \\ 2+6i & 6-5i \end{bmatrix}$

75. $(\sigma_1)^2 = \sigma_1 \cdot \sigma_1 = \begin{bmatrix} 0 & 1 \\ 1 & 0 \end{bmatrix}\begin{bmatrix} 0 & 1 \\ 1 & 0 \end{bmatrix} = \begin{bmatrix} 0(0)+1(1) & 0(1)+1(0) \\ 1(0)+0(1) & 1(1)+0(0)) \end{bmatrix} = \begin{bmatrix} 1 & 0 \\ 0 & 1 \end{bmatrix} = I_2$

$(\sigma_2)^2 = \sigma_2 \cdot \sigma_2 = \begin{bmatrix} 0 & -i \\ i & 0 \end{bmatrix}\begin{bmatrix} 0 & -i \\ i & 0 \end{bmatrix} = \begin{bmatrix} 0(0)+(-i)(i) & 0(-i)+(-i)(0) \\ i(0)+0(i) & i(-i)+0(0) \end{bmatrix} = \begin{bmatrix} 1 & 0 \\ 0 & 1 \end{bmatrix} = I_2$

$(\sigma_3)^2 = \sigma_3 \cdot \sigma_3 = \begin{bmatrix} 1 & 0 \\ 0 & -1 \end{bmatrix}\begin{bmatrix} 1 & 0 \\ 0 & -1 \end{bmatrix} = \begin{bmatrix} 1(1)+0(0) & 1(0)+0(-1) \\ 0(1)+(-1)(0) & 0(0)+(-1)(-1) \end{bmatrix} = \begin{bmatrix} 1 & 0 \\ 0 & 1 \end{bmatrix} = I_2$

77. $\sigma_1 \cdot \sigma_2 + \sigma_2 \cdot \sigma_1 = \begin{bmatrix} 0 & 1 \\ 1 & 0 \end{bmatrix}\begin{bmatrix} 0 & -i \\ i & 0 \end{bmatrix} + \begin{bmatrix} 0 & -i \\ i & 0 \end{bmatrix}\begin{bmatrix} 0 & 1 \\ 1 & 0 \end{bmatrix} = \begin{bmatrix} 0(0)+1(-i) & 0(-i)+1(0) \\ 1(0)+0(i) & 1(-i)+0(0) \end{bmatrix} + \begin{bmatrix} 0(0)+(-i)(1) & 0(1)+(-i)(0) \\ i(0)+0(1) & i(1)+0(0) \end{bmatrix}$

$= \begin{bmatrix} i & 0 \\ 0 & -i \end{bmatrix} + \begin{bmatrix} -i & 0 \\ 0 & i \end{bmatrix} = \begin{bmatrix} 0 & 0 \\ 0 & 0 \end{bmatrix} = O$

79. $a(bA) = a\left(b\begin{bmatrix} a_{11} & a_{12} \\ a_{21} & a_{22} \end{bmatrix}\right) = a\begin{bmatrix} b \cdot a_{11} & b \cdot a_{12} \\ b \cdot a_{21} & b \cdot a_{22} \end{bmatrix} = \begin{bmatrix} ab \cdot a_{11} & ab \cdot a_{12} \\ ab \cdot a_{21} & ab \cdot a_{22} \end{bmatrix} = ab\begin{bmatrix} a_{11} & a_{12} \\ a_{21} & a_{22} \end{bmatrix} = (ab)A$

Prepare for Section 7.3

80. $-\dfrac{3}{2}$

81. $\begin{bmatrix} 1 & 0 & 0 \\ 0 & 1 & 0 \\ 0 & 0 & 1 \end{bmatrix}$

82.
1. Interchange any two rows.
2. Multiply all elements in a row by the same nonzero number.
3. Replace a row by the sum of that row and a nonzero multiple of any other row.

83. $\begin{bmatrix} 1 & -2 & 3 \\ 2 & -1 & 4 \\ -3 & 2 & 2 \end{bmatrix} \xrightarrow[\;3R_1+R_3\;]{\;-2R_1+R_2\;} \begin{bmatrix} 1 & -2 & 3 \\ 0 & 3 & -2 \\ 0 & -4 & 11 \end{bmatrix}$

84.
$$AX = B$$
$$A^{-1}AX = A^{-1}B$$
$$X = A^{-1}B$$

85. $\begin{cases} 2x + 3y = 9 \\ 4x - 5y = 7 \end{cases}$

Section 7.3

1. $\begin{bmatrix} 1 & -3 & | & 1 & 0 \\ -2 & 5 & | & 0 & 1 \end{bmatrix} \xrightarrow{2R_1+R_2} \begin{bmatrix} 1 & -3 & | & 1 & 0 \\ 0 & -1 & | & 2 & 1 \end{bmatrix} \xrightarrow{-1R_2} \begin{bmatrix} 1 & -3 & | & 1 & 0 \\ 0 & 1 & | & -2 & -1 \end{bmatrix} \xrightarrow{3R_2+R_1} \begin{bmatrix} 1 & 0 & | & -5 & -3 \\ 0 & 1 & | & -2 & -1 \end{bmatrix}$

The inverse matrix is $\begin{bmatrix} -5 & -3 \\ -2 & -1 \end{bmatrix}$.

3. $\begin{bmatrix} 1 & 4 & | & 1 & 0 \\ 2 & 10 & | & 0 & 1 \end{bmatrix} \xrightarrow{-2R_1+R_2} \begin{bmatrix} 1 & 4 & | & 1 & 0 \\ 0 & 2 & | & -2 & 1 \end{bmatrix} \xrightarrow{(1/2)R_2} \begin{bmatrix} 1 & 4 & | & 1 & 0 \\ 0 & 1 & | & -1 & \frac{1}{2} \end{bmatrix} \xrightarrow{-4R_2+R_1} \begin{bmatrix} 1 & 0 & | & 5 & -2 \\ 0 & 1 & | & -1 & \frac{1}{2} \end{bmatrix}$

The inverse matrix is $\begin{bmatrix} 5 & -2 \\ -1 & \frac{1}{2} \end{bmatrix}$.

5. $\begin{bmatrix} 1 & 2 & -1 & | & 1 & 0 & 0 \\ 2 & 5 & 1 & | & 0 & 1 & 0 \\ 3 & 6 & -2 & | & 0 & 0 & 1 \end{bmatrix} \xrightarrow[-3R_1+R_3]{-2R_1+R_2} \begin{bmatrix} 1 & 2 & -1 & | & 1 & 0 & 0 \\ 0 & 1 & 3 & | & -2 & 1 & 0 \\ 0 & 0 & 1 & | & -3 & 0 & 1 \end{bmatrix}$

$\xrightarrow{-2R_2+R_1} \begin{bmatrix} 1 & 0 & -7 & | & 5 & -2 & 0 \\ 0 & 1 & 3 & | & -2 & 1 & 0 \\ 0 & 0 & 1 & | & -3 & 0 & 1 \end{bmatrix} \xrightarrow[-3R_3+R_2]{7R_3+R_1} \begin{bmatrix} 1 & 0 & 0 & | & -16 & -2 & 7 \\ 0 & 1 & 0 & | & 7 & 1 & -3 \\ 0 & 0 & 1 & | & -3 & 0 & 1 \end{bmatrix}$

The inverse matrix is $\begin{bmatrix} -16 & -2 & 7 \\ 7 & 1 & -3 \\ -3 & 0 & 1 \end{bmatrix}$.

7. $\begin{bmatrix} 1 & 2 & -1 & | & 1 & 0 & 0 \\ 2 & 6 & 1 & | & 0 & 1 & 0 \\ 3 & 6 & -4 & | & 0 & 0 & 1 \end{bmatrix} \xrightarrow[-3R_1+R_3]{-2R_1+R_2} \begin{bmatrix} 1 & 2 & -1 & | & 1 & 0 & 0 \\ 0 & 2 & 3 & | & -2 & 1 & 0 \\ 0 & 0 & -1 & | & -3 & 0 & 1 \end{bmatrix} \xrightarrow{(1/2)R_2} \begin{bmatrix} 1 & 2 & -1 & | & 1 & 0 & 0 \\ 0 & 1 & \frac{3}{2} & | & -1 & \frac{1}{2} & 0 \\ 0 & 0 & -1 & | & -3 & 0 & 1 \end{bmatrix}$

$\xrightarrow{-1R_3} \begin{bmatrix} 1 & 2 & -1 & | & 1 & 0 & 0 \\ 0 & 1 & \frac{3}{2} & | & -1 & \frac{1}{2} & 0 \\ 0 & 0 & 1 & | & 3 & 0 & -1 \end{bmatrix} \xrightarrow{-2R_2+R_1} \begin{bmatrix} 1 & 0 & -4 & | & 3 & -1 & 0 \\ 0 & 1 & \frac{3}{2} & | & -1 & \frac{1}{2} & 0 \\ 0 & 0 & 1 & | & 3 & 0 & -1 \end{bmatrix} \xrightarrow[(-3/2)R_3+R_2]{4R_3+R_1} \begin{bmatrix} 1 & 0 & 0 & | & 15 & -1 & -4 \\ 0 & 1 & 0 & | & -\frac{11}{2} & \frac{1}{2} & \frac{3}{2} \\ 0 & 0 & 1 & | & 3 & 0 & -1 \end{bmatrix}$

The inverse matrix is $\begin{bmatrix} 15 & -1 & -4 \\ -\frac{11}{2} & \frac{1}{2} & \frac{3}{2} \\ 3 & 0 & -1 \end{bmatrix}$.

9. $\begin{bmatrix} 2 & 4 & -4 & | & 1 & 0 & 0 \\ 1 & 3 & -4 & | & 0 & 1 & 0 \\ 2 & 4 & -3 & | & 0 & 0 & 1 \end{bmatrix} \xrightarrow{(1/2)R_1} \begin{bmatrix} 1 & 2 & -2 & | & \frac{1}{2} & 0 & 0 \\ 1 & 3 & -4 & | & 0 & 1 & 0 \\ 2 & 4 & -3 & | & 0 & 0 & 1 \end{bmatrix} \xrightarrow[-2R_1+R_3]{-1R_1+R_2} \begin{bmatrix} 1 & 2 & -2 & | & \frac{1}{2} & 0 & 0 \\ 0 & 1 & -2 & | & -\frac{1}{2} & 1 & 0 \\ 0 & 0 & 1 & | & -1 & 0 & 1 \end{bmatrix}$

$\xrightarrow{-2R_2+R_1} \begin{bmatrix} 1 & 0 & 2 & | & \frac{3}{2} & -2 & 0 \\ 0 & 1 & -2 & | & -\frac{1}{2} & 1 & 0 \\ 0 & 0 & 1 & | & -1 & 0 & 1 \end{bmatrix} \xrightarrow[2R_3+R_2]{-2R_3+R_1} \begin{bmatrix} 1 & 0 & 0 & | & \frac{7}{2} & -2 & -2 \\ 0 & 1 & 0 & | & -\frac{5}{2} & 1 & 2 \\ 0 & 0 & 1 & | & -1 & 0 & 1 \end{bmatrix}$

The inverse matrix is $\begin{bmatrix} \frac{7}{2} & -2 & -2 \\ -\frac{5}{2} & 1 & 2 \\ -1 & 0 & 1 \end{bmatrix}$.

11.

$$\left[\begin{array}{cccc|cccc} 1 & -1 & 2 & 1 & 1 & 0 & 0 & 0 \\ 2 & -1 & 5 & 1 & 0 & 1 & 0 & 0 \\ 3 & -3 & 7 & 5 & 0 & 0 & 1 & 0 \\ -2 & 3 & -4 & -1 & 0 & 0 & 0 & 1 \end{array}\right] \xrightarrow[\substack{2R_1+R_4}]{\substack{2R_1+R_2 \\ -3R_1+R_3}} \left[\begin{array}{cccc|cccc} 1 & -1 & 2 & 1 & 1 & 0 & 0 & 0 \\ 0 & 1 & 1 & -1 & -2 & 1 & 0 & 0 \\ 0 & 0 & 1 & 2 & -3 & 0 & 1 & 0 \\ 0 & 1 & 0 & 1 & 2 & 0 & 0 & 1 \end{array}\right]$$

$$\xrightarrow{-1R_2+R_4} \left[\begin{array}{cccc|cccc} 1 & -1 & 2 & 1 & 1 & 0 & 0 & 0 \\ 0 & 1 & 1 & -1 & -2 & 1 & 0 & 0 \\ 0 & 0 & 1 & 2 & -3 & 0 & 1 & 0 \\ 0 & 0 & -1 & 2 & 4 & -1 & 0 & 1 \end{array}\right] \xrightarrow{1R_3+R_4} \left[\begin{array}{cccc|cccc} 1 & -1 & 2 & 1 & 1 & 0 & 0 & 0 \\ 0 & 1 & 1 & -1 & -2 & 1 & 0 & 0 \\ 0 & 0 & 1 & 2 & -3 & 0 & 1 & 0 \\ 0 & 0 & 0 & 4 & 1 & -1 & 1 & 1 \end{array}\right]$$

$$\xrightarrow{(1/4)R_4} \left[\begin{array}{cccc|cccc} 1 & -1 & 2 & 1 & 1 & 0 & 0 & 0 \\ 0 & 1 & 1 & -1 & -2 & 1 & 0 & 0 \\ 0 & 0 & 1 & 2 & -3 & 0 & 1 & 0 \\ 0 & 0 & 0 & 1 & \frac{1}{4} & -\frac{1}{4} & \frac{1}{4} & \frac{1}{4} \end{array}\right] \xrightarrow{R_2+R_1} \left[\begin{array}{cccc|cccc} 1 & 0 & 3 & 0 & -1 & 1 & 0 & 0 \\ 0 & 1 & 1 & -1 & -2 & 1 & 0 & 0 \\ 0 & 0 & 1 & 2 & -3 & 0 & 1 & 0 \\ 0 & 0 & 0 & 1 & \frac{1}{4} & -\frac{1}{4} & \frac{1}{4} & \frac{1}{4} \end{array}\right]$$

$$\xrightarrow[\substack{-R_3+R_2}]{\substack{-3R_3+R_1}} \left[\begin{array}{cccc|cccc} 1 & 0 & 0 & -6 & 8 & 1 & -3 & 0 \\ 0 & 1 & 0 & -3 & 1 & 1 & -1 & 0 \\ 0 & 0 & 1 & 2 & -3 & 0 & 1 & 0 \\ 0 & 0 & 0 & 1 & \frac{1}{4} & -\frac{1}{4} & \frac{1}{4} & \frac{1}{4} \end{array}\right] \xrightarrow[\substack{-2R_4+R_3}]{\substack{6R_4+R_1 \\ 3R_4+R_2}} \left[\begin{array}{cccc|cccc} 1 & 0 & 0 & 0 & \frac{19}{2} & -\frac{1}{2} & -\frac{3}{2} & \frac{3}{2} \\ 0 & 1 & 0 & 0 & \frac{7}{4} & \frac{1}{4} & -\frac{1}{4} & \frac{1}{4} \\ 0 & 0 & 1 & 0 & -\frac{7}{2} & \frac{1}{2} & \frac{1}{2} & -\frac{1}{2} \\ 0 & 0 & 0 & 1 & \frac{1}{4} & -\frac{1}{4} & \frac{1}{4} & \frac{1}{4} \end{array}\right]$$

The inverse matrix is $\left[\begin{array}{cccc} \frac{19}{2} & -\frac{1}{2} & -\frac{3}{2} & \frac{3}{2} \\ \frac{7}{4} & \frac{1}{4} & -\frac{1}{4} & \frac{3}{4} \\ -\frac{7}{2} & \frac{1}{2} & \frac{1}{2} & -\frac{1}{2} \\ \frac{1}{4} & -\frac{1}{4} & \frac{1}{4} & \frac{1}{4} \end{array}\right].$

13.

$$\left[\begin{array}{cccc|cccc} 1 & -1 & 1 & 3 & 1 & 0 & 0 & 0 \\ 2 & -1 & 4 & 8 & 0 & 1 & 0 & 0 \\ 1 & 1 & 6 & 10 & 0 & 0 & 1 & 0 \\ -1 & 5 & 5 & 4 & 0 & 0 & 0 & 1 \end{array}\right] \xrightarrow[\substack{1R_1+R_4}]{\substack{-2R_1+R_2 \\ -1R_1+R_3}} \left[\begin{array}{cccc|cccc} 1 & -1 & 1 & 3 & 1 & 0 & 0 & 0 \\ 0 & 1 & 2 & 2 & -2 & 1 & 0 & 0 \\ 0 & 2 & 5 & 7 & -1 & 0 & 1 & 0 \\ 0 & 4 & 6 & 7 & 1 & 0 & 0 & 1 \end{array}\right]$$

$$\xrightarrow[\substack{-4R_2+R_4}]{\substack{-2R_2+R_3}} \left[\begin{array}{cccc|cccc} 1 & -1 & 1 & 3 & 1 & 0 & 0 & 0 \\ 0 & 1 & 2 & 2 & -2 & 1 & 0 & 0 \\ 0 & 0 & 1 & 3 & 3 & -2 & 1 & 0 \\ 0 & 0 & -2 & -1 & 9 & -4 & 0 & 1 \end{array}\right] \xrightarrow{2R_3+R_4} \left[\begin{array}{cccc|cccc} 1 & -1 & 1 & 3 & 1 & 0 & 0 & 0 \\ 0 & 1 & 2 & 2 & -2 & 1 & 0 & 0 \\ 0 & 0 & 1 & 3 & 3 & -2 & 1 & 0 \\ 0 & 0 & 0 & 5 & 15 & -8 & 2 & 1 \end{array}\right]$$

$$\xrightarrow{(1/5)R_4} \left[\begin{array}{cccc|cccc} 1 & -1 & 1 & 3 & 1 & 0 & 0 & 0 \\ 0 & 1 & 2 & 2 & -2 & 1 & 0 & 0 \\ 0 & 0 & 1 & 3 & 3 & -2 & 1 & 0 \\ 0 & 0 & 0 & 1 & 3 & -\frac{8}{5} & \frac{2}{5} & \frac{1}{5} \end{array}\right] \xrightarrow{R_2+R_1} \left[\begin{array}{cccc|cccc} 1 & 0 & 3 & 5 & -1 & 1 & 0 & 0 \\ 0 & 1 & 2 & 2 & -2 & 1 & 0 & 0 \\ 0 & 0 & 1 & 3 & 3 & -2 & 1 & 0 \\ 0 & 0 & 0 & 1 & 3 & -\frac{8}{5} & \frac{2}{5} & \frac{1}{5} \end{array}\right]$$

$$\xrightarrow[\substack{-2R_3+R_2}]{\substack{-3R_3+R_1}} \left[\begin{array}{cccc|cccc} 1 & 0 & 0 & -4 & -10 & 7 & -3 & 0 \\ 0 & 1 & 0 & -4 & -8 & 5 & -2 & 0 \\ 0 & 0 & 1 & 3 & 3 & -2 & 1 & 0 \\ 0 & 0 & 0 & 1 & 3 & -\frac{8}{5} & \frac{2}{5} & \frac{1}{5} \end{array}\right] \xrightarrow[\substack{-3R_4+R_3}]{\substack{4R_4+R_1 \\ 4R_4+R_2}} \left[\begin{array}{cccc|cccc} 1 & 0 & 0 & 0 & 2 & \frac{3}{5} & -\frac{7}{5} & \frac{4}{5} \\ 0 & 1 & 0 & 0 & 4 & -\frac{7}{5} & -\frac{2}{5} & \frac{4}{5} \\ 0 & 0 & 1 & 0 & -6 & \frac{14}{5} & -\frac{1}{5} & -\frac{3}{5} \\ 0 & 0 & 0 & 1 & 3 & -\frac{8}{5} & \frac{2}{5} & \frac{1}{5} \end{array}\right]$$

The inverse matrix is $\left[\begin{array}{cccc} 2 & \frac{3}{5} & -\frac{7}{5} & \frac{4}{5} \\ 4 & -\frac{7}{5} & -\frac{2}{5} & \frac{4}{5} \\ -6 & \frac{14}{5} & -\frac{1}{5} & -\frac{3}{5} \\ 3 & -\frac{8}{5} & \frac{2}{5} & \frac{1}{5} \end{array}\right].$

15. $\begin{bmatrix} 1 & 4 \\ 2 & 7 \end{bmatrix}\begin{bmatrix} x \\ y \end{bmatrix} = \begin{bmatrix} 6 \\ 11 \end{bmatrix}$ (1)

Find the inverse of $\begin{bmatrix} 1 & 4 \\ 2 & 7 \end{bmatrix}$.

$\left[\begin{array}{cc|cc} 1 & 4 & 1 & 0 \\ 2 & 7 & 0 & 1 \end{array}\right] \xrightarrow{-2R_1 + R_2} \left[\begin{array}{cc|cc} 1 & 4 & 1 & 0 \\ 0 & -1 & -2 & 1 \end{array}\right] \xrightarrow{-1R_2} \left[\begin{array}{cc|cc} 1 & 4 & 1 & 0 \\ 0 & 1 & 2 & -1 \end{array}\right] \xrightarrow{-4R_2 + R_1} \left[\begin{array}{cc|cc} 1 & 0 & -7 & 4 \\ 0 & 1 & 2 & -1 \end{array}\right]$

The inverse of $\begin{bmatrix} 1 & 4 \\ 2 & 7 \end{bmatrix}$ is $\begin{bmatrix} -7 & 4 \\ 2 & -1 \end{bmatrix}$. Multiply each side of Eq. (1) by the inverse matrix.

$\begin{bmatrix} -7 & 4 \\ 2 & -1 \end{bmatrix}\begin{bmatrix} 1 & 4 \\ 2 & 7 \end{bmatrix}\begin{bmatrix} x \\ y \end{bmatrix} = \begin{bmatrix} -7 & 4 \\ 2 & -1 \end{bmatrix}\begin{bmatrix} 6 \\ 11 \end{bmatrix}$

$\begin{bmatrix} x \\ y \end{bmatrix} = \begin{bmatrix} 2 \\ 1 \end{bmatrix}$

The solution is (2, 1).

17. $\begin{bmatrix} 1 & -2 \\ 3 & 2 \end{bmatrix}\begin{bmatrix} x \\ y \end{bmatrix} = \begin{bmatrix} 8 \\ -1 \end{bmatrix}$ (1)

Find the inverse matrix of $\begin{bmatrix} 1 & -2 \\ 3 & 2 \end{bmatrix}$.

$\left[\begin{array}{cc|cc} 1 & -2 & 1 & 0 \\ 3 & 2 & 0 & 1 \end{array}\right] \xrightarrow{-3R_1 + R_2} \left[\begin{array}{cc|cc} 1 & -2 & 1 & 0 \\ 0 & 8 & -3 & 1 \end{array}\right] \xrightarrow{(1/8)R_2} \left[\begin{array}{cc|cc} 1 & -2 & 1 & 0 \\ 0 & 1 & -\frac{3}{8} & \frac{1}{8} \end{array}\right] \xrightarrow{2R_2 + R_1} \left[\begin{array}{cc|cc} 1 & 0 & \frac{1}{4} & \frac{1}{4} \\ 0 & 1 & -\frac{3}{8} & \frac{1}{8} \end{array}\right]$

The inverse matrix is $\begin{bmatrix} \frac{1}{4} & \frac{1}{4} \\ -\frac{3}{8} & \frac{1}{8} \end{bmatrix}$. Multiply each side of Eq. (1) by the inverse matrix.

$\begin{bmatrix} \frac{1}{4} & \frac{1}{4} \\ -\frac{3}{8} & \frac{1}{8} \end{bmatrix}\begin{bmatrix} 1 & -2 \\ 3 & 2 \end{bmatrix}\begin{bmatrix} x \\ y \end{bmatrix} = \begin{bmatrix} \frac{1}{4} & \frac{1}{4} \\ -\frac{3}{8} & \frac{1}{8} \end{bmatrix}\begin{bmatrix} 8 \\ -1 \end{bmatrix}$

$\begin{bmatrix} x \\ y \end{bmatrix} = \begin{bmatrix} \frac{7}{4} \\ -\frac{25}{8} \end{bmatrix}$

The solution is $\left(\frac{7}{4}, -\frac{25}{8}\right)$.

19.
$$\begin{bmatrix} 1 & 1 & 2 \\ 2 & 3 & 3 \\ 3 & 3 & 7 \end{bmatrix} \begin{bmatrix} x \\ y \\ z \end{bmatrix} = \begin{bmatrix} 4 \\ 5 \\ 14 \end{bmatrix} \quad (1)$$

Find the inverse matrix of $\begin{bmatrix} 1 & 1 & 2 \\ 2 & 3 & 3 \\ 3 & 3 & 7 \end{bmatrix}$.

$$\left[\begin{array}{ccc|ccc} 1 & 1 & 2 & 1 & 0 & 0 \\ 2 & 3 & 3 & 0 & 1 & 0 \\ 3 & 3 & 7 & 0 & 0 & 1 \end{array}\right] \xrightarrow[\;-3R_1 + R_3\;]{2R_1 + R_2} \left[\begin{array}{ccc|ccc} 1 & 1 & 2 & 1 & 0 & 0 \\ 0 & 1 & -1 & -2 & 1 & 0 \\ 0 & 0 & 1 & -3 & 0 & 1 \end{array}\right] \xrightarrow{-R_2 + R_1} \left[\begin{array}{ccc|ccc} 1 & 0 & 3 & 3 & -1 & 0 \\ 0 & 1 & -1 & -2 & 1 & 0 \\ 0 & 0 & 1 & -3 & 0 & 1 \end{array}\right]$$

$$\xrightarrow[\;R_3 + R_2\;]{3R_2 + R_1} \left[\begin{array}{ccc|ccc} 1 & 0 & 0 & 12 & -1 & -3 \\ 0 & 1 & 0 & -5 & 1 & 1 \\ 0 & 0 & 1 & -3 & 0 & 1 \end{array}\right]$$

The inverse matrix is $\begin{bmatrix} 12 & -1 & -3 \\ -5 & 1 & 1 \\ -3 & 0 & 1 \end{bmatrix}$.   Multiply each side of Eq. (1) by the inverse matrix.

$$\begin{bmatrix} 12 & -1 & -3 \\ -5 & 1 & 1 \\ -3 & 0 & 1 \end{bmatrix} \begin{bmatrix} 1 & 1 & 2 \\ 2 & 3 & 3 \\ 3 & 3 & 7 \end{bmatrix} \begin{bmatrix} x \\ y \\ z \end{bmatrix} = \begin{bmatrix} 12 & -1 & -3 \\ -5 & 1 & 1 \\ -3 & 0 & 1 \end{bmatrix} \begin{bmatrix} 4 \\ 5 \\ 14 \end{bmatrix}$$

$$\begin{bmatrix} x \\ y \\ z \end{bmatrix} = \begin{bmatrix} 1 \\ -1 \\ 2 \end{bmatrix}$$

The solution is $(1, -1, 2)$.

21.
$$\begin{bmatrix} 1 & 2 & 2 \\ -2 & -5 & -2 \\ 2 & 4 & 7 \end{bmatrix} \begin{bmatrix} x \\ y \\ z \end{bmatrix} = \begin{bmatrix} 5 \\ 8 \\ 19 \end{bmatrix} \quad (1)$$

Find the inverse matrix of $\begin{bmatrix} 1 & 2 & 2 \\ -2 & -5 & -2 \\ 2 & 4 & 7 \end{bmatrix}$.

$$\left[\begin{array}{ccc|ccc} 1 & 2 & 2 & 1 & 0 & 0 \\ -2 & -5 & -2 & 0 & 1 & 0 \\ 2 & 4 & 7 & 0 & 0 & 1 \end{array}\right] \xrightarrow[\;-2R_1 + R_3\;]{2R_1 + R_2} \left[\begin{array}{ccc|ccc} 1 & 2 & 2 & 1 & 0 & 0 \\ 0 & -1 & 2 & 2 & 1 & 0 \\ 0 & 0 & 3 & -2 & 0 & 1 \end{array}\right] \xrightarrow{-1R_2} \left[\begin{array}{ccc|ccc} 1 & 2 & 2 & 1 & 0 & 0 \\ 0 & 1 & -2 & -2 & -1 & 0 \\ 0 & 0 & 3 & -2 & 0 & 1 \end{array}\right]$$

$$\xrightarrow{(1/3)R_3} \left[\begin{array}{ccc|ccc} 1 & 2 & 2 & 1 & 0 & 0 \\ 0 & 1 & -2 & -2 & -1 & 0 \\ 0 & 0 & 1 & -\frac{2}{3} & 1 & \frac{1}{3} \end{array}\right] \xrightarrow{-2R_2 + R_1} \left[\begin{array}{ccc|ccc} 1 & 0 & 6 & 5 & 2 & 0 \\ 0 & 1 & -2 & -2 & -1 & 0 \\ 0 & 0 & 1 & -\frac{2}{3} & 0 & \frac{1}{3} \end{array}\right] \xrightarrow[\;-6R_3 + R_1\;]{2R_3 + R_2} \left[\begin{array}{ccc|ccc} 1 & 0 & 0 & 9 & 2 & -2 \\ 0 & 1 & 0 & -\frac{10}{3} & -1 & \frac{2}{3} \\ 0 & 0 & 1 & -\frac{2}{3} & 0 & \frac{1}{3} \end{array}\right]$$

The inverse matrix is $\begin{bmatrix} 9 & 2 & -2 \\ -\frac{10}{3} & -1 & \frac{2}{3} \\ -\frac{2}{3} & 0 & \frac{1}{3} \end{bmatrix}$.   Multiply each side of Eq. (1) by the inverse matrix.

$$\begin{bmatrix} 9 & 2 & -2 \\ -\frac{10}{3} & -1 & \frac{2}{3} \\ -\frac{2}{3} & 0 & \frac{1}{3} \end{bmatrix} \begin{bmatrix} 1 & 2 & 2 \\ -2 & -5 & -2 \\ 2 & 4 & 7 \end{bmatrix} \begin{bmatrix} x \\ y \\ z \end{bmatrix} = \begin{bmatrix} 9 & 2 & -2 \\ -\frac{10}{3} & -1 & \frac{2}{3} \\ -\frac{2}{3} & 0 & \frac{1}{3} \end{bmatrix} \begin{bmatrix} 5 \\ 8 \\ 19 \end{bmatrix}$$

$$\begin{bmatrix} x \\ y \\ z \end{bmatrix} = \begin{bmatrix} 23 \\ -12 \\ 3 \end{bmatrix}$$

The solution is $(23, -12, 3)$.

23.

$$\begin{bmatrix} 1 & 2 & 0 & 1 \\ 2 & 5 & 1 & 2 \\ 2 & 4 & 1 & 1 \\ 3 & 6 & 0 & 4 \end{bmatrix} \begin{bmatrix} w \\ x \\ y \\ z \end{bmatrix} = \begin{bmatrix} 6 \\ 10 \\ 8 \\ 16 \end{bmatrix} \quad (1)$$

Find the inverse matrix of $\begin{bmatrix} 1 & 2 & 0 & 1 \\ 2 & 5 & 1 & 2 \\ 2 & 4 & 1 & 1 \\ 3 & 6 & 0 & 4 \end{bmatrix}$.

$$\begin{bmatrix} 1 & 2 & 0 & 1 & | & 1 & 0 & 0 & 0 \\ 2 & 5 & 1 & 2 & | & 0 & 1 & 0 & 0 \\ 2 & 4 & 1 & 1 & | & 0 & 0 & 1 & 0 \\ 3 & 6 & 0 & 4 & | & 0 & 0 & 0 & 1 \end{bmatrix} \xrightarrow[\substack{-2R_1 + R_3 \\ -3R_1 + R_4}]{-2R_1 + R_2} \begin{bmatrix} 1 & 2 & 0 & 1 & | & 1 & 0 & 0 & 0 \\ 0 & 1 & 1 & 0 & | & -2 & 1 & 0 & 0 \\ 0 & 0 & 1 & -1 & | & -2 & 0 & 1 & 0 \\ 0 & 0 & 0 & 1 & | & -3 & 0 & 0 & 1 \end{bmatrix} \xrightarrow{-2R_2 + R_1} \begin{bmatrix} 1 & 0 & -2 & 1 & | & 5 & -2 & 0 & 0 \\ 0 & 1 & 1 & -0 & | & -2 & 1 & 0 & 0 \\ 0 & 0 & 1 & -1 & | & -2 & 0 & 1 & 0 \\ 0 & 0 & 0 & 1 & | & -3 & 0 & 0 & 1 \end{bmatrix}$$

$$\xrightarrow[\substack{-1R_3 + R_2}]{2R_3 + R_1} + \begin{bmatrix} 1 & 0 & 0 & -1 & | & 1 & -2 & 2 & 0 \\ 0 & 1 & 0 & 1 & | & 0 & 1 & -1 & 0 \\ 0 & 0 & 1 & -1 & | & -2 & 0 & 1 & 0 \\ 0 & 0 & 0 & 1 & | & -3 & 0 & 0 & 1 \end{bmatrix} \xrightarrow[\substack{-R_4 + R_2 \\ R_4 + R_3}]{R_4 + R_1} \begin{bmatrix} 1 & 0 & 0 & 0 & | & -2 & -2 & 2 & 1 \\ 0 & 1 & 0 & 0 & | & 3 & 1 & -1 & -1 \\ 0 & 0 & 1 & 0 & | & -5 & 0 & 1 & 1 \\ 0 & 0 & 0 & 1 & | & -3 & 0 & 0 & 1 \end{bmatrix}$$

The inverse matrix is $\begin{bmatrix} -2 & -2 & 2 & 1 \\ 3 & 1 & -1 & -1 \\ -5 & 0 & 1 & 1 \\ -3 & 0 & 0 & 1 \end{bmatrix}$. Multiply each side of Eq. (1) by the inverse matrix.

$$\begin{bmatrix} -2 & -2 & 2 & 1 \\ -3 & 1 & -1 & -1 \\ -5 & 0 & 1 & 1 \\ -3 & 0 & 0 & 1 \end{bmatrix} \begin{bmatrix} 1 & 2 & 0 & 1 \\ 2 & 5 & 1 & 2 \\ 2 & 4 & 1 & 1 \\ 3 & 6 & 0 & 4 \end{bmatrix} \begin{bmatrix} w \\ x \\ y \\ z \end{bmatrix} = \begin{bmatrix} -2 & -2 & 2 & 1 \\ 3 & 1 & -1 & -1 \\ -5 & 0 & 1 & 1 \\ -3 & 0 & 0 & 1 \end{bmatrix} \begin{bmatrix} 6 \\ 10 \\ 8 \\ 16 \end{bmatrix}$$

$$\begin{bmatrix} w \\ x \\ y \\ z \end{bmatrix} = \begin{bmatrix} 0 \\ 4 \\ -6 \\ -2 \end{bmatrix}$$

The solution is $(0, 4, -6, -2)$.

25. The average temperature for the two points,

$$x_1 = \frac{35 + 50 + x_2 + 60}{4} = \frac{145 + x_2}{4} \text{ or } 4x_1 - x_2 = 145$$

$$x_2 = \frac{x_1 + 50 + 55 + 60}{4} = \frac{165 + x_1}{4} \text{ or } -x_1 + 4x_2 = 165$$

The system of equations and associated matrix equation are

$$\begin{cases} 4x_1 - x_2 = 145 \\ -x_1 + 4x_2 = 165 \end{cases} \qquad \begin{bmatrix} 4 & -1 \\ -1 & 4 \end{bmatrix} \begin{bmatrix} x_1 \\ x_2 \end{bmatrix} = \begin{bmatrix} 145 \\ 165 \end{bmatrix}$$

Solving the matrix equation by using an inverse matrix gives $\begin{bmatrix} x_1 \\ x_2 \end{bmatrix} = \begin{bmatrix} 49.7 \\ 53.7 \end{bmatrix}$

The temperatures are $x_1 = 49.7°F$, $x_2 = 53.7°F$.

27. The average temperature for the two points,

$$x_1 = \frac{50+60+x_2+x_3}{4} = \frac{110+x_2+x_3}{4} \text{ or } 4x_1 - x_2 - x_3 = 110$$

$$x_2 = \frac{x_1+60+60+x_4}{4} = \frac{120+x_1+x_4}{4} \text{ or } -x_1 + 4x_2 - x_4 = 120$$

$$x_3 = \frac{50+x_1+x_4+50}{4} = \frac{100+x_1+x_4}{4} \text{ or } -x_1 + 4x_3 - x_4 = 100$$

$$x_4 = \frac{x_3+x_2+60+50}{4} = \frac{110+x_2+x_3}{4} \text{ or } -x_2 - x_3 + 4x_4 = 110$$

The system of equations and associated matrix equation are

$$\begin{cases} 4x_1 - x_2 - x_3 = 110 \\ -x_1 + 4x_2 - x_4 = 120 \\ -x_1 + 4x_3 - x_4 = 100 \\ -x_2 - x_3 + 4x_4 = 110 \end{cases} \quad \begin{bmatrix} 4 & -1 & -1 & 0 \\ -1 & 4 & 0 & -1 \\ -1 & 0 & 4 & -1 \\ 0 & -1 & -1 & 4 \end{bmatrix} \begin{bmatrix} x_1 \\ x_2 \\ x_3 \\ x_4 \end{bmatrix} = \begin{bmatrix} 110 \\ 120 \\ 100 \\ 110 \end{bmatrix}$$

Solving the matrix equation by using an inverse matrix gives $\begin{bmatrix} x_1 \\ x_2 \\ x_3 \\ x_4 \end{bmatrix} = \begin{bmatrix} 55 \\ 57.5 \\ 52.5 \\ 55 \end{bmatrix}$

The temperatures are $x_1 = 55°F$, $x_2 = 57.5°F$, $x_3 = 52.5°F$, $x_4 = 55°F$.

29. A = number of adult tickets
C = number of child tickets

Saturday $\quad A + C = 100$
$\qquad\qquad 20A + 15C = 1900$

$$\begin{bmatrix} 1 & 1 \\ 20 & 15 \end{bmatrix} \begin{bmatrix} A \\ C \end{bmatrix} = \begin{bmatrix} 100 \\ 1900 \end{bmatrix}$$

$$\begin{bmatrix} -3 & \frac{1}{5} \\ 4 & -\frac{1}{5} \end{bmatrix} \begin{bmatrix} 1 & 1 \\ 20 & 15 \end{bmatrix} \begin{bmatrix} A \\ C \end{bmatrix} = \begin{bmatrix} -3 & \frac{1}{5} \\ 4 & -\frac{1}{5} \end{bmatrix} \begin{bmatrix} 100 \\ 1900 \end{bmatrix}$$

$$\begin{bmatrix} A \\ C \end{bmatrix} = \begin{bmatrix} 80 \\ 20 \end{bmatrix}$$

On Saturday, 80 adults and 20 children took the tour.

Sunday $\quad A + C = 120$
$\qquad\qquad 20A + 15C = 2275$

$$\begin{bmatrix} 1 & 1 \\ 20 & 15 \end{bmatrix} \begin{bmatrix} A \\ C \end{bmatrix} = \begin{bmatrix} 120 \\ 2275 \end{bmatrix}$$

$$\begin{bmatrix} -3 & \frac{1}{5} \\ 4 & -\frac{1}{5} \end{bmatrix} \begin{bmatrix} 1 & 1 \\ 20 & 15 \end{bmatrix} \begin{bmatrix} A \\ C \end{bmatrix} = \begin{bmatrix} -3 & \frac{1}{5} \\ 4 & -\frac{1}{5} \end{bmatrix} \begin{bmatrix} 120 \\ 2275 \end{bmatrix}$$

$$\begin{bmatrix} A \\ C \end{bmatrix} = \begin{bmatrix} 95 \\ 25 \end{bmatrix}$$

On Sunday, 95 adults and 25 children took the tour.

31. $x_1 =$ number of 100-gram portions of additive 1

$x_2 =$ number of 100-gram portions of additive 2

$x_3 =$ number of 100-gram portions of additive 3

$$30x_1 + 40x_2 + 50x_3 = 380$$

Sample 1: $10x_1 + 15x_2 + 5x_3 = 95$

$$10x_1 + 10x_2 + 5x_3 = 85$$

$$\begin{bmatrix} 30 & 40 & 50 \\ 10 & 15 & 5 \\ 10 & 10 & 5 \end{bmatrix} \begin{bmatrix} x_1 \\ x_2 \\ x_3 \end{bmatrix} = \begin{bmatrix} 380 \\ 95 \\ 85 \end{bmatrix}$$

$$\begin{bmatrix} -\frac{1}{70} & -\frac{6}{35} & \frac{11}{35} \\ 0 & \frac{1}{5} & -\frac{1}{5} \\ \frac{1}{35} & -\frac{2}{35} & -\frac{1}{35} \end{bmatrix} \begin{bmatrix} 30 & 40 & 50 \\ 10 & 15 & 5 \\ 10 & 10 & 5 \end{bmatrix} \begin{bmatrix} x_1 \\ x_2 \\ x_3 \end{bmatrix} = \begin{bmatrix} -\frac{1}{70} & -\frac{6}{35} & \frac{11}{35} \\ 0 & \frac{1}{5} & -\frac{1}{5} \\ \frac{1}{35} & -\frac{2}{35} & -\frac{1}{35} \end{bmatrix} \begin{bmatrix} 380 \\ 95 \\ 85 \end{bmatrix}$$

$$\begin{bmatrix} S \\ D \end{bmatrix} = \begin{bmatrix} 50 \\ 50 \end{bmatrix}$$

For Sample 1, 500 g of additive 1, 200 g of additive 2, and 300 g of additive 3 are required.

$$30x_1 + 40x_2 + 50x_3 = 380$$

Sample 2: $10x_1 + 15x_2 + 5x_3 = 110$

$$10x_1 + 10x_2 + 5x_3 = 90$$

$$\begin{bmatrix} 30 & 40 & 50 \\ 10 & 15 & 5 \\ 10 & 10 & 5 \end{bmatrix} \begin{bmatrix} x_1 \\ x_2 \\ x_3 \end{bmatrix} = \begin{bmatrix} 380 \\ 100 \\ 90 \end{bmatrix}$$

$$\begin{bmatrix} -\frac{1}{70} & -\frac{6}{35} & \frac{11}{35} \\ 0 & \frac{1}{5} & -\frac{1}{5} \\ \frac{1}{35} & -\frac{2}{35} & -\frac{1}{35} \end{bmatrix} \begin{bmatrix} 30 & 40 & 50 \\ 10 & 15 & 5 \\ 10 & 10 & 5 \end{bmatrix} \begin{bmatrix} x_1 \\ x_2 \\ x_3 \end{bmatrix} = \begin{bmatrix} -\frac{1}{70} & -\frac{6}{35} & \frac{11}{35} \\ 0 & \frac{1}{5} & -\frac{1}{5} \\ \frac{1}{35} & -\frac{2}{35} & -\frac{1}{35} \end{bmatrix} \begin{bmatrix} 380 \\ 110 \\ 90 \end{bmatrix}$$

$$\begin{bmatrix} x_1 \\ x_2 \\ x_3 \end{bmatrix} = \begin{bmatrix} 4 \\ 4 \\ 2 \end{bmatrix}$$

For Sample 2, 400 g of additive 1, 400 g of additive 2, and 200 g of additive 3 are required.

33. Using a calculator,

$$\begin{bmatrix} 2 & -2 & 3 & 1 \\ 5 & 2 & -2 & 3 \\ 6 & -1 & 2 & 3 \\ 2 & 3 & -1 & 5 \end{bmatrix}^{-1} \approx \begin{bmatrix} -5.667 & -3.667 & 5 & 0.333 \\ -27.667 & -18.667 & 24 & 2.333 \\ -19.333 & -13.333 & 17 & 1.667 \\ 15 & 10 & -13 & -1 \end{bmatrix}$$

35. Using a calculator,

$$\begin{bmatrix} -\frac{2}{7} & 4 & -\frac{1}{6} \\ -2 & \sqrt{2} & -3 \\ \sqrt{3} & 3 & -\sqrt{5} \end{bmatrix}^{-1} \approx \begin{bmatrix} -0.150 & -0.217 & 0.302 \\ 0.248 & -0.024 & 0.013 \\ 0.217 & -0.200 & -0.195 \end{bmatrix}$$

37. $X = (I - A)^{-1}D$, where X is consumer demand, I is the identity matrix, A is the input-output matrix, and D is the final demand.

Thus

$$X = \left(\begin{bmatrix} 1 & 0 & 0 \\ 0 & 1 & 0 \\ 0 & 0 & 1 \end{bmatrix} - \begin{bmatrix} 0.20 & 0.15 & 0.10 \\ 0.10 & 0.30 & 0.25 \\ 0.20 & 0.10 & 0.10 \end{bmatrix} \right)^{-1} \begin{bmatrix} 120 \\ 60 \\ 55 \end{bmatrix}$$

$$= \begin{bmatrix} 0.80 & -0.15 & -0.10 \\ -0.10 & 0.70 & -0.25 \\ -0.20 & -0.10 & 0.90 \end{bmatrix}^{-1} \begin{bmatrix} 120 \\ 60 \\ 55 \end{bmatrix}$$

$$\approx \begin{bmatrix} 194.67 \\ 157.03 \\ 121.82 \end{bmatrix}$$

$194.67 million worth of manufacturing, $157.03 million worth of transportation, $121.82 million worth of services.

39.   The input-output matrix, A, is given by

$$A = \begin{bmatrix} 0.05 & 0.20 & 0.15 \\ 0.02 & 0.03 & 0.25 \\ 0.10 & 0.12 & 0.05 \end{bmatrix}$$

Consumer demand is given by

$$X = (I - A)^{-1} D$$

$$X = \left(\begin{bmatrix} 1 & 0 & 0 \\ 0 & 1 & 0 \\ 0 & 0 & 1 \end{bmatrix} - \begin{bmatrix} 0.05 & 0.20 & 0.15 \\ 0.02 & 0.03 & 0.25 \\ 0.10 & 0.12 & 0.05 \end{bmatrix} \right)^{-1} \begin{bmatrix} 30 \\ 5 \\ 25 \end{bmatrix}$$

$$= \begin{bmatrix} 0.95 & -0.20 & -0.15 \\ -0.02 & 0.97 & -0.25 \\ -0.10 & -0.12 & 0.95 \end{bmatrix}^{-1} \begin{bmatrix} 30 \\ 5 \\ 25 \end{bmatrix}$$

$$\approx \begin{bmatrix} 39.69 \\ 14.30 \\ 32.30 \end{bmatrix}$$

$39.69 million worth of coal, $14.30 million worth of iron, $32.30 million worth of steel.

···   **Connecting Concepts**

41.
$$AB = \begin{bmatrix} 2 & -3 \\ -6 & 9 \end{bmatrix} \begin{bmatrix} -3 & 15 \\ -2 & 10 \end{bmatrix} = \begin{bmatrix} 2(-3) + (-3)(-2) & 2(15) + (-3)(10) \\ -6(-3) + 9(-2) & -6(15) + 9(10) \end{bmatrix} = \begin{bmatrix} 0 & 0 \\ 0 & 0 \end{bmatrix} = O$$

43.
$$AB = \begin{bmatrix} 2 & -1 \\ -4 & 2 \end{bmatrix} \begin{bmatrix} 3 & 4 \\ 1 & 5 \end{bmatrix} = \begin{bmatrix} 2(3) + (-1)(1) & 2(4) + (-1)(5) \\ -4(3) + 2(1) & -4(4) + 2(5) \end{bmatrix} = \begin{bmatrix} 5 & 3 \\ -10 & -6 \end{bmatrix}$$

$$AC = \begin{bmatrix} 2 & -1 \\ -4 & 2 \end{bmatrix} \begin{bmatrix} 4 & 7 \\ 3 & 11 \end{bmatrix} = \begin{bmatrix} 2(4) + (-1)(3) & 2(7) + (-1)(11) \\ -4(4) + 2(3) & -4(7) + 2(11) \end{bmatrix} = \begin{bmatrix} 5 & 3 \\ -10 & -6 \end{bmatrix}$$

45.
$$\begin{bmatrix} a & b & | & 1 & 0 \\ c & d & | & 0 & 1 \end{bmatrix} \xrightarrow{\frac{1}{a}R_1} \begin{bmatrix} 1 & \frac{b}{a} & | & \frac{1}{a} & 0 \\ c & d & | & 0 & 1 \end{bmatrix} \xrightarrow{(-c)R_1 + R_2} \begin{bmatrix} 1 & \frac{b}{a} & | & \frac{1}{a} & 0 \\ 0 & \frac{ad - bc}{a} & | & -\frac{c}{a} & 1 \end{bmatrix} \xrightarrow{\frac{a}{ad - bc}R_2} \begin{bmatrix} 1 & \frac{b}{a} & | & \frac{1}{a} & 0 \\ 0 & 1 & | & -\frac{c}{ad - bc} & \frac{a}{ad - bc} \end{bmatrix}$$

$$\xrightarrow{-\frac{b}{a}R_2 + R_1} \begin{bmatrix} 1 & 0 & | & \frac{d}{ad - bc} & -\frac{b}{ad - bc} \\ 0 & 1 & | & -\frac{c}{ad - bc} & \frac{a}{ad - bc} \end{bmatrix}$$

$$A^{-1} = \begin{bmatrix} \frac{d}{ad - bc} & -\frac{b}{ad - bc} \\ -\frac{c}{ad - bc} & \frac{a}{ad - bc} \end{bmatrix} = \frac{1}{ad - bc} \begin{bmatrix} d & -b \\ -c & a \end{bmatrix}$$

47. **a.** $a = 2, b = -3, c = 4, d = -5$

$$\frac{1}{ad-bc}\begin{bmatrix} d & -b \\ -c & a \end{bmatrix} = \frac{1}{2(-5)-(-3)(4)}\begin{bmatrix} -5 & 3 \\ -4 & 2 \end{bmatrix} = \frac{1}{2}\begin{bmatrix} -5 & 3 \\ -4 & 2 \end{bmatrix} = \begin{bmatrix} -\frac{5}{2} & \frac{3}{2} \\ -2 & 1 \end{bmatrix}$$

b. $a = 5, b = 6, c = 3, d = 4$

$$\frac{1}{ad-bc}\begin{bmatrix} d & -b \\ -c & a \end{bmatrix} = \frac{1}{5(4)-(6)(3)}\begin{bmatrix} 4 & -6 \\ -3 & 5 \end{bmatrix} = \frac{1}{2}\begin{bmatrix} 4 & -6 \\ -3 & 5 \end{bmatrix} = \begin{bmatrix} 2 & -3 \\ -\frac{3}{2} & \frac{5}{2} \end{bmatrix}$$

c. $a = 0, b = -1, c = 4, d = 4$

$$\frac{1}{ad-bc}\begin{bmatrix} d & -b \\ -c & a \end{bmatrix} = \frac{1}{0(4)-(-1)(4)}\begin{bmatrix} 4 & 1 \\ -4 & 0 \end{bmatrix} = \frac{1}{4}\begin{bmatrix} 4 & 1 \\ -4 & 0 \end{bmatrix} = \begin{bmatrix} 1 & \frac{1}{4} \\ -1 & 0 \end{bmatrix}$$

49. $(AB)(AB)^{-1} = I$

$A^{-1}(AB)(AB)^{-1} = A^{-1}I$

$(A^{-1}A)B(AB)^{-1} = A^{-1}$

$IB(AB)^{-1} = A^{-1}$

$B(AB)^{-1} = A^{-1}$

$B^{-1}B(AB)^{-1} = B^{-1}A^{-1}$

$I(AB)^{-1} = B^{-1}A^{-1}$

$(AB)^{-1} = B^{-1}A^{-1}$

•••

Prepare for Section 7.4

50. 2

51. $(-1)^{i+j}$

$(-1)^{2+6} = (-1)^8 = 1$

52. $(-1)^{1+1}(-3)+(-1)^{1+2}(-2)+(-1)^{1+3}(5)$

$=(-1)^2(-3)+(-1)^3(-2)+(-1)^4(5)$

$=-3+(-1)(-2)+5$

$=-3+2+5$

$=4$

53. $a_{23} = 1$

54. $3\begin{bmatrix} -2 & 1 \\ 3 & -5 \end{bmatrix} = \begin{bmatrix} -6 & 3 \\ 9 & -15 \end{bmatrix}$

55. $\begin{bmatrix} 1 & 3 & -2 \\ -2 & -1 & 1 \\ 4 & 0 & 1 \end{bmatrix} \xrightarrow[\substack{2R_1+R_2 \\ -4R_1+R_3}]{} \begin{bmatrix} 1 & 3 & -2 \\ 0 & 5 & -3 \\ 0 & -12 & 9 \end{bmatrix}$

Section 7.4

1. $\begin{vmatrix} 2 & -1 \\ 3 & 5 \end{vmatrix} = 2(5)-(-1)(3) = 10-(-3) = 13$

3. $\begin{vmatrix} 5 & 0 \\ 2 & -3 \end{vmatrix} = 5(-3)-(2)(0) = -15-0 = -15$

5. $\begin{vmatrix} 4 & 6 \\ 2 & 3 \end{vmatrix} = 4(3)-(2)(6) = 12-12 = 0$

7. $\begin{vmatrix} 0 & 9 \\ 0 & -2 \end{vmatrix} = 0(-2)-(0)(9) = 0-0 = 0$

9. $M_{11} = \begin{vmatrix} 4 & -1 \\ -5 & 6 \end{vmatrix} = 4(6)-(-5)(-1) = 19$

$C_{11} = (-1)^{1+1}M_{11} = M_{11} = 19$

11. $M_{32} = \begin{vmatrix} 5 & -3 \\ 2 & -1 \end{vmatrix} = 5(-1)-2(-3) = 1$

$C_{32} = (-1)^{3+2}M_{32} = -M_{32} = -1$

13. $M_{22} = \begin{vmatrix} 3 & 3 \\ 6 & 3 \end{vmatrix} = 3(3)-6(3) = -9$

$C_{22} = (-1)^{2+2}M_{22} = M_{22} = -9$

14. $M_{13} = \begin{vmatrix} 1 & 3 \\ 6 & -2 \end{vmatrix} = 1(-2)-6(3) = -20$

$C_{13} = (-1)^{1+3}M_{13} = M_{13} = -20$

15. $M_{31} = \begin{vmatrix} -2 & 3 \\ 3 & 0 \end{vmatrix} = -2(0) - 3(3) = -9$

$C_{31} = (-1)^{3+1} M_{31} = M_{31} = -9$

17. $\begin{vmatrix} 2 & -3 & 1 \\ 2 & 0 & 2 \\ 3 & -2 & 4 \end{vmatrix} = -2 \begin{vmatrix} -3 & 1 \\ -2 & 4 \end{vmatrix} + 0 \begin{vmatrix} 2 & 1 \\ 3 & 4 \end{vmatrix} - 2 \begin{vmatrix} 2 & -3 \\ 3 & -2 \end{vmatrix}$

$\qquad = -2(-10) + 0 - 2(5)$
$\qquad = 20 - 10$
$\qquad = 10$

19. $\begin{vmatrix} -2 & 3 & 2 \\ 1 & 2 & -3 \\ -4 & -2 & 1 \end{vmatrix} = -2 \begin{vmatrix} 2 & -3 \\ -2 & 1 \end{vmatrix} - 3 \begin{vmatrix} 1 & -3 \\ -4 & 1 \end{vmatrix} + 2 \begin{vmatrix} 1 & 2 \\ -4 & -2 \end{vmatrix}$

$\qquad = -2(-4) - 3(-11) + 2(6)$
$\qquad = 8 + 33 + 12$
$\qquad = 53$

21. $\begin{vmatrix} 2 & -3 & 10 \\ 0 & 2 & -3 \\ 0 & 0 & 5 \end{vmatrix} = 2 \begin{vmatrix} 2 & -3 \\ 0 & 5 \end{vmatrix} - 0 \begin{vmatrix} -3 & 10 \\ 0 & 5 \end{vmatrix} + 0 \begin{vmatrix} -3 & 10 \\ 2 & -3 \end{vmatrix}$

$\qquad = 2(10) - 0 + 0$
$\qquad = 20$

23. $\begin{vmatrix} 0 & -2 & 4 \\ 1 & 0 & -7 \\ 5 & -6 & 0 \end{vmatrix} = 0 \begin{vmatrix} 0 & -7 \\ -6 & 0 \end{vmatrix} - (-2) \begin{vmatrix} 1 & -7 \\ 5 & 0 \end{vmatrix} + 4 \begin{vmatrix} 1 & 0 \\ 5 & -6 \end{vmatrix}$

$\qquad = 0 + 2(35) + 4(-6)$
$\qquad = 70 - 24$
$\qquad = 46$

25. $\begin{vmatrix} 4 & -3 & 3 \\ 2 & 1 & -4 \\ 6 & -2 & -1 \end{vmatrix} = 4 \begin{vmatrix} 1 & -4 \\ -2 & -1 \end{vmatrix} - (-3) \begin{vmatrix} 2 & -4 \\ 6 & -1 \end{vmatrix} + 3 \begin{vmatrix} 2 & 1 \\ 6 & -2 \end{vmatrix}$

$\qquad = 4(-9) + 3(22) + 3(-10)$
$\qquad = -36 + 66 - 30$
$\qquad = 0$

27. Row 2 consists entirely of zeros. Therefore, the determinant is zero.

29. 2 was factored from row 2.

31. Row 1 was multiplied by −2 and added to row 2.

33. 2 was factored from column 1.

35. The matrix is in triangular form.
The product of the elements on the main diagonal is −12. Therefore, the value of the determinant is −12.

37. Row 1 and row 3 were interchanged.
Therefore, the sign of the determinant was changed.

39. Each row of the first determinant was multiplied by a to produce the second determinant.

41. $\begin{vmatrix} 2 & 4 & 1 \\ 1 & 2 & -1 \\ 1 & 2 & 2 \end{vmatrix} = - \begin{vmatrix} 1 & 2 & -1 \\ 2 & 4 & -1 \\ 1 & 2 & 2 \end{vmatrix} \, R_1 \leftrightarrow R_2$

$\qquad = - \begin{vmatrix} 1 & 2 & -1 \\ 0 & 0 & 1 \\ 0 & 0 & 3 \end{vmatrix} \begin{matrix} -2R_1 + R_2 \\ -R_1 + R_3 \end{matrix}$

$\qquad = -(1)(0)(3) = 0$

43. $\begin{vmatrix} 1 & 2 & -1 \\ 2 & 3 & 1 \\ 3 & 4 & 3 \end{vmatrix} = \begin{vmatrix} 1 & 2 & -1 \\ 0 & -1 & 3 \\ 0 & -2 & 6 \end{vmatrix} \begin{matrix} -2R_1 + R_2 \\ -3R_1 + R_3 \end{matrix}$

$\qquad = \begin{vmatrix} 1 & 2 & -1 \\ 0 & -1 & 3 \\ 0 & 0 & 0 \end{vmatrix} -2R_2 + R_3$

$\qquad = (-1)(0) = 0$

45. $\begin{vmatrix} 0 & -1 & 1 \\ 1 & 0 & -2 \\ 2 & 2 & 0 \end{vmatrix} = - \begin{vmatrix} 1 & 0 & -2 \\ 0 & -1 & 1 \\ 2 & 2 & 0 \end{vmatrix} \, R_1 \leftrightarrow R_2$

$\qquad = - \begin{vmatrix} 1 & 0 & -2 \\ 0 & -1 & 1 \\ 0 & 2 & 4 \end{vmatrix} -2R_1 + R_3$

$\qquad = - \begin{vmatrix} 1 & 0 & -2 \\ 0 & -1 & 1 \\ 0 & 0 & 6 \end{vmatrix} 2R_2 + R_3$

$\qquad = -(1)(-1)(6) = 6$

47.
$$\begin{vmatrix} 1 & 2 & -1 & 2 \\ 1 & -2 & 0 & 3 \\ 3 & 0 & 1 & 5 \\ -2 & -4 & 1 & 6 \end{vmatrix} = \begin{vmatrix} 1 & 2 & -1 & 2 \\ 0 & -4 & 1 & 1 \\ 0 & -6 & 4 & -1 \\ 0 & 0 & -1 & 10 \end{vmatrix} \quad \begin{matrix} -1R_1 + R_2 \\ -3R_1 + R_3 \\ 2R_1 + R_4 \end{matrix}$$

$$= \begin{vmatrix} 1 & 2 & -1 & 2 \\ 0 & -4 & 1 & 1 \\ 0 & 0 & \frac{5}{2} & -\frac{5}{2} \\ 0 & 0 & -1 & 10 \end{vmatrix} \quad -\frac{3}{2}R_2 + R_3$$

$$= \begin{vmatrix} 1 & 2 & -1 & 2 \\ 0 & -4 & 1 & 1 \\ 0 & 0 & \frac{5}{2} & -\frac{5}{2} \\ 0 & 0 & 0 & 9 \end{vmatrix} \quad \frac{2}{5}R_3 + R_4$$

$$= 1(-4)\left(\frac{5}{2}\right)(9) = -90$$

49.
$$\begin{vmatrix} 1 & 2 & 3 & -1 \\ 6 & 5 & 9 & 8 \\ 2 & 4 & 12 & -1 \\ 1 & 2 & 6 & -1 \end{vmatrix} = 3\begin{vmatrix} 1 & 2 & 1 & -1 \\ 6 & 5 & 3 & 8 \\ 2 & 4 & 4 & -1 \\ 1 & 2 & 2 & -1 \end{vmatrix} \quad \text{Factor 3 from } C_3$$

$$= 3\begin{vmatrix} 1 & 2 & 1 & -1 \\ 0 & -7 & -3 & 14 \\ 0 & 0 & 2 & 1 \\ 0 & 0 & 1 & 0 \end{vmatrix} \quad \begin{matrix} -6R_1 + R_2 \\ -2R_1 + R_3 \\ -1R_1 + R_4 \end{matrix}$$

$$= 3\begin{vmatrix} 1 & 2 & 1 & -1 \\ 0 & -7 & -3 & 14 \\ 0 & 0 & 2 & 1 \\ 0 & 0 & 0 & -\frac{1}{2} \end{vmatrix} \quad -\frac{1}{2}R_3 + R_4$$

$$= 3(1)(-7)(2)\left(-\frac{1}{2}\right) = 21$$

51. Using a calculator,
$$\begin{vmatrix} 2 & -2 & 3 & 1 \\ 5 & 2 & -2 & 3 \\ 6 & -1 & 2 & 3 \\ 2 & 3 & -1 & 5 \end{vmatrix} = 3$$

53. Using a calculator,
$$\begin{vmatrix} -\frac{2}{7} & 4 & -\frac{1}{6} \\ -2 & \sqrt{2} & -3 \\ \sqrt{3} & 3 & -\sqrt{5} \end{vmatrix} \approx -38.933$$

Connecting Concepts

55.
$$\frac{1}{2}\begin{vmatrix} 2 & 3 & 1 \\ -1 & 0 & 1 \\ 4 & 8 & 1 \end{vmatrix} = \frac{1}{2}[3C_{12} + 0C_{22} + 8C_{32}]$$

$$= \frac{1}{2}\left[-3\begin{vmatrix} -1 & 1 \\ 4 & 1 \end{vmatrix} + 0 - 8\begin{vmatrix} 2 & 1 \\ -1 & 1 \end{vmatrix}\right]$$

$$= \frac{1}{2}[-3(5) - 8(3)] = \frac{1}{2}(15 - 24) = \frac{1}{2}(-9) = -\frac{9}{2}$$

$$\left|-\frac{9}{2}\right| = \frac{9}{2}$$

The area of the triangle is $4\frac{1}{2}$ square units.

57.
$$\frac{1}{2}\begin{vmatrix} 4 & 9 & 1 \\ 8 & 2 & 1 \\ -3 & -2 & 1 \end{vmatrix} = \frac{1}{2}[4C_{11} + 8C_{21} + (-3)C_{31}]$$

$$= \frac{1}{2}[4M_{11} - 8M_{21} - 3M_{31}]$$

$$= \frac{1}{2}\left[4\begin{vmatrix} 2 & 1 \\ -2 & 1 \end{vmatrix} - 8\begin{vmatrix} 9 & 1 \\ -2 & 1 \end{vmatrix} - 3\begin{vmatrix} 9 & 1 \\ 2 & 1 \end{vmatrix}\right]$$

$$= \frac{1}{2}[4(4) - 8(11) - 3(7)]$$

$$= \frac{1}{2}[16 - 88 - 21] = \frac{1}{2}(-93) = -\frac{93}{2}$$

$$\left|-\frac{93}{2}\right| = \frac{93}{2}$$

The area of the triangle is $46\frac{1}{2}$ square units.

59.
$$\begin{vmatrix} a & b & c \\ na & nb & nc \\ d & e & f \end{vmatrix} = \begin{vmatrix} a & b & c \\ a & b & c \\ d & e & f \end{vmatrix}$$

Since two rows are identical, the determinant is 0.

61.
$$\begin{vmatrix} x & y & 1 \\ x_1 & y_1 & 1 \\ x_2 & y_2 & 0 \end{vmatrix} = xC_{11} + yC_{12} + 1C_{13} = 0$$

$$= xM_{11} - yM_{12} + 1M_{13} = 0$$

$$= x(y_1 - y_2) - y(x_1 - x_2) + (x_1y_2 - x_2y_1) = 0$$

Since x_1, x_2, y_1 and y_2 are constants, $x(y_1 - y_2) - y(x_1 - x_2) + (x_1y_2 - x_2y_1) = 0$ is a line in the form $ax + by + c = 0$, and (x_1, y_1) and (x_2, y_2) satisfy this equation.

63.

$$\begin{vmatrix} x & y & 1 \\ -3 & 4 & 1 \\ 2 & -3 & 1 \end{vmatrix} = xC_{11} + yC_{12} + 1C_{13} = 0$$

$$= xM_{11} - yM_{12} + 1M_{13} = 0$$
$$= x(7) - y(-5) + 1(1) = 0$$
$$= 7x + 5y + 1 = 0$$

$7x + 5y = -1$ is the equation of the line passing through the points $(-3, 4)$ and $(2, -3)$.

65.

$$A = \frac{1}{2}\left(\begin{vmatrix} 8 & 25 \\ -4 & 5 \end{vmatrix} + \begin{vmatrix} 25 & 15 \\ 5 & 9 \end{vmatrix} + \begin{vmatrix} 15 & 17 \\ 9 & 20 \end{vmatrix} + \begin{vmatrix} 17 & 0 \\ 20 & 10 \end{vmatrix} + \begin{vmatrix} 0 & 8 \\ 10 & -4 \end{vmatrix} \right)$$

$$= \frac{1}{2}\left[140 + 150 + 147 + 170 + (-80) \right]$$

$$= \frac{1}{2}(527) = 263.5 \text{ square units}$$

·   **Prepare for Section 7.5**

66. $\begin{vmatrix} -5 & 2 \\ 3 & 1 \end{vmatrix} = -5(1) - 3(2) = -5 - 6 = -11$

67.

$$\begin{vmatrix} 3 & -1 & 6 \\ 2 & 9 & 0 \\ 1 & -2 & 3 \end{vmatrix} = 3\begin{vmatrix} 9 & 0 \\ -2 & 3 \end{vmatrix} + 1\begin{vmatrix} 2 & 0 \\ 1 & 3 \end{vmatrix} + 6\begin{vmatrix} 2 & 9 \\ 1 & -2 \end{vmatrix}$$

$$= 3(27) + 1(6) + 6(-13)$$
$$= 81 + 6 - 78$$
$$= 9$$

68. $\begin{bmatrix} 2 & -7 \\ 3 & 5 \end{bmatrix}$

69.

$$\begin{vmatrix} 1 & -2 & 1 \\ -1 & 1 & -2 \\ 2 & 3 & -1 \end{vmatrix} = 1\begin{vmatrix} 1 & -2 \\ 3 & -1 \end{vmatrix} + 2\begin{vmatrix} -1 & -2 \\ 2 & -1 \end{vmatrix} + 1\begin{vmatrix} -1 & 1 \\ 2 & 3 \end{vmatrix}$$

$$= (5) + 2(5) + (-5)$$
$$= 5 + 10 - 5$$
$$= 10$$

70.

$$\begin{vmatrix} 3 & -1 \\ 2 & -3 \end{vmatrix} = -9 + 2 = -7 \qquad \begin{vmatrix} 1 & 4 \\ -2 & 5 \end{vmatrix} = 5 + 8 = 13 \qquad \dfrac{\begin{vmatrix} 3 & -1 \\ 2 & -3 \end{vmatrix}}{\begin{vmatrix} 1 & 4 \\ -2 & 5 \end{vmatrix}} = -\dfrac{7}{13}$$

71. No

Section 7.5

1.

$$x_1 = \frac{\begin{vmatrix} 8 & 4 \\ 1 & -5 \end{vmatrix}}{\begin{vmatrix} 3 & 4 \\ 1 & -5 \end{vmatrix}} = \frac{-44}{-31} = \frac{44}{31}$$

$$x_2 = \frac{\begin{vmatrix} 3 & 8 \\ 4 & 1 \end{vmatrix}}{\begin{vmatrix} 3 & 4 \\ 4 & -5 \end{vmatrix}} = \frac{-29}{-31} = \frac{29}{31}$$

3.

$$x_1 = \frac{\begin{vmatrix} -1 & 4 \\ 5 & -6 \end{vmatrix}}{\begin{vmatrix} 5 & 4 \\ 3 & -6 \end{vmatrix}} = \frac{-14}{-42} = \frac{1}{3}$$

$$x_2 = \frac{\begin{vmatrix} 5 & -1 \\ 3 & 5 \end{vmatrix}}{\begin{vmatrix} 5 & 4 \\ 3 & -6 \end{vmatrix}} = \frac{28}{-42} = -\frac{2}{3}$$

5.

$$x_1 = \frac{\begin{vmatrix} 0 & 2 \\ -3 & 1 \end{vmatrix}}{\begin{vmatrix} 7 & 2 \\ 2 & 1 \end{vmatrix}} = \frac{6}{3} = 2$$

$$x_2 = \frac{\begin{vmatrix} 7 & 0 \\ 2 & -3 \end{vmatrix}}{\begin{vmatrix} 7 & 2 \\ 2 & 1 \end{vmatrix}} = \frac{-21}{3} = -7$$

7.

$$x_1 = \frac{\begin{vmatrix} 0 & -7 \\ 0 & 4 \end{vmatrix}}{\begin{vmatrix} 3 & -7 \\ 2 & 4 \end{vmatrix}} = \frac{0}{26} = 0$$

$$x_2 = \frac{\begin{vmatrix} 3 & 0 \\ 2 & 0 \end{vmatrix}}{\begin{vmatrix} 3 & -7 \\ 2 & 4 \end{vmatrix}} = \frac{0}{26} = 0$$

9.

$$x_1 = \frac{\begin{vmatrix} 2.1 & 0.3 \\ -1.6 & -1.4 \end{vmatrix}}{\begin{vmatrix} 1.2 & 0.3 \\ 0.8 & -1.4 \end{vmatrix}} = \frac{-2.46}{-1.92} = 1.28125$$

$$x_2 = \frac{\begin{vmatrix} 1.2 & 2.1 \\ 0.8 & -1.6 \end{vmatrix}}{\begin{vmatrix} 1.2 & 0.3 \\ 0.8 & -1.4 \end{vmatrix}} = \frac{-3.6}{-1.92} = 1.875$$

11.

$$D = \begin{vmatrix} 3 & -4 & 2 \\ 1 & -1 & 2 \\ 2 & 2 & 3 \end{vmatrix} = -17$$

$$D_1 = \begin{vmatrix} 1 & -4 & 2 \\ -2 & -1 & 2 \\ -3 & 2 & 3 \end{vmatrix} = -21$$

$$D_2 = \begin{vmatrix} 3 & 1 & 2 \\ 1 & -2 & 2 \\ 2 & -3 & 3 \end{vmatrix} = 3$$

$$D_3 = \begin{vmatrix} 3 & -4 & 1 \\ 1 & -1 & -2 \\ 2 & 2 & -3 \end{vmatrix} = 29$$

$$x_1 = \frac{D_1}{D} = \frac{-21}{-17} = \frac{21}{17}$$

$$x_2 = \frac{D_2}{D} = \frac{3}{-17} = -\frac{3}{17}$$

$$x_3 = \frac{D_3}{D} = \frac{29}{-17} = -\frac{29}{17}$$

13.

$$D = \begin{vmatrix} 1 & 4 & -2 \\ 3 & -2 & 3 \\ 2 & 1 & -3 \end{vmatrix} = 49$$

$$D_1 = \begin{vmatrix} 0 & 4 & -2 \\ 4 & -2 & 3 \\ -1 & 1 & -3 \end{vmatrix} = 32$$

$$D_2 = \begin{vmatrix} 1 & 0 & -2 \\ 3 & 4 & 3 \\ 2 & -1 & -3 \end{vmatrix} = 13$$

$$D_3 = \begin{vmatrix} 1 & 4 & 0 \\ 3 & -2 & 4 \\ 2 & 1 & -1 \end{vmatrix} = 42$$

$$x_1 = \frac{D_1}{D} = \frac{32}{49}$$

$$x_2 = \frac{D_2}{D} = \frac{13}{49}$$

$$x_3 = \frac{D_3}{D} = \frac{42}{49} = \frac{6}{7}$$

15.

$$D = \begin{vmatrix} 0 & 2 & -3 \\ 3 & -5 & 1 \\ 4 & 0 & 2 \end{vmatrix} = -64$$

$$D_1 = \begin{vmatrix} 1 & 2 & -3 \\ 0 & -5 & 1 \\ -3 & 0 & 2 \end{vmatrix} = 29$$

$$D_2 = \begin{vmatrix} 0 & 1 & -3 \\ 3 & 0 & 1 \\ 4 & -3 & 2 \end{vmatrix} = 25$$

$$D_3 = \begin{vmatrix} 0 & 2 & 1 \\ 3 & -5 & 0 \\ 4 & 0 & -3 \end{vmatrix} = 38$$

$$x_1 = \frac{D_1}{D} = \frac{29}{-64} = -\frac{29}{64}$$

$$x_2 = \frac{D_2}{D} = \frac{25}{-64} = -\frac{25}{64}$$

$$x_3 = \frac{D_3}{D} = \frac{38}{-64} = -\frac{19}{32}$$

17.

$$D = \begin{vmatrix} 4 & -5 & 1 \\ 3 & 1 & 0 \\ 1 & -1 & 3 \end{vmatrix} = 53$$

$$D_1 = \begin{vmatrix} -2 & -5 & 1 \\ 4 & 1 & 0 \\ 0 & -1 & 3 \end{vmatrix} = 50$$

$$D_2 = \begin{vmatrix} 4 & -2 & 1 \\ 3 & 4 & 0 \\ 1 & 0 & 3 \end{vmatrix} = 62$$

$$D_3 = \begin{vmatrix} 4 & -5 & -2 \\ 3 & 1 & 4 \\ 1 & -1 & 0 \end{vmatrix} = 4$$

$$x_1 = \frac{D_1}{D} = \frac{50}{53}$$

$$x_2 = \frac{D_2}{D} = \frac{62}{53}$$

$$x_3 = \frac{D_3}{D} = \frac{4}{53}$$

19.
$$D = \begin{vmatrix} 2 & 2 & -3 \\ 1 & -3 & 2 \\ 4 & -1 & 3 \end{vmatrix} = -37$$

$$D_1 = \begin{vmatrix} 0 & 2 & -3 \\ 0 & -3 & 2 \\ 0 & -1 & 3 \end{vmatrix} = 0$$

$$D_2 = \begin{vmatrix} 2 & 0 & -3 \\ 1 & 0 & 2 \\ 4 & 0 & 3 \end{vmatrix} = 0$$

$$D_3 = \begin{vmatrix} 2 & 2 & 0 \\ 1 & -3 & 0 \\ 4 & -1 & 0 \end{vmatrix} = 0$$

$$x_1 = \frac{D_1}{D} = \frac{0}{-37} = 0$$

$$x_2 = \frac{D_2}{D} = \frac{0}{-37} = 0$$

$$x_3 = \frac{D_3}{D} = \frac{0}{-37} = 0$$

21.
$$D = \begin{vmatrix} 2 & -3 & 4 & -1 \\ 1 & 2 & 0 & 2 \\ 3 & 1 & 0 & -2 \\ 1 & -3 & 2 & -1 \end{vmatrix} = -38$$

$$D_2 = \begin{vmatrix} 2 & 1 & 4 & -1 \\ 1 & -1 & 0 & 2 \\ 3 & 2 & 0 & -2 \\ 1 & 3 & 2 & -1 \end{vmatrix} = 70$$

$$x_2 = \frac{D_2}{D} = \frac{70}{-38} = -\frac{35}{19}$$

23.
$$D = \begin{vmatrix} 1 & -3 & 2 & 4 \\ 3 & 5 & -6 & 2 \\ 2 & -1 & 9 & 8 \\ 1 & 1 & 1 & -8 \end{vmatrix} = -1310$$

$$D_1 = \begin{vmatrix} 0 & -3 & 2 & 4 \\ -2 & 5 & -6 & 2 \\ 0 & -1 & 9 & 8 \\ -3 & 1 & 1 & -8 \end{vmatrix} = 1210$$

$$x_1 = \frac{D_1}{D} = \frac{1210}{-1310} = -\frac{121}{131}$$

25.
$$D = \begin{vmatrix} 0 & 3 & -1 & 2 \\ 5 & 1 & 3 & -1 \\ 1 & -2 & 0 & 9 \\ 2 & 0 & 2 & 0 \end{vmatrix} = 120, \quad D_4 = \begin{vmatrix} 0 & 3 & -1 & 1 \\ 5 & 1 & 3 & -4 \\ 1 & -2 & 0 & 5 \\ 2 & 0 & 2 & 3 \end{vmatrix} = 160, \quad x_4 = \frac{D_4}{D} = \frac{160}{120} = \frac{4}{3}$$

Connecting **C**oncepts

27.
$$D = \begin{vmatrix} 2 & -3 & 1 \\ 1 & 1 & -2 \\ 4 & -1 & -3 \end{vmatrix} = 0$$

In order for us to use Cramer's Rule, the determinant of the coefficient matrix cannot be zero. The system of equations has infinitely many solutions.

29.
$$D = \begin{vmatrix} k & 3 \\ k & -2 \end{vmatrix} = -5k$$

For the system of equations to have a unique solution, the determinant of the coefficient matrix cannot be zero.

$-5k = 0$

$k = 0$

The system of equations has a unique solution for all values of k except $k = 0$.

31.
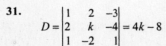
$$D = \begin{vmatrix} 1 & 2 & -3 \\ 2 & k & -4 \\ 1 & -2 & 1 \end{vmatrix} = 4k - 8$$

For the system of equations to have a unique solution, the determinant of the coefficient matrix cannot be zero.

$4k - 8 = 0$

$4(k - 2) = 0$

$k - 2 = 0$

$k = 2$

The system of equations has a unique solution for all values of k except $k = 2$.

33.
$$ru + sv = w$$
$$(2+3i)r + (4-2i)s = -6+15i$$
$$2r + 3ri + 4s - 2si = -6+15i$$
$$(2r + 4s) + (3r - 2s)i = -6+15i$$
$$2r + 4s = -6$$
$$3r - 2s = 15$$
$$D = \begin{vmatrix} 2 & 4 \\ 3 & -2 \end{vmatrix} = -16$$
$$D_r = \begin{vmatrix} -6 & 4 \\ 15 & -2 \end{vmatrix} = -48$$
$$D_s = \begin{vmatrix} 2 & -6 \\ 3 & 15 \end{vmatrix} = 48$$
$$r = \frac{D_r}{D} = \frac{-48}{-16} = 3$$
$$s = \frac{D_s}{D} = \frac{48}{-16} = -3$$

1. False. $A^2 = A \cdot A = \begin{bmatrix} 2 & 3 \\ 1 & 4 \end{bmatrix} \begin{bmatrix} 2 & 3 \\ 1 & 4 \end{bmatrix} = \begin{bmatrix} 7 & 18 \\ 6 & 19 \end{bmatrix} \neq \begin{bmatrix} 4 & 9 \\ 1 & 16 \end{bmatrix}$ **2.** True.

3. False. A singular matrix does not have a multiplicative inverse.

4. False. As an example, $A = \begin{bmatrix} 2 & -1 \\ -4 & 2 \end{bmatrix}$, $B = \begin{bmatrix} 3 & 4 \\ 1 & 5 \end{bmatrix}$ and $C = \begin{bmatrix} 4 & 7 \\ 3 & 11 \end{bmatrix}$. $AB = AC$ but $B \neq C$.

5. True.

6. False. For example, if $A = \begin{bmatrix} 1 & 4 \\ -2 & 3 \end{bmatrix}$ and $B = \begin{bmatrix} 2 & 0 \\ -1 & 5 \end{bmatrix}$, then $\det(A) = 11$ and $\det(B) = 10$.

Therefore, $\det(A) + \det(B) = 21$ and $\det(A + B) = \det\begin{bmatrix} 3 & 4 \\ -3 & 8 \end{bmatrix} = \begin{bmatrix} 3 & 4 \\ -3 & 8 \end{bmatrix} = 36$.

Thus, $\det(A) + \det(B) \neq \det(A + B)$.

7. False. If the determinant of the coefficient matrix is zero, Cramer's Rule cannot be used to solve the system of equations.

8. False, since matrix multiplication is not commutative. That is, in general, $AB \neq BA$, so $AB - BA \neq 0$.

9. True.

10. False. By the Associative Property of Matrix Multiplication, given A, B, and C square matrices of order n, $(AB)C = A(BC)$.

11. False. If the number of equations is less than the number of variables, the Gaussian method can be used to solve the system of linear equations. If the system of equations has a solution, the solutions will be given in terms of one or more of the variables.

12. False. For example, for a 2×2 matrix, $\det(2A) = 2 \cdot 2 \det(A)$; and for a 3×3 matrix, $\det(2A) = 4 \cdot 2 \det(A)$.

13. True.

14. False. For example, given $A = \begin{bmatrix} -3 & 2 \\ -6 & 4 \end{bmatrix}$ and $B = \begin{bmatrix} 2 & 4 \\ 3 & 6 \end{bmatrix}$, then $AB = \begin{bmatrix} -3 & 2 \\ -6 & 4 \end{bmatrix} \begin{bmatrix} 2 & 4 \\ 3 & 6 \end{bmatrix} = \begin{bmatrix} 0 & 0 \\ 0 & 0 \end{bmatrix} = 0$, but $A \neq O$ and $B \neq O$.

15. True.

1. $3A = 3\begin{bmatrix} 2 & -1 & 3 \\ 3 & 2 & -1 \end{bmatrix} = \begin{bmatrix} 6 & -3 & 9 \\ 9 & 6 & -3 \end{bmatrix}$ [7.2]

2. $-2B = -2\begin{bmatrix} 0 & -2 \\ 4 & 2 \\ 1 & -3 \end{bmatrix} = \begin{bmatrix} 0 & 4 \\ -8 & -4 \\ -2 & 6 \end{bmatrix}$ [7.2]

3. $-A + D = -\begin{bmatrix} 2 & -1 & 3 \\ 3 & 2 & -1 \end{bmatrix} + \begin{bmatrix} -3 & 4 & 2 \\ 4 & -2 & 5 \end{bmatrix}$ [7.2]

$= \begin{bmatrix} -2 & 1 & -3 \\ -3 & -2 & 1 \end{bmatrix} + \begin{bmatrix} -3 & 4 & 2 \\ 4 & -2 & 5 \end{bmatrix}$

$= \begin{bmatrix} -5 & 5 & -1 \\ 1 & -4 & 6 \end{bmatrix}$

4. $2A - 3D = 2\begin{bmatrix} 2 & -1 & 3 \\ 3 & 2 & -1 \end{bmatrix} - 3\begin{bmatrix} -3 & 4 & 2 \\ 4 & -2 & 5 \end{bmatrix}$ [7.2]

$= \begin{bmatrix} 4 & -2 & 6 \\ 6 & 4 & -2 \end{bmatrix} - \begin{bmatrix} -9 & 12 & 6 \\ 12 & -6 & 15 \end{bmatrix}$

$= \begin{bmatrix} 13 & -14 & 0 \\ -6 & 10 & -17 \end{bmatrix}$

5. $AB = \begin{bmatrix} 2 & -1 & 3 \\ 3 & 2 & -1 \end{bmatrix} \begin{bmatrix} 0 & -2 \\ 4 & 2 \\ 1 & -3 \end{bmatrix} = \begin{bmatrix} -1 & -5 \\ 7 & 1 \end{bmatrix}$ [7.2]

6. $DB = \begin{bmatrix} -3 & 4 & 2 \\ 4 & -2 & 5 \end{bmatrix} \begin{bmatrix} 0 & -2 \\ 4 & 2 \\ 1 & -3 \end{bmatrix} = \begin{bmatrix} 18 & 8 \\ -3 & -27 \end{bmatrix}$ [7.2]

7.
$$BA = \begin{bmatrix} 0 & -2 \\ 4 & 2 \\ 1 & -3 \end{bmatrix} \begin{bmatrix} 2 & -1 & 3 \\ 3 & 2 & -1 \end{bmatrix} = \begin{bmatrix} -6 & -4 & 2 \\ 14 & 0 & 10 \\ -7 & -7 & 6 \end{bmatrix} \quad [7.2]$$

8.
$$BD = \begin{bmatrix} 0 & -2 \\ 4 & 2 \\ 1 & -3 \end{bmatrix} \begin{bmatrix} -3 & 4 & 2 \\ 4 & -2 & 5 \end{bmatrix} = \begin{bmatrix} -8 & 4 & -10 \\ -4 & 12 & 18 \\ -15 & 10 & -13 \end{bmatrix} \quad [7.2]$$

9.
$$C^2 = C \cdot C = \begin{bmatrix} 2 & 6 & 1 \\ 1 & 2 & -1 \\ 2 & 4 & -1 \end{bmatrix} \begin{bmatrix} 2 & 6 & 1 \\ 1 & 2 & -1 \\ 2 & 4 & -1 \end{bmatrix} \quad [7.2]$$
$$= \begin{bmatrix} 12 & 28 & -5 \\ 2 & 6 & 0 \\ 6 & 16 & -1 \end{bmatrix}$$

10.
$$C^3 = C \cdot C \cdot C = \begin{bmatrix} 2 & 6 & 1 \\ 1 & 2 & -1 \\ 2 & 4 & -1 \end{bmatrix} \begin{bmatrix} 2 & 6 & 1 \\ 1 & 2 & -1 \\ 2 & 4 & -1 \end{bmatrix} \begin{bmatrix} 2 & 6 & 1 \\ 1 & 2 & -1 \\ 2 & 4 & -1 \end{bmatrix} \quad [7.2]$$
$$= \begin{bmatrix} 12 & 28 & -5 \\ 2 & 6 & 0 \\ 6 & 16 & -1 \end{bmatrix} \begin{bmatrix} 2 & 6 & 1 \\ 1 & 2 & -1 \\ 2 & 4 & -1 \end{bmatrix}$$
$$= \begin{bmatrix} 42 & 108 & -11 \\ 10 & 24 & -4 \\ 26 & 64 & -9 \end{bmatrix}$$

11.
$$BAC = \begin{bmatrix} 0 & -2 \\ 4 & 2 \\ 1 & -3 \end{bmatrix} \begin{bmatrix} 2 & -1 & 3 \\ 3 & 2 & -1 \end{bmatrix} \begin{bmatrix} 2 & 6 & 1 \\ 1 & 2 & -1 \\ 2 & 4 & -1 \end{bmatrix} = \begin{bmatrix} -6 & -4 & 2 \\ 14 & 0 & 10 \\ -7 & -7 & 6 \end{bmatrix} \begin{bmatrix} 2 & 6 & 1 \\ 1 & 2 & -1 \\ 2 & 4 & -1 \end{bmatrix} = \begin{bmatrix} -12 & -36 & -4 \\ 48 & 124 & 4 \\ -9 & -32 & -6 \end{bmatrix} \quad [7.2]$$

12. Not possible since A is of order 2×3 and D is of order 2×3. [7.2]

13.
$$AB - BA = \begin{bmatrix} 2 & -1 & 3 \\ 3 & 2 & -1 \end{bmatrix} \begin{bmatrix} 0 & -2 \\ 4 & 2 \\ 1 & -3 \end{bmatrix} - \begin{bmatrix} 0 & -2 \\ 4 & 2 \\ 1 & -3 \end{bmatrix} \begin{bmatrix} 2 & -1 & 3 \\ 3 & 2 & -1 \end{bmatrix} = \begin{bmatrix} -1 & -15 \\ 7 & 1 \end{bmatrix} - \begin{bmatrix} -6 & -4 & 2 \\ 14 & 0 & 10 \\ -7 & -7 & 6 \end{bmatrix}$$

Not possible since AB is of order 2×2 and BA is of order 3×3. [7.2]

14.
$$DB - BD = \begin{bmatrix} -3 & 4 & 2 \\ 4 & -2 & 5 \end{bmatrix} \begin{bmatrix} 0 & -2 \\ 4 & 2 \\ 1 & -3 \end{bmatrix} - \begin{bmatrix} 0 & -2 \\ 4 & 2 \\ 1 & -3 \end{bmatrix} \begin{bmatrix} -3 & 4 & 2 \\ 4 & -2 & 5 \end{bmatrix} = \begin{bmatrix} 18 & 8 \\ -3 & -27 \end{bmatrix} - \begin{bmatrix} -8 & 4 & -10 \\ -4 & 12 & 18 \\ -15 & 10 & -13 \end{bmatrix}$$

Not possible since DB is of order 2×2 and BD is of order 3×3. [7.2]

15.
$$(A - D)C = \left(\begin{bmatrix} 2 & -1 & 3 \\ 3 & 2 & -1 \end{bmatrix} - \begin{bmatrix} -3 & 4 & 2 \\ 4 & -2 & 5 \end{bmatrix} \right) \begin{bmatrix} 2 & 6 & 1 \\ 1 & 2 & -1 \\ 2 & 4 & -1 \end{bmatrix} = \begin{bmatrix} 5 & -5 & 1 \\ -1 & 4 & -6 \end{bmatrix} \begin{bmatrix} 2 & 6 & 1 \\ 1 & 2 & -1 \\ 2 & 4 & -1 \end{bmatrix} = \begin{bmatrix} 7 & 24 & 9 \\ -10 & -22 & 1 \end{bmatrix} \quad [7.2]$$

16.
$$AC - DC = \begin{bmatrix} 2 & -1 & 3 \\ 3 & 2 & -1 \end{bmatrix} \begin{bmatrix} 2 & 6 & 1 \\ 1 & 2 & -1 \\ 2 & 4 & -1 \end{bmatrix} - \begin{bmatrix} -3 & 4 & 2 \\ 4 & -2 & 5 \end{bmatrix} \begin{bmatrix} 2 & 6 & 1 \\ 1 & 2 & -1 \\ 2 & 4 & -1 \end{bmatrix} = \begin{bmatrix} 9 & 22 & 0 \\ 6 & 18 & 2 \end{bmatrix} \begin{bmatrix} 2 & -2 & -9 \\ 16 & 40 & 1 \end{bmatrix} = \begin{bmatrix} 7 & 24 & 9 \\ -10 & -22 & 1 \end{bmatrix} \quad [7.2]$$

17.
$$\begin{bmatrix} 2 & 6 & 1 & | & 1 & 0 & 0 \\ 1 & 2 & -1 & | & 0 & 1 & 0 \\ 2 & 4 & -1 & | & 0 & 0 & 1 \end{bmatrix} \xrightarrow{\frac{1}{2}R_1} \begin{bmatrix} 1 & 3 & \frac{1}{2} & | & \frac{1}{2} & 0 & 0 \\ 1 & 2 & -1 & | & 0 & 1 & 0 \\ 2 & 4 & -1 & | & 0 & 0 & 1 \end{bmatrix} \xrightarrow[-2R_1+R_3]{-1R_1+R_2} \begin{bmatrix} 1 & 3 & \frac{1}{2} & | & \frac{1}{2} & 0 & 0 \\ 0 & -1 & -\frac{3}{2} & | & -\frac{1}{2} & 1 & 0 \\ 0 & -2 & -2 & | & -1 & 0 & 1 \end{bmatrix}$$

$$\xrightarrow[\substack{-3R_2+R_1 \\ 2R_2+R_3}]{-1R_2} \begin{bmatrix} 1 & 0 & -4 & | & -1 & 3 & 0 \\ 0 & 1 & \frac{3}{2} & | & \frac{1}{2} & -1 & 0 \\ 0 & 0 & 1 & | & 0 & -2 & 1 \end{bmatrix} \xrightarrow[(-3/2)R_3+R_2]{4R_3+R_1} \begin{bmatrix} 1 & 0 & 0 & | & -1 & -5 & 4 \\ 0 & 1 & 0 & | & \frac{1}{2} & 2 & -\frac{3}{2} \\ 0 & 0 & 1 & | & 0 & -2 & 1 \end{bmatrix}$$

$$C^{-1} = \begin{bmatrix} -1 & -5 & 4 \\ \frac{1}{2} & 2 & -\frac{3}{2} \\ 0 & -2 & 1 \end{bmatrix} \quad [7.3]$$

18.

Determinant of $C = \begin{bmatrix} 2 & 6 & 1 \\ 1 & 2 & -1 \\ 2 & 4 & -1 \end{bmatrix} = 2C_{11} + 1C_{21} + 2C_{31}$ [7.4]

$= 2M_{11} - 1M_{21} + 2M_{31}$

$= 2\begin{vmatrix} 2 & -1 \\ 4 & -1 \end{vmatrix} - 1\begin{vmatrix} 6 & 1 \\ 4 & -1 \end{vmatrix} + 2\begin{vmatrix} 6 & 1 \\ 2 & -1 \end{vmatrix} = 2(2) - 1(-10) + 2(-8) = 4 + 10 - 16 = -2$

19.

$\begin{bmatrix} 2 & -3 & | & 7 \\ 3 & -4 & | & 10 \end{bmatrix} \xrightarrow{-1R_1 + R_2} \begin{bmatrix} 2 & -3 & | & 7 \\ 1 & -1 & | & 3 \end{bmatrix} \xleftarrow{R_1 + R_2} \begin{bmatrix} 1 & -1 & | & 3 \\ 2 & -3 & | & 7 \end{bmatrix} \xrightarrow{-2R_1 + R_2} \begin{bmatrix} 1 & -1 & | & 3 \\ 0 & -1 & | & 1 \end{bmatrix} \xrightarrow{-1R_2} \begin{bmatrix} 1 & -1 & | & 3 \\ 0 & 1 & | & -1 \end{bmatrix}$

$\begin{cases} x - y = 3 \\ \quad y = -1 \end{cases}$ $\begin{aligned} x - (-1) &= 3 \\ x &= 2 \end{aligned}$

The solution is $(2, -1)$. [7.1]

20.

$\begin{bmatrix} 3 & 4 & | & -9 \\ 2 & 3 & | & -7 \end{bmatrix} \xrightarrow{-R_2 + R_1} \begin{bmatrix} 1 & 1 & | & -2 \\ 2 & 3 & | & -7 \end{bmatrix} \xrightarrow{-2R_1 + R_2} \begin{bmatrix} 1 & 1 & | & -2 \\ 0 & 1 & | & -3 \end{bmatrix}$

$\begin{cases} x + y = -2 \\ \quad y = -3 \end{cases}$ $\begin{aligned} x + (-3) &= -2 \\ x &= 1 \end{aligned}$

The solution is $(1, -3)$. [7.1]

21.

$\begin{bmatrix} 4 & -5 & | & 12 \\ 3 & 1 & | & 9 \end{bmatrix} \xrightarrow{-1R_2 + R_1} \begin{bmatrix} 1 & -6 & | & 3 \\ 3 & 1 & | & 9 \end{bmatrix} \xrightarrow{-3R_1 + R_2} \begin{bmatrix} 1 & -6 & | & 3 \\ 0 & 19 & | & 0 \end{bmatrix} \xrightarrow{\frac{1}{19}R_2} \begin{bmatrix} 1 & -6 & | & 3 \\ 0 & 1 & | & 0 \end{bmatrix}$

$\begin{cases} x - 6y = 3 \\ \quad y = 0 \end{cases}$ $\begin{aligned} x - 6(0) &= 3 \\ x &= 3 \end{aligned}$

The solution is $(3, 0)$. [7.1]

22.

$\begin{bmatrix} 2 & -5 & | & 10 \\ 5 & 2 & | & 4 \end{bmatrix} \xrightarrow{-2R_1 + R_2} \begin{bmatrix} 2 & -5 & | & 10 \\ 1 & 12 & | & -16 \end{bmatrix} \xleftrightarrow{R_1 \leftrightarrow R_2} \begin{bmatrix} 1 & 12 & | & -16 \\ 2 & -5 & | & 10 \end{bmatrix} \xrightarrow{-2R_1 + R_2} \begin{bmatrix} 1 & 12 & | & -16 \\ 0 & -29 & | & 42 \end{bmatrix}$

$\xrightarrow{-\frac{1}{29}R_2} \begin{bmatrix} 1 & 12 & | & -16 \\ 0 & 1 & | & -\frac{42}{29} \end{bmatrix}$

$\begin{cases} x + 12y = -16 \\ \quad y = -\frac{42}{29} \end{cases}$ $\begin{aligned} x + 12\left(-\frac{42}{29}\right) &= -16 \\ x - \frac{504}{29} &= -16 \\ x &= \frac{40}{29} \end{aligned}$

The solution is $\left(\frac{40}{29}, -\frac{42}{29}\right)$. [7.1]

23.

$\begin{bmatrix} 1 & 2 & 3 & | & 5 \\ 3 & 8 & 11 & | & 17 \\ 2 & 6 & 7 & | & 12 \end{bmatrix} \xrightarrow[-2R_1 + R_3]{-3R_1 + R_2} \begin{bmatrix} 1 & 2 & 3 & | & 5 \\ 0 & 2 & 2 & | & 2 \\ 0 & 2 & 1 & | & 2 \end{bmatrix} \xrightarrow{(1/2)R_2} \begin{bmatrix} 1 & 2 & 3 & | & 5 \\ 0 & 1 & 1 & | & 1 \\ 0 & 2 & 1 & | & 2 \end{bmatrix} \xrightarrow{-2R_2 + R_3} \begin{bmatrix} 1 & 2 & 3 & | & 5 \\ 0 & 1 & 1 & | & 1 \\ 0 & 0 & -1 & | & 0 \end{bmatrix} \xrightarrow{-1R_3} \begin{bmatrix} 1 & 2 & 3 & | & 5 \\ 0 & 1 & 1 & | & 1 \\ 0 & 0 & 1 & | & 0 \end{bmatrix}$

$\begin{cases} x + 2y + 3z = 5 \\ \quad y + z = 1 \\ \qquad z = 0 \end{cases}$ $\begin{aligned} y + 0 &= 1 \\ y &= 1 \end{aligned}$ $\begin{aligned} x + 2(1) + 3(0) &= 5 \\ x &= 3 \end{aligned}$

The solution is $(3, 1, 0)$. [7.1]

24.

$$\begin{bmatrix} 1 & -1 & 3 & | & 10 \\ 2 & -1 & 7 & | & 24 \\ 3 & -6 & 7 & | & 21 \end{bmatrix} \xrightarrow[\substack{-2R_1+R_2 \\ -3R_1+R_3}]{} \begin{bmatrix} 1 & -1 & 3 & | & 10 \\ 0 & 1 & 1 & | & 4 \\ 0 & -3 & -2 & | & -9 \end{bmatrix} \xrightarrow{3R_2+R_3} \begin{bmatrix} 1 & -1 & 3 & | & 10 \\ 0 & 1 & 1 & | & 4 \\ 0 & 0 & 1 & | & 3 \end{bmatrix}$$

$$\begin{cases} x - y + 3z = 10 \\ \quad y + z = 4 \\ \qquad z = 3 \end{cases} \qquad \begin{aligned} y + 3 &= 4 \\ y &= 1 \end{aligned} \qquad \begin{aligned} x - 1 + 3(3) &= 10 \\ x &= 2 \end{aligned}$$

The solution is (2, 1, 3). [7.1]

25.

$$\begin{bmatrix} 2 & -1 & -1 & | & 4 \\ 1 & -2 & -2 & | & 5 \\ 3 & -3 & -8 & | & 19 \end{bmatrix} R_1 \longleftrightarrow R_2 \begin{bmatrix} 1 & -2 & -2 & | & 5 \\ 2 & -1 & -1 & | & 4 \\ 3 & -3 & -8 & | & 19 \end{bmatrix} \xrightarrow[\substack{-2R_1+R_2 \\ -3R_1+R_3}]{} \begin{bmatrix} 1 & -2 & -2 & | & 5 \\ 0 & 3 & 3 & | & -6 \\ 0 & 3 & -2 & | & 4 \end{bmatrix} \xrightarrow{\frac{1}{3}R_2} \begin{bmatrix} 1 & -2 & -2 & | & 5 \\ 0 & 1 & 1 & | & -2 \\ 0 & 3 & -2 & | & 4 \end{bmatrix}$$

$$\xrightarrow{-3R_2+R_3} \begin{bmatrix} 1 & -2 & -2 & | & 5 \\ 0 & 1 & 1 & | & -2 \\ 0 & 0 & -5 & | & 10 \end{bmatrix} \xrightarrow{-\frac{1}{5}R_3} \begin{bmatrix} 1 & -2 & -2 & | & 5 \\ 0 & 1 & 1 & | & -2 \\ 0 & 0 & 1 & | & -2 \end{bmatrix}$$

$$\begin{cases} x - 2y - 2z = 5 \\ \quad y + z = -2 \\ \qquad z = -2 \end{cases} \qquad \begin{aligned} y + (-2) &= -2 \\ y &= 0 \end{aligned} \qquad \begin{aligned} x - 2(0) - 2(-2) &= 5 \\ x &= 1 \end{aligned}$$

The solution is (1, 0, −2). [7.1]

26.

$$\begin{bmatrix} 3 & -7 & 8 & | & 10 \\ 1 & -3 & 2 & | & 0 \\ 2 & -8 & 7 & | & 5 \end{bmatrix} R_1 \longleftrightarrow R_2 \begin{bmatrix} 1 & -3 & 2 & | & 0 \\ 3 & -7 & 8 & | & 10 \\ 2 & -8 & 7 & | & 5 \end{bmatrix} \xrightarrow[\substack{-3R_1+R_2 \\ -2R_1+R_3}]{} \begin{bmatrix} 1 & -3 & 2 & | & 0 \\ 0 & 2 & 2 & | & 10 \\ 0 & -2 & 3 & | & 5 \end{bmatrix} \xrightarrow{\frac{1}{2}R_2} \begin{bmatrix} 1 & -3 & 2 & | & 0 \\ 0 & 1 & 1 & | & 5 \\ 0 & -2 & 3 & | & 5 \end{bmatrix}$$

$$\xrightarrow{2R_2+R_3} \begin{bmatrix} 1 & -3 & 2 & | & 0 \\ 0 & 1 & 1 & | & 5 \\ 0 & 0 & 5 & | & 15 \end{bmatrix} \xrightarrow{\frac{1}{5}R_3} \begin{bmatrix} 1 & -3 & 2 & | & 0 \\ 0 & 1 & 1 & | & 5 \\ 0 & 0 & 1 & | & 3 \end{bmatrix}$$

$$\begin{cases} x - 3y + 2z = 0 \\ \quad y + z = 5 \\ \qquad z = 3 \end{cases} \qquad \begin{aligned} y + 3 &= 5 \\ y &= 2 \end{aligned} \qquad \begin{aligned} x - 3(2) + 2(3) &= 0 \\ x &= 0 \end{aligned}$$

The solution is (0, 2, 3). [7.1]

27.

$$\begin{bmatrix} 4 & -9 & 6 & | & 54 \\ 3 & -8 & 8 & | & 49 \\ 1 & -3 & 2 & | & 17 \end{bmatrix} R_1 \longleftrightarrow R_3 \begin{bmatrix} 1 & -3 & 2 & | & 17 \\ 3 & -8 & 8 & | & 49 \\ 4 & -9 & 6 & | & 54 \end{bmatrix} \xrightarrow[\substack{-3R_1+R_2 \\ -4R_1+R_3}]{} \begin{bmatrix} 1 & -3 & 2 & | & 17 \\ 0 & 1 & 2 & | & -2 \\ 0 & 3 & -2 & | & -14 \end{bmatrix} \xrightarrow{-3R_2+R_3} \begin{bmatrix} 1 & -3 & 2 & | & 17 \\ 0 & 1 & 2 & | & -2 \\ 0 & 0 & -8 & | & -8 \end{bmatrix}$$

$$\xrightarrow{(-1/8)R_3} \begin{bmatrix} 1 & -3 & 2 & | & 17 \\ 0 & 1 & 2 & | & -2 \\ 0 & 0 & 1 & | & 1 \end{bmatrix}$$

$$\begin{cases} x - 3y + 2z = 17 \\ \quad y + 2z = -2 \\ \qquad z = 1 \end{cases} \qquad \begin{aligned} y + 2(1) &= -2 \\ y &= -4 \end{aligned} \qquad \begin{aligned} x - 3(-4) + 2(1) &= 17 \\ x &= 3 \end{aligned}$$

The solution is (3, −4, 1). [7.1]

28.

$$\begin{bmatrix} 3 & 8 & -5 & | & 6 \\ 2 & 9 & -1 & | & -8 \\ 1 & -4 & -2 & | & 16 \end{bmatrix} R_1 \longleftrightarrow R_3 \begin{bmatrix} 1 & -4 & -2 & | & 16 \\ 2 & 9 & -1 & | & -8 \\ 3 & 8 & -5 & | & 6 \end{bmatrix} \xrightarrow[\substack{-2R_1+R_2 \\ -3R_1+R_3}]{} \begin{bmatrix} 1 & -4 & -2 & | & 16 \\ 0 & 17 & 3 & | & -40 \\ 0 & 20 & 1 & | & -42 \end{bmatrix} \xrightarrow{\frac{1}{17}R_2} \begin{bmatrix} 1 & -4 & -2 & | & 16 \\ 0 & 1 & \frac{3}{17} & | & -\frac{40}{17} \\ 0 & 20 & 1 & | & -42 \end{bmatrix}$$

$$\xrightarrow{-20R_2+R_3} \begin{bmatrix} 1 & -4 & -2 & | & 16 \\ 0 & 1 & \frac{3}{17} & | & -\frac{40}{17} \\ 0 & 0 & -\frac{43}{17} & | & \frac{86}{17} \end{bmatrix} \xrightarrow{-\frac{17}{43}R_3} \begin{bmatrix} 1 & -4 & -2 & | & 16 \\ 0 & 1 & \frac{3}{17} & | & -\frac{40}{17} \\ 0 & 0 & 1 & | & -2 \end{bmatrix}$$

$$\begin{cases} x - 4y - 2z = 16 \\ \quad\quad y + \frac{3}{17}z = -\frac{40}{17} \\ \quad\quad\quad\quad z = -2 \end{cases} \qquad \begin{aligned} y + \frac{3}{17}(-2) &= -\frac{40}{17} \\ y &= -2 \end{aligned} \qquad \begin{aligned} x - 4(-2) - 2(-2) &= 16 \\ x &= 4 \end{aligned}$$

The solution is $(4, -2, -2)$. [7.1]

29.

$$\begin{bmatrix} 1 & 1 & 2 & | & -5 \\ 2 & 3 & 5 & | & -13 \\ 2 & 5 & 7 & | & -19 \end{bmatrix} \xrightarrow[\substack{-2R_1+R_2 \\ -2R_1+R_3}]{} \begin{bmatrix} 1 & 1 & 2 & | & -5 \\ 0 & 1 & 1 & | & -3 \\ 0 & 3 & 3 & | & -9 \end{bmatrix} \xrightarrow{-3R_2+R_3} \begin{bmatrix} 1 & 1 & 2 & | & -5 \\ 0 & 1 & 1 & | & -3 \\ 0 & 0 & 0 & | & 0 \end{bmatrix}$$

$$\begin{cases} x + y + 2z = -5 \\ \quad\; y + \;\; z = -3 \end{cases} \qquad y = -z - 3 \qquad \begin{aligned} x + (-z - 3) + 2z &= -5 \\ x &= -z - 2 \end{aligned}$$

Let z be any real number c.
The solution is $(-c-2, -c-3, c)$. [7.1]

30.

$$\begin{bmatrix} 1 & -2 & 3 & | & 9 \\ 3 & -5 & 8 & | & 25 \\ 1 & 0 & -1 & | & 5 \end{bmatrix} \xrightarrow[\substack{-3R_1+R_2 \\ -1R_1+R_3}]{} \begin{bmatrix} 1 & -2 & 3 & | & 9 \\ 0 & 1 & -1 & | & -2 \\ 0 & 2 & -4 & | & -4 \end{bmatrix} \xrightarrow{-2R_2+R_3} \begin{bmatrix} 1 & -2 & 3 & | & 9 \\ 0 & 1 & -1 & | & -2 \\ 0 & 0 & -2 & | & 0 \end{bmatrix} \xrightarrow{(-1/2)R_3} \begin{bmatrix} 1 & -2 & 3 & | & 9 \\ 0 & 1 & -1 & | & -2 \\ 0 & 0 & 1 & | & 0 \end{bmatrix}$$

$$\begin{cases} x - 2y + 3z = 9 \\ \quad\; y - \;\; z = -2 \\ \quad\quad\quad\; z = 0 \end{cases} \qquad \begin{aligned} y - 0 &= -2 \\ y &= -2 \end{aligned} \qquad \begin{aligned} x - 2(-2) + 3(0) &= 9 \\ x &= 5 \end{aligned}$$

The solution is $(5, -2, 0)$. [7.1]

31.

$$\begin{bmatrix} 1 & 2 & -1 & 2 & | & 1 \\ 3 & 8 & 1 & 4 & | & 1 \\ 2 & 7 & 3 & 2 & | & 0 \\ 1 & 3 & -2 & 5 & | & 6 \end{bmatrix} \xrightarrow[\substack{-3R_1+R_2 \\ -2R_1+R_3 \\ -1R_1+R_4}]{} \begin{bmatrix} 1 & -2 & -1 & 2 & | & 1 \\ 0 & 2 & 4 & -2 & | & -2 \\ 0 & 3 & 5 & -2 & | & -2 \\ 0 & 1 & -1 & 3 & | & 5 \end{bmatrix} \xrightarrow{(-1/2)R_2} \begin{bmatrix} 1 & 2 & -1 & 2 & | & 1 \\ 0 & 1 & 2 & -1 & | & -1 \\ 0 & 3 & 5 & -2 & | & -2 \\ 0 & 1 & -1 & 3 & | & 5 \end{bmatrix}$$

$$\xrightarrow[\substack{-3R_2+R_3 \\ -1R_2+R_4}]{} \begin{bmatrix} 1 & 2 & -1 & 2 & | & 1 \\ 0 & 1 & 2 & -1 & | & -1 \\ 0 & 0 & -1 & 1 & | & 1 \\ 0 & 0 & -3 & 4 & | & 6 \end{bmatrix} \xrightarrow{-1R_3} \begin{bmatrix} 1 & 2 & -1 & 2 & | & 1 \\ 0 & 1 & 2 & -1 & | & -1 \\ 0 & 0 & 1 & -1 & | & -1 \\ 0 & 0 & -3 & 4 & | & 6 \end{bmatrix} \xrightarrow{-3R_3+R_4} \begin{bmatrix} 1 & 2 & -1 & 2 & | & 1 \\ 0 & 1 & 2 & -1 & | & -1 \\ 0 & 0 & 1 & -1 & | & -1 \\ 0 & 0 & 0 & 1 & | & 3 \end{bmatrix}$$

$$\begin{cases} w + 2x - y + 2z = 1 \\ \quad\;\; x + 2y - \;\; z = -1 \\ \quad\quad\quad\; y - \;\; z = -1 \\ \quad\quad\quad\quad\quad z = 3 \end{cases} \qquad \begin{aligned} y - 3 &= -1 \\ y &= 2 \end{aligned} \qquad \begin{aligned} x + 2(2) - 3 &= -1 \\ x &= -2 \end{aligned} \qquad \begin{aligned} w + 2(-2) - 2 + 2(3) &= 1 \\ w &= 1 \end{aligned}$$

The solution is $(1, -2, 2, 3)$. [7.1]

32.

$$\begin{bmatrix} 1 & -3 & -2 & 1 & | & -1 \\ 2 & -5 & 0 & 3 & | & 1 \\ 3 & -7 & 3 & 0 & | & -18 \\ 2 & -3 & -5 & -2 & | & -8 \end{bmatrix} \xrightarrow[\substack{-3R_1+R_3 \\ -2R_1+R_4}]{-2R_1+R_2} \begin{bmatrix} 1 & -3 & -2 & 1 & | & -1 \\ 0 & 1 & 4 & 1 & | & 3 \\ 0 & 2 & 9 & -3 & | & -15 \\ 0 & 3 & -1 & -4 & | & -6 \end{bmatrix} \xrightarrow[-3R_2+R_4]{-2R_2+R_3} \begin{bmatrix} 1 & -3 & -2 & 1 & | & -1 \\ 0 & 1 & 4 & 1 & | & 3 \\ 0 & 0 & 1 & -5 & | & -21 \\ 0 & 0 & -13 & -7 & | & -15 \end{bmatrix}$$

$$\xrightarrow{13R_3+R_4} \begin{bmatrix} 1 & -3 & -2 & 1 & | & -1 \\ 0 & 1 & 4 & 1 & | & 3 \\ 0 & 0 & 1 & -5 & | & -21 \\ 0 & 0 & 0 & -72 & | & -288 \end{bmatrix} \xrightarrow{(-1/72)R_4} \begin{bmatrix} 1 & -3 & -2 & 1 & | & -1 \\ 0 & 1 & 4 & 1 & | & 3 \\ 0 & 0 & 1 & -5 & | & -21 \\ 0 & 0 & 0 & 1 & | & 4 \end{bmatrix}$$

$$\begin{cases} w-3x-2y+ z = -1 \\ x+4y+ z = 3 \\ y-5z = -21 \\ z = 4 \end{cases}$$

$$\begin{aligned} y-5(4) &= -21 & x+4(-1)+4 &= 3 & w-3(3)-2(-1)+4 &= -1 \\ y &= -1 & x &= 3 & w &= 2 \end{aligned}$$

The solution is $(2, 3, -1, 4)$. [7.1]

33.

$$\begin{bmatrix} 1 & 3 & 1 & -4 & | & 3 \\ 1 & 4 & 3 & -6 & | & 5 \\ 2 & 8 & 7 & -5 & | & 11 \\ 2 & 5 & 0 & -6 & | & 4 \end{bmatrix} \xrightarrow[\substack{-2R_1+R_3 \\ -2R_1+R_4}]{-1R_1+R_2} \begin{bmatrix} 1 & 3 & 1 & -4 & | & 3 \\ 0 & 1 & 2 & -2 & | & 2 \\ 0 & 2 & 5 & 3 & | & 5 \\ 0 & -1 & -2 & 2 & | & -2 \end{bmatrix} \xrightarrow[1R_2+R_4]{-2R_2+R_3} \begin{bmatrix} 1 & 3 & 1 & -4 & | & 3 \\ 0 & 1 & 2 & -2 & | & 2 \\ 0 & 0 & 1 & 7 & | & 1 \\ 0 & 0 & 0 & 0 & | & 0 \end{bmatrix}$$

$$\begin{cases} w+3x+ y-4z = 3 \\ x+2y-2z = 2 \\ y+7z = 1 \end{cases}$$

$$\begin{aligned} y &= -7z+1 & x+2(-7z+1)-2z &= 2 & w+3(16z)+(-7z+1)-4z &= 3 \\ & & x &= 16z & w &= -37z+2 \end{aligned}$$

Let z be any real number c.

The solution is $(-37c+2, 16c, -7c+1, c)$. [7.1]

34.

$$\begin{bmatrix} 1 & 4 & -2 & 3 & | & 6 \\ 2 & 9 & -1 & 5 & | & 13 \\ 1 & 7 & 6 & 5 & | & 9 \\ 3 & 14 & 0 & 7 & | & 20 \end{bmatrix} \xrightarrow[\substack{-1R_1+R_3 \\ -3R_1+R_4}]{-2R_1+R_2} \begin{bmatrix} 1 & 4 & -2 & 3 & | & 6 \\ 0 & 1 & 3 & -1 & | & 1 \\ 0 & 3 & 8 & 2 & | & 3 \\ 0 & 2 & 6 & -2 & | & 2 \end{bmatrix} \xrightarrow[-2R_2+R_4]{-3R_2+R_3} \begin{bmatrix} 1 & 4 & -2 & 3 & | & 6 \\ 0 & 1 & 3 & -1 & | & 1 \\ 0 & 0 & -1 & 5 & | & 0 \\ 0 & 0 & 0 & 0 & | & 0 \end{bmatrix} \xrightarrow{-1R_3} \begin{bmatrix} 1 & 4 & -2 & 3 & | & 6 \\ 0 & 1 & 3 & -1 & | & 1 \\ 0 & 0 & 1 & -5 & | & 0 \\ 0 & 0 & 0 & 0 & | & 0 \end{bmatrix}$$

$$\begin{cases} w+4x-2y+3z = 6 \\ x+3y- z = 1 \\ y-5z = 0 \end{cases}$$

$$\begin{aligned} y &= 5z & x+3(5z)-z &= 1 & w+4(-14z+1)-2(5z)+3z &= 6 \\ & & x &= -14z+1 & w &= 63z+2 \end{aligned}$$

Let z be any real number c.
The solution is $(63c+2, -14c+1, 5c, c)$. [7.1]

35. Because there are three points, the degree of the interpolating polynomial is at most 2.

The form of the polynomial is $p(x) = a_2 x^2 + a_1 x + a_0$.

Use this polynomial and the given points to find the system of equations.

$$p(-1) = a_2(-1)^2 + a_1(-1) + a_0 = -4$$
$$p(2) = a_2(2)^2 + a_1(2) + a_0 = 8$$
$$p(3) = a_2(3)^2 + a_1(3) + a_0 = 16$$

The system of equations and the associated augmented matrix are $\begin{cases} a_2 - a_1 + a_0 = -4 \\ 4a_2 + 2a_1 + a_0 = 8 \\ 9a_2 + 3a_1 + a_0 = 16 \end{cases}$ $\begin{bmatrix} 1 & -1 & 1 & -4 \\ 4 & 2 & 1 & 8 \\ 9 & 3 & 1 & 16 \end{bmatrix}$

The ref (row echelon form) feature of a graphing calculator can be used to rewrite the augmented matrix in echelon form. Consider using the function of your calculator that converts a decimal to a fraction.

The augmented matrix in echelon form and resulting system of equations are $\begin{bmatrix} 1 & 1/3 & 1/9 & 16/9 \\ 0 & 1 & -2/3 & 13/3 \\ 0 & 0 & 1 & -2 \end{bmatrix}$ $\begin{cases} a_2 + \dfrac{1}{3}a_1 + \dfrac{1}{9}a_0 = \dfrac{16}{9} \\ a_1 - \dfrac{2}{3}a_0 = \dfrac{13}{2} \\ a_0 = -2 \end{cases}$

Solving by back substitution yields $a_0 = -2$, $a_1 = 3$, and $a_2 = 1$.

The interpolating polynomial is $p(x) = x^2 + 3x - 2$. [7.1]

36. Because there are three points, the degree of the interpolating polynomial is at most 2.

The form of the polynomial is $p(x) = a_2 x^2 + a_1 x + a_0$.

Use this polynomial and the given points to find the system of equations.

$$p(-1) = a_2(-1)^2 + a_1(-1) + a_0 = 4$$
$$p(1) = a_2(1)^2 + a_1(1) + a_0 = 0$$
$$p(2) = a_2(2)^2 + a_1(2) + a_0 = -5$$

The system of equations and the associated augmented matrix are $\begin{cases} a_2 - a_1 + a_0 = 4 \\ a_2 + a_1 + a_0 = 0 \\ 4a_2 + 2a_1 + a_0 = -5 \end{cases}$ $\begin{bmatrix} 1 & -1 & 1 & 4 \\ 1 & 1 & 1 & 0 \\ 4 & 2 & 1 & -5 \end{bmatrix}$

The ref (row echelon form) feature of a graphing calculator can be used to rewrite the augmented matrix in echelon form. Consider using the function of your calculator that converts a decimal to a fraction.

The augmented matrix in echelon form and resulting system of equations are $\begin{bmatrix} 1 & 1/2 & 1/4 & -5/4 \\ 0 & 1 & -1/2 & -7/2 \\ 0 & 0 & 1 & 3 \end{bmatrix}$ $\begin{cases} a_2 + \dfrac{1}{2}a_1 + \dfrac{1}{4}a_0 = -\dfrac{5}{4} \\ a_1 - \dfrac{1}{2}a_0 = -\dfrac{7}{2} \\ a_0 = 3 \end{cases}$

Solving by back substitution yields $a_0 = 3$, $a_1 = -2$, and $a_2 = -1$.

The interpolating polynomial is $p(x) = -x^2 - 2x + 3$. [7.1]

37.

$$\begin{bmatrix} 2 & -2 & 1 & 0 \\ 3 & -2 & 0 & 1 \end{bmatrix} \xrightarrow{(1/2)R_1} \begin{bmatrix} 1 & -1 & \frac{1}{2} & 0 \\ 3 & -2 & 0 & 1 \end{bmatrix} \xrightarrow{-3R_1 + R_2} \begin{bmatrix} 1 & -1 & \frac{1}{2} & 0 \\ 0 & 1 & -\frac{3}{2} & 1 \end{bmatrix} \xrightarrow{R_2 + R_1} \begin{bmatrix} 1 & 0 & -1 & 1 \\ 0 & 1 & -\frac{3}{2} & 1 \end{bmatrix}$$

The inverse matrix is $\begin{bmatrix} -1 & 1 \\ -\frac{3}{2} & 1 \end{bmatrix}$. [7.3]

334   Chapter 7: Matrices

38.
$$\begin{bmatrix} 3 & 4 & | & 1 & 0 \\ 2 & 3 & | & 0 & 1 \end{bmatrix} \xrightarrow{\frac{1}{3}R_1} \begin{bmatrix} 1 & \frac{4}{3} & | & \frac{1}{3} & 0 \\ 2 & 3 & | & 0 & 1 \end{bmatrix} \xrightarrow{-2R_1+R_2} \begin{bmatrix} 1 & \frac{4}{3} & | & \frac{1}{3} & 0 \\ 0 & \frac{1}{3} & | & -\frac{2}{3} & 1 \end{bmatrix} \xrightarrow{3R_2} \begin{bmatrix} 1 & \frac{4}{3} & | & \frac{1}{3} & 0 \\ 0 & 1 & | & -2 & 3 \end{bmatrix} \xrightarrow{-\frac{4}{3}R_2+R_1} \begin{bmatrix} 1 & 0 & | & 3 & -4 \\ 0 & 1 & | & -2 & 3 \end{bmatrix}$$

The inverse matrix is $\begin{bmatrix} 3 & -4 \\ -2 & 3 \end{bmatrix}$. [7.3]

39.
$$\begin{bmatrix} -2 & 3 & | & 1 & 0 \\ 2 & 4 & | & 0 & 1 \end{bmatrix} \xrightarrow{=\frac{1}{2}R_1} \begin{bmatrix} 1 & -\frac{3}{2} & | & -\frac{1}{2} & 0 \\ 2 & 4 & | & 0 & 1 \end{bmatrix} \xrightarrow{-2R_1+R_2} \begin{bmatrix} 1 & -\frac{3}{2} & | & -\frac{1}{2} & 0 \\ 0 & 7 & | & 1 & 1 \end{bmatrix} \xrightarrow{\frac{1}{7}R_2} \begin{bmatrix} 1 & -\frac{3}{2} & | & -\frac{1}{2} & 0 \\ 0 & 1 & | & \frac{1}{7} & \frac{1}{7} \end{bmatrix}$$

$$\xrightarrow{\frac{3}{2}R_2+R_1} \begin{bmatrix} 1 & 0 & | & -\frac{2}{7} & \frac{3}{14} \\ 0 & 1 & | & \frac{1}{7} & \frac{1}{7} \end{bmatrix}$$

The inverse matrix is $\begin{bmatrix} -\frac{2}{7} & \frac{3}{14} \\ \frac{1}{7} & \frac{1}{7} \end{bmatrix}$. [7.3]

40.
$$\begin{bmatrix} 5 & -4 & | & 1 & 0 \\ 3 & 2 & | & 0 & 1 \end{bmatrix} \xrightarrow{(1/5)R_1} \begin{bmatrix} 1 & -\frac{4}{5} & | & \frac{1}{5} & 0 \\ 3 & 2 & | & 0 & 1 \end{bmatrix} \xrightarrow{-3R_1+R_2} \begin{bmatrix} 1 & -\frac{4}{5} & | & \frac{1}{5} & 0 \\ 0 & \frac{22}{5} & | & -\frac{3}{5} & 1 \end{bmatrix} \xrightarrow{(5/22)R_2} \begin{bmatrix} 1 & -\frac{4}{5} & | & \frac{1}{5} & 0 \\ 0 & 1 & | & -\frac{3}{22} & \frac{5}{22} \end{bmatrix}$$

$$\xrightarrow{(4/5)R_2+R_1} \begin{bmatrix} 1 & 0 & | & \frac{1}{11} & \frac{2}{11} \\ 0 & 1 & | & -\frac{3}{22} & \frac{5}{22} \end{bmatrix}$$

The inverse matrix is $\begin{bmatrix} \frac{1}{11} & \frac{2}{11} \\ -\frac{3}{22} & \frac{5}{22} \end{bmatrix}$. [7.3]

41.
$$\begin{bmatrix} 1 & 2 & 1 & | & 1 & 0 & 0 \\ 2 & 6 & 4 & | & 0 & 1 & 0 \\ 3 & 8 & 6 & | & 0 & 0 & 1 \end{bmatrix} \xrightarrow[\substack{-3R_1+R_3}]{-2R_1+R_2} \begin{bmatrix} 1 & 2 & 1 & | & 1 & 0 & 0 \\ 0 & 2 & 2 & | & -2 & 1 & 0 \\ 0 & 2 & 3 & | & -3 & 0 & 1 \end{bmatrix} \xrightarrow{(1/2)R_2} \begin{bmatrix} 1 & 2 & 1 & | & 1 & 0 & 0 \\ 0 & 1 & 1 & | & -1 & \frac{1}{2} & 0 \\ 0 & 2 & 3 & | & -3 & 0 & 1 \end{bmatrix}$$

$$\xrightarrow{-2R_2+R_3} \begin{bmatrix} 1 & 2 & 1 & | & 1 & 0 & 0 \\ 0 & 1 & 1 & | & -1 & \frac{1}{2} & 0 \\ 0 & 0 & 1 & | & -1 & -1 & 1 \end{bmatrix} \xrightarrow{-2R_2+R_1} \begin{bmatrix} 1 & 0 & -1 & | & 3 & -1 & 0 \\ 0 & 1 & 1 & | & -1 & \frac{1}{2} & 0 \\ 0 & 0 & 1 & | & -1 & -1 & 1 \end{bmatrix} \xrightarrow[\substack{-R_3+R_2}]{R_3+R_1} \begin{bmatrix} 1 & 0 & 0 & | & 2 & -2 & 1 \\ 0 & 1 & 0 & | & 0 & \frac{3}{2} & -1 \\ 0 & 0 & 1 & | & -1 & -1 & 1 \end{bmatrix}$$

The inverse matrix is $\begin{bmatrix} 2 & -2 & 1 \\ 0 & \frac{3}{2} & -1 \\ -1 & -1 & 1 \end{bmatrix}$. [7.3]

42.
$$\begin{bmatrix} 1 & -3 & 2 & | & 1 & 0 & 0 \\ 3 & -8 & 7 & | & 0 & 1 & 0 \\ 2 & -3 & 6 & | & 0 & 0 & 1 \end{bmatrix} \xrightarrow[\substack{-2R_1+R_3}]{-3R_1+R_2} \begin{bmatrix} 1 & -3 & 2 & | & 1 & 0 & 0 \\ 0 & 1 & 1 & | & -3 & 1 & 0 \\ 0 & 3 & 2 & | & -2 & 0 & 1 \end{bmatrix} \xrightarrow{-3R_2+R_3} \begin{bmatrix} 1 & -3 & 2 & | & 1 & 0 & 0 \\ 0 & 1 & 1 & | & -3 & 1 & 0 \\ 0 & 0 & -1 & | & 7 & -3 & 1 \end{bmatrix}$$

$$\xrightarrow{-1R_3} \begin{bmatrix} 1 & -3 & 2 & | & 1 & 0 & 0 \\ 0 & 1 & 1 & | & -3 & 1 & 0 \\ 0 & 0 & 1 & | & -7 & 3 & -1 \end{bmatrix} \xrightarrow{3R_2+R_1} \begin{bmatrix} 1 & 0 & 5 & | & -8 & 3 & 0 \\ 0 & 1 & 1 & | & -3 & 1 & 0 \\ 0 & 0 & 1 & | & -7 & 3 & -1 \end{bmatrix} \xrightarrow[\substack{-R_3+R_2}]{-5R_3+R_1} \begin{bmatrix} 1 & 0 & 0 & | & 27 & -12 & 5 \\ 0 & 1 & 0 & | & 4 & -2 & 1 \\ 0 & 0 & 1 & | & -7 & 3 & -1 \end{bmatrix}$$

The inverse matrix is $\begin{bmatrix} 27 & -12 & 5 \\ 4 & -2 & 1 \\ -7 & 3 & -1 \end{bmatrix}$. [7.3]

43.

$$\left[\begin{array}{ccc|ccc} 3 & -2 & 7 & 1 & 0 & 0 \\ 2 & -1 & 5 & 0 & 1 & 0 \\ 3 & 0 & 10 & 0 & 0 & 1 \end{array}\right] \xrightarrow{(1/3)R_1} \left[\begin{array}{ccc|ccc} 1 & -\frac{2}{3} & \frac{7}{3} & \frac{1}{3} & 0 & 0 \\ 2 & -1 & 5 & 0 & 1 & 0 \\ 3 & 0 & 10 & 0 & 0 & 1 \end{array}\right] \xrightarrow[-3R_1+R_3]{-2R_1+R_2} \left[\begin{array}{ccc|ccc} 1 & -\frac{2}{3} & \frac{7}{3} & \frac{1}{3} & 0 & 0 \\ 0 & \frac{1}{3} & \frac{1}{3} & -\frac{2}{3} & 1 & 0 \\ 0 & 2 & 3 & -1 & 0 & 1 \end{array}\right]$$

$$\xrightarrow{3R_2} \left[\begin{array}{ccc|ccc} 1 & -\frac{2}{3} & \frac{7}{3} & \frac{1}{3} & 0 & 0 \\ 0 & 1 & 1 & -2 & 3 & 0 \\ 0 & 2 & 3 & -1 & 0 & 1 \end{array}\right] \xrightarrow{-2R_2+R_3} \left[\begin{array}{ccc|ccc} 1 & -\frac{2}{3} & \frac{7}{3} & \frac{1}{3} & 0 & 0 \\ 0 & 1 & 1 & -2 & 3 & 0 \\ 0 & 0 & 1 & 3 & -6 & 1 \end{array}\right] \xrightarrow{(2/3)R_2+R_1} \left[\begin{array}{ccc|ccc} 1 & 0 & 3 & -1 & 2 & 0 \\ 0 & 1 & 1 & -2 & 3 & 0 \\ 0 & 0 & 1 & 3 & -6 & 1 \end{array}\right]$$

$$\xrightarrow[-1R_3+R_2]{-3R_3+R_1} \left[\begin{array}{ccc|ccc} 1 & 0 & 0 & -10 & 20 & -3 \\ 0 & 1 & 0 & -5 & 9 & -1 \\ 0 & 0 & 1 & 3 & -6 & 1 \end{array}\right]$$

The inverse matrix is $\begin{bmatrix} -10 & 20 & -3 \\ -5 & 9 & -1 \\ 3 & -6 & 1 \end{bmatrix}$. [7.3]

44.

$$\left[\begin{array}{ccc|ccc} 4 & 9 & -11 & 1 & 0 & 0 \\ 3 & 7 & -8 & 0 & 1 & 0 \\ 2 & 6 & -3 & 0 & 0 & 1 \end{array}\right] \xrightarrow{(1/4)R_1} \left[\begin{array}{ccc|ccc} 1 & \frac{9}{4} & -\frac{11}{4} & \frac{1}{4} & 0 & 0 \\ 3 & 7 & -8 & 0 & 1 & 0 \\ 2 & 6 & -3 & 0 & 0 & 1 \end{array}\right] \xrightarrow[-2R_1+R_3]{-3R_1+R_2} \left[\begin{array}{ccc|ccc} 1 & \frac{9}{4} & -\frac{11}{4} & \frac{1}{4} & 0 & 0 \\ 0 & \frac{1}{4} & \frac{1}{4} & -\frac{3}{4} & 1 & 0 \\ 0 & \frac{3}{2} & \frac{5}{2} & -\frac{1}{2} & 0 & 1 \end{array}\right]$$

$$\xrightarrow{4R_2} \left[\begin{array}{ccc|ccc} 1 & \frac{9}{4} & -\frac{11}{4} & \frac{1}{4} & 0 & 0 \\ 0 & 1 & 1 & -3 & 4 & 0 \\ 0 & \frac{3}{2} & \frac{5}{2} & -\frac{1}{2} & 0 & 1 \end{array}\right] \xrightarrow{(-3/2)R_2+R_3} \left[\begin{array}{ccc|ccc} 1 & \frac{9}{4} & -\frac{11}{4} & \frac{1}{4} & 0 & 0 \\ 0 & 1 & 1 & -3 & 4 & 0 \\ 0 & 0 & 1 & 4 & -6 & 1 \end{array}\right]$$

$$\xrightarrow{(-9/4)R_2+R_1} \left[\begin{array}{ccc|ccc} 1 & 0 & -5 & 7 & -9 & 0 \\ 0 & 1 & 1 & -3 & 4 & 0 \\ 0 & 0 & 1 & 4 & -6 & 1 \end{array}\right] \xrightarrow[-1R_3+R_2]{5R_3+R_1} \left[\begin{array}{ccc|ccc} 1 & 0 & 0 & 27 & -39 & 5 \\ 0 & 1 & 0 & -7 & 10 & -1 \\ 0 & 0 & 1 & 4 & -6 & 1 \end{array}\right]$$

The inverse matrix is $\begin{bmatrix} 27 & -39 & 5 \\ -7 & 10 & -1 \\ 4 & -6 & 1 \end{bmatrix}$. [7.3]

45.

$$\left[\begin{array}{cccc|cccc} 1 & -1 & 2 & 3 & 1 & 0 & 0 & 0 \\ 2 & -1 & 6 & 5 & 0 & 1 & 0 & 0 \\ 3 & -1 & 9 & 6 & 0 & 0 & 1 & 0 \\ 2 & -2 & 4 & 7 & 0 & 0 & 0 & 1 \end{array}\right] \xrightarrow[\substack{-3R_1+R_3 \\ -2R_1+R_4}]{-2R_1+R_2} \left[\begin{array}{cccc|cccc} 1 & -1 & 2 & 3 & 1 & 0 & 0 & 0 \\ 0 & 1 & 2 & -1 & -2 & 1 & 0 & 0 \\ 0 & 2 & 3 & -3 & -3 & 0 & 1 & 0 \\ 0 & 0 & 0 & 1 & -2 & 0 & 0 & 1 \end{array}\right] \xrightarrow{-2R_2+R_3} \left[\begin{array}{cccc|cccc} 1 & -1 & 2 & 3 & 1 & 0 & 0 & 0 \\ 0 & 1 & 2 & -1 & -2 & 1 & 0 & 0 \\ 0 & 0 & -1 & -1 & 1 & -2 & 1 & 0 \\ 0 & 0 & 0 & 1 & -2 & 0 & 0 & 1 \end{array}\right]$$

$$\xrightarrow{-1R_3} \left[\begin{array}{cccc|cccc} 1 & -1 & 2 & 3 & 1 & 0 & 0 & 0 \\ 0 & 1 & 2 & -1 & -2 & 1 & 0 & 0 \\ 0 & 0 & 1 & 1 & -1 & 2 & -1 & 0 \\ 0 & 0 & 0 & 1 & -2 & 0 & 0 & 1 \end{array}\right] \xrightarrow{R_2+R_1} \left[\begin{array}{cccc|cccc} 1 & 0 & 4 & 2 & -1 & 1 & 0 & 0 \\ 0 & 1 & 2 & -1 & -2 & 1 & 0 & 0 \\ 0 & 0 & 1 & 1 & -1 & 2 & -1 & 0 \\ 0 & 0 & 0 & 1 & -2 & 0 & 0 & 1 \end{array}\right]$$

$$\xrightarrow[-2R_3+R_2]{-4R_3+R_1} \left[\begin{array}{cccc|cccc} 1 & 0 & 0 & -2 & 3 & -7 & 4 & 0 \\ 0 & 1 & 0 & -3 & 0 & -3 & 2 & 0 \\ 0 & 0 & 1 & 1 & -1 & 2 & -1 & 0 \\ 0 & 0 & 0 & 1 & -2 & 0 & 0 & 1 \end{array}\right] \xrightarrow[\substack{3R_4+R_2 \\ -1R_4+R_3}]{2R_4+R_1} \left[\begin{array}{cccc|cccc} 1 & 0 & 0 & 0 & -1 & -7 & 4 & 2 \\ 0 & 1 & 0 & 0 & -6 & -3 & 2 & 3 \\ 0 & 0 & 1 & 0 & 1 & 2 & -1 & -1 \\ 0 & 0 & 0 & 1 & -2 & 0 & 0 & 1 \end{array}\right]$$

The inverse matrix is $\begin{bmatrix} -1 & -7 & 4 & 2 \\ -6 & -3 & 2 & 3 \\ 1 & 2 & -1 & -1 \\ -2 & 0 & 0 & 1 \end{bmatrix}$. [7.3]

46.

$$\begin{bmatrix} 1 & 2 & -2 & 1 & | & 1 & 0 & 0 & 0 \\ 3 & 7 & -3 & 1 & | & 0 & 1 & 0 & 0 \\ 2 & 7 & 4 & 3 & | & 0 & 0 & 1 & 0 \\ 1 & 4 & 2 & 4 & | & 0 & 0 & 0 & 1 \end{bmatrix} \xrightarrow[\substack{-2R_1+R_3 \\ -1R_1+R_4}]{-3R_1+R_2} \begin{bmatrix} 1 & 2 & -2 & 1 & | & 1 & 0 & 0 & 0 \\ 0 & 1 & 3 & -2 & | & -3 & 1 & 0 & 0 \\ 0 & 3 & 8 & 1 & | & -2 & 0 & 1 & 0 \\ 0 & 2 & 4 & 3 & | & -1 & 0 & 0 & 1 \end{bmatrix}$$

$$\xrightarrow[-2R_2+R_4]{-3R_2+R_3} \begin{bmatrix} 1 & 2 & -2 & 1 & | & 1 & 0 & 0 & 0 \\ 0 & 1 & 3 & -2 & | & -3 & 1 & 0 & 0 \\ 0 & 0 & -1 & 7 & | & 7 & -3 & 1 & 0 \\ 0 & 0 & -2 & 7 & | & 5 & -2 & 0 & 1 \end{bmatrix} \xrightarrow{-1R_3} \begin{bmatrix} 1 & 2 & -2 & 1 & | & 1 & 0 & 0 & 0 \\ 0 & 1 & 3 & -2 & | & -3 & 1 & 0 & 0 \\ 0 & 0 & 1 & -7 & | & -7 & 3 & -1 & 0 \\ 0 & 0 & -2 & 7 & | & 5 & -2 & 0 & 1 \end{bmatrix}$$

$$\xrightarrow{2R_3+R_4} \begin{bmatrix} 1 & 2 & -2 & 1 & | & 1 & 0 & 0 & 0 \\ 0 & 1 & 3 & -2 & | & -3 & 1 & 0 & 0 \\ 0 & 0 & 1 & -7 & | & -7 & 3 & -1 & 0 \\ 0 & 0 & 0 & -7 & | & -9 & 4 & -2 & 1 \end{bmatrix} \xrightarrow{-2R_2+R_1} \begin{bmatrix} 1 & 0 & -8 & 5 & | & 7 & -2 & 0 & 0 \\ 0 & 1 & 3 & -2 & | & -3 & 1 & 0 & 0 \\ 0 & 0 & 1 & -7 & | & -7 & 3 & -1 & 0 \\ 0 & 0 & 0 & -7 & | & -9 & 4 & -2 & 1 \end{bmatrix}$$

$$\xrightarrow[-3R_3+R_2]{8R_3+R_1} \begin{bmatrix} 1 & 0 & 0 & -51 & | & -49 & 22 & -8 & 0 \\ 0 & 1 & 0 & 19 & | & 18 & -8 & 3 & 0 \\ 0 & 0 & 1 & -7 & | & -7 & 3 & -1 & 0 \\ 0 & 0 & 0 & -7 & | & -9 & 4 & -2 & 1 \end{bmatrix} \xrightarrow{(-1/7)R_4} \begin{bmatrix} 1 & 0 & 0 & -51 & | & -49 & 22 & -8 & 0 \\ 0 & 1 & 0 & 19 & | & 18 & -8 & 3 & 0 \\ 0 & 0 & 1 & -7 & | & -7 & 3 & -1 & 0 \\ 0 & 0 & 0 & 1 & | & \frac{9}{7} & -\frac{4}{7} & \frac{2}{7} & -\frac{1}{7} \end{bmatrix}$$

$$\xrightarrow[\substack{-19R_4R_2 \\ 51R_4+R_1}]{7R_4+R_3} \begin{bmatrix} 1 & 0 & 0 & 0 & | & \frac{116}{7} & -\frac{50}{7} & \frac{46}{7} & -\frac{51}{7} \\ 0 & 1 & 0 & 0 & | & -\frac{45}{7} & \frac{20}{7} & -\frac{17}{7} & \frac{19}{7} \\ 0 & 0 & 1 & 0 & | & 2 & -1 & 1 & -1 \\ 0 & 0 & 0 & 1 & | & \frac{9}{7} & -\frac{4}{7} & \frac{2}{7} & -\frac{1}{7} \end{bmatrix}$$

The inverse matrix is $\begin{bmatrix} \frac{116}{7} & -\frac{50}{7} & \frac{46}{7} & -\frac{51}{7} \\ -\frac{45}{7} & \frac{20}{7} & -\frac{17}{7} & \frac{19}{7} \\ 2 & -1 & 1 & -1 \\ \frac{9}{7} & -\frac{4}{7} & \frac{2}{7} & -\frac{1}{7} \end{bmatrix}$. [7.3]

47.

$$\begin{bmatrix} 3 & 7 & -1 & 8 & | & 1 & 0 & 0 & 0 \\ 2 & 5 & 0 & 5 & | & 0 & 1 & 0 & 0 \\ 3 & 6 & -4 & 8 & | & 0 & 0 & 1 & 0 \\ 2 & 4 & -4 & 4 & | & 0 & 0 & 0 & 1 \end{bmatrix} \xrightarrow{(1/3)R_1} \begin{bmatrix} 1 & \frac{7}{3} & -\frac{1}{3} & \frac{8}{3} & | & \frac{1}{3} & 0 & 0 & 0 \\ 2 & 5 & 0 & 5 & | & 0 & 1 & 0 & 0 \\ 3 & 6 & -4 & 8 & | & 0 & 0 & 1 & 0 \\ 2 & 4 & -4 & 4 & | & 0 & 0 & 0 & 1 \end{bmatrix} \xrightarrow[\substack{-3R_1+R_3 \\ -2R_1+R_4}]{-2R_1+R_2} \begin{bmatrix} 1 & \frac{7}{3} & -\frac{1}{3} & \frac{8}{3} & | & \frac{1}{3} & 0 & 0 & 0 \\ 0 & \frac{1}{3} & \frac{2}{3} & -\frac{1}{3} & | & -\frac{2}{3} & 1 & 0 & 0 \\ 0 & -1 & -3 & 0 & | & -1 & 0 & 1 & 0 \\ 0 & -\frac{2}{3} & -\frac{10}{3} & -\frac{4}{3} & | & -\frac{2}{3} & 0 & 0 & 1 \end{bmatrix}$$

$$\xrightarrow{3R_2} \begin{bmatrix} 1 & \frac{7}{3} & -\frac{1}{3} & \frac{8}{3} & | & \frac{1}{3} & 0 & 0 & 0 \\ 0 & 1 & 2 & -1 & | & -2 & 3 & 0 & 0 \\ 0 & -1 & -3 & 0 & | & -1 & 0 & 1 & 0 \\ 0 & -\frac{2}{3} & -\frac{10}{3} & -\frac{4}{3} & | & -\frac{2}{3} & 0 & 0 & 1 \end{bmatrix} \xrightarrow[\substack{(2/3)R_2+R_4}]{1R_2+R_3} \begin{bmatrix} 1 & \frac{7}{3} & -\frac{1}{3} & \frac{8}{3} & | & \frac{1}{3} & 0 & 0 & 0 \\ 0 & 1 & 2 & -1 & | & -2 & 3 & 0 & 0 \\ 0 & 0 & -1 & -1 & | & -3 & 3 & 1 & 0 \\ 0 & 0 & -2 & -2 & | & -2 & 2 & 0 & 1 \end{bmatrix}$$

$$\xrightarrow{-1R_3} \begin{bmatrix} 1 & \frac{7}{3} & -\frac{1}{3} & \frac{8}{3} & | & \frac{1}{3} & 0 & 0 & 0 \\ 0 & 1 & 2 & -1 & | & -2 & 3 & 0 & 0 \\ 0 & 0 & 1 & 1 & | & 3 & -3 & -1 & 0 \\ 0 & 0 & -2 & -2 & | & -2 & 2 & 0 & 1 \end{bmatrix} \xrightarrow{2R_3+R_4} \begin{bmatrix} 1 & \frac{7}{3} & -\frac{1}{3} & \frac{8}{3} & | & \frac{1}{3} & 0 & 0 & 0 \\ 0 & 1 & 2 & -1 & | & -2 & 3 & 0 & 0 \\ 0 & 0 & 1 & 1 & | & 3 & -3 & -1 & 0 \\ 0 & 0 & 0 & 0 & | & 4 & -4 & -2 & 1 \end{bmatrix}$$

The matrix does not have an inverse. [7.3]

48.

$$\left[\begin{array}{cccc|cccc} 3 & 1 & 5 & -5 & 1 & 0 & 0 & 0 \\ 2 & 1 & 4 & -3 & 0 & 1 & 0 & 0 \\ 3 & 0 & 4 & -3 & 0 & 0 & 1 & 0 \\ 4 & 1 & 8 & 1 & 0 & 0 & 0 & 1 \end{array}\right] \xrightarrow{(1/3)R_1} \left[\begin{array}{cccc|cccc} 1 & \frac{1}{3} & \frac{5}{3} & -\frac{5}{3} & \frac{1}{3} & 0 & 0 & 0 \\ 2 & 1 & 4 & -3 & 0 & 1 & 0 & 0 \\ 3 & 0 & 4 & -3 & 0 & 0 & 1 & 0 \\ 4 & 1 & 8 & 1 & 0 & 0 & 0 & 1 \end{array}\right]$$

$$\xrightarrow[\substack{-2R_1+R_2 \\ -3R_1+R_3 \\ -4R_1+R_4}]{} \left[\begin{array}{cccc|cccc} 1 & \frac{1}{3} & \frac{5}{3} & -\frac{5}{3} & \frac{1}{3} & 0 & 0 & 0 \\ 0 & \frac{1}{3} & \frac{2}{3} & \frac{1}{3} & -\frac{2}{3} & 1 & 0 & 0 \\ 0 & -1 & -1 & 2 & -1 & 0 & 1 & 0 \\ 0 & -\frac{1}{3} & \frac{4}{3} & \frac{23}{3} & -\frac{4}{3} & 0 & 0 & 1 \end{array}\right]$$

$$\xrightarrow[\substack{3R_2 \\ 1R_2+R_3 \\ (1/3)R_2+R_4}]{} \left[\begin{array}{cccc|cccc} 1 & \frac{1}{3} & \frac{5}{3} & -\frac{5}{3} & \frac{1}{3} & 0 & 0 & 0 \\ 0 & 1 & 2 & 1 & -2 & 3 & 0 & 0 \\ 0 & 0 & 1 & 3 & -3 & 3 & 1 & 0 \\ 0 & 0 & 2 & 8 & -2 & 1 & 0 & 1 \end{array}\right] \xrightarrow{-2R_3+R_4} \left[\begin{array}{cccc|cccc} 1 & \frac{1}{3} & \frac{5}{3} & -\frac{5}{3} & \frac{1}{3} & 0 & 0 & 0 \\ 0 & 1 & 2 & 1 & -2 & 3 & 0 & 0 \\ 0 & 0 & 1 & 3 & -3 & 3 & 1 & 0 \\ 0 & 0 & 0 & 2 & 4 & -5 & -2 & 1 \end{array}\right]$$

$$\xrightarrow{(1/2)R_4} \left[\begin{array}{cccc|cccc} 1 & \frac{1}{3} & \frac{5}{3} & -\frac{5}{3} & \frac{1}{3} & 0 & 0 & 0 \\ 0 & 1 & 2 & 1 & -2 & 3 & 0 & 0 \\ 0 & 0 & 1 & 3 & -3 & 3 & 1 & 0 \\ 0 & 0 & 0 & 1 & 2 & -\frac{5}{2} & -1 & \frac{1}{2} \end{array}\right] \xrightarrow{(-1/3)R_2+R_1} \left[\begin{array}{cccc|cccc} 1 & 0 & 1 & -2 & 1 & -1 & 0 & 0 \\ 0 & 1 & 2 & 1 & -2 & 3 & 0 & 0 \\ 0 & 0 & 1 & 3 & -3 & 3 & 1 & 0 \\ 0 & 0 & 0 & 1 & 2 & -\frac{5}{2} & -1 & \frac{1}{2} \end{array}\right]$$

$$\xrightarrow[\substack{-2R_3+R_2 \\ -1R_3+R_1}]{} \left[\begin{array}{cccc|cccc} 1 & 0 & 0 & -5 & 4 & -4 & -1 & 0 \\ 0 & 1 & 0 & -5 & 4 & -3 & -2 & 0 \\ 0 & 0 & 1 & 3 & -3 & 3 & 1 & 0 \\ 0 & 0 & 0 & 1 & 2 & -\frac{5}{2} & -1 & \frac{1}{2} \end{array}\right] \xrightarrow[\substack{5R_4+R_1 \\ 5R_4+R_2 \\ -3R_4+R_3}]{} \left[\begin{array}{cccc|cccc} 1 & 0 & 0 & 0 & 14 & -\frac{33}{2} & -6 & \frac{5}{2} \\ 0 & 1 & 0 & 0 & 14 & -\frac{31}{2} & -7 & \frac{5}{2} \\ 0 & 0 & 1 & 0 & -9 & \frac{21}{2} & 4 & -\frac{3}{2} \\ 0 & 0 & 0 & 1 & 2 & -\frac{5}{2} & -1 & \frac{1}{2} \end{array}\right]$$

The inverse matrix is $\begin{bmatrix} 14 & -\frac{33}{2} & -6 & \frac{5}{2} \\ 14 & -\frac{31}{2} & -7 & \frac{5}{2} \\ -9 & \frac{21}{2} & 4 & -\frac{3}{2} \\ 2 & -\frac{5}{2} & -1 & \frac{1}{2} \end{bmatrix}$. [7.3]

49. a.

$$\begin{bmatrix} 3 & 4 \\ 2 & 3 \end{bmatrix}\begin{bmatrix} x \\ y \end{bmatrix} = \begin{bmatrix} 2 \\ -3 \end{bmatrix}$$

$$\begin{bmatrix} 3 & -4 \\ -2 & 3 \end{bmatrix}\begin{bmatrix} 3 & 4 \\ 2 & 3 \end{bmatrix}\begin{bmatrix} x \\ y \end{bmatrix} = \begin{bmatrix} 3 & -4 \\ -2 & 3 \end{bmatrix}\begin{bmatrix} 2 \\ -3 \end{bmatrix}$$

$$\begin{bmatrix} x \\ y \end{bmatrix} = \begin{bmatrix} 18 \\ -13 \end{bmatrix}$$

The solution is $(18, -13)$.

b.

$$\begin{bmatrix} 3 & 4 \\ 2 & 3 \end{bmatrix}\begin{bmatrix} x \\ y \end{bmatrix} = \begin{bmatrix} -2 \\ 4 \end{bmatrix}$$

$$\begin{bmatrix} 3 & -4 \\ -2 & 3 \end{bmatrix}\begin{bmatrix} 3 & 4 \\ 2 & 3 \end{bmatrix}\begin{bmatrix} x \\ y \end{bmatrix} = \begin{bmatrix} 3 & -4 \\ -2 & 3 \end{bmatrix}\begin{bmatrix} -2 \\ 4 \end{bmatrix}$$

$$\begin{bmatrix} x \\ y \end{bmatrix} = \begin{bmatrix} -22 \\ 16 \end{bmatrix}$$

The solution is $(-22, 16)$. [7.3]

50. a.

$$\begin{bmatrix} 2 & -5 \\ 3 & -7 \end{bmatrix}\begin{bmatrix} x \\ y \end{bmatrix} = \begin{bmatrix} -3 \\ 4 \end{bmatrix}$$

$$\begin{bmatrix} -7 & 5 \\ -3 & 2 \end{bmatrix}\begin{bmatrix} 2 & -5 \\ 3 & -7 \end{bmatrix}\begin{bmatrix} x \\ y \end{bmatrix} = \begin{bmatrix} -7 & 5 \\ -3 & 2 \end{bmatrix}\begin{bmatrix} -3 \\ 4 \end{bmatrix}$$

$$\begin{bmatrix} x \\ y \end{bmatrix} = \begin{bmatrix} 41 \\ 17 \end{bmatrix}$$

The solution is $(41, 17)$.

b.

$$\begin{bmatrix} 2 & -5 \\ 3 & -7 \end{bmatrix}\begin{bmatrix} x \\ y \end{bmatrix} = \begin{bmatrix} 2 \\ -5 \end{bmatrix}$$

$$\begin{bmatrix} -7 & 5 \\ -3 & 2 \end{bmatrix}\begin{bmatrix} 2 & -5 \\ 3 & -7 \end{bmatrix}\begin{bmatrix} x \\ y \end{bmatrix} = \begin{bmatrix} -7 & 5 \\ -3 & 2 \end{bmatrix}\begin{bmatrix} 2 \\ -5 \end{bmatrix}$$

$$\begin{bmatrix} x \\ y \end{bmatrix} = \begin{bmatrix} -39 \\ -16 \end{bmatrix}$$

The solution is $(-39, -16)$. [7.3]

51. **a.**
$$\begin{bmatrix} 2 & -5 \\ 3 & -7 \end{bmatrix} \begin{bmatrix} x \\ y \end{bmatrix} = \begin{bmatrix} -3 \\ 4 \end{bmatrix}$$

$$\begin{bmatrix} 1 & -\frac{1}{14} & -\frac{5}{14} \\ -1 & \frac{2}{7} & \frac{3}{7} \\ 0 & \frac{1}{7} & -\frac{2}{7} \end{bmatrix} \begin{bmatrix} 2 & 1 & -1 \\ 4 & 4 & 1 \\ 2 & 2 & -3 \end{bmatrix} \begin{bmatrix} x \\ y \\ z \end{bmatrix} = \begin{bmatrix} 1 & -\frac{1}{14} & -\frac{5}{14} \\ -1 & \frac{2}{7} & \frac{3}{7} \\ 0 & \frac{1}{7} & -\frac{2}{7} \end{bmatrix} \begin{bmatrix} -1 \\ 2 \\ 4 \end{bmatrix}$$

$$\begin{bmatrix} x \\ y \\ z \end{bmatrix} = \begin{bmatrix} -\frac{18}{7} \\ \frac{23}{7} \\ -\frac{6}{7} \end{bmatrix}$$

The solution is $\left(-\dfrac{18}{7}, \dfrac{23}{7}, -\dfrac{6}{7}\right)$.

b.
$$\begin{bmatrix} 2 & 1 & -1 \\ 4 & 4 & 1 \\ 2 & 2 & -3 \end{bmatrix} \begin{bmatrix} x \\ y \\ z \end{bmatrix} = \begin{bmatrix} -2 \\ 3 \\ 0 \end{bmatrix}$$

$$\begin{bmatrix} 1 & -\frac{1}{14} & -\frac{5}{14} \\ -1 & \frac{2}{7} & \frac{3}{7} \\ 0 & \frac{1}{7} & -\frac{2}{7} \end{bmatrix} \begin{bmatrix} 2 & 1 & -1 \\ 4 & 4 & 1 \\ 2 & 2 & -3 \end{bmatrix} \begin{bmatrix} x \\ y \\ z \end{bmatrix} = \begin{bmatrix} 1 & -\frac{1}{14} & -\frac{5}{14} \\ -1 & \frac{2}{7} & \frac{3}{7} \\ 0 & \frac{1}{7} & -\frac{2}{7} \end{bmatrix} \begin{bmatrix} -2 \\ 3 \\ 0 \end{bmatrix}$$

$$\begin{bmatrix} x \\ y \\ z \end{bmatrix} = \begin{bmatrix} -\frac{31}{14} \\ \frac{20}{7} \\ \frac{3}{7} \end{bmatrix}$$

The solution is $\left(-\dfrac{31}{14}, \dfrac{20}{7}, \dfrac{3}{7}\right)$. [7.3]

52. **a.**
$$\begin{bmatrix} 3 & -2 & 1 \\ 3 & -1 & 3 \\ 6 & -4 & 1 \end{bmatrix} \begin{bmatrix} x \\ y \\ z \end{bmatrix} = \begin{bmatrix} 0 \\ 3 \\ -2 \end{bmatrix}$$

$$\begin{bmatrix} -\frac{11}{3} & \frac{2}{3} & \frac{5}{3} \\ -5 & 1 & 2 \\ 2 & 0 & -1 \end{bmatrix} \begin{bmatrix} 3 & -2 & 1 \\ 3 & -1 & 3 \\ 6 & -4 & 1 \end{bmatrix} \begin{bmatrix} x \\ y \\ z \end{bmatrix} = \begin{bmatrix} -\frac{11}{3} & \frac{2}{3} & \frac{5}{3} \\ -5 & 1 & 2 \\ 2 & 0 & -1 \end{bmatrix} \begin{bmatrix} 0 \\ 3 \\ -2 \end{bmatrix}$$

$$\begin{bmatrix} x \\ y \\ z \end{bmatrix} = \begin{bmatrix} -\frac{4}{3} \\ -1 \\ 2 \end{bmatrix}$$

The solution is $\left(-\dfrac{4}{3}, -1, 2\right)$.

b.
$$\begin{bmatrix} 3 & -2 & 1 \\ 3 & -1 & 3 \\ 6 & -4 & 1 \end{bmatrix} \begin{bmatrix} x \\ y \\ z \end{bmatrix} = \begin{bmatrix} 1 \\ 2 \\ -4 \end{bmatrix}$$

$$\begin{bmatrix} -\frac{1}{13} & \frac{2}{3} & \frac{5}{3} \\ -5 & 1 & 2 \\ 2 & 0 & -1 \end{bmatrix} \begin{bmatrix} 3 & -2 & 1 \\ 3 & -1 & 3 \\ 6 & -4 & 1 \end{bmatrix} \begin{bmatrix} x \\ y \\ z \end{bmatrix} = \begin{bmatrix} -\frac{1}{13} & \frac{2}{3} & \frac{5}{3} \\ -5 & 1 & 2 \\ 2 & 0 & -1 \end{bmatrix} \begin{bmatrix} 1 \\ 2 \\ -4 \end{bmatrix}$$

$$\begin{bmatrix} x \\ y \\ z \end{bmatrix} = \begin{bmatrix} -9 \\ -11 \\ 6 \end{bmatrix}$$

The solution is $(-9, -11, 6)$. [7.3]

53.

$$\begin{vmatrix} 2 & 6 & 4 \\ 1 & 2 & 1 \\ 3 & 8 & 6 \end{vmatrix} \xrightarrow{\text{Factor 2 from row 1}} 2\begin{vmatrix} 1 & 3 & 2 \\ 1 & 2 & 1 \\ 3 & 8 & 6 \end{vmatrix}$$

$$\xrightarrow[\begin{array}{c} -3R_1+R_3 \end{array}]{-1R_1+R_2} 2\begin{vmatrix} 1 & 3 & 2 \\ 0 & -1 & -1 \\ 0 & -1 & 0 \end{vmatrix}$$

$$\xrightarrow{-R_2+R_3} 2\begin{vmatrix} 1 & 3 & 2 \\ 0 & -1 & -1 \\ 0 & 0 & 1 \end{vmatrix}$$

$$=2(1)(-1)(1)=-2 \quad [7.4]$$

54.

$$\begin{vmatrix} 3 & 0 & 10 \\ 3 & -2 & 7 \\ 2 & -1 & 5 \end{vmatrix} \xrightarrow{(-10/3)C_1+C_3} \begin{vmatrix} 3 & 0 & 0 \\ 3 & -2 & -3 \\ 2 & -1 & -\frac{5}{3} \end{vmatrix}$$

$$\xrightarrow{(-3/2)C_2+C_3} \begin{vmatrix} 3 & 0 & 0 \\ 3 & -2 & 0 \\ 2 & -1 & -\frac{1}{6} \end{vmatrix}$$

$$=3(-2)\left(-\frac{1}{6}\right)=1 \quad [7.4]$$

55.

$$\begin{vmatrix} 3 & -8 & 7 \\ 2 & -3 & 6 \\ 1 & -3 & 2 \end{vmatrix} \xrightarrow[\begin{array}{c}(-1/3)R_1+R_3\end{array}]{(-2/3)R_1+R_2} \begin{vmatrix} 3 & -8 & 7 \\ 0 & \frac{7}{3} & \frac{4}{3} \\ 0 & -\frac{1}{3} & -\frac{1}{3} \end{vmatrix}$$

$$\xrightarrow{(1/7)R_2+R_3} \begin{vmatrix} 3 & -8 & 7 \\ 0 & \frac{7}{3} & \frac{4}{3} \\ 0 & 0 & -\frac{1}{7} \end{vmatrix}$$

$$=3\frac{7}{3}\left(-\frac{1}{7}\right)=-1 \quad [7.4]$$

56.

$$\begin{vmatrix} 4 & 9 & -11 \\ 2 & 6 & -3 \\ 3 & 7 & -8 \end{vmatrix} \xrightarrow[\begin{array}{c}(-3/4)R_1+R_3\end{array}]{(-1/2)R_1+R_2} \begin{vmatrix} 4 & 9 & -11 \\ 0 & \frac{3}{2} & \frac{5}{2} \\ 0 & \frac{1}{4} & \frac{1}{4} \end{vmatrix}$$

$$\xrightarrow{(-1/6)R_2+R_3} \begin{vmatrix} 4 & 9 & -11 \\ 0 & \frac{3}{2} & \frac{5}{2} \\ 0 & 0 & -\frac{1}{6} \end{vmatrix}$$

$$=4\left(\frac{3}{2}\right)\left(-\frac{1}{6}\right)=-1 \quad [7.4]$$

57.

$$\begin{vmatrix} 1 & -1 & 2 & 1 \\ 2 & -1 & 6 & 3 \\ 3 & -1 & 8 & 7 \\ 3 & 0 & 9 & 9 \end{vmatrix} \xrightarrow{\text{Factor 3 from row 4}} 3\begin{vmatrix} 1 & -1 & 2 & 1 \\ 2 & -1 & 6 & 3 \\ 3 & -1 & 8 & 7 \\ 1 & 0 & 3 & 3 \end{vmatrix}$$

$$\xrightarrow[\begin{array}{c} -3R_1+R_3 \\ -1R_1+R_4 \end{array}]{-R_1+R_2} 3\begin{vmatrix} 1 & -1 & 2 & 1 \\ 0 & 1 & 2 & 1 \\ 0 & 2 & 2 & 4 \\ 0 & 1 & 1 & 2 \end{vmatrix}$$

$$\xrightarrow[\begin{array}{c} -1R_2+R_4 \end{array}]{-2R_2+R_3} 3\begin{vmatrix} 1 & -1 & 2 & 1 \\ 0 & 1 & 2 & 1 \\ 0 & 0 & -2 & 2 \\ 0 & 0 & -1 & 1 \end{vmatrix}$$

$$\xrightarrow[\begin{array}{c} R_3+R_4 \end{array}]{\text{Factor } -2 \text{ from row 3}} -6\begin{vmatrix} 1 & -1 & 2 & 1 \\ 0 & 1 & 2 & 1 \\ 0 & 0 & 1 & -1 \\ 0 & 0 & 0 & 0 \end{vmatrix}$$

$$=-6(1)(1)(1)(0)=0 \quad [7.4]$$

58.

$$\begin{vmatrix} 1 & 2 & -2 & 3 \\ 3 & 7 & -3 & 11 \\ 2 & 3 & -5 & 11 \\ 2 & 6 & 1 & 8 \end{vmatrix} \xrightarrow[\substack{-3R_1+R_2 \\ -2R_1+R_3 \\ -2R_1+R_4}]{} \begin{vmatrix} 1 & 2 & -2 & 3 \\ 0 & 1 & 3 & 2 \\ 0 & -1 & -1 & 5 \\ 0 & 2 & 5 & 2 \end{vmatrix}$$

$$\xrightarrow[\substack{R_2+R_3 \\ -2R_2+R_4}]{} \begin{vmatrix} 1 & 2 & -2 & 3 \\ 0 & 1 & 3 & 2 \\ 0 & 0 & 2 & 7 \\ 0 & 0 & -1 & -2 \end{vmatrix}$$

$$\xrightarrow[\;(1/2)R_3+R_4\;]{} \begin{vmatrix} 1 & 2 & -2 & 3 \\ 0 & 1 & 3 & 2 \\ 0 & 0 & 2 & 7 \\ 0 & 0 & 0 & \frac{3}{2} \end{vmatrix}$$

$$=1(1)(2)\left(\frac{3}{2}\right)=3 \quad [7.4]$$

59.

$$\begin{vmatrix} 1 & 2 & -2 & 1 \\ 2 & 5 & -3 & 1 \\ 2 & 0 & -10 & 1 \\ 3 & 8 & -4 & 1 \end{vmatrix} \xrightarrow[\substack{-R_4+R_1 \\ -R_4+R_2 \\ -R_4+R_3}]{} \begin{vmatrix} -2 & -6 & 2 & 0 \\ -1 & -3 & 1 & 0 \\ -1 & -8 & -6 & 0 \\ 3 & 8 & -4 & 1 \end{vmatrix}$$

$$\xrightarrow[\substack{(1/6)R_3+R_2 \\ (1/3)R_3+R_1}]{} \begin{vmatrix} -\frac{7}{3} & -\frac{26}{3} & 0 & 0 \\ -\frac{7}{6} & -\frac{13}{3} & 0 & 0 \\ -1 & -8 & -6 & 0 \\ 3 & 8 & -4 & 1 \end{vmatrix}$$

$$\xrightarrow[\;-2R_2+R_1\;]{} \begin{vmatrix} 0 & 0 & 0 & 0 \\ -\frac{7}{6} & -\frac{13}{3} & 0 & 0 \\ -1 & -8 & -6 & 0 \\ 3 & 8 & -4 & 1 \end{vmatrix}$$

$$=0\left(-\frac{13}{3}\right)(-6)(-1)=0 \quad [7.4]$$

60.

$$\begin{vmatrix} 1 & 3 & -2 & 0 \\ 3 & 11 & -4 & 4 \\ 2 & 9 & -8 & 2 \\ 3 & 12 & -10 & 2 \end{vmatrix} \xrightarrow[\substack{\text{Factor } -2 \text{ from column 3} \\ \text{Factor } 2 \text{ from column 4}}]{} -4\begin{vmatrix} 1 & 3 & 1 & 0 \\ 3 & 11 & 2 & 2 \\ 2 & 9 & 4 & 1 \\ 3 & 12 & 5 & 1 \end{vmatrix}$$

$$\xrightarrow[\substack{-2R_4+R_2 \\ -1R_4+R_3}]{} -4\begin{vmatrix} 1 & 3 & 1 & 0 \\ -3 & -13 & -8 & 0 \\ -1 & -3 & -1 & 0 \\ 3 & 12 & 5 & 1 \end{vmatrix}$$

$$\xrightarrow[\substack{R_3+R_1 \\ -8R_3+R_2}]{} -4\begin{vmatrix} 0 & 0 & 0 & 0 \\ 5 & 11 & 0 & 0 \\ -1 & -3 & -1 & 0 \\ 3 & 12 & 5 & 1 \end{vmatrix}$$

$$=-4(0)(11)(-1)(1)=0 \quad [7.4]$$

61.

$$x_1 = \frac{\begin{vmatrix} 2 & -3 \\ 2 & 5 \end{vmatrix}}{\begin{vmatrix} 2 & -3 \\ 3 & 5 \end{vmatrix}} = \frac{16}{19}$$

$$x_2 = \frac{\begin{vmatrix} 2 & 2 \\ 3 & 2 \end{vmatrix}}{\begin{vmatrix} 2 & -3 \\ 3 & 5 \end{vmatrix}} = \frac{-2}{19} = -\frac{2}{19} \quad [7.5]$$

62.

$$x_1 = \frac{\begin{vmatrix} -3 & 4 \\ 2 & -2 \end{vmatrix}}{\begin{vmatrix} 3 & 4 \\ 5 & -2 \end{vmatrix}} = \frac{-2}{-26} = \frac{1}{13}$$

$$x_2 = \frac{\begin{vmatrix} 3 & -3 \\ 5 & 2 \end{vmatrix}}{\begin{vmatrix} 3 & 4 \\ 5 & -2 \end{vmatrix}} = \frac{21}{-26} = -\frac{21}{26} \quad [7.5]$$

63.

$$D = \begin{vmatrix} 2 & 1 & -3 \\ 3 & 2 & 1 \\ 1 & -3 & 4 \end{vmatrix} = 44 \quad [7.5]$$

$$D_1 = \begin{vmatrix} 2 & 1 & -3 \\ 1 & 2 & 1 \\ -2 & -3 & 4 \end{vmatrix} = 13$$

$$D_2 = \begin{vmatrix} 2 & 2 & -3 \\ 3 & 1 & 1 \\ 1 & -2 & 4 \end{vmatrix} = 13$$

$$D_3 = \begin{vmatrix} 2 & 1 & 2 \\ 3 & 2 & 1 \\ 1 & -3 & 4 \end{vmatrix} = -17$$

$$x_1 = \frac{D_1}{D} = \frac{13}{44}$$

$$x_2 = \frac{D_2}{D} = \frac{11}{44} = \frac{1}{4}$$

$$x_3 = \frac{D_3}{D} = \frac{-17}{44} = -\frac{17}{44}$$

64.

$$D = \begin{vmatrix} 3 & 2 & -1 \\ 1 & 3 & -2 \\ 4 & -1 & -5 \end{vmatrix} = -44 \quad [7.5]$$

$$D_1 = \begin{vmatrix} 0 & 2 & -1 \\ 3 & 3 & -2 \\ -1 & -1 & -5 \end{vmatrix} = 34$$

$$D_2 = \begin{vmatrix} 3 & 0 & -1 \\ 1 & 3 & -2 \\ 4 & -1 & -5 \end{vmatrix} = -38$$

$$D_3 = \begin{vmatrix} 3 & 2 & 0 \\ 1 & 3 & 3 \\ 4 & -1 & -1 \end{vmatrix} = 26$$

$$x_1 = \frac{D_1}{D} = \frac{34}{-44} = -\frac{17}{22}$$

$$x_2 = \frac{D_2}{D} = \frac{-38}{-44} = \frac{19}{22}$$

$$x_3 = \frac{D_3}{D} = \frac{26}{-44} = -\frac{13}{22}$$

65.

$$D = \begin{vmatrix} 0 & 2 & 5 \\ 2 & -5 & 1 \\ 4 & 3 & 0 \end{vmatrix} = 138 \quad [7.5]$$

$$D_1 = \begin{vmatrix} 2 & 2 & 5 \\ 4 & -5 & 1 \\ 2 & 3 & 0 \end{vmatrix} = 108$$

$$D_2 = \begin{vmatrix} 0 & 2 & 5 \\ 2 & 4 & 1 \\ 4 & 2 & 0 \end{vmatrix} = -52$$

$$D_3 = \begin{vmatrix} 0 & 2 & 2 \\ 2 & -5 & 4 \\ 4 & 3 & 2 \end{vmatrix} = 76$$

$$x_1 = \frac{D_1}{D} = \frac{108}{138} = \frac{54}{69} = \frac{18}{23}$$

$$x_2 = \frac{D_2}{D} = \frac{-52}{138} = -\frac{26}{69}$$

$$x_3 = \frac{D_3}{D} = \frac{76}{138} = \frac{38}{69}$$

66.

$$D = \begin{vmatrix} 2 & -3 & -4 \\ 1 & -2 & 2 \\ 2 & 7 & -1 \end{vmatrix} = -83 \quad [7.5]$$

$$D_1 = \begin{vmatrix} 2 & -3 & -4 \\ -1 & -2 & 2 \\ 2 & 7 & -1 \end{vmatrix} = -21$$

$$D_2 = \begin{vmatrix} 2 & 2 & -4 \\ 1 & -1 & 2 \\ 2 & 2 & -1 \end{vmatrix} = -12$$

$$D_3 = \begin{vmatrix} 2 & -3 & 2 \\ 1 & -2 & -1 \\ 2 & 7 & 2 \end{vmatrix} = 40$$

$$x_1 = \frac{D_1}{D} = \frac{-21}{-83} = \frac{21}{83}$$

$$x_2 = \frac{D_2}{D} = \frac{-12}{-83} = \frac{12}{83}$$

$$x_3 = \frac{D_3}{D} = \frac{40}{-83} = -\frac{40}{83}$$

67.

$$D = \begin{vmatrix} 1 & -3 & 1 & 2 \\ 2 & 7 & -3 & 1 \\ -1 & 4 & 2 & -3 \\ 3 & 1 & -1 & -2 \end{vmatrix} = -252 \quad [7.5]$$

$$D_3 = \begin{vmatrix} 1 & -3 & 3 & 2 \\ 2 & 7 & 2 & 1 \\ -1 & 4 & -1 & -3 \\ 3 & 1 & 0 & -2 \end{vmatrix} = -230$$

$$x_3 = \frac{D_3}{D} = \frac{-230}{-252} = \frac{115}{126}$$

68.

$$D = \begin{vmatrix} 2 & 3 & -2 & 1 \\ 1 & -1 & -3 & 2 \\ 3 & 3 & -4 & -1 \\ 5 & -5 & -1 & 2 \end{vmatrix} = -230 \quad [7.5]$$

$$D_2 = \begin{vmatrix} 2 & -2 & -2 & 1 \\ 1 & 2 & -3 & 2 \\ 3 & 4 & -4 & -1 \\ 5 & 7 & -1 & 2 \end{vmatrix} = 289$$

$$x_2 = \frac{D_2}{D} = \frac{289}{-230} = -\frac{289}{230}$$

69. The input-output matrix A is given by

$$A = \begin{bmatrix} 0.05 & 0.06 & 0.08 \\ 0.02 & 0.04 & 0.04 \\ 0.03 & 0.03 & 0.05 \end{bmatrix}$$

Consumer demand X is given by $X = (I - A)^{-1} D$.

$$X = \left(\begin{bmatrix} 1 & 0 & 0 \\ 0 & 1 & 0 \\ 0 & 0 & 1 \end{bmatrix} - \begin{bmatrix} 0.05 & 0.06 & 0.08 \\ 0.02 & 0.04 & 0.04 \\ 0.03 & 0.03 & 0.05 \end{bmatrix} \right)^{-1} \begin{bmatrix} 30 \\ 12 \\ 21 \end{bmatrix}$$

$$= \begin{bmatrix} 0.95 & -0.06 & -0.08 \\ -0.02 & 0.96 & -0.04 \\ -0.03 & -0.03 & 0.95 \end{bmatrix}^{-1} \begin{bmatrix} 30 \\ 12 \\ 21 \end{bmatrix}$$

$$\approx \begin{bmatrix} 34.47 \\ 14.20 \\ 23.64 \end{bmatrix}$$

$34.47 million computer division, $14.20 million monitor division, $23.64 million disk drive division. [7.3]

70. The input-output matrix A is given by

$$A = \begin{bmatrix} 0.07 & 0.04 & 0.07 \\ 0.03 & 0.07 & 0.04 \\ 0.03 & 0.03 & 0.02 \end{bmatrix}$$

The consumer demand X is given by $X = (I - A)^{-1} D$.

$$X = \left(\begin{bmatrix} 1 & 0 & 0 \\ 0 & 1 & 0 \\ 0 & 0 & 1 \end{bmatrix} - \begin{bmatrix} 0.07 & 0.04 & 0.07 \\ 0.03 & 0.07 & 0.04 \\ 0.03 & 0.03 & 0.02 \end{bmatrix} \right)^{-1} \begin{bmatrix} 27 \\ 18 \\ 10 \end{bmatrix}$$

$$= \begin{bmatrix} 0.93 & -0.04 & -0.07 \\ -0.03 & 0.93 & -0.04 \\ -0.03 & -0.03 & 0.98 \end{bmatrix}^{-1} \begin{bmatrix} 27 \\ 18 \\ 10 \end{bmatrix}$$

$$= \begin{bmatrix} 30.82 \\ 20.86 \\ 11.79 \end{bmatrix}$$

$30.82 million lumber division, $20.86 million paper division, $11.79 million prefabricated wall division. [7.3]

•••

Chapter Test

1. $\begin{bmatrix} 2 & 3 & -3 & | & 4 \\ 3 & 0 & 2 & | & -1 \\ 4 & -4 & 2 & | & 3 \end{bmatrix}, \begin{bmatrix} 2 & 3 & -3 \\ 3 & 0 & 2 \\ 4 & -4 & 2 \end{bmatrix}, \begin{bmatrix} 4 \\ -1 \\ 3 \end{bmatrix}$ [7.1]

2. $\begin{cases} 3x - 2y + 5z - w = 9 \\ 2x + 3y - z + 4w = 8 \\ x + 3z + 2w = -1 \end{cases}$ [7.1]

3. $\begin{bmatrix} 1 & -2 & 3 & | & 10 \\ 2 & -3 & 8 & | & 23 \\ -1 & 3 & -2 & | & -9 \end{bmatrix} \xrightarrow[R_1 + R_3]{-2R_1 + R_2} \begin{bmatrix} 1 & -2 & 3 & | & 10 \\ 0 & 1 & 2 & | & 3 \\ 0 & 1 & 1 & | & 1 \end{bmatrix} \xrightarrow{-2R_2 + R_3} \begin{bmatrix} 1 & -2 & 3 & | & 10 \\ 0 & 1 & 2 & | & 3 \\ 0 & 0 & -1 & | & -2 \end{bmatrix} \xrightarrow{-R_3} \begin{bmatrix} 1 & -2 & 3 & | & 10 \\ 0 & 1 & 2 & | & 3 \\ 0 & 0 & 1 & | & 2 \end{bmatrix}$

$\begin{cases} x - 2y + 3z = 10 \\ y + 2z = 3 \\ z = 2 \end{cases}$ $\begin{aligned} y + 2(2) &= 3 \\ y &= -1 \end{aligned}$ $\begin{aligned} x - 2(-1) + 3(2) &= 10 \\ x &= 2 \end{aligned}$

The solution is $(2, -1, 2)$. [7.1]

4. $\begin{bmatrix} 2 & 6 & -1 & | & 1 \\ 1 & 3 & -1 & | & 1 \\ 3 & 10 & -2 & | & 1 \end{bmatrix} R_1 \leftrightarrow R_2 \begin{bmatrix} 1 & 3 & -1 & | & 1 \\ 2 & 6 & -1 & | & 1 \\ 3 & 10 & -2 & | & 1 \end{bmatrix} \xrightarrow[-3R_1 + R_3]{-2R_1 + R_2} \begin{bmatrix} 1 & 3 & -1 & | & 1 \\ 0 & 0 & 1 & | & -1 \\ 0 & 1 & 1 & | & -2 \end{bmatrix} R_2 \leftrightarrow R_3 \begin{bmatrix} 1 & 3 & -1 & | & 1 \\ 0 & 1 & 1 & | & -2 \\ 0 & 0 & 1 & | & -1 \end{bmatrix}$

$\begin{cases} x + 3y - z = 1 \\ y + z = -2 \\ z = -1 \end{cases}$ $\begin{aligned} y + (-1) &= -2 \\ y &= -1 \end{aligned}$ $\begin{aligned} x + 3(-1) - (-1) &= 1 \\ x &= 3 \end{aligned}$

The solution is $(3, -1, -1)$. [7.1]

5. $\begin{bmatrix} 1 & 2 & -3 & 2 & | & 11 \\ 2 & 5 & -8 & 5 & | & 28 \\ -2 & -4 & 7 & -1 & | & -18 \end{bmatrix} \xrightarrow[2R_1 + R_3]{-2R_1 + R_2} \begin{bmatrix} 1 & 2 & -3 & 2 & | & 11 \\ 0 & 1 & -2 & 1 & | & 6 \\ 0 & 0 & 1 & 3 & | & 4 \end{bmatrix}$

$\begin{cases} w + 2x - 3y + 2z = 11 \\ x - 2y + z = 6 \\ y + 3z = 4 \end{cases}$ $y = 4 - 3z$ $\begin{aligned} x - 2(4 - 3z) + z &= 6 \\ x &= -7z + 14 \end{aligned}$ $\begin{aligned} w + 2(-7z + 14) - 3(4 - 3z) + 2z &= 11 \\ w &= 3z - 5 \end{aligned}$

Let z be any real number c.

The solution is $(3c - 5, \ -7c + 14, \ 4 - 3c, \ c)$ [7.1]

6.

$$-3A = -3\begin{bmatrix} -1 & 3 & 2 \\ 1 & 4 & -1 \end{bmatrix} = \begin{bmatrix} 3 & -9 & -6 \\ -3 & -12 & 3 \end{bmatrix}$$ [7.2]

7.

$$A + B = \begin{bmatrix} -1 & 3 & 2 \\ 1 & 4 & -1 \end{bmatrix} + \begin{bmatrix} 2 & -1 & 3 \\ 4 & -2 & -1 \\ 3 & 2 & 2 \end{bmatrix}$$

$A + B$ is not defined because the matrices do not have the same order. [7.2]

8.

$$3B - 2C = 3\begin{bmatrix} 2 & -1 & 3 \\ 4 & -2 & -1 \\ 3 & 2 & 2 \end{bmatrix} - 2\begin{bmatrix} 1 & -2 & 3 \\ 2 & -3 & 8 \\ -1 & 3 & -2 \end{bmatrix} = \begin{bmatrix} 6 & -3 & 9 \\ 12 & -6 & -3 \\ 9 & 6 & 6 \end{bmatrix} - \begin{bmatrix} 2 & -4 & 6 \\ 4 & -6 & 16 \\ -2 & 6 & -4 \end{bmatrix} = \begin{bmatrix} 4 & 1 & 3 \\ 8 & 0 & -19 \\ 11 & 0 & 10 \end{bmatrix}$$ [7.2]

9.

$$AB = \begin{bmatrix} -1 & 3 & 2 \\ 1 & 4 & -1 \end{bmatrix}\begin{bmatrix} 2 & -1 & 3 \\ 4 & -2 & -1 \\ 3 & 2 & 2 \end{bmatrix} = \begin{bmatrix} (-1)(2)+3(4)+2(3) & (-1)(-1)+3(-2)+2(2) & (-1)3+3(-1)+2(2) \\ 1(2)+4(4)+(-1)(3) & 1(-1)+4(-2)+(-1)(2) & 1(3)+4(-1)+(-1)(2) \end{bmatrix} = \begin{bmatrix} 16 & -1 & -2 \\ 15 & -11 & -3 \end{bmatrix}$$ [7.2]

10.

Use AB from Problem 9. $AB - A = \begin{bmatrix} 16 & -1 & -2 \\ 15 & -11 & -3 \end{bmatrix} - \begin{bmatrix} -1 & 3 & 2 \\ 1 & 4 & -1 \end{bmatrix} = \begin{bmatrix} 17 & -4 & -4 \\ 14 & -15 & -2 \end{bmatrix}$ [7.2]

11.

$$CA = \begin{bmatrix} 1 & -2 & 3 \\ 2 & -3 & 8 \\ -1 & 3 & -2 \end{bmatrix}\begin{bmatrix} -1 & 3 & 2 \\ 1 & 4 & -1 \end{bmatrix}$$ [7.2]

The number of columns of the first matrix is not equal to the number of rows of the second matrix. The product is not possible.

12.

$$BC - CB = \begin{bmatrix} 2 & -1 & 3 \\ 4 & -2 & -1 \\ 3 & 2 & 2 \end{bmatrix}\begin{bmatrix} 1 & -2 & 3 \\ 2 & -3 & 8 \\ -1 & 3 & -2 \end{bmatrix} - \begin{bmatrix} 1 & -2 & 3 \\ 2 & -3 & 8 \\ -1 & 3 & -2 \end{bmatrix}\begin{bmatrix} 2 & -1 & 3 \\ 4 & -2 & -1 \\ 3 & 2 & 2 \end{bmatrix}$$

$$= \begin{bmatrix} -3 & 8 & -8 \\ 1 & -5 & -2 \\ 5 & -6 & 21 \end{bmatrix} - \begin{bmatrix} 3 & 9 & 11 \\ 16 & 20 & 25 \\ 4 & -9 & -10 \end{bmatrix}$$

$$= \begin{bmatrix} -6 & -1 & -19 \\ -15 & -25 & -27 \\ 1 & 3 & 31 \end{bmatrix}$$ [7.2]

13.

$$A^2 = \begin{bmatrix} -1 & 3 & 2 \\ 1 & 4 & -1 \end{bmatrix}\begin{bmatrix} -1 & 3 & 2 \\ 1 & 4 & -1 \end{bmatrix}$$

The number of columns of the first matrix is not equal to the number of rows of the second matrix. The product is not possible. [7.2]

14.

$$B^2 = \begin{bmatrix} 2 & -1 & 3 \\ 4 & -2 & -1 \\ 3 & 2 & 2 \end{bmatrix}\begin{bmatrix} 2 & -1 & 3 \\ 4 & -2 & -1 \\ 3 & 2 & 2 \end{bmatrix} = \begin{bmatrix} 9 & 6 & 13 \\ -3 & -2 & 12 \\ 20 & -3 & 11 \end{bmatrix}$$ [7.2]

15.

$$\begin{bmatrix} 1 & -2 & 3 & | & 1 & 0 & 0 \\ 2 & -3 & 8 & | & 0 & 1 & 0 \\ -1 & 3 & -2 & | & 0 & 0 & 1 \end{bmatrix} \xrightarrow[R_1+R_3]{-2R_1+R_2} \begin{bmatrix} 1 & -2 & 3 & | & 1 & 0 & 0 \\ 0 & 1 & 2 & | & -2 & 1 & 0 \\ 0 & 1 & 1 & | & 1 & 0 & 1 \end{bmatrix} \xrightarrow{-2R_2+R_3} \begin{bmatrix} 1 & -2 & 3 & | & 1 & 0 & 0 \\ 0 & 1 & 2 & | & -2 & 1 & 0 \\ 0 & 0 & -1 & | & 3 & -1 & 1 \end{bmatrix}$$

$$\xrightarrow{2R_2+R_1} \begin{bmatrix} 1 & 0 & 7 & | & -3 & 2 & 0 \\ 0 & 1 & 2 & | & -2 & 1 & 0 \\ 0 & 0 & -1 & | & 3 & -1 & 1 \end{bmatrix} \xrightarrow[\substack{2R_3+R_2 \\ -R_3}]{7R_3+R_1} \begin{bmatrix} 1 & 0 & 0 & | & 18 & -5 & 7 \\ 0 & 1 & 0 & | & 4 & -1 & 2 \\ 0 & 0 & 1 & | & -3 & 1 & -1 \end{bmatrix}$$

The inverse matrix is $\begin{bmatrix} 18 & -5 & 7 \\ 4 & -1 & 2 \\ -3 & 1 & -1 \end{bmatrix}$. [7.3]

16.

$$M_{21} = \begin{vmatrix} -1 & 3 \\ 2 & 2 \end{vmatrix} = -2 - 6 = -8 \quad [7.4]$$

$$C_{21} = (-1)^{2+1} M_{21} = -(-8) = 8$$

17.

$$|B| = \begin{vmatrix} 2 & -1 & 3 \\ 4 & -2 & -1 \\ 3 & 2 & 2 \end{vmatrix} = 3C_{31} + 2C_{32} + 2C_{33} \quad [7.4]$$

$$= 3(-1)^{3+1}\begin{vmatrix} -1 & 3 \\ -2 & -1 \end{vmatrix} + 2(-1)^{3+2}\begin{vmatrix} 2 & 3 \\ 4 & -1 \end{vmatrix} + 2(-1)^{3+3}\begin{vmatrix} 2 & -1 \\ 4 & -2 \end{vmatrix}$$

$$= 3(1+6) - 2(-2-12) + 2(-4+4) = 21 + 28 + 0 = 49$$

18.
$$\begin{vmatrix} 1 & -2 & 3 \\ 2 & -3 & 8 \\ -1 & 3 & -2 \end{vmatrix} = \begin{matrix} -2R_1 + R_2 \\ R_1 + R_3 \end{matrix} \begin{vmatrix} 1 & -2 & 3 \\ 0 & 1 & 2 \\ 0 & 1 & 1 \end{vmatrix} = -R_2 + R_3 \begin{vmatrix} 1 & -2 & 3 \\ 0 & 1 & 2 \\ 0 & 0 & -1 \end{vmatrix} = (1)(1)(-1) = -1 \quad [7.4]$$

19.
$$D = \begin{vmatrix} 3 & 2 & -1 \\ 2 & -3 & 2 \\ 5 & 6 & 3 \end{vmatrix} = -82 \qquad D_3 = \begin{vmatrix} 3 & 2 & 12 \\ 2 & -3 & -1 \\ 5 & 6 & 4 \end{vmatrix} = 280 \qquad z = \frac{D_3}{D} = \frac{280}{-82} = -\frac{140}{41} \quad [7.5]$$

20. $X = (I - A)^{-1} D \quad [7.3]$

$$\left(\begin{bmatrix} 1 & 0 & 0 \\ 0 & 1 & 0 \\ 0 & 0 & 1 \end{bmatrix} - \begin{bmatrix} 0.15 & 0.23 & 0.11 \\ 0.08 & 0.10 & 0.05 \\ 0.16 & 0.11 & 0.07 \end{bmatrix} \right)^{-1} \begin{bmatrix} 50 \\ 32 \\ 8 \end{bmatrix}$$

•••

1.
$$(x+2)^2 + (y-4)^2 = 25 \quad [2.1]$$
$$x^2 + 4x + 4 + y^2 - 8y + 16 = 25$$
$$x^2 + y^2 + 4x - 8y - 5 = 0$$

2.
$$24x^2 - 14x - 24 = 2(12x^2 - 7x - 12) \quad [P.4]$$
$$= 2(4x + 3)(3x - 4)$$

3.
$$y - 5 = -\frac{1}{2}(x - (-4)) \quad [2.3]$$
$$y - 5 = -\frac{1}{2}x - 2$$
$$y = -\frac{1}{2}x + 3$$

4.
$$\begin{array}{r} 2x^2 + x - 10 \\ x - 3 \overline{) 2x^3 - 5x^2 - 13x + 30} \\ \underline{2x^3 - 6x^2} \\ x^2 - 13x \\ \underline{x^2 - 3x} \\ -10x + 30 \\ \underline{-10x + 30} \\ 0 \end{array} \quad [3.1]$$

5.
$$h[k(0)] = h[3^0] \quad [4.2]$$
$$= h[1]$$
$$= e^{-1}$$
$$\approx 0.3679$$

6.
$$2x^2 - 4x + 3y - 1 = 0 \quad [5.1]$$
$$2x^2 - 4x = -3y + 1$$
$$2(x^2 - 2x) = -3y + 1$$
$$2(x - 1)^2 = -3y + 3$$
$$2(x - 1)^2 = -3(y - 1)$$
Vertex = (1, 1)

7.
$$\begin{cases} 3x - 4y = 4 & (1) \\ 2x - 3y = 1 & (2) \end{cases}$$
Solve (2) for x and substitute into (1).
$$2x - 3y = 1$$
$$2x = 3y + 1$$
$$x = \frac{3y + 1}{2}$$
$$3\left(\frac{3y + 1}{2}\right) - 4y = 4$$
$$9y + 3 - 8y = 8$$
$$y = 5$$
$$x = \frac{3(5) + 1}{2} = 8$$
The solution is (8, 5). [6.1]

8.
$$\frac{1 - i}{4 + i} \cdot \frac{4 - i}{4 - i} = \frac{4 - 5i + i^2}{16 + 1} = \frac{3}{17} - \frac{5}{17}i \quad [P.6]$$

9.   Domain: $\{x \mid -3 \le x \le 3\} \quad [2.2]$

10.   Yes, since
$$(-x)(-y) - (-x)^2 + (-y)^2 = 0$$
simplifies to the original equation.
[2.5]

11.
$$x^2 + 4x - 5 = (x + 5)(x - 1) \quad [3.5]$$
$$x + 5 = 0 \qquad x - 1 = 0$$
$$x = -5 \qquad x = 1$$
Vertical asymptotes: $x = -5, x = 1$

12.

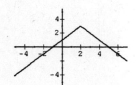

[2.5]

---

13. $\dfrac{x+2}{x+1}>0$

The quotient $\dfrac{x+2}{x+1}$ is positive.

The critical values are -2 and -1.

$\dfrac{x+2}{x+1}$ $\quad$ $+\ +\ +\ +\ +\ +\ +\ +\ -\ -\ -\ +\ +\ +\ +\ +\ +\ +$

$\qquad\qquad$ $-4\qquad-3\qquad-2\qquad-1\qquad0\qquad1$

$(-\infty,-2)\cup(-1,\infty)$ [1.5]

14. $2a=12$

$a=6$

$a^2=b^2+c^2$

$(6)^2=b^2+(4)^2$

$36-16=b^2$

$20=b^2$

$\dfrac{(x-3)^2}{36}+\dfrac{(y+4)^2}{20}=1$ [5.2]

15. $\begin{cases} x-y+z=-1 & (1) \\ 2x+3y-z=1 & (2) \\ 3x-2y+3z=12 & (3) \end{cases}$

$\begin{array}{ll} x-y+z=-1 & (1) \\ 2x+3y-z=1 & (2) \\ \hline 3x+2y\quad\ \ =0 & (4) \end{array}$

$\begin{array}{ll} 6x+9y-3z=3 & 3\text{ times }(2) \\ 3x-2y+3z=12 & (3) \\ \hline 9x+7y\quad\ \ =15 & (5) \end{array}$

$\begin{array}{ll} -9x-6y=0 & -3\text{ times }(4) \\ 9x+7y=15 & (5) \\ \hline \quad\ \ y=15 \end{array}$

$9x+7(15)=15$

$9x+105=15$

$9x=-90$

$x=-10$

$-10-15+z=-1$

$z=24$

The solution is $(-10,\ 15,\ 24)$. [6.2]

16. $\dfrac{f(x+h)-f(x)}{h}=\dfrac{(x+h)^2-3(x+h)+2-(x^2-3x+2)}{h}$ [2.6]

$\qquad\qquad\qquad\quad =\dfrac{x^2+2xh+h^2-3x-3h+2-x^2+3x-2}{h}$

$\qquad\qquad\qquad\quad =\dfrac{h^2+2xh-3h}{h}$

$\qquad\qquad\qquad\quad =2x-3+h$

17. $125^x=\dfrac{1}{25}$ [4.5]

$5^{3x}=5^{-2}$

$3x=-2$

$x=-\dfrac{2}{3}$

18. $\dfrac{x-2}{x^2-5x-6}=\dfrac{x-2}{(x+1)(x-6)}$

$\dfrac{x-2}{(x+1)(x-6)}=\dfrac{A}{x+1}+\dfrac{B}{x-6}$

$x-2=A(x-6)+B(x+1)$

$x-2=Ax-6A+Bx+B$

$x-2=(A+B)x+(-6A+B)$

$\begin{cases} 1=A+B & (1) \\ -2=-6A+B & (2) \end{cases}$

$\begin{array}{ll} -1=-A-B & -1\text{ times }(1) \\ -2=-6A+B & (2) \\ \hline -3=-7A \end{array}$

$\dfrac{3}{7}=A$

$1=\dfrac{3}{7}+B$

$\dfrac{4}{7}=B$

$\dfrac{x-2}{x^2-5x-6}=\dfrac{4}{7(x+1)}+\dfrac{3}{7(x-6)}$ [6.4]

19.

$$10^x - 10^{-x} = 2 \qquad [4.5]$$

$$10^x(10^x - 10^{-x}) = 2(10^x)$$

$$(10^x)^2 - 2(10^x) - 1 = 0$$

Let $u = 10^x$

$$u^2 - 2u - 1 = 0$$

$$u = \frac{2 \pm \sqrt{4 - 4(1)(-1)}}{2}$$

$$= \frac{2 \pm \sqrt{8}}{2}$$

$$= 1 \pm \sqrt{2}$$

$$10^x = 1 + \sqrt{2}$$

$$\log 10^x = \log(1 + \sqrt{2})$$

$$x = \log(1 + \sqrt{2}) \approx 0.3828$$

20. Rate of canoeist with the current: 8
Rate of canoeist against the current: 2

$$d = rt$$

Distance upstream equals distance downstream

$$8t = 2(4 - t)$$

$$8t = 8 - 2t$$

$$10t = 8$$

$$t = \frac{4}{5}$$

$$d = rt = 8\frac{4}{5} = 6.4 \text{ mi} \quad [6.1]$$

Chapter 8
Sequences, Series, and Probability

Section 8.1

1.
$$a_1 = 1(1-1) = 1 \cdot 0 = 0$$
$$a_2 = 2(2-1) = 2 \cdot 1 = 2$$
$$a_3 = 3(3-1) = 3 \cdot 2 = 6$$
$$a_8 = 8(8-1) = 8 \cdot 7 = 56$$

3.
$$a_1 = 1 - \frac{1}{1} = 0$$
$$a_2 = 1 - \frac{1}{2} = \frac{1}{2}$$
$$a_3 = 1 - \frac{1}{3} = \frac{2}{3}$$
$$a_8 = 1 - \frac{1}{8} = \frac{7}{8}$$

5.
$$a_1 = \frac{(-1)^{1+1}}{1^2} = \frac{(-1)^2}{1} = 1$$
$$a_2 = \frac{(-1)^{2+1}}{2^2} = \frac{(-1)^3}{4} = -\frac{1}{4}$$
$$a_3 = \frac{(-1)^{3+1}}{3^2} = \frac{(-1)^4}{9} = \frac{1}{9}$$
$$a_8 = \frac{(-1)^{8+1}}{8^2} = \frac{(-1)^9}{64} = -\frac{1}{64}$$

7.
$$a_1 = \frac{(-1)^{2 \cdot 1 - 1}}{3 \cdot 1} = \frac{(-1)^{2-1}}{3} = -\frac{1}{3}$$
$$a_2 = \frac{(-1)^{2 \cdot 2 - 1}}{3 \cdot 2} = \frac{(-1)^{4-1}}{6} = -\frac{1}{6}$$
$$a_3 = \frac{(-1)^{2 \cdot 3 - 1}}{3 \cdot 3} = \frac{(-1)^{6-1}}{9} = -\frac{1}{9}$$
$$a_8 = \frac{(-1)^{2 \cdot 8 - 1}}{3 \cdot 8} = \frac{(-1)^{16-1}}{24} = -\frac{1}{24}$$

9.
$$a_1 = \left(\frac{2}{3}\right)^1 = \frac{2}{3}$$
$$a_2 = \left(\frac{2}{3}\right)^2 = \frac{4}{9}$$
$$a_3 = \left(\frac{2}{3}\right)^3 = \frac{8}{27}$$
$$a_8 = \left(\frac{2}{3}\right)^8 = \frac{256}{6561}$$

11.
$$a_1 = 1 + (-1)^1 = 1 + (-1) = 0$$
$$a_2 = 1 + (-1)^2 = 1 + 1 = 2$$
$$a_3 = 1 + (-1)^3 = 1 + (-1) = 0$$
$$a_8 = 1 + (-1)^8 = 1 + 1 = 2$$

13.
$$a_1 = (1.1)^1 = 1.1$$
$$a_2 = (1.1)^2 = 1.21$$
$$a_3 = (1.1)^3 = 1.331$$
$$a_8 = (1.1)^8 = 2.14358881$$

15.
$$a_1 = \frac{(-1)^{1+1}}{\sqrt{1}} = \frac{(-1)^2}{1} = 1$$
$$a_2 = \frac{(-1)^{2+1}}{\sqrt{2}} = \frac{(-1)^3}{\sqrt{2}} = -\frac{1}{\sqrt{2}} = -\frac{\sqrt{2}}{2}$$
$$a_3 = \frac{(-1)^{3+1}}{\sqrt{3}} = \frac{(-1)^4}{\sqrt{3}} = \frac{1}{\sqrt{3}} = \frac{\sqrt{3}}{3}$$
$$a_8 = \frac{(-1)^{8+1}}{\sqrt{8}} = \frac{(-1)^9}{2\sqrt{2}} = -\frac{1}{2\sqrt{2}} = -\frac{\sqrt{2}}{4}$$

17.
$$a_1 = 1! = 1$$
$$a_2 = 2! = 2 \cdot 1 = 2$$
$$a_3 = 3! = 3 \cdot 2 \cdot 1 = 6$$
$$a_8 = 8! = 8 \cdot 7 \cdot 6 \cdot 5 \cdot 4 \cdot 3 \cdot 2 \cdot 1 = 40,320$$

19.
$$a_1 = \log 1 = 0$$
$$a_2 = \log 2 \approx 0.3010$$
$$a_3 = \log 3 \approx 0.4771$$
$$a_8 = \log 8 \approx 0.9031$$

21.
$$a_1 = 1 \qquad \frac{1}{7} = 0.\overline{142857}$$
$$a_2 = 4$$
$$a_3 = 2$$
$$a_8 = 4$$

23.
$$a_1 = 3$$
$$a_2 = 3$$
$$a_3 = 3$$
$$a_8 = 3$$

25.
$$a_1 = 5$$
$$a_2 = 2 \cdot a_1 = 2 \cdot 5 = 10$$
$$a_3 = 2 \cdot a_2 = 2 \cdot 10 = 20$$

27.
$$a_1 = 2$$
$$a_2 = 2 \cdot a_1 = 2 \cdot 2 = 4$$
$$a_3 = 3 \cdot a_2 = 3 \cdot 4 = 12$$

29.
$$a_1 = 2$$
$$a_2 = (a_1)^2 = (2)^2 = 4$$
$$a_3 = (a_2)^2 = (4)^2 = 16$$

31.
$$a_1 = 2$$
$$a_2 = 2 \cdot 2 \cdot a_1 = 4 \cdot 2 = 8$$
$$a_3 = 2 \cdot 3 \cdot a_2 = 6 \cdot 8 = 48$$

33. $a_1 = 3$

$a_2 = (a_1)^{1/2} = (3)^{1/2} = \sqrt{3}$

$a_3 = (a_2)^{1/3} = \left(3^{1/2}\right)^{1/3} = 3^{1/6} = \sqrt[6]{3}$

35. $a_1 = 1$

$a_2 = 3$

$a_3 = \frac{1}{2}(a_2 + a_1) = \frac{1}{2}(3+1) = \frac{1}{2}(4) = 2$

$a_4 = \frac{1}{2}(a_3 + a_2) = \frac{1}{2}(2+3) = \frac{1}{2}(5) = \frac{5}{2}$

$a_5 = \frac{1}{2}(a_4 + a_3) = \frac{1}{2}\left(\frac{5}{2}+2\right) = \frac{1}{2}\left(\frac{9}{2}\right) = \frac{9}{4}$

37. $7! - 6! = 7 \cdot 6! - 6! = 6!(7-1) = 6! \cdot 6 = 6 \cdot 5 \cdot 4 \cdot 3 \cdot 2 \cdot 1 \cdot 6 = 4320$

39. $\dfrac{9!}{7!} = \dfrac{9 \cdot 8 \cdot 7!}{7!} = 72$

41. $\dfrac{8!}{3!5!} = \dfrac{8 \cdot 7 \cdot 6 \cdot 5!}{3 \cdot 2 \cdot 1 \cdot 5!} = 56$

43. $\dfrac{100!}{99!} = \dfrac{100 \cdot 99!}{99!} = 100$

45. $\displaystyle\sum_{i}^{5} i = 1 + 2 + 3 + 4 + 5 = 15$

47. $\displaystyle\sum_{i}^{5} i(i-1) = 1(1-1) + 2(2-1) + 3(3-1) + 4(4-1) + 5(5-1)$

$= 1 \cdot 0 + 2 \cdot 1 + 3 \cdot 2 + 4 \cdot 3 + 5 \cdot 4$

$= 0 + 2 + 6 + 12 + 20 = 40$

49. $\displaystyle\sum_{k=1}^{4} \frac{1}{k} = \frac{1}{1} + \frac{1}{2} + \frac{1}{3} + \frac{1}{4} = \frac{12}{12} + \frac{6}{12} + \frac{4}{12} + \frac{3}{12} = \frac{25}{12}$

51. $\displaystyle\sum_{j=1}^{8} 2j = 2\sum_{j=1}^{8} j = 2(1+2+3+4+5+6+7+8) = 2(36) = 72$

53. $\displaystyle\sum_{i=3}^{5} (-1)^i 2^i = (-1)^3 2^3 + (-1)^4 2^4 + (-1)^5 2^5 = (-1)8 + (1)16 + (-1)32 = -8 + 16 - 32 = -24$

55. $\displaystyle\sum_{n=1}^{7} \log\left(\frac{n+1}{n}\right) = \log\left(\frac{1+1}{1}\right) + \log\left(\frac{2+1}{2}\right) + \log\left(\frac{3+1}{3}\right) + \log\left(\frac{4+1}{4}\right) + \log\left(\frac{5+1}{5}\right) + \log\left(\frac{6+1}{6}\right) + \log\left(\frac{7+1}{7}\right)$

$= \log\left(2 \cdot \frac{3}{2} \cdot \frac{4}{3} \cdot \frac{5}{4} \cdot \frac{6}{5} \cdot \frac{7}{6} \cdot \frac{8}{7}\right) = \log 8 = 3\log 2 \approx 0.9031$

57. $\displaystyle\sum_{k=0}^{8} \frac{8!}{k!(8-k)!} = \frac{8!}{0!(8-0)!} + \frac{8!}{1!(8-1)!} + \frac{8!}{2!(8-2)!} + \frac{8!}{3!(8-3)!} + \frac{8!}{4!(8-4)!} + \frac{8!}{5!(8-5)!} + \frac{8!}{6!(8-6)!} + \frac{8!}{7!(8-7)!} + \frac{8!}{8!(8-8)!}$

$= \frac{8!}{0!8!} + \frac{8!}{1!7!} + \frac{8!}{2!6!} + \frac{8!}{3!5!} + \frac{8!}{4!4!} + \frac{8!}{5!3!} + \frac{8!}{6!2!} + \frac{8!}{7!1!} + \frac{8!}{8!0!}$

$= 1 + 8 + \frac{8 \cdot 7}{2} + \frac{8 \cdot 7 \cdot 6}{3 \cdot 2} + \frac{8 \cdot 7 \cdot 6 \cdot 5}{4 \cdot 3 \cdot 2} + \frac{8 \cdot 7 \cdot 6}{3 \cdot 2 \cdot 1} + \frac{8 \cdot 7}{2} + 8 + 1$

$= 1 + 8 + 28 + 56 + 70 + 56 + 28 + 8 + 1 = 256$

59. $\dfrac{1}{1} + \dfrac{1}{4} + \dfrac{1}{9} + \dfrac{1}{16} + \dfrac{1}{25} + \dfrac{1}{36} = \dfrac{1}{1^2} + \dfrac{1}{2^2} + \dfrac{1}{3^2} + \dfrac{1}{4^2} + \dfrac{1}{5^2} + \dfrac{1}{6^2} = \displaystyle\sum_{i=1}^{6} \frac{1}{i^2}$

61.

$$2-4+8-16+32-64+128=2^1(-1)^{1+1}+2^2(-1)^{2+1}+2^3(-1)^{3+1}+2^4(-1)^{4+1}+2^5(-1)^{5+1}+2^6(-1)^{6+1}+2^7(-1)^{7+1}=\sum_{i=1}^{7}2^i(-1)^{i+1}$$

63.

$$7+10+13+16+19=7+(7+3)+(7+3\cdot2)+(7+3\cdot3)+(7+3\cdot4)=\sum_{i=0}^{4}(7+3i)$$

65.

$$\frac{1}{2}+\frac{1}{4}+\frac{1}{8}+\frac{1}{16}=\frac{1}{2}+\frac{1}{2^2}+\frac{1}{2^3}+\frac{1}{2^4}=\sum_{i=1}^{4}\frac{1}{2^i}$$

••

Connecting Concepts

67. Let $N = 7$.

$a_1 = \dfrac{7}{2} = 3.5$

$a_2 = \dfrac{1}{2}\left(3.5 + \dfrac{7}{3.5}\right) = 2.75$

$a_3 = \dfrac{1}{2}\left(2.75 + \dfrac{7}{2.75}\right) \approx 2.6477273$

$a_4 \approx \dfrac{1}{2}\left(2.6477273 + \dfrac{7}{2.6477273}\right) \approx 2.6457520$

69. $a_{20} \approx 1.0000037$

$a_{100} \approx 1$

71.

$a_1 = \dfrac{1}{2}\left(-1 + i\sqrt{3}\right)$; $a_2 = \left(\dfrac{1}{2}\right)^2\left(-1 + i\sqrt{3}\right)^2 = \dfrac{1}{2}\left(-1 - i\sqrt{3}\right)$; $a_3 = 1$

$a_4 = \dfrac{1}{2}\left(-1 + i\sqrt{3}\right)$; $a_5 = \dfrac{1}{2}\left(-1 - i\sqrt{3}\right)$; $a_6 = 1$

Notice that the sequence repeats itself in groups of 3.

To find a_{99}, divide 99 by 3. $a_{99} = \left[\dfrac{1}{2}\left(-1 + i\sqrt{3}\right)\right]^r$ where r is the remainder after division.

Thus $a_{99} = \left[\dfrac{1}{2}\left(-1 + i\sqrt{3}\right)\right]^0 = 1$.

73.

$$\sum_{i=1}^{n}ca_i = ca_1 + ca_2 + ca_3 + \cdots + ca_n$$

$$= c(a_1 + a_2 + a_3 + \cdots + a_n)$$

$$= c\sum_{i=1}^{n}a_i$$

••

Prepare for Section 8.2

74. $-3 = 25 + (15-1)d$

$-3 = 25 + 14d$

$-28 = 14d$

$-2 = d$

75. $13 = 3 + (5-1)d$

$13 = 3 + 4d$

$10 = 4d$

$\dfrac{5}{2} = d$

76.
$$S = \frac{50\left[2(2)+(50-1)\frac{5}{4}\right]}{2} = \frac{50\left[4+\frac{245}{4}\right]}{2}$$

$$= \frac{50\left[\frac{261}{4}\right]}{2} = \frac{6525}{4}$$

77. $a_5 = 5 + (5-1)4 = 21$

78. $a_{20} = 52 + (20-1)(-3) = -5$

79.
$5 - 2 = 3$
$8 - 5 = 3$
Yes

Section 8.2

1. $d = 10 - 6 = 4$

$a_n = 6 + (n-1)4 = 6 + 4n - 4 = 4n + 2$
$a_9 = 4 \cdot 9 + 2 = 36 + 2 = 38$
$a_{24} = 4 \cdot 24 + 2 = 98$

3. $d = 4 - 6 = -2$

$a_n = 6 + (n-1)(-2) = 6 - 2n + 2 = 8 - 2n$
$a_9 = 8 - 2 \cdot 9 = 8 - 18 = -10$
$a_{24} = 8 - 2 \cdot 24 = 8 - 48 = -40$

5. $d = -5 - (-8) = 3$

$a_n = -8 + (n-1)3 = -8 + 3n - 3$
$\quad = 3n - 11$
$a_9 = 3 \cdot 9 - 11 = 27 - 11 = 16$
$a_{24} = 3 \cdot 24 - 11 = 72 - 11 = 61$

7. $d = 4 - 1 = 3$

$a_n = 1 + (n-1)3 = 1 + 3n - 3 = 3n - 2$
$a_9 = 3 \cdot 9 - 2 = 27 - 2 = 25$
$a_{24} = 3 \cdot 24 - 2 = 72 - 2 = 70$

9. $d = (a + 2) - a = 2$

$a_n = a + (n-1)2 = a + 2n - 2$
$a_9 = a + 2 \cdot 9 - 2 = a + 18 - 2 = a + 16$
$a_{24} = a + 2 \cdot 24 - 2 = a + 48 - 2 = a + 46$

11. $d = \log 14 - \log 7 = \log\frac{14}{7} = \log 2$

$a_n = \log 7 + (n-1)\log 2$
$a_9 = \log 7 + 8\log 2$
$a_{24} = \log 7 + 23\log 2$

13. $d = \log a^2 - \log a = \log\frac{a^2}{a} = \log a$

$a_n = \log a + (n-1)\log a$
$\quad = (1 + n - 1)\log a = n\log a$
$a_9 = 9\log a$
$a_{24} = 24\log a$

15. $d = 15 - 13 = 2$
$a_4 = a_1 + (4-1)2 = 13$
$\qquad a_1 + 6 = 13$
$\qquad\quad a_1 = 7$
$a_{20} = 7 + (20-1)2 = 7 + (19)2 = 7 + 38 = 45$

17. $a_5 = -19 = a_1 + (5-1)d \qquad a_7 = -29 = a_1 + (7-1)d$
$\quad -19 = a_1 + 4d \qquad\qquad -29 = a_1 + 6d$
$-19 - 4d = a_1 \qquad\qquad\quad -29 = (-19 - 4d) + 6d$
$\qquad\qquad\qquad\qquad\qquad -29 = -19 + 2d$
$\qquad\qquad\qquad\qquad\qquad -10 = 2d$
$\qquad\qquad\qquad\qquad\qquad\quad d = -5$

$a_1 = -4(-5) - 19 = 1$
$a_{17} = 1 + (17-1)(-5) = 1 + 16(-5) = 1 - 80 = -79$

19.
$a_1 = 3(1) + 2 = 5$
$a_{10} = 3(10) + 2 = 32$

$S_{10} = \frac{10}{2}(a_1 + a_{10}) = 5(5 + 32) = 185$

21.
$a_1 = 3 - 5(1) = -2$
$a_{15} = 3 - 5(15) = -72$

$S_{15} = \frac{15}{2}(a_1 + a_{15}) = \frac{15}{2}(-2 + (-72)) = \frac{15}{2}(-74) = -555$

23.
$a_1 = 6(1) = 6$
$a_{12} = 6(12) = 72$

$S_{12} = \frac{12}{2}(a_1 + a_{12}) = 6(6 + 72) = 6(78) = 468$

25. $a_1 = 1 + 8 = 9$

$a_{25} = 25 + 8 = 33$

$S_{25} = \dfrac{25}{2}(a_1 + a_{25}) = \dfrac{25}{2}(9 + 33) = \dfrac{25}{2}(42) = 525$

27. $a_1 = -1$

$a_{30} = -30$

$S_{30} = \dfrac{30}{2}(a_1 + a_{30}) = 15(-1 + (-30)) = 15(-31) = -465$

29. $a_1 = 1 + x$

$a_{12} = 12 + x$

$S_{12} = \dfrac{12}{2}(a_1 + a_{12}) = 6(1 + x + 12 + x) = 78 + 12x$

31. $a_1 = (1)x = x$

$a_{20} = (20)x = 20x$

$S_{20} = \dfrac{20}{2}(a_1 + a_{20}) = 10(x + 20x) = 210x$

33. $-1,\ c_2,\ c_3,\ c_4,\ c_5,\ c_6,\ 23$

$a_1 = -1$

$a_7 = a_1 + (n - 1)d$

$23 = -1 + (7 - 1)d$

$23 = -1 + 6d$

$24 = 6d$

$d = 4$

$c_2 = -1 + (2 - 1)4 = -1 + 4 = 3$

$c_3 = -1 + (3 - 1)4 = -1 + (2)4 = 7$

$c_4 = -1 + (4 - 1)4 = -1 + (3)4 = 11$

$c_5 = -1 + (5 - 1)4 = -1 + (4)4 = 15$

$c_6 = -1 + (6 - 1)4 = -1 + (5)4 = 19$

35. $3,\ c_2,\ c_3,\ c_4,\ c_5,\ \dfrac{1}{2}$

$a_1 = 3$

$a_6 = a_1 + (n - 1)d$

$\dfrac{1}{2} = 3 + (6 - 1)d$

$-\dfrac{5}{2} = 5d$

$d = -\dfrac{1}{2}$

$c_2 = 3 + (2 - 1)\left(-\dfrac{1}{2}\right) = 3 - \dfrac{1}{2} = \dfrac{5}{2}$

$c_3 = 3 + (3 - 1)\left(-\dfrac{1}{2}\right) = 3 - 1 = 2$

$c_4 = 3 + (4 - 1)\left(-\dfrac{1}{2}\right) = 3 - \dfrac{3}{2} = \dfrac{3}{2}$

$c_5 = 3 + (5 - 1)\left(-\dfrac{1}{2}\right) = 3 - 2 = 1$

37. $a_1 = 1,\ d = 2$

$S_n = \dfrac{n[2(1) + (n - 1)2]}{2} = \dfrac{n}{2}[2n] = n^2$

39. $a_1 = 25,\ d = -1$

$a_6 = 25 + (6 - 1)(-1) = 25 - 5 = 20$

$S_6 = \dfrac{6}{2}(25 + 20) = 3(45) = 135$

20 logs stacked on sixth row,
135 logs in the six rows

41. $a_1 = 5000, d = -250$

$a_{15} = 5000 + (15 - 1)(-250) = 5000 - 3500 = 1500$

The fifteenth prize is $1500.

$S_{15} = \dfrac{15}{2}(5000 + 1500) = \dfrac{15}{2}(6500) = 48,750$

The total amount of money distributed is $48,750.

43. $a_1 = 16, d = 32$

$S_7 = \dfrac{7}{2}\big[2(16) + (7 - 1)32\big] = \dfrac{7}{2}[32 + 192] = \dfrac{7}{2}[224] = 784$

The total distance the object falls is 784 ft.

Connecting Concepts

45. If $f(x)$ is a linear function, then $f(x) = mx + b$. To show that $f(n)$, where n is a positive integer, is an arithmetic sequence, we must show that $f(n + 1) - f(n)$ is a constant. We have

$$f(n + 1) - f(n) = (m(n + 1) + b) - (m(n) + b)$$
$$= mn + m + b - mn - b$$
$$= m$$

Thus, the difference between any two successive terms is m, the slope of the linear function.

47. $a_1 = 4,\ a_n = a_{n-1} - 3$

Rewriting $a_n = a_{n-1} - 3$ as $a_n - a_{n-1} = -3$, we find that the difference between successive terms is the same constant -3. Thus the sequence is an arithmetic sequence with $a_1 = 4$ and $d = -3$.

$a_n = a_1 + (n - 1)d$

Substituting,

$a_n = 4 + (n - 1)(-3) = 4 - 3n + 3 = 7 - 3n$

49. $a_1 = 1, a_n = b_{n-1} + 7; b_1 = -2, b_n = a_{n-1} + 1$

To show that a_n is an arithmetic sequence, we must show that $a_n - a_{n-1} = d$, where d is a constant. We begin by finding a relationship between a_n and a_{n-2}.

$a_n = b_{n-1} + 7 = a_{n-2} + 1 + 7$

$a_n = a_{n-2} + 8$

This establishes a relationship between *alternate* successive terms. We now examine some terms of a_n.

$a_1 = 1$

$a_2 = b_1 + 7 = -2 + 7 = 5$

$a_3 = a_1 + 8$ $(a_n = a_{n-2} + 8)$

$a_4 = a_2 + 8$

$a_5 = a_3 + 8 = (a_1 + 8) + 8 = a_1 + 2(8)$

$a_6 = a_4 + 8 = (a_2 + 8) + 8 = a_2 + 2(8)$

$a_7 = a_5 + 8 = (a_1 + 2(8)) + 8 = a_1 + 3(8)$

$a_8 = a_6 + 8 = (a_2 + 2(8)) = a_2 + 3(8)$

Now consider two cases. First, n is an even integer, $n = 2k$.

$a_{2k} = a_2 + (k-1)8 \qquad k \geq 2$

When n is an odd integer, $n = 2k - 1$.

$a_{2k-1} = a_1 + (k-1)8 \qquad k \geq 2$

Thus $a_{2k} - a_{2k-1} = (a_2 + (k-1)8) - (a_1 + (k-1)8) = a_2 - a_1 = 5 - 1 = 4$

Therefore, the difference between successive terms is the constant. To find a_{50}, use $a_n = a_1 + (n-1)d$.

$a_{50} = 1 + (49)(4) = 197$

To show that b_n is an arithmetic sequence, we have

$b_n - b_{n-1} = (a_{n-1} + 1) - (a_{n-2} + 1) = a_{n-1} - a_{n-2}$

Because a_n is an arithmetic sequence, $a_{n-1} - a_{n-2}$ is a constant. Thus b_n is an arithmetic sequence.

••   **Prepare for Section 8.3**

50. $\dfrac{4}{2} = 2, \quad \dfrac{8}{4} = 2$
The ratio is 2.

51. $\displaystyle\sum_{n=1}^{4} \dfrac{1}{2^{n-1}} = \dfrac{1}{2^0} + \dfrac{1}{2^1} + \dfrac{1}{2^2} + \dfrac{1}{2^3} = \dfrac{15}{8}$

52. $S = \dfrac{3(1-(-2)^5)}{1-(-2)} = 33$

53. $S - rS = a - ar^2$

$S(1-r) = a(1-r^2)$

$S = \dfrac{a(1+r)(1-r)}{(1-r)}$

$S = a(1+r)$

54. $a_1 = 3\left(-\dfrac{1}{2}\right)^1 = -\dfrac{3}{2}$

$a_2 = 3\left(-\dfrac{1}{2}\right)^2 = \dfrac{3}{4}$

$a_3 = 3\left(-\dfrac{1}{2}\right)^3 = -\dfrac{3}{8}$

55. $S_1 = 2$

$S_2 = 2 + 4 = 6$

$S_3 = 2 + 4 + 8 = 14$

Section 8.3

1. $\dfrac{4^{i+1}}{4^i} = 4$, geometric, $r = 4$

3. $\dfrac{\frac{1}{i+1}}{\frac{1}{i}} = \dfrac{i}{i+1}$, not geometric

5. $\dfrac{2^{(i+1)x}}{2^{ix}} = \dfrac{2^{ix+x}}{2^{ix}} = 2^x$, geometric, $r = 2^x$

7. $\dfrac{3(2^{(i+1)-1})}{3(2^{i-1})} = \dfrac{2^i}{2^{i-1}} = 2$, geometric, $r = 2$

9. $\dfrac{x^{2(i+1)}}{x^{2i}} = \dfrac{x^{2i+2}}{x^{2i}} = x^2$, geometric, $r = x^2$

11. $\dfrac{\ln 5(i+1)}{\ln 5i} = \left(\dfrac{\ln 5}{\ln 5i}\right)\left(\dfrac{\ln(i+1)}{\ln 5i}\right)$, not geometric

13. $r = \dfrac{8}{2} = 4$,

$a_n = 2 \cdot 4^{n-1} = 2 \cdot 2^{2(n-1)} = 2^{2n-1}$

15. $r = \dfrac{12}{-4} = -3, a_n = -4(-3)^{n-1}$

17. $r = \dfrac{4}{6} = \dfrac{2}{3}, a_n = 6\left(\dfrac{2}{3}\right)^{n-1}$

19. $r = -\dfrac{5}{6}, a_n = -6\left(-\dfrac{5}{6}\right)^{n-1}$

21. $r = \dfrac{-3}{9} = -\dfrac{1}{3}, a_n = 9\left(-\dfrac{1}{3}\right)^{n-1} = \left(-\dfrac{1}{3}\right)^{n-3}$

23. $r = \dfrac{-x}{1} = -x, a_n = 1(-x)^{n-1} = (-x)^{n-1}$

25. $r = \dfrac{c^5}{c^2} = c^3, a_n = c^2\left(c^3\right)^{n-1} = c^2 c^{3n-3} = c^{3n-1}$

27. $r = \dfrac{\frac{3}{10,000}}{\frac{3}{100}} = \dfrac{1}{100}, a_n = \dfrac{3}{100}\left(\dfrac{1}{100}\right)^{n-1} = 3\left(\dfrac{1}{100}\right)^n$

29. $r = \dfrac{0.05}{0.5} = 0.1, a_n = 0.5(0.1)^{n-1} = 5(0.1)^n$

31. $r = \dfrac{0.0045}{0.45} = 0.01, a_n = 0.45(0.01)^{n-1} = 45(0.01)^n$

33. $a_1 = 2, \qquad a_5 = 162, \qquad a_n = a_1 r^{n-1}$

$162 = 2r^{5-1}$

$r^4 = 81$

$r = 3$

$a_3 = 2(3)^{3-1} = 2 \cdot 9 = 18$

35. $a_3 = \dfrac{4}{3}, \qquad a_6 = -\dfrac{32}{81}$

$\dfrac{\frac{4}{3}}{-\frac{32}{81}} = \dfrac{a_1(r)^{3-1}}{a_1(r)^{6-1}}$

$\dfrac{-27}{8} = \dfrac{1}{r^3}$

$r^3 = -\dfrac{8}{27}$

$r = \dfrac{-2}{3}$

$\dfrac{4}{3} = a_1\left(-\dfrac{2}{3}\right)^{3-1}$

$a_1 = \dfrac{4}{3}\left(\dfrac{9}{4}\right) = 3$

$a_2 = 3\left(\dfrac{-2}{3}\right) = -2$

37. $a_1 = 3, \qquad a_2 = 9, \qquad r = \dfrac{9}{3} = 3$

$S_5 = \dfrac{3(1-3^5)}{1-3} = \dfrac{3(-242)}{-2} = 363$

39. $a_1 = \dfrac{2}{3}, \qquad a_2 = \dfrac{4}{9}, \qquad r = \dfrac{\frac{4}{9}}{\frac{2}{3}} = \dfrac{2}{3}$

$S_6 = \dfrac{\frac{2}{3}\left[1-\left(\frac{2}{3}\right)^6\right]}{1-\frac{2}{3}} = \dfrac{\frac{2}{3}\left(\frac{665}{729}\right)}{\frac{1}{3}} = \dfrac{1330}{729}$

41. $a_1 = 1, a_2 = -\dfrac{2}{5}, r = -\dfrac{2}{5}$

$$S_9 = \frac{1\left[1 - \left(-\dfrac{2}{5}\right)^9\right]}{1 - \left(-\dfrac{2}{5}\right)} = \frac{\dfrac{1{,}953{,}637}{1{,}953{,}125}}{\dfrac{7}{5}} = \frac{279{,}091}{390{,}625}$$

43. $a_1 = 1, a_2 = -2, r = -2$

$$S_7 = \frac{1[1 - (-2)^{10}]}{1 - (-2)} = -341$$

45. $a_1 = 5, a_2 = 15, r = 3$

$$S_{10} = \frac{5[1 - 3^{10}]}{1 - 3} = 147{,}620$$

47. $a_1 = \dfrac{1}{3}, a_2 = \dfrac{1}{9}, r = \dfrac{1}{3}$

$$S = \frac{\dfrac{1}{3}}{1 - \dfrac{1}{3}} = \frac{\dfrac{1}{3}}{\dfrac{2}{3}} = \frac{1}{2}$$

49. $a_1 = -\dfrac{2}{3}, r = -\dfrac{2}{3}$

$$S = \frac{-\dfrac{2}{3}}{1 - \left(-\dfrac{2}{3}\right)} = \frac{-\dfrac{2}{3}}{\dfrac{5}{3}} = -\frac{2}{5}$$

51. $a_1 = \dfrac{9}{100}, r = \dfrac{9}{100}$

$$S = \frac{\dfrac{9}{100}}{1 - \dfrac{9}{100}} = \frac{\dfrac{9}{100}}{\dfrac{91}{100}} = \frac{9}{91}$$

53. $a_1 = 0.1, r = 0.1$

$$S = \frac{0.1}{1 - 0.1} = \frac{0.1}{0.9} = \frac{1}{9}$$

55. $a_1 = 1, r = -0.4$

$$S = \frac{1}{1 - (-0.4)} = \frac{1}{1.4} = \frac{5}{7}$$

57. $0.\overline{3} = \dfrac{3}{10} + \dfrac{3}{100} + \dfrac{3}{1000} + \cdots$

$a_1 = \dfrac{3}{10}, r = \dfrac{\dfrac{3}{100}}{\dfrac{3}{10}} = \dfrac{1}{10}$

$0.\overline{3} = \dfrac{\dfrac{3}{10}}{1 - \dfrac{1}{10}} = \dfrac{\dfrac{3}{10}}{\dfrac{9}{10}} = \dfrac{1}{3}$

59. $0.\overline{45} = \dfrac{45}{100} + \dfrac{45}{10{,}000} + \dfrac{45}{1{,}000{,}000} + \cdots$

$a_1 = \dfrac{45}{100}, r = \dfrac{\dfrac{45}{10{,}000}}{\dfrac{45}{100}} = \dfrac{1}{100}$

$0.\overline{45} = \dfrac{\dfrac{45}{100}}{1 - \dfrac{1}{100}} = \dfrac{\dfrac{45}{100}}{\dfrac{99}{100}} = \dfrac{5}{11}$

61. $0.\overline{123} = \dfrac{123}{100} + \dfrac{123}{1{,}000{,}000} + \dfrac{123}{1{,}000{,}000{,}000} + \cdots$

$a_1 = \dfrac{123}{1000}, r = \dfrac{1}{1000}$

$0.\overline{123} = \dfrac{\dfrac{123}{1000}}{1 - \dfrac{1}{1000}} = \dfrac{123}{999} = \dfrac{41}{333}$

63. $0.\overline{422} = \dfrac{422}{1000} + \dfrac{422}{1{,}000{,}000} + \dfrac{422}{1{,}000{,}000{,}000} + \cdots$

$a_1 = \dfrac{422}{1000}, r = \dfrac{1}{1000}$

$0.\overline{422} = \dfrac{\dfrac{422}{1000}}{1 - \dfrac{1}{1000}} = \dfrac{422}{999}$

65. $0.25\overline{4} = \dfrac{25}{100} + \left[\dfrac{4}{1{,}000} + \dfrac{4}{10{,}000} + \dfrac{4}{100{,}000} + \cdots\right]$

$a_1 = \dfrac{4}{1000}, r = \dfrac{1}{10}$

$0.25\overline{4} = \dfrac{25}{100} + \dfrac{\dfrac{4}{1000}}{1 - \dfrac{1}{10}} = \dfrac{25}{100} + \dfrac{4}{900} = \dfrac{229}{900}$

67. $1.20\overline{84} = 1 + \dfrac{2}{10} + \left[\dfrac{84}{10{,}000} + \dfrac{84}{1{,}000{,}000} + \dfrac{84}{100{,}000{,}000} + \cdots\right]$

$a_1 = \dfrac{84}{10{,}000}, r = \dfrac{1}{100}$

$1.20\overline{84} = 1 + \dfrac{2}{10} + \dfrac{\dfrac{84}{10{,}000}}{1 - \dfrac{1}{100}} = \dfrac{12}{10} + \dfrac{7}{825} = \dfrac{1994}{1650} = \dfrac{997}{825}$

69. $A = 100, i = 0.09, n = 2, r = 8, r = \dfrac{i}{n} = \dfrac{0.09}{2} = 0.049, m = nt = 2 \cdot 8 = 16$

$$P = 100\frac{\left[(1 + 0.045)^{16} - 1\right]}{0.045} \approx 2271.93367$$

The future value is \$2271.93.

71. Let a_n be a geometric sequence. Thus

$$a_n = a_1 r^{n-1}, a_1 \neq 0, \quad r \neq 0$$

and $\log a_n = \log a_1 r^{n-1} = \log a_1 + \log r^{n-1}$
$$= \log a_1 + (n-1)\log r$$

Since r is a constant, $\log r$ is a constant. Conjecture: The sequence $\log a_n$ is an arithmetic sequence. To prove this conjecture, we must show that $\log a_n - \log a_{n-1}$ is a constant.

$$\log a_n - \log a_{n-1} = \big(\log a_1 + (n-1)\log r\big) - \big(\log a_1 + (n-2)\log r\big)$$
$$= \log r$$

Since $\log r$ is a constant, the sequence $\log a_n$ is an arithmetic sequence.

73. Yes. Because $x \neq 0$, the first term is 1 and the common ratio is x. If $|x| < 1$, the geometric series converges to $\dfrac{1}{1-x}$. If $|x| \geq 1$, the geometric series does not converge.

75. If a_n is a geometric sequence, then $a_n = a_1 r^{n-1}$

Since $a_n = ar^{n-1}$, then $a_1 = a$.

$$\begin{aligned}
P_n &= a_1 \cdot a_2 \cdot a_3 \cdot \ \cdots \ \cdot a_n \\
&= a \cdot a_2 \cdot a_3 \cdot \ \cdots \ \cdot a_n \\
&= a \cdot ar \cdot ar^2 \cdot \ \cdots \ \cdot ar^{n-1} \\
&= a^n r^{[(n-1)n]/2}
\end{aligned}$$

The exponent on r is found by using the sum of an arithmetic series formula. Note that

$$a \cdot ar \cdot ar^2 \cdot ar^3 \cdot \ \cdots \ \cdot ar^{n-1} = a^n \cdot r^{1+2+3+\cdots+n-1} \text{ and } 1+2+3+ \ \cdots \ + n-1 = \frac{(n-1)n}{2}.$$

77. The distance the ball travels each bounce is given by

$a_1 = 5$

$a_2 = 2(0.8)5$ Multiply by 2 for the distance up and down.

$a_3 = 2(0.8)(0.8)(5) = 2(0.8)^2 5$

$a_4 = 2(0.8)(0.8)^2 5 = 2(0.8)^3 5$

$\vdots$

$a_n = 2(0.8)^{n-1} \cdot 5$

This is a geometric sequence (after a_1). The sum of this sequence is the total distance travelled by the ball.

$$\frac{a_{n+1}}{a_n} = \frac{2(0.8)^n (5)}{2(0.8)^{n+1}(5)} = 0.8$$

Because $0.8 < 1$, the geometric series converges.

$$S = 5 + \frac{8}{1-0.8} = 5 + \frac{8}{0.2} = 5 + 40 = 45$$

The distance traveled is 45 feet. Note from our calculation that the geometric series begins with a_2. The first term ($a_1 = 5$) is added to the series.

79. The nth generation has $a_n = 2^n$ grandparents. Since this is a geometric sequence, the sum can be found by a formula.

$$S_n = \frac{a_1(1-r^n)}{1-r}$$

$$S_{10} = \frac{2(1-2^{10})}{1-2} = \frac{2(1-1024)}{-1} = 2046$$

When $n = 1, a_n = 2$ and there are no grandparents.

Therefore there are $2046 - 2 = 2044$ grandparents
by the 10th generation.

80.
$$\sum_{i=1}^{4}\frac{1}{i(i+1)}=\frac{1}{1(1+1)}+\frac{1}{2(2+1)}+\frac{1}{3(3+1)}+\frac{1}{4(4+1)}$$
$$=\frac{1}{2}+\frac{1}{6}+\frac{1}{12}+\frac{1}{20}=\frac{4}{5}=\frac{4}{4+1}$$

81.
$$k(k+1)(2k+1)+6(k+1)^2=(k+1)[k(2k+1)+6(k+1)]$$
$$=(k+1)[2k^2+k+6k+6]$$
$$=(k+1)[2k^2+7k+6]$$
$$=(k+1)(k+2)(2k+3)$$

82.
$$\frac{k}{k+1}+\frac{1}{(k+1)(k+2)}=\frac{k+2}{k+2}\cdot\frac{k}{k+1}+\frac{1}{(k+1)(k+2)}$$
$$=\frac{k^2+2k+1}{(k+1)(k+2)}=\frac{(k+1)(k+1)}{(k+1)(k+2)}=\frac{k+1}{k+2}$$

83.
$$1^2\not>2(1)+1=3$$
$$2^2\not>2(2)+1=5$$
$$3^2>2(3)+1=7$$
$$3$$

84.
$$S_n+a_{n+1}=\frac{n(n+1)}{2}+n+1$$
$$=\frac{n^2+n}{2}+\frac{2n+2}{2}=\frac{n^2+3n+2}{2}$$
$$=\frac{(n+1)(n+2)}{2}$$

85.
$$S_n+a_{n+1}=2^{n+1}-2+2^{n+1}$$
$$=2^{n+2}-2$$
$$=2(2^{n+1}-1)$$

Section 8.4

1.

1. Let $n=1$. $S_1=3\cdot\ -2=1=\dfrac{1(3\cdot 1-1)}{2}$

2. Assume the statement is true for some positive integer k.

$S_k=1+4+7+\cdots+3k-2=\dfrac{k(3k-1)}{2}$ (Induction Hypothesis)

Verify that the statement is true when $n=k+1$

$S_{k+1}=\dfrac{(k+1)(3k+2)}{2}$.

$a_k=3k-2,\ a_{k+1}=3k+1$

$S_{k+1}=S_k+a_{k+1}$

$=\dfrac{k(3k-1)}{2}+3k+1=\dfrac{3k^2-k}{2}+\dfrac{6k+2}{2}$

$=\dfrac{3k^2+5k+2}{2}=\dfrac{(k+1)(3k+2)}{2}$

By the Principle of Mathematical Induction, the statement is true for all positive integers.

3.

1. Let $n=1$. $S_1=1^3=1=\dfrac{1^2(1+1)^2}{4}$

2. Assume $S_k=1+8+27+\cdots+k^3=\dfrac{k^2(k+1)^2}{4}$ is true for some positive integer k.(Induction Hypothesis).

Verify that $S_{k+1}=\dfrac{(k+1)^2(k+2)^2}{4}$.

$a_k=k^3,\ a_{k+1}=(k+1)^3$

$S_{k+1}=S_k+a_{k+1}=\dfrac{k^2(k+1)^2}{4}+(k+1)^3=\dfrac{k^2(k+1)^2+4(k+1)^3}{4}$

$=\dfrac{(k+1)^2(k^2+4k+4)}{4}=\dfrac{(k+1)^2(k+2)^2}{4}$

By the Principle of Mathematical Induction, the statement is true for all positive integers.

5. 1. Let $n = 1$. $S_1 = 4 \cdot 1 - 1 = 3 = 1(2 \cdot 1 + 1)$

2. Assume that $S_k = 3 + 7 + 11 + \cdots + 4k - 1 = k(2k + 1)$ is true for some positive integer k (Induction Hypothesis).

Verify that $S_{k+1} + (k + 1)(2k + 3)$.

$a_k = 4k - 1, \quad a_{k+1} = 4k + 3$

$S_{k+1} = S_k + a_{k+1}$

$\quad = k(2k + 1) + 4k + 3$

$\quad = 2k^2 + 5k + 3 = (k + 1)(2k + 3)$

By the Principle of Mathematical Induction, the statement is true for all positive integers.

7. 1. Let $n = 1$. $S_1 = (2 \cdot 1 - 1)^3 = 1 = 1^2(2 \cdot 1^2 - 1)$

2. Assume that $S_k = 1 + 27 + 125 + \cdots + (2k - 1)^3 = k^2(2k^2 - 1)$ is true for some positive integer k (Induction Hypothesis).

Verify that $S_{k+1} = (k + 1)^2(2k^2 + 4k + 1)$.

$a_k = (2k - 1)^3, \quad a_{k+1} = (2k + 1)^3$

$S_{k+1} = S_k + a_{k+1} = k^2(2k^2 - 1) + (2k + 1)^3 = 2k^4 - k^2 + 8k^3 + 12k^2 + 6k + 1$

$= 2k^4 + 8k^3 + 11k^2 + 6k + 1 = (k + 1)(2k^3 + 6k^2 + 5k + 1)$

$= (k + 1)^2(2k^2 + 4k + 1)$

By the Principle of Mathematical Induction, the statement is true for all positive integers.

9. 1. Let $n = 1$. $S_1 = \dfrac{1}{(2 \cdot 1 - 1)(1 \cdot 1 + 1)} = \dfrac{1}{3} = \dfrac{1}{2 \cdot 1 + 1}$

2. Assume that $S_k = \dfrac{1}{1 \cdot 3} + \dfrac{1}{3 \cdot 5} + \dfrac{1}{5 \cdot 7} + \cdots + \dfrac{1}{(2k - 1)(2k + 1)} = \dfrac{k}{2k + 1}$ for some positive integer k (Induction Hypothesis).

Verify that $S_{k+1} = \dfrac{k + 1}{2k + 3}$.

$a_k = \dfrac{1}{(2k - 1)(2k + 1)}, \quad a_{k+1} = \dfrac{1}{(2k + 1)(2k + 3)}$

$S_{k+1} = \dfrac{k}{2k + 1} + \dfrac{1}{(2k + 1)(2k + 3)} = \dfrac{2k^2 + 3k + 1}{(2k + 1)(2k + 3)} = \dfrac{(2k + 1)(k + 1)}{(2k + 1)(2k + 3)} = \dfrac{k + 1}{2k + 3}$

By the Principle of Mathematical Induction, the statement is true for all positive integers.

11. 1. Let $n = 1$. $S_1 = 1^4 = 1 = \dfrac{1(1 + 1)(2 \cdot 1 + 1)(3 \cdot 1^2 + 3 \cdot 1 - 1)}{30} = \dfrac{2 \cdot 3 \cdot 5}{30} = 1$

2. Assume that $S_k = 1 + 16 + 81 + \cdots + k^4 = \dfrac{k(k + 1)(2k + 1)(3k^2 + 3k - 1)}{30}$ for some positive integer k (Induction Hypothesis).

Verify that $S_{k+1} = \dfrac{(k + 1)(k + 2)(2k + 3)(3k^2 + 9k + 5)}{30}$.

$a_k = k^4, \quad a_{k+1} = (k + 1^4)$

$S_{k+1} = \dfrac{k(k + 1)(2k + 1)(3k^2 + 3k - 1)}{30} + (k + 1)^4$

$\quad = \dfrac{(k + 1)[k(2k + 1)(3k^2 + 3k - 1) + 30(k + 1)^3]}{30}$

$\quad = \dfrac{(k + 1)[6k^4 + 39k^3 + 91k^2 + 89k + 30]}{30} = \dfrac{(k + 1)(k + 2)(6k^3 + 27k^2 + 37k + 15)}{30}$

$\quad = \dfrac{(k + 1)(k + 2)(2k + 3)(3k^2 + 9k + 5)}{30}$

By the Principle of Mathematical Induction, the statement is true for all positive integers.

13.

1.   Let $n = 4$. Then $\left(\dfrac{3}{2}\right)^4 = \dfrac{81}{16} = 5\dfrac{1}{16}$; $4 + 1 = 5$

     Thus, $\left(\dfrac{3}{2}\right)^n > n + 1$ for $n = 4$.

2.   Assume $\left(\dfrac{3}{2}\right)^k > k + 1$ is true for some positive integer $k \geq 4$ (Induction Hypothesis).

     Verify that $\left(\dfrac{3}{2}\right)^{k+1} > k + 2$.

$$\left(\frac{3}{2}\right)^{k+1} = \left(\frac{3}{2}\right)^k \left(\frac{3}{2}\right) > (k+1)\left(\frac{3}{2}\right) = \frac{1}{2}(3k+3) = \frac{1}{2}(2k+k+3) > \frac{1}{2}(2k+1+3) = k+2$$

     Thus $\left(\dfrac{3}{2}\right)^{k+1} > k + 2$. By the Principle of Mathematical Induction, $\left(\dfrac{3}{2}\right)^n > n + 1$ for all $n \geq 4$.

15.

1.   Let $n = 1$.
$$0 < a < 1$$
$$0 < a \cdot a < a \cdot 1$$
$$a^{1+1} = a^2 < 1$$
     Thus, if $0 < a < 1$, then $a^{1+1} < a^n$ for $n = 1$.

2.   Assume $a^{k+1} < a^k$ is true for some positive integer k, if $0 < a < 1$ (Induction Hypothesis).

     Verify $a^{k+2} < a^{k+1}$.
$$0 < a < 1$$
$$0 < a \cdot a^{k+1} < 1 \cdot a^{k+1}$$
$$a^{k+2} < a^{k+1}$$

     By the Principle of Mathematical Induction, if $0 < a < 1$, then $a^{n+1} < a^n$ for all positive integers.

17.

1.   Let $n = 4$. $1 \cdot 2 \cdot 3 \cdot 4 = 24$, $2^4 = 16$

     Thus, $1 \cdot 2 \cdot 3 \cdot 4 > 2^n$ for $n = 4$.

2.   Assume $1 \cdot 2 \cdot 3 \cdot 4 \cdot \;\cdots\; \cdot k > 2^k$ is true for some positive integer $k \geq 4$ (Induction Hypothesis).

     Verify $1 \cdot 2 \cdot 3 \cdot \;\cdots\; \cdot k \cdot (k+1) > 2^{k+1}$.

$$1 \cdot 2 \cdot 3 \cdot \;\cdots\; \cdot k \cdot (k+1) > 2^k(k+1) > 2^k \cdot 2 = 2^{k+1}$$

     Thus, $1 \cdot 2 \cdot 3 \cdot \;\cdots\; \cdot k \cdot (k+1) > 2^{k+1}$. By the Principle of Mathematical Induction, $1 \cdot 2 \cdot 3 \cdot \;\cdots\; \cdot n > 2^n$ for all $n \geq 4$.

19.

1.   Let $n = 1$ and $a > 0$. $(1+a)^1 = 1 + a = 1 + 1 \cdot a$

     Thus $(1+a)^n \geq 1 + na$ for $n = 1$.

2.   Assume $(1+a)^k \geq 1 + ka$ is true for some positive integer k (Induction Hypotheses).

     Verify $(1+a)^{k+1} > 1 + (k+1)a$.

$$(1+a)^{k+1} = (1+a)^k(1+a) \geq (1+ka)(1+a) = 1 + (k+1)a + ka^2 > 1 + (k+1)a$$

     Thus $(1+a)^{k+1} > 1 + (k+1)a$. By the Principle of Mathematical Induction, $(1+a)^n > 1 + na$ for all positive integers n.

21.

1. Let $n = 1$. $1^2 + 1 = 2$, $2 = 2 \cdot 1$

   Thus 2 is a factor of $n^2 + n$ for $n = 1$.

2. Assume 2 is a factor of $k^2 + k$ for some positive integer k (Induction Hypothesis).

   Verify 2 is a factor of $(k+1)^2 + k + 1$.

   $(k+1)^2 + k + 1 = (k+1)(k+1+1) = (k+1)(k+2)$

   Since $k^2 + k = k(k+1)$, 2 is a factor of k or $k + 1$.

   If 2 is a factor of $k + 1$, then 2 is a factor of $(k+1)(k+2)$.

   If 2 is a factor of k, then 2 is a factor of $k + 2$.

Thus, 2 is a factor of $(k+1)^2 + k + 1$. By the Principle of Mathematical Induction, 2 is a factor of $n^2 + n$ for all positive integers.

23.

1. Let $n = 1$. $5^1 - 1 = 4$, $4 = 4 \cdot 1$

   Thus, 4 is a factor of $5^n - 1$ for $n = 1$.

2. Assume 4 is a factor of $5^k - 1$ for some positive integer k (Induction Hypothesis).

   Verify 4 is a factor of $5^{k+1} - 1$.

   Now $5^{k+1} - 1 = 5 \cdot 5^k - 5 + 4 = 5(5^k - 1) + 4$ which is the sum of two multiples of 4.

Thus, 4 is a factor of $5^{k+1} - 1$. By the Principle of Mathematical Induction, 4 is a factor of $5^n - 1$ for all positive integers.

25.

1. Let $n = 1$. $(xy)^1 = xy = x^1 y^1$

   Thus, $(xy)^n = x^n y^n$ for $n = 1$.

2. Assume $(xy)^k = x^k y^k$ is true for some positive integer k (Induction Hypothesis).

   Verify $(xy)^{k+1} = x^{k+1} y^{k+1}$.

   $(xy)^{k+1} = (xy)^k (xy)^1 = x^k y^k \cdot xy = x^{k+1} y^{k+1}$

Thus $(xy)^{k+1} = x^{k+1} y^{k+1}$. By the Principle of Mathematical Induction, $(xy)^n = x^n y^n$ for all positive integers.

27.

1. Let $n = 1$. $a^1 - b^1 = a - b$

   Thus $a - b$ is a factor of $a^n - b^n$ for $n = 1$.

2. Assume $a - b$ is a factor of $a^k - b^k$ for some positive integer k (Induction Hypothesis).

   Verify $a - b$ is a factor of $a^{k+1} - b^{k+1}$.

   $a^{k+1} - b^{k+1} = (a \cdot a^k - ab^k) + (ab^k - b \cdot b^k) = a(a^k - b^k) + b^k(a - b)$

The sum of two multiples of $a - b$ is a multiple of $a - b$. Thus, $a - b$ is a factor of $a^{k+1} - b^{k+1}$. By the Principle of Mathematical Induction, $a - b$ is a factor of $a^n - b^n$ for all positive integers.

29.

1.   Let $n = 1$. $ar^{1-1} = a \cdot 1 = a = \dfrac{a(1-r^1)}{1-r}$

Thus, the statement is true for $n = 1$.

2.   Assume $\displaystyle\sum_{k=1}^{j} ar^{k-1} = \dfrac{a(1-r^j)}{1-r}$ is true for some positive integer j.

Verify $\displaystyle\sum_{k=1}^{j+1} ar^{k-1} = \dfrac{a(1-r^{j+1})}{1-r}$ is true for $n = j+1$.

$$\sum_{k=1}^{j+1} ar^{k-1} = \sum_{k=1}^{j} (ar^{k+1} - 1) = \dfrac{a(1-r^j)}{1-r} + ar^j$$

$$= \dfrac{a(1-r^j) + ar^j(1-r)}{1-r} = \dfrac{a[1-r^j + r^j - r^{j+1}]}{1-r}$$

$$= \dfrac{a(1-r^{j+1})}{1-r}$$

By the Principle of Mathematical Induction, $\displaystyle\sum_{k=1}^{n} ar^{k-1} = \dfrac{a(1-r^n)}{1-r}$

Connecting Concepts

31.

1.   If $N = 25$, then $\log 25! \approx 25.19 > 25$.

2.   Assume $\log k! > k$ for $k > 25$ (Induction Hypothesis).
     Prove $\log(k+1)! > k+1$.
     $\log(k+1)! = \log[(k+1)k!] = \log(k+1) + \log k! > \log(k+1) + k$
     Because $k > 25$, $\log(k+1) > 1$. Thus, $\log(k+1)! > k+1$.
     Therefore, $\log n! > n$ for all $n > 25$.

33.

1.   When $n = 1$, we have $(x^m)^1 = x^m$ and $x^{m \cdot 1} = x^m$.
     Therefore, the statement is true for $n = 1$.

2.   Assume the statement is true for $n = k$. That is, assume $(x^m)^k = x^{mk}$ (Induction Hypothesis).
     Prove the statement is true for $n = k + 1$.
     $x^{m(k+1)} = x^{mk+m} = x^{mk} \cdot x^m = (x^m)^k \cdot x^m = (x^m)^{k+1}$
     Thus, the statement is true for all positive integers n and m.

35.

1. When $n = 3$, we have $\left(\dfrac{3+1}{3}\right)^3 = \left(\dfrac{4}{3}\right)^3 = \dfrac{64}{27} < 3$.

Thus the statement is true for $n = 3$.

2. Assume the statement is true for $n = k$. That is, assume $\left(\dfrac{k+1}{k}\right)^k < k$ (Induction Hypothesis).

Prove the statement is true for $n = k + 1$. That is, prove $\left(\dfrac{k+2}{k+1}\right)^{k+1} < k+1$.

We begin by noting that $\left(\dfrac{k+2}{k+1}\right) < \dfrac{k+1}{k}$. Therefore

$$\left(\dfrac{k+2}{k+1}\right)^{k+1} < \left(\dfrac{k+1}{k}\right)^{k+1} = \left(\dfrac{k+1}{k}\right)^k \left(\dfrac{k+1}{k}\right)$$

By the Induction Hypothesis, $\left(\dfrac{k+1}{k}\right)^k < k$; thus

$$\left(\dfrac{k+1}{k}\right)^k \left(\dfrac{k+1}{k}\right) < k\left(\dfrac{k+1}{k}\right) = k+1$$

We now have $\left(\dfrac{k+2}{k+1}\right)^{k+1} < k+1$. The induction is complete.

Thus $\left(\dfrac{n+1}{n}\right)^n < n$ is true for all $n \geq 3$.

•   **Prepare for Section 8.5**

36. $(a+b)^3 = (a+b)(a+b)(a+b)$
$\qquad = a^3 + 3a^2b + 3ab^2 + b^3$

37. $5! = 5 \cdot 4 \cdot 3 \cdot 2 \cdot 1 = 120$

38. $0! = 1$

39. $\dfrac{6!}{2!(6-2)!} = \dfrac{720}{2(24)} = 15$

40. $\dfrac{7!}{3!(7-3)!} = \dfrac{5040}{6(24)} = 35$

41. $\dfrac{10!}{10!(10-10)!} = \dfrac{3,628,800}{3,628,000(1)} = 1$

Section 8.5

1. $\dbinom{7}{4} = \dfrac{7!}{4!(7-4)!} = \dfrac{7 \cdot 6 \cdot 5 \cdot 4!}{4!(3 \cdot 2 \cdot 1)} = 35$

3. $\dbinom{9}{2} = \dfrac{9!}{2!(9-2)!} = \dfrac{9 \cdot 8 \cdot 7!}{2 \cdot 1 \cdot 7!} = 36$

5. $\dbinom{12}{9} = \dfrac{12!}{9!(12-9)!} = \dfrac{12 \cdot 11 \cdot 10 \cdot 9!}{9! \cdot 3 \cdot 2 \cdot 1} = 220$

7. $\dbinom{11}{0} = \dfrac{11!}{0!(11-0)!} = \dfrac{11!}{1 \cdot 11!} = 1$

9. $(x-y)^6 = \dbinom{6}{0}x^6 + \dbinom{6}{1}x^5(-y) + \dbinom{6}{2}x^4(-y)^2 + \dbinom{6}{3}x^3(-y)^3 + \dbinom{6}{4}x^2(-y)^4 + \dbinom{6}{5}x(-y)^5 + \dbinom{6}{6}(-y)^6$
$\qquad = x^6 - 6x^5y + 15x^4y^2 - 20x^3y^3 + 15x^2y^4 - 6xy^5 + y^6$

11. $(x+3)^5 = \dbinom{5}{0}x^5 + \dbinom{5}{1}x^4 \cdot 3 + \dbinom{5}{2}x^3 \cdot 3^2 + \dbinom{5}{3}x^2 \cdot 3^3 + \dbinom{5}{4}x \cdot 3^4 + \dbinom{5}{5}3^5$
$\qquad = x^5 + 15x^4 + 90x^3 + 270x^2 + 405x + 243$

13. $(2x-1)^7 = \binom{7}{0}(2x)^7 + \binom{7}{1}(2x)^6(-1) + \binom{7}{2}(2x)^5(-1)^2 + (-1)^2 + \binom{7}{3}(2x)^4(-1)^3 + \binom{7}{4}(2x)^3(-1)^4 + \binom{7}{5}(2x)^2(-1)^5$

$\qquad + \binom{7}{6}(2x)(-1)^6 + \binom{7}{7}(-1)^7$

$\qquad = 128x^7 - 448x^6 + 672x^5 - 560x^4 + 280x^3 - 84x^2 + 14x - 1$

15. $(x+3y)^6 = \binom{6}{0}x^6 + \binom{6}{1}x^5(3y) + \binom{6}{2}x^4(3y)^2 + \binom{6}{3}x^3(3y)^3 + \binom{6}{4}x^2(3y)^4 + \binom{6}{5}x(3y)^5 + \binom{6}{6}(3y)^6$

$\qquad = x^6 + 18x^5y + 135x^4y^2 + 540x^3y^3 + 1215x^2y^4 + 1458xy^5 + 729y^6$

17. $(2x-5y)^4 = \binom{4}{0}(2x)^4 + \binom{4}{1}(2x)^3(-5y) + \binom{4}{2}(2x)^2(-5y)^2 + \binom{4}{3}(2x)(-5y)^3 + \binom{4}{4}(-5y)^4$

$\qquad = 16x^4 - 160x^3y + 600x^2y^2 - 1000xy^3 + 625y^4$

19. $\left(x+\dfrac{1}{x}\right)^6 = \binom{6}{0}x^6 + \binom{6}{1}x^5\left(\dfrac{1}{x}\right) + \binom{6}{2}x^4\left(\dfrac{1}{x}\right)^2 + \binom{6}{3}x^3\left(\dfrac{1}{x}\right)^3 + \binom{6}{4}x^2\left(\dfrac{1}{x}\right)^4 + \binom{6}{5}x\left(\dfrac{1}{x}\right)^5 + \binom{6}{6}\left(\dfrac{1}{x}\right)^6$

$\qquad = x^6 + 6x^4 + 15x^2 + 20 + \dfrac{15}{x^2} + \dfrac{6}{x^4} + \dfrac{1}{x^6}$

21. $(x^2-4)^7 = \binom{7}{0}(x^2)^7 + \binom{7}{1}(2x)^6(-4) + \binom{7}{2}(x^2)^5(-4)^2 + \binom{7}{3}(x^2)^4(-4)^3 + \binom{7}{4}(x^2)^3(-4)^4 + \binom{7}{5}(x^2)^2(-4)^5$

$\qquad + \binom{7}{6}(x^2)(-4)^6 + \binom{7}{7}(-4)^7$

$\qquad = x^{14} - 28x^{12} + 336x^{10} - 2240x^8 + 8960x^6 - 21504x^4 + 28672x^2 - 16384$

23. $(2x^2+y^3)^5 = \binom{5}{0}(2x^2)^5 + \binom{5}{1}(2x^2)^4(y^3) + \binom{5}{2}(2x^2)^3(y^3)^2 + \binom{5}{3}(2x^2)^2(y^3)^3 + \binom{5}{4}(2x^2)(y^3)^4 + \binom{5}{5}(y^3)^5$

$\qquad = 32x^{10} + 80x^8y^3 + 80x^6y^6 + 40x^4y^9 + 10x^2y^{12} + y^{15}$

25. $\left(\dfrac{2}{x}-\dfrac{x}{2}\right)^4 = \binom{4}{0}\left(\dfrac{2}{x}\right)^4 + \binom{4}{1}\left(\dfrac{2}{x}\right)^3\left(-\dfrac{x}{2}\right) + \binom{4}{2}\left(\dfrac{2}{x}\right)^2\left(-\dfrac{x}{2}\right)^2 + \binom{4}{3}\left(\dfrac{2}{x}\right)\left(-\dfrac{x}{2}\right)^3 + \binom{4}{4}\left(-\dfrac{x}{2}\right)^4 = \dfrac{16}{x^4} - \dfrac{16}{x^2} + 6 - x^2 + \dfrac{x^4}{16}$

27. $(s^{-2}+s^2)^6 = \binom{6}{0}(s^{-2})^6 + \binom{6}{1}(s^{-2})^5(s^2) + \binom{6}{2}(s^{-2})^4(s^2)^2 + \binom{6}{3}(s^{-2})^3(s^2)^3 + \binom{6}{4}(s^{-2})^2(s^2)^4 + \binom{6}{5}(s^{-2})(s^2)^5 + \binom{6}{6}(s^2)^6$

$\qquad = s^{-12} + 6s^{-8} + 15s^{-4} + 20 + 15s^4 + 6s^8 + s^{12}$

29. eighth term is $\binom{10}{7}(3x)^3(-y)^7 = -3240x^3y^7$

31. third term is $\binom{12}{2}x^{10}(4y)^2 = 1056x^{10}y^2$

33. fifth term is $\binom{9}{4}(\sqrt{x})^5(-\sqrt{y})^4 = 126x^2y^2\sqrt{x}$

35. ninth term is $\binom{11}{8}\left(\dfrac{a}{b}\right)^3\left(\dfrac{b}{a}\right)^8 = \dfrac{165b^5}{a^5}$

37. $\binom{n}{i-1}a^{n-(i-1)}b^{i-1}$, if $b^{i-1} = b^8$, then $i = 9$.

ninth term is $\binom{10}{8}(2a)^2(-b)^8 = 180a^2b^8$

39. $(y^2)^{i-1} = y^8$, if $2i - 2 = 8$, then $2i = 10$ or $i = 5$.

fifth term is $\binom{6}{4}(2x)^2(y^2)^4 = 60x^2y^8$

41. sixth term is $\binom{10}{5}(3a)^5(-b)^5 = -61,236a^5b^5$

43. fifth term is $\binom{9}{4}(s^{-1})^5(s)^4 = 126s^{-1}$

sixth term is $\binom{9}{5}(s^{-1})^4(s)^5 = 126s$

45.
$$(2-i)^4 = \binom{4}{0}(2^4) + \binom{4}{1}(2)^3(-i)^1 + \binom{4}{2}(2)^2(-i)^2 + \binom{4}{3}2(-i)^3 + \binom{4}{4}(-i)^4$$
$$= 16 + 32(-i) + 24(-1) + 8(-i)^3 + 1$$
$$= 16 - 32i - 24 + 8i + 1$$
$$= -7 - 24i$$

47.
$$(1+2i)^5 = \binom{5}{0}(1)^5 + \binom{5}{1}(1)^4(2i)^1 + \binom{5}{2}(1)^2(2i)^2 + \binom{5}{3}(1)^2(2i)^3 + \binom{5}{4}(1)(2i)^4 + \binom{5}{5}(2i)^5$$
$$= 1 + 10i - 40 - 80i + 80 + 32i$$
$$= 41 - 38i$$

49.
$$\left(\frac{\sqrt{2}}{2} + i\frac{\sqrt{2}}{2}\right)^8 = \left(\frac{\sqrt{2}}{2}\right)^8 (1+i)^8 + \frac{1}{16}(1 + 8i - 28 - 56i + 70 + 56i - 28 - 8i + 1) = \frac{1}{16}(16) = 1$$

Connecting Concepts

51.
$$\frac{(x+h)^n - x^n}{h} = \frac{x^n + nx^{n-1}h + \frac{n(n-1)x^{n-2}h^2}{2} + \frac{n(n-1)(n-2)x^{n-3}h^3}{6} + \cdots + h^n - x^n}{h}$$
$$= nx^{x-1} + \frac{(n)(n-1)x^{n-2}h}{2} + \frac{n(n-1)(n-2)x^{n-3}h^2}{6} + \cdots + h^{n-1}$$

53.
$$(x+y)^n = \sum_{k=0}^{n}\binom{n}{k}x^{n-k}y^k. \text{ With } x = 1 \text{ and } y = 1, \text{ we have } (1+1)^n = \sum_{k=0}^{n}\binom{n}{k}(1)^{n-k}(1)^k$$
$$2^n = \sum_{k=0}^{n}\binom{n}{k}$$

55. Let $x = 1$ and $y = -1$ in the expansion of $(x+y)^n$.
$$(x+y)^n = \sum_{i=0}^{n}\binom{n}{i}x^{n-i}y^i$$
$$(1+(-1))^n = 0^n = 0 = \sum_{i=0}^{n}\binom{n}{i}1^{n-i}(-1)^i = \sum_{i=0}^{n}(-1)^i\binom{n}{i}$$
Thus $\sum_{i=0}^{n}(-1)^i\binom{n}{i} = 0$

57.
$$(1.02)^8 = (1 + 0.02)^8 = \sum_{8-i}^{8}\binom{8}{i}(1)^{8-1}(0.02)^i$$
The sum of the first three terms is
$$\binom{8}{0}(0.02)^0 + \binom{8}{1}(0.02)^1 + \binom{8}{2}(0.02)^2 = 1 + 0.16 + 0.0112$$
$$(1.02)^8 \approx 1.1712$$

59. $\dfrac{9!}{5!2!2!} = 756$

61. $\dfrac{8!}{3!5!0!} = 56$

Prepare for Section 8.6

62. $7! = 7 \cdot 6 \cdot 5 \cdot 4 \cdot 3 \cdot 2 \cdot 1 = 5040$

63. $0! = 1$

64. $\dbinom{7}{1} = \dfrac{7!}{1!(7-1)!} = \dfrac{7 \cdot 6!}{1(6!)} = 7$

65. $\dbinom{8}{5} = \dfrac{8!}{5!(8-5)!} = \dfrac{8 \cdot 7 \cdot 6 \cdot 5!}{5!(3 \cdot 2 \cdot 1)} = 56$

66. $\dfrac{10!}{(10-2)!} = \dfrac{10 \cdot 9 \cdot 8!}{8!} = 90$

67. $\dfrac{6!}{(6-6)!} = \dfrac{6 \cdot 5 \cdot 4 \cdot 3 \cdot 2 \cdot 1}{0!} = 720$

Section 8.6

1. $P(6,2) = \dfrac{6!}{(6-2)!} = \dfrac{6 \cdot 5 \cdot 4!}{4!} = 30$

3. $C(8,4) = \dfrac{8!}{4!(8-4)!} = \dfrac{8 \cdot 7 \cdot 6 \cdot 5 \cdot 4!}{4! \cdot 4 \cdot 3 \cdot 2 \cdot 1} = 70$

5. $P(8,0) = \dfrac{8!}{(8-0)!} = \dfrac{8!}{8!} = 1$

7. $C(7,7) = \dfrac{7!}{7!(7-7)!} = \dfrac{7!}{7! \cdot 1} = 1$

9. $C(10,4) = \dfrac{10!}{4!(10-4)!} = \dfrac{10 \cdot 9 \cdot 8 \cdot 7 \cdot 6!}{4 \cdot 3 \cdot 2 \cdot 1 \cdot 6!} = 210$

11. Use the counting principle.
$3 \cdot 2 \cdot 2 = 12$
There are 12 different possible computer systems.

13. Use the counting principle.
$2 \cdot 2 \cdot 2 \cdot 2 = 16$
There are 16 possible light switch configurations.

15. $P(6,6) = 6! = 720$

17. $5 \cdot 5 \cdot 5 = 125$ ways

19. Use the combination formula with $n = 25$, $r = 5$.
$C(25,5) = \dfrac{25!}{5!(20)!} = 53,130$

21. There are 676 ways to arrange 26 letters taken two at a time ($26 \cdot 26 = 676$). Now if there are more than 676 employees, then at least two employees have the same first and last initials.

23. $C(6,3) \cdot C(8,3) = 1120$

25. $2^{10} = 1024$

27. $C(40,6) = 3,838,380$

29. **a.** $C(7,5) = 21$
b. $C(7,4) \cdot C(3,1) = 35 \cdot 3 = 105$
c. $C(7,2) \cdot C(3,3) = 21 \cdot 1 = 21$

31. $3 \cdot 12 \cdot 5 \cdot 10^7 = 1.8 \times 10^9$

33. $C(10,3) - C(8,1) = 120 - 8 = 112$

35. $P(5,5) = 120$

37. $C(7,2) = 21$

39. $\dfrac{16 \cdot 14}{2} = 112$

41. $C(20,10) = 184,756$

43. $C(20,12) \cdot C(12,4) = 125,970 \cdot 495 = 62,355,150$

45. A triple-decker cone could have all one flavor ice cream, or two different flavors with one scoop of the first flavor and two scoops of the second flavor (such as one scoop of vanilla and two scoops of chocolate), or two different flavors with two scoops of the first flavor and one scoop of the second flavor (such as two scoops of vanilla and one scoop of chocolate), or three different flavors.

$$C(31, 1) + C(31, 2) + C(31, 2) + C(31, 3) = \frac{31!}{1!30!} + \frac{31!}{2!29!} + \frac{31!}{2!29!} + \frac{31!}{3!28!}$$
$$= 31 + 465 + 465 + 4495$$
$$= 5456$$

47. $19!$

49. **a.** $12 \cdot 11 \cdot 10 \cdot 9 \cdot 8 \cdot 7 \cdot 6 = 3,991,680$

b. $12^7 - 12 \cdot 11 \cdot 10 \cdot 9 \cdot 8 \cdot 7 \cdot 6 = 31,840,128$

51. Let $a_1, a_2, \ldots, a_5$ be the long pieces and $b_1, b_2, \ldots, b_5$ be the short pieces. The pairs must have one a with one b. For a_1 there are 5 b's, for a_2 there are 4 b's, $\ldots$. Thus there are $5 \cdot 4 \cdot 3 \cdot 2 \cdot 1 = 120$ pairs consisting of a long piece and a short piece.

53. To return to the original spot, the tourist must toss an equal number of heads and tails. This is $C(10, 5) = 252$. There are 252 different toss combinations that return the tourist to the origin.

••

54. See 8.6.

55. Use the counting principle.
$4 \cdot 3 = 12$
There are 12 different possible two-digit numbers.

56. $P(7,2) = \dfrac{7!}{(7-2)!} = \dfrac{7 \cdot 6 \cdot 5!}{5!} = 42$

57. $C(7,2) = \dfrac{7!}{2!(7-2)!} = \dfrac{7 \cdot 6 \cdot 5!}{2! \cdot 5!} = 21$

58. $\dbinom{8}{5}\left(\dfrac{1}{4}\right)^5\left(\dfrac{3}{4}\right)^{8-5} = \dfrac{8!}{5!(8-5)!}\left(\dfrac{1}{4}\right)^5\left(\dfrac{3}{4}\right)^3 = \dfrac{189}{8192}$

59. Use the counting principle.
$2 \cdot 2 \cdot 2 \cdot 2 = 16$
There are 16 possible light switch configurations.

Section 8.7

1. Label senators S_1, S_2 and representatives R_1, R_2, R_3.
The sample space is $S = \{S_1R_1,\ S_1R_2,\ S_1R_3,\ S_2R_1,\ S_2R_2,\ S_2R_3,\ R_1R_2,\ R_1R_3,\ R_2R_3,\ S_1S_2\}$

3. Label coin H, T and integers 1, 2, 3, 4.
$S = \{H1,\ H2,\ H3,\ H4,\ T1,\ T2,\ T3,\ T4\}$

5. Let the three cans be represented by A, B, and C and (x, y) represent the cans that balls 1 and 2 are placed in; e.g., (A, B) means ball 1 is in can A and ball 2 is in can B.
$S = \{(A,A),\ (A,B),\ (A,C),\ (B,A),\ (B,B),\ (B,C),\ (C,A),\ (C,B),\ (C,C)\}$

7. $S = \{HSC, HSD, HCD, SCD\}$

9. $S = \{ae, ai, ao, au, ei, eo, eu, io, iu, ou\}$

11. $E = \{HHHH\}$

13. $E = \{TTTT, HTTT, THTT, TTHT, TTTH, TTHH, THTH, HTHT, THHT, HTTH, HHTT\}$

15. $E = \varnothing$

The sample space S for the events in Exercises 16—20 is
$S = \{(1,1),\ (1,2),\ (1,3),\ (1,4),\ (1,5),\ (1,6),\ (2,1),\ (2,2),\ (2,3),\ (2,4),\ (2,5),\ (2,6),\ (3,1),\ (3,2),\ (3,3),\ (3,4),\ (3,5),\ (3,6),$
$(4,1),\ (4,2),\ (4,3),\ (4,4),\ (4,5),\ (4,6),\ (5,1),\ (5,2),\ (5,3),\ (5,4),\ (5,5),\ (5,6),\ (6,1),\ (6,2),\ (6,3),\ (6,4),\ (6,5),\ (6,6)\}$

17. $E = \{(1,1),(2,2),(3,3),(4,4),(5,5),(6,6)\}$

19. $E = \{(1,4),(2,4),(3,4),(4,4),(5,4),(6,4)\}$

21.
   a. $P(\text{king}) = \dfrac{4}{52} = \dfrac{1}{13}$
   b. $P(\text{spade}) = \dfrac{13}{52} = \dfrac{1}{4}$

23. $P(\text{increase GNP}) + P(\text{increase inflation}) - P(\text{increase GNP and inflation}) = 0.64 + 0.55 - 0.22 = 0.97$

25. $P(\text{1st}) + P(\text{2nd}) - P(\text{1st and 2nd}) = \dfrac{1}{2} + \dfrac{1}{5} - \dfrac{1}{10} = \dfrac{6}{10} = \dfrac{3}{5}$

27. Because sampling is with replacement, the events are independent. On one trial, the probability of not selecting a 0 is $\dfrac{9}{10}$. Therefore, the probability of not selecting a 0 on five trials is

$$\left(\dfrac{9}{10}\right)^5 = 0.59.$$

29. To receive at least $50, an envelope with $50 in cash or $100 in cash must be selected. The probability is

$$\dfrac{75}{500} + \dfrac{50}{500} = \dfrac{125}{500} = \dfrac{1}{4} = 0.25.$$

31. There are $P(6, 6) = 720$ seating arrangements for the 6 children. There are $2 \cdot 3! \cdot 3!$ ways to have boys and girls alternate. Therefore the probability of boys and girls alternating is

$$\dfrac{2 \cdot 3! \cdot 3!}{720} = \dfrac{72}{720} = \dfrac{1}{10} = 0.1.$$

33. The subject can select $C(5, 2) = 10$ different sets of 2 cards. The magician must name the set the subject has drawn. Therefore, the probability that a magician can guess the answers is $\dfrac{1}{10}$ or 0.1.

35. The probability of choosing Monday is $\dfrac{1}{5}$. The probability of choosing 8:00 A.M. is $\dfrac{1}{8}$. Therefore the probability of choosing Monday at 8:00 A.M. is

$$\dfrac{1}{5} \cdot \dfrac{1}{8} = \dfrac{1}{40} \text{ or } 0.025.$$

37. The probability of at least one unprofitable
$$= 1 - \text{probability of all profitable}$$
$$= 1 - \left[(0.10)(0.10)(0.10)(0.10)\right]$$
$$= 1 - 0.0001 = 0.9999$$

39. Assuming there is no preference, then the probability of choosing program A is $\dfrac{1}{2}$. The probability of all four companies choosing program A is $\left(\dfrac{1}{2}\right)^4 = \dfrac{1}{16}$.

41. The probability of at least one defective equals 1 minus the probability of no defectives. The probability of no defectives is $(0.95)^5$. Therefore the probability of at least one defective is
$$1 - (0.95)^5 \approx 0.2262$$

43. This is a binomial probability with $p = \dfrac{3}{4}$, $q = \dfrac{1}{4}$, $n = 25$, and $k = 21, 22, 23, 24,$ and 25.

$$P = \binom{25}{21}\left(\dfrac{3}{4}\right)^{21}\left(\dfrac{1}{4}\right)^4 + \binom{25}{22}\left(\dfrac{3}{4}\right)^{22}\left(\dfrac{1}{4}\right)^3 + \binom{25}{23}\left(\dfrac{3}{4}\right)^{23}\left(\dfrac{1}{4}\right)^2 + \binom{25}{24}\left(\dfrac{3}{4}\right)^{24}\left(\dfrac{1}{4}\right)^1 + \binom{25}{25}\left(\dfrac{3}{4}\right)^{25}$$

The probability is approximately 0.2137.

• •

Connecting Concepts

45. Let the originator tell a member of the club. (Rumor told once.) This person repeats it to any of 7 remaining members with probability $\dfrac{7}{8}$. (Rumor told twice.) That person repeats it to any of 7 members with probability $\dfrac{7}{8}$. Probability of both events is $\left(\dfrac{7}{8}\right)^2$.

47. Let a, b, c, d be the first number chosen. Then event E is choosing a second number such that the first digit is not a, the second digit is not b, the third digit is not c, and the fourth digit matches the third. Since there are 9 digits available (digits 1 through 9), the probability that the first digit is not a is $\dfrac{8}{9}$, the probability that the second digit is not b is $\dfrac{8}{9}$, the probability that the third digit is not c is $\dfrac{8}{9}$, and the probability that the fourth digit matches the third is $\dfrac{1}{9}$.

Thus, $P(E) = \dfrac{8}{9} \cdot \dfrac{8}{9} \cdot \dfrac{8}{9} \cdot \dfrac{1}{9} = \dfrac{512}{6561} \approx 0.078.$

1. False, $0! \cdot 4! = 1 \cdot 4 \cdot 3 \cdot 2 \cdot 1 = 24$

2. False, $\left(\sum_{i=1}^{3} i\right)\left(\sum_{i=1}^{3} i\right) = 6 \cdot 6 = 36$

$\sum_{i=1}^{3} i^2 = 1 + 4 + 9 = 14$

Thus, $\left(\sum_{i=1}^{3} i\right)\left(\sum_{i=1}^{3} i\right) \neq \sum_{i=1}^{3} i^2$

3. True

4. False, a constant sequence has all terms equal.

5. False, $\dfrac{(k+1)^3}{k^3} = \left(1 + \dfrac{1}{k}\right)^3$ is not a constant.

6. True

7. True

8. False, for example the geometric series

$\sum_{i=1}^{\infty} \dfrac{1}{2^i} = \dfrac{\dfrac{1}{2}}{1 - \dfrac{1}{2}} = 1$

9. False; see Project 1, Section 8.4.

10. False, the exponent is 4.

11. False, there are $m \cdot n$ ways.

12. False, $P(n,r) = \dfrac{n!}{(n-r)!}$

13. True

14. False, $P(A \cap B) = P(\varnothing) = 0$

15. True

1. $a_n = n^2$ [8.1]
$a_3 = 3^2 = 9$
$a_7 = 7^2 = 49$

2. $a_n = n!$ [8.1]
$a_3 = 3! = 6$
$a_7 = 7! = 5040$

3. $a_n = 3n + 2$ [8.1]
$a_3 = 11$
$a_7 = 23$

4. $a_n = 1 - 2n$ [8.1]
$a_3 = 1 - 2(3) = 1 - 6 = -5$
$a_7 = 1 - 2(7) = 1 - 14 = -13$

5. $a_n = 2^{-n}$ [8.1]
$a_3 = 2^{-3} = \dfrac{1}{8}$
$a_7 = 2^{-7} = \dfrac{1}{128}$

6. $a_n = 3n$ [8.1]
$a_3 = 3^3 = 27$
$a_7 = 3^7 = 2187$

7. $a_n = \dfrac{1}{n!}$ [8.1]
$a_3 = \dfrac{1}{3!} = \dfrac{1}{6}$
$a_7 = \dfrac{1}{7!} = \dfrac{1}{5040}$

8. $a_n = \dfrac{1}{n}$ [8.1]
$a_3 = \dfrac{1}{3}$
$a_7 = \dfrac{1}{7}$

9. $a_n = \left(\dfrac{2}{3}\right)^n$ [8.1]
$a_3 = \left(\dfrac{2}{3}\right)^3 = \dfrac{8}{27}$
$a_7 = \left(\dfrac{2}{3}\right)^7 = \dfrac{128}{2187}$

10. $a_n = \left(-\dfrac{4}{3}\right)^n$ [8.1]
$a_3 = \left(-\dfrac{4}{3}\right)^3 = -\dfrac{64}{27}$
$a_7 = \left(-\dfrac{4}{3}\right)^7 = -\dfrac{16,384}{2187}$

11. $a_1 = 2, a_n = 3a_{n-1}$ [8.1]
$a_2 = 3a_1 = 3 \cdot 2 = 6$
$a_3 = 3a_2 = 3 \cdot 6 = 18$ •
$a_4 = 3a_3 = 3 \cdot 18 = 54$
$a_5 = 3a_4 = 3 \cdot 54 = 162$
$a_6 = 3a_5 = 3 \cdot 162 = 486$
$a_7 = 3a_6 = 3 \cdot 486 = 1458$ •

12. $a_1 = -1, a_n = 2a_{n-1}$ [8.1]
$a_2 = 2a_1 = 2(-1) = -2$
$a_3 = 2a_2 = 2(-2) = -4$ •
$a_4 = 2a_3 = 2(-4) = -8$
$a_5 = 2a_4 = 2(-8) = -16$
$a_6 = 2a_5 = 2(-16) = -32$
$a_7 = 2a_6 = 2(-32) = -64$ •

13. $a_1 = 1, a_n = -na_{n-1}$ [8.1]

$a_2 = -2a_1 = -2 \cdot 1 = -2$

$a_3 = -3a_2 = -3 \cdot (-2) = 6$ •

$a_4 = -4a_3 = -4 \cdot 6 = -24$

$a_5 = -5a_4 = -5 \cdot (-24) = 120$

$a_6 = -6a_5 = -6 \cdot 120 = -720$

$a_7 = -7a_6 = -7 \cdot (-720) = 5040$ •

14. $a_1 = 2, a_n = n^2 a_{n-1}$ [8.1]

$a_2 = 2^2 a_1 = 2^2 \cdot 2 = 8$

$a_3 = 3^2 a_2 = 9 \cdot 8 = 72$ •

$a_4 = 4^2 a_3 = 16 \cdot 72 = 1152$

$a_5 = 5^2 a_4 = 25 \cdot 1152 = 28,800$

$a_6 = 6^2 a_5 = 36 \cdot 28,800 = 1,036,800$

$a_7 = 7^2 a_6 = 49 \cdot 1,036,800 = 50,803,200$ •

15. $a_1 = 4, a_n = a_{n-1} + 2$ [8.1]

$a_2 = a_1 + 2 = 4 + 2 = 6$

$a_3 = a_2 + 2 = 6 + 2 = 8$ •

$a_4 = a_3 + 2 = 8 + 2 = 10$

$a_5 = a_4 + 2 = 10 + 2 = 12$

$a_6 = a_5 + 2 = 12 + 2 = 14$

$a_7 = a_6 + 2 = 14 + 2 = 16$ •

16. $a_1 = 3, a_n = a_{n-1} - 3$ [8.1]

$a_2 = a_1 - 3 = 3 - 3 = 0$

$a_3 = a_2 - 3 = 0 - 3 = -3$ •

$a_4 = a_3 - 3 = -3 - 3 = -6$

$a_5 = a_4 - 3 = -6 - 3 = -9$

$a_6 = a_5 - 3 = -9 - 3 = -12$

$a_7 = a_6 - 3 = -12 - 3 = -15$ •

17. $a_1 = 1, a_2 = 2, a_n = a_{n-1}a_{n-2}$ [8.1]

$a_3 = a_2 \cdot a_1 = 2 \cdot 1 = 2$ •

$a_4 = a_3 \cdot a_2 = 2 \cdot 2 = 4$

$a_5 = a_4 \cdot a_3 = 4 \cdot 2 = 8$

$a_6 = a_5 \cdot a_4 = 8 \cdot 4 = 32$

$a_7 = a_6 \cdot a_5 = 32 \cdot 8 = 256$ •

18. $a_1 = 1, a_2 = 2, a_n = \dfrac{a_n - 1}{a_n - 2}$ [8.1]

$a_3 = \dfrac{a_2}{a_1} = \dfrac{2}{1} = 2$ •

$a_4 = \dfrac{a_3}{a_2} = \dfrac{2}{2} = 1$

$a_5 = \dfrac{a_4}{a_3} = \dfrac{1}{2}$

$a_6 = \dfrac{a_5}{a_4} = \dfrac{1/2}{1} = \dfrac{1}{2}$

$a_7 = \dfrac{a_6}{a_5} = \dfrac{1/2}{1/2} = 1$ •

19. $a_1 = -1, a_n = 3_n a_{n-1}$ [8.1]

$a_2 = 3(2)a_1 = 3(2)(-1) = -6$

$a_3 = 3(3)a_2 = 3(3)(-6) = -54$ •

$a_4 = 3(4)a_3 = 3(4)(-54) = -648$

$a_5 = 3(5)a_4 = 3(5)(-648) = -9720$

$a_6 = 3(6)a_5 = 3(6)(-9720) = -174,960$

$a_7 = 3(7)a_6 = 3(7)(-174,960) = -3,674,160$ •

20. $a_1 = 2, a_n = -2na_{n-1}$ [8.1]

$a_2 = -2(2)a_1 = -2(2)(2) = -8$

$a_3 = -2(3)a_2 = -2(3)(-8) = 48$ •

$a_4 = -2(4)a_3 = -2(4)(48) = -384$

$a_5 = -2(5)a_4 = -2(5)(-384) = 3840$

$a_6 = -2(6)a_5 = -2(6)(3840) = -46,080$

$a_7 = -2(7)a_6 = -2(7)(-46,080) = 645,120$ •

21. $a_{n+1} - a_n = (n+1)^2 - n^2 = 2n + 1 \neq$ constant.

Thus not an arithmetic sequence.

$\dfrac{a_{n+1}}{a_n} = \dfrac{(n+1)^2}{n^2} = \left(1 + \dfrac{1}{n}\right)^2 \neq$ constant.

Thus not a geometric sequence.

Neither an arithmetic nor a geometric sequence.   [8.1]

22. $a_{n+1} - a_n = (n+1)! - n!$

$= (n+1)n! - n! = n \cdot n! \neq$ constant.

Thus not an arithmetic sequence.

$\dfrac{a_{n+1}}{a_n} = \dfrac{(n+1)!}{n!} = \dfrac{(n-1)n!}{n!} = n + 1 \neq$ constant.

Thus not a geometric sequence.

Neither an arithmetic nor a geometric sequence.   [8.1]

23. $a_{n+1} - a_n = 3(n+1) + 2 - (3n+2) = 3 =$ constant.   [8.2]

Arithmetic sequence.

24. $a_{n+1} - a_n = (1 - 2(n+1)) - (1 - 2n) = -2 =$ constant.   [8.2]

Arithmetic sequence.

25. $\dfrac{a_{n+1}}{a_n} = \dfrac{2^{-(n+1)}}{2^{-n}} = \dfrac{2^{-n} \cdot 2^{-1}}{2^{-n}} = 2^{-1} = \dfrac{1}{2} =$ constant.   [8.3]

Geometric sequence.

26. $\dfrac{a_{n+1}}{a_n} = \dfrac{3^{n+1}}{3^n} = \dfrac{3^n \cdot 3}{3^n} = 3 =$ constant.   [8.3]

Geometric sequence.

27.

$$a_{n+1} - a_n = \frac{1}{(n+1)!} - \frac{1}{n!}$$

$$= \frac{1}{(n+1)n!} - \frac{1}{n!} = \frac{1}{n!}\left(\frac{1}{n+1} - 1\right) \neq \text{constant}$$

$$\frac{a_{n+1}}{a_n} = \frac{\frac{1}{(n+1)!}}{\frac{1}{n!}} = \frac{n!}{(n+1)!} = \frac{n!}{(n+1)n!} = \frac{1}{n+1} \neq \text{constant}$$

Neither an arithmetic nor a geometric sequence. [8.1]

28.

$$a_{n+1} - a_n = \frac{1}{n+1} - \frac{1}{n} = -\frac{1}{n(n+1)} \neq \text{constant}$$

$$\frac{a_{n+1}}{a_n} = \frac{\frac{1}{n+1}}{\frac{1}{n}} = \frac{n}{n+1} \neq \text{constant}$$

Neither an arithmetic nor a geometric sequence. [8.1]

29.

$$\frac{a_{n+1}}{a_n} = \frac{\left(\frac{2}{3}\right)^{n+1}}{\left(\frac{2}{3}\right)^n} = \frac{2}{3} = \text{constant.}$$

Geometric sequence. [8.3]

30.

$$\frac{a_{n+1}}{a_n} = \frac{\left(-\frac{4}{3}\right)^{n+1}}{\left(-\frac{4}{3}\right)^n} = -\frac{4}{3} = \text{constant.}$$

Geometric sequence [8.3]

31. Since each successive term is 3 times the previous term, the sequence has a common ratio of 3.
Geometric sequence. [8.1]

32. Since each successive term is 2 times the previous term, the sequence has a common ratio of 2.
Geometric sequence. [8.1]

33. Examining the terms of the sequence reveals that there is no common difference and no common ratio.
Neither an arithmetic nor a geometric sequence. [8.1]

34. Examining the terms of the sequence reveals that there is no common difference and no common ratio.
Neither an arithmetic nor a geometric sequence. [8.1]

35. Since each successive term is 2 more than the preceding term, the sequence has a common difference of 2.
Arithmetic sequence. [8.2]

36. Since each successive term is 3 less than the preceding term, the sequence has a common difference of -3.
Arithmetic sequence. [8.2]

37. Examining the terms of the sequence reveals that there is no common difference and no common ratio.
Neither an arithmetic nor a geometric sequence. [8.1]

38. Examining the terms of the sequence reveals that there is no common difference and no common ratio.
Neither an arithmetic nor a geometric sequence. [8.1]

39. Examining the terms of the sequence reveals that there is no common difference and no common ratio.
Neither an arithmetic nor a geometric sequence. [8.1]

40. Examining the terms of the sequence reveals that there is no common difference and no common ratio.
Neither an arithmetic nor a geometric sequence. [8.1]

41.

$$\sum_{n=1}^{9}(2n-3) \text{ is an arithmetic series with common difference 2. } a_1 = -1, a_9 = 15, n = 9 \quad [8.2]$$

$$S_n = \frac{n}{2}(a_1 + a_n)$$

$$S_9 = \frac{9}{2}(-1 + 15) = \frac{9}{2}(14) = 63$$

42.

$$\sum_{i=1}^{11}(1-3i) \text{ is an arithmetic series with common difference } -3. \ a_1 = -2, a_{11} = -32, n = 11 \quad [8.2]$$

$$S_n = \frac{n}{2}(a_1 + a_n)$$

$$S_{11} = \frac{11}{2}(-2 + (-32)) = \frac{11}{2}(-34) = -187$$

43.

$\displaystyle\sum_{k=1}^{8} (4k+1)$ is an arithmetic series with common difference 4. $a_1 = 5, a_8 = 33, n = 8$ [8.2]

$S_n = \dfrac{n}{2}(a_1 + a_n)$

$S_8 = \dfrac{8}{2}(5 + 33) = 4(38) = 152$

44.

$\displaystyle\sum_{i=1}^{10} (i^2 + 3)$ is neither an arithmetic nor a geometric series. [8.1]

$\displaystyle\sum_{i=1}^{10} (i^2 + 3) = (1+3) + (4+3) + (9+3) + (16+3) + (25+3) + (36+3) + (49+3) + (64+3) + (81+3) + (100+3) = 415$

45.

$\displaystyle\sum_{n=1}^{6} 3 \cdot 2^n$ is a geometric series with common ratio 2. $a_1 = 6, n = 6, r = 2$ [8.3]

$S_n = \dfrac{a_1(1 - r^n)}{1 - r}$

$S_6 = \dfrac{6(1 - 2^6)}{1 - 2} = \dfrac{6(-63)}{-1} = 378$

46.

$\displaystyle\sum_{i=1}^{5} 2 \cdot 4^{i-1}$ is a geometric series with common ratio 4. $a_1 = 2, n = 5, r = 4$ [8.3]

$S_n = \dfrac{a_1(1 - r^n)}{1 - r}$

$S_5 = \dfrac{2(1 - 4^5)}{1 - 4} = \dfrac{2(-1023)}{-3} = 682$

47.

$\displaystyle\sum_{k=1}^{9} (-1)^k (3^k)$ is a geometric series with common ratio -3. $a_1 = -3, n = 9, r = -3$ [8.3]

$S_n = \dfrac{a_1(1 - r^n)}{1 - r}$

$S_9 = \dfrac{-3(1 - (-3)^9)}{1 - (-3)} = \dfrac{-3(19{,}684)}{4} = -14{,}763$

48.

$\displaystyle\sum_{i=1}^{8} (-1)^{i+1} 2^i$ is a geometric series with common ratio -2. $a_1 = 2, n = 8, r = -2$ [8.3]

$S_n = \dfrac{a_1(1 - r^n)}{1 - r}$

$S_8 = \dfrac{2(1 - (-2)^8)}{1 - (-2)} = \dfrac{2(-255)}{3} = -170$

49.

$\displaystyle\sum_{i=1}^{10}\left(\frac{2}{3}\right)^{i}$ is a geometric series with common ratio $\frac{2}{3}$. $a_1 = \frac{2}{3}$, $n = 10$, $r = \frac{2}{3}$ [8.3]

$$S_n = \frac{a_1(1-r^n)}{1-r}$$

$$S_{10} = \frac{\frac{2}{3}\left(1-\left(\frac{2}{3}\right)^{10}\right)}{1-\frac{2}{3}} = \frac{\frac{2}{3}\left(1-\left(\frac{2}{3}\right)^{10}\right)}{\frac{1}{3}} = 2\left(1-\left(\frac{2}{3}\right)^{10}\right) = 2\left(1-\frac{1{,}024}{59{,}049}\right) = 2\left(\frac{58{,}025}{59{,}049}\right) = \frac{116{,}050}{59{,}049} \approx 1.9653$$

50.

$\displaystyle\sum_{i=1}^{11}\left(\frac{3}{2}\right)^{i}$ is a geometric series with common ratio $\frac{3}{2}$. $a_1 = \frac{3}{2}$, $n = 11$, $r = \frac{3}{2}$ [8.3]

$$S_n = \frac{a_1(1-r^n)}{1-r}$$

$$S_{11} = \frac{\frac{3}{2}\left(1-\left(\frac{3}{2}\right)^{11}\right)}{1-\frac{3}{2}} \approx \frac{\frac{3}{2}(-85.4976)}{-\frac{1}{2}} \approx 256.4927$$

51.

$\displaystyle\sum_{n=1}^{9}\frac{(-1)^{n+1}}{n^2}$ is neither a geometric nor an arithmetic series. [8.1]

$$\sum_{n=1}^{9}\frac{(-1)^{n+1}}{n^2} = 1 - \frac{1}{4} + \frac{1}{9} - \frac{1}{16} + \frac{1}{25} - \frac{1}{26} + \frac{1}{49} - \frac{1}{64} + \frac{1}{81} \approx 0.8280$$

52.

$\displaystyle\sum_{k=1}^{5}\frac{(-1)^{k+1}}{k!}$ is neither an arithmetic nor a geometric series. [8.1]

$$\sum_{k=1}^{5}\frac{(-1)^{k+1}}{k!} = 1 - \frac{1}{2} + \frac{1}{6} - \frac{1}{24} + \frac{1}{120} = \frac{19}{30} \approx 0.6\overline{3}$$

53.

$\displaystyle\sum_{n=1}^{\infty}\left(\frac{1}{4}\right)^{n}$ is an infinite geometric series with common ratio $\frac{1}{4}$. $a_1 = \frac{1}{4}$, $r = \frac{1}{4}$ [8.3]

$$S = \frac{a_1}{1-r}$$

$$S = \frac{\frac{1}{4}}{1-\frac{1}{4}} = \frac{\frac{1}{4}}{\frac{3}{4}} = \frac{1}{3}$$

54.

$\displaystyle\sum_{i=1}^{\infty}\left(-\frac{5}{6}\right)^{i}$ is an infinite geometric series with common ratio $-\frac{5}{6}$. $a_1 = -\frac{5}{6}$, $r = -\frac{5}{6}$ [8.3]

$$S = \frac{a_1}{1-r}$$

$$S = \frac{-\frac{5}{6}}{1-\left(-\frac{5}{6}\right)} = \frac{-\frac{5}{6}}{\frac{11}{6}} = -\frac{5}{11}$$

55. $\displaystyle\sum_{k=1}^{\infty}\left(-\frac{4}{5}\right)^k$ is an infinite geometric series with common ratio $-\frac{4}{5}$. $a_1 = -\frac{4}{5}$, $r = -\frac{4}{5}$ [8.3]

$$S = \frac{a_1}{1-r}$$

$$S = \frac{-\dfrac{4}{5}}{1-\left(-\dfrac{4}{5}\right)} = \frac{-\dfrac{4}{5}}{\dfrac{9}{5}} = -\frac{4}{9}$$

56. $\displaystyle\sum_{j=0}^{\infty}\left(\frac{1}{5}\right)^j$ is an infinite geometric series with common ratio $\frac{1}{5}$. $a_1 = 1$, $r = \frac{1}{5}$ [8.3]

$$S = \frac{a_1}{1-r}$$

$$S = \frac{1}{1-\dfrac{1}{5}} = \frac{1}{\dfrac{4}{5}} = \frac{5}{4}$$

57. $\displaystyle\sum_{i=1}^{n}(5i+1) = \frac{n(5n+7)}{2}$ [8.4]

1. For $n=1$, we have $\displaystyle\sum_{i=1}^{1}(5i+1) = 6$ and $\dfrac{1(5+7)}{2} = 6$. Therefore that statement is true for $n=1$.

2. Assume the statement is true for $n=k$.

$$\sum_{i=1}^{k}(5i+1) = \frac{k(5k+7)}{2} \quad \text{Induction Hypothesis}$$

Prove the statement is true for $n=k+1$. That is, prove

$$\sum_{i=1}^{k+1}(5i+1) = \frac{(k+1)(5k+12)}{2}$$

$$\sum_{i=1}^{k+1}(5i+1) = \sum_{i=1}^{k}(5i+1) + 5(k+1) + 1 = \sum_{i=1}^{k}(5i+1) + 5k + 6$$

$$= \frac{k(5k+7)}{2} + 5k + 6 \quad \text{Using the Induction Hypothesis}$$

$$= \frac{k(5k+7) + 10k + 12}{2} = \frac{5k^2 + 7k + 10k + 12}{2}$$

$$= \frac{5k^2 + 17k + 12}{2} = \frac{(k+1)(5k+12)}{2}$$

Thus the statement is true for $n=k+1$. By the Induction Axiom, the statement is true for all positive integers.

58.

$$\sum_{i=1}^{n}(3-4i)=n(1-2n) \quad [8.4]$$

1.   For $n=1$, we have $\displaystyle\sum_{i=1}^{1}(3-4i)=-1$ and $1[1-2(1)]=-1$.

Therefore the statement is true for $n=1$.

2.   Assume the statement is true for $n=k$.

$$\sum_{i=1}^{k}(3-4i)=k(1-2k) \text{ Induction Hypothesis}$$

Prove the statement is true for $n=k+1$. That is, prove

$$\sum_{i=1}^{k+1}(3-4i)=(k+1)(-1-2k)=-(k+1)(2k+1)$$

$$\sum_{i=1}^{k+1}(3-4i)=\sum_{i=1}^{k}(3-4i)+3-4(k+1)=\sum_{i=1}^{k}(3-4i)-1-4k$$

$$=k(1-2k)-1-4k \quad \text{Using the Induction Hypothesis}$$

$$=k-2k^2-1-4k=-2k^2-3k-1$$

$$=-(2k^2+3k+1)=-(k+1)(2k+1)$$

Thus the statement is true for $n=k+1$. By the Induction Axiom, the statement is true for all positive integers.

59.

$$\sum_{i=0}^{n}\left(-\frac{1}{2}\right)^i=\frac{2\left(1-\left(-\frac{1}{2}\right)^{n+1}\right)}{3} \quad [8.4]$$

1.   This induction begins with $n=0$.

$$\sum_{i=0}^{0}\left(-\frac{1}{2}\right)^i=\left(-\frac{1}{2}\right)^0=1 \text{ and } \frac{2\left(1-\left(-\frac{1}{2}\right)^1\right)}{3}=1$$

Thus the statement is true when $n=0$.

2.   Assume the statement is true for $n=k$.

$$\sum_{i=0}^{k}\left(-\frac{1}{2}\right)^i=\frac{2\left(1-\left(-\frac{1}{2}\right)^{k+1}\right)}{3} \text{ Induction Hypothesis}$$

Prove the statement is true for $n=k+1$. That is, prove

$$\sum_{i=0}^{k+1}\left(-\frac{1}{2}\right)^i=\frac{2\left(1-\left(-\frac{1}{2}\right)^{k+2}\right)}{3}=\frac{2-2\left(-\frac{1}{2}\right)^{k+2}}{3}=\frac{2-2\left(-\frac{1}{2}\right)\left(-\frac{1}{2}\right)^{k+1}}{3}=\frac{2+\left(-\frac{1}{2}\right)^{k+1}}{3}$$

$$\sum_{i=0}^{k+1}\left(-\frac{1}{2}\right)^i=\sum_{i=0}^{k}\left(-\frac{1}{2}\right)^i+\left(-\frac{1}{2}\right)^{k+1}$$

$$=\frac{2\left(1-\left(-\frac{1}{2}\right)^{k+1}\right)}{3}+\left(-\frac{1}{2}\right)^{k+1}$$

$$=\frac{2\left(1-\left(-\frac{1}{2}\right)^{k+1}\right)+3\left(-\frac{1}{2}\right)^{k+1}}{3}=\frac{2-2\left(-\frac{1}{2}\right)^{k+1}+3\left(-\frac{1}{2}\right)^{k+1}}{3}$$

$$=\frac{2+\left(-\frac{1}{2}\right)^{k+1}}{3}$$

Thus the statement is true for all integers $n\geq 0$.

60.

$$\sum_{i=0}^{n}(-1)^i = \frac{1-(-1)^{n+1}}{2} \quad [8.4]$$

1.   This induction begins with $n = 0$.

$$\sum_{i=0}^{0}(-1)^i = (-1)^0 = 1 \text{ and } \frac{1-(-1)}{2} = \frac{1+1}{2} = 1$$

Thus the statement is true for $n = 0$.

2.   Assume the statement is true for $n = k$.

$$\sum_{i=0}^{k}(-1)^i = \frac{1-(-1)^{k+1}}{2}$$

Prove the statement is true for $n = k + 1$. That is, prove

$$\sum_{i=0}^{k+1}(-1)^i = \frac{1-(-1)^{k+2}}{2} = \frac{1-(-1)(-1)^{k+1}}{2} = \frac{1+(-1)^{k+1}}{2}$$

$$\sum_{i=0}^{k+1}(-1)^i = \sum_{i=0}^{k}(-1)^i + (-1)^{k+1}$$

$$= \frac{1-(-1)^{k+1}}{2} + (-1)^{k+1} \quad \text{Using the Induction Hypothesis}$$

$$= \frac{1-(-1)^{k+1}+2(-1)^{k+1}}{2}$$

$$= \frac{1+(-1)^{k+1}}{2}$$

Thus the statement is true for all integers $n \geq 0$.

61. $n^n \geq n!$ [8.4]

1.   When $n = 1$, $1^1 = 1$ and $n! = 1$. The statement is true for $n = 1$.

2.   Assume the statement is true for $n = k$.

$k^k \geq k!$ Induction Hypothesis

Prove the statement is true for $n = k + 1$. That is, prove

$(k+1)^{k+1} \geq (k+1)!$

$(k+1)^{k+1} = (k+1)(k+1)^k > (k+1)k^k$

By Induction Hypothesis $k^k \geq k!$. We have

$(k+1)k^k \geq (k+1)k! = (k+1)!$

Therefore $(k+1)^{k+1} \geq (k+1)!$

Therefore the statement is true for all integers $n \geq 1$.

62.

1.   For $n = 9$, $9! = 362,880$, $4^9 = 262,144$ [8.4]

Since $362,880 > 262,144$, the statement is true for $n = 9$.

2.   Assume the statement is true for $n = k$.

$k! > 4^k$ Induction Hypothesis

Prove the statement is true for $n = k + 1$. That is, prove

$(k+1)! > 4^{k+1}$

$(k+1)! = (k+1)k! > (k+1)4^k$ By Induction Hypothesis

Since $k \geq 9$, $k+1 \geq 4$. Thus

$(k+1)4^k > 4 \cdot 4^k = 4^{k+1}$

Thus $(k+1)! > 4^{k+1}$

The statement is true for all integers $n \geq 9$.

63.

1. When $n = 1$, we have $1^3 + 2(1) = 3$. Since 3 is a factor of 3, the statement is true for $n = 1$. [8.4]

2. Assume the statement is true for $n = k$.

3 is a factor of $k^3 + 2k$ Induction Hypothesis

Prove the statement is true for $n = k + 1$. That is, prove

3 is a factor of $(k + 1)^3 + 2(k + 1)$.

$$(k + 1)^3 + 2(k + 1) = k^3 + 3k^2 + 3k + 1 + 2k + 2$$
$$= (k^3 + 2k) + 3(k^2 + k + 1)$$

By Induction Hypothesis, 3 is a factor of $k^3 + 2k$. Three is also a factor of $3(k^2 + k + 1)$. Thus 3 is a factor of $(k + 1)^3 + 2(k + 1)$.
The statement is true for all positive integers n.

64.

1. When $n = 1$, $a_1 = \sqrt{2} < 2$. The statement is true for $n = 1$. [8.4]

2. Assume the statement is true for some integer k.

$a_k < 2$ Induction Hypothesis

Prove the statement is true for $n = k + 1$. That is, prove

$a_{k+1} < 2$.

By the Induction Hypothesis, $a_k < 2$. Thus

$$(\sqrt{2})^{a_k} < (\sqrt{2})^2 = 2$$

But $(\sqrt{2})^{a_k} = a_{k+1}$. Thus

$a_{k+1} < 2$

The statement is true for all positive integers n.

65.

$$(4a - b)^5 = \sum_{i=0}^{5} \binom{5}{i}(4a)^{5-i}(-b)^i$$ [8.5]

$$= \binom{5}{0}(4a)^5 + \binom{5}{1}(4a)^4(-b)^1 + \binom{5}{2}(4a)^3(-b)^2 + \binom{5}{3}(4a)^2(-b)^3 + \binom{5}{4}(4a)(-b)^4 + \binom{5}{5}(-b)^5$$

$$= 1(1024a^5) + 5(-256a^4b) + 10(64a^3b^2) + 10(-16a^2b^3) + 5(4ab^4) + (-b^5)$$

$$= 1024a^5 - 1280a^4b + 640a^3b^2 - 160a^2b^3 + 20ab^4 - b^5$$

66.

$$(x + 3y)^6 = \sum_{i=0}^{6} \binom{6}{i}x^{6-i}(3y)^i$$ [8.5]

$$= \binom{6}{0}x^6 + \binom{6}{1}x^5(3y) + \binom{6}{2}x^4(3y)^2 + \binom{6}{3}x^3(3y)^3 + \binom{6}{4}x^2(3y)^4 + \binom{6}{5}x(3y)^5 + \binom{6}{6}(3y)^6$$

$$= x^6 + 6x^5(3y) + 15x^4(9y^2) + 20x^3(27y^3) + 15x^2(81y^4) + 6x(243y^5) + 1(729y^6)$$

$$= x^6 + 18x^5y + 135x^4y^2 + 540x^3y^3 + 1215x^2y^4 + 1458xy^5 + 729y^6$$

67.

$$\left(\sqrt{a} + 2\sqrt{b}\right)^8 = \sum_{i=0}^{8} \binom{8}{i}\left(\sqrt{a}\right)^{8-i}\left(2\sqrt{b}\right)^i$$ [8.5]

$$= \binom{8}{0}(\sqrt{a})^8 + \binom{8}{1}(\sqrt{a})^7(2\sqrt{b}) + \binom{8}{2}(\sqrt{a})^6(2\sqrt{b})^2 + \binom{8}{3}(\sqrt{a})^5(2\sqrt{b})^3 + \binom{8}{4}(\sqrt{a})^4(2\sqrt{b})^4 + \binom{8}{5}(\sqrt{a})^3(2\sqrt{b})^5$$

$$+ \binom{8}{6}(\sqrt{a})^2(2\sqrt{b})^6 + \binom{8}{7}(\sqrt{a})(2\sqrt{b})^7 + \binom{8}{8}(2\sqrt{b})^8$$

$$= 1(a^4) + 8a^{7/2}(2b^{1/2}) + 28a^3(4b) + 56a^{5/2}(8b^{3/2}) + 70a^2(16b^2) + 56a^{3/2}(32b^{5/2}) + 28a(64b^3)$$

$$+ 8a^{1/2}(128b^{7/2}) + 1(256b^4)$$

$$= a^4 + 16a^{7/2}b^{1/2} + 112a^3b + 448a^{5/2}b^{3/2} + 1120a^2b^2 + 1792a^{3/2}b^{5/2} + 1792ab^3 + 1024a^{1/2}b^{7/2} + 256b^4$$

68.

$$\left(2x - \frac{1}{2x}\right)^7 = \sum_{i=0}^{7} \binom{7}{i}(2x)^{7-i}\left(-\frac{1}{2x}\right)^i \quad [8.5]$$

$$= \binom{7}{0}(2x)^7 + \binom{7}{1}(2x)^6\left(-\frac{1}{2x}\right) + \binom{7}{2}(2x)^5\left(-\frac{1}{2x}\right)^2 + \binom{7}{3}(2x)^4\left(-\frac{1}{2x}\right)^3 + \binom{7}{4}(2x)^3\left(-\frac{1}{2x}\right)^4 + \binom{7}{5}(2x)^2\left(-\frac{1}{2x}\right)^5$$

$$+ \binom{7}{6}(2x)\left(-\frac{1}{2x}\right)^6 + \binom{7}{7}\left(-\frac{1}{2x}\right)^7$$

$$= 1(128x^7) - 7(64x^6)\left(\frac{1}{2x}\right) + 21(32x^5)\left(\frac{1}{4x^2}\right) - 35(16x^4)\left(\frac{1}{8x^3}\right) + 35(8x^3)\left(\frac{1}{16x^4}\right) - 21(4x^2)\left(\frac{1}{32x^5}\right)$$

$$+ 7(2x)\left(\frac{1}{64x^6}\right) - 1\left(\frac{1}{128x^7}\right)$$

$$= 128x^7 - 224x^5 + 168x^3 - 70x + \frac{35}{2x} - \frac{21}{8x^3} + \frac{7}{32x^5} - \frac{1}{128x^7}$$

69.

The fifth term of $(3x - 4y)^7$ is $\binom{7}{4}(3x)^3(-4y)^4 = 35(27x^3)(256y^4) = 241,920x^3y^4.$ [8.5]

70.

The eighth term of $(1 - 3x)^9$ is $\binom{9}{7}(1)^2(-3x)^7 = 36 \cdot 1 \cdot (-2187x^7) = -78,732x^7.$ [8.5]

71.

There are 26 choices for each letter. By the Fundamental Counting Principle, there are 26^8 possible passwords. [8.6]

72.

Using the Fundamental Counting Principle, we have $10^6 \cdot 26$ possible serial numbers. [8.6]

73.

This is a permutation with $n = 15$ and $r = 3$. [8.6]

$$P(15,3) = \frac{15!}{(15-3)!} = \frac{15!}{12!} = 2730$$

74.

There are $\binom{4}{1}$ ways to choose a supervisor and $\binom{12}{3}$ ways to choose 3 regular employees. Thus, there are $\binom{4}{1}\binom{12}{3}$ ways to do both.

$$\binom{4}{1}\binom{12}{3} = 4 \cdot 220 = 880 \text{ shifts have 1 supervisor. [8.6]}$$

75.

This problem is solved in stages. First, there are $\binom{10}{5}$ ways to choose a committee excluding both people who refuse to serve

together. Second, there are $\binom{10}{4}\binom{2}{1}$ ways to choose a committee that includes one person but not the other.

Altogether there are $\binom{10}{5} + \binom{10}{4}\binom{2}{1}$ ways to choose the committee.

$$\binom{10}{5} + \binom{10}{4}\binom{2}{1} = 252 + 210(2) = 672 \text{ possible committees [8.6]}$$

76.

There are $\binom{10}{4} = 210$ ways of choosing 4 calculators from 10. If the inspector is to choose 1 defective calculator, then 3 nondefective

calculators must also be chosen. There are $\binom{2}{1}\binom{8}{3} = 2(56) = 112$ ways to accomplish that. Therefore, the probability of the event is

$\frac{112}{210} = \frac{8}{15}$. [8.7]

77.

The probability is $\frac{1}{2} \cdot \frac{1}{2} \cdot \frac{1}{2} = \frac{1}{8}$.

The probability of one tail and therefore two heads is $3\left(\frac{1}{2} \cdot \frac{1}{2} \cdot \frac{1}{2}\right) = \frac{3}{8}$. [8.4]

78. There are $\binom{10}{4}$ ways to draw 4 cards from 10. There are $\binom{5}{2}\binom{5}{2}$ ways to draw 2 red and 2 black cards The probability of drawing 2 red

and 2 black cards is $\dfrac{\binom{5}{2}\binom{5}{2}}{\binom{10}{4}} = \dfrac{10\cdot 10}{210} = \dfrac{10}{21}$. [8.7]

79. We look at the possibility for each case.

If the middle digit is zero, there are	0	numbers
If the middle digit is one, there is	1	numbers
If the middle digit is two, there are	4	numbers
If the middle digit is three, there are	9	numbers
If the middle digit is four, there are	16	numbers
If the middle digit is five, there are	25	numbers
If the middle digit is six, there are	36	numbers
If the middle digit is seven, there are	49	numbers
If the middle digit is eight, there are	64	numbers
If the middle digit is nine, there are	81	numbers
	Total 285	numbers

The probability is $\dfrac{285}{1000} = 0.285$. [8.7]

80. The probability that the sum of two numbers is 9 when the numbers are selected with replacement from 1, 2, 3, 4, 5, 6 is $\dfrac{4}{36} = \dfrac{1}{9}$.

The probability that the sum is 7 is $\dfrac{6}{36} = \dfrac{1}{6}$. Therefore the probability that it is not 7 and not 9 is

$1 - \left(\dfrac{1}{9} + \dfrac{1}{6}\right) = 1 - \dfrac{10}{36} = \dfrac{13}{18}$

First selection, sum is 9.

Second selection, probability of 9 is $\dfrac{1}{9}$.

Third selection, probability is $\dfrac{13}{18} \cdot \dfrac{1}{9}$.

Fourth selection, probability is $\dfrac{13}{18} \cdot \dfrac{13}{18} \cdot \dfrac{1}{9}$.

$\vdots$

The total probability is the sum of this infinite process.

$\dfrac{1}{9} + \dfrac{13}{18} \cdot \dfrac{1}{9} + \left(\dfrac{13}{18}\right)^2 \left(\dfrac{1}{9}\right) + \cdots$

This is a geometric series with $a_1 = \dfrac{1}{9}, r = \dfrac{13}{18}$.

$S = \dfrac{\frac{1}{9}}{1 - \frac{13}{18}} = \dfrac{\frac{1}{9}}{\frac{5}{18}} = \dfrac{2}{5}$

The probability is $\dfrac{2}{5}$. [8.7]

81. Probability of drawing an ace and a 10 card from one regular deck of playing cards is

$\dfrac{\binom{4}{1}\binom{16}{1}}{\binom{52}{2}} = \dfrac{4\cdot 16}{\frac{52\cdot 51}{2}} \approx 0.0483$

The probability of drawing an ace and a 10 card from two regular decks of playing cards is

$\dfrac{\binom{8}{1}\binom{32}{1}}{\binom{104}{2}} = \dfrac{8\cdot 32}{\frac{104\cdot 103}{2}} \approx 0.0478$

Drawing an ace and a 10 card from *one* deck has the greater probability. [8.7]

82. Probability = (probability of 2)(probability of 1) [8.7]

$\qquad$ + (probability of 3)(probability of 1 or 2)

$\qquad$ + (probability of 4)(probability of 1 or 2 or 3)

$\qquad$ + (probability of 5)

$$= \frac{1}{5}\cdot\frac{1}{4} + \frac{1}{5}\cdot\frac{2}{4} + \frac{1}{5}\cdot\frac{3}{4} + \frac{1}{5}\cdot\frac{4}{4}$$

$$= \frac{1}{20} + \frac{2}{20} + \frac{3}{20} + \frac{4}{20} = \frac{10}{20} = \frac{1}{2}$$

83. There are $\binom{12}{3}$ ways of choosing 3 people from 12. There are $\binom{11}{2}\cdot 1$ ways of choosing 2 people and the person with [8.7]

badge number 6.

$$\text{Probability} = \frac{\binom{11}{2}\cdot 1}{\binom{12}{3}} = \frac{\dfrac{11\cdot 10}{2}}{\dfrac{12\cdot 11\cdot 10}{3\cdot 2}} = \frac{1}{4}$$

•••

Chapter Test

1.
$$a_3 = \frac{2^3}{3!} = \frac{8}{6} = \frac{4}{3} \quad [8.1]$$

$$a_5 = \frac{2^5}{5!} = \frac{32}{120} = \frac{4}{15}$$

2.
$$a_3 = \frac{(-1)^{3+1}}{2(3)} = \frac{1}{6} \quad [8.1]$$

$$a_5 = \frac{(-1)^{5+1}}{2(5)} = \frac{1}{10}$$

3.
$a_2 = 2\cdot a_1 = 2\cdot 3 = 6$ [8.1]

$a_3 = 2\cdot a_2 = 12$ •

$a_4 = 2\cdot a_3 = 24$

$a_5 = 2\cdot a_4 = 48$ •

4.
$$a_{n+1} - a_n = [-2(n+1)+3] - (-2n+3) \quad [8.3]$$
$$= -2n - 2 + 3 + 2n - 3$$
$$= -2 = \text{constant}$$

arithmetic

5.
$$a_{n+1} - a_n = 2(n+1)^2 - 2n^2 \quad [8.1]$$
$$= 4n + 2 \neq \text{constant}$$

$$\frac{a_{n+1}}{a_n} = \frac{2(n+1)^2}{2n^2}$$

$$= 1 + \frac{2}{n} + \frac{1}{n^2} \neq \text{constant}$$

neither

6.
$$\frac{a_{n+1}}{a_n} = \frac{\dfrac{(-1)^{n+1-1}}{3^{n+1}}}{\dfrac{(-1)^{n-1}}{3^n}} = \frac{-1}{3} = \text{constant} \quad [8.3]$$

geometric

7.
$$\sum_{i=1}^{6} \frac{1}{i} = 1 + \frac{1}{2} + \frac{1}{3} + \frac{1}{4} + \frac{1}{5} + \frac{1}{6} = \frac{120}{120} + \frac{60}{120} + \frac{40}{120} + \frac{30}{120} + \frac{24}{120} + \frac{20}{120} \quad [8.1]$$

$$= \frac{294}{120} = \frac{49}{20}$$

8.
$$\sum_{j=1}^{10} \frac{1}{2^j} = \frac{1}{2} + \frac{1}{4} + \frac{1}{8} + \frac{1}{16} + \cdots \frac{1}{1024} = \frac{\dfrac{1}{2}\left(1-\left(\dfrac{1}{2}\right)^{10}\right)}{1-\dfrac{1}{2}} = 1 - \left(\frac{1}{2}\right)^{10} \quad [8.3]$$

$$= 1 - \frac{1}{1024} = \frac{1023}{1024}$$

9.

$$\sum_{k=1}^{20}(3k-2)=1+4+7+10+\cdots+58=\frac{20}{2}(1+58)=10(59) \quad \text{[8.2]}$$
$$=590$$

10.

$$a_3=a_1+(3-1)d=7, \qquad a_1+2d=7 \qquad a_1=a_3-2(3) \qquad a_{20}=a_1+(20-1)d \quad \text{[8.2]}$$
$$a_8=a_1+(8-1)d=22 \qquad \underline{a_1+7d=22} \qquad =7-6 \qquad =1+(19)(3)$$
$$-5d=-15 \qquad =1 \qquad =58$$
$$d=3$$

11.

$$\sum_{k=1}^{\infty}\left(\frac{3}{8}\right)^k=\frac{a_1}{1-r}=\frac{\frac{3}{8}}{1-\left(\frac{3}{8}\right)}=\frac{\frac{3}{8}}{\frac{5}{8}}=\frac{3}{5} \quad \text{[8.3]}$$

12.

$$0.\overline{15}=0.15+0.0015+0.000015+\ldots=\frac{0.15}{1-0.01}=\frac{0.15}{0.99}=\frac{15}{99}=\frac{5}{33} \quad \text{[8.3]}$$

13.

1. Let $n=1$. $2-3(1)=-1$ $\dfrac{1(1-3(1))}{2}=-1$ [8.4]

   Thus the statement is true for $n=1$.

2. Assume $\displaystyle\sum_{i=1}^{k}(2-3i)=\frac{k(1-3k)}{2}$ is true for some positive number k.

   Verify $\displaystyle\sum_{i=1}^{k+1}(2-3i)=\frac{(k+1)[1-3(k+1)]}{2}=\frac{(k+1)(1-3k-3)}{2}=\frac{(k+1)(-3k-2)}{2}=-\frac{(k+1)(3k+2)}{2}$

   $$\frac{k(1-3k)}{2}+[2-3(k+1)]=\frac{k(1-3k)}{2}+(-3k-1)$$
   $$=\frac{k-3k^2-6k-2}{2}$$
   $$=-\frac{(3k^2+5k+2)}{2}$$
   $$=-\frac{(k+1)(3k+2)}{2}$$

   Thus the formula has been established by the extended principle of mathematical induction.

14.

1. Let $n=7$ [8.4]

   $7!=50,407$ $3^7=2187$

   Thus $n!>3^n$ for $n=7$.

2. Assume $k!>3^k$

   Verify $(k+1)!>3^{k+1}$

   $$k!>3^k$$
   $$k+1>3$$
   $$(k+1)k!>3\cdot 3^k$$
   $$(k+1)!>3^{k+1}$$

   Thus the formula has been established by the extended principle of mathematical induction.

15.

$$(x-2y)^5=x^5-5(x)^4(2y)+10(x)^3(2y)^2-10(x)^2(2y)^3+5(x)(2y)^4-(2y)^5$$
$$=x^5-10x^4y+40x^3y^2-80x^2y^3+80xy^4-32y^5 \quad \text{[8.5]}$$

16. $(a+b)^6 = a^6 + 6a^5b + 15a^4b^2 + 20a^3b^3 + 15a^2b^4 + 6ab^5 + b^6$ [8.5]

$$\left(x + \frac{1}{x}\right)^6 = x^6 + 6(x)^5\left(\frac{1}{x}\right) + 15(x)^4\left(\frac{1}{x}\right)^2 + 20(x)^3\left(\frac{1}{x}\right)^3 + 15(x)^2\left(\frac{1}{x}\right)^4 + 6x\left(\frac{1}{x}\right)^5 + \left(\frac{1}{x}\right)^6$$

$$= x^6 + 6x^4 + 15x^2 + 20 + \frac{15}{x^2} + \frac{6}{x^4} + \frac{1}{x^6}$$

17. 6th term of $(3x + 2y)^8 = \binom{8}{6-1}(3x)^3(2y)^{6-1}$ [8.5]

$$= \binom{8}{5}(3x)^3(2y)^5$$

$$= 56 \cdot 27x^3 \cdot 32y^5$$

$$= 48,384x^3y^5$$

18. $52 \cdot 51 \cdot 50 = 132,600$ [8.6]

19. $26 \cdot 25 \cdot 24 \cdot 9 \cdot 8 \cdot 23 \cdot 22 = 568,339,200$ [8.6]

20. $\dfrac{C(8,\ 3)C(10,\ 2)}{C(18,\ 5)} = \dfrac{56 \cdot 45}{8568} = \dfrac{5}{17} \approx 0.294118$ [8.7]

....

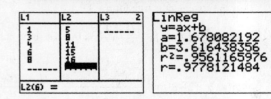

Cumulative Review

1. $|3 - 5x| \le 4$

$-4 \le 3 - 5x \le 4$

$-7 \le -5x \le 1$

$\dfrac{7}{5} \ge x \ge -\dfrac{1}{5}$

The solution set is $\left[-\dfrac{1}{5}, \dfrac{7}{5}\right]$. [1.5]

2.

$y = 1.7x + 3.6$ [2.7]

3.

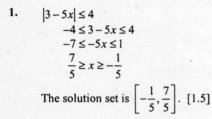

[2.1]

4. $5 + \dfrac{x}{3} = -3$ [2.3]

$\dfrac{x}{3} = -8$

$x = -24$

5.

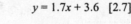

$$\dfrac{x^3 - 1}{x + 1} = x^2 - x + 1 - \dfrac{2}{x + 1}$$ [3.1]

6. $2x^2 - 3x = 4$ [1.3]

$2x^2 - 3x - 4 = 0$

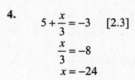

$x = \dfrac{3 \pm \sqrt{(-3)^2 - 4(2)(-4)}}{2(2)} = \dfrac{3 \pm \sqrt{9 + 32}}{4}$

$$= \dfrac{3 \pm \sqrt{41}}{4}$$

7.
$$\log_b\left(\frac{xy^2}{z^3}\right) = \log_b x + \log_b y^2 - \log_b z^3 \quad [4.4]$$
$$= \log_b x + 2\log_b y - 3\log_b z$$

8.
$$16x^2 + 25y^2 - 96x + 100y - 156 = 0$$
$$16(x^2 - 6x) + 25(y^2 + 4y) = 156$$
$$16(x-3)^2 + 25(y+2)^2 = 156 + 144 + 100$$
$$16(x-3)^2 + 25(y+2)^2 = 400$$
$$\frac{16(x-3)^2}{400} + \frac{25(y+2)^2}{400} = 1$$
$$\frac{(x-3)^2}{25} + \frac{(y+2)^2}{16} = 1$$
$$a^2 = 25, b^2 = 16$$
$$c^2 = a^2 - b^2 = 25 - 16 = 9$$
$$c = 3$$
$$e = \frac{c}{a} = \frac{3}{5} \quad [5.2]$$

9.
$$\begin{cases} 2x - 3y = 8 & (1) \\ x + 4y = -7 & (2) \end{cases}$$

Solve (2) for x and substitute into (1).
$$x = -4y - 7$$
$$2(-4y - 7) - 3y = 8$$
$$-8y - 14 - 3y = 8$$
$$-11y = 22$$
$$y = -2$$
$$x = -4(-2) - 7 = 1$$
The solution is $(1, -2)$. [6.1]

10.
$$3A - 2B = 3\begin{bmatrix} -1 & 2 \\ 5 & 3 \\ 0 & 3 \end{bmatrix} - 2\begin{bmatrix} 7 & -3 \\ 6 & 5 \\ 1 & -2 \end{bmatrix} \quad [7.2]$$
$$= \begin{bmatrix} -3 & 6 \\ 15 & 9 \\ 0 & 9 \end{bmatrix} - \begin{bmatrix} 14 & -6 \\ 12 & 10 \\ 2 & -4 \end{bmatrix} = \begin{bmatrix} -17 & 12 \\ 3 & -1 \\ -2 & 13 \end{bmatrix}$$

11. $-2\sqrt[4]{80} + 3\sqrt[4]{405} = -4\sqrt[4]{5} + 9\sqrt[4]{5} = 5\sqrt[4]{5}$ [P.2}

12. No [2.2]

13.
$$-\frac{b}{2a} = -\frac{5}{2(-2)} = \frac{5}{4} \quad [2.4]$$
$$F\left(\frac{5}{4}\right) = -2\left(\frac{5}{4}\right)^2 + 5\left(\frac{5}{4}\right) - 2 = \frac{9}{8}$$
Vertex: $\left(\frac{5}{4}, \frac{9}{8}\right)$

14.
$$\left(\frac{h}{g}\right)(-3) = \frac{h(-3)}{g(-3)} = \frac{-3 - 2}{(-3)^2 - (-3) + 4} = \frac{-5}{16} \quad [2.6]$$

15. $y = 0$ [3.5]

16. $\log_{1/2} 64 = -6$ [4.3]

17.

$$4^{2x+1} = 3^{x-2} \qquad [4.5]$$

$$\ln 4^{2x+1} = \ln 3^{x-2}$$

$$(2x+1)\ln 4 = (x-2)\ln 3$$

$$2x\ln 4 + \ln 4 = x\ln 3 - 2\ln 3$$

$$x\ln 4^2 - x\ln 3 = -2\ln 3 - \ln 4$$

$$x(\ln 16 - \ln 3) = -2\ln 3 - \ln 4$$

$$x = \frac{-2\ln 3 - \ln 4}{\ln 16 - \ln 3} \approx -2.1$$

18.

$$\begin{cases} x^2 + y^2 + xy = 10 & (1) \\ x - y = 1 & (2) \end{cases}$$

Solve (2) for x and substitute into (1).

$$x = y+1$$

$$(y+1)^2 + y^2 + (y+1)y = 10$$

$$y^2 + 2y + 1 + y^2 + y^2 + y = 10$$

$$3y^2 + 3y - 9 = 0$$

$$3(y^2 + y - 3) = 0$$

$$y = \frac{-1 \pm \sqrt{1^2 - 4(1)(-3)}}{2(1)} = \frac{-1 \pm \sqrt{1+12}}{2} = \frac{-1 \pm \sqrt{13}}{2}$$

$$x = \frac{-1 \pm \sqrt{13}}{2} + 1 = \frac{1 \pm \sqrt{13}}{2}$$

The solutions are $\left(\dfrac{1+\sqrt{13}}{2}, \dfrac{-1+\sqrt{13}}{2} \right)$ and

$\left(\dfrac{1-\sqrt{13}}{2}, \dfrac{-1-\sqrt{13}}{2} \right)$. [6.3]

19.

$$\begin{bmatrix} 3 & 2 \\ -2 & 1 \\ 1 & -4 \end{bmatrix} \begin{bmatrix} 2 & 3 & 1 & 1 \\ -2 & 0 & 4 & -3 \end{bmatrix} = \begin{bmatrix} 2 & 9 & 11 & -3 \\ -6 & -6 & 2 & -5 \\ 10 & 3 & -15 & 13 \end{bmatrix} \quad [7.2]$$

20. Let $t = 5$, [4.5]

$$5 = -\frac{175}{32}\ln\left(1 - \frac{v}{175}\right)$$

$$5\left(-\frac{32}{175}\right) = \ln\left(1 - \frac{v}{175}\right)$$

$$e^{-32/35} = 1 - \frac{v}{175}$$

$$-175\left(e^{-32/35} - 1\right) = v$$

$$v \approx 105 \text{ mph}$$

Chapter Tests

Preliminary Concepts

1. For real numbers a, b, and c, identify the property that is illustrated by $a(b + c) = a(c + b)$.

2. Given $A = \{1, 4, 9, 16\}$ and $B = \{2, 4, 8, 16\}$, find $A \cap B$.

3. Find the distance between the points 7 and -4 on the number line.

4. Simplify: $\left(3x^{-1}y^2\right)^{-2}\left(-5x^{-3}y^0\right)^2$

5. Simplify: $\dfrac{\left(5ab^3c^{-1}\right)^4}{\left(2^{-3}a\right)\left(3^{-2}bc^{-3}\right)^2}$

6. Write 186,000,000 in scientific notation.

7. Simplify: $(2x^2 + 3y)(x^2 + x - 2y)$

8. Evaluate the polynomial $-2x^4 + x^3 + 3x^2 - x - 4$ for $x = -2$.

9. Factor: $12x^2 - x - 6$

10. Factor: $2ax + 4ay - bx - 2by$

11. Factor: $64x^4y + 27xy^4$

12. Simplify: $\dfrac{16 - 6x - x^2}{x^2 - 10x + 16}$

13. Simplify: $\dfrac{2x}{x^2 - 3x + 2} + \dfrac{3}{x^2 - x - 2}$

14. Simplify: $\dfrac{x^2 + x - 2}{x^2 - 3x - 10} \div \dfrac{x^2 + 6x + 9}{x^2 - 2x - 15}$

15. Simplify: $\dfrac{3}{b} - \dfrac{a+b}{3a-b} \cdot \dfrac{3}{3a^2\,4ab + b^2}$

16. Simplify: $2x + \dfrac{4x}{x - \dfrac{1}{3}}$

17. Simplify: $\dfrac{x^{-1/2}y^{2/3}}{x^{-3/4}y^{-1/6}}$

18. Simplify: $2b\sqrt[3]{16a^4b^3c^7} - 5ac\sqrt[3]{2ab^6c^4}$

19. Simplify: $\dfrac{3x}{\sqrt[3]{3x^2}}$

20. Simplify: $\dfrac{2}{\sqrt{x} - 4}$

Equations and Inequalities

1. Solve: $4 - \dfrac{x}{5} = \dfrac{3}{2}$

2. Solve: $\dfrac{x}{x-3} - \dfrac{2}{5} = \dfrac{1}{x-3}$

3. Solve: $2ax - b = cx + 2d$ for x.

4. Solve $x^2 - 10x + 22 = 0$ by completing the square.

5. Solve: $2x^2 - 6x + 1 = 0$

6. Solve: $x^4 - 2x^3 + 8x - 16 = 0$

7. Solve: $\sqrt{x-6} + \sqrt{2x-5} = 4$

8. Solve: $x^6 - 4x^3 - 12 = 0$

9. Solve: $2(x-1)^{2/3} + 5(x-1)^{1/3} = 12$

10. Solve: $2(3 - x) \le 5x + 2$

11. Solve: $\dfrac{x^2 + x - 2}{x^2 + 2x - 15} \le 0$

12. Solve: $|3x - 4| = 8$

13. Solve: $|x - 5| \le 2$

14. Solve: $|4x - 3| > 9$

15. Simplify: $\dfrac{3 - 5i}{1 + 2i}$

16. A bus leaves a tourist site and travels at an average rate of 50 miles per hour. One hour later, a car leaves the same site and travels the same route at an average rate of 60 miles per hour. How long will it take the car to catch up with the bus?

17. A total of $12,000 is deposited into two simple interest accounts. On one account the annual simple interest rate is 4%, and on the second account, the annual simple interest rate is 6%. The amount of interest earned for 1 year was $650. How much was invested in each account?

18. Pump A can fill a pool in 4 hours and pump B can fill the same pool in 12 hours. How long would it take to fill the pool if both pumps are used?

19. A bank offers two checking account plans. Plan A charges $4 per month and $0.04 per check. Plan B charges no monthly fee and $0.10 per check. Under what conditions is it less expensive to use Plan A?

20. The load L a horizontal beam can safely support varies jointly as the width w and the square of the depth d and inversely as the length l. If an 8-foot beam with width 2 inches and depth 4 inches safely supports 150 pounds, how many pounds can a 12-foot beam with width 6 inches and depth 8 inches be expected to support?

Functions and Graphs

1. Find the midpoint and the length of the line segment with endpoints $(-3, 4)$ and $(-7, -5)$.

2. Determine the x- and y-intercepts, and then graph the equation $x + y^2 = 6$.

3. Graph the equation $y = -2|x + 3| + 4$.

4. Find the center and radius of the circle that has the general form $x^2 + 6x + y^2 - 8y - 11 = 0$.

5. Determine the domain of the function $f(x) = \sqrt{25 - x^2}$.

6. Use the formula $d = \dfrac{|mx_1 + b - y_1|}{\sqrt{1 + m^2}}$ to find the distance from the point $(-2, 5)$ to the line given by the equation $y = 4x - 3$.

7. Graph $f(x) = \begin{cases} x^2 & \text{if } x \le -1 \\ |x| & \text{if } -1 < x < 1 \\ 1 & \text{if } x \ge 1 \end{cases}$.

   Identify the intervals over which the function is
   a. increasing
   b. constant
   c. decreasing

8. Graph the function $f(x) = (x - 2)^2 - 1$. From the graph, find the domain and range of the function.

9. Use the graph of $f(x) = x^2$ to graph $y = 3f(x + 1) + 2$.

10. Classify each of the following as either an even function, an odd function, or neither an even nor an odd function.
    a. $f(x) = x^2 + 3$
    b. $f(x) = x^2 + 2x$
    c. $f(x) = 4x$

11. Let $f(x) = 4x^2 - 3$ and $g(x) = x + 6$. Find $(f - g)$ and (fg).

12. Find the difference quotient of the function $f(x) = x^2 - x - 4$.

13. Evaluate $(f \circ g)$, where $f(x) = \sqrt{2x}$ and $g(x) = \frac{1}{2}x^2$.

14. Find the inverse of $f(x) = \frac{2}{3}x - 4$. Graph f and f^{-1} on the same coordinate axes.

15. Find the inverse of $f(x) = \dfrac{x - 3}{3x + 6}$. State the domain and the range of f^{-1}.

16. The distance traveled by a ball rolling down a ramp is given by $s(t) = 4t^2$, where t is the time in seconds after the ball is released and $s(t)$ is measured in feet. Evaluate the average velocity of the ball for each of the following time intervals.
    a. $[1, 2]$ b. $[1, 1.5]$ c. $[1, 1.01]$

17. a. Determine the linear regression equation for the given set.

x	2	3	4	6	10
y	3	4	6	10	16

    b. Using the linear model from part **a**, find the expected y-value when the x-value is 8.

Polynomial and Rational Functions

1. Use synthetic division to divide:

$$(4x^3 - 2x^2 - 3x + 6) \div (x - 3)$$

2. Use the Remainder Theorem to find $P(4)$ if

$$P(x) = 5x^4 - 2x^3 + x - 8$$

3. Show that $x - 2$ is a factor of

$$3x^4 - 10x^3 + 14x^2 - 15x + 6.$$

4. Examine the leading term of the function given by the equation $P(x) = 2x^4 - x^3 + 5x^2 + 12x - 20$ and determine the far-left and far-right behavior of the graph of P.

5. Find the real solutions of $3x^3 - 2x^2 - 8x = 0$.

6. Use the Zero Location Theorem to verify that

$$P(x) = 5x^3 + 4x^2 - 3x + 2 \text{ has a zero between } -1 \text{ and } -2.$$

7. Find the zeros of the polynomial

$$P(x) = (x^2 - 9)^3(4x - 1)^2(5x + 1)(x - 3)^2$$

and state the multiplicity of each.

8. Use the Rational Zero Theorem to list the possible rational zeros for the polynomial $P(x) = 4x^3 - 2x^2 - 3x + 8$.

9. Find, by using the Upper- and Lower-Bound Theorem, the smallest positive integer and the largest negative integer that are upper and lower bounds for the polynomial

$$P(x) = 3x^4 - 2x^3 - 4x^2 + 9x - 12$$

10. Use Descartes' Rule of Signs to state the number of possible positive and negative real zeros of

$$P(x) = -3x^4 - 4x^3 - 6x^2 + 5x + 8.$$

11. Find the zeros of the polynomial

$$P(x) = 4x^3 - 12x^2 + 9x - 2.$$

12. Given that $3 - i$ is a zero of $4x^4 - 24x^3 + 31x^2 + 54x - 90$, find the remaining zeros.

13. Find all the zeros of the polynomial

$$P(x) = x^6 + x^5 - 5x^4 - 15x^3 - 18x^2$$

14. Find a polynomial of lowest degree that has real coefficients and zeros $2 - i$, -3, and 4.

15. Find all vertical asymptotes of the graph of

$$f(x) = \frac{2x^2 - 3x + 5}{x^2 - x - 20}.$$

16. Find the horizontal asymptote of the graph of

$$f(x) = \frac{2x^2 - 5x + 8}{4x^2 + x - 12}$$

17. Graph $f(x) = \dfrac{x^2 - 2x - 3}{x^2 - 5x + 6}$ and label the open circle that appears on the graph with its coordinates.

18. Graph $f(x) = \dfrac{3x^2 - 5x + 4}{x - 2}$ and label the slant asymptote with its equation.

19. Graph $f(x) = \dfrac{x + 2}{x^2 + 4}$.

20. Use a graphing utility to approximate the zero in the interval $1 < x < 2$ of the polynomial $P(x) = x^3 + 2x^2 - 6$ to within one-tenth of a unit.

Exponential and Logarithmic Functions

1. Graph : $f(x) = 2^{-x}$

2. Graph : $f(x) = e^{2x}$

3. Write $\log_4 (3x + 2) = d$ in exponential form.

4. Write $4^{x+3} = y$ in logarithmic form.

5. Write $\log_b \dfrac{\sqrt{y}}{x^3 z^2}$ in terms of logarithms x, y, and z.

6. Write $\log_b (x - 1) + \frac{1}{2}\log_b (y + 2) - 4\log_b (z + 3)$ as a single logarithm with a coefficient of 1.

7. Use the change-of-base formula and a calculator to approximate $\log_5 15$. Round your result to the nearest 0.0001.

8. Graph: $f(x) = \ln (x + 2)$

9. Solve: $6^x = 60$. Round your solution to the nearest 0.0001.

10. Find the *exact* solution(s) of
$$\frac{10^x - 10^{-x}}{10^x + 10^{-x}} = \frac{1}{4}$$

11. Solve: $\log (2x + 1) - 2 = \log (3x - 1)$

12. Solve: $\ln (x + 1) + \ln(x - 2) = \ln (4x - 8)$

13. Find the balance on $12,000 invested at an annual interest rate of 6.7% for 3 years:
    a. compounded quarterly.
    b. compounded continuously

14. a. What, to the nearest 0.1, will an earthquake measure on the Richter scale if it has an intensity of $I = 35{,}792{,}000 I_0$?

    b. Compare the intensity of an earthquake that measures 6.4 on the Richter scale to the intensity of an earthquake that measures 5.1 on the Richter scale by finding the ratio of the larger intensity to the smaller intensity. Round to the nearest whole number.

15. a. Find the exponential growth function for a city whose population was 51,300 in 1980 and 240,500 in 2000. Use $t = 0$ to represent the year 1980.
    b. Use the growth function to predict the population of the city in 2010. Round to the nearest 100.

16. Determine, to the nearest 10 years, the age of a bone if it now contains 89% of its original amount of carbon-14. The half-life of carbon-14 is 5730 years.

17. a. Use a graphing utility to find the exponential regression function for the following data:
    $\{(1.4, 3), (2.6, 7), (3.9, 15), (4.3, 20), (5.2, 26)\}$
    b. Use the function to predict, to the nearest whole number, the y-value associated with $x = 8.2$.

18. An altimeter is used to determine the height of an airplane above sea level. The following table shows the values for the pressure p and altitude h of an altimeter.

Pressure p in pounds per square inch	13.1	12.7	12.3	11.4	10.9
Altitude h in feet	3000	3900	4800	6800	8000

    a. Find the logarithmic regression function for the data and use the function to estimate, to the nearest 100 feet, the height of the airplane when the pressure is 12.0 pounds per square inch.
    b. According to your function, what will the pressure be, to the nearest 0.1 per square inch, when the airplane is 6200 feet above sea level?

Topics in Analytic Geometry

1. Find the vertex, focus, and directrix of the parabola given by the equation $x = \frac{1}{12}y^2$.

2. Find the vertex, focus, and directrix of the parabola given by the equation $x^2 - 6x + 8y - 3 = 0$

3. Find the equation in standard form of the parabola with directrix $y = 1$ and focus $(-5, 2)$.

4. Graph the parabola with focus $(3, 1)$ and directrix $x = 5$.

5. Find the vertices and foci of the ellipse given by the equation $\frac{x^2}{25} + \frac{y^2}{36} = 1$

6. Graph $\frac{x^2}{9} + \frac{y^2}{4} = 1$

7. Find the vertices and foci of the ellipse given by the equation $4x^2 - 8x + y^2 + 6y - 3 = 0$

8. Find the equation in standard form of the ellipse with center $(4, -1)$, foci $(4, 3)$ and $(4, -5)$, and major axis of length 10.

9. Find the eccentricity of the ellipse given by the equation $16x^2 + 9y^2 = 144$.

10. Graph $\frac{x^2}{9} - \frac{y^2}{4} = 1$

11. Find the vertices, foci, and asymptotes of the hyperbola given by the equation $\frac{y^2}{16} - \frac{x^2}{64} = 1$

12. Graph $9x^2 + 36x - 4y^2 + 24y = 36$

13. Find the vertices and foci of the hyperbola given by the equation $\frac{(x+5)^2}{25} - \frac{(y-1)^2}{4} = 1$

14. Find the equation in standard form of the hyperbola with vertices at $(-2, 3)$ and $(-2, 9)$, and foci $\left(-2, 6 + 3\sqrt{5}\right)$ and $\left(-2, 6 - 3\sqrt{5}\right)$

15. Find the equation in standard form of the parabola with focus $(4, -8)$ and directrix $y = 0$.

Systems of Equations

In Exercises 1 to 12, solve each system of equations. If a system of equations is inconsistent, so state.

1. $\begin{cases} 4x + 3y = 29 \\ y = 9 \end{cases}$

2. $\begin{cases} 5x - 2y = 2 \\ 15x - 7y = 12 \end{cases}$

3. $\begin{cases} 8x - 5y = 7 \\ 3x + 4y = 32 \end{cases}$

4. $\begin{cases} \frac{1}{3}x + y = 2 \\ x + 2y = 1 \end{cases}$

5. $\begin{cases} 3x + 4y = 12 \\ \frac{3}{4}x + y = \frac{5}{4} \end{cases}$

6. $\begin{cases} x + 2y = 6 \\ y = -\frac{1}{2}x + 3 \end{cases}$

7. $\begin{cases} x + 2y + 3z = 12 \\ 2x - y + 2z = 3 \\ 3x + 3y - z = -7 \end{cases}$

8. $\begin{cases} 6x - 2y - z = 0 \\ x + 2y - 3z = 0 \\ 5x - 4y + 2z = 0 \end{cases}$

9. $\begin{cases} 4x + 3y = 17 \\ 5x - 4y = 19 \end{cases}$

10. $\begin{cases} 3x + y - 4z = 12 \\ 2x - 3y + 6z = 10 \end{cases}$

11. $\begin{cases} x^2 + y^2 = 9 \\ 2x^2 - y^2 = 3 \end{cases}$

12. $\begin{cases} y = 2x \\ y = x^2 - 3x + 4 \end{cases}$

In Exercises 13 and 14, graph each inequality.

13. $3x - 2y > 10$

14. $x \geq y^2 - 1$

In Exercises 15 and 16, graph each system of inequalities. If the solution set is empty, so state.

15. $\begin{cases} x^2 + y^2 \leq 16 \\ x^2 + 36y^2 \geq 36 \end{cases}$

16. $\begin{cases} 2x + 3y \leq 9 \\ x - y \geq -1 \\ x - 2y \leq 3 \\ x \geq 0, y \geq 0 \end{cases}$

In Exercises 17 and 18, find the partial fraction decomposition.

17. $\dfrac{8x + 31}{(x + 2)(x + 5)}$

18. $\dfrac{4x - 7}{(x - 1)^2}$

19. Maximize $P = 14x + 42y$ with the constraints

$\begin{cases} x + y \leq 5 \\ x - 2y \geq -7 \\ 3x + 2y \leq 12 \\ 2x - y \leq 4 \\ x \geq 0, y \geq 0 \end{cases}$

20. Use $x^2 + y^2 + ax + by + c = 0$ to find an equation of the circle that passes through the points $(2, -7)$, $(8, 1)$, and $(1, 0)$.

Matrices

1. Write the augmented matrix, the coefficient matrix, and the constant matrix, for the system of equations

$$\begin{cases} 2x + 5y - 2z = -3 \\ 3x - 2y - 4z = 1 \\ 5x + 3y - 3z = 10 \end{cases}$$

2. Write a system of equations that is equivalent to the augmented matrix $\begin{bmatrix} 3 & 0 & -1 & | & 4 \\ 5 & 6 & -2 & | & -8 \\ 0 & -1 & 1 & | & 2 \end{bmatrix}$.

In Exercises 3 to 5, solve the system of equations by using the Gaussian elimination method.

3. $\begin{cases} x + 3y + 2z = 8 \\ 2x - y + 3z = 3 \\ 3x + 2y + 12z = 4 \end{cases}$

4. $\begin{cases} 2x - y + 3z = -8 \\ 5x + 2y + 6z = 1 \\ x + y + z = 3 \end{cases}$

5. $\begin{cases} w + 2x + 3y - z = 7 \\ 2w - x - y + z = 2 \\ 3w - 3x + 2y - 4z = 13 \\ 4w + x + 3y + 2z = 5 \end{cases}$

In Exercises 6 to 19, let $A = \begin{bmatrix} 1 & 4 & 2 \\ 2 & -1 & 0 \\ -1 & -3 & 2 \end{bmatrix}$, $B = \begin{bmatrix} 2 & 0 & -3 \\ 3 & -4 & -1 \\ 2 & 1 & 1 \end{bmatrix}$, $C = \begin{bmatrix} 3 & 0 & 1 \\ -3 & -1 & -2 \end{bmatrix}$, and $D = \begin{bmatrix} 2 & 3 \\ -4 & -5 \end{bmatrix}$. Perform each possible operation. If an operation is not possible, so state.

6. $A + B$

7. $A + C$

8. $3A - B$

9. $-4C$

10. $DC + C$

11. B^2

12. $2D$

13. D^2

14. AB

15. CB

16. BC

17. C^{-1}

18. A^{-1}

19. D^{-1}

20. Find the minor of a_{32} for matrix A.

21. Find the cofactor of a_{32} for matrix A.

22. Find the determinant of B by expanding cofactors of column 2.

23. Find the determinant of A by using elementary row-operations.

24. Find the value of y for the following system of equations by using Cramer's Rule.

$$\begin{cases} 3x - 2y - 4z = 1 \\ 2x + 5y - 2z = -3 \\ 5x + 3y - 3z = 10 \end{cases}$$

25. A simplified economy has three industries: manufacturing, transportation and service. The input-output matrix for this economy is

$$\begin{bmatrix} 0.10 & 0.15 & 0.10 \\ 0.05 & 0.30 & 0.25 \\ 0.10 & 0.10 & 0.10 \end{bmatrix}$$

Set up, but do not solve, a matrix equation that, when solved, will determine the gross output needed to satisfy consumer demand of $26 million worth of mining, $38 million worth of manufacturing, and $22 million worth of transportation.

Sequences, Series, and Probability

In Exercises 1 to 3, find the fourth and sixth terms of the sequence defined by a_n.

1. $a_n = \dfrac{n^3}{3^n}$

2. $a_n = \dfrac{(-1)^n}{n!}$

3. $a_1 = -2,\ a_n = 3a_{n-1}$

In Exercises 4 to 6, classify each sequence as an arithmetic sequence, a geometric sequence, or neither.

4. $a_n = 2n$

5. $a_n = 2^n$

6. $a_n = n^2$

In Exercises 7 to 9, find the indicated sum of the series.

7. $\displaystyle\sum_{i=1}^{5} (-1)^{i+1} i^2$

8. $\displaystyle\sum_{j=1}^{8} \left(\dfrac{1}{3}\right)^{j}$

9. $\displaystyle\sum_{k=1}^{27} (4k+3)$

10. The fourth term of an arithmetic sequence is 5 and the ninth term is 20. Find the twenty-first term.

11. Find the sum of the infinite geometric series given by
$$\sum_{k=1}^{\infty} \left(\dfrac{2}{5}\right)^{k}.$$

12. Write $0.1\overline{08}$ as the quotient of integers in simplest form.

13. Write the binomial expansion of $(3x - y)^4$.

14. Write the binomial expansion of $\left(2x - \dfrac{1}{2x}\right)^3$.

15. Find the eighth term in the expansion of $(2x - 5y)^{10}$.

In Exercises 16 and 17, prove the statement by mathematical induction.

16. $\displaystyle\sum_{i=1}^{n} 3i = \dfrac{3n(n+1)}{2}$

17. $\left(\dfrac{1}{2}\right)^{n} < n, \quad n \geq 1$

18. A serial number consists of three letters of the alphabet followed by five digits. How many serial numbers are possible if no letter can be used twice in the same serial number?

19. How many different committees of five people can be selected from 12 people?

20. Five cards are randomly chosen from a regular deck of playing cards. What is the probability that all are the same suit?

Solutions to
Chapter Tests

Preliminary Concepts

1. The commutative property of addition   2. $A \cap B = \{4, 16\}$ 3. $|7 - (-4)| = |7 + 4| = |11| = 11$

4. $\left(3x^{-1}y^2z^{-3}\right)^{-2}\left(-5x^{-3}y^0z^{-2}\right)^2 = \left(3^{-2}x^2y^{-4}z^6\right)\left[(-5)^2x^{-6}z^{-4}\right] = \left(\dfrac{x^2z^6}{3^2y^4}\right)\left(\dfrac{(-5)^2}{x^6z^4}\right) = \left(\dfrac{x^2z^6}{9y^4}\right)\left(\dfrac{25}{x^6z^4}\right) = \dfrac{25z^2}{9x^4y^4}$

5. $\dfrac{\left(5ab^3c^{-1}\right)^4}{\left(2^{-1}a\right)\left(3^{-2}bc^{-3}\right)^{-2}} = \dfrac{5^4a^4b^{12}c^{-4}}{2^{-1}a \cdot 3^4b^{-2}c^6} = \dfrac{5^4a^4b^{12} \cdot 2^1b^2}{a \cdot 3^4c^6 \cdot c^4} = \dfrac{625a^4b^{12} \cdot 2b^2}{81ac^{10}} = \dfrac{1250a^4b^{14}}{81ac^{10}} = \dfrac{1250a^3b^{14}}{81c^{10}}$

6. $186{,}000{,}000 = 1.86 \times 10^8$

7. $(2x^2 + 3y)(x^2 + x - 2y) = 2x^4 + 2x^3 - 4x^2y + 3x^2y + 3xy - 6y^2 = 2x^4 + 2x^3 - x^2y + 3xy - 6y^2$

8. If $x = -2$, then $-2x^4 + x^3 + 3x^2 - x - 4 = -2(-2)^4 + (-2)^3 + 3(-2)^2 - (-2) - 4 = -2(16) - 8 + 3(4) + 2 - 4 = -32 - 8 + 12 + 2 - 4 = -30$.

9. $12x^2 - x - 6 = (4x - 3)(3x + 2)$ 10. $2ax + 4ay - bx - 2by = 2a(x + 2y) - b(x + 2y) = (x + 2y)(2a - b)$

11. $64x^4y + 27xy^4 = xy(64x^3 + 27y^3) = xy(4x + 3y)(16x^2 - 12xy + 9y^2)$

12. $\dfrac{16 - 6x - x^2}{x^2 - 10x + 16} = \dfrac{(8 + x)(2 - x)}{(x - 8)(x - 2)} = -\dfrac{(x + 8)(x - 2)}{(x - 8)(x - 2)} = -\dfrac{(x + 8)\cancel{(x - 2)}}{(x - 8)\cancel{(x - 2)}} = -\dfrac{x + 8}{x - 8}$

13. $\dfrac{2x}{x^2 - 3x + 2} + \dfrac{3}{x^2 - x - 2} = \dfrac{2x}{(x - 2)(x - 1)} + \dfrac{3}{(x - 2)(x + 1)} = \dfrac{2x(x + 1) + 3(x - 1)}{(x - 2)(x - 1)(x + 1)} = \dfrac{2x^2 + 2x + 3x - 3}{(x - 2)(x - 1)(x + 1)}$

$= \dfrac{2x^2 + 5x - 3}{(x - 2)(x - 1)(x + 1)} = \dfrac{(2x - 1)(x + 3)}{(x - 2)(x - 1)(x + 1)}$

14. $\dfrac{x^2 + x - 2}{x^2 - 3x - 10} \div \dfrac{x^2 + 6x + 9}{x^2 - 2x - 15} = \dfrac{x^2 + x - 2}{x^2 - 3x - 10} \cdot \dfrac{x^2 - 2x - 15}{x^2 + 6x + 9} = \dfrac{(x + 2)(x - 1)}{(x - 5)(x + 2)} \cdot \dfrac{(x - 5)(x + 3)}{(x + 3)(x + 3)} = \dfrac{\cancel{(x + 2)}(x - 1)}{\cancel{(x - 5)}\cancel{(x + 2)}} \cdot \dfrac{\cancel{(x - 5)}\cancel{(x + 3)}}{(x + 3)\cancel{(x + 3)}} = \dfrac{x - 1}{x + 3}$

15. $\dfrac{3}{b} - \dfrac{a + b}{3a - b} \cdot \dfrac{3}{3a^2 + 4ab + b^2} = \dfrac{3}{b} - \dfrac{a + b}{3a - b} \cdot \dfrac{3}{(3a + b)(a + b)} = \dfrac{3}{b} - \dfrac{\cancel{a + b}}{3a - b} \cdot \dfrac{3}{(3a + b)\cancel{(a + b)}} = \dfrac{3}{b} - \dfrac{3}{(3a - b)(3a + b)}$

$= \dfrac{3(3a - b)(3a + b) - 3b}{b(3a - b)(3a + b)} = \dfrac{3(9a^2 - b^2) - 3b}{b(3a - b)(3a + b)} = \dfrac{3[(9a^2 - b^2) - b]}{b(3a - b)(3a + b)} = \dfrac{3(9a^2 - b - b^2)}{b(3a - b)(3a + b)}$

16. $2x + \dfrac{4x}{x - \frac{1}{3}} = 2x + \dfrac{4x}{\frac{3x - 1}{3}} = 2x + 4x \cdot \dfrac{3}{3x - 1} = 2x + \dfrac{12x}{3x - 1} = \dfrac{2x(3x - 1) + 12x}{3x - 1} = \dfrac{6x^2 - 2x + 12x}{3x - 1} = \dfrac{6x^2 + 10x}{3x - 1} = \dfrac{2x(3x + 5)}{3x - 1}$

17. $\dfrac{x^{-1/2}y^{2/3}}{x^{-3/4}y^{-1/6}} = \dfrac{x^{3/4}y^{2/3}y^{1/6}}{x^{1/2}} = \dfrac{x^{3/4}y^{4/6}y^{1/6}}{x^{2/4}} = x^{3/4 - 2/4}y^{4/6 + 1/6} = x^{1/4}y^{5/6}$

18. $2b\sqrt[3]{16a^4b^3c^7} - 5ac\sqrt[3]{2ab^6c^4} = 2b\sqrt[3]{2^4a^4b^3c^7} - 5ac\sqrt[3]{2ab^6c^4} = 2b\sqrt[3]{2^3a^3b^3c^6 \cdot 2ac} - 5ac\sqrt[3]{b^6c^3 \cdot 2ac}$

$= 2b(2abc^2)\sqrt[3]{2ac} - 5ac(b^2c)\sqrt[3]{2ac} = 4ab^2c^2\sqrt[3]{2ac} - 5ab^2c^2\sqrt[3]{2ac} = -ab^2c^2\sqrt[3]{2ac}$

19. $\dfrac{3x}{\sqrt[3]{3x^2}} = \dfrac{3x}{\sqrt[3]{3x^2}} \cdot \dfrac{\sqrt[3]{3^2x}}{\sqrt[3]{3^2x}} = \dfrac{3x\sqrt[3]{3^2x}}{\sqrt[3]{3^3x^3}} = \dfrac{3x\sqrt[3]{9x}}{3x} = \sqrt[3]{9x}$ 20. $\dfrac{2}{\sqrt{x} - 4} = \dfrac{2}{\sqrt{x} - 4} \cdot \dfrac{\sqrt{x} + 4}{\sqrt{x} + 4} = \dfrac{2(\sqrt{x} + 4)}{x - 16}$

Equations and Inequalities

1. $4 - \dfrac{x}{5} = \dfrac{3}{2}$

$10\left(4 - \dfrac{x}{5}\right) = 10\left(\dfrac{3}{2}\right)$

$40 - 2x = 15$

$-2x = 15 - 40$

$-2x = -25$

$x = \dfrac{-25}{-2}$

$x = \dfrac{25}{2}$

The solution is $\dfrac{25}{2}$.

2. $\dfrac{x}{x-3} - \dfrac{2}{5} = \dfrac{1}{x-3}$

$5(x-3)\left(\dfrac{x}{x-3} - \dfrac{2}{5}\right) = 5(x-3)\left(\dfrac{1}{x-3}\right)$

$5x - 2(x-3) = 5$

$5x - 2x + 6 = 5$

$3x = -1$

$x = -\dfrac{1}{3}$

The solution is $-\dfrac{1}{3}$.

3. $2ax - b = cx + 2d$

$2ax - cx = b + 2d$

$x(2a - c) = b + 2d$

$x = \dfrac{b + 2d}{2a - c}, \; 2a \neq c$

4. $x^2 - 10x + 22 = 0$

$x^2 - 10x = -22$

$x^2 - 10x + 25 = -22 + 25$

$(x - 5)^2 = 3$

$x - 5 = \pm\sqrt{3}$

$x = 5 \pm \sqrt{3}$

$x = 5 + \sqrt{3}$ or $x = 5 - \sqrt{3}$

The solutions are $5 + \sqrt{3}$ and $5 - \sqrt{3}$.

5. $2x^2 - 6x + 1 = 0$

$x = \dfrac{-(-6) \pm \sqrt{(-6)^2 - 4(2)(1)}}{2(2)}$

$x = \dfrac{6 \pm \sqrt{36 - 8}}{4}$

$x = \dfrac{6 \pm \sqrt{28}}{4}$

$x = \dfrac{6 \pm 2\sqrt{7}}{4}$

$x = \dfrac{3 \pm \sqrt{7}}{2}$

$x = \dfrac{3 + \sqrt{7}}{2}$ or $x = \dfrac{3 - \sqrt{7}}{2}$

The solutions are $\dfrac{3 + \sqrt{7}}{2}$ and $\dfrac{3 - \sqrt{7}}{2}$.

6. $x^4 - 2x^3 + 8x - 16 = 0$

$x^3(x - 2) + 8(x - 2) = 0$

$(x - 2)(x^3 + 8) = 0$

$(x - 2)(x + 2)(x^2 - 2x + 4) = 0$

$x - 2 = 0 \Rightarrow x = 2$

$x + 2 = 0 \Rightarrow x = -2$

$x^2 - 2x + 4 = 0 \Rightarrow x = \dfrac{-(-2) \pm \sqrt{(-2)^2 - 4(1)(4)}}{2(1)}$

$x = \dfrac{2 \pm \sqrt{4 - 16}}{2}$

$x = \dfrac{2 \pm \sqrt{-12}}{2}$

$x = \dfrac{2 \pm 2i\sqrt{3}}{2}$

$x = 1 \pm i\sqrt{3}$

The solutions are $2, \, -2, \, 1 + i\sqrt{3}, 1 - i\sqrt{3}$.

7. $\sqrt{x-6}+\sqrt{2x-5}=4$

$\sqrt{x-6}=4-\sqrt{2x-5}$

$\left(\sqrt{x-6}\right)^2=\left(4-\sqrt{2x-5}\right)^2$

$x-6=16-8\sqrt{2x-5}+2x-5$

$8\sqrt{2x-5}=x+17$

$\left(8\sqrt{2x-5}\right)^2=(x+17)^2$

$64(2x-5)=x^2+34x+289$

$128x-320=x^2+34x+289$

$0=x^2-94x+609$

$x=\dfrac{-(-94)\pm\sqrt{94^2-4(1)(609)}}{2(1)}$

$x=\dfrac{94\pm\sqrt{6400}}{2}$

$x=\dfrac{94\pm80}{2}$

$x=\dfrac{94+80}{2}$ or $x=\dfrac{94-80}{2}$

$x=\dfrac{174}{2}$ $x=\dfrac{14}{2}$

$x=87$ $x=7$

Check $\sqrt{87-6}+\sqrt{2(87)-5}=4$

$\sqrt{81}+\sqrt{169}=4$

$9+13=4$

$22=4$ (No)

$\sqrt{7-6}+\sqrt{2(7)-5}=4$

$\sqrt{1}+\sqrt{9}=4$

$1+3=4$

$4=4$

The solution is 7.

9. $2(x-1)^{2/3}+5(x-1)^{1/3}=12$

Let $u=(x-1)^{1/3}$

$2u^2+5u=12$

$2u^2+5u-12=0$

$(2u-3)(u+4)=0$

$2u-3=0$ or $u+4=0$

$u=\dfrac{3}{2}$ $u=-4$

$(x-1)^{1/3}=\dfrac{3}{2}$ $(x-1)^{1/3}=-4$

$\left[(x-1)^{1/3}\right]^3=\left(\dfrac{3}{2}\right)^3$ $\left[(x-1)^{1/3}\right]^3=(-4)^3$

$x-1=\dfrac{27}{8}$ $x-1=-64$

$x=\dfrac{35}{8}$ $x=-63$

8. $x^4-4x^2-12=0$

Let $u=x^2$

$u^2-4u-12=0$

$(u-6)(u+2)=0$

$u=6$ or $u=-2$

$x^2=6$ $x^2=-2$

$x=\pm\sqrt6$ $x=\pm\sqrt{-2}$

$x=\pm i\sqrt2$

The solutions are $\sqrt6$, $-\sqrt6$, $i\sqrt2$, and $-i\sqrt2$.

10. $2(3-x)\le5x+2$

$6-2x\le5x+2$

$-7x\le-4$

$x\ge\dfrac{-4}{-7}$

$x\ge\dfrac{4}{7}$

11. $\dfrac{x^2 + x - 2}{x^2 + 2x - 15} \le 0$

$\dfrac{(x-1)(x+2)}{(x-3)(x+5)} \le 0$

The quotient is negative or zero.

$x - 1 = 0 \Rightarrow x = 1$

$x + 2 = 0 \Rightarrow x = -2$

$x - 3 = 0 \Rightarrow x = 3$

$x + 5 = 0 \Rightarrow x = -5$

Critical values are 1, −2, 3 and −5.

$\dfrac{(x-1)(x+2)}{(x-3)(x+5)} \le 0$

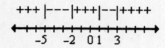

$+++ \; |--- \; |+++|-- \; |++++$

$-5 \quad -2 \quad 0\,1 \quad 3$

Denominator $\ne 0 \Rightarrow x \ne 3, x \ne -5$.

$(-5, -2] \cup [1, 3)$

12. $|3x - 4| = 8$

$3x - 4 = 8$ or $3x - 4 = -8$

$3x = 12$ $\qquad\qquad$ $3x = -4$

$x = 4$ $\qquad\qquad$ $x = -\dfrac{4}{3}$

13. $|x - 5| \le 2$

$-2 \le x - 5 \le 2$

$3 \le \;\; x \;\; \le 7$

$[3, 7]$

14. $|4x - 3| > 9$

$4x - 3 > 9$ or $4x - 3 < -9$

$4x > 12$ $\qquad\qquad$ $4x < -6$

$x > 3$ $\qquad\qquad$ $x < -\dfrac{3}{2}$

$\left(-\infty, -\dfrac{3}{2}\right) \cup (3, \infty)$

15. $\dfrac{3 - 5i}{1 + 2i} = \dfrac{3 - 5i}{1 + 2i} \cdot \dfrac{1 - 2i}{1 - 2i}$

$= \dfrac{3 - 6i - 5i + 10i^2}{1 - 4i^2}$

$= \dfrac{3 - 11i - 10}{1 + 4}$

$= \dfrac{-7 - 11i}{5}$

$= -\dfrac{7}{5} - \dfrac{11}{5}i$

16.

	rate	time
bus	50	$t + 1$
car	60	t

Use $rt = d$

bus distance = car distance

$50(t + 1) = 60t$

$50t + 50 = 60t$

$50 = 10t$

$5 = t$

The car catches up with the bus in 5 hours.

17.

	principal	rate
4% account	x	0.04
6% account	$12{,}000 - x$	0.06

Use $I = Prt$, with $t = 1$.

$0.04x + 0.06(12{,}000 - x) = 650$

$0.04x + 720 - 0.06x = 650$

$-0.02x = -70$

$x = 3500$

$12{,}000 - x = 8500$

$3500 is invested at 4%; $8500 is invested at 6%.

18. Let $x =$ the number of hours to fill the pool together. Pump A fills $\dfrac{1}{4}$ of the pool per hour. Pump B fills $\dfrac{1}{12}$ of the pool per hour. Both pumps work for x hours. Therefore, pump A completes $\dfrac{x}{4}$ of the job and pump B completes $\dfrac{x}{12}$ of the job.

$\dfrac{x}{4} + \dfrac{x}{12} = 1$

$12\left(\dfrac{x}{4} + \dfrac{x}{12}\right) = 12(1)$

$3x + x = 12$

$4x = 12$

$x = 3$

It takes 3 hours to fill the pool with both pumps working.

19. Let x = the number of checks written per month.

Plan A costs $4 + 0.04x$ per month.

Plan B costs $0.10x$ per month.

If plan A is less expensive than plan B, then

$$4 + 0.04x < 0.10x$$

$$4 < 0.06x$$

$$\frac{4}{0.06} < x$$

$$66\frac{2}{3} < x$$

$$x > 66\frac{2}{3}$$

Plan A is less expensive if 67 or more checks are written per month.

20. $L = \dfrac{kwd^2}{l}$

$$150 = \frac{k(2)(4)^2}{8}$$

$$8(150) = 8\left(\frac{k(2)(4)^2}{8}\right)$$

$$1200 = k(2)(4^2)$$

$$1200 = 32k$$

$$37.5 = k$$

$$L = \frac{37.5(6)(8^2)}{12}$$

$$L = \frac{14400}{12}$$

$$L = 1200$$

The beam can be expected to safely support 1200 pounds.

Functions and Graphs

1. midpoint = $\left(\dfrac{x_1+x_2}{2},\ \dfrac{y_1+y_2}{2}\right) = \left(\dfrac{-3+(-7)}{2},\ \dfrac{4+(-5)}{2}\right) = \left(\dfrac{-3-7}{2},\ \dfrac{4-5}{2}\right) = \left(\dfrac{-10}{2},\ \dfrac{-1}{2}\right) = \left(-5,\ -\dfrac{1}{2}\right)$

length = $d = \sqrt{(x_1-x_2)^2+(y_1-y_2)^2} = \sqrt{[-3-(-7)]^2+[4-(-5)]^2} = \sqrt{(-3+7)^2+(4+5)^2} = \sqrt{(4)^2+(9)^2} = \sqrt{16+81} = \sqrt{97}$

2. $x+y^2=6$

$y=0 \Rightarrow x+(0)^2 = 6 \Rightarrow x = 6$
Thus the x-intercept is $(6, 0)$.
$x=0 \Rightarrow 0+y^2 = 6$
$\qquad\qquad y^2 = 6$
$\qquad\qquad y = \pm\sqrt{6}$
Thus the y-intercepts are $\left(0,\ -\sqrt{6}\right)$ and $\left(0,\ \sqrt{6}\right)$.

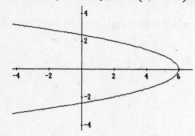

3. $y = -2|x+3|+4$

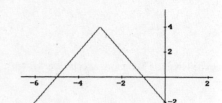

4. $\qquad x^2+6x+y^2-8y-11=0.$
$\qquad (x^2+6x)+(y^2-8y) = 11$
$(x^2+6x+9)+(y^2-8y+16) = 11+9+16$
$\qquad\quad (x+3)^2+(y-4)^2 = 36$
$\qquad\quad (x+3)^2+(y-4)^2 = 6^2$
center $(-3, 4)$, radius 6

5. $\qquad 25-x^2 \ge 0$
$\qquad (5-x)(5+x) \ge 0$
The product is positive or zero.
The critical values are 5 and -5.

The domain is $\{x | -5 \le x \le 5\}$.

6. $y = 4x-3,\ (x_1, y_1) = (-2, 5)$

$d = \dfrac{|mx_1+b-y_1|}{\sqrt{1+m^2}} = \dfrac{|4(-2)+(-3)-5|}{\sqrt{1+4^2}} = \dfrac{|-8-3-5|}{\sqrt{1+16}} = \dfrac{|-16|}{\sqrt{17}} = \dfrac{16}{\sqrt{17}} = \dfrac{16\sqrt{17}}{17}$

7.
$f(x) = \begin{cases} x^2 & \text{if } x \le -1 \\ |x| & \text{if } -1 < x < 1 \\ 1 & \text{if } x \ge 1 \end{cases}$

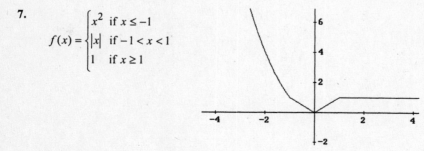

a. increasing on $[0, 1]$
b. constant on $[1, \infty)$
c. decreasing on $(-\infty, 0]$

8. $f(x) = (x-2)^2 - 1$

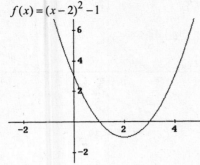

domain: all real numbers
range: $\{y | y \geq -1\}$

9. The graph is shifted 1 unit to the left and 2 units up, and is stretched vertically by multiplying each y-coordinate by 3.

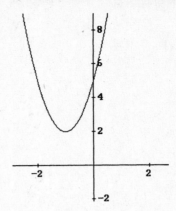

10. a. $f(x) = x^2 + 3$

$f(-x) = (-x)^2 + 3 = x^2 + 3 = f(x)$

$f(x)$ is an even function.

b. $f(x) = x^2 + 2x$

$f(-x) = (-x)^2 + 2(-x) = x^2 - 2x$

$f(-x) = x^2 - 2x \neq f(x)$ not an even function

$f(-x) = x^2 - 2x \neq -f(x)$ not an odd function

$f(x)$ is neither an even function nor an odd function.

c. $f(x) = 4x$

$f(-x) = 4(-x) = -4x = -f(x)$

$f(x)$ is an odd function.

$f(3) = -(3)^2 + 6(3) + 7$

$\qquad = -9 + 18 + 7$

$\qquad = 16$

The maximum value of the function is 16.

11. $(f - g)(x) = f(x) - g(x)$

$\qquad = (4x^2 - 3) - (x + 6)$

$\qquad = 4x^2 - 3 - x - 6$

$\qquad = 4x^2 - x - 9$

$(fg) = f(x) \cdot g(x)$

$\qquad = (4x^2 - 3)(x + 6)$

$\qquad = 4x^3 + 24x^2 - 3x - 18$

12. $\qquad f(x) = x^2 - x - 4$

$\dfrac{f(x+h) - f(x)}{h} = \dfrac{(x+h)^2 - (x+h) - 4 - (x^2 - x - 4)}{h}$

$\qquad = \dfrac{x^2 + 2xh + h^2 - x - h - 4 - x^2 + x + 4}{h}$

$\qquad = \dfrac{2xh + h^2 - h}{h}$

$\qquad = \dfrac{h(2x + h - 1)}{h}$

$\qquad = 2x + h - 1$

13. $f(x) = \sqrt{2x}$ and $g(x) = \frac{1}{2}x^2$

$(f \circ g)(x) = f[g(x)] = f\left(\frac{1}{2}x^2\right)$

$\qquad = \left(\sqrt{2\left(\frac{1}{2}x^2\right)}\right)$

$\qquad = \sqrt{x^2}$

$\qquad = x$

14. $y = \frac{2}{3}x - 4$

Interchange x and y, then solve for y.

$$x = \frac{2}{3}y - 4$$

$$3(x) = 3\left(\frac{2}{3}y - 4\right)$$

$$3x = 2y - 12$$

$$3x + 12 = 2y$$

$$\frac{1}{2}(3x + 12) = \frac{1}{2}(2y)$$

$$\frac{3}{2}x + 6 = y$$

$$f^{-1}(x) = \frac{3}{2}x + 6$$

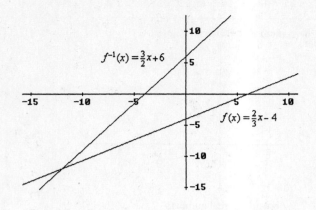

15. $y = \dfrac{x - 3}{3x + 6}$

Interchange x and y, then solve for y.

$$x = \frac{y - 3}{3y + 6}$$

$$x(3y + 6) = y - 3$$

$$3xy + 6x = y - 3$$

$$3xy - y = -6x - 3$$

$$y(3x - 1) = -6x - 3$$

$$y = \frac{-6x - 3}{3x - 1}$$

$$f^{-1}(x) = \frac{-6x - 3}{3x - 1}$$

Domain $f^{-1}(x)$: all real numbers except $\frac{1}{3}$

Range $f^{-1}(x)$: all real numbers except -2

16. $s(t) = 4t^2$

a. Average velocity $= \dfrac{4(2)^2 - 4(1)^2}{2 - 1}$

$$= \frac{4(4) - 4(1)}{1}$$

$$= 16 - 4$$

$$= 12 \text{ ft/sec}$$

b. Average velocity $= \dfrac{4(1.5)^2 - 4(1)^2}{1.5 - 1}$

$$= \frac{4(2.25) - 4(1)}{1.5 - 1}$$

$$= \frac{9 - 4}{0.5}$$

$$= \frac{5}{0.5}$$

$$= 10 \text{ ft/sec}$$

c. Average velocity $= \dfrac{4(1.01)^2 - 4(1)^2}{1.01 - 1}$

$$= \frac{4(1.0201) - 4(1)}{0.01}$$

$$= \frac{4.0804 - 4}{0.01}$$

$$= \frac{0.0804}{0.01}$$

$$= 8.04 \text{ ft/sec}$$

17. a.   Enter the data on your calculator. The technique for a TI-83 calculator is illustrated here.

```
EDIT CALC TESTS
1:Edit
2:SortA(
3:SortD(
4:ClrList
5:SetUpEditor
```

```
L1    L2    L3    2
2     3     ------
3     4
4     6
6     10
10    16
------ ------
L2(6)=
```

```
EDIT CALC TEST
1:1-Var Stats
2:2-Var Stats
3:Med-Med
4:LinReg (ax+b)
5:QuadReg
6:CubicReg
7↓QuartReg
```

```
LinReg
y=ax+b
a=1.675
b=-.575
r2=.9949024823
r=.9974479847
```

$y = 1.675x - 0.575$

b. $y = 1.675(8) - 0.575$

$\quad\ = 12.825$

Polynomial and Rational Functions

1.
$$
\begin{array}{r|rrrr}
3 & 4 & -2 & -3 & 6 \\
  &   & 12 & 30 & 81 \\
\hline
  & 4 & 10 & 27 & 87
\end{array}
$$

$$4x^2 + 10x + 27 + \frac{87}{x-3}$$

2.
$$
\begin{array}{r|rrrrr}
4 & 5 & -2 & 0 & 1 & -8 \\
  &   & 20 & 72 & 288 & 1156 \\
\hline
  & 5 & 18 & 72 & 289 & 1148
\end{array}
$$

$$P(4) = 1148$$

3.
$$
\begin{array}{r|rrrrr}
2 & 3 & -10 & 14 & -15 & 6 \\
  &   & 6 & -8 & 12 & -6 \\
\hline
  & 3 & -4 & 6 & -3 & 0
\end{array}
$$

A remainder of 0 implies that $x - 2$ is a factor of
$$3x^4 - 10x^3 + 14x^2 - 15x + 6.$$

4. $P(x) = 2x^4 - x^3 + 5x^2 + 12x - 20$

Since $A_n = 2$ is positive and $n = 4$ is even, the graph of P goes up to the far left and up to the far right.

5.
$$3x^3 - 2x^2 - 8x = 0$$
$$x(3x^2 - 2x - 8) = 0$$
$$x(3x + 4)(x - 2) = 0$$
$$x = 0, \quad 3x + 4 = 0, \quad \text{or} \quad x - 2 = 0$$
$$x = -\frac{4}{3} \qquad x = 2$$

The real solutions of
$$3x^3 - 2x^2 - 8x = 0$$
are $0, \ -\frac{4}{3}$, and 2.

6. $P(x) = 5x^3 + 4x^2 - 3x + 2$

$$
\begin{array}{r|rrrr}
-1 & 5 & 4 & -3 & 2 \\
   &   & -5 & 1 & 2 \\
\hline
   & 5 & -1 & -2 & 4
\end{array}
$$

$$
\begin{array}{r|rrrr}
-2 & 5 & 4 & -3 & 2 \\
   &   & -10 & 12 & -18 \\
\hline
   & 5 & -6 & 9 & -16
\end{array}
$$

Because $P(-1)$ and $P(-2)$ have different signs, P must have a real zero between -1 and -2.

7. $P(x) = (x^2 - 9)^3(4x - 1)^2(5x + 1)(x - 3)^2$

$$P(x) = (x - 3)^3(x + 3)^3(4x - 1)^2(5x + 1)(x - 3)^2$$

$$P(x) = (x - 3)^5(x + 3)^3(4x - 1)^2(5x + 1)$$

The zeros of P are 3 (multiplicity 5), -3 (multiplicity 3), $\frac{1}{4}$ (multiplicity 2), and $-\frac{1}{5}$ (multiplicity 1).

8. $P(x) = 4x^3 - 2x^2 - 3x + 8$
$$p = \pm 1, \pm 2, \pm 4, \pm 8$$
$$q = \pm 1, \pm 2, \pm 4$$
$$\frac{p}{q} = \pm 1, \pm 2, \pm 4, \pm 8, \pm\frac{1}{2}, \pm\frac{1}{4}$$

9.
$$
\begin{array}{r|rrrrr}
2 & 3 & -2 & -4 & 9 & -12 \\
  &   & 6 & 8 & 8 & 34 \\
\hline
  & 3 & 4 & 4 & 17 & 22
\end{array}
$$
upper bound: 2

$$
\begin{array}{r|rrrrr}
-2 & 3 & -2 & -4 & 9 & -12 \\
   &   & -6 & 16 & -24 & 30 \\
\hline
   & 3 & -8 & 12 & -15 & 18
\end{array}
$$
lower bound: -2

10. $P(x) = -3x^4 - 4x^3 - 6x^2 + 5x + 8$

$$P(-x) = -3x^4 + 4x^3 - 6x^2 - 5x + 8$$

one positive and three or one negative real zeros

11.
$$
\begin{array}{r|rrrr}
\square & 4 & -12 & 9 & -2 \\
  &   & 2 & -5 & 2 \\
\hline
  & 4 & -10 & 4 & 0
\end{array}
$$

$$4x^2 - 10x + 4 = 0$$
$$2(2x^2 - 5x + 2) = 0$$
$$2(2x - 1)(x - 2) = 0$$
$$x = \frac{1}{2} \quad \text{or} \quad x = 2$$

The zeros of $P(x) = 4x^3 - 12x^2 + 9x - 2$ are $\frac{1}{2}$ (multipicity 2) and 2.

12.
$$
\begin{array}{r|rrrr}
3 - i & 4 & -24 & 31 & 54 & -90 \\
  &   & 12 - 4i & -40 & -27 + 9i & 90 \\
\hline
  & 4 & -12 - 4i & -9 & 27 + 9i & 0
\end{array}
$$

$$
\begin{array}{r|rrrr}
3 + i & 4 & -12 - 4i & -9 & 27 + 9i \\
  &   & 12 + 4i & 0 & -27 - 9i \\
\hline
  & 4 & 0 & -9 & 0
\end{array}
$$

$$4x^2 - 9 = (2x + 3)(2x - 3) = 0 \Rightarrow x = -\frac{3}{2} \quad \text{or} \quad x = \frac{3}{2}$$

The zeros of $4x^4 - 24x^3 + 31x^2 + 54x - 90$ are
$3 - i, 3 + i, -\frac{3}{2}$, and $\frac{3}{2}$.

13. $P(x) = x^6 + x^5 - 5x^4 - 15x^3 - 18x^2$

$P(x) = x^2(x^4 + x^3 - 5x^2 - 15x - 18)$

$$
\begin{array}{r|rrrr}
3 & 1 & 1 & -5 & -15 & -18 \\
  &   & 3 & 12 & 21 & 18 \\
\hline
-2 & 1 & 4 & 7 & 6 & 0 \\
   &   & -2 & -4 & -6 & \\
\hline
   & 1 & 2 & 3 & 0 &
\end{array}
$$

$x^2 + 2x + 3 = 0$

$$x = \frac{-2 \pm \sqrt{2^2 - 4(1)(3)}}{2(1)} \quad x = \frac{-2 \pm \sqrt{4 - 12}}{2}$$

$$x = \frac{-2 \pm \sqrt{-8}}{2} = \frac{-2 \pm 2i\sqrt{2}}{2} = -1 \pm i\sqrt{2}$$

The zeros of $x^6 + x^5 - 5x^4 - 15x^3 - 18x^2$ are 0 (multiplicity 2), 3, −2, $-1 + i\sqrt{2}$, and $-1 - i\sqrt{2}$.

14. $P(x) = [x - (2 - i)][x - (2 + i)](x + 3)(x - 4)$

$= (x^2 - 4x + 5)(x^2 - x - 12)$

$= x^4 - x^3 - 12x^2 - 4x^3 + 4x^2 + 48x + 5x^2 - 5x - 60$

$= x^4 - 5x^3 - 3x^2 + 43x - 60$

15. $f(x) = \dfrac{2x^2 - 3x + 5}{x^2 - x - 20}$ $x^2 - x - 20 = 0$

$(x + 4)(x - 5) = 0$

$x = -4 \quad x = 5$

vertical asymptotes: $x = -4$, $x = 5$

16. $f(x) = \dfrac{2x^2 - 5x + 8}{4x^2 + x - 12}$

$\frac{2}{4} = \frac{1}{2} \Rightarrow$ horizontal asymptote: $y = \frac{1}{2}$

17. $f(x) = \dfrac{x^2 - 2x - 3}{x^2 - 5x + 6} = \dfrac{(x-3)(x+1)}{(x-3)(x-2)} = \dfrac{x+1}{x-2}$

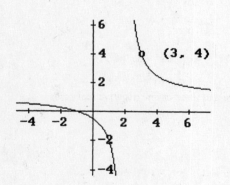

zero at $x = -1$

hole at $x = 3$, $f(3) = 4/1 = 4$

horizontal asymptote at $y = 1$,

vertical asymptote at $x = 2$

18.

$$
\begin{array}{r|rrr}
2 & 3 & -5 & 4 \\
  &   & 6 & 2 \\
\hline
  & 3 & 1 & 6
\end{array}
$$

$f(x) = \dfrac{3x^2 - 5x + 4}{x - 2}$

$= 3x + 1 + \dfrac{6}{x - 2}$

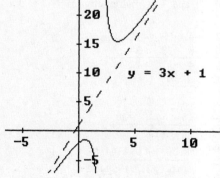

$y = 3x + 1$

19.

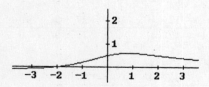

zero at $x = -2$, y-intercept at $y = \frac{1}{2}$

horizontal asymptote at $y = 0$

20.

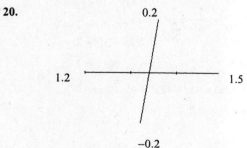

Draw the graph of $P(x) = x^3 + 2x^2 - 6$ and estimate the x-coordinate of the x-intercept. This value is a zero of P The zero between 1 and 2 is 1.3 (to the nearest tenth)

Exponential and Logarithmic Functions

1.

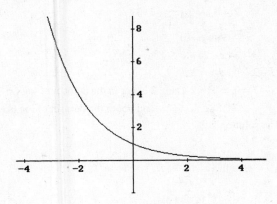

2.

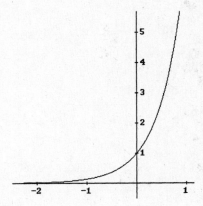

3. $4^d = 3x + 2$

4. $\log_4 y = x + 3$

5. $\frac{1}{2}\log_b y - 3\log_b x - 2\log_b z$

6. $\log_b \frac{(x-1)\sqrt{y+2}}{(z+3)^4}$

7. $\log_5 15 = \frac{\log 15}{\log 5} = \frac{1.176091259}{0.6989700043} \approx 1.6826$

Note that you could also have used natural logarithms.

$\log_5 15 = \frac{\ln 15}{\ln 5} = \frac{2.708050201}{1.609437912} \approx 1.6826$

8.

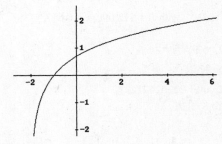

9. $6^x = 60$

$x = \log_6 60$

$x = \frac{\log 60}{\log 6} = \frac{1.77815125}{0.7781512504} \approx 2.2851$

Note that you could also have used natural logarithms.

$x = \log_6 60 = \frac{\ln 60}{\ln 6} = \frac{4.094344562}{1.791759469} \approx 2.2851$

10. $\left(\frac{10^x}{10^x}\right)\left(\frac{10^x - 10^{-x}}{10^x + 10^{-x}}\right) = \frac{1}{4}$

$\frac{10^{2x} - 1}{10^{2x} + 1} = \frac{1}{4}$

$4(10^{2x} - 1) = 10^{2x} + 1$

$4(10^{2x}) - 4 = 10^{2x} + 1$

$4(10^{2x}) - 10^{2x} = 1 + 4$

$10^{2x}(4 - 1) = 1 + 4$

$10^{2x}(3) = 5$

$10^{2x} = \frac{5}{3}$

$\log\left(10^{2x}\right) = \log\left(\frac{5}{3}\right)$

$2x = \log 5 - \log 3$

$x = \frac{1}{2}\log 5 - \frac{1}{2}\log 3$

11. $\log(2x+1) - \log(3x-1) = 2$

$$\log\frac{2x+1}{3x-1} = 2$$

$$10^2 = \frac{2x+1}{3x-1}$$

$$100(3x-1) = 2x+1$$

$$300x - 100 = 2x+1$$

$$298x = 101$$

$$x = \frac{101}{298}$$

12. $\ln[(x+1)(x-2)] = \ln(4x-8)$

$$(x+1)(x-2) = 4x-8$$

$$x^2 - x - 2 = 4x - 8$$

$$x^2 - 5x + 6 = 0$$

$$(x-3)(x-2) = 0$$

$$x-3 = 0 \Rightarrow x = 3$$

$x-2 = 0 \Rightarrow x = 2$ [No; 2 is not in the domain of $\log(x-2)$

and not in the domain of $\log(4x-8)$.]

The solution is 3.

13. a. Use $A = P\left(1+\dfrac{r}{n}\right)^{nt}$ with $P = \$12{,}000$, $r = 0.067$,

$n = 4$, $t = 3$.

$$A = 12{,}000\left(1 + \frac{0.067}{4}\right)^{4(3)}$$

$$= 12{,}000(1 + 0.01675)^{12}$$

$$= 12{,}000(1.01675)^{12}$$

$$= 12{,}000(1.220591027)$$

$$\approx \$14{,}647.09$$

b. Use $A = Pe^{rt}$ with $P = \$12{,}000$, $r = 0.067$,

$t = 3$.

$$A = 12{,}000e^{0.067(3)}$$

$$= 12{,}000e^{0.201}$$

$$= 12{,}000(1.222624772)$$

$$\approx \$14{,}671.50$$

14. a. $M = \log\left(\dfrac{I}{I_0}\right)$

$$= \log\left(\frac{35{,}792{,}000I_0}{I_0}\right)$$

$$= \log 35{,}792{,}000$$

$$\approx 7.6 \text{ on the Richter scale}$$

b. $\log\left(\dfrac{I_1}{I_0}\right) = 6.4$ and $\log\left(\dfrac{I_2}{I_0}\right) = 5.1$

$$\frac{I_1}{I_0} = 10^{6.4} \qquad\qquad \frac{I_2}{I_0} = 10^{5.1}$$

$$I_1 = 10^{6.4}I_0 \qquad\qquad I_2 = 10^{5.1}I_0$$

To compare the intensities, compute the ratio $\dfrac{I_1}{I_2}$.

$$\frac{I_1}{I_2} = \frac{10^{6.4}I_0}{10^{5.1}I_0} = \frac{10^{6.4}}{10^{5.1}} = 10^{6.4-5.1} = 10^{1.3} \approx 20$$

An earthquake that measures 6.4 on the Richter scale is approximately 20 times as intense as an earthquake that measures 5.1 on the Richter scale.

15. a. $N(t) = N_0 e^{kt}$

$$N_0 = N(0) = 51{,}300$$

$$N(20) = 240{,}500$$

To determine k, substitute $t = 20$ and

$N_0 = 51{,}300$ into $N(t) = N_0 e^{kt}$ to produce

$$N(20) = 51{,}300e^{k(20)}$$

$$240{,}500 = 51{,}300e^{20k}$$

$$\frac{240{,}500}{51{,}300} = e^{20k}$$

$$\ln\frac{240{,}500}{51{,}300} = \ln e^{20k}$$

$$\ln\frac{240{,}500}{51{,}300} = 20k$$

$$\frac{1}{20}\ln\frac{240{,}500}{51{,}300} = k$$

$$0.0773 \approx k$$

The exponential growth function is

$N(t) = 51{,}300e^{0.0773t}$.

b. Use $N(t) = 51{,}300e^{0.0773t}$ with $t = 30$.

$$N(30) = 51{,}300e^{0.0773(30)}$$

$$\approx 521{,}500$$

The exponential growth function yields 521,500 as the approximate population of the town in 2010.

16. The percent of carbon-14 present at time t is

$P(t) = 0.5^{t/5730}$.

$$0.89 = 0.5^{t/5730}$$

$$\ln 0.89 = \ln 0.5^{t/5730}$$

$$\ln 0.89 = \left(\frac{t}{5730}\right)\ln 0.5$$

$$5730\left(\frac{\ln 0.89}{\ln 0.5}\right) = t$$

$$960 \approx t$$

The bone is about 960 years old.

17. a.

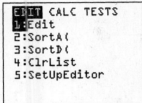

$$y = 1.447348651(1.79279858)^x$$

b. Use $y = 1.447348651(1.79279858)^x$ with $x = 8.2$.

$$y = 1.447348651(1.79279858)^{8.2}$$

$$\approx 174$$

18. a.

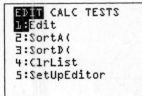

The logarithmic regression function is $h = 72610.5637 - 27040.63079\ln p$.

When $p = 12.0$, $h = 72610.5637 - 27040.63079\ln 12.0 \approx 5400$ feet.

b.

$$6200 = 72610.5637 - 27040.63079\ln p \Rightarrow \frac{6200 - 72610.5637}{-27040.63079} = \ln p$$

$$\ln p = \frac{-66410.5637}{-27040.63079} = 2.455954679 \Rightarrow e^{2.455954679} = e^{\ln p} \Rightarrow e^{2.455954679} = p \approx 11.7$$

CHAPTER 5 of *College Algebra* Chapter Test

Topics in Analytic Geometry

1. The standard form of the equation of a parabola with vertex at $(0, 0)$ and a horizontal axis of symmetry is $y^2 = 4px$.
The focus is $(p, 0)$.
The equation of the directrix is $x = -p$.

$$x = \frac{1}{12}y^2$$

$$12x = y^2$$

$$12x = 4px \Rightarrow 12 = 4p \Rightarrow 3 = p$$

vertex: $(0, 0)$
focus: $(3, 0)$
directrix: $x = -3$

2. The standard form of the equation of a parabola with vertex at (h, k) and a vertical axis of symmetry is
$$(x - h)^2 = 4p(y - k)$$
The focus is $(h, k + p)$.
The equation of the directrix is $y = k - p$.

$$x^2 - 6x + 8y - 3 = 0$$
$$x^2 - 6x = -8y + 3$$
$$x^2 - 6x + 9 = -8y + 3 + 9$$
$$(x - 3)^2 = -8y + 12$$
$$(x - 3)^2 = -8\left(y - \frac{3}{2}\right) \Rightarrow 4p = -8 \Rightarrow p = -2$$

vertex: $\left(3, \frac{3}{2}\right)$

focus: $\left(3, \frac{3}{2} - 2\right) = \left(3, -\frac{1}{2}\right)$

directrix: $y = \frac{3}{2} - (-2) \Rightarrow y = \frac{3}{2} + 2 \Rightarrow y = \frac{7}{2}$

3. Directrix $y = 1$ is vertical axis of symmetry. The standard form of the equation of a parabola with vertical axis of symmetry is $(x - h)^2 = 4p(y - k)$.

The vertex (h, k) is the midpoint of the segment joining $(-5, 2)$ and $(-5, 1)$ on the directrix, so the vertex is $\left(-5, \frac{3}{2}\right)$.

The focus is above the directrix so the parabola opens up.

The distance p from the vertex to the focus is $\frac{1}{2}$. Therefore,

$$4p = 4 \cdot \left(\frac{1}{2}\right) = 2$$

Thus the equation in standard form of the parabola is

$$(x + 5)^2 = 2\left(y - \frac{3}{2}\right).$$

4. Directrix $x = 5$ is horizontal axis of symmetry.
The vertex (h, k) is the midpoint of the segment joining $(3, 1)$ and $(5, 1)$ on the directrix, so the vertex is $(4, 1)$.
The focus is to the left of the directrix so the parabola opens to the left.

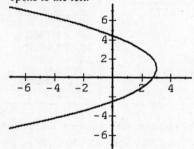

5. The standard equation of an ellipse with the center at the origin and major axis on the y-axis is $\frac{x^2}{b^2} + \frac{y^2}{a^2} = 1$.

$$\frac{x^2}{25} + \frac{y^2}{36} = \frac{x^2}{5^2} + \frac{y^2}{6^2} = 1 \Rightarrow a = 6 \text{ and } b = 5$$

$$c^2 = a^2 - b^2 \Rightarrow c^2 = 36 - 25 = 11 \Rightarrow c = \pm\sqrt{11}$$

The vertices are $(0, -a)$ and $(0, a)$ and the coordinates of The foci are $(0, -c)$ and $(0, c)$.
Vertices: $(0, -6)$ and $(0, 6)$

Foci: $\left(0, \sqrt{11}\right)$ and $\left(0, -\sqrt{11}\right)$

6. Center: $(0, 0)$
Vertices: $(-3, 0)$ and $(3, 0)$
Endpoints of minor axis $(0, -2)$ and $(0, 2)$

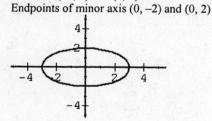

7.

$$4x^2 - 8x + y^2 + 6y = 3$$

$$4(x^2 - 2x) + (y^2 + 6y) = 3$$

$$4(x^2 - 2x + 1) + (y^2 + 6y + 9) = 3 + 4 + 9$$

$$4(x-1)^2 + (y+3)^2 = 16$$

$$\frac{(x-1)^2}{4} + \frac{(y+3)^2}{16} = 1 \Rightarrow \text{center}(1, -3)$$

$$\frac{(x-1)^2}{2^2} + \frac{(y+3)^2}{4^2} = 1 \Rightarrow a = 4 \text{ and } b = 2$$

$$c^2 = a^2 - b^2$$

$$c^2 = 4^2 - 2^2$$

$$c^2 = 16 - 4$$

$$c^2 = 12$$

$$c = \sqrt{12} = 2\sqrt{3}$$

vertices: (1, –7) and (1, 1)

foci: $(1, -3 - 2\sqrt{3})$ and $(1, -3 + 2\sqrt{3})$

8. Foci(4, 3) and (4, –5) vertical major axis

c = distance between (4, –1) and (4, 3), $c = 4$.

Major axis of length $10 \Rightarrow 2a = 10 \Rightarrow a = 5$.

$$c^2 = a^2 - b^2$$

$$4^2 = 5^2 - b^2$$

$$16 = 25 - b^2$$

$$b^2 = 25 - 16 = 9$$

equation in standard form: $\dfrac{(x-4)^2}{9} + \dfrac{(y+1)^2}{25} = 1$

9.

$$16x^2 + 9y^2 = 144$$

$$\frac{16x^2}{144} + \frac{9y^2}{144} = \frac{144}{144}$$

$$\frac{x^2}{9} + \frac{y^2}{16} = 1$$

$$\frac{x^2}{3^2} + \frac{y^2}{4^2} = 1 \Rightarrow a = 4 \text{ and } b = 3$$

$$c^2 = a^2 - b^2$$

$$c^2 = 4^2 - 3^2$$

$$c^2 = 16 - 9$$

$$c^2 = 7$$

$$c = \sqrt{7}$$

eccentricity: $e = \dfrac{c}{a} = \dfrac{\sqrt{7}}{4}$

10.

$$\frac{x^2}{3^2} - \frac{y^2}{2^2} = 1 \Rightarrow a = 3 \text{ and } b = 2$$

hyperbola centered at (0, 0)

vertices: (–3, 0) and (3, 0)

asymptotes: $y = \pm\dfrac{b}{a}x \Rightarrow y = \pm\dfrac{2}{3}x$

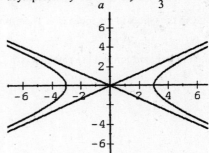

11.

$$\frac{y^2}{4^2} - \frac{x^2}{8^2} = 1 \Rightarrow a = 4 \text{ and } b = 8$$

hyperbola centered at (0, 0)

$$c^2 = a^2 + b^2$$

$$c^2 = 4^2 + 8^2$$

$$c^2 = 16 + 64$$

$$c^2 = 80$$

$$c = \sqrt{80} = 4\sqrt{5}$$

vertices: (0, –4) and (0, 4)

foci: $(0, -4\sqrt{5})$ and $(0, 4\sqrt{5})$

asymptotes: $y = \pm\dfrac{a}{b}x \Rightarrow y = \pm\dfrac{4}{8}x \Rightarrow y = \pm\dfrac{1}{2}x$

12.

$$9(x^2 + 4x) - 4(y^2 - 6y) = 36$$

$$9(x^2 + 4x + 4) - 4(y^2 - 6y + 9) = 36 + 36 - 36$$

$$9(x+2)^2 - 4(y-3)^2 = 36$$

$$\frac{9(x+2)^2}{36} - \frac{4(y-3)^2}{36} = \frac{36}{36}$$

$$\frac{(x+2)^2}{4} - \frac{(y-3)^2}{9} = 1$$

hyperbola centered at (–2, 3)

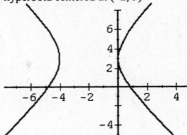

13. $\dfrac{(x+5)^2}{5^2} - \dfrac{(y-1)^2}{2^2} = 1 \Rightarrow a = 5$ and $b = 2$

center: $(h, k) = (-5, 1)$

$c^2 = a^2 + b^2$

$c^2 = 5^2 + 2^2$

$c^2 = 25 + 4$

$c^2 = 29$

$c = \sqrt{29}$

$(h \pm a, k) = (-5 \pm 5, 1)$

$\qquad\quad = (-5 - 5, 1)$ and $(-5 + 5, 1)$

vertices: $(-10, 1)$ and $(0, 1)$

$(h \pm c, k) = (-5 \pm \sqrt{29}, 1)$

foci: $(-5 - \sqrt{29}, 1)$ and $(-5 + \sqrt{29}, 1)$

14. Vertices: $(-2, 3)$ and $(-2, 9) \Rightarrow 2a = |9 - 3| = 6 \Rightarrow a = 3$

Midpoint of segment joining $(-2, 3)$ and $(-2, 9) = (-2, 6)$

Center $= (h, k) = (-2, 6)$

Foci: $\left(-2, 6 + 3\sqrt{5}\right)$ and $\left(-2, 6 - 3\sqrt{5}\right) \Rightarrow c = 3\sqrt{5}$

$c^2 = a^2 + b^2$

$\left(3\sqrt{5}\right)^2 = 3^2 + b^2$

$45 = 9 + b^2$

$36 = b^2$

$6 = b$

Use $\dfrac{(y - k)^2}{a^2} - \dfrac{(x - h)^2}{b^2} = 1$

Equation in standard form: $\dfrac{(y - 6)^2}{9} - \dfrac{(x + 2)^2}{36} = 1$

15. Directrix $y = 0$ is vertical axis of symmetry. The standard Form of the equation of a parabola with vertical axis of symmetry is $(x - h)^2 = 4p(y - k)$

The vertex (h, k) is the midpoint of the segment joining $(4, -8)$ and $(4, 0)$ on the directrix. Therefore the vertex is $(4, -4)$.

The focus is below the directrix so the parabola opens down.

The distance p from the vertex to the focus is 4. Therefore, $4p = 4(4) = 16$.

Thus the equation in standard form of the parabola is $(x - 4)^2 = 16(y + 4)$.

Systems of Equations

1. $\begin{cases} 4x + 3y = 29 & (1) \\ y = 9 & (2) \end{cases}$

The value of y is already known.
Substitute the value of y into Equation (1) and solve for x.

$4x + 3(9) = 29$
$4x + 27 = 29$
$4x = 2$
$x = \dfrac{1}{2}$

The solution is $\left(\dfrac{1}{2},\ 9\right)$.

2. $\begin{cases} 5x - 2y = 2 & (1) \\ 15x - 7y = 12 & (2) \end{cases}$

Multiply Equation (1) by -3.
Add the results to Equation (2) and solve for x.

$-3(5x - 2y = 2) \quad \rightarrow \quad \begin{array}{r} -15x + 6y = -6 \\ + \quad 15x - 7y = 12 \\ \hline -y = 6 \\ y = -6 \end{array}$

Substitute the value of y into Equation (1) and solve for x.

$5x - 2(-6) = 2$
$5x + 12 = 2$
$5x = -10$
$x = -2$

The solution is $(-2, -6)$.

3. $\begin{cases} 8x - 5y = 7 & (1) \\ 3x + 4y = 32 & (2) \end{cases}$

Multiply Equation (1) by 4.
Multiply Equation (2) by 5.
Add the results together and solve for x.

$\begin{array}{l} 4(8x - 5y = 7) \\ 5(3x + 4y = 32) \end{array} \quad \rightarrow \quad \begin{array}{r} 32x - 20y = 28 \\ + \quad 15x + 20y = 160 \\ \hline 47x = 188 \\ x = 4 \end{array}$

Substitute the value of x into Equation (1) and solve for y.

$8(4) - 5y = 7$
$32 - 5y = 7$
$-5y = -25$
$y = 5$

The solution is $(4, 5)$.

4. $\begin{cases} \dfrac{1}{3}x + y = 2 & (1) \\ x + 2y = 1 & (2) \end{cases}$

Multiply Equation (1) by -3.
Add the results to Equation (2) and solve for y.

$-3\left(\dfrac{1}{3}x + y = 2\right) \quad \rightarrow \quad \begin{array}{r} -x - 3y = -6 \\ + \quad x + 2y = 1 \\ \hline -y = -5 \\ y = 5 \end{array}$

Substitute the value of y into Equation (2) and solve for x.

$x + 2(5) = 1$
$x + 10 = 1$
$x = -9$

The solution is $(-9, 5)$.

5. $\begin{cases} 3x + 4y = 12 & (1) \\ \dfrac{3}{4}x + y = \dfrac{5}{4} & (2) \end{cases}$

Multiply Equation (2) by -4.
Add the results to Equation (1) and solve for y.

$-4\left(\dfrac{3}{4}x + y = \dfrac{5}{4}\right) \quad \rightarrow \quad \begin{array}{r} 3x + 4y = 12 \\ + \quad -3x - 4y = -5 \\ \hline 0 = 7 \end{array}$

Because $0 = 7$ is never true, the system is inconsistent.

6. $\begin{cases} x + 2y = 6 & (1) \\ y = -\dfrac{1}{2}x + 3 & (2) \end{cases}$

Substitute $-\dfrac{1}{2}x + 3$ for y into Equation (1) and solve for x.

$x + 2(-\dfrac{1}{2}x + 3) = 6$
$x - x + 6 = 6$
$6 = 6$

Because $6 = 6$ is always true, the system is dependent.
The solution is $\left(a, -\dfrac{1}{2}a + 3\right)$.

7. $\begin{cases} x + 2y + 3z = 12 & (1) \\ 2x - y + 2z = 3 & (2) \\ 3x + 3y - z = -7 & (3) \end{cases}$

Multiply Equation (1) by –2.
Add the results to Equation (2).

$$-2(x + 2y + 3z = 12) \rightarrow \begin{array}{r} -2x - 4y - 6z = -24 \\ + \quad 2x - y + 2z = 3 \\ \hline -5y - 4z = -21 \quad (4) \end{array}$$

Multiply Equation (1) by –3.
Add the results to Equation (3).

$$-3(x + 2y + 3z = 12) \rightarrow \begin{array}{r} -3x - 6y - 9z = -36 \\ + \quad 3x + 3y - z = -7 \\ \hline -3y - 10z = -43 \quad (5) \end{array}$$

Now consider the system of Equation (4) and Equation (5).

$$\begin{cases} -5y - 4z = -21 & (4) \\ -3y - 10z = -43 & (5) \end{cases}$$

Multiply Equation (4) by 3.
Multiply Equation (5) by –5.
Add the resulting equations.

$$\begin{array}{l} 3(-5y - 4z = -21) \\ -5(-3y - 10z = -43) \end{array} \rightarrow \begin{array}{r} -15y - 12z = -63 \\ + \quad 15y + 50z = 215 \\ \hline 38z = 152 \\ z = 4 \end{array}$$

Substitute 4 for z in Equation (4) and solve for y.

$$\begin{aligned} -5y - 4(4) &= -21 \\ -5y - 16 &= -21 \\ -5y &= -5 \\ y &= 1 \end{aligned}$$

Substitute 4 for z and substitute 1 for y in Equation (1).
Solve for x.

$$\begin{aligned} x + 2(1) + 3(4) &= 12 \\ x + 2 + 12 &= 12 \\ x &= -2 \end{aligned}$$

The solution is $(-2, 1, 4)$.

8. $\begin{cases} 6x - 2y - z = 0 & (1) \\ x + 2y - 3z = 0 & (2) \\ 5x - 4y + 2z = 0 & (3) \end{cases}$

Multiply Equation (2) by –6.
Add the results to Equation (1).

$$-6(x + 2y - 3z = 0) \rightarrow \begin{array}{r} -6x - 12y + 18z = 0 \\ + \quad 6x - 2y - z = 0 \\ \hline -14y + 17z = 0 \quad (4) \end{array}$$

Multiply Equation (2) by –5.
Add the results to Equation (3).

$$-5(x + 2y - 3z = 0) \rightarrow \begin{array}{r} -5x - 10y + 15z = 0 \\ + \quad 5x - 4y + 2z = 0 \\ \hline -14y + 17z = 0 \quad (5) \end{array}$$

Now consider the system of Equation (4) and Equation (5).

$$\begin{cases} -14y + 17z = 0 & (4) \\ -14y + 17z = 0 & (5) \end{cases}$$

Since Equation (4) and Equation (5) are identical, the system is dependent.

Solve Equation (4) for y.

$$\begin{aligned} -14y + 17z &= 0 \\ -14y &= -17z \\ y &= \frac{17}{14}z \end{aligned}$$

Substitute $\frac{17}{14}z$ for y in Equation (1) and solve for x.

$$\begin{aligned} x + 2\left(\frac{17}{14}z\right) - 3z &= 0 \\ x + \frac{17}{7}z - \frac{21}{7}z &= 0 \\ x - \frac{4}{7}z &= 0 \\ x &= \frac{4}{7}z \end{aligned}$$

Let z be represented by c.
Then $x = \frac{4}{7}c$ and $y = \frac{17}{14}c$.

The solution is $\left(\frac{4}{7}c, \frac{17}{14}c, c\right)$.

9. $\begin{cases} 4x + 3y = 17 & (1) \\ 5x - 4y = 19 & (2) \end{cases}$

Multiply Equation (1) by 5.
Multiply Equation (2) by –4.
Add the resulting equations.

$\begin{aligned} & 5(4x + 3y = 17) \\ -\, & 4(5x - 4y = 19) \end{aligned}$ $\rightarrow$ $\begin{aligned} 20x + 15y &= \ \ 85 \\ +\ \ -20x + 16y &= -76 \\ \hline 31y &= 9 \\ y &= \tfrac{9}{31} \end{aligned}$

One method of solving for x involves substituting $\tfrac{9}{31}$ for y in Equation (1) or Equation (2). Some students prefer the alternate method of eliminating y using the original system of equations.

$\begin{cases} 4x + 3y = 17 & (1) \\ 5x - 4y = 19 & (2) \end{cases}$

Multiply Equation (1) by 4.
Multiply Equation (2) by 3.
Add the resulting equations.

$\begin{aligned} & 4(4x + 3y = 17) \\ & 3(5x - 4y = 19) \end{aligned}$ $\rightarrow$ $\begin{aligned} 16x + 12y &= 68 \\ +\ \ 15x - 12y &= 57 \\ \hline 31x \quad\ &= 125 \\ x \quad\ &= \tfrac{125}{31} \end{aligned}$

The solution is $\left(\tfrac{125}{31}, \tfrac{9}{31}\right)$.

10. $\begin{cases} 3x + y - 4z = 12 & (1) \\ 2x - 3y + 6z = 10 & (2) \end{cases}$

There are fewer equations than variables—a nonsquare system of equations—so the system has either no solution or an infinite number of solutions.

Multiply Equation (1) by 3.
Add the result to Equation (2) and solve for x.

$3(3x + y - 4z = 12)$ $\rightarrow$ $\begin{aligned} 9x + 3y - 12z &= 36 \\ +\ \ 2x - 3y + 6z &= 10 \\ \hline 11x \quad\ - 6z &= 46 \\ 11x &= 6z + 46 \\ x &= \tfrac{6}{11}z + \tfrac{46}{11} \end{aligned}$

Multiply Equation (1) by 2.
Multiply Equation (2) by –3.
Add the resulting Equations together and solve for y.

$\begin{aligned} & 2(3x + y - 4z = 12) \\ -\, & 3(2x - 3y + 6z = 10) \end{aligned}$ $\rightarrow$ $\begin{aligned} 6x + 2y - \ 8z &= \ \ 24 \\ +\ \ -6x + 9y - 18z &= -30 \\ \hline 11y - 26z &= -6 \\ 11y &= 26z - 6 \\ y &= \tfrac{26}{11}z - \tfrac{6}{11} \end{aligned}$

The solution is $\left(\tfrac{6}{11}c + \tfrac{46}{11}, \tfrac{26}{11}c - \tfrac{6}{11}, c\right)$.

11. $\begin{cases} x^2 + y^2 = 9 & (1) \\ 2x^2 - y^2 = 3 & (2) \end{cases}$

Add Equation (1) to Equation (2) and solve for x.

$\begin{aligned} x^2 + y^2 &= 9 \\ +\ \ 2x^2 - y^2 &= 3 \\ \hline 3x^2 \quad\ &= 12 \Rightarrow x^2 = 4 \Rightarrow x = \pm\sqrt{4} \Rightarrow x = \pm 2 \\ x = 2 \ & \text{ or } \ x = -2 \end{aligned}$

To find y when x is 2, substitute 2 for x in Equation (1).
$(2)^2 + y^2 = 9 \Rightarrow 4 + y^2 = 9 \Rightarrow y^2 = 5 \Rightarrow y = \pm\sqrt{5}$
Thus, when $x = 2$, $y = \sqrt{5}$ or $-\sqrt{5}$.

To find y when x is –2, substitute –2 for x in Equation (1).
$(-2)^2 + y^2 = 9 \Rightarrow 4 + y^2 = 9 \Rightarrow y^2 = 5 \Rightarrow y = \pm\sqrt{5}$
Thus, when $x = -2$, $y = \sqrt{5}$ or $-\sqrt{5}$.

The solutions are $\left(2, \sqrt{5}\right), \left(2, -\sqrt{5}\right), \left(-2, \sqrt{5}\right),$ and $\left(-2, -\sqrt{5}\right)$.

12. $\begin{cases} y = 2x & (1) \\ y = x^2 - 3x + 4 & (2) \end{cases}$

Substitute $2x$ for y in Equation (2) and solve for x.

$\begin{aligned} 2x &= x^2 - 3x + 4 \\ 0 &= x^2 - 5x + 4 \\ 0 &= (x - 4)(x - 1) \\ x = 4 \ & \text{ or } \ x = 1 \end{aligned}$

To find y when x is 4, substitute 4 for x in Equation (1).
$y = 2(4) \Rightarrow y = 8$
Thus, when $x = 4$, $y = 8$.

To find y when x is 1, substitute 1 for x in Equation (1).
$y = 2(1) \Rightarrow y = 2$
Thus, when $x = 1$, $y = 2$.

The solutions are $(4, 8)$ and $(1, 2)$.

13. $3x - 2y > 10$

$\qquad -2y > -3x + 10$

$\qquad y < \dfrac{3}{2}x - 5$

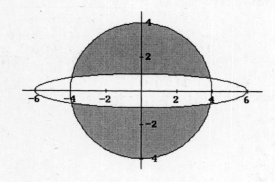

14. $x \geq y^2 - 1$

$\qquad x \geq (y + 1)(y - 1)$

The parabola opens to the right. The shading is to the right.

If $y = 0$, then $x = 0^2 - 1 = -1 \Rightarrow$ the x-intercept is $(-1, 0)$.

If $x = 0$, then $0 = (y + 1)(y - 1)$

$\qquad\qquad\qquad y = -1 \ $ or $\ y = 1$

Therefore the y-intercepts are $(0, -1)$ and $(0, 1)$.

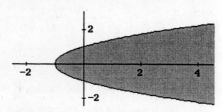

15. $x^2 + y^2 \leq 16$

$\quad x^2 + 36y^2 \geq 36 \Rightarrow \dfrac{x^2}{36} + \dfrac{y^2}{1} \geq 1$

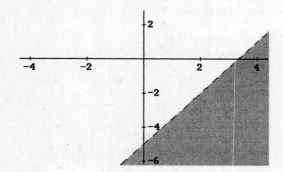

16. $2x + 3y \leq 9 \Rightarrow y \leq -\dfrac{2}{3}x + 3$

$\quad x - y \geq -1 \Rightarrow y \leq x + 1$

$\quad x - 2y \leq 3 \Rightarrow y \geq \dfrac{1}{2}x - \dfrac{3}{2}$

$\quad x \geq 0, y \geq 0$

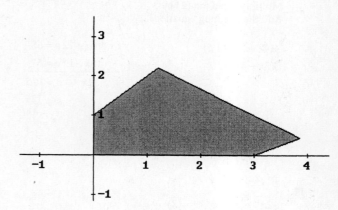

17. $\dfrac{8x + 31}{(x + 2)(x + 5)} = \dfrac{A}{x + 2} + \dfrac{B}{x + 5}$

Multiply by $(x + 2)(x + 5)$.

$8x + 31 = A(x + 5) + B(x + 2)$

$8x + 31 = Ax + 5A + Bx + 2B$

$8x + 31 = (A + B)x + (5A + 2B)$

Equate coefficients of like powers.

$\quad 8 = A + B \qquad\qquad (1)$

$\quad 31 = 5A + 2B \qquad\ (2)$

Solving this system of equations yields $A = 5$ and $B = 3$.

Thus, $\dfrac{8x + 31}{(x + 2)(x + 5)} = \dfrac{5}{x + 2} + \dfrac{3}{x + 5}$.

18. $\dfrac{4x - 7}{(x - 1)^2} = \dfrac{A}{x - 1} + \dfrac{B}{(x - 1)^2}$

Multiply by $(x - 1)^2$.

$4x - 7 = A(x - 1) + B$

$4x - 7 = Ax - A + B$

Equate coefficients of like powers.

$\quad 4 = A \qquad\qquad (1)$

$\quad -7 = -A + B \qquad (2)$

Solving this system of equations yields $A = 4$ and $B = -3$.

Thus, $\dfrac{4x - 7}{(x - 1)^2} = \dfrac{4}{x - 1} + \dfrac{-3}{(x - 1)^2}$.

19. objective function: $P = 14x + 42y$

constraints:
$$\begin{cases} x + y \le 5 \\ x - 2y \ge -7 \\ 3x + 2y \le 12 \\ 2x - y \le 4 \\ x \ge 0, y \ge 0 \end{cases}$$

Graph the solution set of the constraints.

Determine the vertices of the bounded region either by using a graphing utility or by solving systems of equations.

The system $\begin{cases} x + y = 5 \\ x - 2y = -7 \end{cases}$ yields $(1, 4)$.

The system $\begin{cases} x + y = 5 \\ 3x + 2y = 12 \end{cases}$ yields $(2, 3)$.

The system $\begin{cases} 3x + 2y = 12 \\ 2x - y = 4 \end{cases}$ yields $\left(\frac{20}{7}, \frac{12}{7}\right)$.

The system $\begin{cases} 2x - y = 4 \\ y = 0 \end{cases}$ yields $(2, 0)$.

The system $\begin{cases} x - 2y = -7 \\ x = 0 \end{cases}$ yields $\left(0, \frac{7}{2}\right)$.

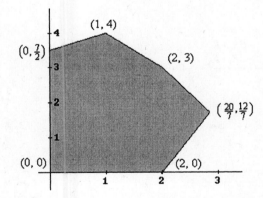

Determine the value of $P = 14x + 42y$ at each vertex.

(x, y) $P = 14x + 42y$
$(0, 0)$ $P = 14(0) + 42(0) = 0$
$\left(0, \frac{7}{2}\right)$ $P = 14(0) + 42(\frac{7}{2}) = 147$
$(1, 4)$ $P = 14(1) + 42(4) = 182$ • maximum
$(2, 3)$ $P = 14(2) + 42(3) = 154$
$\left(\frac{20}{7}, \frac{12}{7}\right)$ $P = 14(\frac{20}{7}) + 42(\frac{12}{7}) = 112$
$(2, 0)$ $P = 14(2) + 42(0) = 28$

The maximum value of the objective function is 182. It occurs when $x = 1$ and $y = 4$.

20. Using $x^2 + y^2 + ax + by + c = 0$ with the points $(2, -7)$, $(8, 1)$, and $(1, 0)$ produces the following system.
$$\begin{cases} 2a - 7b + c = -53 & (1) \\ 8a + b + c = -65 & (2) \\ a + c = -1 & (3) \end{cases}$$

Multiply Equation (2) by 7.
Add the results to Equation (1)

$$7(8a + b + c = -65) \rightarrow \begin{array}{r} 56a + 7b + 7c = -455 \\ + \quad 2a - 7b + c = -53 \\ \hline 58a + 8c = -508 \quad (4) \end{array}$$

Now consider the system of Equation (3) and Equation (4).

$$\begin{cases} a + c = -1 & (3) \\ 58a + 8c = -508 & (4) \end{cases}$$

Multiply Equation (3) by -8.
Add the result to Equation (4) and solve for a.

$$-8(a + c = -1) \rightarrow \begin{array}{r} -8a - 8c = 8 \\ + \quad 58a + 8c = -508 \\ \hline 50a = -500 \\ a = -10 \end{array}$$

Substitute -10 for a in Equation (3) and solve for c.

$$-10 + c = -1$$
$$c = 9$$

Substitute -10 for a and substitute 9 for c in Equation (2). Solve for b.

$$8(-10) + b + 9 = -65$$
$$-80 + b + 9 = -65$$
$$b = 6$$

The equation of the circle is $x^2 + y^2 - 10x + 6y + 9 = 0$.

The equation of the circle may be written in standard form.
$$x^2 + y^2 - 10x + 6y + 9 = 0$$
$$x^2 - 10x + y^2 + 6y = -9$$
$$x^2 - 10x + 25 + y^2 + 6y + 9 = -9 + 25 + 9$$
$$(x - 5)^2 + (y + 3)^2 = 25$$
$$\text{or}$$
$$(x - 5)^2 + (y + 3)^2 = 5^2$$

Matrices

1. $\begin{cases} 2x + 5y - 2z = -3 \\ 3x - 2y - 4z = 1 \\ 5x + 3y - 3z = 10 \end{cases}$

2. $\begin{bmatrix} 3 & 0 & -1 & | & 4 \\ 5 & 6 & -2 & | & -8 \\ 0 & -1 & 1 & | & 2 \end{bmatrix} \rightarrow \begin{cases} 3x \quad\;\; - z = 4 \\ 5x + 6y - 2z = -8 \\ \quad\;\; - y + z = 2 \end{cases}$

augmented matrix: $\begin{bmatrix} 2 & 5 & -2 & | & -3 \\ 3 & -2 & -4 & | & 1 \\ 5 & 3 & -3 & | & 10 \end{bmatrix}$

coefficient matrix: $\begin{bmatrix} 2 & 5 & -2 \\ 3 & -2 & -4 \\ 5 & 3 & -3 \end{bmatrix}$

constant matrix: $\begin{bmatrix} -3 \\ 1 \\ 10 \end{bmatrix}$

3. $\begin{cases} x + 3y + 2z = 8 \\ 2x - y + 3z = 3 \\ 3x + 2y + 12z = 4 \end{cases} \rightarrow \begin{bmatrix} 1 & 3 & 2 & | & 8 \\ 2 & -1 & 3 & | & 3 \\ 3 & 2 & 12 & | & 4 \end{bmatrix} \xrightarrow[\;-3R_1 + R_3\;]{-2R_1 + R_2} \begin{bmatrix} 1 & 3 & 2 & | & 8 \\ 0 & -7 & -1 & | & -13 \\ 0 & -7 & 6 & | & -20 \end{bmatrix} \xrightarrow{-\frac{1}{7}R_2} \begin{bmatrix} 1 & 3 & 2 & | & 8 \\ 0 & 1 & \frac{1}{7} & | & \frac{13}{7} \\ 0 & -7 & 6 & | & -20 \end{bmatrix}$

$\xrightarrow{7R_2 + R_3} \begin{bmatrix} 1 & 3 & 2 & | & 8 \\ 0 & 1 & \frac{1}{7} & | & \frac{13}{7} \\ 0 & 0 & 7 & | & -7 \end{bmatrix} \xrightarrow{\frac{1}{7}R_3} \begin{bmatrix} 1 & 3 & 2 & | & 8 \\ 0 & 1 & \frac{1}{7} & | & \frac{13}{7} \\ 0 & 0 & 1 & | & -1 \end{bmatrix} \rightarrow \begin{cases} x + 3y + 2z = 8 \\ y + \frac{1}{7}z = \frac{13}{7} \\ z = -1 \end{cases}$

$y + \frac{1}{7}(-1) = \frac{13}{7}$ $x + 3(2) + 2(-1) = 8$

$y - \frac{1}{7} = \frac{13}{7}$ $x + 6 - 2 = 8$

$y = \frac{14}{7} = 2$ $x = 4$

The solution is $(4, 2, -1)$.

4. $\begin{cases} 2x - y + 3z = -8 \\ 5x + 2y + 6z = 1 \\ x + y + z = 3 \end{cases} \rightarrow \begin{bmatrix} 2 & -1 & 3 & | & -8 \\ 5 & 2 & 6 & | & 1 \\ 1 & 1 & 1 & | & 3 \end{bmatrix} \;\; R_1 \longleftrightarrow R_3 \;\; \begin{bmatrix} 1 & 1 & 1 & | & 3 \\ 5 & 2 & 6 & | & 1 \\ 2 & -1 & 3 & | & -8 \end{bmatrix} \xrightarrow[\;-2R_1 + R_3\;]{-5R_1 + R_2} \begin{bmatrix} 1 & 1 & 1 & | & 3 \\ 0 & -3 & 1 & | & -14 \\ 0 & -3 & 1 & | & -14 \end{bmatrix}$

$\xrightarrow{-\frac{1}{3}R_2} \begin{bmatrix} 1 & 1 & 1 & | & 3 \\ 0 & 1 & -\frac{1}{3} & | & \frac{14}{3} \\ 0 & -3 & 1 & | & -14 \end{bmatrix} \xrightarrow{3R_2 + R_3} \begin{bmatrix} 1 & 1 & 1 & | & 3 \\ 0 & 1 & -\frac{1}{3} & | & \frac{14}{3} \\ 0 & 0 & 0 & | & 0 \end{bmatrix} \rightarrow \begin{cases} x + y + z = 3 \\ y - \frac{1}{3}z = \frac{14}{3} \end{cases}$

This is a nonsquare system of equations. Solve for y in terms of z.

$y = \frac{1}{3}z + \frac{14}{3}$

Then solve for x in terms of z.

$x + \left(\frac{1}{3}z + \frac{14}{3}\right) + z = 3$

$x = -\frac{4}{3}z - \frac{5}{3}$

The solution is $\left(-\frac{4}{3}c - \frac{5}{3}, \frac{1}{3}c + \frac{14}{3}, c\right)$.

5. $\begin{cases} w+2x+3y-\ z=\ 7 \\ 2w-\ x-\ y+\ z=\ 2 \\ 3w-3x+2y-4z=13 \\ 4w+\ x+3y+2z=\ 5 \end{cases} \rightarrow \begin{bmatrix} 1 & 2 & 3 & -1 & \vline & 7 \\ 2 & -1 & -1 & 1 & \vline & 2 \\ 3 & -3 & 2 & -4 & \vline & 13 \\ 4 & 1 & 3 & 2 & \vline & 5 \end{bmatrix} \xrightarrow[\substack{-2R_1+R_2 \\ -3R_1+R_3 \\ -4R_1+R_4}]{} \begin{bmatrix} 1 & 2 & 3 & -1 & \vline & 7 \\ 0 & -5 & -7 & 3 & \vline & -12 \\ 0 & -9 & -7 & -1 & \vline & -8 \\ 0 & -7 & -9 & 6 & \vline & -23 \end{bmatrix}$

$\xrightarrow{-\frac{1}{5}R_2} \begin{bmatrix} 1 & 2 & 3 & -1 & \vline & 7 \\ 0 & 1 & \frac{7}{5} & -\frac{3}{5} & \vline & \frac{12}{5} \\ 0 & -9 & -7 & -1 & \vline & -8 \\ 0 & -7 & -9 & 6 & \vline & -23 \end{bmatrix} \xrightarrow[\substack{9R_2+R_3 \\ 7R_2+R_4}]{} \begin{bmatrix} 1 & 2 & 3 & -1 & \vline & 7 \\ 0 & 1 & \frac{7}{5} & -\frac{3}{5} & \vline & \frac{12}{5} \\ 0 & 0 & \frac{28}{5} & -\frac{32}{5} & \vline & \frac{68}{5} \\ 0 & 0 & \frac{4}{5} & \frac{9}{5} & \vline & -\frac{31}{5} \end{bmatrix} \xrightarrow{\frac{5}{28}R_3} \begin{bmatrix} 1 & 2 & 3 & -1 & \vline & 7 \\ 0 & 1 & \frac{7}{5} & -\frac{3}{5} & \vline & \frac{12}{5} \\ 0 & 0 & 1 & -\frac{8}{7} & \vline & \frac{17}{7} \\ 0 & 0 & \frac{4}{5} & \frac{9}{5} & \vline & -\frac{31}{5} \end{bmatrix}$

$\xrightarrow{-\frac{4}{5}R_3+R_4} \begin{bmatrix} 1 & 2 & 3 & -1 & \vline & 7 \\ 0 & 1 & \frac{7}{5} & -\frac{3}{5} & \vline & \frac{12}{5} \\ 0 & 0 & 1 & -\frac{8}{7} & \vline & \frac{17}{7} \\ 0 & 0 & 0 & \frac{19}{7} & \vline & -\frac{57}{7} \end{bmatrix} \xrightarrow{\frac{7}{19}R_4} \begin{bmatrix} 1 & 2 & 3 & -1 & \vline & 7 \\ 0 & 1 & \frac{7}{5} & -\frac{3}{5} & \vline & \frac{12}{5} \\ 0 & 0 & 1 & -\frac{8}{7} & \vline & \frac{17}{7} \\ 0 & 0 & 0 & 1 & \vline & -3 \end{bmatrix} \rightarrow \begin{cases} w+2x+3y-\ z=\ 7 \\ x+\frac{7}{5}y-\frac{3}{5}z=\frac{12}{5} \\ y-\frac{8}{7}z=\frac{17}{7} \\ z=-3 \end{cases}$

$\begin{aligned} y-\frac{8}{7}(-3) &= \frac{17}{7} \\ y+\frac{24}{7} &= \frac{17}{7} \\ y &= -\frac{7}{7} = -1 \end{aligned}$
$\qquad$
$\begin{aligned} x+\frac{7}{5}(-1)-\frac{3}{5}(-3) &= \frac{12}{5} \\ x-\frac{7}{5}+\frac{9}{5} &= \frac{12}{5} \\ x &= \frac{10}{5} = 2 \end{aligned}$
$\qquad$
$\begin{aligned} w+2(2)+3(-1)-(-3) &= 7 \\ w+4-3+3 &= 7 \\ w &= 3 \end{aligned}$

The solution is $(3, 2, -1, -3)$.

6. $\begin{bmatrix} 1 & 4 & 2 \\ 2 & -1 & 0 \\ -1 & -3 & 2 \end{bmatrix} + \begin{bmatrix} 2 & 0 & -3 \\ 3 & -4 & -1 \\ 2 & 1 & 1 \end{bmatrix} = \begin{bmatrix} 3 & 4 & -1 \\ 5 & -5 & -1 \\ 1 & -2 & 3 \end{bmatrix}$

7. $\begin{bmatrix} 1 & 4 & 2 \\ 2 & -1 & 0 \\ -1 & -3 & 2 \end{bmatrix} + \begin{bmatrix} 3 & 0 & 1 \\ -3 & -1 & -2 \end{bmatrix}$ is not defined.

8. $\begin{bmatrix} 3 & 12 & 6 \\ 6 & -3 & 0 \\ -3 & -9 & 6 \end{bmatrix} - \begin{bmatrix} 2 & 0 & -3 \\ 3 & -4 & -1 \\ 2 & 1 & 1 \end{bmatrix} = \begin{bmatrix} 1 & 12 & 9 \\ 3 & 1 & 1 \\ -5 & -10 & 5 \end{bmatrix}$

9. $\begin{bmatrix} -12 & 0 & -4 \\ 12 & 4 & 8 \end{bmatrix}$

10. $\begin{bmatrix} 2(3)+3(-3) & 2(0)+3(-1) & 2(1)+3(-2) \\ -4(3)+(-5)(-3) & -4(0)+(-5)(-1) & -4(1)+(-5)(-2) \end{bmatrix} + \begin{bmatrix} 3 & 0 & 1 \\ -3 & -1 & -2 \end{bmatrix} = \begin{bmatrix} -3 & -3 & -4 \\ 3 & 5 & 6 \end{bmatrix} + \begin{bmatrix} 3 & 0 & 1 \\ -3 & -1 & -2 \end{bmatrix} = \begin{bmatrix} 0 & -3 & -3 \\ 0 & 4 & 4 \end{bmatrix}$

11. $\begin{bmatrix} 2(2)+0(3)+(-3)(2) & 2(0)+0(-4)+(-3)(1) & 2(-3)+0(-1)+(-3)(1) \\ 3(2)+(-4)(3)+(-1)(2) & 3(0)+(-4)(-4)+(-1)(1) & 3(-3)+(-4)(-1)+(-1)(1) \\ 2(2)+1(3)+1(2) & 2(0)+1(-4)+1(1) & 2(-3)+1(-1)+1(1) \end{bmatrix} = \begin{bmatrix} -2 & -3 & -9 \\ -8 & 15 & -6 \\ 9 & -3 & -6 \end{bmatrix}$

12. $\begin{bmatrix} 4 & 6 \\ -8 & -10 \end{bmatrix}$

13. $\begin{bmatrix} 2(2)+3(-4) & 2(3)+3(-5) \\ -4(2)+(-5)(-4) & (-4)(3+(-5)(-5) \end{bmatrix} = \begin{bmatrix} -8 & -9 \\ 12 & 13 \end{bmatrix}$

14. $\begin{bmatrix} 1(2)+4(3)+2(2) & 1(0)+4(-4)+2(1) & 1(-3)+4(-1)+2(1) \\ 2(2)+(-1)(3)+0(2) & 2(0)+(-1)(-4)+0(1) & 2(-3)+(-1)(-1)+0(1) \\ -1(2)+(-3)(3)+2(2) & -1(0)+(-3)(-4)+2(1) & -1(-3)+(-3)(-1)+2(1) \end{bmatrix} = \begin{bmatrix} 18 & -14 & -5 \\ 1 & 4 & -5 \\ -7 & 14 & 8 \end{bmatrix}$

15. $\begin{bmatrix} 3(2)+0(3)+1(2) & 3(0)+0(-4)+1(1) & 3(-3)+0(-1)+1(1) \\ -3(2)+(-1)(3)+(-2)(2) & -3(0)+(-1)(-4)+(-2)(1) & -3(-3)+(-1)(-1)+(-2)(1) \end{bmatrix} = \begin{bmatrix} 8 & 1 & -8 \\ -13 & 2 & 8 \end{bmatrix}$

420 **Solutions to Chapter Tests**

16. $\begin{bmatrix} 2 & 0 & -3 \\ 3 & -4 & -1 \\ 2 & 1 & 1 \end{bmatrix} \begin{bmatrix} 3 & 0 & 1 \\ -3 & -1 & -2 \end{bmatrix}$ is not defined. **17.** C^{-1} is not defined..

18. $\begin{bmatrix} 1 & 4 & 2 & | & 1 & 0 & 0 \\ 2 & -1 & 0 & | & 0 & 1 & 0 \\ -1 & -3 & 2 & | & 0 & 0 & 1 \end{bmatrix} \xrightarrow[R_1+R_3]{-2R_1+R_2} \begin{bmatrix} 1 & 4 & 2 & | & 1 & 0 & 0 \\ 0 & -9 & -4 & | & -2 & 1 & 0 \\ 0 & 1 & 4 & | & 1 & 0 & 1 \end{bmatrix} R_2 \longleftrightarrow R_3 \begin{bmatrix} 1 & 4 & 2 & | & 1 & 0 & 0 \\ 0 & 1 & 4 & | & 1 & 0 & 1 \\ 0 & -9 & -4 & | & -2 & 1 & 0 \end{bmatrix}$

$\xrightarrow[9R_2+R_3]{-4R2+R_1} \begin{bmatrix} 1 & 0 & -14 & | & -3 & 0 & -4 \\ 0 & 1 & 4 & | & 1 & 0 & 1 \\ 0 & 0 & 32 & | & 7 & 1 & 9 \end{bmatrix} \xrightarrow{\frac{1}{32}R_3} \begin{bmatrix} 1 & 0 & -14 & | & -3 & 0 & -4 \\ 0 & 1 & 4 & | & 1 & 0 & 1 \\ 0 & 0 & 1 & | & \frac{7}{32} & \frac{1}{32} & \frac{9}{32} \end{bmatrix} \xrightarrow[-4R_3+R_2]{14R_3+R_1} \begin{bmatrix} 1 & 0 & 0 & | & \frac{1}{16} & \frac{7}{16} & -\frac{1}{16} \\ 0 & 1 & 0 & | & \frac{1}{8} & -\frac{1}{8} & -\frac{1}{8} \\ 0 & 0 & 1 & | & \frac{7}{32} & \frac{1}{32} & \frac{9}{32} \end{bmatrix}$

The inverse matrix is $A^{-1} = \begin{bmatrix} \frac{1}{16} & \frac{7}{16} & -\frac{1}{16} \\ \frac{1}{8} & -\frac{1}{8} & -\frac{1}{8} \\ \frac{7}{32} & \frac{1}{32} & \frac{9}{32} \end{bmatrix}$.

19. $\begin{bmatrix} 2 & 3 & | & 1 & 0 \\ -4 & -5 & | & 0 & 1 \end{bmatrix} \xrightarrow{\frac{1}{2}R_1} \begin{bmatrix} 1 & \frac{3}{2} & | & \frac{1}{2} & 0 \\ -4 & -5 & | & 0 & 1 \end{bmatrix} \xrightarrow{4R_1+R_2} \begin{bmatrix} 1 & \frac{3}{2} & | & \frac{1}{2} & 0 \\ 0 & 1 & | & 2 & 1 \end{bmatrix} \xrightarrow{-\frac{3}{2}R_2+R_1} \begin{bmatrix} 1 & 0 & | & -\frac{5}{2} & -\frac{3}{2} \\ 0 & 1 & | & 2 & 1 \end{bmatrix}$

The inverse matrix is $D^{-1} = \begin{bmatrix} -\frac{5}{2} & -\frac{3}{2} \\ 2 & 1 \end{bmatrix}$.

20. M_{32} of $\begin{bmatrix} 1 & 4 & 2 \\ 2 & -1 & 0 \\ -1 & -3 & 2 \end{bmatrix}$ is $\begin{vmatrix} 1 & 2 \\ 2 & 0 \end{vmatrix} = 1(0) - 2(2) = -4$. **21.** C_{32} of $\begin{bmatrix} 1 & 4 & 2 \\ 2 & -1 & 0 \\ -1 & -3 & 2 \end{bmatrix}$ is $(-1)\begin{vmatrix} 1 & 2 \\ 2 & 0 \end{vmatrix} = -1(-4) = 4$.

22. $\begin{vmatrix} 2 & 0 & -3 \\ 3 & -4 & -1 \\ 2 & 1 & 1 \end{vmatrix} = (-1)(0)\begin{vmatrix} 3 & -1 \\ 2 & 1 \end{vmatrix} + (-4)\begin{vmatrix} 2 & -3 \\ 2 & 1 \end{vmatrix} + (-1)(1)\begin{vmatrix} 2 & -3 \\ 3 & -1 \end{vmatrix} = 0 - 4(2+6) - 1(-2+9) = -4(8) - 1(7) = -32 - 7 = -39$

23. $\begin{vmatrix} 1 & 4 & 2 \\ 2 & -1 & 0 \\ -1 & -3 & 2 \end{vmatrix} \xrightarrow[R_1+R_3]{-2R_1+R_2} \begin{vmatrix} 1 & 4 & 2 \\ 0 & -9 & -4 \\ 0 & 1 & 4 \end{vmatrix} R_2 \longleftrightarrow R_3 - \begin{vmatrix} 1 & 4 & 2 \\ 0 & 1 & 4 \\ 0 & -9 & -4 \end{vmatrix} \xrightarrow{9R_2+R_3} - \begin{vmatrix} 1 & 4 & 2 \\ 0 & 1 & 4 \\ 0 & 0 & 32 \end{vmatrix} = -(1)(1)(32) = -32$

24. $y = \dfrac{\begin{vmatrix} 3 & 1 & -4 \\ 2 & -3 & -2 \\ 5 & 10 & -3 \end{vmatrix}}{\begin{vmatrix} 3 & -2 & -4 \\ 2 & 5 & -2 \\ 5 & 3 & -3 \end{vmatrix}} = \dfrac{-57}{57} = -1$

25. $\begin{bmatrix} x \\ y \\ z \end{bmatrix} = \left(\begin{bmatrix} 1 & 0 & 0 \\ 0 & 1 & 0 \\ 0 & 0 & 1 \end{bmatrix} - \begin{bmatrix} 0.10 & 0.15 & 0.10 \\ 0.05 & 0.30 & 0.25 \\ 0.10 & 0.10 & 0.10 \end{bmatrix} \right)^{-1} \begin{bmatrix} 26 \\ 38 \\ 22 \end{bmatrix}$

Sequences, Series, and Probability

1. $a_4 = \dfrac{4^3}{3^4} = \dfrac{64}{81}$

   $a_6 = \dfrac{6^3}{3^6} = \dfrac{216}{729} = \dfrac{8}{27}$

2. $a_4 = \dfrac{(-1)^4}{4!} = \dfrac{1}{24}$

   $a_6 = \dfrac{(-1)^6}{6!} = \dfrac{1}{720}$

3. $a_1 = -2$

   $a_2 = 3(-2) = -6$

   $a_3 = 3(-6) = -18$

   $a_4 = 3(-18) = -54 \ \leftarrow$

   $a_5 = 3(-54) = -162$

   $a_6 = 3(-162) = -486 \ \leftarrow$

4. $a_n = 2n = 2, 4, 6, 8, \dots$

   arithmetic sequence

5. $a_n = 2^n = 2, 4, 8, 16, \dots$

   geometric sequence

6. $a_n = n^2 = 1, 4, 9, 25, \dots$

   neither

7. $\displaystyle\sum_{i=1}^{5} (-1)^{i+1} i^2 = 1 \cdot 1^2 + (-1) \cdot 2^2 + 1 \cdot 3^2 + (-1) \cdot 4^2 + 1 \cdot 5^2$

   $\qquad\qquad\qquad = 1 - 4 + 9 - 16 + 25 = 15$

8. $\displaystyle\sum_{j=1}^{8} \left(\dfrac{1}{3}\right)^j = \dfrac{1}{3} + \dfrac{1}{9} + \dfrac{1}{27} + \dfrac{1}{81} + \dots + \dfrac{1}{3^8}$

   This is the nth partial sum of a geometric sequence with

   $a_1 = \dfrac{1}{3}, r = \dfrac{1}{3},$ and $n = 8$.

   $S_8 = \dfrac{\dfrac{1}{3}\left(1 - \left(\dfrac{1}{3}\right)^8\right)}{1 - \dfrac{1}{3}}$

   $\quad = \dfrac{\dfrac{1}{3}\left(1 - \dfrac{1}{6561}\right)}{\dfrac{2}{3}}$

   $\quad = \dfrac{\dfrac{1}{3}\left(\dfrac{6560}{6561}\right)}{\dfrac{2}{3}}$

   $\quad = \dfrac{3}{2} \cdot \dfrac{1}{3}\left(\dfrac{6560}{6561}\right)$

   $\quad = \dfrac{3280}{6561}$

9. $\displaystyle\sum_{k=1}^{27} (4k + 3) = 4 \sum_{k=1}^{27} k + \sum_{k=1}^{27} 3$

   $\qquad\qquad\quad = 4(1 + 2 + 3 + \dots + 27) + 3(27)$

   $\qquad\qquad\quad = 4\left(\dfrac{27}{2}\right)(1 + 27) + 3(27)$

   $\qquad\qquad\quad = 1512 + 81$

   $\qquad\qquad\quad = 1593$

10. $a_4 = a_1 + (4 - 1)d = 5 \quad \Rightarrow \quad a_1 + 3d = 5 \qquad (1)$

    $a_9 = a_1 + (9 - 1)d = 20 \quad \Rightarrow \quad a_1 + 8d = 20 \qquad (2)$

    Solve the system of equations.

    Multiply Equation (1) by -1.

    Add the results to Equation (2).

    $\quad -a_1 - 3d = -5$

    $+ \quad \underline{a_1 + 8d = 20}$

    $\qquad\qquad 5d = 15$

    $\qquad\qquad\ d = 3$

    Substitute 3 for d in Equation (1) and solve for a_1.

    $a_1 + 3(3) = 5$

    $\quad a_1 + 9 = 5$

    $\qquad a_1 = -4$

    $a_{21} = -4 + (21 - 1)(3) = 56$

11. $\displaystyle\sum_{k=1}^{\infty}\left(\frac{2}{5}\right)^k = S = \frac{a_1}{1-r}$ with $a_1 = \frac{2}{5}$ and $r = \frac{2}{5}$.

$$S = \frac{\frac{2}{5}}{1-\frac{2}{5}} = \frac{\frac{2}{5}}{\frac{3}{5}} = \frac{2}{3}$$

12. $1000x = 108.\overline{108}$ (1)

$x = 0.\overline{108}$ (2)

Subtract Equation (1) from Equation (2).
Solve the resulting equation for x.

$$999x = 108$$

$$x = \frac{108}{999} = \frac{4}{37}$$

13. $(3x-y)^4 = (3x)^4 - 4(3x)^3 y + 6(3x)^2 y^2 - 4(3x)y^3 + y^4$

$ = 81x^4 - 108x^3 y + 54x^2 y^2 - 12xy^3 + y^4$

14. $\displaystyle\left(2x - \frac{1}{2x}\right)^3 = \binom{3}{0}(2x)^3 - \binom{3}{1}(2x)^2\left(\frac{1}{2x}\right) + \binom{3}{2}(2x)\left(\frac{1}{2x}\right)^2 - \binom{3}{3}\left(\frac{1}{2x}\right)^3$

$\displaystyle\phantom{\left(2x-\frac{1}{2x}\right)^3} = (1)\left(8x^3\right) - \left(\frac{3}{1}\right)\left(4x^2\right)\left(\frac{1}{2x}\right) + \left(\frac{3\cdot 2}{2\cdot 1}\right)(2x)\left(\frac{1}{4x^2}\right) - \left(\frac{3\cdot 2\cdot 1}{3\cdot 2\cdot 1}\right)\left(\frac{1}{8x^3}\right)$

$\displaystyle\phantom{\left(2x-\frac{1}{2x}\right)^3} = 8x^3 - 6x + \frac{3}{2x} - \frac{1}{8x^3}$

15. To find the eighth term in the expansion of $(2x-5y)^{10}$, use $\displaystyle\binom{n}{i-1}a^{n-i+1}b^{i-1}$ with $n=10$, $i=8$, $a=2x$, and $b=-5y$.

$$\binom{10}{8-1}(2x)^{10-8+1}(-5y)^{8-1} = \binom{10}{7}(2x)^3(-5y)^7$$

$$= \frac{(10\cdot 9\cdot 8)}{3\cdot 2\cdot 1}\left(8x^3\right)\left(-78125y^7\right)$$

$$= -75{,}000{,}000x^3 y^7$$

16. Prove $3(1) + 3(2) + 3(3) + \cdots + 3(n) = \dfrac{3n(n+1)}{2}$.

Part 1. Prove the statement is true when $n=1$.

$$3(1) = \frac{3(1)(1+1)}{2} = \frac{3(2)}{2} = 3$$

Part 2. Assume $3(1) + 3(2) + 3(3) + \cdots + 3k = \dfrac{3k(k+1)}{2}$.

Prove $3(1) + 3(2) + 3(3) + \cdots + 3(k+1) = \dfrac{3(k+1)(k+2)}{2}$.

$3(1) + 3(2) + \cdots + 3(k+1) = 3(1) + 3(2) + \cdots + 3k + 3(k+1)$

$ = \dfrac{3k(k+1)}{2} + 3(k+1)$

$ = 3(k+1)\left[\dfrac{k}{2} + 1\right]$

$ = 3(k+1)\left[\dfrac{k+2}{2}\right]$

$ = \dfrac{3(k+1)(k+2)}{2}$

17. Part 1. Prove the statement is true when $n=1$.

$$\left(\frac{1}{2}\right)^1 = \frac{1}{2} < 1$$

Part 2. Assume $\left(\dfrac{1}{2}\right)^k < k$. Prove $\left(\dfrac{1}{2}\right)^{k+1} < k+1$.

$$\left(\frac{1}{2}\right)^{k+1} = \left(\frac{1}{2}\right)^k\left(\frac{1}{2}\right) < k\left(\frac{1}{2}\right) = \frac{1}{2}k < k < k+1.$$

18. $26 \cdot 25 \cdot 24 \cdot 10^5 = 1{,}560{,}000{,}000$

19. $C(12,\,5) = \dfrac{12!}{5!\,7!} = \dfrac{12\cdot 11\cdot 10\cdot 9\cdot 8}{5\cdot 4\cdot 3\cdot 2\cdot 1} = 792$

20. $\dfrac{52}{52} \cdot \dfrac{12}{51} \cdot \dfrac{11}{50} \cdot \dfrac{10}{49} \cdot \dfrac{9}{48} = \dfrac{33}{16660} \approx 0.002$